KU-205-849

METHODS OF SOCIAL RESEARCH

FOURTH EDITION

KENNETH D. BAILEY

THE FREE PRESS

THE FREE PRESS
1230 Avenue of the Americas
New York, NY 10020

Copyright © 1994 by The Free Press

All rights reserved,
including the right of reproduction
in whole or in part in any form.

THE FREE PRESS and colophon are trademarks
of Simon & Schuster Inc.

Manufactured in the United States of America

10 9 8 7 6 5

Bailey, Kenneth D.
    Methods of social research / Kenneth D. Bailey. — 4th ed.
        p. cm.
    Includes bibliographical references (p.   ) and indexes.
    ISBN 0–02–901279–1
        1. Sociology—Methodology. I. Title.
HM24.B295 1994   93–36444
301'.072—dc20   CIP

To
JNB
and
SJB

LIVERPOOL
JOHN MOORES UNIVERSITY
I.M. MARSH LIBRARY
BARKHILL ROAD
LIVERPOOL L17 6BD
TEL. 0151 231 5216/5299

LIVERPOOL
JOHN MOORES UNIVERSITY
I.M. MARSH LIBRARY
BARKHILL ROAD
LIVERPOOL L17 6BD
TEL. 0151 231 5216/5299

CONTENTS

v

PREFACE TO
FOURTH EDITION

It seems customary to preface a book on social research methods by stating that the book focuses on the interrelationship between theory and research. The implication seems to be that this will make it clear and easy to read. Unfortunately, things are not so simple. While not de-emphasizing the need to integrate theory and research, I have made it my major objective to write a book that is comprehensive and detailed enough to be useful while plainly written enough to be readable. Students are too often faced either with a book too simple to prepare them for the complexities of the real world of social research, with all its myriad problems, or too complex and abstract to be understood.

I have attempted to integrate the various data collection techniques by discussing the advantages and disadvantages and assessing the reliability and validity of each. I hope that this common framework will allow the student to compare methods more easily and will illuminate the compatibility of otherwise apparently diverse methods, thus dispelling the all too common but erroneous tendency to view the presentation of several methods in a single volume as a "cafeteria" approach having little continuity or depth.

The response from readers of the first three editions has been most gratifying, and I wish to thank all of you.

The chief goal in preparing the fourth edition is to move *Methods of Social Research* firmly into the 1990s. As before, this has meant diligent updating, reflecting steady progress in various areas. Once again, I had the impression of a maturing discipline, still growing, but now involved in refinement in a number of basic areas.

However, in addition to this steady growth and refinement, social research shows evidence of rather dramatic change in at least two areas. One is the growth of a number of new techniques, all new to this edition, and some spawned by technological developments. These include discussions of postmodernism and the "value-full" approach (chapter 2), focus groups and computer and fax surveys (chapter 8), and meta-analysis (chapter 16).

A second major development is the growing recognition that some groups are excluded from social research, and the development of methods for including them. The fourth and earlier editions deal with this problem in a number of chapters. For example, chapter 5 presents snowball sampling as a means of sampling excluded populations, while chapter 8 discusses the effects of race and sex of interviewers and respondents. In addition to such discussions, the fourth edition includes an entirely new chapter designed to study inclusion in a general fashion. This is chapter 17, "Inclusionary Research Methods." This chapter deals with why such groups as women, racial and ethnic groups, alcoholics, homosexuals, the ill and disabled, and others are often excluded from research, and how they can be included.

I think that chapter 17 is a very important chapter. It obviously cannot deal with all groups, but it provides general guidelines for inclusion based on the available literature (which is mostly quite recent). This area will surely grow in importance and will receive increased attention as societies become more pluralistic during the 1990s and beyond.

A number of people worked especially hard in preparing this fourth edition. I wish to thank Leah Robin for reading the entire text and providing many helpful comments, and Charles O'Connell for once again preparing the instructor's manual. Special thanks also go to Joyce Seltzer, senior editor and vice president at The Free Press, for her excellent support at all stages of the project, and to Loretta Denner, Free Press production editor, for her excellent supervision.

ACKNOWLEDGMENTS

We wish to thank the following for the use of their materials in the production of this book:

Patricia Breyer Wild for various questionnaire items, questionnaire portions, cover-letter portions, and descriptions of survey procedure from *Child Health Care Survey* (Los Angeles: University of California, 1973) and from *Sociological Determinants of Utilization of a Prepaid Pediatric Health Care Plan* (Ph.D. dissertation, University of California at Los Angeles, © 1974 Patricia Breyer Wild). Reprinted by the permission of the author.

Gene N. Levine and Robert C. Rhodes for questionnaire items and introductory questionnaire statement from the *Nisei Male Questionnaire Mailed Instrument* (University of California at Los Angeles, Japanese-American Research Project [JARP] by Gene N. Levine and John Modell, 1967), which will be appearing in their forthcoming book, *The Japanese-American Community.* Reprinted by permission.

Leo G. Reeder for questionnaire items, opening statement, and face sheet from *Student Survey: Questionnaire* 1969a; *The UCLA Student Poll* 1969b; *Los Angeles Metropolitan Area Survey: III (LAMAS III): Questionnaire* 1971; and *Los Angeles Metropolitan Area Survey: IV (LAMAS IV): Questionnaire* 1972 by The Survey Research Center (SRC) of the University of California at Los Angeles. Reprinted by permission.

Marjorie N. Donald for material from "Implications of Nonresponse for the Interpretation of Mail Questionnaire Data" in *Public Opinion Quarterly* 24 (Spring): 102. Reprinted by the permission of the author and the publisher, © 1960 American Association for Public Opinion Research.

John R. Raser for material from *Simulation and Society: An Exploration of Scientific Gaming* (Boston: Allyn and Bacon). Reprinted by the permission of the author, © 1969 by John R. Raser.

Otis Dudley Duncan for material from "Path Analysis: Sociological Examples" in *The American Journal of Sociology 72* (July). Reprinted by the permission of the author and the publisher, © 1966 the University of Chicago. All rights reserved.

Robert Brown for material from *Explanation in Social Science* (Chicago: Aldine). Reprinted by the permission of Routledge and Kegan Paul, Ltd. and Aldine Publishing Co., © 1963 Routledge and Kegan Paul, Ltd.

PART ONE

PRINCIPLES OF SOCIAL RESEARCH

CHAPTER 1

THE RESEARCH PROCESS

AS TRADITIONALLY DEFINED, social research has been concerned with gathering data that can help us answer questions about various aspects of society and thus can enable us to understand society. These questions may pertain to very specific problems such as how a social welfare caseworker in city A may better meet the needs of his or her clients, or how conflict among medical professionals in a particular hospital may be lessened. Alternatively, social research may be asked to provide the answers to questions of theoretical interest to a particular social science discipline. Such questions may have no apparent application in the present society. These include such questions as why bureaucracy has increased over time in industrialized countries, why occupational specialization has increased over time, or how peer clique structures come to be formed and later to dissolve.

Thus, the implicit assumption in the traditional use of social science data gathering techniques, such as the survey, experiment, or small group laboratory, was that the research method was a means to an end. The method would be used to gather information that would benefit society either through the direct application of findings to the amelioration of social ills or through the use of the findings to test theoretical issues in social science.

Recently, however, an interesting trend has been emerging. Not only are research methods having an impact upon society through their findings, but the methods *themselves* are being increasingly used by sectors of the society outside of the social sciences. The most obvious example is the increasing use of surveys by newspapers, television networks, and political parties and their candidates for office.

This development has a number of ramifications, some of them quite complex, for both society and social scientists. Consider, for example, the role of survey research methods in determining the proper voting hours in presidential elections. Traditionally, surveys would have been used in two ways to determine voting hours. One way would be for a social scientist to develop a theory concerning the voting hours that would best meet the goals of a democracy. Then the survey could be used to gather data for testing the theory. If the theory were supported, it could be applied in subsequent elections. Alternatively, one could use a survey to ask people when it would be most convenient for them to vote, and to open the polls at those hours to ensure a maximum voter turnout. Both of these are examples of quite standard uses of social research methods.

In the presidential elections of 1980, however, surveys had an impact on voting hours in quite a different, and perhaps serendipitous, manner. Surveys conducted by the major television networks in the afternoon of November 4, 1980, showed that Ronald Reagan was ahead of President Carter in a landslide vote and projected that Reagan would be the winner. In and of itself such reporting would seem to be in the best tradition of broadcast journalism and beneficial to all concerned. However, the effect of these projections was that Carter conceded the election while some people were still at work and had not had a chance to vote. While the polls had closed on the East Coast at the time of the concession, the West Coast polls were scheduled to remain open for nearly three more hours. For the first time in history some potential voters knew for a fact that their vote would not play a part in determining the outcome of the election. This led to talk of changing the voting hours on the West Coast so that the polls would close at the same hour across the nation. Thus we see that surveys had an impact on voting hours in a third way—by negatively affecting the election process so that some people called for changes in voting hours.

4

Another problem in the 1980 presidential election was that the survey generally showed the race to be close until shortly before election day. This led to bickering over whether the polls were in error, or whether there was a massive last-minute change in voting preference. Predictably enough, the pollsters tended to feel that the overall role of the political polls in the election process was not negative. How could they tell? With another poll, of course. The *Los Angeles Times* telephone survey conducted by I. A. Lewis nationwide from November 9 to November 13, 1980, contacted 1,829 adults, including 1,273 who had voted in the presidential election (Skelton 1980). The *Times* concluded from the poll that Carter's concession had had little effect on election results. However, 12 percent of people who had voted earlier said that they would not have voted had they heard that Carter had already lost.

In the 1984 presidential election the effects of survey research were somewhat different from those in 1980. Most of the polls predicted the landslide victory of President Reagan over Senator Mondale quite accurately, so there was little feeling that polling results swayed crucial votes, as was the case in 1980. However, since the results were so clear, the pollsters were able to predict the winner quite quickly, with the result that many persons doubtless felt (and with some justification) that the issue had been settled without them and that the value of their vote had thus been diminished. Further, the debate over the polling hours in the West continued. It was clear in 1984 that the conjunction of sophisticated survey procedures, modern sampling techniques, and rapid information transmission had changed American voting behavior profoundly, so that to some potential voters the election was over almost before it had begun, and they were alienated from the process.

What is the actual magnitude of the effect of exit polls on voting? Although this is very difficult to estimate, Sudman (1986, p. 338) studied voting in congressional districts and concluded that "there is a possibility of a small decrease ranging from 1 to 5 percent in total vote in congressional districts where polls close significantly later than 8 P.M. EST in those elections where the exit polls suggest a clear winner when previously the race had been considered close."

As Milvasky (1985, p. 1) notes, "The saturation of the mass media with exit poll results can produce a backlash of adverse public reactions, ranging from hostility toward polling to political apathy and nonvoting." This has led to calls for laws prohibiting pollsters from interviewing voters as they leave polling places. However, such laws appear currently unresolved in the courts and may not be deemed constitutional. Swift (1985) reports that Congress seeks "voluntary compliance" to withhold projecting results until the polls are closed.

How has voluntary compliance worked? The impact of exit polling on voting was less an issue in the landslide 1988 election but resurfaced in the Bush–Clinton–Perot race of 1992. Again, voters in the West feared that their votes would appear meaningless in the light of "projections" based on exit polls, which declared winners after voting had closed in the East but before it had closed in the West. More ominously, some observers feared that if national elections appeared already decided, some Western voters would stay home from the voting booth, thus affecting the many ballot measures (amendments and propositions) on the ballot in the West, including controversial "gay rights" measures, such as Proposition 6 in Oregon (which was defeated), and Amendment 2 in Colorado (which was passed, resulting in an economic boycott—see Mazanec, 1992).

So, what happened in 1992? What was the effect of more than a decade of nationally televised exit polling? The results were relatively uneventful. People voted in quite large numbers in the West, where, for example, the polls remained open until the customary hour of 8 P.M. in California (11 P.M. Eastern Standard Time). Apparently no laws were passed to prohibit exit polls or the televising of their results, but "voluntary compliance" did seem reasonably successful, with the major networks recognizing the problem of late voting in the West and in consequence delaying their projections in many cases until that voting had closed.

Thus, social science research methods, in the form of exit polls (survey research), did not sabotage voting in the West in the November 1992 elections. Part of the reason was that many people worked to get out the vote, including a successful "Rock the Vote" campaign by MTV (Music Television) targeted at young voters. All this leads to a number of points for 1990s social research: (a) Social research methods and the media remain in a close partnership; (b) research methods can, if used irresponsibly, have a negative effect on such social processes as elections, but voluntary regulation seems to be avoiding this to a large degree; and (c) the media, which were accused of suppressing voting through the use of exit polls, actually aided the voting process, by using surveys showing a high degree of apathy among young people, to target this group, producing an increased voter turnout.

The lesson for the 1990s and the twenty-first century is that research methods are not an indisputable (and indispensable) part of mass-media operations, and thus of society. This is true not only in the United States but also in other countries, such as Israel, where the desire to forecast elections has been labeled an "obsession" (see Weimann 1990). Most newspapers, magazines, and television stations gather news data through personal interviews of eye-witnesses and others, but that is often done in an admittedly "nonscientific" manner. Increasingly, one is seeing scientific, professionally designed surveys becoming a staple of the media, and the public increasingly understands such research jargon as "accurate within three percentage points plus or minus." The Los Angeles riots of 1992, following the highly publicized Rodney King beating trial, not only were widely reported by the international media but also spawned a number of social surveys designed to gather data about not only opinions concerning the underlying causes of the riots but a number of other matters as well.

This does not mean that research methods, including exit polls, are always correct. While recent national polls have been relatively accurate in the United States, exit polls in Virginia (as well as national polls in Nicaragua—see chapter 5) have not been so accurate. The most recent polling problem in the United States was the November, 1989 exit poll in the Virginia gubernatorial election (see Clymer 1989, Davidson 1989, Mitofsky and Waksberg 1989, and Traugott and Price 1992). The exit poll conducted by Mason–Dixon Opinion Research (MDOR) for several television stations in Virginia and Washington accurately predicted the Democrat L. Douglas Wilder (also an early candidate for President in 1992) as the gubernatorial winner over the Republican J. Marshall Coleman. However, it erred in estimating a Wilder victory by ten percentage points (55 to 45 percent) while the actual victory was a very narrow two-tenths of one percentage point. This is a five-percentage-point error, and is outside of the normally accepted standards of sampling error (see Traugott and Price 1992).

Among the probable reasons for the error are sampling errors caused by redistricting (which may have changed not only the size but also the demographic composition of voting districts) and social desirability bias. The latter probably stemmed from some voters' reluctance to admit that they were not voting for the black candidate (Wilder) for fear of being labeled racist. For further discussion, see Traugott and Price (1992) and also Part Two, "Survey Research Methods" (chapters 5–8) in this volume.

The point to be made from all of this is that social research methods have an impact upon us not only as social scientists but also as members of the larger society. Where surveys were once used principally by social scientists, their use by the media may come dangerously close to affecting important processes, such as elections, and thus become a form of social engineering rather than purely a method of research. Thus, it seems more and more important for the social scientist to understand social research methods, both as one who conducts research and as one who is affected by such methods.

Despite their growing use outside of social science, the primary role of research methods is to further the work of social scientists. It is useful in this introductory chapter, therefore, to discuss the logic of social science and then to provide examples of the research process.

Social Science as Science

Even cursory perusal of intellectual history will suffice to show the reader that social science, in comparison to physical science and such other disciplines as philosophy and humanities, is quite a recent development. Modern sociology dates back only to the very late eighteenth or early nineteenth century, with most of the development occurring in the twentieth century. Humans have always studied their world but have often seemed to study distant things (as in ancient astronomy) before they studied their own society. Even within social science, there was an emphasis on the anthropological study of distant societies before there was emphasis on our own sociological backyard.

Why have we studied social science only relatively recently? Why is there much less government funding for social science research than for physical science research in the United States? Even more to the point, why study social science now? These are issues that could preoccupy us for many volumes, and even then would probably defy resolution. In the last century, for example, America was quite rural, and the society seemed relatively simple to understand. Perhaps social issues did not seem to have priority over such fundamental issues as how to grow enough food to survive. Now, however, it is clear to many people that our complex society must be understood in depth, as our social environment effects us just as directly and profoundly as our physical environment, although in different ways.

As a catastrophic but salient example of this point, consider the American space program and the devastating explosion of the space shuttle Challenger on January 28, 1986. For years there has been some friction between the space program and social programs, with adherents of social programs, such as antipoverty programs complaining that government priorities were misplaced, that it was wrong to spend large amounts of money on a perhaps superfluous space program when a more pressing need was to feed the urban hungry. One answer to that has always been that physical scientists could expect more satisfactory results than social scientists. Thus, while dollars spent on the space program were backed by sophisticated scientific theory and sound engineering application, social science was so poorly developed that money spent on social programs would achieve little. An extension of the argument was the notion that perhaps space scientists could apply their principles to social problems.

Against this backdrop, the explosion of Challenger electrified the nation and the world. It showed, for one thing, that despite the sophistication of scientific theory and engineering, physical science applications can also result in devastating (and expensive) failure. While such dramatic loss of life and money in a social program would be likely to cause its abrupt cancellation, no such fate seems in store for the space program, and no subsequent shift in funding from space programs to social programs is likely. Furthermore, the attention of the world was focused not only upon the engineering feats and failures of Challenger but upon the sociological characteristics of the crew. Among the sociological variables noted were the gender of crew members (two were female), their ethnicity, and their occupational roles (particularly the fact that a teacher was on board). Thus, the Challenger tragedy illustrates that our modern world events are not merely technological or scientific but are generally of sociological import as well, and display a mix of interdependent social and technological factors. Thus, while we must continue the study of physical science, we will increasingly recognize the importance of social science and the interdependency of the two.

World events during the 1990s have also focused attention on sociological factors. The riots in Los Angeles in 1992 focused attention on the court system (when the Los Angeles police officers accused of beating Rodney King were acquitted) and on urban poverty, while the 1992 riots in Germany focused on the problem of the adaptation of immigrants in that country. Further, the United States sent troops to Somalia in 1992 and 1993 to help alleviate mass starvation. While it is axiomatic in sociology that in times of famine or mass starvation children are usually the most affected (see the examples of density research later in this chapter), in Somalia more adults died than children, resulting in a large number of orphans. Why did more adults die than children? The answer is simple—the bandits stealing relief supplies were more likely to target "adult" food such as rice and beans than the formula used to feed small children.

A crucial question in social science is what constitutes the proper understanding of society, and how that understanding can be achieved. Krathwohl (1985) deals with those issues in depth. Among the points he emphasizes are the ways in which one's orientation to knowledge affects the research methods used and the different criteria utilized by researchers with different orientations.

Throughout its history, practitioners of social science have sought the proper position of their discipline with respect to physical science and, to a lesser extent, with respect to the humanities. To this day you will find within social science both those who think of themselves as scientists in the strictest sense of the word and those with a more subjective approach to the study of society, who see themselves more as humanists than as scientists.

The founders of sociology grappled with this central issue. The essential problem concerns the nature of social phenomena and how they can best be understood. One of the most extreme positions was espoused by Wilhelm Dilthey, a nineteenth-century sociologist. He believed that humans had free will, and thus no one can predict their actions and generalize about them. In its extreme form, this view would allow only for the study of unique events and not for explanation and prediction. Thus, social science as it is generally conceived today (as an explanatory science) would be precluded.

Emile Durkheim espoused essentially the opposite view. He said that social phenomena are orderly and can be generalized. His viewpoint was based on the assumption that phenomena adhere to underlying social laws, just as physical phenomena follow physical laws. In Durkheim's view, then, there was little difference between physical and natural science and social science except for subject matters. The logic of inquiry was essentially the same. This strictly scientific view is often labeled *positivism*. According to Durkheim, sociologists could use the methods of natural science, such as experimentation, to study and explain social phenomena just as others used them to study physical phenomena. For example, Durkheim discussed the orderly change in suicide rates in European countries. Although rates changed over time, the rank ordering of rates tended to stay the same. That is, if country A had a higher rate than country B at time 1, it generally would have a higher rate at time 2, even if the rates changed in both countries between times 1 and 2. To Durkheim such orderliness was proof that national suicide rates were following some social law. Thus, the task of the social scientist is to use scientific methods to discover this law. Durkheim postulated his law of suicide, i.e., that the suicide rate varies inversely with the degree of social integration.

Not all social scientists, either in Durkheim's time or now, endorse the physical science or positivistic approach as wholeheartedly as did Durkheim. Many sociologists favor an approach modeled after the word of Max Weber. Weber took an intermediate approach between the two extremes espoused by Dilthey on the one hand (that human actions were unpredictable) and Durkheim on the other (that social science should use the methods of the natural sciences). According to Weber, social phenomena were not merely determined by social laws but were the product of human volitional action. In his view, the fact that humans have free will does not mean that their actions are random and entirely unpredictable. Rather, free will is exercised in a rational fashion, and human action can be predicted by understanding rational action.

According to Weber, the use of the methods of natural science plays a role in social research, but not an exclusive role. Physical scientists, he argued, stand in a different relationship to the phenomena they are studying from that of social scientists. For example, the physicist often represents theoretical statements in quantitative terms, generally as mathematical equations. To Weber, the use of mathematics in research means that the mathematical symbols mediate between the researcher and the phenomena being studied. Thus, the understanding that such research yields is in a sense always indirect.

Weber saw the situation in social science to be somewhat different. According to Weber, the use of the scientific methods followed in the physical and natural sciences is legitimate but inadequate for the study of all social phenomena. They should be used when they seem valuable. Beyond that point they can be supplanted with direct understanding. Direct understanding of the sort Weber discusses is not possible in physical science but is possible in social science because of the different relationship between the researcher and his or her data. While the physicist studying gases and the mineralogist studying minerals have nothing in common with their data, and thus cannot understand them directly, the sociologist may actually be a *member* of the very group that he or she is studying. In Weber's view this opens the possibility for a different kind of understanding— direct understanding or *Verstehen*. This is the sort of understanding experienced when you observe a person in a particular situation or predicament and are able to empathize with him or her and understand how he or she feels because you yourself have been in the same or a similar situation.

Among contemporary social scientists, it seems relatively safe to say that Dilthey's extreme view that social phenomena are random and unpredictable is relatively rare, if not completely absent. Most social scientists feel that if human action were indeed random, a scientific social science would be impossible. They tend to think that social phenomena are orderly enough to be explained and predicted. However, many would agree that not all social phenomena can be explained or predicted with complete accuracy at present. Some social scientists think this is because social phenomena themselves are not 100 percent orderly and predictable, but always contain some random element or margin of error. Others contend that the phenomena are orderly and predictable but that the theory, the methods of data collection, and the techniques of data analysis that we have at present are not sufficient to explain these phenomena completely. For example, suppose a team of sociologists and social welfare professionals is concerned with delinquency problems in a community. They conduct a research project and are able to explain to their satisfaction approximately 80 percent of the cases of delinquency by studying such factors as age of parents, type of family relationships between parents (particularly whether both parents are in the home), and peer group relationships. It may be that the other 20 percent of cases arise from random factors that are each unique to a given case and can never be satisfactorily generalized. Nonetheless, most social scientists would prefer to think that 100 percent of cases can be explained but that such a perfect explanation can be attained only after advances in theory, data collection, and data analysis.

While few social scientists believe that social phenomena occur randomly, there is disagreement about how social phenomena should be studied, and even about which phenomena to study. Probably the predominant view among social scientists, in terms of numbers, is an adherence to some form of positivism. Essentially, positivism is the view (as discussed above in conjunction with Durkheim) that social science should use the methods of the physical sciences. This essentially means that social phenomena are considered to be objectively occurring phenomena. As discussed by Bierstedt (1957), this scientific view embodies the notion that sociology is seen as a pure rather than an applied science; its task is thus to gather knowledge rather than to use it. Moreover, sociology is seen as an abstract science rather than a concrete one, and thus should be more concerned with generalizing rather than with particularizing. This latter point dictates that social science does not concern itself with the description or explanation of unique historical events but is primarily concerned with the generation of scientific laws. This is a fundamental principle of positivism. Scientific laws are statements that hold for all times and all places. Those who advocate a positivistic approach are somewhat divided as to whether the laws of social science they seek must be causal laws. Some social scientists feel that it is presumptuous, at least at the present level of development of social science, to demand that we find actual causes of social phenomena. They think it is more realistic to have causal explanations as an ultimate goal, but to seek in the interim simply the correlates or concomitants of social phenomena, and to stop short of referring to these factors as causes. (See chapter 3 for additional discussion of causality.)

Although some researchers would probably resist such labeling, I think it is safe to say that survey researchers (chapters 5 through 8) and experimentalists (chapter 9) are generally regarded as being within the positivistic tradition. The experimentalists generally seek to establish causality, while the survey researchers look for correlates, if not causes. Most positivists tend to use quantitative techniques, including computer simulation (chapter 13) and techniques of data reduction, scaling, and statistical analysis (chapters 14 through 16). They also tend to formulate rather rigorous hypotheses that are amenable to test (verification). Thus, chapters 3, 4, and 20 reflect the general positivistic orientation. Similarly the latter part of the present chapter, along with chapter 2 (choosing the research problem), chapter 18 (ethics), and chapter 19 (applications), largely (but not wholly) reflect the emphasis on this tradition within contemporary social research.

Not all social science is conducted within the tradition of Durkheimian positivism. Chapters 10, 11, 12, and 17 (observation, ethnomethodology, document study, and inclusive research methods) present the other current of research. Observational researchers tend to use an approach more similar to Weber's than to Durkheim's. They have a tendency to eschew rigorous hypotheses and quantification. They rely heavily on verbal analysis and are likely to be interested in a more subjective understanding of their research subjects. Document analysis also tends to rely more upon subjective verbal analysis than upon rigorous, quantitative hypothesis testing. Some observational and documentary research is structured and quantitative, just as some survey research is unstructured, but these are exceptions to the general rule. The chapter on inclusive research methods (chapter 17) seeks ways for including persons whom traditional "positivistic" or conservative methods may have neglected.

Ethnomethodology is probably the most radical of the contemporary schools of thought. Many ethnomethodologists view themselves as rigorous scientists. But while ethnomethodology may share with positivism the label "science," it differs radically from positivism in that it does not seek to formulate general scientific laws. Ethnomethodologists tend to de-emphasize the importance of developing general social laws or even general concepts; they focus instead upon the unique situational nature of the meaning of social phenomena. However, while they do not see the formulation of general laws as a primary focus of social research, they are concerned with studying the ways in which meaning is made of particular phenomena in specific settings.

I hope this book will show that the whole range of approaches to social research presented has value. While a given individual researcher will not be able to use all of these methods in a given study, and perhaps not even in a lifetime, an understanding of the perspectives of alternative approaches will surely allow a less dogmatic understanding of the particular approach that is finally chosen for the research and a clearer understanding of its relation to other approaches.

In the past there has often been altogether too much chauvinism and dogmatism in social research, with adherents of a particular method claiming a superior method for social research and condemning all others. It is my view that such rivalry is detrimental to the development of social research and the pursuit of knowledge. The truth of the matter is that each approach has its strengths and weaknesses. Each approach has instances where it is definitely the method of choice. Conversely, there are times when each particular method is inappropriate. The tendency to tout one method over others can prevent researchers from seeing the essential complementarity of these various methods. I have attempted to show this complementarity in the volume by discussing each approach within a similar framework, analyzing the validity and reliability of each, and by exploring the advantages and disadvantages of each.

Stages of Social Research

I have already indicated that there are a variety of approaches to social research, and a glance at the table of contents of this volume will bear that out. Further, each particular project will be unique in some ways because of the particular time and place in which it is conducted. Nevertheless, all research projects share a common goal of furthering our understanding of society, and thus all share certain basic stages, although there may be some variation in the specific details of these stages. Each research project must have a clearly stated research problem or goal that can be stated in terms of a hypothesis. In addition each project will have a research design that tells how the data will be gathered and analyzed (for example, what the sample size will be, where the observation will take place and for how long, or what the experimental design will be). Further, each project entails gathering data, analyzing data, and interpreting data. These stages are as follows:

1. Choosing the research problem and stating the hypothesis
2. Formulating the research design
3. Gathering the data
4. Coding and analyzing the data
5. Interpreting the results so as to test the hypothesis

Each of these stages is dependent upon the others. It is obvious that one cannot analyze data (stage 4) before one has collected the data (stage 3). It may be less obvious, however, that a researcher who has no knowledge of his or her subject matter and no knowledge of how to analyze data may find himself or herself unable to formulate an adequate hypothesis, formulate the research design, or gather the data. The researcher needs to have adequate knowledge of the later stages before he or she can perform the earlier prerequisites. A researcher can do irreparable harm to the study by performing one of the early steps inadequately—for example, by writing an untestable hypothesis or by securing an inadequate sample. Research, then, is a system of interdependent related stages.

Circularity

The research process is best conceived as a circle, as in figure 1–1. One usually enters the diagram for a particular project at stage 1. However, the researcher generally is able to draw on past studies in formulating his or her hypothesis. After the researcher completes stage 5 he or she may stop, but the research process itself is not completed at this stage. If the study was unsuccessful or only partially successful (that is, if the data did not support or only partially supported the hypothesis), the researcher must return to the early stages of investigation. Often analysis of the data (stage 5) provides the researcher with knowledge useful for revising the hypothesis (stage 1). He or she may decide to revise the hypothesis and then test it exactly as before (stages 2–5). Or the researcher may decide that the hypothesis is adequate and that failure to confirm it is due to error in some other stage—perhaps inadequate sample design (stage 2), inadequate measurement of key concepts in the questionnaire or other data-gathering instrument (stage 3), or inadequate methods of data analysis (stage 4). In these cases the re-

Figure 1–1

Stages in the Research Process

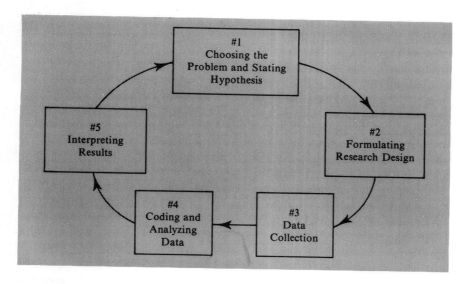

searcher would be able to salvage work done prior to the faulty step but would have to repeat all stages beginning with the faulty stage.

Replication

Even if the research is successful and the findings of stage 5 confirm the hypothesis of stage 1, it is often advisable to repeat the study so as to demonstrate that the findings are not an accident or mere coincidence. If the study is repeated exactly, especially with a different sample, a second confirmation of the findings will lend further support to the contention that the hypothesis cannot be rejected. This exact repetition of a study is called *replication.*

It is important that the researcher so design his study that it can be replicated by himself or someone else. Otherwise the findings will not be so convincing as they would be if others were able to check them through repetition of the study. For example, suppose that I hypothesized that a new birth-control drug does not have any harmful side effects and confirmed this hypothesis by giving the drug to a sample of ten women over a period of a week, with no visible side effects. You would probably feel much better about taking the drug or having a friend or relative take it if other researchers were able to repeat my study many times, with larger samples and over a longer time period, and still conclude that the pill is not harmful.

But despite the importance of making a study potentially replicable—many researchers in social science do so by clearly reporting their hypothesis, the characteristics of their sample, and the question asked—very few studies actually are replicated. One important reason is that a later researcher may find what he considers to be a deficiency in the study and would rather improve on it than replicate it. Another factor that keeps researchers from replicating studies is the lack of money—it is difficult enough to get money to do a study the first time. Some sociologists also may consider the research "old hat" after it has been done once or twice and may prefer to conduct research in a new and previously unstudied area. Rather than a strict replication of a study, it is much more common to find the study repeated in its essentials with some modifications. Nevertheless, the basic point is that research is a never ending cycle. We always accept each finding tentatively, aware that it may be proved wrong in further investigations. For further discussion of the advantages and disadvantages of replication in social science, see Bailey (1987).

Examples: Density Research

While all social research projects share the five basic stages, they exhibit much diversity in the way in which these stages are carried out. Research projects in social science range from highly controlled experimental laboratory studies to uncontrolled observational studies. A brief comparison of two different studies dealing with the same general topic (the effects of population density on individuals) not only will provide examples of research that we can refer to when discussing the five stages of research in detail in subsequent chapters but also will demonstrate the range of permissible activities within each stage.

Researchers have long speculated about the possible negative effects of population density, theorizing that high density levels cause such phenomena as crime and mental illness (Dunham 1937) and anxiety or alienation (Wirth 1938). However, only recently have attempts been made to test these hypotheses in a controlled and systematic fashion.

The father of population theory was the eighteenth-century economist Thomas Malthus, who theorized that overpopulation was a major cause of poverty that if unchecked would lead to mass starvation. Calhoun (1962) tested Malthus's hypothesis that overpopulation causes social pathologies. However, his subjects were rats rather than humans. In studies on both wild and tame rats Calhoun found that a certain density that he determined was about twice the comfortable level caused such negative effects as high infant mortality rates, poor care of the young by mothers, and hyperactivity, cannibalism, and other antisocial behavior among males.

Many social researchers were impressed with these findings. However, finding that population density has negative effects on rats obviously does not mean that this relationship holds to the same degree, or even at all, for humans. In many medical or chemical studies on rats the real population of interest is humans, and rats are used primarily because potentially harmful experiments cannot be performed with humans. Just as researchers cannot give humans an overdose of cyclamate to see if this chemical causes cancer, they cannot expose humans to high degrees of population density for long periods of time to see if harmful effects result. If they were to perform such experiments with foreknowledge of the possible danger to their human subjects, they would be guilty of unethical behavior and might find themselves subject to lawsuits or criminal prosecution. The problem is: How can we design a study adequate to test the hypothesis that overcrowding causes harmful effects on humans without actually harming the population we study? By now, both the challenges and the difficulties of conducting social research should be obvious.

Quite different approaches are evident in two of the best-known recent studies on the effects of density on human populations. One of these studies is "Population Density and Pathology: What Are the Relations for Man?" by Galle, Gove, and McPherson (1972). The second study, by Griffit and Veitch (1971), is entitled "Hot and Crowded: Influences of Population Density and Temperature on Interpersonal Affective Behavior." We can compare these studies in terms of our five stages of research.

Stage 1: Choosing the Problem and Stating the Hypothesis

Choosing the problem was relatively easy in both studies, for both were based upon past research and did not have to be formulated in a vacuum. Both research teams were aware of the evidence showing negative effects of density that had been found by Calhoun and others. In addition, the Griffit team was aware of findings by the U.S. Riot Commission (1968) that most riots (and it was also true for the Los Angeles riots of 1992) occurred under crowded conditions and on hot days. Thus the general research problem and the hypothesis (that density causes harmful effects on humans) were about the same for both studies.

Stage 2: Research Design

In this stage the researcher must decide how to measure the two main variables in his or her hypothesis (density and negative social effects) and on what group of people to test the hypothesis. This involves deciding not only how many people will be used as subjects but also what their particular characteristics should be and under what circumstances the data will be gathered. One of the major problems in social research is control of extraneous factors that might interfere with the study (e.g., by causing effects that would be wrongly attributed to density). For example, one would not conduct a density study in a hospital and probably not in a prison, for the researcher would have no assurance that any negative effects he or she found were due to density. Thus in selecting the sample ideally he or she would choose a group of people free of harmful effects caused by factors other than density. It is at this stage of research that the two studies diverge radically.

Griffit and Veitch decided to conduct a laboratory study. This involved a decision to take people out of their natural everyday environment and put them in an artificial setting, in this case a Sherer-Gillet environmental chamber, seven feet wide, nine feet long, and nine feet high. The advantages of such a design for controlling density are obvious. The researcher can easily vary density from high to low simply by controlling the number of persons admitted to the chamber at any one time. Griffit and Veitch (1971, p. 94) defined low density as three to five persons in the chamber (12.7 square feet of space for each person) and high density as twelve to sixteen persons in the chamber (only four square feet for each person, or an area of floor space two feet long and two feet wide).

While it facilitates the measurement of density, the use of such a chamber makes the measurement of harmful effects more difficult. For example, Calhoun found extreme aggressive

behavior such as cannibalism among rats. It would be unethical for Griffit and Veitch to attempt to create such effects among humans, even if these effects could be brought about by
long exposure. It is possible that even short exposure to high density could cause some measurable degree of aggressiveness, but this behavior will generally be nonphysical and nonvisi-
ble, and thus difficult to measure. Griffit and Veitch (1971, p. 94) used a questionnaire called
the Interpersonal Judgment Scale that measures aggressiveness by how well the subject likes
a hypothetical stranger. Their hypothesis that density causes aggression will therefore be supported if people show more dislike of strangers, as measured by this questionnaire, under the
high-density conditions than under the low-density conditions. Since Griffit and Veitch
thought that heat as well as density might affect aggression, they used eight different combinations. As their sample they chose a "captive audience" of 121 male and female students in
introductory psychology classes at Kansas State University.

Like Griffit and Veitch, the Galle team also studied the effects of density of humans. However, their research design for testing their hypotheses was radically different, and different
measures of harmful effects were used. They discovered that data for Chicago in 1960 were
available in the *Local Community Fact Book for Chicago* (Kitagawa and Taeuber, 1963). Use
of such data has obvious advantages in addition to the money saved by not having to interview.
One advantage is that "natural" data on actual urban density are used, rather than the contrived
artificial setting used by Griffit and Veitch. Thus it is much more likely that the long-term
effects of density can be shown, even though data were collected only on a cross-section of the
Chicago population at one point in time. A further advantage is that the sample size is much
larger than in the Griffit and Veitch study. Thus there will be a firmer basis for generalizing the
results of this study than there would be for the results of a study with a small sample. The data
used by Galle cover all of Chicago, with data given for each of 75 community areas (statistical
divisions within the city).

Disadvantages of this type of design are also obvious. The chief one is that the researchers
are not free to design the best possible measures of population density and its effects but are
limited solely to the data contained in the *Fact Book*. Further disadvantages are that the data
are old, relate to only one point in time (although some of the statistics, such as the data on
juvenile delinquency, cover a period of time), and the researchers have no direct control over
the study. Rather than being on the scene, able to manipulate density, the Galle team simply
studied things that had already happened. In addition, Galle et al. did not have data recorded
for each individual but had only summary data, such as the number of juvenile delinquents for
each 100 males in the community area.

The *Fact Book* lists the number of residents per acre, and this was used as the measure of
population density. The hypothesis was tested not by actually controlling and changing density
as Griffit and Veitch did but by observing whether areas that had higher density also had
higher levels of harmful effects. The effects of density that Galle et al. tried to measure are
modeled after the effects found by Calhoun. They are: (1) a measure of mortality (standard
mortality rate); (2) a measure of fertility (general fertility rate); (3) a measure of ineffectual
care of the young (percent of persons under 18 who were recipients of public assistance in May
1962); (4) a measure of asocial, aggressive behavior (percent of males aged 12–16 in 1960
who were brought before the family court during the period 1958–1961; in other words, the
juvenile delinquency rate); and (5) a measure of psychiatric disorders (the number of admis-

sions to mental hospitals per 100,000 persons). Obviously the Galle study is attempting to measure different negative effects from those in the Griffit study.

Stage 3: Gathering the Data

The persons in the sample in the Griffit study were randomly assigned to one of eight experimental conditions formed by varying density and heat. All subjects were dressed alike and were told that the experiment was intended to investigate "judgmental processes under altered environmental conditions" (Griffit and Veitch 1971, p. 94). While in the chamber, each group was given a number of pencil and paper tests in addition to the Interpersonal Judgment Scale. The subjects were asked to rate their attraction to a hypothetical stranger. Half of the subjects were told that the stranger agreed with their answers to 25 percent of a 24-item questionnaire they had filled out; the other half were told that the stranger agreed with them 75 percent of the time.

In the Galle study data had already been collected. The researchers could not collect exactly the data they needed but had to use what was available in the *Fact Book*.

Stage 4: Coding and Analyzing the Data

Griffit and Veitch used answers to two items on the Interpersonal Judgment Scale (subjects' probable liking of the stranger and desirability of a stranger as a working partner) to obtain a measure of attraction toward the stranger. This measure yielded scores ranging from 2 (low attraction) to 14 (high attraction). The results were computed for strangers with 75 percent and 25 percent similarity to the subjects' answers for both high and low density. As expected, subjects showed more attraction to strangers more similar to themselves, regardless of density. But the most important finding was that subjects in the high-density group showed a lower attraction level to strangers in 75 percent agreement with them than did subjects in the low-density group. Similarly, for strangers with 25 percent similarity there was lower attraction (more dislike) in the high-density group than in the low-density group. This supports the hypothesis that high density increases the tendency of people to dislike one another.

Data analysis was more complicated in the Galle study, not only because more variables were involved but also because there were many confounding factors that might affect the relationship between density and pathology, thus making it difficult to ascertain whether density really caused pathology. This problem was less acute in the Griffit study because the experimental environment was strictly controlled, and in the Calhoun study because rats were being studied. While rat societies do not exhibit much social structure, human societies do, and social-structural variables such as occupation, education, income, and ethnicity can affect the relationship between density and pathology. Thus if Galle et al. find differences among the various community areas in rates of juvenile delinquency and admission to mental hospitals, it is not clear that these differences are due to different levels of density. They might be due to differences in social class or ethnicity. Without including social class and ethnicity in the analysis, Galle et al. found an apparent relationship between density measured as number of persons per acre and the pathology measures. However, when social class and ethnicity measures were included in the analysis, the relationship between density and the pathologies disappeared. Thus the researchers concluded that density does not cause pathology, but that differences in *both* density and pathologies are caused by differences in social class (it is well known, for example, that poor people live in more crowded areas and also have higher juvenile delinquency rates).

Stage 5: Interpreting the Results and Testing the Hypothesis

Griffit and Veitch found evidence to support their hypothesis that increasing the level of population density increases the level of aggression. The next step is to replicate the study, perhaps with a large sample, to make sure that their finding was not a fluke. The study could also be redone with some changes. The Galle study would indicate that class should be controlled for. A sample of persons other than students could be used to see if this would affect the results. Further, Griffit and Veitch tested males and females separately; studying a sample composed of both females and males might affect the results. Freedman (1971) found results different for mixed-sex groups than for single-sex groups in his density research.

Evidence in the Galle study seems to indicate that density does not cause pathology but that both density level and pathology level vary with social class. If the researchers still feel that density causes pathology, they need to revise the study. This is exactly what happened. They left the hypothesis unchanged but changed the measure of density (stage 2) and redid the study. They decided that persons per acre was too crude a measure of density, so they created four separate measures of density: (1) number of persons per room; (2) number of rooms per housing unit: (3) number of housing units per structure; and (4) number of structures per acre. They then redid the study and found that when density is measured by persons per room there *is* a relationship between density and pathology, and the hypothesis is supported.

Discussion of these two studies has shown how interesting and challenging social research can be, and what wide differences exist in social research. However, these studies also show how difficult social research can be. We have seen some of the main reasons for this difficulty; the need to collect a lot of data from a lot of people; the difficulty of collecting data over a long period of time; the difficulty of controlling extraneous factors that contaminate the hypothesis test; and the researcher's ethical obligation to avoid doing anything that might harm his or her subjects in any way, physically or emotionally.

Summary

Chapter 1 discussed social science as science and provided an overview of the social research project. Although social research is often difficult, it can be fun. A major difficulty in conducting social research is that we often must study social behavior in its natural surroundings, where there are many extraneous factors that are difficult to control. For example, although it would be easier to study a youth gang in a laboratory setting, placing the gang in such an artificial environment would alter the very behavior we wished to study.

Although each research project is unique in some ways, all projects involve the same basic stages. These are: choosing the problem; formulating the research design; gathering the data;

coding and analyzing the data; and interpreting the results. Each of these stages is dependent upon the others, and the total research process is quite circular. If the hypothesis is rejected, the researcher must revise the study and begin again. Even if the hypothesis is not rejected, the researcher often wishes to replicate or repeat the study, to make sure the findings are accurate.

This chapter used population density research as an example to illustrate the various stages in social research. Two quite different density studies, one laboratory and one nonlaboratory, were presented to show the range of alternative approaches to similar research problems.

LIVERPOOL
JOHN MOORES UNIVERSITY
I.M. MARSH LIBRARY
BARKHILL ROAD
LIVERPOOL L17 6BD
TEL. 0151 231 5216/5299

LIVERPOOL
JOHN MOORES UNIVERSITY
I.M. MARSH LIBRARY
BARKHILL ROAD
LIVERPOOL L17 6BD
TEL. 0151 231 5216/5299

CHAPTER 2

CHOOSING THE RESEARCH PROBLEM

STUDENTS OFTEN WISH to conduct a research project that is new, different, and vitally important. This is an admirable goal, of course, but it often leads to the choice of an exotic project for which data sources and references are limited. It should be clear from chapter 1 that replicating research or reworking an old project with a new twist can be very important. It also should be clear that research projects are not selected in a vacuum but that the researcher is stimulated by the ideas and the research of others. Efforts to come up with creative ideas in isolation often lead to feelings that one has lost creative powers. However, if the researcher starts by reading other studies in his or her area of interest, he or she can often see new things that need to be done to improve the research or for new applications for old research.

Factors Affecting Problem Selection

Several factors influence the ultimate selection of the problem for study. These factors are all defined in this chapter. They include (1) the sociological paradigm (a model or school of thought with which the researcher identifies; there are a number of distinct paradigms within social science, and most of these differ in values, methodology, degree of reactivity involved, scope, and time); (2) the researcher's values (values affect not only the problem deemed worthy of research but also the method considered appropriate and the way the researcher views the relationship between him- or herself and his or her subjects); (3) the degree of reactivity inherent in the particular method deemed appropriate for gathering data on the research problem that is chosen (by reactivity we mean that the study can affect the data, as when the group being observed acts one way in the presence of an observer and differently when the observer is not present); (4) the researcher's methodology, including the degree of proof he or she requires in order to consider the hypothesis proven (e.g., some researchers require a correlation coefficient of a certain level of statistical significance, while others are content with a statement of behavior as observed and recorded in field notes); (5) the unit of analysis chosen (e.g., whether the unit of analysis is small, such as an individual person, or large, such as a country); and (6) the time factor (whether the study deals with a cross-section of the population at one point in time or is a longitudinal study conducted over time). In addition to discussing these factors, we will also distinguish between pure and applied research and will provide examples of several areas of research interest in sociology.

Although we will not discuss data-gathering methods in this chapter, the reader should not be left with the mistaken impression that choice of a research problem and of the method of researching that problem are independent, uncorrelated decisions. The same considerations that lead a researcher to choose a certain problem for study often also lead him or her to choose one method of data collection over others. Further, some methods are simply inappropriate for researching certain problems. For example, a researcher whose goal is to understand the day-to-day life of a juvenile gang member would find participant observation to be superior to the survey, while someone interested in predicting voting behavior in a national election would find the survey the preferred method.

Examples of Current Research

Social researchers often choose problem areas that they feel are of particular relevance for their own lives. Thus researchers who are members of minority groups often study race relations, and female researchers in large numbers are turning to the study of sex roles and women in the labor force.

Many interesting theories are contending for imaginative testing in the various specialties. Most of these studies have practical applications as well as being contributions to the theoretical literature. In my view some of the most interesting, in addition to the density and social pathology relationship discussed in chapter 1, are (1) the theory of status inconsistency; (2) the theory of women's fear of success; (3) the labeling theory of deviancy; (4) the theory of middleman minorities; (5) the study by Mazur and his colleagues (1980) of the physiological effects of eye contact; (6) the work by Harris (1986) on the effects of human culture on adaptation to life in space; and in the 1990s (7) the Soviet transition from socialism to capitalism.

Briefly put, the theory of status inconsistency states that each person holds a number of different statuses or positions in society, most of which are consistent with each other. For example, in terms of income status, occupational status, and educational status, a consistent person would be at about the same level in all three (e.g., high education, prestigious occupation, and high income; or low education, unskilled job, and low income). This consistency occurs because there is obviously a correlation among these statuses, inasmuch as high education is generally required for a prestigious, well-paying job. But occasionally status inconsistency occurs. For example, the person might have a rather high education but a low income (teachers, bank clerks, secretaries, librarians) or a low education but high income. The theory of status inconsistency hypothesizes that a person with status inconsistency, particularly one with high education and low occupation and low income, will receive psychological pressure from friends and relatives who feel that he or she should "do better" economically, given his or her high level of education. Such psychological stress is hypothesized to be the cause of all sorts of conduct from political behavior such as voting liberal (Lenski 1954) to prejudice (Treiman and Hodge 1966). Some of the latest inconsistency research has focused upon inconsistencies among the status characteristics of people working together on tasks (Berger et al. 1992).

The theory of women's fear of success stems largely from the work of Matina Horner (1969), drawing on the earlier work of McClelland (1953). McClelland found in studies on males that the need to achieve (symbolized by "N Ach") was very strong. Success was welcomed, but failure aroused fear and tension. Horner, in a series of interesting studies, replicated McClelland's studies on women and concluded that women not only feared failure, as men did, but also feared success. She theorized that this might be due to women's early childhood socialization, which teaches them that to be aggressive and competitive is "un-ladylike" and that they should be subordinate to men.

The labeling theory of deviancy says that to a certain extent deviancy or mental illness may result from an individual's being defined and labeled as deviant or mentally ill by society, and subsequently acting accordingly. That is, the individual accepts society's label and acts as society expects him or her to act (see Becker 1963).

The theory of middleman minorities (Blalock 1967, pp. 79–84) asserts that certain minorities (e.g., Jews in Europe, Armenians in Turkey) are forced into middle positions in the social structure, where they concentrate in middle-income positions such as trade and commerce and play the role of middleman between producer and consumer and between the elite and the masses (Bonacich 1973).

Another interesting area for study is the relationship between social interaction and physiology.

Mazur et al. (1980) studied the degree to which eye contact had physiological effects on persons. Their experimental work resulted in quite reliable findings. For example, they found that when a person stares, his or her pulse rate consistently drops during the first 10 seconds of the stare. This is true whether the person is staring at another person or at an inanimate object.

A largely unprobed frontier for social science research was opened up in the late 1980s by thoughts of human colonies in space. Harris (1986) presented a pioneer study of the salient sociological factors that will have to be considered if human families are to live safely on space stations. Among the factors he studied in his analysis of "the new space culture" are values and norms; beliefs, customs, and traditions; dress and appearance; communication and language; and time and time consciousness.

In the 1990s a phenomenon that is of great interest to both scholars and laypersons alike is the dissolution of the Soviet Union, and the transition in Eastern Europe from state socialism toward capitalism. Burawoy and Krotov (1992) use a case study of the Soviet wood industry to argue that the transition from socialism to capitalism revolves around two crucial features: anarchy in production and bargaining in external relations.

These studies represent only a few of the major areas of social research. Common specialties within sociology include the study of formal organizations, work, occupations, stratification, the family, juvenile delinquency, crime, deviance, social change, small groups, mass communication, sociology of law, demography (population), and race relations. There are numerous other areas of research within sociology as well as in other social sciences.

Applied Versus Pure Research

Applied Research

Research can be roughly classified as applied or pure. Pure research (sometimes called "basic" research) involves developing and testing theories and hypotheses that are intellectually interesting to the investigator and might thus have some social application in the future, but have no application to social problems in the present time. Applied research covers a wide range of social science areas, including education, busing to achieve racial integration, drug addiction and use, alcoholism, crime and delinquency, women in the labor force, and problems of the aged. Applied research also deals with problems only partially in the area of social science, including the energy crisis and air, water, and noise pollution.

Applied research often entails large-scale studies with subsequent data-collection problems. Such studies are expensive and often cannot be conducted without support from some funding agency such as the federal government or a charitable foundation. Thus selection of a problem is limited to those areas that the granting agencies are willing to fund. Agencies often publish lists of projects they are interested in funding. For example, the Center for Population Research of the National Institute of Child Health and Human Development (which is in the U.S. Department of Health and Human Services) circulated in 1971 a list of projects for which it was interested in providing research grant money. The list, which is quite general and extensive, includes a wide range of areas, such as: "Antecedents and consequences of abortion and sterilization," "Medical and psychological effects of family planning and contraception," "Social, psychological, and economic factors causing variation in sexual behavior, attitudes, and norms," "Role of family and other institutions in rearing children," and "Effects of selected legislation (e.g., tax or housing legislation) on population phenomena." Thus any researcher with the training and facilities to carry out such research has his or her research problem virtually chosen. All he or she need do is write an explicit research proposal that details the hypotheses, the sample, the method by which data will be gathered and analyzed, and the cost of each facet of the study. The granting agency will upon request send the researcher an application form and detailed instructions on filing a proposal.

The main criticism of such lists of research topics and notices of available money is that they often attract researchers whose main interests and skills lie elsewhere, and who do not have the necessary commitment or experience to do the research, but are motivated by the money. An idealistic demographer who conducts his or her research solely because he or she feels the work is worthwhile and for the good of society may understandably react negatively toward some newly self-styled "expert" in demography who had no interest in the field until the research money in his or her area of interest dried up. The research conducted by such newcomers may be excellent, but this does not satisfy researchers who were committed to the field long before the money was available.

Probably the strictest from of applied research funding is the research contract, a form used increasingly by U.S. government funding agencies. In a contract, in contrast to a grant, the investigator makes a binding legal agreement with the funding agency to perform a certain study, with a certain sample size, for a certain amount of money, and by a certain deadline. In such an arrangement the application of findings is given first priority, although this does not mean that the researcher cannot be intellectually motivated or that his or her findings cannot be theoretically important.

The researcher working under a research grant has much more leeway than one operating in accordance with a contract. To secure a grant, he or she must also write a proposal telling the purpose of the study, the sample, the data-collection and analysis methods, the cost, and so on. However, grants usually give the researcher more freedom to pursue his or her intellectual interests and to test hypotheses that have theoretical importance but few practical applications.

Pure Research

Pure research deals with questions that are intellectually challenging to the researcher but may or may not have practical applications at the present time or in the future. Thus such work often involves testing hypotheses containing very abstract and specialized concepts. A person wishing to do pure research in any specialized area of social science generally must have studied the concepts and assumptions of that specialization enough to know what has been done and what remains to be done. Most pure research cannot be done in isolation but must be conducted within a unifying conceptual framework so that it can build upon past research in the area.

Pure and Applied Research

Although it is customary to distinguish between pure and applied research in both the physical and social sciences, these two categories are not mutually exclusive in the sense that any study that is pure cannot have practical applications (and vice versa). Some researchers feel that the ultimate goal is a study that is helpful in solving social problems and at the same time makes a valuable contribution to the theoretical social-science literature. For example, suppose that a governmental agency contracts with a social demographer to conduct research on fertility control. The agency may not know or care about demographic theory but may be interested solely in whether or not the results of the study can be applied so as actually to limit population growth in the country. But even though the agency is interested solely in practical applications (and the policy implications of such application), the demographer's colleagues might view the study results as being of great theoretical importance and might be much less interested in any practical applications.

The fact that governments and laypersons tend to give a higher priority to social applications than to abstract theory, while social scientists often give priority to a "contribution to knowledge" and feel that applications are of secondary importance, can lead to criticism of the scientists if laypersons fail to see the theoretical importance of a study. It is a favorite game of politicians and others these days to read the titles of studies funded by the U.S. government and ridicule the studies as a waste of the taxpayers' money. The same study that seems unimportant to such a critic may seem of utmost importance to a scientist who views it not in terms of its potential applications but as a needed theoretical breakthrough.

Research Paradigms

In addition to the number of different areas of interest from which one can choose a research problem, there are distinct paradigms that coexist within the same area of specialization. *Webster's New World Dictionary* (1968, p. 1060) defines a paradigm as "a pattern, example, or model." As the term is used in social science, a paradigm is a perspective or frame of reference for viewing the social world, consisting of a set of concepts and assumptions.

The concept of a paradigm is an old one in social research, but it received new emphasis through the publication of Thomas Kuhn's *The Structure of Scientific Revolutions* (1962). This book has been the inspiration for a number of analyses of social science in terms of paradigms, notably Friedrichs's *A Sociology of Sociology* (1970) and Ritzer's *Sociology: A Multiple Paradigm Science* (1975).

A paradigm is the mental window through which the researcher views the world. Generally, what he or she sees in the social world is what is objectively out there, as interpreted by his or her paradigm of concepts, categories, assumptions, and biases. Thus two researchers describing the same thing from two different paradigms may produce considerably different accounts. For example, if a house is built at the halfway point of a hill and I am standing at the top of the hill and you are standing at the bottom, I will describe the house as being halfway down the hill and you will describe it as being halfway up the hill. Both descriptions are accurate in terms of where each of us stands, because we have different vantage points or paradigms from which to observe the same phenomenon. Further examples of two distinct paradigms for viewing the same phenomenon are the Malthusian paradigm and the Marxian paradigm. The phenomenon viewed is the same for each paradigm—the overpopulation problem. However, the perspectives from which this question is viewed are quite different.

Malthus said that population growth on a generational basis was geometric (e.g., 1, 2, 4, 8, 16, 32 . . .), while the food supply could grow only at an arithmetic rate (e.g., 1, 2, 3, 4, 5,

6 . . .). Thus if population growth remained unchecked, starvation was inevitable. Malthus called this the natural law of population growth and said that this law would hold regardless of the political system of the country. Malthus, a minister, flatly rejected birth control as a means of population limitation as immoral. Thus the real hope of limiting population was for each individual to exercise moral restraint, to refrain from sex (especially premarital and extramarital), and to delay marriage. He opposed socialism and welfare programs, because he felt that individualism must be promoted to avoid overpopulation, and he feared that welfare and socialism would destroy the individual's initiative.

In contrast, Marx said that there was no natural law of population but that each form of control of production had its own law of population. Overpopulation was caused by capitalism, which needed a surplus labor supply to exploit. The Marxist position was that overpopulation would disappear with a transition from capitalism to socialism.

Thus these two schools of thought, Malthusian and Marxist, look at the same phenomenon (population) from greatly different paradigms or perspectives and arrive at different conclusions. To this day there is no agreement between the two paradigms with regard to population, and the issue has never been definitely settled.

Each paradigm has its own set of concepts or jargon. The Malthusian paradigm uses such concepts as arithmetic rate, geometric rate, positive check, preventive check, vice, and misery. The Marxist paradigm uses such concepts as class, class consciousness, means of production, surplus labor, exploitation, and the dialectic.

Paradigms differ not only in concepts and assumptions but also in the research problems they consider important. For example, in the Malthusian paradigm overpopulation is a central problem, perhaps the most important one the world faces. Malthus felt that poverty was due to overpopulation (e.g., as in India) and was not a function of politics, class conflict, or means of production. To Marxists, however, the central problem is the class struggle and exploitation of the lower classes by those in control of the means of production. Overpopulation is a false problem—an epiphenomenon or function of the real problem, capitalism. In the Marxian view, when the real problem is solved by eliminating capitalism and replacing it with socialism, the overpopulation problem will disappear.

There are a number of competing paradigms within social science today, especially within sociology. I think that this is a healthy phenomenon, since no single paradigm will suffice to solve all of the problems of social science. Further, Kuhn (1962) said that scientists typically work within the reigning paradigm, accumulating findings within this perspective until the paradigm's limit is reached. At this point anomalies, or findings that cannot be adequately explained within the reigning paradigm, appear. If there are enough anomalies or paradoxes, the paradigm may be overthrown in favor of a newer one. However, the older adherents of the old paradigm often do not readily abandon it. Instead, the old paradigm simply ceases to win new adherents as younger scientists flock to the new paradigm. Thus as long as the old scientists are active, multiple paradigms exist simultaneously.

But although competition between paradigms may be healthy and may stimulate research, problems arise when proponents of different paradigms are unable to communicate effectively with each other or when each group insists that only its view is correct. Paradigms offer a splendid opportunity for people to talk past each other, even about the most obvious things. For example, in the uphill/downhill example, adherents of competing paradigms might insist that the others were wrong simply because they started from such different reference points that they were unable to ascertain that they were talking about the same thing.

Further, division of a discipline into a number of distinct paradigms makes the accumulation of research findings difficult, for there is no common language for discussing research findings. In this book we will be concerned with research paradigms such as ethnography, experimental research, survey research, etc. (all discussed below). For discussion of substantive paradigms in social sciences, refer to Ritzer (1975), Friedrichs (1970), and Ritzer (1990).

Values

Paradigms differ in terms of assumptions and values. By values we simply mean conceptions of the desirable and undesirable (Wilson 1971, p. 672). Values certainly exist in both the Malthusian and the Marxist paradigms, although they may be hidden or "latent," and even the authors themselves may not be aware of all their own values. Malthus's values are a combination of conservative Protestantism, with its emphasis on independence, hard work, and the view that birth control and sex are largely immoral and logico-positivistic science, with its view that social problems can be objectively and rationally explored and dealt with scientifically. The Marxist paradigm embodies the feeling that capitalism is evil, exploits the masses, and harms the many to help the few, and that capitalistic countries should become socialistic.

Thus both the Malthusian and the Marxist paradigms include not only assumptions about the way things are in the empirical world but also value judgments or statements about the way things *should be*. Examples of such value judgments are that people *should not* use birth control, or that capitalism is bad and should be abolished. Virtually all people have many such values, some that they are aware of and some that they are unaware of, and they make many value judgments every day. There is nothing wrong with having values and making value judgments. The main problem with value judgements in social research is that they are essentially untestable. For example, the value judgment that persons should not use birth control is an opinion, not a testable statement. No study can be designed to test such an opinion. We can test many statements about birth control, such as whether the extent of birth-control usage is correlated with social class or whether a particular birth-control usage is morally wrong. All we can do is argue with Malthus—perhaps that birth control is "unnatural," as Malthus thinks, and so immoral in that sense, but that failure to use it will result in mass starvation and death, which is even more immoral (Thou shall not kill). But even if we win the argument, we have not gained new knowledge that can be accumulated into a body of knowledge.

Another problem with strongly held values is that they are not only untestable but may so prejudice a researcher that he or she loses all semblance of objectivity. For example, if one believes strongly, as Malthus did, that birth control is undesirable, one will probably be unimpressed with research findings showing that birth control is an important factor in controlling overpopulation and will try to minimize their importance.

The chief thing to remember about values and value judgments is that all researchers have them and that they are different for different paradigms. Since researchers espousing different paradigms will have different values, they will choose different problems to research and will interpret the findings differently. Since values are not amenable to testing and since they are possible sources of bias, or at least of failure to communicate, what should be done about values? There are at least two alternatives. We may attempt to suppress values and conduct "value-free research." Proponents of this position say that a researcher is perfectly free to express his or her political and moral values at home with his or her family, but when at work he or she should leave these values behind. Proponents of the other position say that it is impossible to suppress one's values and that it is better for a researcher to state his or her values explicitly and use them in conjunction with facts rather than deny that he or she has a value position, only to have the values enter unconsciously, in a somewhat covert and perhaps dishonest manner.

Value-free Sociology

The first possibility mentioned above is for the researcher to display "ethical neutrality," to attempt to be purely objective in his or her research regardless of personal feelings. Weber (1949) suggested that this could be accomplished if a researcher took care to separate his or her everyday life, with the particular set of values he or she displays every day, from his or her professional role as social scientist in which he or she tries to refrain from making value judgments.

This is the tactic that has been predominant so far in the development of sociology, especially among the more "scientific" researchers who have identified more closely with the physical sciences. For example, Bierstedt says:

> Sociology is a *categorical,* not a *normative,* discipline; that is, it confines itself to statements about what is, not what should or ought to be. As a science, sociology is necessarily silent about questions of value; it cannot decide the directions in which society ought to go, and it makes no recommendations on matters of social policy. This is not to say that sociological knowledge is useless for purposes of social and political judgment, but only that sociology cannot itself deal with problems of good and evil, right and wrong, better or worse, or any others that concern human values. . . . It is this canon that distinguishes sociology, as a science, from social and political philosophy and from ethics and religion (Bierstedt 1957, p. 11).

It is clear that Bierstedt advocates physical science as a model for sociology, because of its several principles of objectivity and ethical neutrality. He defines these principals as follows:

> *Objectivity* means that the conclusions arrived at as the result of inquiry and investigation are independent of the race, color, creed, occupation, nationality, religion, moral preferences, and political predispositions of the investigator. If his research is truly objective, it is independent of any subjective elements, any personal desires, that he may have. This kind of objectivity is difficult to achieve, because factors of many varieties distort the process of inquiry (Bierstedt 1957, p. 17).

> *Ethical neutrality* . . . means that the scientist, in his professional capacity, does not take sides on issues of moral or ethical significance. . . . The scientist, *as such,* has no ethical, religious, political, literary, philosophical, moral, or marital preferences. That he has these preferences as a citizen makes it all the more important that he dispense with them as a scientist. As a scientist he is interested not in what is right or wrong or good or evil, but only in what is true or false (Bierstedt 1957, p. 10).

Bierstedt further remarks that sociology is solely a pure science, not an applied science, and that social work is the applied science facet of sociology (1957, p. 12).

The Myth of Value-free Sociology

That a social researcher can and must suppress his values and conduct value-free social research is probably the prevailing view in social research today. This view was championed in Lundberg's (1947) classic *Can Science Save Us?* Certainly most statisticians and researchers who utilize quantitative methods adhere more or less to the value-free perspective.

However, an increasing number of social scientists, including adherents from several methodological paradigms, reject (or at least question) the notion that it is possible or even desirable to separate values from either the selection of the research problem or the application of findings. These persons tend to advocate use of qualitative rather than quantitative methods and to reject the physical-science model of research. Rather than label themselves scientific, they would be more likely to drop the terms "humanistic," "qualitative," or "radical."

The best statement of this position is Gouldner's (1962) article, "Anti-Minotaur: The Myth of a Value-free Sociology." Gouldner feels that strict adherence to the value-free position tends to ignore the distinction between good and evil potentials always present in science. He says: "Before Hiroshima, physicists also talked of a value-free science; they, too, vowed to make no value judgments. Today, many of them are not so sure." Gouldner suggests that a teacher should state his or her personal values as honestly as he or she can lest these values be introduced in a covert or disguised fashion, perhaps without the teacher's awareness. Gouldner also notes that the value-free position can cause researchers to avoid researching social problems that are of vital importance to society but controversial, so as to render them difficult to study without some explicit moral commitment.

The obvious problem with attempting to make one's own values explicit and use them in research is that the researcher may not be able to recognize and control all of his or her own values. Another problem is that some adherents of this position (chiefly Marxists or "radical sociologists") can use it as an excuse to introduce Marxist politics into the classroom, with the rationale that since there is no such thing as a value-free statement, they cannot be prohibited from making political statements in the course of their teaching and research. Recent work on the value-free issue has noted, among other things, the difficulty in maintaining a value-free position and the shifts that some social scientists make in their thinking regarding this issue (for example, from early adherence to a value-free position to later cynicism regarding the feasibility of a truly value-free position in social science). For more discussion of this matter see Lloyd (1983) and Garfinkel (1981, pp. 140–41).

Postmodernism and Value-full Sociology

The 1980s and 1990s have seen the maturation of postmodernism. This approach is prevalent not only in social science but in art, music, literature, and other areas as well. Many postmodern scholars are highly critical of positivism and of science in general. Not only do they often reject its emphasis on causality and its claim of objectivity, but they also critique what they see as its dominance by Europeans and elite white males, characterizing it thus as an "Euro-centered white-male-dominated, elitist approach." Writing as a postmodernist, Young (1993) advocates scholarship that is "value-full" rather than "value free". The value-full approach views scholarship as not only value-laden but also inherently political. Thus, according to this position, a researcher can never be value free but in reality is always representing some political position, be it overt or covert. For one example of the value-full position, see chapter 17 on inclusive methods. While still using the language of positivism (as does Young, 1993, with his use of chaos theory), chapter 17 takes a postmodern stance in the sense that it examines the degree to which much contemporary social science research represents the interests of white males of European heritage, while relatively neglecting the interests of females, non-Europeans, and others. Chapter 17 is new for the fourth edition of this volume and represents currents that will continue to be prominent in social science throughout the 1990s and beyond.

For a clearer definition of value-full research, we can quote Young, who says:

> If modern science and its claims of objectivity are insupportable, the task of postmodern sociologists is to frame a sociology that is value-full. By value-full, I simply mean that the researcher acknowledges the value agenda from which concepts are selected and research is done. We may not share the same set of values in every scientific enterprise; indeed, it would be most surprising were that the case. However, in the postmodern epoch, science and the knowledge process writ large must face up to its partisan and its creative nature (Young, 1993, p. 3).

A related postmodern idea is the notion of deconstruction. Deconstruction is the dismantling of the dominant, white, European-centered perspective. For further discussion of this view, and reactions to it, see Chapter 17.

Effects of Values in Social Research

I adopt a moderate position on the value-free sociology controversy, which recognizes in summary:

1. Different paradigms representing different sets of values and beliefs (whether overt or covert) exist in social science.
2. Two or more different paradigms will have compatible beliefs and values with regard to certain research topics but incompatible beliefs and values for other potential research areas.
3. In those areas in which beliefs are incompatible, there may be violent disagreement between paradigms concerning suitability of the topic for study, appropriate hypothesis, and interpretation of the findings.

We can illustrate briefly the effects of different value systems on such research tasks as choosing the area of study, formulating the hypothesis, and interpreting the results. Consider the sensitive topic of whether racial differences in intelligence exist. The democratic principle that all men and women are created equal leads to the hypothesis that there are no racially based differences in intelligence. Yet many people in our society contend that some races are intellectually inferior to others. Social scientists are by and large politically liberal and thus eager to study the matter in order to prove that there are not racial differences in intelligence. Curiously, social scientists who are committed to the ideal of objectivity must admit the possibility that racial differences may exist. However, they also wish to study this problem to add to general social knowledge.

Thus persons from most value systems may agree that research on racial differences in intelligence is a worthwhile topic and yet disagree violently on the correct hypothesis. Bierstedt's scientific position, with its emphasis on ethical neutrality and value-free objectivity, would lead to the hypothesis that various racial groups may display differing levels of intelligence. Persons who do not believe in the possibility of a value-free sociology and who feel that attempts to attribute lower intelligence to racial minorities, even in scientific studies, are no more than thinly disguised racism, would hypothesize that no racial differences in intelligence exist.

When it comes time to interpret findings, differences between value systems may again become apparent. For example, suppose that a (purely hypothetical) study reveals that black persons with lighter skin color achieve higher educational levels than black persons with darker skin. One who believes that racial differences in intelligence do not exist will say that the lighter person was less discriminated against by whites, and that this relative lack of prejudice enabled him or her to achieve more than his or her darker fellows. However, one who believes that blacks are intellectually inferior to whites will find it equally obvious that the lighter person's greater achievement is due not to relative lack of prejudice but rather to a greater amount of "white blood."

A number of researchers who have conducted studies dealing with racial differences have encountered pressure from critics who refused to accept their findings. For example, Arthur R. Jensen, who claims that his research shows lower IQ levels for blacks than for whites, has been barred from speaking on some college campuses. For an introduction to his controversial research see Jensen (1969).

Values and Perception

Even objective findings may be criticized by people who find them morally reprehensible. And many findings are *not* objectively neutral. Further, one's perception of evidence may depend upon one's values, beliefs, and past experiences. As McCain and Segal (1969, p. 70) put it: "There is a major difference between saying that someone sees a phenomenon and then interprets it and saying that someone sees interpreted phenomena. The latter view seems correct." These authors say that rather than first observing a phenomenon (step 1) and then interpreting it (step 2), we actually interpret as we observe.

In figure 2–1 (McCain and Segal 1969, p. 71), for example, you probably see only a set of dark objects. If you concentrate on the unenclosed areas, however, you can see the word "THE." After you once see this word you will probably find it difficult ever to see the figure as containing merely blank objects. Thus in the view of McCain and Segal such representations are not objective in the sense that all observers will see them the same way. On the contrary, there is a real chance that observers with different value sets or different past experiences will see an ostensibly "objective" figure differently. That is, persons who have seen the figure before will always see "THE," while persons who have not seen the figure before will almost surely see only a group of blank objects.

Figure 2–1

Illustration of Effect of Values and Experiences on Perception

SOURCE: From *The Game of Science,* by G. McCain and E. M. Segal. Copyright © 1969 by Wadsworth, Inc. Reprinted by permission of the publisher, Brooks/Cole Publishing Company, Monterey, California.

All of this does not mean that there is no ground on which followers of different paradigms can agree as to the interpretation of particular research results, but it does mean that findings that "obviously" mean one thing to you may "obviously" mean something entirely different to a researcher with a different paradigm. It can also mean that a social phenomenon that is "obviously" important to one researcher is "obviously" unimportant and not worthy of study to another.

Reactivity

Another issue on which social paradigms differ is reactivity. A reactive research technique is one whose application causes a reaction on the part of the persons being studied in such a way that the data are affected. A reactive technique can change the very social situation that the researcher wishes to study. The reactive effect of research on the social phenomena being studied is often known as the "Hawthorne effect," deriving its name from the study of the Hawthorne Plant of the Western Electric Company in Chicago in which reactive effect was found (see Roethlisberger and Dickson 1959). The investigators were interested in the effects of various factors such as rest periods, quitting time, and hot lunches on work performance among female employees whose task was assembling telephone relays. They found that output increased when rest periods were eliminated and later quitting times were instituted. The investigators were at first at a loss to explain what caused this higher productivity. They finally decided that it was a reactive effect. That is, the workers' morale was increased by having attention paid to them and their suggestions sought in solving plant problems (such as increasing productivity). This attention from the researchers altered the very behavior (worker productivity) that the researchers wished to study.

The reactivity problem exists in other fields (and perhaps in all fields), but it is acute in social research. If persons know that they are being observed by a social researcher, they often will feel self-conscious and alter their behavior (either consciously or unconsciously). Thus, ironically, the normal behavior that the researcher wishes to observe will not occur merely because of his or her presence. Also, survey researchers often find that their questions are reactive in that they may stimulate a person to think about a topic that he or she has not previously considered, thus causing him or her to form an opinion where none existed; or the questions may lead a respondent to answer the way he or she feels the researcher wished him or her to answer, or to state an opinion when none exists, simply to please the researcher.

Unlike physical scientists, who study nonhuman and often inanimate objects, social scientists study humans and are often members of the very groups that they are studying. Social interaction with their respondents accounts for much of the reactivity in social research. In contrast, the physical scientist testing minerals for hardness may affect them in the sense that he or she may leave scratches or marks on them, but their degree of hardness will not be altered through research manipulations, and thus the behavior being studied will not be affected.

The fact that he or she is a member of the society he or she is studying poses additional problems for the social scientist. Being a member of the group being studied can affect one's own values, biasing one's interpretation of the data in favor of the group members. However, membership in the group being studied can also have advantages. Some researchers feel that only by thinking exactly as a group member thinks can one ever really understand social phenomena. According to this view, to understand a particular ethnic group one must live as a group member, speak the group's language, and learn the group's norms, values, and customs. This is the prevailing premise underlying the observational, or ethnographic, paradigm, which is discussed in detail in chapter 10.

Methodology Versus Method

The fact that the physical scientist is generally not a participant in the phenomenon he or she is studying while the social scientist is leads many researchers to question whether social science can ever be conducted in the same way as physical science. The controversy over the differences between the physical sciences and the social sciences centers around *methodology,* not around *method.* By "method" we simply mean the research technique or tool used to gather data. There is no doubt that different tools are used in the physical sciences than in the social sciences—physicists do not use public opinion polls and sociologists do not use electron microscopes. However, it is also true that tools differ widely within the physical sciences and within the social sciences. Furthermore, some of the differences in method between the physical and social sciences are differences of degree rather than of kind. For example, whether the researcher uses a radiotelescope, an electron microscope, a bathysphere, a one-way mirror, or participant observation, he is using the same technique—observation.

By "methodology" we mean the philosophy of the research process. This includes the assumptions and values that serve as a rationale for research and the standards or criteria the researcher uses for interpreting data and reaching conclusions. A researcher's methodology determines such factors as how he or she writes hypotheses and what level of evidence is necessary to make the decision whether or not to reject a hypothesis. The methodology of the physical sciences is currently somewhat more rigorous and elegant than the methodology of the social sciences, but this may not always be the case. Specifically, physical scientists are much more likely than social scientists to state the relationships between variables in exact terms, usually in the form of mathematical equations. The social scientist is often satisfied to be able to prove the existence of a relationship between two variables, while saying nothing about the nature of the relationship.

Further, the fact that the physical scientist's methodology results in formulations that are more quantitative and precise than the results of the sociologist's methodology does not necessarily mean that the former's explanation is superior. In fact, some sociologists feel that quantitative explanations are artificial and tend to dehumanize, or at least oversimplify, social phenomena. These researchers feel that the more emotional kind of understanding that can be gained through interaction with the subject or through sharing his or her experiences may yield more satisfactory explanations than the more logically precise explanations that may be achieved through mathematical modeling.

Such sympathetic or vicarious understanding, if not a substitute for logical explanation, may be a supplement to it. Weber labeled such use of "sympathetic empathy" as "the method of *Verstehen.*" As Martindale says:

> To the degree that behavior is rational (in a logical or scientific sense, according to logical or scientific standards), it is understandable directly without further ado. Beyond this, empathic understanding . . . is of great assistance in explaining conduct. One does not have to have been Caesar to understand Caesar (Martindale 1960, p. 385).

The question of whether social science methodology will ever duplicate physical science methodology is a philosophical issue that we need not attempt to resolve here, and is probably unimportant. The main point is that there is a wide range of alternative methodologies, or approaches and criteria for understanding social phenomena, in social science. These range from qualitative to quantitative. Some researchers will first choose a research problem and then decide that one methodological perspective is superior to others for studying it. Other researchers may be intellectually committed to a particular methodological perspective and will choose a research problem suited to that perspective.

The Unit of Analysis

Social research also varies by the unit of analysis. Both the personality theorist and the learning theorist, for example, use the same level of analysis or unit of analysis—i.e., an individual person. Different characteristics of the person are studied, in one case his or her personality development and in another case his or her learning ability, but in each case the units from which the study sample is drawn consist of a population of persons.

However, in a social science that deals with groups as well as individuals, social research can vary not only in terms of subject matter but also in terms of the unit of analysis. For example, many social researchers study death or mortality, but these studies may differ greatly in terms of the scope or size of the units being compared. Thus Glaser and Strauss (1963;1967) take the individual as the unit of analysis. Using a sample of terminally ill individuals, they study the adjustment to death of each individual. Other researchers interested in the same characteristic (death) compare death rates from various countries. For example, they might hypothesize that a country's mortality rate, as measured by the number of deaths per 1,000 persons per year, is inversely related to the country's degree of urbanization. In this case the unit of analysis for which comparisons are made is not an individual person but an entire country.

We call large-scale studies *macro* research. Any study that compares large geographical areas or large aggregates of persons such as continents, countries, states, counties, or census tracts is obviously macro. Studies with an individual person as the unit of analysis are called *micro* research. Generally one would refer to small group studies involving two, three, or four persons as micro, but there is no consensus on the borderline between micro and macro. It is probably not necessary to set an exact dividing line. What is important is that a researcher attempting to choose a suitable research project make a decision concerning the unit of analysis of the project, and thus realize the range of units of analysis that exists in social research.

A related notion is the scope of the study. Scope refers to the breadth of concrete instances to which a theory applies. For example, consider studies in which the unit of analysis is the individual. If the study cannot be generalized beyond the specific data being gathered (e.g., a class in a university), then the scope of the study is small. However, if it is thought that the results found for the particular sample of individuals studied can be generalized to a much larger group of individuals (even the entire world population, for example), then the scope of the study is large.

Cross-sectional Versus Longitudinal Studies

Studies also differ in the way they deal with time, a distinction often made between cross-sectional studies and longitudinal studies. A cross-sectional study is one that studies a cross-section of the population at a single point in time. By a "cross- section" we mean a broad sampling of persons of different ages, different educational and income levels, different races, different religions, and so on. In contrast, a longitudinal study involves data gathered over an extended period of time, generally several weeks or months but often several years. Because of the difficulty and expense of encompassing different points in time, longitudinal studies generally cannot use as broad a cross-section but must settle for studying fewer respondents. If the same respondents are studied over time the study is called a panel study. If different respondents are studied and compared at different points in time the study is sometimes called a trend study. Longitudinal studies may also use data gathered by different researchers at different points in time.

Survey studies are studies that ask a sample of respondents questions (often about opinions but commonly about factual matters as well). Such surveys generally either interview respondents in the field, mail questionnaires to the respondents' households, or pass out questionnaires to a group such as a class. Most survey studies are in theory cross-sectional, even though in practice it may take several weeks or months for interviewing to be completed. The epitome of the cross-sectional study is the census, in which (at least theoretically) every household in the United States is interviewed on the same day. The basic advantages of a cross-sectional study are that data can be gathered from a large number of people and these data are comparable since they are not affected by changes over time. For example, if one wished to discover whether people thought the Secret Service was doing an adequate job of protecting the president, he or she would not want to survey part of the sample before an assassination attempt and part following such an attempt but would wish to question everyone at the same time.

The advantage of a longitudinal study is that changes over time can be studied. Anyone wishing to examine attitudinal changes, for example, will have to use a longitudinal study. For example, if you wished to study changes in American attitudes toward abortion during the period 1980–2000, your study would be longitudinal. There are two chief ways that longitudinal studies may be designed: as *panel* studies, and as *trend* studies. A panel study uses the same sample of individuals, and follows them throughout the study. In contrast, a trend study would sample different individuals in each time period, although they would be similar to the individuals studied at the other time periods. Each time period studied in either a panel or trend study is called a *wave*.

To illustrate the difference between a panel and a trend study, let us be more specific about the abortion study. A panel study of abortion attitudes for the period 1980–2000 could begin with a panel of 100 Americans aged 20 in 1980, and use three waves or sampling times of 1980, 1990, and 2000. The individuals studied would be aged 20 in 1980 (the first wave), aged 30 in 1990 (the second wave), and aged 40 in 2000 (the third wave). In contrast, the trend study would also begin with 100 Americans aged 20 in 1980, and also use three waves (1980, 1990, and 2000). However, instead of the same individuals each time, it would sample one group of 100 Americans aged 20 in 1980, another 100 aged 20 in 1990, and another group aged 20 in 2000. Thus, you can see that while both designs reveal changes in attitudes, they do so for different groups. The panel design shows how attitudes toward abortion change as people age through their life span (ages 20–40), while the trend study reveals changing trends in twenty-year-old Americans' attitudes towards abortion in the period 1980–2000.

By now the readers should have some idea of the paradigm with which he or she identifies (ethnography, statistical, and so on) and consequently the type of research project he or she is interested in pursuing. In other words, we take as given that researchers have certain values that predispose them to a particular paradigm more than to others, and that this in turn largely determines their particular research interests. Some common sociological paradigms are classified in table 2–1, showing some of the principal concepts, assumptions, levels of analysis (micro or macro), types of data collection, and types of data analysis most frequently employed. Table 2–1 is not exhaustive or definitive, and there may be some overlap in the paradigms listed. However, it does serve to demonstrate that there are many different approaches to social research.

Summary

Chapter 2 discussed selection of the social research problem. There are several factors affecting problem selection, including the research paradigm a researcher identifies with, the researcher's values, the researcher's methodology, the unit of analysis chosen, and whether the study is to be conducted over time or at a single point in time. A number of examples of current social research were discussed, including research on status inconsistency, women's fear of success, labeling theory of deviance, and the theory of middleman minorities.

The difference between pure and applied research was explained, and these two types of research were discussed. This was followed by a discussion of social research paradigms. The Malthusian and Marxian paradigms were presented as examples of social research paradigms. The discussion of paradigms was followed by a discussion of the role of values in social research, specifically the "value-free sociology" controversy. Some researchers feel that an

Table 2–1

Some Common Social Research Paradigms

Paradigm	Unit of Analysis	Data-Collection Method Used	Data-Analysis Technique
"Scientific" or statistical	Usually micro, but may be macro	Survey	Statistical
Social psychology and small-group research	Micro	Usually laboratory experiment or observation	Statistical
Ethnography	From micro to macro (e.g., collective behavior)	Observation and field notes	Verbal or qualitative analysis of field notes
Ethnomethodology	Micro	Observation and tape recording	Verbal analysis of field tapes and notes

investigator's values should be held in abeyance so that the research will not be biased. Others feel that it is not only unnecessary but in fact impossible to keep one's values out of one's research. The latest developments in this area are the rise of postmodernism and the attendant notion of value-full sociology, in which values are explicitly acknowledged and utilized. The notion of reactivity, or the idea that the conduct of research can affect the very data one is attempting to study, was also discussed. The remainder of the chapter was devoted to discussion of various methodological approaches, differences in scope among research projects, and different ways that time is dealt with.

CHAPTER 3

CONSTRUCTING SOCIAL EXPLANATIONS

AFTER THE RESEARCH PROBLEM has been chosen, the next task is to formulate a specific research question or hypothesis. Let us begin our discussion of this problem by distinguishing between descriptive studies, which tell only *what* happened, and explanatory studies, which tell *why* or *how* it happened.

Descriptive Studies

Often the researcher will have no formal hypothesis. This is especially true in an exploratory study. For example, a researcher may be interested in studying a new group or social movement, such as the Jesus People, the Jewish Defense League, the Symbionese Liberation Army, or Scientology. Since the Jesus movement is a relatively recent phenomenon, the researcher probably knows very little about its members at the outset. Thus the researcher's first task is simply to learn more about the Jesus movement in general in order to answer the question, "What is happening?" To answer this question fully the researcher must gather information about specific groups in the movement (who is the leader, how does one become a member, how is discipline maintained, how is the group supported, what is the division of labor) and about individual members (age, gender, income of parents, geographical region of birth). Such explorations are often called *descriptive* studies because they attempt to describe phenomena in detail (to describe *what* happened), in contrast to *explanatory* studies, which generally attempt to explain a social phenomenon by specifying why or how it happened.

Explanatory Studies

Explanation

Many studies go beyond mere description and seek to explain a phenomenon. For example, an explanatory study of the Jesus movement would seek to discover the causes of the movement and why converts are attracted to it. There is consensus that the goal of social research is to increase our understanding of society. However, what is meant by the term "understand" is less clear. How can we judge whether we understand or not? One basic form of explanation is to answer *why* and *how* questions such as "Why does racism exist?" or "How do social movements begin?"

Prediction

In addition to explanation, a related (some say a higher) goal is prediction. The precise nature of the relationship between explanation and prediction has been a subject of debate among philosophers of science. One view is that explanation and prediction are basically the same phenomenon except that prediction precedes the event while explanation takes place after the event has occurred. Another view is that explanation and prediction are fundamentally different processes. We need not be concerned with this debate here but can simply state that in addition to being able to explain an event after it has occurred, we would also like to be able to predict when the event will occur. Further, we would like to control its occurrence. This is

40

sometimes feasible in a laboratory but often very difficult in the street. That is, if we can establish that heat and crowding occurring simultaneously are sufficient to cause rioting, we may be able to predict when riots will occur (or at least pinpoint areas that are susceptible to rioting). However, since we cannot control the climate, our ability to control rioting will depend upon our ability to control crowding.

Theory

Explanations and predictions are provided by theories. Theories attempt to answer the why and how questions. *Theorizing* can be defined as the process of providing explanations and predictions of social phenomena, generally by relating the subject of interest (e.g., riots) to some other phenomena (e.g., heat and crowding). Often, but not always, our theories can be stated in causal terms (crowded ghettos cause riots; broken homes cause juvenile delinquency).

There are a number of different conceptions of theory. The sociological classics (e.g., the nineteenth-century writings of Emile Durkheim, Karl Marx, and Max Weber) are often called theory, as are sets of untestable statements. The term as used in everyday conversation has two basic meanings. One usage defines theory as a possible but untested explanation (as in "I don't know exactly what happened but I've got a theory"). This is basically the sense in which social scientists use the term, except that they apply it to concepts that, although untested, are potentially testable. The other lay definition of theory is an impractical notion, as in "Theoretically speaking, it is possible, but practically speaking it is impossible." We will not use this connotation in social research.

Theory, as we will use the term here, is first an attempt to explain a particular phenomenon. A statement that does not seek to explain or predict anything is not a theory. Second, the theory must be testable, at least ultimately. That is, a group of statements that cannot be tested at present simply because a test would be prohibitively expensive is nevertheless a theory inasmuch as it is inherently testable, while a statement that is true by definition, inherently self-contradictory, or too vague to be understandable is not an adequate theory.

The basic components of theory are concepts and variables, which are related in statements generally known as propositions. As we shall see, a proposition may be an axiom, a postulate, a theorem, an empirical generalization, or a hypothesis. Sets of propositions in turn may be interrelated to form theories, although some theories consist of a single proposition.

Concepts and Variables

Explanatory statements vary greatly in scope and complexity, but all explanatory statements contain concepts and variables. Concepts are simply mental images or perceptions. Concepts may be impossible to observe directly, such as justice or love, or they may have referents that are readily observable, such as a tree or a table. Very often concepts are dichotomous, meaning that they have only two possible values. A familiar example is gender (male/female).

On the other hand, many concepts contain several categories, values, or subconcepts, often falling along a recognizable dimension or continuum. The concept of age, for example, is a continuum containing many different values or categories, such as one year old, ten years old, and so on. Similarly, population density (as discussed in chapter 1) can vary from one person per square mile to many persons per square mile. Concepts (such as age or density) that can take on more than one value along a continuum are called *variables*. A concept that has only a single, never changing value is called a *constant*. Usually the values or categories of a variable are designated quantitatively (that is, signified by numbers, as in the case of age), but some variables have categories designated by word labels rather than by numbers. For example, gender is a variable, with the categories designated by the labels male and female.

Propositions Defined

After the basic concepts are formulated, the next step in theory construction is to write one or more propositions. Generically a proposition is simply a statement about one or more concepts or variables. A proposition that discusses a single variable is called *univariate*. A *bivariate* proposition is one that relates two variables, while a proposition relating more than two variables is called *multivariate*. As an example of a univariate proposition we could state that "45 percent of college students in the United States have used marijuana at least once." A bivariate hypothesis could be: "The higher the density level in a city, the higher the crime rate in that city." A multivariate hypothesis is "The higher the density, the higher the rates of illiteracy and drug addiction."

Multivariate propositions can usually be written as two or more bivariate propositions. This is recommended, especially for inexperienced researchers, as multivariate propositions can be treacherous to work with. For example, in the multivariate proposition above, if density were found to be related to illiteracy but not to drug addiction, would you reject the entire proposition? It would be better to write two propositions: (1) the higher the density, the higher the illiteracy; and (2) the higher the density, the higher the drug addiction. Then, if the data warrant it, one portion of the original hypothesis can be rejected without rejecting the other portion. Most propositions encountered in the social research literature will be bivariate.

Relationships Between Variables

When we say that the variables X and Y are related, we mean simply that they vary together, so that a change in X is accompanied by a change in Y and vice versa. Such variation is often referred to as *concomitant variation* or *correlation*. For example, if we find that as density increases crime rate also increases, we can say that the variables of density and crime are related, or correlated. However, if we find that as density increases there is no recognizable pattern of change in crime, we conclude that density and crime are uncorrelated.

Types of Propositions

Just as concepts are the building blocks of propositions, propositions are the building blocks of theories. As such they have been given different names depending upon their theoretical uses. Subtypes of propositions include hypotheses, empirical generalizations, axioms, postulates, and theorems.

Hypotheses

There are two basic types of propositions that are often used alone rather than in combination with other propositions. These are hypotheses and empirical generalizations. A *hypothesis* is a proposition that is stated in testable form and predicts a particular relationship between two (or more) variables. In other words, if we think that a relationship exists, we first state it as a hypothesis and then test the hypothesis in the field.

Webster's (1968) defines hypothesis as "a tentative assumption made in order to draw out and test its logical or empirical consequences. . . . Hypothesis implies insufficiency of presently attainable evidence and therefore a tentative explanation." Our definition is only slightly different. A hypothesis, as we will use the term, is a tentative explanation for which the evidence necessary for testing is at least potentially available. By *test* we mean either to confirm it to our satisfaction or to prove it wrong. What type of statement fits this definition? First, it must be a statement of fact susceptible to empirical investigation—that is, some statement that we can prove right or wrong through research. This definition excludes all statements that are merely opinions, value judgments, or normative. For example, the statement that every person should attend religious worship services at least once a week is a normative statement. It is a statement of what ought to be, not a factual statement that can be shown through investigation to be right or wrong. The statement that 50 percent or more of the residents of Los Angeles attend worship services at least once a week is a statement of purported fact and can therefore be tested.

A hypothesis is clearly not a statement of wishful thinking or of value (however, it is certainly true, as shown in chapter 2, that the researcher's value may affect his or her choice of hypotheses). The hypothesis is merely a statement, as yet tentative and unproved, of what the researcher thinks the facts are. For the statement to be proved it must be tested; to be tested it must be stated as precisely as possible. Consider, for example, a possible relationship between intelligence and happiness. The simplest question we can ask is, "Is there a relationship between intelligence and happiness?" The simplest answer to this question is "Yes, there is a relationship."

If we assume that some relationship does exist between the two variables, then we can speculate about its form. Such a speculative statement, which is often merely a hunch or an educated guess, is our hypothesis. For example, after hearing many stories about unhappy geniuses, we might speculate that "The more intelligent one is, the more unhappy he or she is." Assuming that intelligence and happiness can be measured satisfactorily, this statement is an adequate hypothesis.

Derivation of Hypotheses.   The inspiration for hypotheses comes form a number of sources. Very often investigators see evidence in their daily lives or in the course of social research indicating that certain phenomena are correlated. The suspected correlation leads the investigator to hypothesize a relationship and to conduct a study to see if his or her suspicions are confirmed. In addition, hypotheses are often inspired by past research or by commonly held lay beliefs. For example, a number of studies have shown that college freshmen are more politically conservative than college seniors, suggesting a correlation between year in school and political belief. Such a hypothesis could be used either to replicate past studies or to extend the test of a familiar hypothesis to a sample of persons with different characteristics (e.g., college students in another country). Alternatively, the researcher might revise the hypothesis or hypothesize that the alleged correlation does not exist for a certain population.

Examples of commonly held lay beliefs that might inspire testable hypotheses are the contentions that fat people are happy, that there is a thin line between genius and insanity, that married people without children are not fulfilled, and that being an only child is detrimental to the child. Although social scientists are often accused of belaboring the obvious, social researchers who test a hypothesis based on "what everybody knows is true" often find that it is not true after all.

Hypotheses may also be generated through direct analysis of data in the field or may be deduced from a formal theory. Three distinct approaches to hypothesis generation and verification are discussed later in this chapter.

Writing a Testable Hypothesis.   The statement that a hypothesis must be testable requires clarification. Consider the contention that geniuses are often unhappy. We might call this purported relationship a proposition (the generic term for statements of relationship) but we would not call it a testable hypothesis until the concepts of intelligence and happiness are adequately measured or defined on an empirical level. The proposition as it now stands is simply too vague to be testable. Bear in mind that when we require a hypothesis to be testable we mean that analysis of data should (at least ideally) clearly either support or refute the hypothesis. Often propositions are so vague, with concepts so poorly defined, that it is difficult to tell whether or not the data support the hypothesis sufficiently. The researcher who conducted the study may argue that the data prove the hypothesis, but critics will not agree. This is one argument in favor of quantitative measurement in variables, for quantification often eliminates vagueness. For example, although the relationship between intelligence and unhappiness as stated above cannot be tested because the meaning of genius and unhappiness is debatable, if we can construct an IQ test to measure intelligence and a comparable scale to measure happiness, then we can state, "The higher the score on the IQ test, the lower the score on the happiness test." This is a testable hypothesis.

Another common error in writing hypotheses is to make the hypothesis "double barreled," or containing two hypotheses in one. The main problem with this is again testability; one of the hypotheses may be rejected and the other not rejected. We presented an example of this in our discussion of multivariate relationships, when we said that density should not be related to both illiteracy and drug addiction in the same proposition, as evidence might show density to be related to one of these variables but not the other. If both hypotheses are combined, interpretation is difficult.

Empirical Generalizations

In contrast to a hypothesis, an *empirical generalization* is a relationship that represents an exercise in induction. Rather than hypothesizing that a relationship exists and then testing this hypothesis, an empirical generalization is a statement of relationship that is constructed by first observing the existence of a relationship (in one or a few instances) and then generalizing to say that the observed relationship holds in all cases (or most cases).

As an example, consider the relationship between population density and crime rate. On the basis of past experience, observation, and reading we may make the educated guess that as the density of a neighborhood rises, its crime rate will rise. This statement is a hypothesis. However, it is too ambiguous and unspecific to be testable. We need to state the ways density and crime rate should be measured, and we should also indicate where the hypothesis holds (e.g., the United States, the world).

Perhaps we may not feel capable of constructing even a tentative hypothesis and may not wish to specify anything about the relationship between density and crime rate prior to field study. In this instance we may choose either to go into the field or to use published statistical data in order to observe what relation, if any, exists between density and crime rate. We may find that as density increases, so does crime rate. If we observe this consistently enough for a large enough number of cases, we may feel justified in generalizing from our study to the entire country or even to the world.

Components of Axiomatic Theory: Postulates, Axioms, Theorems

Although single propositions such as hypotheses or empirical generalizations can certainly be called theoretical statements or minitheories, many researchers reserve the term "theory" for a set of two or more interrelated propositions (Zetterberg 1965). The most common form of such a set of interrelated propositions is the *axiomatic theory*. The axiomatic or deductive theory takes the basic form of the deductive syllogism.

PROPOSITION 1: If A then B.
PROPOSITION 2: If B then C.
Therefore:
PROPOSITION 3: If A then C.

In such a theory, if propositions 1 and 2 are true statements, it follows by deduction that proposition 3 is also true. Such true statements from which other statements are deducted are called *axioms* or *postulates*. Thus propositions 1 and 2 are axioms or postulates. The two terms are used almost interchangeably, the chief difference being that the term "axiom" has a mathematical connotation and is used more often for statements that are true by definition and for propositions involving highly abstract concepts. The term "postulate" is more often used for statements whose truth has been demonstrated empirically. Since all the information in proposition 3 can be deduced from propositions 1 and 2, proposition 3 need not be stated in the main body of the theory. A proposition that can be deduced from a set of postulates is called a *theorem*.

Since postulates are considered to be true, there is little reason to treat them as testable hypotheses. However, often one will wish to write the deduced proposition (the theorem) as a hypothesis and test it, as this is often the only means of testing the entire theory.

We will discuss axiomatic theories in more detail in chapter 20. Our goal here is merely to introduce the notion of a proposition and to show the different types of propositions, as summarized in table 3–1.

Bivariate Relationships

Properties of bivariate relationship include whether the relationship is positive or negative, the strength of the relationship, whether it is symmetrical or asymmetrical, which variable is the

Table 3–1

Types of Proposition

Name of Proposition	How Generated	Directly Testable or Not
Hypothesis	Either deduced or data-generated	Yes
Empirical generalization	Data-generated	Yes
Axiom	True by definition	No
Postulate	Assumed to be true	No
Theorem	Deduced from axioms or postulates	Yes

independent variable and which is the dependent (asymmetrical relationships only), whether the relationship is linear or curvilinear, and whether the relationship is spurious or involves an intervening variable.

Positive Versus Negative Relationships

If an increase in the value of one variable is accompanied by an increase in the value of the second variable, the relationship is called *positive*. Similarly, if a decrease in one variable is accompanied by a decrease in the other variable, the relationship is called positive or direct. That is, a positive relationship is one in which both variables vary in the same direction. However, if increase in one variable is accompanied by decrease in the other variable, the relationship is called *negative* or *inverse*. For example, if an increase in one's educational level is accompanied by an increase in income, the relationship is positive. If an increase in educational level is accompanied by a decrease in the level of ethnic prejudice, the relationship is inverse.

The fact that we can call a relationship negative does not mean that the variables are less strongly related than the variables in a positive relationship but merely that they vary in opposite directions. The minus sign shows the direction of the relationship, not its strength.

Strength of the Relationship

After we have established that two variables are indeed related, the next question is how strongly they are related. We said above that if two variables X and Y are related, a change in X is accompanied by a change in Y, and vice versa. The concept of strength of relationship is clearer if we speak in terms of prediction rather than concomitant change between the two variables. If variables A and B are related, then not only do they change in value together but, by knowing the value of one variable, we are able to make a more accurate prediction of the value of the other variable. If the two are unrelated, knowing the value of one (e.g., variable A)

does not aid our prediction of the value of variable *B*. For example, if density and crime rate are related, then if we know the value of density in a neighborhood we can accurately predict its crime rate. The average prediction is usually correct more than zero but less than 100 percent of the time—unfortunately, generally closer to the former than to the latter. The degree to which a prediction is correct (out of 100 predictions) is called the *strength* of a relationship.

A common statistic for measuring the strength of a relationship is called the *correlation coefficient* or, more formally, Pearson's Product Moment Correlation Coefficient (see Blalock 1972). Symbolized by the letter *r,* the coefficient varies between − 1.00 and + 1.00, with 0.00 signifying no relationship, or zero percent accuracy in prediction; +1.00 meaning 100 percent accuracy in predicting a positive relationship between the two variables; and −1.00 meaning 100 percent accuracy in predicting a negative relationship between the variables.

Symmetrical Versus Asymmetrical Relationships

We have so far been discussing only symmetrical relationships in which change in either variable is accompanied by change in the other variable. In an asymmetrical relationship, change in variable *A* is accompanied by change in variable *B,* but not vice versa. For example, we would assume that a relationship between smoking and lung cancer would be asymmetrical because smoking could cause lung cancer, but lung cancer could not cause smoking.

Independent and Dependent Variables

In an asymmetrical relationship, the variable capable of effecting change in the other variable is called the *independent variable.* The variable whose value is dependent upon the other but which cannot itself affect the other is called the *dependent variable.* In a causal relationship, the cause is the independent variable and the effect is the dependent variable. For example, if we hypothesize that smoking causes lung cancer, smoking is the independent variable and cancer the dependent variable.

It is common in the statistical literature to equate symmetrical relationships with explanation and asymmetrical relationships with prediction. That is, an exploratory step in research is first to identify all variables that are correlated, or symmetrically related to each other. Since weak relationships provide no basis for prediction, it does not make much sense to try to predict unless rather strong correlations can be noted. Once correlations are found, one can use an asymmetrical coefficient such as a regression coefficient to predict the value of one variable from the value of another variable. These procedures are discussed in detail in chapter 16.

Distinguishing Independent from Dependent Variables

Generally the dependent variable is the variable we wish to explain and the independent variable is the hypothesized explanation. However, there may be times, particularly when we are reading an account of someone else's study, when we are not sure which variable is dependent and which is independent.

Often we can recognize one variable as independent simply because it occurs before the other variable. For example, we may find a relationship between region of birth and level of education attained. In this case region of birth clearly comes before schooling and must be the independent variable. The relationship is obviously asymmetrical; educational level can in no way influence region of birth, since birth has already occurred. Similarly, if we use a parent's educational level to predict the child's educational level, the former would clearly be the independent variable and the latter the dependent variable.

In relationships in which one variable does not clearly precede the other, it may be difficult to designate the dependent and independent variables. For example, there may be a relationship between the level of racial group esteem and self-esteem. If a person holds his or her racial group in high regard he or she may hold himself or herself in high regard or vice versa. The question, which develops first, perception of group esteem or perception of self-esteem? Perhaps each influences the other. In this case we have little alternative but to label the relationship symmetrical and consider the question of which variable is independent and which dependent to be moot.

Causal Relationships

The discovery that there is a relationship between two or more variables does not ensure that the relationship is a causal one, that is, that change in one variable causes change in another variable. The concept of causality has long been studied by philosophers and, at least since the time of Hume, has been quite controversial. The concept of causality is interesting. It is not strictly a logical concept but instead applies to a relationship between concrete or empirical events (by "empirical" we mean those phenomena that can be directly gauged by our senses such as sight, touch, or smell). Ironically, though, while the concept applies to empirical phenomena, it is very difficult to "prove" the existence of causality. As Hume argued, we can observe one billiard ball hitting a second, and the second ball falling into the pocket, but cannot "prove" that the first ball "caused" the second to fall into the pocket. Rather, we can only observe the sequence of events.

In spite of this continuing debate, the concept of causation is so strongly ingrained in both science and our everyday thinking that it is doubtful that we could ever expunge it completely even if we wanted to. Thus, it seems best to work with the concept of causality, but to be very careful about how cause is defined and about what means are used to attempt to demonstrate its existence. We say that X causes Y if:

1. There is a relationship between X and Y.
2. The relationship is asymmetrical so that change in X results in change in Y but not vice versa.
3. A change in X results in a change in Y regardless of the actions of other factors.

Generally it is said that the change in the cause (X) must occur before the change in the effect (Y), although some definitions allow for the possibility that the cause and effect occur simultaneously. However, no definition of cause allows for the effect to precede the cause. Thus, the temporal sequence is often one major way that we may determine which factor is the cause and which is the effect. (That is, the one that occurs first is the cause and the one that occurs second is the effect.) Also, it is possible to define cause for symmetrical relationships. This is a case of so-called mutual causation, in which X causes Y and simultaneously Y and X, so that each factor is both a cause and effect. In most cases, however, the causal relationship is asymmetrical, with the cause preceding the effect in time. For example, let us assume that there may be a causal relationship between cigarette smoking and lung cancer and that this is an asymmetrical relationship with the cause preceding the effect in time. Thus, smoking (X) at one point in time causes cancer (Y) at some later point in time, but not vice versa (having cancer does not cause smoking).

It is often useful to talk of causality in terms of necessary and sufficient conditions. We can say that the cause X is *necessary* for the existence of the effect Y if Y never occurs unless X occurs (or has already occurred in the past). We can say that X is *sufficient* for the existence of Y if Y occurs every time that X occurs.

To complicate the matter further, there are three combinations of necessity and sufficiency. One combination is when X is a necessary but *not* sufficient condition for the existence of Y. In this case, X must occur before Y can occur, but X alone is not enough to cause the occurrence of Y. Rather, there must be some other factor that occurs in addition to X before Y can occur. As an example, assume that research shows that only persons who smoke will get lung cancer; persons who do not smoke will never get it. This shows that smoking (X) is necessary for lung cancer (Y). But assume that further research indicates that not all smokers will contract the disease. Actually, only those smokers who also live in a smog-filled area (Z) will get cancer. Thus, smoking (X) is only a partial cause of cancer (Y). It cannot cause cancer by itself, but in combination with smog, which is also a necessary but not sufficient cause, it can lead to cancer. Together, the combined factors of smoking (X) and smog (Z) are sufficient to cause cancer, but each alone is not sufficient even though it is necessary.

A factor can also be a sufficient but *not* necessary condition. For example, now let us change our example and assume that smoking (X) is sufficient to cause cancer by itself every time it exists, and need not be combined with other factors such as smog. Assume further that smog (Z) is also sufficient to cause cancer by itself. However, neither factor is itself necessary for cancer to occur. Smoking is not necessary because cancer can occur without it (if smog is present), and smog is not necessary because cancer can occur without it if smoking is present. However, one of these two must be present. In the case of sufficient but not necessary conditions we can say that X and Z are alternative causes of Y. They are not partial causes, as each is sufficient to cause Y by itself, but they are alternatives.

The third possibility is that the cause (X) is both necessary *and* sufficient simultaneously for the existence of the effect Y. This is the strongest or ideal form of causal relationship. In this case, Y will never exist unless X exists, and will always exist when X exists. There are no other alternative causes. X is the complete cause and the only cause. As an example, if smoking is both necessary and sufficient for cancer, then all smokers will get cancer, and no nonsmokers will ever get it. Since X is necessary there can be no alternative causes, and since X is also sufficient, it is the complete cause and not a partial cause. A necessary and sufficient relationship represents the purest case of causality. It is an instance of unicausality, because X is the only cause of Y, and Y will never occur without the occurrence of X.

In social science we often have a great deal of difficulty in establishing causality, for a number of reasons. One reason is that our theories may not be sufficient to isolate the proper causes. In such cases we may be attempting to prove that the wrong factors are the causes, a task obviously doomed to defeat. Even if our theory can isolate the correct cause or causes, it may be exceedingly difficult to demonstrate to our satisfaction that these variables really are the causes we seek. One problem is that often there are a large number, sometimes seemingly nearly an infinite number, of possible causes. This is one reason why our theories may not isolate the correct ones. Even if the correct causes are hypothesized, we often cannot demonstrate that they are indeed the causes, because we cannot properly control other variables that also might be causes or might be the source of extraneous variation which confounds the relationship we are seeking to establish. We cannot put a riot or a street gang into a laboratory, and this greatly hampers our efforts by lessening our degree of control. Further, since much of the data in social science are gathered via the survey, we often cannot observe which factor occurs first. Without knowledge of the temporal sequence we may not be able to tell which is the cause and which is the effect and may simply have to treat the relationship as though it were symmetrical, and not specify causality. The best method for attempting to demonstrate the existence of causality is the experiment. Experiments are discussed in detail in chapter 9.

Linear Versus Nonlinear (Curvilinear) Relationships

In a *linear* or straight-line relationship the two variables vary at the same rate regardless of whether the scores or values of the variables are low, high, or intermediate. In *nonlinear* or curvilinear relationships the rate at which one variable changes in value may be different for different values of the second variable.

Figure 3–1a depicts a linear relationship in which the rate of change of variable Y is the same regardless of the value of variable X. The rate of change is shown by the slope of the line. A steep slope shows a high rate of change; a less sharp angle indicates a slower rate of change. Figure 3–1b shows a curvilinear relationship in which Y varies much more slowly for high

Figure 3–1

Linear and Curvilinear Relationships

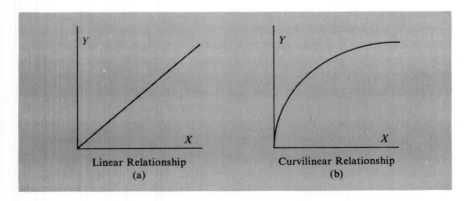

values of *X* than for low values of *X*. A possible example is the relationship between education and income. Up to a certain point, additional education has "marginal utility." To go to school forever would certainly not make one a millionaire. Curvilinear relationships need not take the form shown in figure 3–1b but may take any form except a straight line.

Spurious and Intervening Relationships

Occasionally one will find an apparent relationship between two variables, only to discover ultimately that the two variables are not really affecting each other at all. For example, if we study all the cities in the United States having a population of 300,000 or more, it is quite possible that we will find a correlation between number of animals in the city zoo and crime rate. Can we conclude from this relationship that elephants and tigers are a major cause of crime? The most realistic conclusion is that some third factor that we have not studied is responsible for *both* the size of the zoo and the crime rate, thus causing the two to vary together. It is possible that city size is highly correlated with both zoo size and crime rate and thus causes the two to appear to be correlated. A relationship in which two variables appear to be related only because both are caused by a third variable is called a *spurious relationship*.

Often an apparent relationship between two variables is caused by an *intervening variable*. That is, variables *A* and *B* may be highly correlated, but only because *A* causes a third variable, *C*, which in turn causes *B*. In this case *C* is called an intervening variable. Spurious and intervening relationships are diagrammed in figure 3–2. The variable at the foot of the arrow is the cause of the variable at the head of the arrow. Thus in figure 3–2a, *C* causes both *A* and *B*, while in figure 3–2b, *A* causes *C* which in turn causes *B*.

Suppressor and Distorter Variables

Rosenberg (1968) noted the possibility of a "spurious zero relationship" in which two variables that are actually related appear to be unrelated because each is correlated with a third

Figure 3–2
Spurious and Intervening Relationships

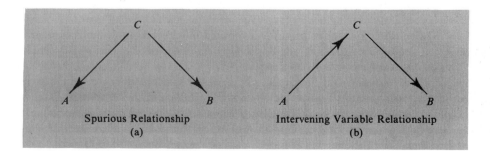

Spurious Relationship
(a)

Intervening Variable Relationship
(b)

variable (which Rosenberg refers to as a "suppressor" variable because it suppresses the relationship between the two other variables). The suppressor variable suppresses the relationship by being positively correlated with one of the variables in the relationship and negatively correlated with the other. The true relationship between the two variables will reappear when the suppressor variable is controlled for. We might hypothesize a positive relationship between level of education completed and income (the higher the education the higher the income), but conduct a study and find no relationship. We might find subsequently that a relationship exists but is being suppressed by the variable of age, which is inversely correlated with education among our sample (the higher the age the less the education) and positively correlated with income (the higher the age the higher the income). Thus a low age pulls education up but income down, while a high age pulls income up but education down, effectively canceling out the relationship between education and income unless age is controlled for. If education and income are studied for a single age group the relationship between them will reappear. The third variable may also be what Rosenberg calls a "distorter" variable, indicating that it distorts the relationship between two variables in some way. For further discussion of distorter variables see Rosenberg (1968).

In the study by Galle, Gove, and McPherson (1972), discussed in chapter 1, the authors investigated whether the apparent relationship between crowding (variable A) and pathology (B) might be spurious, with the variable of socioeconomic status (SES) (C) causing both pathology and density simultaneously. That is, they considered whether high SES areas exhibited low density and also low pathology while low SES areas had high density and high pathology. They also considered whether SES could be an intervening variable, with crowding not causing pathology directly but only causing SES, which in turn caused pathology. They decided that the relationship was spurious. In either case (either intervening or spurious), if the value of the third variable C is held constant, there will be no relationship between A and B. That is, if the relationship between crowding and pathology is due solely to the fact that changes in both variables are caused wholly by changes in SES, then for a given constant value of SES, no relationship between A and B will exist.

Alternate Strategies for Hypothesis Formulation and Verification

On first glance hypothesis construction and testing might seem to be a relatively simple and noncontroversial endeavor. Upon closer analysis we find that the task is not so simple and that researchers disagree upon the proper approach. The difficult thing about writing and testing hypotheses is that this process involves blending theory and data. While explanation is largely a mental or conceptual process, testing to determine whether the explanation is correct (to verify the theory) requires observation and analysis of data.

Following Blalock (1968), we will distinguish between the conceptual or theoretical level and the empirical or data level. By "empirical phenomena" we mean all phenomena that are directly amenable to detection and monitoring by such senses as observation, touch, hearing, and smell. The conceptual-empirical scheme includes the assumption that each social phenomenon being investigated occurs on each level. That is, the concept has an empirical counterpart, and the empirical phenomenon has a conceptual counterpart. For example, you can have a mental image of the color red on the conceptual level (which you can see in your "mind's eye") with your eyes closed, and you can actually observe its empirical counterpart with your eyes open. Similarly, you can define a crowd as a mental concept and you can also observe an actual crowd empirically.

However, some concepts may be so abstract that they are difficult to measure empirically. Consider such concepts as alienation, authoritarianism, intelligence, id, and ego. Since these concepts cannot be observed directly as a crowd can, how can one be sure that one's measure of the concept is error-free? The difficulty of this task has led to three basic approaches to hypothesis construction and testing: (1) the classical approach, (2) grounded theory, and (3) strict operationalism.

The Classical Approach

The *classical approach* consists of three distinct stages. Stage 1, which takes place entirely on the conceptual level, consists of defining the concepts and writing a proposition stating a relationship between them. Stage 2 bridges the gap between the conceptual and empirical levels. It consists of devising ways to measure the concepts empirically. This stage includes writing a testable hypothesis that links the empirical measures of the two concepts. The hypothesis of stage 2 is identical to the proposition of stage 1 except that stage 2 is on the empirical level (relates empirical measures) while stage 1 is on the conceptual level and cannot be tested as it contains no empirical measures. The third and final stage consists of gathering and analyzing data in an attempt to verify the hypothesis.

As an example, suppose that we are interested in the effects of intelligence and, having heard many stories about unhappy and maladjusted geniuses, write a proposition (stage 1 of the classical process) stating that the higher a person's intelligence, the less happy he or she will be. For the present we can accept the dictionary definition of both intelligence and happiness. However, we cannot yet attempt to verify this proposition as we have not yet measured the concepts on the empirical level. In stage 2 we specify a measure of intelligence (an intelligence test) and a measure of happiness (a happiness scale) and write a hypothesis linking these measures. Our hypothesis is that a person's score on the intelligence scale (IQ test) is inversely related to his score on the happiness scale (the higher the IQ the lower the happiness). Now we are ready to gather the data in the field to the test the hypothesis (stage 3).

The relationships between the conceptual and empirical levels are diagrammed in figure 3–3. The empirical measures of the theoretical concepts X and Y are designated by the symbols X' and Y' respectively. For example, X' is the empirical measure of concept X. That is, X is the concept of intelligence and X' is the IQ test that measures this concept. Empirical measures such as X' and Y' are variously called *indicators* of the concept, *measures, scales, indices* (or *indexes*), or *operational definitions,* depending upon their form and the context in which they are used. In figure 3–3 the *r*s signify relationships between concepts. On the conceptual level, r_1 represents the hypothesized causal relationship between intelligence and happiness. The primes simply indicate the empirical level. Thus, r'_1

Figure 3–3

The Classical Approach to Hypothesis Construction and Verification

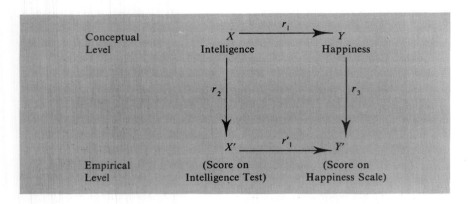

is the empirical-level counterpart of r_1. The value of r'_1 can be computed, but the value of r'_1 cannot be computed because it is on the conceptual level. However, r_1 is the same value as r_1 if X' and Y' are accurate measures of X and Y respectively. The relationship between X and X' is signified by r_2. The relationship between Y and Y' is signified by r_3. These relationships between the conceptual and empirical levels are generally called *epistemic relationships* or epistemic correlations. They cannot be measured directly but must be assumed.

The chief danger with the classical approach is that there is always a chance of measurement error. Measurement error exists if either r_2 or r_3 is less than perfect (that is, if either X' is a less than perfect measure of X or Y' is a less than perfect measure of Y).

In stage 3 we administer both the intelligence scale and the happiness scale to a sample of respondents and then analyze the data to determine whether the hypothesized relationship holds. We might verify the hypothesis on the first attempt. On the other hand, we might find that a relationship does exist and is in the hypothesized direction (inverse) but is very weak. We might also find no relationship or a positive relationship (the more intelligent one is, the happier he or she is). The last three findings all fail to verify the hypothesis developed in stage 2.

There are a number of possible reasons for failure to verify a hypothesis. The most obvious possibility is that the hypothesis as stated is simply incorrect. It is also possible that the proposition stated in stage 1 is correct but the hypothesis of stage 2 is incorrect, or that the measures are inadequate (measurement error). Another possibility is that the proposition, the hypothesis, and the measures are all adequate but that the sample on which the hypothesis was tested was inadequate.

The possibility that the hypothesis will not be verified as first stated but must be either revised or abandoned leads many investigators to state the hypothesis initially in a tentative form. A hypothesis that is designed to be revised if necessary on the basis of findings is called a *working hypothesis.*

Grounded Theory

Grounded theory is theory that is discovered or generated from data rather than being abstract and tentative. Grounded theory is developed by: (1) entering the fieldwork phase without a hypothesis; (2) describing what happens; and (3) formulating explanations as to why it happens on the basis of observation.

Glaser and Strauss (1967), in the most comprehensive explication of grounded theory available to date, say:

> Previous books on methods of social research have focused mainly on how to verify theories. This suggests an overemphasis in current sociology on the verification of theory, and a resultant de-emphasis on the prior step of discovering what concepts and hypotheses are relevant for the area that one wishes to research. Testing theory is, of course, also a basic task confronting sociology. We would all agree that in social research generating theory goes hand in hand with verifying it; but many sociologists have been diverted from this truism in their zeal to test either existing theories or a theory that they have barely started to generate (Glaser and Strauss 1967, pp. 1–2).

Most adherents of the grounded-theory approach utilize observation as their basic data-gathering method.

Glaser and Strauss say that to be optimally useful, theory should utilize concepts readily applicable to the data under study, and that the theory must be able to explain the behavior being studied. They feel that the best way to generate such theory is from the data themselves. They provide examples of the development of grounded theory from their studies of dying patients. Through systematic observation and study of the data they developed the category (variable) of social loss, which they define as the degree of loss the patient's death will represent to his family and employer (Glaser and Strauss 1967, p. 36). This is clearly an "emergent" variable in that it emerges from the data during the course of the study, and Glaser and Strauss say that they probably could not have anticipated it prior to study. One hypothesis that emerges from the data is: The higher the perception of a patient's social loss by hospital staff members, the better his or her care by these staff members.

Classical Versus Grounded-Theory Approach

Unlike the three stages used in the classical approach—(1) concept and proposition construction, (2) concept measurement and hypothesis construction, and (3) verification of the hypothesis—grounded theory essentially blends stages 2 and 3 into a single stage. The only variables and hypotheses utilized are those that emerge from the data. Thus, in a real sense, only those hypotheses that are verified are recognized, and verification as a separate step is unnecessary. Further, instead of proceeding from the conceptual level to the empirical level, as the classical approach does, grounded theory begins at the empirical level and ends at the conceptual level, because the only concepts used are those that are generated through analysis of empirical data.

The grounded-theory approach is diagrammed in figure 3–4. Notice that since all concepts are formed by direct observation of data, there should be no measurement error, or at least only

Figure 3–4

The Grounded-Theory Approach

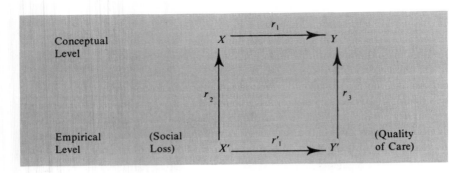

a minimal amount stemming from perceptual (observational) errors on the part of the researcher. However, this lack of measurement error may hold only for the specific time and place in which the study was done and may not be generalizable. If the researcher wishes to utilize a hypothesis developed from grounded theory in some new research setting, he or she may have to utilize a verification stage (stage 3 of the classical approach).

Operationalism

The term "operationalism" refers to operations carried out in the measurement of a concept. It was originally defined by P. W. Bridgman:

> In general, we mean by any concept nothing more than a set of operations; *the concept is synonymous with the corresponding set of operations.* If the concept is physical, as of length, the operations are actual physical operations, namely, those by which length is measured; or if the concept is mental, as of mathematical continuity, the operations are mental operations, namely, those by which we determine whether a given aggregate of magnitudes is continuous (Bridgman 1948, pp. 5–6).

Researchers who emphasize operationalism generally seek quantitative measures of their concepts. Those who take Bridgman literally are called physical or rigid operationalists (Sjoberg 1959, p. 606), and their approach may be called strict operationalism or extreme operationalism (Phillips 1971, p. 51). Perhaps the most famous strict operationalist in sociology was George A. Lundberg, whose *Foundations of Sociology* appeared in 1939. As Blalock puts it:

> Lundberg vigorously denied that certain kinds of variables are inherently unmeasurable or that one should be concerned with hypothetical entities or "common essences." Such a position, claimed Lundberg, is based on the erroneous assumption that "measurement is not a way of defining things, but is a process which can be carried out only after the 'thing' to be

measured has been defined" (Lundberg 1939, p. 68). If one is asked what is meant by the concept "intelligence," he should be told that intelligence is what an IQ test measures (Blalock 1968, pp. 7–8).

To a strict operationalist measurement error is not a major problem, simply because the concept is defined to be that which is measured. Strict operationalism is clearly a pragmatic approach. To a strict operationalist a concept that is not defined clearly enough to be measured is of little or no use in research, and a researcher should not waste time on it.

The strict operationalist approach to hypothesis construction is diagrammed in figure 3–5. While the grounded-theory approach merges stages 2 and 3 of the classical approach (hypothesis construction and verification), the operationalist approach merges stages 1 and 2 (the theoretical and empirical levels of proposition and hypothesis construction). Inasmuch as conceptual level exists at all, it is an outgrowth of the empirical level. Although the first two stages are merged in operationalism, the third state (verification) remains separate and is emphasized.

A Critique of Operationalism

It is all well and good to say that intelligence is what an IQ test measures, no more and no less. However, how do we know that our test is an IQ test and not a test of something else (for example, dexterity, authority, or test-taking ability)? Can we take any series of questions we choose, construct a test from them, and call it an IQ test? The answer is clearly no. If we ask such questions as "What is your favorite color?" "What is your favorite tree?" "What is your favorite fish?" we cannot presume that a certain set of answers shows higher intelligence than another set. If we had started with a completely blank or undefined concept of intelligence, perhaps we would be content to say that intelligence is what an intelligence test measures. However, we began with a rather precise definition of intelligence as the capacity to comprehend facts, so any test we construct to measure intelligence must appear, on the face of it, to

Figure 3–5
The Strict Operationalist Approach

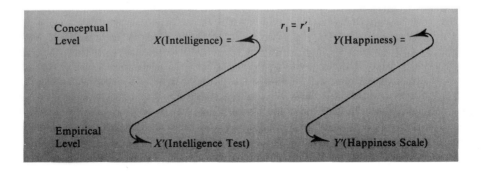

measure the capacity to comprehend facts. Questions about respondents' favorite colors will not even appear to measure ability to comprehend facts and so will not have *face validity*.

In an article criticizing the strict operational position, Adler (1947) discusses a new concept called C_N. The concept of C_N is operationally defined by the following questions:

1. How many hours did you sleep last night?
2. Estimate the length of your nose in inches and multiply by 2.
3. Estimate the number of glasses of ginger ale the inventor of this test drank while inventing it.

Now we know what C_N is: It is what the C_N test measures, no more and no less. The only question is, what good is C_N?

Classical, Grounded-Theory, and Operational Approaches Compared

The advantages of the classical approach are that (1) it is complete, includes all stages, and takes maximum advantage of both theorizing and data analysis; and (2) it can utilize abstract concepts that have generalizability and can make use of the power of deduction to generate concepts. The chief disadvantage of the classical approach is the opportunity for measurement error, which occurs if the measurement does not adequately represent the abstract concept. Some critics (particularly adherents of the grounded-theory approach) also see an overemphasis on deduction and verification as a weakness.

The chief advantages of the ground-theory approach is that the probability of measurement error is reduced, since concepts are mirror images of empirically observed data. Disadvantages are that the emphasis on empirically derived concepts makes it difficult to use abstract concepts and thus limits theorizing to a certain extent. Because deduction is eschewed in this approach, it forfeits all the advantages of deduction. In addition, the emphasis on empirical data in a specific location may make the findings difficult to generalize to another time or place.

The advantage of operationalism is that measurement error is absent (by definition). The disadvantage is that abstract concepts that cannot be operationally defined are not allowed. This may severely limit both theory development and the power to generalize.

Summary

Chapter 3 discussed social explanations, or the goals of social research. That is, what sort of knowledge are we seeking when we study a social phenomenon, and how can we best design our studies to obtain this knowledge? A distinction was made between descriptive and explanatory studies; the former merely describe phenomena in detail, while the latter attempt to explain, generally by answering why, what, or how questions. After defining theories as formulations that attempt to explain or predict, we turned to a discussion of various forms of statements of relationship between variables. Such statements are called propositions. The types of propositions discussed include hypotheses, empirical generalizations, axioms, postulates, and theorems. The difference between independent and dependent variables was explained. We also discussed the meaning of strength of relationship, and distinguished between positive and negative relationships; symmetrical and asymmetrical relationships; linear and nonlinear relationships; and spurious and intervening relationships, including the notion of suppressor and distorter variables.

We next discussed alternative strategies for constructing and verifying hypotheses. One such strategy is the classical approach, in which one first defines concepts (for example, social class and juvenile delinquency), then hypothesizes a relationship between the two, then devises ways of measuring each concept, and finally gathers data and tests the hypothesis. One alternative is the grounded-theory approach popularized by Glaser and Strauss (1967). This approach advocates observation of social phenomena before any hypothesis is constructed. The proper concepts to study and the hypothesized relationship between variables are supposedly derived empirically from examination of actual data. The chapter concluded with a discussion and critique of operationalism, including the notion of strict operationalism that suggests that a concept cannot be defined independently of its measurement.

CHAPTER 4

MEASUREMENT

THE MEASUREMENT PROCESS is an integral part of social research. One can have brilliant theories and research studies that are perfectly constructed in every other detail, yet social research will be a failure if we cannot adequately measure our concepts.

Measurement generally entails the assignment of numbers to concepts or variables. A familiar example is the IQ test in which we attempt to assign a number to a person's intelligence level. The construction of such tests, usually called scales, is discussed in detail in chapter 15. Here we are concerned with the general notion of measurement, with levels of measurement, and with the notion of validity and reliability of measurement. We shall apply the notion of levels of measurement in discussions in subsequent chapters. For example, when we discuss response categories for questionnaire items in chapter 6, it is helpful to distinguish between different levels of measurement such as ordinal and interval in the response categories. Also, we shall use the notions of validity and reliability as a common framework for the comparative assessment of the various methods of data collection.

Concepts differ rather markedly in terms of the ease with which they can be measured. If a property is directly observable, is familiar to virtually all respondents, and is not controversial, then we generally think that it can be measured rather easily. Examples are a person's weight and age. Although perhaps considered sensitive topics by some, these concepts are understandable, and they are even measured quantitatively in everyday life. Other concepts, particularly attitudes, may be much more difficult to measure. Examples are authoritarianism or alienation. Such concepts are not directly observable (although their effects may be), and may even be multidimensional. These concepts are theoretically important for social science but may pose substantial measurement problems.

We discussed the concept of unit of analysis in chapter 2. The most common unit of analysis in social science is the individual, but other units may be used, including the group, county, state, and so forth. In measuring social concepts one first defines the unit of analysis and then specifies the characteristic of that unit to be measured. For example, if the unit of analysis is an individual, many characteristics of that person, some visible and many invisible, can be measured. Visible characteristics include sex, skin color, age, height, weight, eye color, and hair color. Invisible or unobservable characteristics include intelligence, prejudice, authoritarianism, alienation, paranoia, love, and hate. Such potentially measurable features of the unit of analysis are referred to variously as variables, characteristics, properties, or attributes.

The Quantitative/Qualitative Distinction

We will define measurement as the process of determining the value or level, either qualitative or quantitative, of a particular attribute for a particular unit of analysis. Thus measurement is not confined to numerical or quantitative specification but can be qualitative as well. Qualitative attributes have labels or names rather than numbers, assigned to their respective categories. Any attribute that we measure in numbers we will call a quantitative attribute or variable.

A variable such as eye color is qualitative rather than quantitative. We can think of numerous other qualitative variables, such as political affiliation (Republican, Democrat, Independent) or religious affiliation (Protestant, Catholic, Jewish). Qualitative variables are used extensively in observational studies. Although some observers attempt to quantify their observational data, most researchers simply arrange their data into qualitative categories and give each category a name to distinguish it from other categories. For example, Gouldner (1957) classified college teachers into locals (loyal to the organization) and cosmopolitans (loyal to the profession). Davis (1959) classified taxicab customers into five categories: the sport, the blowhard, the businessman, the lady shopper, the live one. Giallombardo (1966) classified male prison inmates as the right guy, wolf, tough, gorilla, hipster, and ball buster. Dalton (1959) classified cliques in organizations as vertical, vertical symbiotic, and vertical parasitic.

The categories of qualitative variables can be labeled with numbers rather than names, but the numbers do not have the properties of the number system; that is, they cannot be added, subtracted, divided, or multiplied. For example, the room numbers of a hotel cannot be used in arithmetic operations. One cannot add room 202 and room 111 the way one would add 202 pounds plus 111 pounds. The only numerical operation that can be conducted on qualitative variables is calculation of the frequency or percentage in each category (e.g., the percentage of persons who have red hair). Other familiar examples of qualitative classifications that use number designations are social security numbers, telephone numbers, and driver's license identification numbers.

Level of Measurement

S. S. Stevens (1951) constructed a widely adopted classification of levels of measurement in which he speaks of nominal measurement, ordinal measurement, interval measurement, and ratio measurement.

Nominal

All qualitative measurement is nominal, regardless of whether the categories are designated by names (quarterback, halfback) or numerals (room 23, room 32). Nominal measurement is essentially a classification system. Basically all we require of a nominally measured variable (skin color, for example) is that there be at least two categories (or else it is not a variable), and that the categories be distinct, mutually exclusive, and exhaustive. By exhaustive we mean that there must be an appropriate category for each case we are measuring. By mutually exclusive we mean that each case appropriately fits in only one category. Thus each case must have a category (exhaustiveness), but only one category (mutual exclusiveness), into which it clearly fits. For example, consider the nominal variable of sex or gender. This is what Stinchcombe (1968) refers to as a natural dichotomy, as only two classes or categories of the variable occur empirically—female and male. The categories of this variable are clearly mutually exclusive and exhaustive, as each person fits into a category, but only one. The best qualitative or nominal variable is one in which the categories are clearly distinct, with few borderline cases.

Ordinal

In addition to qualitative nominal measurement, there are three quantitative levels of measurement: ordinal, interval, and ratio. Each of these levels of measurement from nominal, through ordinal, through interval, through ratio, builds successively upon the other. That is, each new level of measurement has all of the properties of the earlier levels plus some additional properties of its own. Ordinal is like nominal measurement in that it consists of mutually exclusive and exhaustive categories. However, instead of all categories being on the same level and thus equal in value (team A, team B, team C), categories are ranked in order of their value on the property (first place team, second place team; oldest, next oldest, youngest).

Very often in ordinal measurement we will encounter ties, or categories with the same ranking. For example, imagine that we are ranking all of the football teams in the league, from the top team down, solely on the basis of number of games won (assume that all teams played the same number of games and there were no tie games). Imagine that ten teams had the following win-loss records:

Team	Won	Lost
Hornets	4	6
Jets	6	4
Rockets	8	2
Angels	10	0
Falcons	0	10
Indians	5	5
Rams	8	2
Senators	4	6
Puritans	9	1
Outlaws	4	6

On the basis of their record we can rank the teams in the following order: Angels, Puritans, Rockets, Rams, Jets, Indians, Senators, Outlaws, Hornets, and Falcons. However, when we begin assigning numbers to the ranks we run into problems in the form of ties. The Rockets and Rams are tied, as are the Hornets, Outlaws, and Senators:

Team	Ranking
Angels	1
Puritans	2
Rockets	3.5
Rams	3.5
Jets	5
Indians	6
Senators	8
Outlaws	8
Hornets	8
Falcons	10

The usual practice, as shown above, is to rank tied objects equally. Since the Rockets and Rams had the same win-loss record, ranking one of them 3 and one 4 would have concealed the information that the tie had occurred, and it would appear that one team had a better record than the other. Also, it would not seem appropriate to rank them both 3 or both 4 since there is only one of each rank in our ordinal measuring system. The ranks, from 1 through 10, sum to 55. If we used two 3s or two 4s the ranks would sum respectively to 54 or 56. We wish to retain the overall consistency of our measuring system, so we take the ranks affected by ties (3 and 4), sum, and divide by the number of objects tied. This yields a rank of 7/2, or 3.5 for each team. Similarly, when three teams are tied (Senators, Outlaws, Hornets), the rankings 7, 8, and 9 are affected. Again we sum the ranks affected—(7 + 8 + 9) = 24—and divide by the number of teams tied. This time there are no fractions, as 24/3 = 8, giving each of the three tied teams a rank of 8. The student can verify that if an even number of objects are tied the rankings will be fractional, and if an odd number of objects are tied the rankings will be whole numbers.

We can apply more of the properties of the number system to ordinal measurement than to nominal. Specifically, we can say that a person of rank r is higher in value on the property being measured than is a person of rank $r + 1$, and that a person of rank $r + 1$ is higher in value on the property than a person of rank $r + 2$. We cannot claim this with nominal measurement. Further, we know that if $r > r + 1$ and $r + 1 > r + 2$ then it follows that $r > r + 2$. However, we still do not know how much greater the value r is than $r + 1$, and we have no assurance that there is the same difference in value between r and $r + 1$ as between $r + 1$ and $r + 2$. When we do have this information in a measurement system, it is called interval measurement.

Interval

Using age as an example, instead of merely dividing our sample of persons into different age categories or ranking persons from oldest to youngest, if we can measure each person in terms of the number of years he or she has lived, then we have at least interval level measurement. With interval measurement we can determine how many units' difference in age there are from one rank to the next. This information was not available in either nominal or ordinal measurement. Thus, we may find that there is only one unit's difference between the oldest person and the second oldest person (e.g., 90 years old and 89 years old), but 27 units' difference between the second oldest person and the third oldest person (89 years versus 62 years old). One unit's difference means the same wherever it occurs in the scale. That is, one year's difference is one year's difference, whether it occurs between 88 years old and 87 years old or between 16 years old and 15 years old.

As defined here, we shall consider the difference between ordinal and interval to be the fact that in interval measurement we can tell not only which person ranks higher on the measure but also how much higher he or she ranks (how many units). We will assume that when the amount of the difference is known (unless the contrary is obvious), the value of the unit will be consistent wherever it occurs (i.e., one year will mean one year regardless of where it occurs in the scale).

Ratio

In addition to the numerical operations of addition and subtraction that are legitimate with interval measurement, ratio measurement allows multiplication and division. These latter operations require an absolute, fixed, and nonarbitrary zero point. We used the variable "age" to illustrate the notion of an interval scale. Technically, though, age exceeds the requirements of an interval scale as it has an absolute zero point (zero is nonarbitrary, and negative age is not defined). The existence of such a nonarbitrary zero point is the only difference between ratio measurement, which has the zero point, and interval measurement, which does not. Weight also has a nonarbitrary zero point and does not have negative values, and thus is a ratio variable. One cannot be any younger than zero (birth), and one must weigh at least zero. If one has such a clear and nonarbitrary zero point as a reference and the units are constant, then one can multiply or divide. For example, 20 years old is twice as old as 10 years old, and 15 years old is one-half as old as 30 years old. The best test of whether a measurement is ratio, that is, whether the zero point is absolute, is whether zero can be thought of as measuring "none of" the property. Many times such scales do not have negative values (e.g., zero distance means that two points are the same, and negative distance is not defined). Similar statements hold for the number of children in your family, your age, your weight, and your height. You can weigh nothing only if you do not exist, and we cannot measure negative weight.

Many scales are only interval and cannot be considered ratio because their zero point is arbitrarily chosen. The Fahrenheit and centigrade scales of temperatures are good examples. Both of these scales have negative as well as positive values. In centigrade the zero point is chosen to represent freezing (although it makes just as much sense to construct a temperature scale with boiling as the zero point), and in the Fahrenheit scale the zero point is 32° below freezing. However, the Kelvin scale is a ratio scale. As Phillips says:

> The zero points for both the centigrade scale (the temperature at which water freezes) and the Fahrenheit scale (the lowest temperature Fahrenheit could produce—that of a mixture of snow and salt) is an arbitrary one. In the Kelvin scale, however, temperature has a direct interpretation in terms of the motion of molecules, and 0°K is that point at which there is no motion whatsoever. Only with this type of scale is it meaningful to multiply or divide a given temperature. We cannot say that 30°C, for example, is three times as warm as 10°C even though this scale does have interval properties. In the Kelvin scale, however, 30° and 10° are directly translatable into the motion of molecules, which is three times more rapid at the former temperature than at the latter (D. Phillips 1971, p. 243).

Discrete Versus Continuous

An additional distinction is between discrete and continuous variables. Discrete measurement does not contain fractions, while continuous measurement does. The number of children in your family is discrete (unless you are the famous "average American family" having 2.3 children), while your age is continuous (you might be 20.5 years old). Any measurement with a decimal point is continuous. As Johnson (1975, p. 10) says, the difference between discrete and continuous is in many cases as easy as deciding if the data result from a count or a measurement. A count will generally be discrete, while measurement can attempt to measure an underlying continuous variable. The basic difference between the two is that in discrete measurement only certain values are possible, while in continuous measurement an almost infinite number are possible. In general, discrete means from one whole number to the next, while continuous means a large number of potential values in between. Discrete means interrupted or broken measurement, while continuous measurement is unbroken.

We said above that most data gathered by observation will be nominal or qualitative. Johnson has noted that data gathered by counting are generally discrete. You might guess, then, that qualitative data gathered through observation are almost always categorical, and thus discrete. Quantitative data can be either continuous or discrete. Ordinal measurement will generally be discrete, although it may be thought of as measuring some underlying continuum. Interval and ratio data can be either discrete (number of children born in the family) or continuous (age or weight).

By now the reader is undoubtedly anxious to move on to the study of data-collection methods. However we shall pause to study the concepts of reliability and validity, as it is important that we be able to discuss the reliability and validity of the respective data-collection techniques. We shall conclude the chapter with a brief discussion of sources of error.

Measuring the Validity and Reliability of Measurement

In discussing validity of measurement, Selltiz et al. say:

> Certain basic questions must be asked about any measuring instrument: What does it measure? Are the data it provides relevant to the characteristics in which one is interested? To what extent do the differences in scores represent true differences in the characteristic we are trying to measure; to what extent do they reflect also the influence of other factors?
>
> The *validity* of a measuring instrument may be defined as the extent to which differences in scores on it reflects true differences among individuals on the characteristic that we seek to measure, rather than constant or random errors (Selltiz et al. 1976, pp. 168–69).

Derek Phillips (1971, p. 197) says: "In scientific usage a measurement of a given phenomenon (as designated by a given concept) is viewed as a valid measure if it successfully measures the phenomenon."

It is clear that the definition of validity has two parts: (1) that the measuring instrument is actually measuring the concept in question, and not some other concept; and (2) that the concept is being measured accurately. Obviously, one can have the first without the second but not vice versa (the concept cannot be measured accurately if some other concept is being measured).

For example, assume that we wish to measure intelligence, and that John clearly has some actual level of intelligence (say 100 units). We can construct an intelligence test that does measure his intelligence, but measures it with some degree of error. That is, it measures his intelligence as 75 when it is really 100. At least such a test is measuring the right concept (intelligence) and has some potential for being a valid instrument if we are able to refine it so as to remove the error in measurement. On the other hand, if we wish to measure John's intelligence, we may devise a test which does not actually measure intelligence at all. Such a test can never be a valid measure of intelligence as it is measuring some other concept (or maybe is measuring nothing at all), rather than measuring intelligence as we had planned. The difficulty is that this test may still yield a numerical score, and could conceivably even yield a score of 100 for John. However, it still is not valid because it is not measuring the desired phenomenon. Thus, it obviously becomes very important to be able to assess the validity of tests, as all of them will yield some sort of score, but this does not mean that the measurement is valid.

The student should be forewarned that the notion of validity/reliability is not a simple or uncontroversial matter. For one thing there is a disturbing plethora of different types of validity, and discussions of these types often fail to distinguish adequately between the definition of validity and means of attempting to assess or evaluate validity. Some recent (and continuing) work by the present author (Bailey 1984a, 1984b, 1986, 1988c, 1990, 1994a) has shown that the empirical/conceptual distinction as discussed in chapter 3 is really too simple for a thorough analysis of measurement in general and of reliability and validity in particular. I am working with the possibility of distinguishing among conceptual, empirical, and operational levels. These three levels are generally merged into two in most discussions. Keeping all three separate seems to clarify the notion of validity but does not solve all of the problems. This work is beyond the scope of the volume. However, the main points for the student to keep in mind are that validity and reliability are important but complicated notions, and there are often confusion and disagreement in discussions dealing with them. I will try in this chapter to discuss these issues as clearly as possible.

In addition to validity we are also concerned with the reliability of the measuring instrument, by which we simply mean the consistency of the measurement. For example, if you weigh 180 pounds on Monday and still weigh 180 pounds on Tuesday, your scale is reliable if it measures your weight as 180 on both days. It is not reliable if it measures your weight as 180 on Monday and 190 on Tuesday, or 177 on Monday and 168 on Tuesday. By equating reliability with consistency, we allow a scale to be not valid but still consistent (consistently inaccurate) and thus still reliable. Our scale can measure us as 177 on both Monday and Tuesday and still be reliable (although not valid) if we actually weigh 180. Notice, though, that while a measuring instrument can be reliable but not valid, the converse is not true. By definition, if a measure is valid it will be accurate every time, and thus must be reliable also. Thus we can say that the relationship between validity and reliability is asymmetrical, as validity means reliability but not vice versa.

Our degree of success in assessing either validity or reliability is directly dependent upon the degree of accuracy or precision we require. For example, if I weigh 200 pounds and require that my scale be accurate only ± 20 pounds, then if the scale weighs me at 180 pounds one time and 220 pounds the next it is still considered reliable, because it is accurate within the limits I imposed. However, if I actually weigh 200.00 pounds but require accuracy within .10 pounds, then if the scale weighs me at 200.15 pounds or 199.89 pounds it cannot be considered reliable, as it deviates from the true weight by more than the allowable amount.

Assessing Validity

A casual reading of the research literature reveals the existence of many alleged validation procedures. One type is face validation (Selltiz et al. 1976, Phillips 1976, pp. 138–39), also called content validation (Kerlinger 1964, pp. 445–46) and logical validation (Goode and Hatt 1952, p. 237). Another is criterion validation (Phillips 1976, pp. 139–40), also called pragmatic validation by Selltiz et al. Two forms of pragmatic validation distinguished by Selltiz (1976, pp. 179–81) are concurrent validation and predictive validation. Kerlinger (1964, pp. 447–48) also uses the terms "predictive" and "concurrent" validity. The third major form of validation is construct validation.

Face Validity

Face validation is probably the easiest validation procedure to explain but the most difficult to carry out in the course of actual field research. As defined by Selltiz et al., face validity is ultimately a matter of judgment: "Two major questions must be considered: (1) whether the instrument is really measuring the kind of behavior that the investigator assumes it is, and (2) whether it provides an adequate sample of that kind of behavior." It seems to me that these are two separate questions. The first, whether the instrument measures what it is supposed to measure, is, as Selltiz and associates say, ultimately a matter of judgment. This is essentially the area of epistemic correlation, which we have discussed in some detail. Both the grounded theorists and the extreme operationalists equate the concept with the measurement, and so would probably argue that their measures always have complete or almost complete face validity. To know whether a measuring instrument has face validity, we need first to know the definition of the concept being measured, and second whether the information being gathered is germane to that concept. For example, if the concept to be measured is intelligence and the questionaire item ostensibly measuring intelligence asks a respondent for his or her age, this item does not have face validity as a measure of intelligence, as age is not part of the definition of intelligence.

Thus face validity is simply assessed by the evaluator's studying the concept to be measured and determining, in his or her best judgment, whether the instrument arrives at the concept adequately. It is partially a definitional or semantic judgment. If the measure clearly measures another concept, then obviously it does not have face validity. However, if the item does not seem to be measuring any recognizable concept other than the one it is supposed to be measuring, the instrument can be said to have face validity. The major problems with face validity arise when (1) there is no consensus about the definition of the concept to be measured; (2) the concept is a multidimensional one consisting of several subconcepts; (3) the measure is lengthy and complex.

Criterion Validity

Criterion validity, variously called pragmatic validity, concurrent validity, or predictive validity, involves multiple measurements of the same concept. The term "concurrent validity" has been used to describe a measure that is valid for measuring a particular phenomenon at the present time, while "predictive validity" refers to the measure's ability to predict future events. An example of the former would be a prejudice scale that is capable of distinguishing between prejudiced and nonprejudiced respondents. An example of the latter would be a scale or test such as the Law School Aptitude Test (LSAT), which accurately predicts success in law school in the future. Whether the measuring instrument is valid for current or future discrimination is not the central point of criterion validity. The process entails use of a second measure of the concept as a criterion by which the validity of the new measure may be checked. For example, if one had a measuring instrument that one knew to be a valid measure of prejudice, a respondent's score on the new measuring instrument could be compared with his or her score on the old instrument. If the two scores were similar, the new method could be said to have criterion validity or, to be more specific, concurrent criterion (pragmatic) validity. How would one know that the old measure was itself valid and thus acceptable as a criterion for establishing the criterion validity of a new measure? As a first step, the old measure must have face validity. As we said above, face validity cannot be proved but must be assumed; that is, the measure must at least appear to be valid. Beyond that, the old measure should have proved itself through usage. In the case of the prejudice scale, it should have been used successfully many times, to the investigator's satisfaction, to distinguish prejudiced from nonprejudiced people. Further, the researcher might feel that the criterion measure is taken *by definition* to measure what he or she wishes to measure.

Here another question arises. If the old measure were successful, why would the researcher desire another measure? One reason might be that the old measure, while valid and highly accurate, is unwieldly to use. It may consist of too many questions and thus be difficult to administer, or its response categories might be poor and difficult to answer, or it might be difficult to code, or its language might be old and outmoded (for example, containing the word "Negro" rather than "black," in a wording style not easily updated). Another possibility is that the measure does not have what we will refer to as external validity. That is, it works well for one population (e.g., Anglo-Saxons) but not for other groups.

Construct Validity

Imagine that we construct two indices of social class, which we may label index 1 and index 2. Assume that we have a theory that contains a proposition stating an inverse relationship between social class and prejudice—as social class increases, prejudice decreases. Assume further that this proposition has been tested by measuring social class by index 1, and has been substantiated. Construct validity consists of replacing index 1 by index 2 in the theory and retesting the entire theory. If we get the same results for the whole theory (especially for the proposition containing index 2) as when we used index 1 to measure social class, then we say that the new measure (index 2) has construct validity.

The three types of validation, from face validation through criterion validation to construct validation, can be seen as a progression or accumulation, with each of the subsequent types of validation including all of the elements of all former types, along with some new features. In other words, just as interval measurement requires more information about the variable than does ordinal measurement and ordinal requires more than nominal, construct validation requires more information than criterion validation, and criterion requires more than face validation. For this reason, construct validation is often said to be the strongest kind of validation procedure. These three types of validation procedures are illustrated in figure 4–1. Figure 4–1a shows the simplest procedure, face validation, requiring only a single concept and a single measure of it. Criterion validation, shown in figure 4–1b requires only one concept, but re-

Figure 4–1

Three Types of Validation Procedures

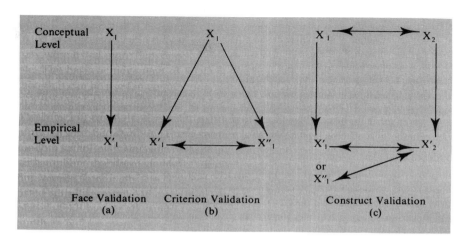

| | Face Validation (a) | Criterion Validation (b) | Construct Validation (c) |

quires two or more measures of that concept. Figure 4–1c shows construct validation, which requires not only a concept with at least two measures (one of which can be substituted for the first in subsequent tests of validity) but also other concepts and their measures that can be related to the concept in question through propositions.

Internal and External Validity

In addition to face validity, criterion validity, and construct validity, two other somewhat different uses of the term "validity" have appeared in the social research literature—internal and external validity. Webb et al. define these terms as follows:

> *Internal validity* asks whether a difference exists at all in any given comparison. It asks whether or not an apparent difference can be explained away as some measurement artifact. . . . *External validity* is the problem of interpreting the difference, the problem of generalization. To what other populations, occasions, stimulus objects, and measures may the obtained results be applied (Webb et al. 1966, pp. 10–11)?

As can be seen, these terms do not refer to the end result of a validation process, as do face validity, criterion validity, and construct validity. These terms were developed within an experimental context and apply to sources of error within the experiment (internal validity) and to problems of generalizing from the experiment to a larger population (external validity).

For example, if one does not encounter contradictions in the data within a given experiment, then the study is said to have internal validity. Contradictory findings signal the absence of internal validity. Even if internal validity is present, the findings are not said to have external validity unless they are held to be valid for additional (external) situations besides the original study that generated the findings.

Assessing Reliability

As we said above, the reliability of a measure is simply its consistency. A measure is reliable if the measurement does not change when the concept being measured remains constant in value. However, if the concept being measured does change in value, the reliable measure will indicate that change. How can a measuring instrument be unreliable? If your weight stays constant at 150 pounds but repeated measurements on your bathroom scale show your weight to fluctuate, the lack of reliability may be due to a weak spring inside the scale. In the case of a social-research instrument such as a questionnaire, the unreliability also lies within the scale and may be due to such things as question or answer categories so ambiguous that the respondent is unsure how he or she should answer, and thus does not answer consistently. A question about which the respondent says "I do not know what he or she wants" is unreliable.

The difficulty in checking for reliability is that when the same question is repeated in a single questionnaire as a consistency check, with no time lag, the respondent tends to see it as a "trick" question. He or she may think that a repeated question is an attempt to make him or her look stupid by answering the question one way in one place and another way later on. Or he or she may feel that a repeated question implies that the researcher is afraid that he or she is lying or giving dishonest answers. In other words, instead of seeing the repeated question as a check on the reliability of the measuring instrument (which it is), the respondent may consider it to be a check on the reliability of the respondent, which is quite a different thing. Thus he or she will feel ego-involved in giving consistent answers even to unreliable questions, and will thereby destroy the use of repeated applications as a test of reliability. This is especially true in the case of "sophisticated" respondents who have had a great deal of experience in answering questionnaires and can anticipate repeated questions. Johnson (1975) observed social workers searching through questionnaires they were answering in order to find the repeated questions, and complaining about the difficulty involved in completing questionnaires containing repeated questions that required consistent answers.

Alternate or Parallel Methods

Methods of testing for reliability have generally taken two forms: (1) alternate or parallel forms of the same measure administered simultaneously or (2) repeated application methods. The first approach is equivalent to using two identical bathroom scales each to weigh the same person (one scale immediately after the other). For example, the researcher could construct two questionnaires each using different items but designed to measure the same concept, and administer them both to the same group of respondents in the same sitting. This is called multiple-forms (Goode and Hatt 1952) or alternate-forms (Selltiz et al. 1976) reliability.

Another popular method is called the split-half method of testing for reliability. Instead of making two distinct but supposedly identical tests or measuring instruments, the researcher constructs a single instrument containing twice as many items as he or she needs, with half of the items being redundant, or a repetition of the first half. This is analogous to a teacher wishing to construct an algebra test of five problems ranging from very easy to very difficult. But instead of making only a five-item test with one item for each degree of difficulty, the teacher makes a ten-item test with two items for each degree of difficulty. Now he or she in effect has twice as many items as he or she needs, and can correlate the student's score on five items with his or her score on the other five parallel items. If the two scores correlate highly the algebra test is said to be reliable. If the student makes a low score on one set of items and a high score on the other set, the test is not a reliable measure of the concept of algebraic knowledge.

The main problem with these methods is making sure that the two halves or the alternate forms actually measure the same thing. If one index measures one concept while the alternate form, supposedly measuring the same concept, actually measures some other concept, then the researcher cannot assess reliability. In a very real sense the use of two alternative measures only assesses the degree to which both measures actually measure the same concept. If there is a high correlation between the two measures, then each measures the same thing; if there is a low correlation, they measure different concepts. Thus one might argue that the use of alternative measuring instruments, rather than testing reliability, really tests criterion validity, as discussed above.

Test/Retest Reliability

Since reliability by definition means consistency in the scores of a single measure, rather than identical scores on two alternate measures, it would seem better to test for reliability through repeated applications of the same measure. This is a view shared by Siegel and Hodge (1968, p. 55), who say, "In order to make any substantial progress on questions of reliability one needs, of course, repeated measurements."

In order to understand fully all of the problems associated with repeated application of the same measurement instrument in social research, we need to examine in more detail exactly how a measuring instrument can be unreliable. If you use your bathroom scale repeatedly over a period of two months, weighing every day, and find that at the end to two months your recorded weight is five pounds heavier than it was two months previously, this is not necessarily evidence of lack of reliability. You may have gained five pounds over the course of two months, so that the accurate scale must show you to be heavier. A reliable scale will show a change in the value of the characteristic being measured whenever such a change occurs. It just should not show a change when none occurs.

Beginning students of research methods sometimes think that in order to be reliable a measuring instrument must show consistent values over each measurement period, but this is true only if no change actually occurs. We have all seen a broken thermometer that shows the same temperature in January as in August; though it shows consistent scores we certainly do not consider it reliable. The problem in social research lies in determining, whenever repeated applications yield inconsistent scores, whether the value of the concept really changed, or whether the measuring instrument is unreliable. For a valuable discussion of the general measurement problem see Blalock (1982). For further discussion of validity and reliability see Carmines and Zeller (1979); Brinberg and McGrath (1985); Bailey (1988c); and Feagin et al. (1991).

Error

Measurement error, as shown by a lack of validity or reliability, is only one of many types of error that we can make in social research. An overview of these different types of error and the stage or research in which each is most likely to be made is provided in table 4–1. Even before research begins, the researcher can in a sense make an error by choosing an irrelevant or unimportant research topic. But by error we mean here the failure to collect the data accurately. In stage 1 of table 4–1, the construction of ambiguous concepts and a poor operational definition of the concept can cause lack of face validity. In addition, an ambiguous or poorly worded hypothesis may never be properly tested, ensuring total error and a worthless study. A lack of face validity resulting from poor work in stage 1 will also ensure lack of reliability, since the latter is dependent upon the former. But even if the concept is clear and well defined and the hypothesis is well written, poorly worded items in the measuring instrument (stage 2) can ensure lack of reliability if the respondent cannot understand them. Further, different respondents may understand the same question to mean different things, thus leading to invalid and unreliable data.

In the third stage poor sampling procedures can lead to unrepresentative data, resulting in

Table 4–1

Types of Errors

Stage of Research	Type of Error
1. Concept and hypothesis construction (including choice of operational definitions)	Lack of face validity
2. Construction of research instrument (questionnaire)	Lack of reliability (faulty or ambiguous wording on questions)
3. Sampling	Lack of external validity (sampling error)
4. Data gathering	Error due to failure to control: (a) Environment (b) Personal characteristics of respondent (fatigue, etc.) (c) Relationship between respondent and researcher (d) Defects of research instrument (faulty sound recording, equipment failure, etc.) (e) Interviewer misunderstood answer
5. Coding	Incorrect information recorded due to missing data, illegible data, or simple coding error
6. Data analysis	Misuse of statistics or faulty interpretation of data

an inability to generalize the findings beyond the specific sample of respondents used in the study. This is more or less the subject of external validity, as Campbell and Stanley (1963, p. 5) use the term. Sampling procedures and means of reducing or eliminating sampling error will be discussed in chapter 5.

In stage 4 many potential sources of error are found in the actual data-gathering situation. These include uncontrolled extraneous factors in the environment, uncontrolled personal factors in the respondent (e.g., he or she is upset about something, or too tired to concentrate), certain aspects of the relationship between researcher and respondent, or equipment failure (e.g., faulty tape recorder). Ways to reduce or eliminate these errors are discussed in chapters 8–11.

In the fifth stage the person coding the data or transferring it from the questionnaires to the computer, or from tape recordings to transcript pages, can make simple clerical errors such as writing an incorrect number. (For that matter, such errors can occur in stage 4.) The interviewer can misunderstand a respondent's answer or write so illegibly that the coder mistakes one answer for another. In the case of questionnaires handled through the mail, the respondent can also make simple clerical errors, such as writing the answer for one question in the space allowed for another. Means of reducing or eliminating coding errors will be discussed in chapter 14.

The final type of error is simply misinterpretation of data during the data-analysis stage. One makes errors at this stage by drawing incorrect conclusions from the data, or by saying that the data show something that they do not show. Such errors can occur because a data analyst is biased or not properly trained. A person who is trained and experienced in the analysis of documents, for example, or of tape transcripts from observation studies, will analyze such data in a much more valid and reliable fashion than an untrained or inexperienced observer. Similarly, a more quantitatively oriented survey researcher can take perfectly valid and reliable data and draw absolutely erroneous conclusions from them simply by choosing the wrong statistics for data analysis, or by using the correct statistics incorrectly. Ways of reducing or eliminating errors of analysis will be discussed in chapters 9–12 and chapter 15.

In discussing these sources of error we are of course referring only to honest mistakes, or inaccuracies resulting from the actions of persons attempting to be accurate. This is quite apart from the problem of deliberate falsification of data, whether it be by the survey interviewer who sits in a bar and fills our 100 questionnaires because, in his or her words, "I know by now what the people will say and it is a waste of time and effort for me to go to 100 houses and be bitten by three dogs," or by the frustrated researcher driven to falsify data or "lie with statistics" because he or she is still sure that his or her hypothesis is correct even though the data indicate otherwise. We will have occasion in various chapters to discuss ways of reducing or eliminating such intentional inaccuracies.

The various errors one can make in social research are not all equal either in terms of seriousness (damage they can do to our findings) or in our ability to remove them or correct for them. Errors can be either random or systematic. In many cases we like to assume that errors, such as those caused by uncontrolled factors in the experimental setting, are random, or without any particular pattern. Thus some errors will consist of estimating the value of a variable to be higher than it actually is, while other errors will estimate the value of the same variable to be lower than it actually is. Such random errors tend to cancel each other out if the sample size is large enough. While we would prefer to have no error whatsoever, random errors can be tolerated, as they should have little or no effect on our overall conclusions.

LIVERPOOL JOHN MOORES UNIVERSITY
LEARNING & INFORMATION SERVICES

Systematic errors, on the other hand, are not random but fall in a pattern, and so have the disadvantage of not canceling each other out. However, since such errors are in a pattern, they can sometimes be detected and removed or, if not removed, corrected for. For example, suppose that you are conducting a study using a mail-out questionnaire that must be filled out by the respondent and returned. One of your primary variables in the study is the respondent's educational level. However, you have a response rate of only 60 percent, meaning that four out of every ten persons who receive a questionnaire do not return it. You suspect that your nonresponse is not random with respect to education but in fact fits a pattern—persons with lower educational levels are overrepresented among the nonrespondents. By interviewing nonrespondents you may be able to estimate the amount of error involved and correct for it.

Other systematic errors might arise from such things as a faulty keypunch machine that always punches a 2 instead of a 1. If detected, such errors may be easily corrected. Even if undetected they may not be very serious, as altering the value of a certain variable by a constant amount will not affect the value of the correlation coefficient relating that variable to another variable, just as adding a constant to both sides of an algebraic equation will not affect the relationship.

In general, then, researchers deal with error by removing it if possible. If it cannot be removed, it can sometimes be estimated and corrected for. In other cases error can be assumed to be random and ignored. A common example of error that can be removed is clerical error, such as keypunch error, that results in values for a particular variable that are outside the allowable range for the variable. For example, the values of a particular questionnaire item might range from 1 through 5, yet the computer printout reveals a number of other values such as 6, 9, and so on. These values are obviously keypunch errors, coding errors, or respondent's errors, and can generally be corrected by rechecking the questionnaire. However, clerical errors falling within the acceptable range of values (3 instead of 2) cannot be distinguished. While this type of error is not systematic, the coder can also make systematic errors such as coding the responses for item 4 (age) in the column for item 5 (weight). Such systematic errors should be easily spotted by thorough examination of the data (e.g., in this example weight would be systematically underestimated).

Summary

Chapter 4 discussed problems of measuring social concepts. We discussed this topic at this point in the book to provide necessary background for subsequently commenting on the reliability and validity of the various data collection techniques. We first distinguished between qualitative data, which is symbolized by nonnumerical symbols (for example, colors), and quantitative data, which is represented by numbers (for example, age or number of years of schooling completed). Next, the four levels of measurement—nominal, ordinal, interval, and ratio—were discussed. The distinction between continuous and noncontinuous variables was also made.

Following this, we turned to a discussion of the validity and reliability of social measuring instruments. For example, if someone constructs an intelligence test, and you take it and score very low, before admitting to a lack of intelligence you may wish to assess the validity and reliability of the measure. After defining validity, we turned to a discussion of various methods of assessing validity, including face validity, criterion validity, and construct validity. The distinction between internal and external validity was also discussed. We next defined reliability, and then discussed methods of reliability assessment. We distinguished between parallel and test-retest methods of reliability assessment, and discussed a prominent parallel method, the split-half method. The chapter concluded with a discussion of the various types of error that can occur at the various stages of research and that the researcher must be continually on guard against.

PART TWO

SURVEY RESEARCH METHODS

LIVERPOOL
JOHN MOORES UNIVERSITY
I.M. MARSH LIBRARY
BARKHILL ROAD
LIVERPOOL L17 6BD
TEL. 0151 231 5216/5299

LIVERPOOL
JOHN MOORES UNIVERSITY
I.M. MARSH LIBRARY
BARKHILL ROAD
LIVERPOOL L17 6BD
TEL. 0151 231 5216/5299

CHAPTER 5

SURVEY SAMPLING

THE USE OF SAMPLING, a relative rarity in social research only fifty years ago, has mushroomed greatly in recent years until it has become very commonplace. Technological developments such as computerization have facilitated surveys of the entire nation, and virtually all these surveys have relied upon sampling. Modern sampling theory based upon modern statistics and probability theory is quite accurate, and when error is present, its extent is generally known.

The logic of sampling is relatively straightforward. We first designate a population of interest, such as all registered voters in the United States. Then we attempt to select a subset of some predetermined size from this population. This subset should adequately represent the entire population so that the information gathered from the subset ideally will be just as accurate as the data that we could gather from the entire population. There are a number of obvious advantages of sampling, especially savings in time and money.

It is not necessary that the population be homogeneous for us to sample successfully from it, but it is necessary that the range of data or information in the population is represented in the sample. For example, suppose we select a national sample from among the nation's registered voters and ask each person in the sample for his or her views on whether the United States military should expand their intervention in Somalia in the current year. It is not necessary that all persons have the same opinion. For example, if only 20 percent of the national population believe in expanded intervention, we can still sample successfully. However, it is obviously imperative that this 20 percent not be neglected in the sample, and conversely that the 20 percent not be overrepresented in the sample.

One key to choosing an adequate sample is the sample size. Statistical sampling theory is so developed that national samplings routinely utilize sample sizes of only a few thousand. According to Sudman (1976, p. 86), common samples for national samples in finance, medicine, and attitudes have modal (the most frequent size encountered) samples sizes of "1000+," with 25 percent of national studies in medicine and attitudes reporting sample sizes of 500. Much larger samples may be required in specialized studies. For example, Freeman et al. (1982) report that the California Disability Survey necessitated a sample of 30,000 households (0.4 percent of all California households) in order to develop statistically reliable disability rates.

In my view, probability theory can definitely assure us that a relatively small sample size is adequate and can allow us to estimate our sampling error. However, it still seems intuitively clear that small sample sizes, no matter how much money they may save in interviewing costs and no matter how quickly they may be processed, still have a number of costs. For one thing, the public at large is often not statistically sophisticated and may not share the specialist's view that the sample is adequate. Even those who might believe our assurances that the study is sound may feel some resentment if they or their friends and acquaintances are never included in the samples. Further, it seems to me that small sample sizes obviously leave smaller margins for other sorts of errors, such as simple coding errors. Unfortunately, in this age of specialization there is often a highly specialized division of labor in large-scale surveys. Thus, a sampling specialist may design a sample with a perfectly adequate, although minimal, sample size. However, the sample size that was adequate from a technical standpoint may not be sufficient if the other persons involved in the study prove incompetent or simply have a run of bad luck.

The smugness that some political surveyors, generally using quite small samples, seem to have felt because of their continued successes ever since the *Literary Digest* debacle (discussed later in this chapter) was shaken somewhat by the fact that many of them failed, as late as the week before the November 1980 U.S. presidential election, to predict the Reagan land-slide. Many of the pollsters continued to predict that the race would be close only a few days before the actual election. There is still disagreement as to whether this failure was due to survey inadequacies or simply to massive last minute changes in voter attitudes.

In the 1984 U.S. presidential election the situation was quite different. President Reagan won by such a large margin that even a relatively poor sample should have been sufficient to predict the winner. In 1988 George Bush was elected even though he had been far behind in the polls some weeks before the election. This did not seem to indicate polling error, but simply that Bush gained in popularity. In 1992, as in 1984, the outcome of the election was probably clear enough to be easily predicted in the polls, with Bill Clinton beating George Bush rather easily. However, this does not justify relaxation of sampling standards. The position we shall take here is that sampling is a very important, often necessary tool that we can generally use with confidence. However, it is important that we do not become so smug with its use that we become careless and fail to pay attention to details, as this can easily lead to erroneous results. Further discussion of the purpose of sampling, as well as guidelists for various aspects of sample design (including sample size) are provided by Alreck and Settle (1985).

In this chapter we shall discuss the selection of respondents for large-scale survey studies, both those that use mailed questionnaires and those that use interviewers. Selection of respondents for other types of study such as observation and experiments will be considered in later chapters, although much of this chapter will apply to those studies as well.

Technical Terms

The first step is to specify the group of persons or things to be studied. The objects of study are called the *units of analysis.* The unit of analysis most often is the individual person, but it may also be a club, an industry, a city, county, or state. The sum total of all the units of analysis is called the *population* or *universe.* Each entity from the population that is the ultimate sampling objective is called a *sampling element.* In a fertility study each element would be a person, more specifically a married women of childbearing age. A *sampling unit* is either a single sampling element or a collection of elements. A *sampling frame* is the complete list of all units from which the sample is drawn.

Sample Versus Population

Ideally we would like to study the entire population or universe, to give more weight to our findings. If we found a strong inverse relationship between education and prejudice for *all* Americans, we would have more faith in our findings than if we got the same results from a study of only ten Americans. Often, however, we are unable to study the entire population and must settle for a sample. We can define sample as a subset or portion of the total population. A 100 percent sample would be the entire population; a 1 percent sample would consist of only 1 out of every 100 entities in the population.

The sample must always be viewed as an approximation of the whole rather than as a whole in itself. Indeed, much statistical effort is directed to the task of determining, given a particular value of a variable for a sample (e.g., mean income), the probability that this value prevails throughout the total population. In other words, how good an estimate of the true population value is the sample value?

Thus a good researcher starts from the top (population) and works down (to the sample, or partial population). He or she may begin with 200 million as potential respondents and finish with a random sample of 40,000 or less.

In contrast, novice researchers often work from the bottom up. Rather than beginning with too many respondents and paring the list down to something manageable, they attempt to determine the minimum number of respondents they need to conduct a successful study. The problem is that unless the total population is identified in advance it is difficult if not impossible to assess the adequacy of the sample. The researcher has a sample, but a sample of what?

For example, one might think that a random sampling can be conducted by standing on a street corner and choosing at random from among passersby. However, if the people are chosen during working hours, the researcher may have a random sample of people on the street at certain times, but not a random sample of all Americans, for the sample may be heavily weighted in favor of unemployed or retired people. The people passing the street corner do constitute a sample of Americans, but not a random or representative one. This sample would be adequate only if the population of interest were weekday street-corner people. If one has a list of the population to begin with, his or her sample is much more likely to be representative. At the very least its adequacy will be easier to judge.

Sampling Efficiency

Some students of social research may have misgivings about the use of samples, feeling that they are a major source of error. Consider national samples such as the Nielsen rating or the Gallup poll. Have you ever been included in either of these polls? Do you know anyone who has been? Some people might feel that a poll that leads to the removal of their favorite television show from the air does not accurately reflect the opinion of the majority of Americans, since there are many whose opinions are never asked. In fact, there has recently been considerable dissatisfaction with the Nielsen rating (see Milvasky 1992).

Notorious Sampling Failures

Those who doubt the accuracy of surveys based on samples can also cite the *Literary Digest* poll of 1936, which predicted that Alf Landon would win the presidential election over Franklin D. Roosevelt (Babbie 1973, pp. 74–75). Babbie says the incorrect prediction was due to an inadequate sampling frame. The *Literary Digest* survey was conducted by mail. The researchers did not have a list of all registered voters in the United States, but instead compiled lists from telephone directories and automobile registrations. It seems probable that many persons in the midst of the Depression did not have an automobile or even a telephone and so were not represented in the poll, but voted overwhelmingly for Roosevelt. Apparently a majority of the poorer people, who were not included in the survey, voted for Roosevelt, while a majority of the richer people, who were included, probably voted for Landon as predicted. Thus the poll was an accurate poll of rich people, but did not represent poorer people very well.

For a recent discussion of the *Digest* failure see Squire (1988) and Cahalan (1989). According to Cahalan a significantly higher proportion of Roosevelt supporters (67 percent) than Landon supporters (52 percent) said that they had *not* received a *Digest* ballot or were unsure, even though their names were on the mailing list.

A similar survey debacle occurred during the 1948 election campaign, in which the Gallup poll predicted that Dewey would be the winner when Truman actually won in late returns. According to Babbie (1973, p. 75) this failure was caused by a number of things, including the fact that pollsters stopped surveying too soon to catch the considerable number of switchovers to Truman, and the fact that the quota-sampling procedure used was inadequate.

The two most recent polling failures did not involve national elections in the United States. One involved the 1989 Virginia gubernatorial election (see the discussion in chapter 1, and Traugott and Price 1992). The other involved the 1990 Nicaraguan national election. In the Virginia election, Democrat Douglas Wilder experienced a much narrower victory than predicted in the exit polls, perhaps due to redistricting and the fact that he was black, perhaps leading some voters (particularly Democrats) to be reluctant in admitting that they were failing to vote for their party's candidate for racial reasons.

The second recent prediction failure was the notorious "polling debacle" of the 1990 Nicaraguan presidential election. In the election of February 25, 1990, Violeta Chamorro was elected president with nearly 55 percent of the vote, while Daniel Ortega was second with nearly 41 percent of the vote (other candidates received the remainder). Only half of 29 polls taken within a year before the election even predicted the correct party. Among the reasons hypothesized for this failure were fraud (poll results may have been fabricated), sampling problems, and data collection problems (see P. Miller 1991). For a discussion of sample designs for preelection surveys see Traugott (1987).

Sampling Successes

Recent political polls using modern probability sampling techniques and accurate sampling frames have been quite accurate, and the 1984, 1988, and 1992 presidential elections are good examples of this. A glaring exception to those successes is the 1980 presidential election, as discussed in chapter 1. Actually, some polls did correctly predict the 1980 election, but not until only a very few days before election day. Until 1980 the polls had correctly predicted not only the winner of every presidential election since 1948 but also his percentage of the vote. For example, in the 1968 election the Gallup poll predicted that Richard Nixon would receive 43 percent of the vote and the Harris poll predicted 41 percent. His actual total was 42.9 percent. Furthermore, these predictions were made using only 2,000 of the approximately 73 million voters as respondents. By contrast, 2 million respondents were used to make the incorrect prediction in the 1936 *Literary Digest* poll (Babbie 1973, p. 76).

Advantages of Sampling

If done with care, sampling can be highly accurate. In addition, the savings in time and money should be obvious. But the sample has certain other advantages as well. Surveying an entire population would take much longer than a sample study, and time is often very important. In a survey, unlike an observation or document study, at least theoretically, the research is conducted at a single point in time so that the opinions of all respondents are comparable. If a total population is to be surveyed, it is difficult to conduct the interviews in a short period of time without using an enormous number of interviewers. And using a large number of interviewers, as Babbie (1973, pp. 73–74) notes, may actually decrease the accuracy of the data because one may be obliged to employ marginal interviewers rather than selecting the most competent.

In addition, it will be difficult to supervise all interviewers adequately and to pay the necessary attention to such details as follow-ups and finding respondents. It may be better to have fewer but more careful interviews. If one does choose to conduct a large number of interviews that take a long period of time, he or she will not know whether or not differences in respondents are due to external events occurring during the course of the study. Opinions polled during the beginning of the study may not be comparable with opinions gathered later. Also, as Babbie notes, problems of record keeping are much greater if an entire population is used, and more paperwork simply provides an opportunity for greater error and temptation for laxity in procedures.

Another possible advantage of the sample over the full population survey is that the sample may achieve a greater response rate and greater cooperation in general from respondents and thus may be more accurate. This is especially true in the case of sensitive questions. A good example is provided by the U.S. Census. A census, by definition, is a survey of the entire population. The census was originally designed to provide population data needed for apportionment of representatives. However, over the years many items have been added, so that now some questions are asked that some respondents consider an invasion of privacy or at least pointless—for example, how many toilets there are in their home. Such questions can engender widespread nonresponse or even deliberate falsification of answers. Irritation of respondents can be disastrous for a private survey not backed by the power of the U.S. government. At best it is poor public relations, and at worst it can cause a storm of protests resulting in cancellation of the survey. If the survey is continued the data may be suspect, as the respondents may sabotage the study by falsifying their answers.

By using a sample instead of the entire population, the researcher can keep a low profile. With a sample he or she does not offend as many people, and those who are offended have less chance to organize in their common interest because no respondent knows the identity of other respondents who have been asked the same question. The census now uses a form on which some of the basic inoffensive questions are the same for every household, but other questions are not included on every form but only on every kth form, forming a sample. This undoubtedly increases accuracy over that which could be achieved by questioning the entire population about sensitive issues.

But to say a sample can yield information that is just as accurate as, or conceivably even more accurate than, information received from a survey of the entire population assumes a carefully drawn sample. Effective design of a sample can involve a tremendous amount of work and expense.

Constructing the Sampling Frame

A sample cannot be more accurate than the sampling frame from which it is drawn. If the sampling elements are the same as the sampling units, then in theory the sampling frame is simply a list of all objects (e.g., persons) in the sample. Every person in the population should be listed (but only once). Listing a person more than once will increase his or her probability of selection. In the case of a larger study, it is virtually impossible to obtain a complete and accurate list. People die and are born daily; they also change their addresses or give the incorrect address or telephone number so that they cannot be contacted. It is virtually impossible for an investigator to list all the people in a city at one point in time. The researcher often must depend upon one or more existing lists. If the study is small the researcher should, if at all possible, construct the list personally, as existing lists have generally been compiled for non-survey purposes and will invariably contain omissions and repetitions that can cause dangerous biases. We have already seen how the use of existing lists of telephone and car owners biased the *Literary Digest* sampling frame by oversampling the rich and undersampling the poor. Any sampling frame compiled from an existing list that excludes a portion of the intended population should itself be viewed as a sample, and sometimes a very biased one. Anyone constructing a sampling frame from existing lists should attempt to determine the number of persons excluded from the population, and whether these excluded persons differ in any systematic way from the ones included on the list. If the people excluded are a random sample of the total population, the damage will not be serious, even if their number is large. In one study, Kviz (1984) concludes that telephone directories often appear useful as sampling frames for general population surveys of rural areas. He compared a telephone directory sample with a listed sample and found that they did not differ significantly.

Unfortunately, however, that may not always be the case. The excluded persons may constitute some distinguishable and homogeneous group or groups that are not representative of the persons on the list. For example, telephone directories can exclude both the poor who do not have telephones and the more affluent who have unlisted numbers. Also, some people have two telephones or multiple listings and thus stand a greater chance of being selected, unless some entries can be culled so that each person appears on the list only a single time. As another example, social researchers wishing to study Chicanos in America are often forced to compile their sampling frame from lists of persons with Spanish surnames. The biases here are that non-Chicano persons with Spanish surnames are included in these lists, while persons who have changed their names, or the rather substantial group of Chicanos who have changed their names through marriage to Anglos, are excluded from the sampling frame.

The situation is similar for other minority groups such as Jews, where sampling by surname alone may lead to biases. However, Himmelfarb et al. (1983) concluded that a random sample of "distinctly Jewish names" (DJN) may provide a fairly representative sample of American Jews, with the advantage of lower cost (see also Cohn 1984; Himmelfarb et al. 1984).

There are some instances in which we can list the entire population satisfactorily, and other instances in which existing lists are perfectly adequate. The biggest problems of constructing an adequate sampling frame arises in large-scale samples, or in state-, county-, or citywide studies. Listing problems are especially acute if the study involves mobile populations, as in migration studies, or if it is a panel study, that is, one that involves interviewing the same respondents again at a later date.

While it is generally too costly in both time and money to list individual persons for moderately large-scale studies, such as one that is citywide, one may be able to list households or residence addresses and use these as the sampling frame from which the sample can be drawn.

Unlike individuals, residences are relatively stable. Such a direct listing procedure has the great advantage of being as up-to-date as possible in addition to being (supposedly) a complete list with no biases and no groups excluded.

If such a listing cannot be undertaken, the next-best alternative is to use information provided by the U.S. Census. Census information is quite accurate, and of course how up-to-date it is depends on how long it has been since the last census (they are conducted every ten years in years ending in zero). The great advantage of the census is that it can pinpoint the location of persons with special characteristics (e.g., it can show which census tracts within Los Angeles County have high concentrations of persons with Spanish surnames and which have low concentrations). Aside from the census or direct listing, we are pretty much dependent upon existing lists for large-scale studies.

For a smaller-scale study, particularly one not encompassing an entire geographic area, our listing problems may be much less. If we are studying something such as membership in a voluntary organization (e.g., the Kiwanis or local V.F.W. branch), we can probably use membership lists with a minimum of error, particularly if we attempt to check whether the names on the list are members and all members are listed.

A study conducted by UCLA will serve to illustrate how difficult and how important it is to construct a sampling frame. Wild (1973) wished to study health care of the children of UCLA students. She planned to send a questionnaire by mail to two comparison groups—married students whose children were enrolled in a UCLA prepaid pediatric health-care plan, and students whose children were not enrolled in the program. The administrators of the program were able to provide her with a fairly adequate list of persons enrolled. Her problem was to secure a random sample of students who had children but had not enrolled them in the plan.

At substantial cost, she was able to obtain a list of currently enrolled married students from the registrar's office. However, the list included students who did not have children and some students who were not married; undoubtedly some married students were not listed. The first departure from the theoretical population (extent unknown) undoubtedly occurred in this list. In addition, some students had withdrawn from school and could not be contacted, while others provided an incorrect address or telephone number.

Wild had to determine which of the students on the list had children. She decided that the only way to do this was to telephone each name on the list and ask. Persons who did not have telephones, whose telephone numbers were incorrect, or who could not be reached by telephone after repeated attempts had to be marked off. Among those who could be reached, there was still the problem of systematic response bias. Only a few respondents were listed incorrectly as having children when they did not. However, the investigator learned that a number of students, perhaps sizable, actually had children but denied this over the telephone. (Apparently parents had frequently been harassed by telephone solicitors attempting to sell them baby food or diaper services.)

Thus, before the formal sampling procedure actually began, some members of the population to be studied had already been lost through informal, but unavoidable, sampling procedures, which unfortunately were not random but were biased. These persons were lost in several stages through (1) not being on the initial list of students; (2) being on the list but not reachable because of incorrect address; (3) being on the list but not having a telephone, or having an incorrect telephone number on the list, or having an unlisted number, or not answering the telephone; and (4) answering the telephone but denying that they had children.

rooms rapidly with additional variables, especially if these variables contain more than two categories.

Cluster Sampling

Mendenhall, Ott, and Scheaffer (1971, p. 121) define a *cluster sample* as a simple random sample in which each sampling unit is a collection, or cluster, or elements. For example, an investigator wishing to study students might first sample groups or clusters of students such as classes or dormitories, and then select the final sample of students from among the clusters. Unlike stratified sampling, in which every stratum is sampled, cluster sampling samples among clusters. Cluster sampling, sometimes called area sampling, is generally used when it is impossible or impractical to construct a sampling frame in which the sampling units are the sampling elements themselves.

For example, for a study of median educational levels of all adult females in Los Angeles County, no adequate list of all females would be available, and direct field listing would be exorbitantly expensive and impractical. (By the time the list was completed half of the potential respondents could have moved out of town unless a tremendous number of listers were employed at great expense.) By multistage cluster sampling the investigator can first randomly sample census tracts from a sampling frame that lists all tracts in the county. Then in the second stage he or she can randomly sample city blocks from a sampling frame consisting of all city blocks within the census tracts drawn in the first stage of the sample. The third stage samples households from a sampling frame of all households contained in the blocks drawn in the second stage of the cluster sample. The fourth stage consists of choosing the adult females within each household drawn in the third stage (if two or more adult females reside in the same household, one of them is randomly selected).

The obvious advantage of cluster sampling is the great saving in time and money that it affords. The obvious disadvantage is that it is not a single sample but two or more, with a possibility for sampling error in each. For example, in simple random sampling there is always the possibility that the sample is not representative of the entire population. But in cluster sampling, if the first stage is representative, the second stage might not be. This means that the investigator must be concerned about sample size and sampling accuracy not once but in every stage of the cluster sample. (Choosing the sample size in cluster sampling will be discussed in the section on sample size later in this chapter.)

It should be clear that the sampling methods discussed heretofore are not mutually exclusive. For example, clusters and then later elements can be drawn by either simple random or systematic procedures. In addition, stratified sampling and cluster sampling can be combined in a single procedure—stratified cluster sampling, in which one chooses the strata as before, then conducts cluster sampling procedures within each stratum.

Nonprobability Sampling

In addition to probability sampling, in which the probability that an element will be chosen from the universe is known, many studies (generally smaller ones) use nonprobability sampling. The obvious disadvantage of nonprobability sampling is that, since the probability that a person will be chosen is not known, the investigator generally cannot claim that his or her sample is representative of the larger population. This greatly limits the investigator's ability to generalize his or her findings beyond the specific sample studied. In addition, he or she is unable to estimate the degree of departure from representation (sampling error). The obvious advantage of nonprobability sampling is that it is much less complicated, much less expensive, and may be done on a spur-of-the-moment basis to take advantage of available (and perhaps unanticipated) respondents without the statistical complexity of a probability sample. A non-probability sample may prove perfectly adequate if the researcher has no desire to generalize his or her findings beyond the sample, or if the study is merely a trial run for a larger study. If the investigator plans to repeat the study at a later date, he or she may initially be more inter-ested in perfecting the questionnaire than in the sample and may find a nonprobability sample adequate.

Convenience Sampling

In convenience or accidental sampling, the investigator merely chooses the closest live per-sons as respondents. What is lost in sampling accuracy is saved in time and money. A common example is "captive audience" sampling, as in the use of introductory social-science students as questionnaire respondents.

Quota Sampling

Quota sampling is the nonprobability sampling equivalent of stratified sampling, with the added requirement that each stratum is generally represented in the sample in the same propor-tion as in the entire population.

In a quota sample one first decides which strata may be relevant for the study to be con-ducted (e.g., Republicans and Democrats for a study of voting behavior; blacks, whites, and Chicanos for a study of race relations). Then the investigator sets a quota for each stratum that is proportionate to its representation in the entire population. For example, if lists of registered voters in a city show that 60 percent are Democrats and 40 percent Republicans, one would not wish to conduct a study of voting preferences using either all Democrats or all Republicans. Rather, the researcher would want a sample reflecting the same proportions. After the quota is set, quota sampling consists merely of finding persons with the requisite characteristics. In the voters' preference study, a total of 200 respondents would mean 80 Republicans and 120 Democrats. Although neither the Democrats nor the Republicans represent a random selection of the population, at least the two groups are in the same proportion in the sample as within the total population.

Even though quota sampling is not probabilistic, the investigator obviously must take every precaution to keep from biasing selection and thus make sure that the sample is as representa-tive and generalizable as possible. The major biasing factor is that interviewers may take the path of least resistance when sampling, avoiding houses with unfriendly dogs or unfriendly people. They may also avoid climbing stairs or hills, and may underselect from certain race, sex, or age groups. Or they may confine their sampling to their friends or to habitués of the neighborhood bar. These tactics will lend a false homogeneity to the data and keep them from being random.

Dimensional Sampling

Dimensional sampling is basically a multidimensional form of quota sampling. The idea is to specify all dimensions (variables) of interest in the population and then to make sure that every combination of these dimensions is represented by at least one case. As David O. Arnold says:

> (1) explicitly delineate the universe to which you eventually wish to generalize; (2) spell out what appear to be the most important dimensions along which the members of this universe vary and develop a typology that includes the various combinations of values on these dimensions; (3) use this typology as a sampling frame for selecting a small number of cases from the universe, typically drawing one case from each cell of the typology (Arnold 1970, p. 147).

This method is designed for studies in which only a small sample is desired so that each case drawn can be studied in more detail than is possible in a large-scale study. However, if the sample is small there is the danger that some needed values of variables will not be represented. The dimensional-sampling method is designed to overcome this danger. An example is Kornhauser's (!962) study of political commitment. The important dimensions were (1) degree of political commitment and (2) whether the commitment was still intact. The combination of these two dimensions provided the typology shown in figure 5–1. Dimensional sampling ensures that each of these four cells is represented even in a very small sample.

Figure 5–1

Important Dimensions in a Study of Political Commitment

Whether Intact or Not	Degree of Commitment	
	Strong	Moderate
Intact	Communist Party leaders	Leaders of Independent Voters of Illinois
Not intact	Former CP leaders	Former leaders of IVI

SOURCE: W. Kornhauser, "Social Bases of Political Commitment," from Rose (ed.), *Human Behavior and Social Processes.* Copyright © 1962 by Houghton Mifflin Company.

Purposive Sampling

In purposive or judgmental sampling the investigator does not necessarily have a quota to fill from within various strata, as in quota sampling, but neither does he or she just pick the nearest warm bodies, as in convenience sampling. Rather, the researcher uses his or her own judgment about which respondents to choose, and picks only those who best meet the purposes of the study.

The advantage of purposive sampling is that the researcher can use his or her research skill and prior knowledge to choose respondents. For example, he or she may seek the "average American housewife" or the "all-American boy." A common technique in purposive sampling dealing with election predictions is to find the average or common-denominator election district, such as one that has cast a majority vote for the winning president for many years. Another ploy is to seek deviant cases rather than average respondents, in order to see what makes them depart from the norm.

Snowball Sampling

Snowball sampling has achieved increased use in recent years, particularly by researchers conducting observational research and in community studies. Although snowball sampling is generally considered a nonprobability sampling technique, TenHouten et al. (1971) have developed a strategy for drawing a probabilistic snowball sample, thus allowing computation of estimates of sampling error and the use of statistical tests of significance.

Snowball sampling, whether probabilistic or nonprobabilistic, is conducted in stages. In the first stage a few persons having the requisite characteristics are identified and interviewed. These persons are used as informants to identify others who qualify for inclusion in the sample. The second stage involves interviewing these persons, who in turn lead to still more persons who can be interviewed in the third stage, and so on. The term "snowball" stems from the analogy of a snowball, which begins small but becomes bigger and bigger as it rolls downhill.

If one wishes the snowball sample to be probabilistic, one should sample randomly within each stage. If a nonprobabilistic sample is sufficient, some method such as quota sampling can be used at each stage.

Some recent authors have referred to snowball sampling as "chain referral sampling" (Biernacki and Waldorf 1981). Like the former term, the newer term is generally descriptive of the sampling process. Snowball or chain referral sampling is particularly useful in the study of deviant subcultures where respondents may not be visible, and routine sampling procedure may be impractical (for example, the study of heroin addicts). Snowball sampling procedures have been rather loosely codified, resulting in a lack of rigor. Biernacki and Waldorf (1981) have attempted to rectify this situation through a methodological analysis of snowball sampling. Among the topics they discuss are finding respondents and beginning referral chains, verifying the eligibility of respondents, and controlling the types of chains and number of cases in each chain.

Sample Size

Introductory students of social research often have no conception of a minimally adequate sample size. Obviously the correct sample size is dependent upon the nature of the population and the purpose of the study. Some studies deal with small, esoteric populations (e.g., all Nobel Prize winners in Oregon). For such studies the entire population may number only six or seven, and a 100 percent sample is desirable. Usually the size of the sample depends on the size of the population to be sampled. Although general rules are hard to make without knowledge of the specific population, around 30 cases seems to be the bare minimum for studies in which statistical data analysis is to be done, although some techniques can be used with fewer than 30 cases (Champion 1970, p. 89). However, many researchers regard 100 cases as the minimum. One reason is that there are often several subpopulations the researcher wishes to study separately or several variables to be controlled for. For example, suppose that you are conducting a study of the relationship between education and income. You decide that 30 cases are sufficient and gather the data shown in figure 5–2. There are enough cases in each cell of the figure to meet the assumptions of standard statistical tests such as χ^2. However, suppose that the researcher submits an article containing these data to a sociological journal for publication and is told by the editor that since a person's race and sex affect his or her income, the figure should show these variables in addition to income and education. Upon breaking down the data by race, sex, education, and income, the researcher finds to his or her dismay that some cells of the figure contain too few cases for reliable data analysis. For example, he or she may find that the total sample of 30 contains only one black male college graduate and two black female college graduates. Thus it is important when deciding upon sample size to estimate how many times the sample may have to be subdivided during data analysis and to ensure an adequate sample size for each subdivision.

The researcher must also remember that, regardless of the theoretical sample size decided upon, the actual number of cases from which data are ultimately collected may be substantially fewer because of respondents who cannot be located, refuse to be interviewed, or return illegible or otherwise unusable questionnaires. A further point easily overlooked is that the sample size available for data analysis actually varies from question to question, depending on the percentage of respondents who fail to answer each particular question. Respondents who are

Figure 5–2

Relationship Between Education and Income

Income	Educational Level		Total
	College	No College	
$20,000+	10	5	15
Less than $20,000	5	10	15
Total	15	15	30

in a hurry to complete the questionnaire may inadvertently omit some items. Other respondents may deliberately leave blank questions that they feel are an invasion of privacy (e.g., questions about finances, sex, or religion). A question that requires much thought before it can be answered properly may also be left unanswered. Other questions may be ambiguous or have unclear answer categories, causing respondents to refuse to answer. It is not inconceivable that a particularly sensitive question could have a response rate of only 50 percent. In addition, some questions are not applicable to all respondents, thus lowering the sample size for that question. For example, a question asking for the number of past pregnancies could obviously be answered only by female respondents.

Statistical Considerations of Sample Size

Apart from the necessity of having a minimum number of cases for analyzing all combinations of groups or variables of interest, one must have the minimum sample size needed to represent accurately the population from which one is sampling. Lack of accurate representation can be referred to as sampling error. Although nonprobability sampling provides no basis for estimating sampling error, probability sampling does. The following discussion applies to simple random sampling only.

The sample size required to reflect the population value of a particular variable depends not only upon the size of the population but also on the amount of heterogeneity of the variable within the population. For populations of equal heterogeneity, as a general rule, the larger the population, the larger the sample required. However, for populations of equal size, the greater the heterogeneity on a variable, the larger the sample required. For populations in which there is no variability or heterogeneity on a variable, a sample of any size (even one) will suffice, regardless of the population size (that is, in cases of complete homogeneity the population size is immaterial in determining sample size).

For samples of any size, the most likely (most frequent) mean sample value on a particular variable, if many samples are drawn, is the population mean (see Selltiz et al. 1976, p. 525). Sampling theory assures us that we are more likely to estimate the population mean correctly from the sample mean than to estimate it incorrectly. If we draw many samples of a given size from a single population, most values of our sample mean will be near the population mean, and only a few will be very far from the population mean.

By drawing a large number of samples of a given size (e.g., five) from a single population, we can create a *sampling distribution*. In theory, if we draw enough samples of a given size, sooner or later we would draw all possible combinations of individuals in the population. The distribution of values of a sample statistic (such as a mean) produced through such repeated random sampling is called a sampling distribution. The Central Limit Theorem states that the sample means will be normally distributed around the population mean. The normal distribution is the familiar bell-shaped curve (figure 5–3). According to the Central Limit Theorem, the mean of all the sample means will be equal to the population mean value. Thus in a large number of samples of the same size, it is possible to obtain a sample mean value drastically different from the population mean value, but most of the sample mean values will be near the population mean value, and the average or mean of all the mean sample values will be the population mean value.

Figure 5–3
Normal Distribution of Sample Means

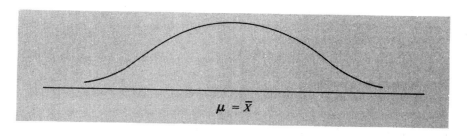

$$\mu = \overline{X}$$

To calculate the error involved in such sampling we first look at variation within the entire population. Suppose we are talking of only a single variable (e.g., height) for a population of 100 persons. For all 100 persons we calculate mean or average height by adding up the heights of all 100 and dividing by 100. Let X, be the height of person i, where i can vary from 1 to 100, representing all 100 persons in the population. Let N = the number of people in the population. In this case $N = 100$. The mean for a population (parameter) is generally symbolized by μ (the Greek letter mu). The mean of the sampling distribution (the mean of all sample means) is symbolized by $\mu_{\overline{x}}$, and the mean for a single sample is symbolized by $\overline{X}$. The population mean μ is calculated by the formula $\mu = \Sigma_{i=1}^{100} X_i / N$.

Assume that our population is a hypothetical one of 100 persons with a mean height of six feet, but with no two persons of the same height. We need some way to express the variation in this population. We can do it by simply determining how much each person (X_i) differs in height from the mean height (μ or $\overline{X}$). For example, if the population mean μ is six feet, and person number 3 (X_3) is five feet six inches tall, then the difference is $X_3 - \overline{X}$ or 66 inches – 72 inches which is –6 inches, with the minus sign indicating that person number 3 is shorter than the mean. If person number 33 is six feet six inches (78 inches) tall, then $X_{33} - \overline{X} = 78 - 72$ inches, or +6 inches.

But simply knowing the amount of variation from the mean for two different individuals is not enough. We need some summary measure of deviation for the entire group of people with whom we are dealing. The most obvious summary measure is derived by simply summing all of the deviations from the mean, or $\Sigma_{i=1}^{100} (X_i - \overline{X})$. However, since $\overline{X}$ is in the middle (is the mean), the plus and minus deviations will cancel each other out, resulting in a sum of zero. We can avoid this by squaring each deviation before summing. This average, $\Sigma_{i=1}^{100}(X_i - X)^2/N$, is known as the variance, and symbolized by σ^2 for the population and s^2 for the sample. By squaring we render all deviations positive, so that the sum will always be greater than zero. We can remove the square from the units by taking the square root. This statistic is known as the standard deviation (σ for populations, s for samples) = $\sqrt{(X - \overline{X})^2/N}$.

The standard deviation gives us a good summary measure of the average deviation from the mean. The greater the heterogeneity (the greater the standard deviation), the larger the sample size must be for the sample mean to be an accurate estimate of the population mean. We can also compute the standard deviation of the sample distribution of sample means around the population mean. This is called the standard error of the mean and is symbolized by σ_x and = $\sigma/\sqrt{N}$, where σ = the standard deviation for the population and N = the sample size. The standard error of the mean is the best estimate of the sampling error. It is clear that sampling error is dependent upon the variability of heterogeneity in the population as measured by σ and also upon the sample size N. The smaller the σ, the smaller the sampling error; the larger the N, the smaller the sampling error. If σ is very large, then N must be very large to counteract it. If σ is smaller, then N can be small and still provide a reasonably small sampling error.

Sample Size Versus Sampling Proportion

Notice that the formula for the standard error includes only the standard deviation (σ) and the sample size (N) and not the *sampling fraction,* which is the proportion of the total population size that is included in the sample. In theory, the sampling fraction should be included in the formula for the standard error, but it is generally excluded because it is usually irrelevant. The complete formula for the standard error is: S.E. = $(\sigma/\sqrt{N})(\sqrt{(1-f)/1}\,)$, where f is the sampling fraction. One would think intuitively that if only a small proportion of the population were in the sample, then the standard error would be greatly affected. That is, a few thousand households would not seem sufficient to represent the entire U.S. population of over 200 million. But the formula shows that for very large populations, the opposite is true. That is, if the sample contains only a very small proportion of the population, then f is very near zero, so that the multiplier $\sqrt{1-f}$ becomes simply $\sqrt{1}$, or 1, which makes no difference in the standard error. Notice that this applies only to large populations, since in a small population a small f would imply a small N, which would result automatically in a large standard error. Thus it is easy to see why for a national poll of the United States, for example, it is the sample size rather than the sampling fraction that is most important in determining the amount of sampling error, and we can rest comfortably with a sample that includes only a small proportion of all Americans *as long as* the sample N is sufficiently large. Remember that this is especially true for a very homogeneous population.

Sample Size for Stratified Sampling

The sample within each stratum (if randomly drawn) can be considered an independent sample of the population of that stratum. That is, if university professors are being sampled in three strata of assistant professors, associate professors, and full professors, then the sample of associate professors is a random sample of the population of all associate professors in the university, and the formula for the standard error given above applies in this case.

Remember that the degree of sampling error depends not only on the sample size but also on the degree of heterogeneity in the population being sampled. Stratified sampling offers the possibility that a very heterogeneous population (which would require a large sample size without stratification) can be stratified into a number of relatively homogeneous strata, each requiring a relatively small sample.

Often stratified random sampling is *disproportionate,* meaning that a higher proportion of the population is sampled in one stratum than in another. The sampling error formula given above points out at least two possible reasons for making a stratified random sample dispro-portionate—differences in population size and homogeneity among strata. If the population of a particular stratum is very small we may have to sample the entire population in order to gain an acceptable sample size (an acceptably low degree of sampling error). Similarly, a larger proportion of the population will have to be sampled in a very heterogeneous stratum than in a more homogeneous stratum. For example, if we are drawing a stratified sample of Catholics, Protestants, and Jews in a Southern town that contains 800 Catholics, 1,000 Protestants, but only 200 Jews, obviously we would have to sample a higher proportion of Jews than of either Catholics or Protestants merely to maintain the sample size necessary to ensure a sufficient degree of sampling accuracy.

Weighted Samples

The major problem with disproportionate sampling arises when one wishes to combine the subsamples into one overall sample for purposes of data analysis. Since the strata were dis-proportionately sampled, with random sampling within strata, the sample was not random overall, as elements within some strata had a higher probability of selection than elements within other strata. This problem can be overcome by the use of weights when combining the samples from the respective strata. In the example above, suppose that we draw random sam-ples respectively of 100 Jews, 100 Protestants, and 100 Catholics. When we combine these into an overall sample we will be combining sampling elements with a one out of two proba-bility of selection (Jews), a one out of eight probability (Catholics), and a one out of ten prob-ability (Protestants). Thus each Jew has a probability of selection four times that of each Cath-olic and five times that of each Protestant. For each sampling element to be represented with the same probability of selection there should be four times as many Catholics in the sample as there now are (400) and five times as many Protestants (500). Short of resampling, the only way to ensure that all three groups are proportionately represented is through unequal weight-ing. In general, proportionate representation can be achieved by noting the probability of se-lection for a group and assigning a weight equal to the inverse of this probability of selection. Since Jews have a one out of two probability of selection, the weight for the Jewish strata is two (the denominator in the probability selection). Similarly, the weight for Catholics is eight and for Protestants ten. In this particular case, since all of these weights are divisible by two we would simply divide by two and assign a weight of one to Jews (that is, not weight them), four to Catholics, and five to Protestants.

Examples of Weighted Samples

To see more clearly what is happening, assume that we administered a questionnaire to each person in the sample for each stratum and entered the data for each person into the computer (via a computer terminal), so that we had one data line per person. Thus each of the 100 Jews has his or her own data line, each of the 100 Catholics has a data line, and each of the 100 Protestants has a data line. The problem is that if we had sampled in the same proportion from each stratum (say one out of two), we would have sampled 400 Catholics instead of only 100, and therefore would have 400 data lines for them. Similarly, we would have 500 data lines for Protestants. Is there any way we can get 300 more data lines for Catholics and 400 more for Protestants without resampling? This can be done simply by duplicating each of the 100 Catholic data lines three times, and adding these 300 duplicates to the original 100. Similarly, each of the 100 Protestants data lines is duplicated four times, and the 400 duplicates are added to the 100 originals for a total sample size of 500 data lines. Alternatively, weighting can be achieved simply by multiplying the number of cases in the stratum by the weight for that stratum (four for Catholics, five for Protestants) during data analysis. For example, suppose we used our unweighted data to construct the following table showing educational levels by religion:

	Religion		
Educational Level	Jewish	Catholic	Protestant
Eighth grade or less	19	23	20
High school	21	38	40
College	60	39	40
Total	100	100	100

To construct a weighted table that represents all strata with a probability of selection of one out of two we multiply all figures in the Catholic column by four and all figures in the Protestant column by five, yielding the following weighted table:

	Religion		
Educational Level	Jewish	Catholic	Protestant
Eighth grade or less	19	92	100
High school	21	152	200
College	60	156	200
Total	100	400	500

Notice that such weighting does not change the average values of the data. For example, the mean level of education is not changed and is the same in the weighted as in the unweighted table. That is, the percentage of Catholics with a college education is the same in the weighted and unweighted tables. Disproportionate stratified sampling combined with weighting ensures adequate and equal representation of all strata.

Weighting is also frequently used when different geographical areas are sampled. For example, suppose we wish to draw a sample of Chicano households in the Los Angeles area. Census tract maps prepared by the Bureau of the Census will show us the areas of Los Angeles that contain dense concentrations of Mexican Americans. However, these are relatively low-income areas, and if we confine our sample to them we will exclude the more affluent Chicanos living in the suburbs. The problem is that the suburban Chicano populations are generally much sparser, and to ensure an adequate sample size we must resort to disproportionate sampling and then use weights when combining the suburban population with the inner-city population for overall data analysis.

Sample Size for Cluster Sampling

The logic of sample size is a little different for cluster sampling from that in stratified sampling. In stratified sampling every stratum is sampled, and each is of interest in itself. Stratified random sampling is thus in a real sense a number of separate random samples. However, cluster sampling is performed chiefly for efficiency and economy. We do not sample every cluster but sample among clusters. The only sample size in which we are really interested is the size of the ultimate sample of sampling elements. We are interested in the number of clusters sampled and the sample size within each cluster only as they affect this ultimate sample size.

Since cluster sampling consists of a number of random samples in consecutive stages, it is important that a sufficiently large N be achieved in each of the samples. If the first stage requires sampling from a population of 100 city blocks, then the larger the number of blocks sampled, the better. However, we must remember that if more blocks are sampled and total sample size is fixed, fewer households per block can be sampled. A more complicated statistical discussion of sampling size for cluster sampling is beyond the scope of this book. For further discussion and specific formulae see Mendenhall, Ott, and Scheaffer (1971, pp. 132–37).

Special Sampling Problems

Special kinds of studies often lead to special sampling problems. One persistent problem is the sampling of rare populations. For discussion of this and other issues see Frankel and Frankel (1987). Other special sampling problems have been spawned by recent research innovations. These include the special problems inherent in securing samples for exit polling or preelection surveys (Traugott 1987).

Telephone surveys also have special sampling problems (see Traugott et al. 1987, as well as chapter 8 in this volume). A very recent development is the computer survey or electronic survey (see chapter 8) in which the respondent types answers directly into a computer terminal. In addition to the obvious requirement that everyone in the sample must have access to a computer terminal, there are other special sampling problems as well. For further discussion of computer-survey sampling see Walsh et al. 1992).

Summary

Chapter 5 dealt with survey sampling. We first distinguished between a population and a sample and defined such technical terms as unit of analysis, sampling element, and sampling frame. The advantages and disadvantages of sampling were discussed, along with examples of prominent sampling failures and successes.

After distinguishing between probability sampling methods—in which the probability of selection of each element is known in advance—and nonprobability methods—in which probability of selection is not known—we discussed a number of well-known methods of each type. In general, only the probability methods yield data suitable for statistical analysis. Probability methods discussed in detail were random sampling, systematic sampling, stratified sampling, and cluster sampling. Nonprobability methods discussed were convenience sampling, quota sampling, dimensional sampling, purposive sampling, and snowball sampling. The chapter ended with a discussion of weighted samples, of sample size for the various sampling methods, and of special sampling problems.

CHAPTER 6

QUESTIONNAIRE CONSTRUCTION

BEFORE BEGINNING OUR DISCUSSION of questionnaire construction, a brief look at the survey method in general (discussed in detail herein and in chapters 7 and 8) is in order. A *survey* consists of asking questions of a (supposedly) representative cross-section of the population at a single point in time. The persons of whom the questions are asked are called survey *respondents*. The questions are often mailed to respondents (see chapter 7), asked by an interviewer in the person's home or elsewhere (chapter 8), asked over the telephone by an interviewer (chapter 8), or handed out (as in a classroom setting) for the respondent to answer and return. Surveys are usually conducted on samples (see chapter 5) simply because it is generally not feasible to interview everyone in the population. Surveys that do interview everyone are called *censuses*. Surveys that question respondents about some topic of public opinion (for example, attitudes toward marijuana or war in the Middle East) are called *public opinion polls*.

When we say that surveys are conducted at a single point in time we obviously do not mean that every single respondent is interviewed at exactly the same instant. We simply mean that data collection is completed in as short a time period as possible, usually in a single week or month, but certainly in a single year. Some surveys are exceptions to the "single point in time" rule. Surveys that are conducted over a longer period of time, with the same respondents being reinterviewed, are called *panel studies* (see chapter 8). Studies in which the same topic (for example, attitudes toward abortion) is studied by reinterviewing over a period of time, but with no attempt to reinterview the same individual respondents each time, are called *trend studies*. All studies conducted over time are called *longitudinal studies*.

If the researcher merely wishes to study general trends, this can be done with two or more (repeated) surveys that ask the same questions of the same general type of sample (e.g., to all registered voters), without any conscious attempt to reinterview in a subsequent survey the same respondents that were interviewed earlier. Thus, we could interview a sample of all registered voters in the United States in 1940, 1950, 1960, 1970, 1980, and 1990 concerning their attitudes toward women in the labor force and doubtless discern a trend, over the decades, of increased acceptance of female employment. Notice that while it is conceivable that some persons would be interviewed in every study, some of the persons interviewed in 1940 would doubtless be deceased in 1990. Further, using a constant minimum voting age of 21, some of the younger voters interviewed in 1990 would not have been born when the first three surveys (1940, 1950, and 1960) were conducted.

In a panel study, however, one follows the same group of respondents and reinterviews them at every phase (usually called a "wave") of the study. This is not practical for a long-range study but can be very useful for such things as determining exactly the point at which undecided voters make up their minds about whom to vote for or for determining the exact age at which teenaged respondents develop certain attitudes about marriage and reproduction. The most difficult thing about a panel study, particularly a large study conducted over a long period, is "panel mortality." Some members of the panel will actually die during the course of the study, while others will move long distances away or otherwise be difficult to reinterview without great cost.

In addition to being conducted at a single point in time, other characteristics of the survey that distinguish it from methods such as document analysis and observation are that (1) there is a fixed set of questions and (2) responses are systematically classified, so that quantitative comparisons can be made. However, these are characteristics of the "pure" survey, and actual surveys vary both in the degree of structure in their questions (for example, from structured to semistructured; see chapter 8) and in how their responses are coded (see this chapter and chapter 14). A good history of survey research, along with a clear discussion of some advantages and disadvantages of surveys, is provided by Marsh (1982). Also see Converse (1987), Bradburn and Sudman (1988), and Singer and Presser (1989).

Constructing Questionnaires

Once the concepts and hypotheses have been carefully formulated and a good sample drawn, the next link in the research chain is the data-collection instrument (questionnaire or interview schedule). A *questionnaire* is generally mailed or handed to the respondent and filled in by him or her with no help from the interviewer. An instrument that is not given directly to the respondent but is filled in by an interviewer who reads the questions to the respondent is generally called an *interview schedule*. We shall use the term "questionnaire" as the generic name for both types.

A good way to begin writing the questionnaire, anticipating possible sources of error, is first to list some of the reasons why a respondent might give erroneous information or might even fail to answer a question altogether. Unfortunately, the reasons are numerous. Some of the problems and their possible remedies are as follows:

1. Respondent feels the interview is not legitimate but is a subterfuge either to sell him or her something (encyclopedia salespersons often gain entry by first conducting a brief survey) or for some other commercial purpose such as conducting a credit check. Remedy: A well-written cover letter or introductory statement legitimizing the study. If the problem is really acute, more drastic measures such as a prior announcement in a newspaper may be necessary.
2. Respondent feels that the information will be used against him or her or is an invasion of privacy (e.g., he or she fears that income information will be released to IRS). Remedy: Omit unnecessarily sensitive questions. Necessary sensitive questions can be used in a subsample only, or put last on the questionnaire after other questions have been answered. Assure the respondent of anonymity.
3. Respondent refuses to cooperate, saying that he or she has "done his or her share" by being interviewed in a previous survey.
4. Respondent is an ethnic-minority member who says he or she is tired of "being a guinea pig" and refuses to be interviewed, suggesting that the respondent study rich people for a while.
5. Respondent is "sophisticated" (e.g., head of a county department), gets many questionnaires, and knows what the investigator wants to hear and where the reliability checks are located in the questionnaire. Remedy for 3, 4, and 5: Survey saturation has become a problem of major proportions with the proliferation of polling and survey organizations. Although sampling helps to ensure that the same person will not be interviewed over and over again, some surveys such as panel studies require resampling, and other respondents may have unique characteristics that make them in demand for surveys. In such cases the investigator can try "sampling around" a particular respondent. For ex-

ample, in a cluster sample he or she could simply not draw a cluster if it has been studied previously. If the respondent must be interviewed, the researcher must make a special appeal, assuring him or her that the interview is necessary and that no one else can be substituted. The interviewer can say that his or her sample is a scientific one that does not allow substitutions.

6. Respondent answers "normatively," the way he or she thinks he or she should answer, whether it is an honest answer or not. Remedy: The same as 2.

7. Respondent is afraid that his or her responses will reveal lack of education or that he or she will appear stupid. Remedy: Emphasize that there are no right and wrong answers, assure anonymity.

8. Respondent says that his or her time is too valuable to waste on the study, that the study is not applicable to him or her. He or she argues that it is not important that he or she be studied anyway and that a relative or neighbor who has more free time should be substituted. Remedy: Same as 5.

9. Respondent says he or she cannot answer because the question is too general and vague, or because he or she has never thought about the topic. Remedy: Use more specific probing questions to guide the answer.

There are many other excuses that respondents give for refusing to answer, such as that the answer categories are insufficient or inappropriate, or that there are too many redundant questions, or that the researcher did not ask the correct questions. This list is obviously not exhaustive, and the remedies are not presented in detail. These items, however, illustrate the threats to reliability and validity that are present in the survey method. We are now ready to discuss questionnaire design more specifically.

Questionnaire Relevance

The key word in questionnaire construction is "relevance." Although relevance can sometimes be an overworked catchword, the term has real meaning for questionnaire construction. Prior to questionnaire construction the researcher has had to see that the operational definitions matched the theoretical concepts (chapters 3 and 4) and that the sample matched the population from which it was drawn (chapter 5). In questionnaire design he or she must combine both spheres, making sure that the questions measure the theoretical concepts adequately and that the sample of respondents answers the questions adequately. The word "relevance" has three different facets here: (1) relevance of the study's goals; (2) relevance of questions to the goals of the study; and (3) relevance of the questions to the individual respondent.

Relevance of the Study

First, the entire goal or raison d'être of the study must seem relevant to the respondent. This is sometimes a problem, for research goals are not always clear outside of their scientific context, especially to a lay respondent. The obvious procedure is to clarify, explain, and justify the goals of the study to the respondent, and this is one of the chief purposes of the cover letter accompanying the questionnaire. However, sometimes the nature of the study is too complex to be explained in a cover letter or cannot be revealed without biasing the responses.

The importance of making the research project seem relevant, worthwhile, legitimate, or whatever word one wishes to use cannot be overemphasized. The researcher must remember that except in those rare cases in which respondents are paid for the interview, the respondent is working for free. He or she is donating his or her time, which he or she considers very valuable, as most people have more things to do than they have time for. (How can a college-student respondent explain to her lonely aged mother that she had 20 minutes free to answer your questionnaire but did not have 20 minutes to write her mother a letter?) A favorite pastime on talk shows these days is to discuss the list of research topics for which U.S. government grants have been given and which appear to the layperson to be a ludicrous and shocking waste of the taxpayer's money. Any researcher with such a project is going to be faced not only with numerous refusals but with sabotaged data, and maybe even with lectures or threats of violence.

On the other hand, experienced researchers have found that most people are willing to aid in projects they feel to be worthwhile and to have scientific value. Convincing the respondent that the project is worthwhile can be more effective than paying him or her money in getting him or her to respond. People who will not take money to answer a questionnaire they consider to be a waste of their time and an insult to their intelligence will answer a lengthy and time-consuming questionnaire that they feel serves a good purpose.

Relevance of Questions to the Study

After the respondents are convinced that the purpose of the study is relevant, they must be convinced that all the questions (often called *items*) in the questionnaire are relevant to the stated goals of the study. Again, to the inexperienced researcher this might not seem a serious problem, but it is. Virtually all questionnaires contain wasted questions. Especially if more than one researcher is submitting questions, there is a tendency to include a number of items that sound important without thinking through how they will ultimately be used. A good tactic is to decide, before including an item in the questionnaire, exactly how the answers will be analyzed (what statistical techniques will be used) and how the data will be published or otherwise presented. If you cannot decide in advance how the data will be used, do not ask the question. Also, since the process of sampling and interviewing is very expensive, there is a tendency for researchers to reason that since the survey is being conducted anyway, it will involve little or no additional cost to let a few marginal questions or questions pertaining to a different study "piggyback" on the questionnaire.

The respondent, however, considers his or her time to be precious and does not want to waste it on needless questions. Further, he or she may, whether or not it is "realistic" to do so, look upon the questionnaire as a reflection upon himself or herself and his or her ego. Although the researcher assures them that there are no right or wrong answers, only opinions, and that the answers will remain anonymous, many respondents will regard the questionnaire as a kind of test and attempt to answer so that they do not appear to be stupid. At the same time they are judging the questionnaire, just as many students judge their professor's examinations and tell their peers whether they consider the exam fair, unfair, easy, and so on. Many a novice researcher has discovered to his or her chagrin that the respondents were judging him or her, by having a questionnaire returned anonymously with such comments as "This question is so stupid that I refuse to answer it." Of course, lack of relevance to the study is not the only reason for refusal to respond (a poorly worded question can also elicit the "stupid" label), but it is one of the main ones.

Remember when writing questions that we see ourselves as others see us. As in Cooley's (1922, p. 184) looking-glass self, we feel constantly that we are being judged by others and look to them for some clue as to how they see us. A questionnaire provides a concrete basis for negative as well as positive evaluation of a respondent. Many respondents feel that they have more to lose than to gain by completing a questionnaire and so become easily frustrated by questions they consider irrelevant, ambiguous, or just plain dumb.

Relevance of Questions to Respondents

The relevance of each question to the particular respondent can be a severe problem when two or more populations are being served by the same questionnaire (e.g., men and women, or citizens and noncitizens).

Often the study is a comparative one whose chief purpose is to compare the views of one group (for example, those in a prepaid health-care plan) with those of another group (persons not in the plan). There are three main ways to make sure that a respondent is not asked a question that does not apply to him or her: (1) use of two or more separate questionnaires for the respective populations (female questionnaire, male questionnaire); (2) use of multiple wording, so that the respondent or interviewer can pick the appropriate phrase ("Have you [your wife, girlfriend] every had an abortion?"); and (3) skips or contingency questions ("If your answer is yes, skip to question 55"). The third alternative is probably the most common, and of course it can be used along with each of the others. The first alternative (separate forms of the questionnaires) is very expensive, and the second (alternate wording) is confusing and can lead to error, especially in self-administered questionnaires, when the respondent has had no previous experience with this type of question. However, this problem cannot be ignored, for irrelevant or inapplicable questions can be very frustrating, especially to authoritarian or rigid personality types, and may account for many unreturned questionnaires. Some respondents are even upset by inapplicable questions that the instructions clearly tell them to skip, especially if there are many such questions.

Pitfalls in Questionnaire Construction: Wording the Questions

Double-barreled Questions

Do not include two or more questions in one. For example, how should the respondent answer the question "Does your department have a special recruitment policy for racial minorities and women?" when his or her department makes a strong attempt to recruit ethnic minorities but does not attempt to recruit women? A negative answer implies that the department recruits neither group, while a positive answer implies that the department recruits both groups. Such a question typically leads to hesitation and indecision on the part of the respondent. Frustration builds up (particularly if there is more than one such question), and the respondent often decides that the question is inadequate, that he or she could have constructed a better questionnaire, and that answering this one is beneath his or her dignity.

Questions with "or" or "and" in them should be checked to see if they consist of two questions with only one answer expected. "And" questions are particularly vulnerable to this. "Or" questions may be adequate, especially if "either" is added and if the two subjects covered by the question can be assumed to be mutually exclusive. For example, "Do you regularly attend religious services at a church or synagogue?" may not be a double-barreled question if the researcher can assume that the two religious services are mutually exclusive, and a respondent who attends a church will not attend a synagogue. Alternatively, the researcher may merely want to classify respondents into the groups "religious" (attends some sort of service) or "not religious" (does not attend services). All he or she needs in this case is an "either-or" answer— "Do you attend either a church or a synagogue?" A person who attends neither would answer no. A person who attends one or the other (but not both) would answer yes. The rare person who attends both would also answer yes and could not be distinguished from the person who attends only one. However, if this information were not needed by the researcher the question would still work, as long as it did not confuse or frustrate the respondent.

Ambiguous Questions

Obviously no researcher would purposely make questions ambiguous. However, ambiguity is sometimes difficult to avoid. Some words are themselves vague and ambiguous (see Labaw 1980, pp. 1–11 and 154–161). Terms such as "social integration," for example, may not be well known to the respondents. The meaning of some words may be known only to highly educated respondents. Slang or colloquial phrases may be known only to one group, or may have different meanings for different groups. Word meanings can vary with geographical area, age group ("the generation gap"), or subculture. Such differences can present a real communication problem if the group of respondents is not homogeneous. For example, the word "bad" has negative connotations in standard usage but in black slang can have either positive or negative connotations depending upon inflection and context. Similarly, "punk," though consistently a derogatory label, refers to a cheap criminal as used on television police shows or in general slang usage but means a homosexual in prison slang; "bread" can mean both something to eat and something you spend.

One possible solution is to avoid slang in question wording. The best precaution is to word each question carefully and to pretest all questions before the actual study by trying them out on people of as many ages, educational levels, ethnic groups, and so on, as possible, to see if they are clear to the respondents.

One problem with ambiguously worded questions, as in double-barreled questions, is that the researcher may be getting answers to what are really two or more different questions, as different respondents interpret a question in different ways. Such errors are devastating to a study, for they are very difficult to detect and correct. Simple failure to answer the question would be preferable, for then the researcher at least would know where he or she stands.

To show how easily ambiguities can arise, consider the question, "In which class do you belong, male or female?" While the wording is rather awkward, the question probably will not be interpreted ambiguously by respondents. Most respondents will simply interpret it as an invitation to specify their gender, and they will respond. But now consider a similarly worded question concerned with a different topic: "In which social class do your parents belong, upper class, upper middle, middle class, lower middle, or lower class?" The word "belong" is here ambiguous. Some respondents would interpret this question as they would the gender question, as asking which social class the respondent's parents *are* currently in. However, others interpret the question as asking which class they *deserve* to be in, or *ought* to be in, either now or ultimately. Thus you can have two respondents, both with middle-class parents, but one answering "middle class" and the other "upper class" (the rightful place from which his or her parents were cheated by fate). These are really two questions passing ambiguously as one. Unfortunately, questions similar to this have been used more than once on expensive surveys.

Another unfortunate example that has actually been used on a survey concerns race or skin color. Questions on race are often sensitive and should be carefully worded. Many researchers are unsure even where to begin. They do not know whether to conceptualize the question in terms of skin color, race, or ethnicity. They may be unable to list all categories but are afraid of offending persons in the residual or "other" category (as in black, white, Chicano, other). Nobody wants to be "other." Fortunately, the question is by now rather standard, having been asked so many times that one does not have to worry too much about wording. The researcher can merely write: "7. Circle one. Black, Chicano, Native American, Asian American, Anglo, Other," and be fairly sure of being understood. However, one study overworded the question by asking "Which of the following do you identify with: Black, Chicano . . . ?" The responses to this question were devastating. More than one respondent answered that he or she identified with all of the races mentioned, while others answered that they did not identify with any of them. Others were unsure of what sort of "identification" was meant: symbolic, emotional, or intellectual. Some respondents simply gave their race, as intended by the researcher. Others, however, felt that something more was intended ("If that's all they wanted they wouldn't have said identify"), and answered in terms of their interpretation of "identify." Many respondents were so frustrated or angered by the poor wording of this question that they simply stopped right there and did not answer the remainder of the questions or return the questionnaire. Other respondents returned the questionnaire with scathing comments.

Apparently the word "identify" was intended to show awareness on the part of the researcher that the racial label was a subjective decision, but the results were unfortunate. The researcher would have been better off with the open-ended question, "What is your race?" He or she would have had to code and group the many responses received and would have had to put up with the usual immature answers (hundred-yard dash, 440) from the same people who always answer "sex" with "yes," but most of the answers received would have been more valid and reliable.

Lack of knowledge on the part of the researcher can cause him or her to write a question that contains no ambiguous words but is ambiguous in the sense that the respondent does not know how to answer. For example, one study asked the seemingly unambiguous question: "Is your union affiliated with the AFL or the CIO?" Unbeknown to the researcher, one union had formerly been affiliated with the AFL but no longer had any affiliation with either group.

Members of that union were unsure how to answer. Some answered that they were affiliated with the AFL, some that they were not. Again, a single question received answers to two different questions. Such occurrences can be avoided only through homework, chiefly through exploratory studies.

Another kind of ambiguity can arise if the item is stated not as a question but as a statement to be agreed or disagreed with, or labeled true or false. Take the statement, "Abortions should be legal for women who want them." The majority of Americans, even Catholics, feel that abortions are justifiable in some extreme cases such as tubal pregnancies, in which the baby has no chance of survival and the mother's life is in danger. However, the number agreeing with the statement when the mother's life is not endangered is substantially lower. Thus the answer for many to such a question is "Yes and no, depending upon the circumstances." Some respondents will try to second-guess what the researcher meant, others answer in terms of what they feel to be the most likely, frequent, or probable case, and others simply refuse to answer the question (and if their frustration level is high enough, throw the questionnaire away). Once again we have two or more questions being answered where only one was intended, and no clue as to which one the respondent is answering (unless he or she indicates as much in a marginal notation, which happens quite frequently).

Level of Wording

The wording of the question, including such concerns as the difficulty of the words used, the degree of formality of the language, and whether slang or colloquialisms are used, is a difficult matter and depends not only upon the educational level and characteristics of the respondent but also upon the characteristics of the researcher. Question wording can greatly affect the answers received (see Schuman and Duncan 1974). In addition to clarity, the key factor in question writing is parsimony. A general rule for writing questionnaire items is that the shortest version that conveys what is intended is best. Never use two or three words when one would suffice. Longer questions take up more of the respondent's time, make him or her less willing to cooperate and increase the probability that he or she will not understand the question. This is perhaps more important in a mailed-out questionnaire, where the respondent must read the questions himself or herself, than in an interview situation in which the question is read to him or her. However, when a lengthy question is read to him or her he may have trouble understanding and remembering and may ask the interviewer to repeat it. Repetition not only increases interview time and thus adds to the cost of the study but is also frustrating for both respondent and interviewer.

Sometimes the use of apparently similar words can make a significant difference in response. Smith (1987) found that respondents' opinions on assistance for the needy were significantly different when the word "welfare" was used instead of "poor." "Welfare" elicits more negative and less generous responses, and seems to imply notions of waste and bureaucracy. Rasinski (1989) found similar effects of different wordings. For example, "dealing with drug addiction" elicits a more favorable response than "drug rehabilitation," while "halting rising crime rate" is viewed more favorably than "law enforcement."

In a study of national health surveys, Fowler (1992) analyzed seven questions that were found to include ambiguous or poorly defined terms. When the questions were revised to clarify the definitions of key terms, the results were improved. For example, one question was, "What is the average number of days each week that you have butter?" (Fowler 1992, p. 222). The problem was that some respondents ate margarine, and were unsure whether it counted. The clarification was to say the question was just about butter, and did not include margarine. For further discussion of wording effects, see also Converse and Presser (1986, pp. 41–42). They note that while "forbid" and "allow" seem to be opposites, in a question regarding speeches against democracy in the United States, many more people are willing to "not allow" such speeches than to forbid them.

After resolving to avoid ambiguous wordings and to keep questions as short as possible, the researcher must decide what level of wording is appropriate. If he or she is researching drinking behavior, the researcher should not ask, "Is anyone in your family a dipsomaniac?" However neither should he or she ask, "Is anyone in your family a drunk (or sot or wino)?" The term "dipsomaniac" will not be understood by all respondents, while words such as "drunk" or "wino" have negative connotations that many respondents might resent, just as they might resent derogatory ethnic labels.

The level of word difficulty depends upon the educational level of the respondents. Words such as "hiatus" and "preclude" can probably be safely used with a college-educated sample but not with persons with less than a high-school education. In general, a mailed-out questionnaire requires simpler wording than the interview, because there is no recourse (other than unanswered or incorrectly answered questions) if words are not understood. But even in an interview study it is important that questions not be above the educational level of the sample, as many respondents are embarrassed to admit they do not understand a word (especially if they think persons of their educational level should know it) and will give any answer instead of requesting clarification. Further, the practice of having interviewers interpret questions should be avoided; it destroys standardization, since some respondents ask for clarification and others do not. Clarification of questions by interviewers can also bias the respondent's answer.

Many researchers feel that they should phrase their questions in the respondent's everyday slang so as to maximize rapport between respondent and researcher. This is perhaps one of those matters for which there is no right or wrong choice. However, several things should be borne in mind when contemplating the use of slang (see the discussion under "Ambiguous Questions" above). One is the level of generalizability of such terms. If the questionnaire is meant for only a small subpopulation, such terms may suffice, but if the study is to be replicated using populations of different age groups or geographic areas, use of these terms may lead to lack of understanding. Another thing to remember is that just as there is a difference between the average person's public and private personality, there is also a difference between the average person's written and spoken language. A person who would conversationally say "I ain't gonna do it" would write, "I am not going to do it." Thus if you mail him or her a questionnaire saying "I ain't going to do such and such in the near future" (agree or disagree) he or she might find the wording peculiar and may feel uncomfortable replying, even though he or she regularly uses such wording conversationally.

Surveying is a two-way street—a social interaction between researcher and respondent. Many subcultures are protective of their argot and discourage its use by outsiders. In fact, when a word achieves common usage in the larger host or outgroup population it generally loses its value as a symbol of in-group solidarity and is often discarded by the in-group. If the interviewer happens to be a member of the in-group, he or she may be allowed to use the words. But survey researchers generally represent entities such as universities, government agencies, or market-research organizations—i.e., the "establishment" rather than various in-groups. Their attempts to use in-group argot may be regarded derisively by respondents (just as teenagers may resent dad's attempt to imitate their hairstyle, dress, and speech). Often the speech and other subcultural manifestations such as dress are the only unique characteristics in which the in-group can take pride, and they resent attempts by others to "steal" their words.

A related issue is that in order to secure the cooperation of respondents the researcher will have to convince them that he or she is a legitimate researcher. Generally he or she will emphasize that he or she is a "scientist." Often he or she will have the backing of considerable authority, such as the U.S. government. The norm dictates that such respectable and highly educated people as scientists should not use bad grammar or colloquialisms. The survey, as a form of social interaction, is a formal or secondary relationship that is conducted not for the purpose of making the interviewer and the respondent buddies, but only to gather scientific information. If it were an in-group interaction between peers or family members, informal language would be appropriate. But in a secondary relationship between a scientist or government official and a respondent, with the interaction initiated by the researcher, more formal language is in order.

Abstract Versus Factual Questions

Questions should refer to concrete and specific matters and have specific answers, if possible. Questions concerning matters such as age or sex are specific. The respondent not only is familiar with the concept, he or she is also familiar with the appropriate response categories. Questions about historical events such as the Kennedy assassinations are also concrete. The main problems that arise with such questions are due to memory failure, especially for events that occurred long ago. Questions about abstract concepts such as happiness or love or justice are much more difficult to answer. Although the respondent is probably familiar with the concept of happiness, he or she may find it difficult to answer a question about his or her "happiness level." Questions such as "How happy are you?—very happy, moderately happy, unhappy," may have low reliability.

Opinion questions are especially difficult. The respondent often does not have an opinion because he or she has never thought about the topic. He or she is concerned about appearing stupid, and must be reassured that there is no right or wrong answer. Such questions generally call for an agree-disagree response, as true or false would imply a single correct answer.

Leading Questions

Questions should be carefully structured in order to minimize the probability of biasing the respondent's answer by leading him or her and thus artificially increasing the probability of a particular response. The question should be asked in its more neutral form. For example, one would ask, "Do you smoke?" rather than "You don't smoke, do you?" Another way to bias a question is by citing an authority, such as "The majority of physicians in America feel that smoking is harmful; do you agree?" According to Selltiz et al. (1959, p. 564), in a study conducted some 30 years ago the mention of President Roosevelt's name caused around a 5 percent increase in affirmative answers in the second question: "Do you like the idea of having Thanksgiving a week earlier this year?" compared with "Do you like President Roosevelt's idea of having Thanksgiving a week earlier this year?" Additional examples of leading questions, utilizing explicitly nonneutral terms, are given by Sudman and Bradburn (1982, pp. 2–4).

In more recent research, Smith and Squire (1990) noted that while survey researchers are often warned against using "prestige names" (such as names of presidents) in research, they nevertheless are used quite frequently. They concluded that when prestige names are used, people respond not only on the content of the issue, but also on the basis of the name used. In another study, Lockerbie and Borrelli (1990), support for U.S. action to overthrow the government of Nicaragua was 13 percent. But when President Reagan's name was added, along with the term "pro-Soviet" government of Nicaragua, support rose to 23 percent.

Sensitive or Threatening Questions

Sensitive topics such as sex, or taboo topics such as suicide, are prone to normative answers—that is, answers that are consistent with a norm even though they are false answers for the particular respondents. This is also known as social-desirability bias. A norm is a statement of what one should or should not do. Norms can be prescriptive, telling what one should do (wait until the light turns green before walking, respect your elders), or proscriptive, telling what one should not do (Thou shalt not kill, you should not steal, you should not lie). Failure to adhere to norms is negatively sanctioned (punished) in ways varying in degree from gossip and social disapproval all the way to prison or even the electric chair. Social surveyors do not have the privilege of immunity, and if they elicited a response from a respondent that constituted admission to a crime they would have to report it to authorities or be a party to the crime. A respondent does not usually have to worry about legal repercussions from his or her answers, but he or she does have to worry about social disapproval if his or her answer fails to meet the norm. Since the respondent often has little to gain from answering the questionnaire (other than the social approval of aiding science), he or she often feels that there is more to lose by revealing anormative or deviant behavior. Thus he or she will feel under great pressure not to admit to proscribed behavior (masturbation, homosexuality, adultery) and to say that he or she does prescribed things that he or she does not do (e.g., attend church regularly).

How can a researcher encourage the respondent to provide the true answer even if that answer is socially undesirable (violates social norms)? Bernard Phillips (1971, p. 140) lists several strategies for dealing with normative answers. Questions that require the respondent to admit that he or she engages in socially undesirable behavior should be phrased in a manner that assumes that he or she engages in that behavior, forcing him or her to deny the behavior if he or she really does not engage in it (or if he or she does but will not admit it), rather than making it easy for the respondent to say that he or she does not engage in the behavior even if he or she really does. For example, one could ask a two-part question such as:

1. Do you masturbate? Yes ___ No ___ If yes, how often? Once a week, once a month, every day?

However, it is preferable to ask:

1. How frequently do you masturbate: Once a week, once a month, every day, never?

A second approach to reducing normative answers to sensitive questions is to word the question so as to presume that there is no consensus regarding the norm ("Some doctors feel that drinking is harmful while others feel that it is beneficial; what do you think?"). A third ploy is to indicate that the behavior is not deviant but is widely practiced, even though it may violate a norm ("Most people have masturbated at one time or another; have you?").

Two other suggestions are made by Phillips for dealing with sensitive issues. One is to use euphemisms (e.g., sanitation engineer rather than garbage man, or custodian rather than janitor). For questions that call upon the respondent to criticize some person or group, one can allow him or her also to praise the person or group, so that he will not feel that he or she is being unfair or discourteous.

Sometimes the respondent simply does not know the answer or does not have an opinion. This is also a normative situation. The respondent feels uncomfortable in not being able to respond. He or she fears that the investigator will consider him or her unintelligent or will withhold social approval. Thus the respondent will search for every possible clue to the appropriate response in the question wording or format and in the interviewer's phrasing, tone of voice, and facial expression. It is in situations such as this that the question must be neutrally worded with no hints or biases and no appeals to authorities. "I don't know" should be presented as an appropriate response.

Sudman and Bradburn (1974) and Bradburn and Sudman (1979) have conducted very detailed analyses of responses to sensitive or threatening questions. Sudman and Bradburn (1974, p. 47) investigated the role of question structure (open or closed—discussed in the next section), question length, question difficulty, and the position of the question in the questionnaire. For nonthreatening questions they found little difference in whether the question was open or closed, worded in a difficult fashion, long or short, or placed early or late in the questionnaire. For threatening questions, these factors did affect responses. Sudman and Bradburn (1974, p. 50) conclude that short questions of 12 words or less are more threatening than questions of 33 words or more, that more difficult questions receive inferior responses for threatening behavioral questions, and that threatening behavioral questions yield worse responses if placed early in the questionnaire than if placed later (see our discussion of question order later in this chapter).

In their later work, Bradburn and Sudman (1979) found a difference in the degree of threat that questions posed to respondents, depending upon whether the questions ask about performing a behavior even once within some time span and are answered "yes" or "no," or ask about the frequency of the behavior. For a simple yes or no, such factors as question format and question length seem to make little difference. However, for questions about frequency, open-ended questions with familiar wording obtained higher levels of response than short, closed, standard questions (Bradburn and Sudman 1979, p. 19). The questions were on gambling, drinking, and sex; they asked, for example, whether the respondent had played dice games for money, drunk hard liquor, or engaged in masturbation or sexual intercourse.

In their latest book on the subject, entitled *Asking Questions*, Sudman and Bradburn (1982) discuss both threatening and nonthreatening questions in great detail, and provide many examples. They also provide checklists of major points for asking both nonthreatening and threatening questions. They discuss determination of whether the question is threatening to the respondent or not, and various mechanisms for securing adequate answers. Their checklist of recommendations for asking threatening questions (Sudman and Bradburn 1982, pp. 55–56) includes the suggestion that open questions are preferable to closed for obtaining frequencies of socially undesirable behavior; the recommendation that long questions are better than short for undesirable behavior and the suggestion that threatening questions should be embedded into a list of more or less nonthreatening topics.

Sudman and Bradburn (1982) also recommend use of randomized response techniques (RRT) with sensitive questions. Originally introduced by Warner (1965), randomized response utilizes both the sensitive question (e.g., Have you ever used heroin?) and its negation (e.g., Have you never used heroin?). The respondent is given a randomizing device so that he or she can randomly determine the question to be asked, without the interviewer's knowledge of the outcome. In this way, the interviewer cannot directly determine the respondent's culpability, thus sparing him or her the embarrassment of the interviewer's knowledge. Although the technique may seem cumbersome, and although further research has shown that it may still contain bias and the respondent may still be embarrassed (Edgell et al. 1982), RRT can be an effective means of asking questions that otherwise perhaps could not be successfully asked.

Open and Closed Response Categories

Wording of the question itself is only part of the picture. Careful attention must be given to the response categories accompanying the question. A distinction is generally made between *open-ended* questions, or questions in which response categories are not specified, and fixed-alternative or *closed-ended* questions, in which the respondent selects one or more of the specific categories provided by the researcher. Like most things, each form has its advantages and disadvantages.

Closed-ended Questions

The advantages of fixed-alternative questions are: (1) The answers are standard, and can be compared from person to person. (2) The answers are much easier to code and analyze, and often can be coded directly from the questionnaire, saving time and money. (3) The respondent is often clearer about the meaning of the question (that is, a respondent who is unsure about the meaning of the question can often tell from the answer categories what is expected). Thus there are fewer frustrated respondents who answer "don't know" or fail to answer at all. This helps the return rate, since frustration over a single question can lead the respondent to discard the entire questionnaire. (4) The answers are relatively complete (if all appropriate answer categories are provided), and a minimum of irrelevant responses are received. For example, asking rural respondents the open-ended question, "How often do you go to town?" may provide such irrelevant and unusable answers as "Whenever I wish" or "When I can get a ride," when what is required is an estimate of the frequency. A closed-ended question with the response categories "once a week or less, two to five times a week, every day," will be more likely to elicit usable information. (5) Another often overlooked advantage of closed-ended questions arises when dealing with variables that are sensitive topics, the answers to which are numbers, such as income, number of years of school completed, and age. Such variables can generally be dealt with in open-ended questions ("How much money did you make last year?"). This is preferable from a data-analysis standpoint, because income is an intervally measured variable, and to change it to a closed-ended set of categories would require collapsing into income ranges (such as $8,000 to $10,000). When such categories are constructed the income variable is in effect changed from interval to ordinal, with a resulting loss of information. If such collapsing is required later, it can always be done, even if the question was originally asked as open-ended. However, if the question is originally asked as closed-ended but the answer categories prove to be inadequate, the interval information can never be restored. But the advantage of closed-ended income questions is that a respondent who would refuse to provide his or her exact income in response to an open-ended question may be willing to identify the range in which his or her income falls. Thus for a variable that has a number for an answer, an open-ended question is preferred from a data-analysis standpoint, but a closed-ended question is preferable if it is the only way the respondent will cooperate. (6) A sixth and final advantage is that the closed-ended question is often easier for a respondent to answer as he or she merely has to choose a category, while formulating an original answer for an open-ended question can be much more difficult.

Some disadvantages of closed-ended questions are: (1) It is very easy for a respondent who does not know the answer or has no opinion to try to guess the appropriate answer or even to answer randomly. (2) The respondent may feel frustrated because the appropriate category for his or her answer either is not provided at all or is not provided in sufficient detail, and there is no opportunity for the respondent to clarify or qualify his or her answer. (3) There may be too many answer categories to print on the questionnaire, or there may be so many categories that the respondent could not remember them all if they were read aloud by the interviewer. This causes rereading and repetition, can lead to errors, and results in a much lengthier and more expensive interview. Obviously one would not ask age as a closed-ended question by listing 100 categories from one to 100. The chief alternatives are to ask an open-ended question or to collapse categories into ranges (0–10 years, 11–20 years). Another alternative when there are too many answer categories to be remembered in an interview is to show the respondent a card listing the alternatives. For example, for the question, "Which of these birth-control methods have you used?" the interviewer's instruction would read "Hand respondent card A." Card A would list the various methods, which would be difficult to remember if merely read aloud (the pill, condom, douche, diaphragm, etc.). (4) Differences in interpretation of what was meant by the question may go undetected, whereas in an open-ended question one might be able to tell from the written answer that the respondent misinterpreted the question. (5) Variations in answers among the different respondents may be eliminated artificially by forced-choice responses. (6) There is more likelihood of a clerical error as the respondent may circle a three when he or she meant to circle a two. Such mistakes do not occur with open-ended responses.

We said above that one disadvantage of closed-ended questions is that an answer is provided for a respondent who has no opinion or does not know, but is tempted to choose one of the convenient responses. This being the case, the question arises as to whether a "Don't Know" (DK) response category should be included. Schuman and Presser (1979, p. 251) studied the assessment of "no opinion" in surveys. They used what they called DK filters, which are questions which specifically state that not everyone has an opinion and say further, "If you do *not* have an opinion, just say so." Such questions induced about a fourth or a fifth of the sample of respondents to shift from one of the answer categories to the DK category. This can be seen as a rationale for omitting the DK category, and this is commonly done. On the other hand, if the respondent really has no opinion, little may be gained by forcing his or her answer into another category through omission of the DK category. I prefer in general to include the DK category. However, it is sometimes worrisome to analyze, as some researchers might feel that DK is not a "real answer" and prefer a firm yes or no, for example. In my view the issue has not been resolved definitively one way or the other and is a decision that each researcher must make in constructing his or her particular questionnaire.

Presser and Schuman (1980) also studies the effect of placing a middle position in answer categories (such as Liberal, Middle [of the road], Conservative). They concluded that placing a middle position in a closed-ended question increases the number of respondents who give a middle response by about 10 to 20 percent (some respondents will choose a middle position even if one is not offered, for example by marking between two categories). Although use of an explicit middle reduced the number of DK answers slightly, Presser and Schuman found that most of the persons choosing the middle category would have answered a polar (extreme) category if the middle category had not been included. Also see Schuman and Presser (1981).

In a more recent study (but building upon the work of Schuman and Presser 1981), Bishop (1987) conducted a series of experiments on the middle response category. He concluded that (a) respondents are more likely to select a middle response when it is offered than when it is omitted; (b) mere mention of a middle alternative in the preface to the question improves its probability of selection, and (c) the order in which a middle alternative is presented in the question makes a difference. In related research, Krosnick and Alwin (1987) tested the effect of question-category order (item order) in the categories of closed questions. Their results showed a clear "primary effect," with items presented early in the list disproportionately chosen as among the three most important qualities of a child.

Open-ended Questions

The advantages of open-ended questions are: (1) They can be used when all of the possible answer categories are not known, or when the investigator wishes to see what the respondent views as appropriate answer categories. For example, the open-ended question, What are the major problems confronting Los Angeles at the present time? may reveal some findings that the researcher did not anticipate, in addition to the expected ones (smog, crime, taxes). (2) They allow the respondent to answer adequately, in all the detail he or she likes, and to clarify and qualify his or her answer. (3) They can be used when there are too many potential answer categories to list on the questionnaire. For example, one might receive 75 answers to the question on problems facing Los Angeles, many of which have a frequency of only a few each. It would be awkward to list all 75 problems on a questionnaire (even if all could be anticipated), but if some were omitted, then there would not be appropriate answers available for all respondents. (4) They are preferable for complex issues that cannot be condensed into a few small categories. (5) They allow more opportunity for creativity or self-expression by the respondent. He or she feels the answers are uniquely his or hers instead of being forced upon him or her by the researcher. Some persons feel that closed-ended questions impose an artificial structure on the data by putting words in the respondent's mouth rather than allowing the respondent to structure his or her own response in a more natural fashion.

Research by Geer (1988) has shown that open-ended questions are quite efficacious. Most people respond to them. The ones that do not generally fail to respond because they are uninterested in the specific question. Geer argues that most people are used to being asked open-ended questions (rather than closed-ended questions) in everyday life. Thus, he argues that closed-ended questions put people in an unnatural position. In later research (Geer 1991) the same author argues that open-ended questions measure the important concerns of respondents, and urges pollsters to use more open-ended questions in public opinion surveys (where they are relatively uncommon).

Disadvantages of open-ended questions include: (1) They may lead to collection of worthless and irrelevant information. The open-ended format is designed to ensure that all relevant information is included in sufficient detail, but there is no way to ensure that much irrelevant information is not also included. (2) Data are often not standardized from person to person, making comparison or statistical analysis such as computation of percentages difficult. (3) Coding is often very difficult and subjective, leading to low intercoder reliability. (4) Open-ended questions require superior writing skills, better ability to express one's feelings verbally, and generally a higher educational level than do closed-ended questions. (5) Open-ended questions designed to be general and to explore all dimensions of the subject may be too general for the respondent to understand what is meant, requiring the use of probes or of more specific follow-up questions administered by the interviewer. This feature makes open-ended questions generally unacceptable for mailed-out or other self-administered questionnaires, which generally rely upon less complex closed-ended questions. (6) Open-ended questions can require much more of the respondent's time and effort, and may engender a high refusal rate. (7) Open-ended questions require more paper and make the questionnaire look longer, possibly discouraging some respondents who do not wish to answer a lengthy questionnaire.

Open and Closed Questions Compared

Closed-ended questions should be used when the answer categories are discrete, distinct, and relatively few in number. Most closed-ended questions measure variables that are nominal (e.g., gender or skin color), ordinal (e.g., educational level), or intervally measured questions that have been collapsed into relatively few ordinal categories. Being by definition continuous and with many categories, ratio and interval variables do not lend themselves to closed-ended questions. The disadvantage of collapsing is that the researcher stands to lose a lot of information if his or her categories are too broad, or if they are split at the wrong points. Like nominal variables, the categories for closed-ended questions should be exhaustive (no categories omitted), and mutually exclusive (only one correct answer). Closed-ended questions are generally self-contained, can be answered quickly, and require fewer instructions than open-ended. Thus closed-ended questions can be used with a sample that has a lower educational level and are generally considered more appropriate for mailed-out and self-administered questionnaires.

Open-ended questions are used for complex questions that cannot be answered in a few simple categories but require more detail and discussion. They are used to elicit the respondent's unique views, philosophy, or goals. Open-ended questions are especially helpful in preliminary investigations in which the researcher has not yet decided which characteristics of the phenomenon are relevant to his or her study and needs to describe all potentially relevant characteristics in detail. Open-ended questions are preferred wherever accuracy, detail, and exhaustiveness are more important than time or simplification of coding and data processing. Also, ratio and intervally scaled variables will generally be measured by open-ended questions, as it is impractical to list all possible answers.

Many questionnaires contain a mixture of both. Most contain a number of questions on simple nominal background variables (e.g., gender), which are fixed-alternative, and perhaps a number of other closed-ended questions (agree/disagree or true/false). They may contain a number of open-ended thought questions as well. A questionnaire containing primarily fixed-alternative questions should contain at least one open-ended question (at the end of the questionnaire) to determine whether anything of importance to the respondent has been omitted. For example, a questionnaire sent to graduate students to determine their opinions of their department contained 49 fixed-alternative (agree/disagree) questions (such as, Are departmental requirements realistic?) and one open-ended question (Please provide any additional comments which will help the Graduate Council to evaluate your department or program) (Graduate Council, UCLA, 1974).

Schuman and Presser (1979) compared open and closed questions on such topics as work values (e.g., chances for advancement and working hours) and the most important problems facing the country (crime, inflation, etc.). Some of the comparisons were done in face-to-face interviews and some in telephone interviews. Schuman and Presser (1979, p. 709) concluded that they could not definitively say when open/closed differences would occur or that one form would always be more valid than the other. However, they do suggest that researchers who wish to use closed questions can begin with open questions administered to large samples of respondents. The responses can then be analyzed and used to construct closed-question categories using the wording and substance of the answers that the respondents gave to the open questions.

Although Schuman and Presser (1979) fail to demonstrate the superiority of open questions, Bradburn and Sudman, as we saw earlier, do report that open questions are rather consistently superior when threatening issues are being studied (Bradburn and Sudman 1979, p. 19). For further discussion of open and closed questions (including the use of precoded answers with open-ended questions, see Labaw (1980, pp. 131–53), Sudman and Bradburn (1982, pp. 148–73), and Converse and Presser 1986, pp. 33–35).

Response-category Format

The response categories for open-ended questions generally consist of only a blank space in which the respondent can write his or her answer. The researcher can regulate the amount the respondent writes by how much space is allowed. However, the researcher must be careful to provide enough space for a complete answer and to keep the respondent from writing in margins and on the back. Some open-ended questions, particularly those requiring a single number (age at last birthday) for an answer, may require only a blank (_____) for a response category.

Response categories for closed-ended or fixed-alternative questions are somewhat more complicated. Most answers are variables having two or more discrete categories. Category style depends at least partially upon whether the variable is (1) nominal (discrete nonnumerical categories such as male or female, (2) ordinal (rank-ordered categories such as most favorable, neutral, least favorable), (3) interval (ordered categories for which intervals between all ranks are equal, such as the Fahrenheit temperature scale); and (4) ratio (which is merely interval measurement with a fixed zero point, such as age). For a more detailed discussion of levels of measurement see chapter 4.

The basic rule for writing answer categories is to provide all possible answers in as clear and uncluttered a fashion as possible. The means of answering the question (check a box, circle a number) should be explicit. For nominal questions with factual answers (as opposed to opinion), the general practice is to list each alternative, providing a blank, a box to be checked, or a number to be circled. For example:

```
Check the appropriate blank
1. Sex: Male  X  ; Female ____
Check the appropriate box
1. Sex: Male ☒; Female ☐
Circle the appropriate number
1. Sex: Male ①: Female 2
```

Boxes are generally superior to blanks for checkmarking answers. When the check is contained within the walls of the box there is little doubt about which response it refers to. With blanks, especially if they are placed side by side with the response labels above them, or printed only once at the top of the page so that no words are between the blanks (_____ _____ _____), the respondent may carelessly check between two blanks, so that the correct response cannot be determined. The circling of numbers or letters is even less ambiguous and is preferable especially when precoding (discussed below) is used. Instead of entering the word "male" or "female" into the computer, the researcher can store the same information by merely assigning a number (1) to the male response category and another (2) to the female response category. The numbers are easily circled and can be entered into a computer directly from the questionnaire, with no further coding nor transferral to a coding sheet.

The trouble with interspersing response-category labels and answer categories on the same line, whether the answer categories are blanks or boxes to be checked or numbers or letters to be circled, is that the respondent often cannot tell at a glance whether a particular blank refers to the label to its left (e.g., male) or to its right (e.g., female). This problem is not so acute for a variable such as gender, which has only two responses, but can be a real problem if there are a large number of possible answers. The respondent typically glances over all answers until he or she finds the appropriate one, then searches for the correct blank to check. Many times he or she must return to the beginning of the answers and count all the blanks to determine whether a blank refers to the answer on its left or its right. Such confusion not only causes error but is frustrating to the respondent and may result in an unreturned questionnaire, especially if the respondent were already looking for some excuse not to respond. The problem can be at least partially remedied through spacing:

```
1. Sex: Male_____ Female_____
```

through use of parentheses:

```
1. Sex: (Male_____) (Female_____)
```

or through dotted lines:

```
1. Sex: Male ... (_____) Female ... (_____)
```

However, the most common format is to place the response categories below one another, thereby greatly reducing the confusion (JARP 1967):

```
79. How often do you read Japanese-American newspapers? (CHECK ONE)
Regularly . . . . . . . . . . . . . ☐
Occassionally.. . . . . . . . . . ☐
Hardly Ever . . . . . . . . . . . ☐
Never  . . . . . . . . . . . . . . ☐
```

The chief problem with this format is that it requires more space than placing items horizontally. Not only is this more expensive because it requires more paper, but it can also make the questionnaire appear longer, which may cause the respondent to refuse the interview or to hurry through it without taking time to consider each question carefully. Space could be better utilized by placing two or more questions side by side on the same line, but this is not recommended as it greatly increases the likelihood that some questions will be missed by the respondent. Also, if the lines are very close together (single-spaced instead of double-spaced), the respondent is more likely to check the incorrect box.

Another way to align each question with its appropriate answer categories is to box in the categories. Such boxed-in answer categories are very effective in eliminating confusion over which response refers to which answer. Although they are quite space-consuming, this disadvantage can often be overcome by combining more than one question in a chart, as in the following (Wild 1973, p. 2, question 2):

2. Please give the name, age, and sex of each of your children and indicate whether or not that child is enrolled in the UCLA Child Health Care Prepayment Plan (CHCPP). Begin with the youngest child. (CIRCLE THE NUMBER IN THE APPROPRIATE COLUMN)

		SEX		CHCPP	
CHILD'S NAME	**AGE**	**MALE**	**FEMALE**	**ENROLLED**	**NOT ENROLLED**
		1	2	1	2
		1	2	1	2
		1	2	1	2
		1	2	1	2
		1	2	1	2
		1	2	1	2

Such a boxed set of response categories is quite efficient, as data about more than one person can be recorded for a single question. This uses less space on the questionnaire than repetition of the question for each person. However, questions in which one respondent answers for other people in the household must be used carefully, generally for factual information only. The respondent often does not know another person's opinion and is likely to give a biased answer that is similar to the respondent's own opinion. For example, one questionnaire I saw had the following format:

1. Contraceptives should be made available on request to females under the age of 18

            Person #1   Person #2
Agree _____ Disagree _____   Agree _____ Disagree _____

There were no clear instructions about who the two persons are, or whether one person could answer for both persons (presumably man and wife) in the household. If one person did answer for another person on such a question, the opinion could easily be incorrect or biased. But even if the second person answers personally he or she may be biased by the first person's answer. The rule to follow here is to only allow one person to answer each questionnaire, especially if opinions are polled. If the information sought involves factual items that are accurately known by the respondent, such as his or her children's names or sex, then a box such as the one above is appropriate.

An inventory is a list of items to be checked or marked by the respondent. For example:

```
Check all the ways in which you have learned some bit of news or information
in the last month.
________ Television
________ Radio
________ Newspaper
________ Magazine
________ Word of mouth
________ Other
```

The box format, often called a *grid,* is frequently used with inventories (see Oppenheim 1966, pp. 81–104). A grid is a boxed format for an inventory that provides an evaluation for each item, or may even be a two-way inventory. For example, see figure 6–1 (from Oppenheim 1966, p. 99).

It is often desirable, where possible, to construct the same answer format for a whole series of questions. If this can be done, one set of response-category labels can serve for a whole set of categories if the labels are placed above the categories like titles. For example:

Figure 6–1

A Grid Gathering Information on Both the Type of Illness and Type of Treatment

	Nose Drops	Chest Rub	Gargle	Inhalants	Throat Sprays	Syrup	Throat Candy	Throat Tablets	Cough Medicine
Chest cough									
Dry cough									
Smoker's cough									
Severe cough									
Sinus pains									
Common cold									
Sore throat									
Infected tonsils									
Dry throat									
Catarrh									
For a lost voice									
Bad taste in mouth									
Help to sleep									
Indigestion									
Bronchitis									
Asthma									

SOURCE: From *Questionnaire Design and Attitude Measurement,* by A. N. Oppenheim, Copyright © 1966 by A. N. Oppenheim. Published by Basic Books, Inc., Publishers, New York, and Heinemann Educational Books Ltd. Reprinted by permission.

	Agree	Disagree
1. If you start trying to change things very much, you usually make them worse.	_____	_____
2. All groups can live in harmony in this country without changing the system in any way.	_____	_____

Another advantage of such a design is that the instructions for completing all questions in the series can be stated only once, at the beginning, and need not be repeated. Generally not all questions in the questionnaire will have the same response series. But often there will be several different sets of fixed-alternative questions, each set having a different set of answer categories. For example, one set of questions may use agree/disagree response categories, while another may use categories such as unimportant/important/very important, while still another group uses categories such as terrible/poor/fair/good/very good.

Number of Categories

So far we have been concerned mainly with answer categories for questions measuring nominal variables. The number of response categories for nominal variables is clear and well known. The easiest variables to measure are those such as male and female in which the categories are conceptually distinct, commonly known and few in number. In other cases there may be a great number of categories. Remember that the answer categories for a nominal variable must be mutually exclusive (only one correct category for each respondent) and exhaustive (a category for every respondent). If there are many possible response categories, it may be difficult if not impossible to list all of them. Furthermore, it may seem unnecessary, as out of 100 categories, for example, there might be only five or six that have many entries, while the rest are rare. In such a case one commonly uses one of two approaches: (1) all alternatives are listed on a card (but not printed on the questionnaire) and shown to the respondent, who then answers, and his or her single answer is written on the questionnaire; or (2) only the most common or most important categories are printed on the questionnaire, and an "other" category is provided to make the answer exhaustive. That is, persons who do not fit in any of the categories provided are thrown together into the residual "other" category. This category provides minimal information but does serve the function of allowing every person to answer. However, "other" categories can cause problems. For example, an important category might inadvertently get lumped into "other," or some persons could object to being labeled as "other," saying it is humiliating and dehumanizing, as in "black/white/other." For a recent study on the effects of category range on responses in Germany, see Schwarz et al. (1985).

Ordinal Variables

A large number, probably a majority, of questionnaire items are opinion or attitude questions in which the answers are ordinal, or somewhat ordinal. Such response categories are generally marked like the nominal categories, that is, by checking a blank or a box or circling a number.

However, in contrast to nominal variables in which the categories are empirically determined, the categories for an ordinal scale are often more subjective and must be defined by the researcher. For example, a question asking about the quality of teaching in the respondent's college may be answered with a scale ranging from terrible to excellent. However, the researcher must decide how fine the gradations on the scale are to be. In other words, he or she must decide how many categories there will be between the lowest and highest, and generally he or she will provide means for these categories. Some commonly used response scales are:

1. strongly agree/agree/neutral/disagree/strongly disagree/unable to answer
2. excellent/adequate/barely adequate/inadequate/terrible/unable to answer
3. excellent/good/all right/poor/bad/unable to answer
4. often/sometimes/almost never
5. radical left/very liberal/somewhat liberal/middle/somewhat conservative/very conservative/radical right (notice that this is actually a nominal variable but is treated as ordinal)
6. certainly true/quite often true/seldom true/never true/don't know
7. very important/important/somewhat important/not important/don't know

Each of these examples can be marked with all of the common types of response marking. Generally the questions are presented in a series so that the labels are listed only once for the whole series, but some questionnaires repeat the categories for every question.

Research by Carp (1974) on such "serial order preferences" (preference for a certain ordering of responses) indicated that whichever responses were listed first were responded to more frequently on attitudinal items. However, more recent research by Powers et al. (1977) challenged Carp's findings. Powers et al. concluded that the ordering of responses did not affect the results, and implied that Carp's earlier findings might have been due to some statistical considerations.

An alternative format for ordinal questions is to list responses as a continuum with labels only at the extremes, such as the following (Survey Research Center 1969a, p. 9):

4. To what extent do you feel students should have a voice in determining course content and degree requirements?

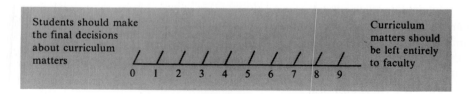

As another example (Wild 1973, p. 17, question 57):

57. Some people like to see their good friends very often, others really only seldom like to see people. Relatively speaking, do you like to see your friends very frequently or very seldom? (CIRCLE THE APPROPRIATE NUMBER)

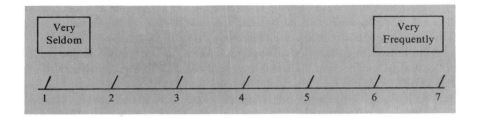

In such "thermometer"-type answers the categories are generally repeated for each question, rather than being printed only once at the top of the page. An alteration that can be made on thermometer-type response scales is to place a zero category in the middle, with negative points on the left and positive points on the right, as in the following:

The advantage of this design is that often a respondent will feel absolutely neutral on an item and simply have no opinions. "No opinion" responses are common and arise either because the respondent has not developed an opinion on the issue or because he or she does not feel strongly enough about the item to express an opinion. Also, many people will have an opinion but will not agree or disagree strongly. If an item is scored zero through ten, then they will not know whether to mark the space between the four and the five or between the five and the six.

It is up to the researcher to decide how many categories are needed. It seems from a cursory examination of a number of questionnaires that the thermometer-type tends to use more categories, from a low of six or seven to a high of nine or more. It is easier to use more categories with this format because it is not necessary to think up names for all of them. Examination of the examples provided above, all taken from actual questionnaires, shows that the modal (most frequent) number of categories for non-thermometer-type ordinal questions seems to be about five (not counting the "unable to answer" category), although as few as two (agree/disagree) or three (above average/average/below average) are often used, and as many as seven or more are also common. If one has too few response categories, each will be very diverse, grouping people with quite different opinions or different levels of commitment into the same-category. This is equivalent to labeling all temperatures under 32° as cold and all over 32° as hot. Thus a temperature of 33° could not be distinguished from a temperature of 212°, as each would be called hot. This is obviously not measuring with much precision. On the other hand, if too many categories are used, the respondent will not be able to distinguish between adjacent categories and may get frustrated and refuse to answer. For example, my fondness for baseball is definitely intermediate. On a scale of high, intermediate, or low, I could easily answer intermediate. However, on a 100-point scale from low to high I would find the question difficult. I know my answer would be somewhere in the middle, but I don't know whether it would be, say, 53 or 54, and I would just have to guess at an answer. Respondents with a low tolerance for ambiguity would be frustrated by such an answer scale and might refuse to answer, especially if there were many such questions on the questionnaire.

Notice that on the thermometer-type response categories, the intervals between numbers are made equal. To make the intervals unequal would only confuse respondents, increasing the likelihood that larger intervals would be checked more frequently and decreasing the likelihood that smaller intervals would be checked at all. However, the question arises as to whether the distances between numbers can really be assumed to be equal—that is, whether the scale is in fact interval (equal intervals) rather than ordinal. We have no way to support the assumption that the intervals are actually equal. Conservatively, we must assume that the scale is ordinal. However, most researchers will treat the scale as if it were interval and will compute a mean (average) score on that scale for the sample of respondents. In theory, computation of the mean requires an interval scale. But the mean is a fairly "robust" statistic, that is, a statistic whose assumptions can be "bent" without dire consequences. Thus there is probably little harm done in computing means and treating such answer categories as interval, even though we have no way to show that they are more than ordinal.

The main thing to remember is that the response categories should be easy for the respondent to answer and should provide just enough detail but not too much. It is generally a good idea to provide a category such as "don't know" or "no opinion" or "unable to answer," so that people who are really unable to answer will not feel frustrated and thus refuse to complete the questionnaire. The "don't know" or "no opinion" categories are often used as neutral categories, as in strongly agree/agree/don't know/disagree/strongly disagree, while the "unable to answer" category is not included as part of the scale but is placed to one side (usually to the right of the scale). The use of two of these terms simultaneously is unnecessary and confusing. For example, one questionnaire used "don't know" between "agree" and "disagree," and then also used "unable to answer" on the side. Respondents were confused about the distinction between these two categories. The problem was solved by changing "don't know" to "neutral," and retaining "unable to answer."

Another response-category format for ordinal variables is to present a list of topics and have the respondent rank-order them. For example:

```
1. The following are some of the problems faced by citizens of Los Angeles
County. Please order them in terms of importance, from 1 (most important) to
5 (less important).
_____ Smog
_____ Traffic
_____ Taxes
_____ Crime
_____ Drug Addiction
```

One problem with this type of answer format is that the order in which the categories are listed can affect the ranking given them by respondents. For example, respondents may rank the first category presented as number 1, or assign adjacent numbers to adjacent categories.

These tendencies can be at least partially remedied (although admittedly at some expense), by listing categories in random or alphabetical order and by rotating the category listed first on different copies of the questionnaire, as is often done on election ballots. If there are four different categories, each could be listed first on 25 percent of the questionnaires administered, second on another 25 percent, and so on. We will consider construction of ordinal scales in much greater detail in chapter 15. For further examples of response-category formats, including some very novel designs, such as feeling thermometers, rating "ladders," and pictorial representations, see Sudman and Bradbury (1982, pp. 148–206), and Alreck and Settle (1985, pp. 97–190). See also Converse and Presser (1986) and Bishop (1987).

Another issue here is whether to use ratings (such as five-point scales) or rankings (such as from highest to lowest). In one study, Alwin and Krosnick (1985) analyzed parental values for children and obtained similar results in regard to the relative importance of value choices in the aggregate.

Interval Scales

As noted above, intervally scaled variables will by definition generally be continuous rather than discrete and thus will have a large number of response categories, often too many to include in a closed-ended question. However, sometimes the researcher will not be interested in all possible values, and at other times will be content with just the approximate group in which the respondent falls rather than the exact value (e.g., only in certain income ranges or age groups rather than exact age or income). The advantage of this is that if a respondent is sensitive about giving his or her exact age or income, he or she may be willing to specify an approximate age or income within a certain range.

Both income and age are commonly asked in such a fashion. Age is generally grouped by demographers into either five- or ten-year groups. The trick is to reduce the number of categories as much as possible (in the interest of parsimony) without making each category too broad. Generally age groups are begun with a number whose last digit is zero, and end with either a four (for five-year age groups) or nine (for ten-year age groups). For example, 0–4/5–9/10–14/15–19; or 0–9/10–19/20–29. All age groups are generally made the same size (e.g., five years), with the exception of the first year of life. The group 0–1 is generally studied separately in mortality studies because of the high mortality rate at this age. Another exception is the oldest age group, which is generally made open-ended (e.g., 65 +).

Income groupings are commonly used but are a little more difficult to construct. Often researchers do not attempt to make all income groups the same size but vary them depending upon the average amount of income. For example, a study of students conducted in 1969 (SRC 1969a) asked about both their parents' income and their estimate of their own future income. The question on parents' income covered a lower income range than the question on the student's individual future income because it reflected an earlier time period when incomes were lower and because parents' income was more precisely known, while the student's future income was merely a guess. The parents' question was (SRC 1969a):

```
8. What is (was) the approximate annual income of your parents?
_____ Under $5,000
_____ $5,000-7,499
_____ $7,500-9,999
_____ $10,000-14,999
_____ $15,000-19,999
_____ $20,000-24,999
_____ $25,000 or more
```

The student's question was (SRC 1969a):

```
5. How much money do you expect to make annually at your peak?
_____ Less than $10,000
_____ $10,000-14,000
_____ $15,000-24,000
_____ $25,000-39,000
_____ $40,000 or more
```

Notice that the parents' question uses mostly $5,000 groups but also contains two $2,500 groups under $10,000, while the student question uses groups of $10,000, $4,000, and $14,000. The student question yields only a rough estimate of income, as the groups are less precise than in the parents' question. For some reason researchers generally feel that it is more important to set ranges in which they are most interested, or where most people fall, rather than to keep all groups of equal size. It is important that critical income values be used as boundary points for income groups. That is, if one is studying poverty for a year in which the official government poverty level is $4,000 for a family of four, one would not use a group of $0–$5,000, as this would mix the respondent officially in poverty (under $4,000) with those making over $4,000 and thus not officially impoverished.

As average incomes rise through the years, the income range covered must be revised upward lest the income groups provided are too low for inflationary times. For example, if the average respondent made $15,000 but the researcher's highest income group was $15,000 +, much information would be lost. This problem can be largely solved through careful pretesting.

Question Order

When combining questions to form the final questionnaire the researcher must decide how many questions to include and in which order to present them. A few general rules for question order may be given.

1. Put sensitive questions and open-ended questions late in the questionnaire. If sensitive questions, such as those about sexual behavior, income, or religion, are placed first, the respondent may react to them adversely and refuse to continue. If these questions are encountered later, the information on all the nonsensitive questions already answered is saved, even if he or she refuses to answer the sensitive questions (see our discussion of sensitive questions earlier in this chapter).

Open-ended questions should also be placed late, even if they deal with nonsensitive issues, because they generally require more thought and writing from the respondent and therefore take longer to answer than fixed-alternative questions. If the respondent takes 15 minutes to answer the first of 100 questions or finds the first question difficult to answer, he or she may decide that he or she does not have time to complete the questionnaire or that it might require too much thought and effort. Thus the respondent may refuse to continue.

2. Ask easy-to-answer questions first. The first questions on the questionnaire should be easy to answer. They should not be a threat to the respondent, and should be clear, with distinct answer categories. The first question should generally be about a fact rather than an opinion or a belief and should require little thought. A question about gender or age is preferable to one about philosophy of life. Opening questions commonly deal with such facts as age, gender, marital status, occupation, and education (but not income, religion, or race). If possible, the opening questions should be interesting ones that will stimulate the respondent to complete the questionnaire.

3. Ask information needed for subsequent questions, first. It is often helpful, particularly for questions that may tax the respondent's memory or that deal with other members of the family, to first elicit information, such as family members' names, to be used in asking subsequent questions. For example, a fertility study in which I participated desired information not only on the number of pregnancies but also on the type of contraception used before the first pregnancy and between subsequent pregnancies. Such information can sometimes be very difficult for the respondent to remember, especially if she is elderly or has had many children. If the researcher asked what type of contraception she was using in 1959 she probably would not remember. If asked what she was using between her third and fourth pregnancies, she probably would figure it out by remembering which child was born third, when he or she was born, and what she used before the next baby was born. Such a question is easier to answer, and rapport is better, if the interviewer asks for the names of all children in order of birth as one of the first questions in the questionnaire. Then, by looking back at the response to this question, the interviewer can personalize the contraception question, as "What type of contraception did you use after Billy was born and before Suzie was born?" (or "between Billy and Suzie?").

4. Place questions in logical order. The average person probably arranges his or her responses to questions in some general order, such as a time sequence. Thus the researcher should follow this practice when constructing a questionnaire. It should go without saying that when the questionnaire asks for the respondent's occupational history, the respondent will find it much easier to respond if a time sequence is followed, either from the first job to the present job or from present job to first job—for example, the questionnaire should not first ask about the second job, then about the fifth job, and then about the fourth job.

Aside from a time sequence, most questionnaires have some organization or "frame of reference," generally determined by the topic being studied. Often there are several subframes of reference within a particular questionnaire. One frame of reference might be occupational history, another marital history, another children's birth dates, and another contraceptive practices, all within a single fertility survey. It is generally a good idea to deal with each of these individual frames of reference completely before moving to the next one. For example, ask questions about all the respondent's jobs before moving to questions about contraceptive practices. If one asked about the respondent's first job, then asked a sex question, then went back to job number two, the respondent's concentration and train of thought might be broken.

5. *Avoid establishing a response set.* The rule just discussed advocates establishing a logical order such as a time sequence and cautions against mixing topics or frames of reference and against jumping abruptly from one frame of reference to another. This is not a hard-and-fast rule; it may be broken whenever the researcher feels that establishing a logical order or asking many consecutive questions on the same topic may establish a response set. A *response set* is a tendency to reply to items in a particular way, regardless of the question's content or the correct answer. One response set already mentioned is "social desirability," the tendency to agree with statements that are socially desirable or supported by norms. This response set is more amenable to correction by question wording than by question order. Another response set that is corrected largely by question wording is "acquiescence," the tendency to answer yes rather than no or to agree rather than disagree. Still another response set corrected by question wording is "a preference for strong statements versus moderate or indecisive ones" (Webb et al. 1966, p. 20).

Other response sets can be caused by question order. Webb et al. (1966, p. 20) say: "Sequences of questions asked in a very similar format produce stereotyped responses, such as a tendency to endorse the righthand or the lefthand response, or to alternate in some simple fashion." It is entirely possible, for example, that when asked about the income derived from each job from first to current, the respondent will have a tendency to increase the income with each subsequent job, whether or not income really increased.

If response bias due to question sequence is suspected or demonstrated in a pretest, the researcher has little recourse but to change the order. He or she can randomize question order or vary the question and/or answer format from question to question. The disadvantages of this are that the respondent's train of thought may be broken, he or she may be confused by having to switch from one format to another, and much more labeling of response categories may be required. However, it may be worthwhile to do so if the response set can be broken. Another possible advantage of mixing question types and orders is that the added variation may make the questionnaire less boring for the respondent and motivate him or her to finish it.

6. *Separate reliability-check question pairs.* Pairs of questions, one stated positively and one negatively, are often used to check reliability. For example, we might ask "Abortion should be legalized (agree/disagree)" at one point in the questionnaire and "Abortion should not be legalized (agree/disagree)" later. If the question is unreliable, because of ambiguity or some other reason, a respondent might disagree with both questions or agree with both questions. (The acquiescence response set just discussed might lead to agreement with both questions.) Use of such question pairs will not solve the problem of acquiescence response set, but it will enable the researcher to detect unreliable questions and to remove them from the data analysis, for a single respondent or for the entire sample.

Obviously one would not place both questions in the pair together, as virtually all respondents would then make sure that their responses were consistent (again so as not to appear "stupid"), and the purpose of using a repeated question would be negated. Also, if there are many such pairs, there should be no orderly sequence, such as the positive form always first; choice of the first question should be random. Even though the questions are separated in the questionnaire, they will often be detected, especially if there are many such pairs or if the respondent has answered many questionnaires and knows in advance that there will be such positive and negative pairs. Detection of pairs by respondents is unfortunate and should be avoided if possible for at least three reasons: (a) the respondent will deliberately answer both questions consistently, thus defeating the purpose; (b) the respondent will spend too much time flipping through the questionnaire to see how he answered the earlier question in the pair, thus possibly causing him or her to become frustrated and to quit before completing the questionnaire; and (c) the respondent may interpret the pairs as a trick to catch him or her cheating, and this may seem to contradict the researcher's contention that there are no right or wrong answers.

7. Place scale items according to response required. Very often a number of the questions included in a questionnaire will be scale items (see chapter 15 for a discussion of scaling and examples). The researcher must decide whether to present the scale items in a single group or to divide them. If he or she is able to present them in one group, he or she will be able to use, for example, agree/disagree as the title for the entire group and will not have to repeat the response categories for every question. This is no problem if the non-scale items also have the same response categories. One of the principal arguments for scattering the scale items is that if they were all presented together the respondent might look for a pattern of answers, or might try to guess what is being measured and answer accordingly.

8. Vary questions by length and type. As mentioned briefly in the discussion of response sets, the researcher may wish to vary questions as to question format, response format, length, and whether open- or closed-ended. This may help maintain respondent interest but could also make the questionnaire more difficult to answer.

9. Determine whether funnel technique is applicable. Some social researchers (see B. Phillips 1971, p. 141; Oppenheim 1966, pp. 38–39) advocate use of the funnel technique of question sequencing. In the funnel technique broad, general, or even open-ended questions are asked first, and then the funnel is narrowed by asking more specific questions. This technique puts the respondent at ease by first asking nonthreatening (even irrelevant) questions. By using the funnel technique in conjunction with "filter" questions, the researcher can determine whether specific questions apply to the respondent, and thus avoid asking questions that do not. A filter or screening question is one that determines whether future questions are applicable to the respondent. For example, instead of asking the respondent how many cigarettes he or she smokes or what brand, the researcher first asks whether the respondent smokes. If the answer is no, then the specific smoking questions are skipped. The funnel technique can work if the general or open-ended questions asked first are easy to answer. But I think it is preferable to ask easy-to-answer, closed-ended factual questions first and the specific sensitive questions and open-ended questions later. In any event, there is consensus that the beginning of the questionnaire should serve to put the respondent at ease. See Sudman and Bradburn (1982, pp. 207–28) for a valuable checklist of points to remember regarding question order.

For more recent studies of question order see McClendon and O'Brien (1988) and Benton and Daly (1991). Their interesting research has focused on the question order of general and specific questions. Their research is consistent in showing that response to general questions is improved if preceded by specific questions on the same topic. Apparently, the specific questions raise the respondent's knowledge and awareness of general issues. This effect is correlated with education, and is particularly pronounced for more poorly educated respondents (see Benton and Daly 1991).

Contingency Questions

A contingency question is a question whose relevance to the respondent is determined by his or her response to an earlier filter or screening question. For example, a study of abortion might first ask the filter question "Have you ever had an abortion?" The next question is: "How old were you when you had your first abortion?" The second question is a contingency question, since whether or not one answers it is contingent upon the answer to the first question. The directions for the filter question will read, "If Yes (did have abortion), answer question 2, if No (no abortion) skip to question 3."

The need to use filter and contingency questions and to skip some questions arises chiefly from the fact that a sample of respondents is often heterogeneous in terms of personal characteristics such as age, sex, race, and marital status, and also in terms of opinions and attitudes. Remember we said that one of the most important goals in questionnaire construction is to make all questions relevant to the respondent. We generally cannot ensure that every question will be relevant to every respondent. If a particular question is relevant to only a small number of respondents, asking the question would yield only a small number of usual responses and a large number of "don't knows" or "not applicables." There would not be sufficient data for analysis, and the question should not be asked. In other cases the question will not be relevant to all respondents, but will be considered too important to discard. The logical procedure in this case is to utilize filter and contingency questions.

The need to use contingency questions can often be reduced by drawing a homogeneous sample. However, in a great many cases one of the primary reasons for the study is to compare two or more groups—for example, black and white professors, or persons enrolled in a prepaid health-care plan and persons not enrolled. In such a study it is necessary, for purposes of data analysis, to have a substantial sample size (preferably 100 or more) of each population to be compared. The questionnaire must be relevant for each respondent (as discussed above). The basic choice the researcher must make is whether to use a different questionnaire for each group or to use only one questionnaire for both groups. The use of separate questionnaires is preferable from the standpoint of interviewing, coding, and data processing and analysis. But sometimes researchers feel that the use of one questionnaire with filter and contingency questions is preferable to two questionnaires each containing some of the same questions but necessitating two different cover letters, sets of instructions, and interviewers. Also, diversity of opinion within any sample of respondents cannot be avoided in any event, and may require filter and contingency questions.

There are several different formats for filter and contingency questions. A common one is to write beside each response category the directions telling which question to answer next in the event of the category being chosen as the answer. For example (SRC 1971):

```
25. In the past two months did you have any illness that kept you in bed,
    indoors, or away from your usual activities?
                          Yes.......... ....(ASK A) ...............1
                          No...........(SKIP TO Q. 26) .........2
         A. About how many days was that? _____
```

Or similarly (SRC 1971):

> 19. There are lots of different types of Americans--for example, black and white and Oriental, and people whose families came from many nations like Mexicans, Italians, and Armenians. Do you and your family feel a part of any particular group like these or any other type of American group?
>
>   Yes . . . . ( ) ASK A
>
>   No . . . . ( )SKIP TO Q. 20
>
>   A. What group is that? _____

Another format that can be used either alone or with skip directions (as in the examples immediately above) involves arrows (JARP 1967):

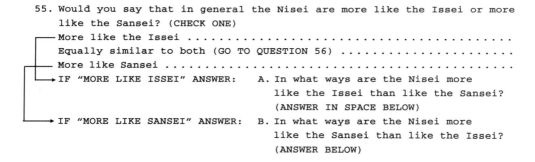

Babbie (1973, p. 147) prefers the use of boxed contingency questions with no arrows leading to them:

> 1. Have you ever had an abortion?
>   ( ) Yes
>   ( ) No

> If Yes: How old were you when you had your first abortion? _____

The boxing sets the contingency question apart from the ordinary or noncontingency questions and makes it clear that this is a special question that is not to be answered by everybody. However, some researchers get carried away with the use of arrows and charts and construct overly elaborate flowcharts that can become very confusing and difficult to use. One questionnaire I examined contained many such charts. The following example is the *least* complicated one in the entire questionnaire (Health and Welfare Agency 1967):

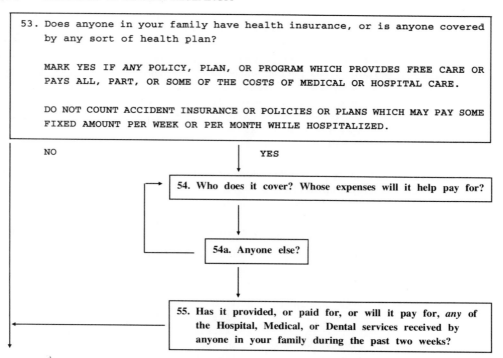

Cover Letter or Introductory Statement

After the questions have been written and their order decided upon, the remaining tasks in questionnaire construction consist of writing the introductory statement or cover letter, writing instructions to interviewers or respondents, precoding (discussed in chapter 14), and pretesting. The introductory statement is important because it justifies the study to the respondent and often determines whether he or she cooperates or not. The introductory statement is essentially a selling or public relations job. In the interview questionnaire it is generally a rather brief statement that is read to the respondent. In the case of the mailed questionnaire the introductory statement is generally in the form of a letter accompanying the questionnaire, although it can be mailed separately. The cover letter is usually written on the letterhead of the organization conducting or sponsoring the survey in order to help legitimize the survey to the respondent.

Whether for a mailed questionnaire or an interview study, the introductory statement should: (1) identify the persons or organization conducting the study; (2) tell why the study is important and should be conducted: (3) tell why it is important that the respondent answer the questionnaire; and (4) assure the respondent that there are no right or wrong answers, that he or she will not be identified, and that his or her answers will be treated confidentially. The first function is usually achieved simply by identifying the organization conducting the study. The second is achieved by describing briefly the study's goals and stressing their importance. The third is often achieved by stressing that the respondent was chosen by a scientific sampling procedure that will not allow another person to be substituted for him or her. It can also be stressed that since only a small sample of the larger population is being studied, the respondent is actually answering for hundreds of fellow citizens who were not selected in the sample, and therefore his or her opinion is very important. This third function is important since many respondents feel that the results of the study, though perhaps important, will not be affected if they fail to take time out from their busy schedules to answer the questionnaire. The fourth function is achieved through various assurances designed to allay the respondent's fears that information provided on the questionnaire will make him or her look stupid or deviant, or will be revealed to others.

Here is an example of the introductory or opening statement to be read by the interviewer (SRC 1971):

> Good morning/afternoon/evening; I am from the UCLA Survey Research Center. In our research, we ask the people of Los Angeles County to tell us how they feel about various issues and problems that are affecting their lives. This information is valuable both for planning and for scientific research. Your household is very important to this survey because it represents hundreds of others which are not in our sample. EVERYTHING YOU TELL US WILL BE STRICTLY CONFIDENTIAL. YOUR NAME WILL BE IN NO WAY CONNECTED TO THE FINDINGS OF THIS IMPORTANT STUDY.

Our next example is from a mailed questionnaire (JARP 1967). The introductory statement is not on stationery but is printed inside the front cover of the questionnaire booklet. The first two functions are fulfilled on the outside front cover, which bears a title identifying the nature of the study (Japanese-American Research Project, University of California at Los Angeles). Authority is further provided by the statement that the survey is supported by a grant from the U.S. Public Health Service. The statement inside the cover is titled "TO OUR RESPONDENT" and is concerned primarily with fulfillment of the third and fourth functions:

> Most of the questions we are asking you to answer in this questionnaire ask you for *facts* about yourself or others you know. Please answer each of these to the best of your ability. We appreciate accuracy, but it will not be necessary for you anywhere on this questionnaire to refer to your records. Just use your memory as best you can. Some other questions ask for your *opinions.* On these questions, obviously there are no right or wrong answers. What we want to know is *just what you think.* When you aren't quite certain what your answer should be, please give us the choice that appeals to you more at the moment. Please record any additional comments you may have about particular questions or the questionnaire as a whole. Such comments are often invaluable in interpreting your answers to other questions.

> None of the questions should be hard or tricky; you will find most are both short and easy. Please remember that it is *you* we are trying to find out about. It will be best, therefore, if you will fill out the entire questionnaire *before* you discuss any of the questions with anyone else. After you are finished with the questionnaire, please feel free to discuss it; but be sure you promptly return the filled-out questionnaire to us in the envelope provided.

It is also common in introductory statements to stress that the questionnaire will not take long to complete. One questionnaire (Wild 1973) used the following statement: "And although the questionnaire looks rather long, it will only take about twenty minutes of your time to complete." This same introductory statement stressed the importance of returning the questionnaire, "since your reply counts for those many others whom we cannot afford to contact." It also urged prompt return for the questionnaire as the results of the study could help improve the respondent's health care.

Many introductory statements offer to send the respondent the results of the study, and provide a blank to be checked, usually as the last question, if the respondent wishes a summary of the results. A typical statement reads: "If you would like a copy of the completed research, be sure to indicate this at the end of the questionnaire." Sending results to respondents costs time and money. However, it helps allay the feeling on the respondent's part that he or she is "alienated labor" who cannot see the fruits of his or her endeavors. It also convinces the respondent that the study is legitimate, and not some subterfuge, the results of which will never be analyzed. Further, some respondents are genuinely interested in the study, and giving them the results constitutes partial payment for their time.

It is also important to say in the introductory statement for what purpose the data will be used and in what form. Wild's (1973) health-care study included the following statement:

> Your responses will be completely confidential. We use identification numbers only to check on our returns; you will never be identified by name. The results of this survey will appear largely in the form of statistical reports.

The U.S. Census Bureau, troubled by charges of invasion of privacy, takes great pains to show how the data will be released. A sample table is included in the introductory statement to show that, for example, median income for a state or city will be made public, but an individual's income will not. It is clear from the example table that an individual's income cannot be determined by his or her neighbors, the IRS, or anyone else.

Sobal (1984) recently analyzed the content of survey introductions. His research showed a considerable degree of variety in the content of introductions used by American survey researchers. He concluded that since survey research depends upon the good will of the public, and since the increasing volume of research is creating a respondent burden, survey researchers need to standardize introductions so that both methodological and ethical needs are filled.

Instructions for Interviewers or Respondents

It is usually necessary to include instructions for respondents in a mail-out questionnaire. In an interview study the person in charge of interviewers usually goes over the questionnaire in detail with them to make sure that they understand all questions. In the course of the discussion the questions are clarified, difficult questions identified, and detailed instruction sheets compiled. Instructions of this sort generally state what the interviewer should do if the respondent answers a certain way. Thus such instructions are generally unique to each question. Rather than try to offer general rules for writing instructions for interviewers, it seems better simply to remind the researcher that such instructions are necessary, and that they are usually compiled during the process of pretesting and interviewer training sessions as specific problems or questions arise.

Questions that necessitate instructions generally include filter questions with many contingencies and skips, historical questions such as occupational or educational career, and any other very long or complicated questions. Questions that require information from former questions to be entered as part of the wording of the present question are generally not even attempted on mail-out questionnaires and can be used in interview studies only after careful training of interviewers. Mailed questionnaires are generally limited to items that require only simple instructions for answering.

Very often in mailed questionnaires the instructions for answering will be repeated with each individual question, such as the following (Wild 1973):

```
39. The doctor can't help you keep your child from getting sick with TB if
it runs in your family (CIRCLE ONE)
                                        Strongly agree . . . . . . . . . . . .1
                                        Agree . . . . . . . . . . . . . . . . . .2
                                        Disagree . . . . . . . . . . . . . . . 3
                                        Strongly disagree . . . . . . . . 4
```

In addition to this repetition of instructions for individual questions, general instructions including worked examples are usually included at the beginning of the questionnaire, either as part of the introductory statement or just after it. For example (Wild 1973):

```
GENERAL INSTRUCTIONS: Most of the questions ask you only to circle the number
that represents the answer of your choice. For example:
                                        Often . . . . . . . . . . . .1
                                        Sometimes . . . . . . . .2
                                        Rarely . . . . . . . . . . 3
                                        Never . . . . . . . . . . 4
Some questions ask you to fill in an appropriate number, word, or phrase on
the line provided:
                        _____ years
Some questions are to be answered by some, but not all, people. Explanations
are provided in every case. For example:
                        Yes . . . . . . . . . . . .ANSWER A . . . . . . . . . . . .1
                        No . . . . . . . . . . . .GO TO Q. 2 . . . . . . . . . . .2
The person who answers "Yes" would continue with the next part of that
question, labeled "A," while the person who answers "NO" would skip "A" and
proceed to Question 2.
You may wonder about the purpose of the numbers in the right-hand column on
each page. These numbers are there only to assist us in tabulating your
responses statistically.
THANK YOU VERY MUCH FOR YOUR ASSISTANCE TO US IN CONDUCTING THIS STUDY. WE
HOPE YOU ENJOY THE QUESTIONNAIRE, AND WE LOOK FORWARD EAGERLY TO RECEIVING
YOUR ANSWERS.
```

In addition to instructions to the interviewer, interview schedules often include up to two pages of items to be answered by the interviewer without the respondent's knowledge. The first of these is the face sheet (figure 6–2).

Figure 6–2

Questionnaire Face Sheet

BEGIN DECK 01

A1. Interviewer: _____

07-11/   12-15/

16-18/

A2. ID _____ TRACT # _____ BLOCK # _____

A3. CALL RECORD:

	Date	Day-of-week	Time	Results	If interview taken:	
					Time start	Time end
1.	19-22/	23/	24-27/			
2.						
3.						
4.	28-31/	32/	33-36/		37-40/	41-44/

Interviewer notes for appointments/call backs

A4. REASON FOR NO INTERVIEW (CIRCLE ONLY ONE. ADVISE SRC OF
LANGUAGE BARRIER AND MORE THAN
ONE DWELLING UNIT AT ADDRESS BY
PHONE)

Vacant 01   Initial contact refused 09 45-46/
Address not a dwelling 02   WHY _____
No such address 03
No one at home, 3 calls 04   _____
Respondent not at home,   Respondent refused 10
    3 calls 05   WHY _____
Language barrier 06
    (What language _____)   _____
Respondent incapable 07   Other 11
WHY _____   SPECIFY: _____

Initial contact incapable 08
WHY _____

ID # _____ TRACT # _____ BLOCK # _____

Name of Respondent _____

Address of Respondent _____
                              number and street   town

Phone # of Respondent _____ Date of Interview _____

SOURCE: From the Los Angeles Metropolitan Area Survey: III (LAMAS III) Questionnaire, 1971. Survey Research Center (SRC). Los Angeles: University of California. Reprinted by permission.

142

The face sheet (SRC 1971) identifies the household in terms of census tract and block, identifies the interviewer, and provides a record of all attempts to interview the respondent. If the interviewer is successful in obtaining the interview, he or she records the time the interview began and the time it ended. If not successful, he or she merely records the dates he or she attempted to obtain interviews and marks the reason for not succeeding. In the case of no interview this is the only sheet of the questionnaire that is completed. In addition to the face sheet, many interview schedules have a final page that is filled in by the interviewer immediately after leaving the interview. This sheet, also completed without the respondent's knowledge, can include such information as the interviewer's estimation of the respondent's household (middle class, lower class), type of dwelling unit, and respondent's race (see figure 6–3, from SRC 1971).

Pretesting

Pretesting is the final stage in questionnaire construction—and one of the most important. The initial effort is merely a rough draft. It can be administered to a few respondents so that its

Figure 6–3

Example of Questions to Be Completed by Interviewer Immediately After Interview

```
                                                              Confidential
                                                                 DECK 13

       TO BE COMPLETED IMMEDIATELY AFTER LEAVING INTERVIEW


87.  Housing type:              single family residence  ............. 1      68/
                                duplex  .......................... 2
                                apt. building (under 20 units)  ........ 3
                                apt. building (20 units or more)  ...... 4
                                mobile home  ..................... 5
                                other  .......................... 6
                                    SPECIFY: _____


88.  Respondent was:            Black, non-Spanish surname  ........ 1     69/
                                Spanish surname  .................. 2
                                White Anglo  ..................... 3
                                Oriental  ........................ 4
                                other  .......................... 5
                                    SPECIFY: _____


89.  Interview was conducted in:  English  .......................... 1    70/
                                Spanish  ......................... 2
                                other  .......................... 3
                                    SPECIFY: _____

                                            CODER I.D. _____       71/
```

Source: From the Los Angeles Metropolitan Area Survey: III (LAMAS III) Questionnaire, 1971. Survey Research Center (SRC), Los Angeles: University of California. Reprinted by permission.

flaws can be identified and corrected. Rather than worry because his or her questionnaire is not perfect, the beginner would be better off constructing a draft questionnaire as well as he or she can, pretesting it, revising, and pretesting again.

The sample for a pretest is usually some "captive audience" such as office staff, coworkers, family, or fellow students. The rule that each question must be relevant for the respondent is usually bent somewhat in a pretest, as researchers need not be careful that the pretest respondents have the exact characteristics of the respondents in the final study. Obviously, however, there are some limits as to how far the relevancy rule can be bent: You would not use male respondents to pretest a questionnaire dealing with pregnancies unless there were absolutely no choice.

The pretest instrument is a complete questionnaire but may be typed triple-spaced or with larger margins than usual to allow and encourage comments by respondents. I generally tell the respondents (at least on the initial pretest) that they are participating in a pretest. In addition to completing the questions as instructed, I ask for their critical analysis of all aspects of the questionnaire, such as question wording; question order; redundant questions (pretest respondents are generally especially helpful in identifying redundant questions); missing questions; inappropriate, inadequate, redundant, or confusing response categories, poor scale items; poor reliability checks; insufficient space for answering open-ended questions; and any other aspects of the questionnaire that they find inadequate.

The pretest should be conducted in the same manner as the final study. If it is a mailed questionnaire, the pretest should also be mailed. If it is an interview study, the pretest should be an interview. During the interview the interviewer can probe for the respondent's understanding of the various questions. Among the most common problems are that the respondent considers some questions redundant, finds some answer categories inadequate, and objects to the manner in which questions are worded. Respondents will also frequently offer additional questions that they feel should have been asked.

It is my feeling that priority in analyzing pretest data should be given to respondents' marginal comments and opinions. If more than one or two respondents label a particular question "stupid" or seem highly offended by it, the researcher should feel obligated to rectify the situation by revising the question wording or answer categories or even eliminating the question if necessary. The researcher need not accept all of the respondents' recommendations, but these comments are generally perceptive and helpful.

After the critical comments are dealt with, the researcher must turn to the more subjective task of seeking clues to problems that were not commented upon by the respondents. This is especially acute in mailed questionnaires. One can begin by tabulating the number of "no responses," "unable to answer," and "don't knows" for each question. Remember that completed sample size varies from question to question, depending upon the number of responses for the question. A large number of nonresponses for a question may reduce sample size below the minimum for data analysis, and DK (don't know) and "unable to answer" or NA (not applicable) answers are generally not of theoretical interest and must be coded as nonresponses.

When a question calls forth a substantial number of nonresponses, the researcher should first look to see if it is a contingency question. If the pretest sample is small and not representative of the ultimate sample, it may well be that everyone in the pretest was instructed to skip the question and that the question is perfectly sound. On the other hand, if the question is not supposed to be skipped, the researcher must attempt to determine why it yielded so little information. If the answer is not obvious, he or she should readminister the item to a pretest sample, taking special pains to interview people if the original pretest was mailed out. In interviewing he or she can ask people outright why they did not or could not answer the question.

After the unanswered questions are dealt with, attention can be turned to patterns of responses. If a series of questions are answered identically, or if there is a clear pattern of answers such as a sequence of agree, disagree, agree, disagree, the researcher must suspect response set. The series of questions can be redistributed in the questionnaire in random order to eliminate response set. Respondents can also be questioned about why their answers formed a pattern.

The researcher should also look for questions in which there is no variation in the answers, with virtually all persons in the sample answering the same way (e.g., 98 percent agree). This may or may not reflect a problem. The researcher should first examine the nature and number of response categories. It may be that the categories are not precise enough to yield useful information. Additional categories might solve the problem, yielding answers in several small categories where previously all answers were in one large category. Another possibility is that the question was adequate as originally written but there is simply an overwhelming consensus on that particular issue. Imagine that the researcher hypothesizes a relationship between gender and agreement on question 1 but finds no correlation because everyone agrees on question 1. Babbie (1973, pp. 216–17) advocates creating variance by increasing the number of categories in order to improve the correlation. However, although increasing the number of categories generally will increase variance, if the opinions are really constant there still will be no statistically significant relationship, as all answers will be constant in a few categories instead of just in one.

After unanswered questions and patterns of answers are examined, the researcher can look for questions that are answered with qualifications (marginal clarifications by the respondent) or do not yield useful data. One subject that frequently yields unsatisfactory information is occupation. The novice researcher may ask "What is your occupation?" and get answers such as "Acme Aircraft Company." This is unsatisfactory as it does not tell the respondent's actual work title, which may range from janitor to vice president. An answer such as "clerical" or "teacher" includes a wide variety of clerical jobs or levels of teaching. After the pretest the researcher may rewrite the question as "Describe your actual duties in your job."

Respondents will often qualify or clarify their answers on a pretest, and these qualifications can help the researcher to improve question wording. For example, if the question asks the respondents to list the duties, dates, and salary of his or her first job, he or she may ask, "Do summer jobs count?" "Do temporary jobs for a few days or weeks count?" "Do part-time jobs count?" If you ask for salary per month, the respondent might say that he or she was paid by the hour, or by the amount of work accomplished, and so on. These qualifications and questions help the researcher to refine question wording and response categories for the final questionnaire. For further discussion of pretesting see Converse and Presser (1986, pp. 51–75).

At least two aspects of questionnaire construction remain to be considered: physical aspects of the questionnaire, such as questionnaire length, type of paper, type of printing, color of paper, type of cover, and precoding. The first is most acute for mailed questionnaires and will be discussed in chapter 7, on mailed questionnaires. The latter will be reserved for our discussion of coding in chapter 14.

Summary

Chapter 6 discussed questionnaire construction. A distinction is often made between question-naires that are self administered and interview schedules that are completed by an interviewer. In this chapter we used the term *questionnaire* for both types and discussed questionnaire construction for both interviews and mailed studies.

We emphasized that each questionnaire is somewhat unique, but that there are certain general pitfalls that can be avoided if they are anticipated in advance. In general, the chief goal of questionnaire construction is to construct an instrument that will not only minimize non-response, but that will also ensure that the information collected is complete, valid, and reliable. The best questionnaire for accomplishing this goal is generally relevant, nonambiguous, and has clear answer categories that are easy to respond to. We discussed in some detail the topics of question relevance, double-barreled questions, ambiguous questions, level of question wording, abstract questions, and leading questions.

After a discussion of question wording, we turned to the problem of constructing proper answer categories. Answer categories can be classified as either open—in which no formal response categories are given (the respondent is merely provided space in which to compose his or her own answer)—or closed (fixed choice)—in which the respondent is forced to choose from among a number of specific answer categories provided. After a discussion of the advantages and disadvantages of each form, various types of closed-ended formats were discussed in detail.

We next turned to the problem of determining proper question order. Improper order can cause problems such as response set (the tendency for the respondent to answer in a certain manner regardless of the appropriate answer). Another problem is that sensitive questions may decrease the respondent's willingness to cooperate further with the study.

The detailed discussion of various criteria for determining question order was followed by a discussion of contingency questions. Contingency questions are not answered by all respondents. Whether or not a respondent answers a given contingency question is determined by his or her response to a prior question called a filter question. The use of filter and contingency questions enables respondents to skip those questions not relevant for them.

The chapter concluded by discussing instructions for interviewers, cover letters for mailed studies, and pretesting. Pretesting is an important step in which the questionnaire is tested on a few respondents in an attempt to discover any problems in the questionnaire, such as ambiguous or extraneous questions.

CHAPTER 7

MAILED QUESTIONNAIRES

ONE OF THE FIRST decisions a survey researcher must make, even before he or she selects his or her sample and constructs a questionnaire, is whether to conduct a self-administered study (usually by means of a mailed questionnaire) or an interview study. There are advantages and disadvantages to each form. Much of our discussion in chapter 6 is relevant to our discussion in this chapter.

Advantages of Mailed Questionnaires

1. *Considerable savings of money.* Interview costs are rising these days, as are all labor costs. Costs of $15 or more per interview (not including sampling or data analysis) are common, and costs of $30 or more per interview are not unusual. Many interview study directors conduct long and costly interviewer-training sessions, hire one or more project supervisors or interview supervisors, and even open field offices in the community to recruit and train interviewers and to conduct public relations. Although the questionnaire in a mailed study generally has to be more expensive than the instrument used in an interview study, perhaps with high-quality paper and printing and an elaborate cover, a mailed study still costs far less than an interview study with the same sample size. This is true even if first-class or airmail postage is used and there are several follow-up mailings, including more than one questionnaire sent to the same respondent.

2. *Time savings.* Mailed questionnaires can be sent to all respondents simultaneously, and most of the replies will be received within a week or so (although the final returns may take several weeks or longer), while interviews are generally performed sequentially and may take months to complete.

3. *The questionnaire may be completed at the respondent's convenience.* The respondent may spend more total time on it than he or she might in an interview study, as he or she is not forced to complete all questions at one time. With the mailed questionnaire the respondent is free to answer a question or two whenever he or she has a spare moment. The respondent is also able to answer the easy questions first and take time to think about answers to the more difficult ones.

4. *Greater assurance of anonymity.* Since there is no interviewer present who can identify him or her later, the respondent may be more willing to provide socially undesirable answers, or answers that violate norms. Montero (1974) compared response rates to mailed questionnaires and interviews for 23 socially undesirable questions among a sample of Japanese Americans. He found a higher percentage of socially undesirable responses on the mailed questionnaires for 18 out of the 23 questions.

5. *Standardized wording.* Comparison of respondents' answers is facilitated by the fact that each respondent is exposed to exactly the same wording. However, this advantage may be lessened by differential understanding of questions due to differences in educational levels among respondents.

6. *No interviewer bias.* There is no opportunity for the respondent to be biased by an interviewer. An interviewer can bias answers in many ways, such as prompting, through voice inflection, assuming that the respondent will answer a certain way, or telling the respondent his or her personal opinion. There is also the possibility that the interviewer will misread the

question, the respondent will misunderstand the interviewer, the interviewer will misunderstand the respondent, or the interviewer will make a clerical error.

7. *Securing information.* The mailed questionnaire allows the respondent to consult his or her records, confer with colleagues, or conduct research before answering, while the interview generally does not.

8. *Accessibility.* Respondents who are widely separated geographically can all be reached for the price of a postage stamp, as compared to expensive travel costs for interviewers.

Disadvantages of Mailed Questionnaires

1. *Lack of flexibility.* With no interviewer present, there can be no variation in questions asked and no probing for a more specific answer if the respondent's first answer is too vague or general to be useful. Also, if the respondent misunderstands the question he or she cannot be corrected. Further, there is no interviewer present to "save" the situation by mollifying an irate respondent who dislikes a particular question. Mail surveys not only often receive higher response rates to socially undesirable questions, they also get more than their share of insults and obscenities from irate respondents who feel strongly about a question or the subject being studied.

2. *Low response rate.* In an interview study the vast majority of interviews are successfully completed, and the reasons for nonresponses are generally known (e.g., respondent's death, language problems). However, mailed studies sometimes receive response rates as low as 10 percent, and 50 percent is considered "adequate" by Babbie (1973, p. 165). Furthermore, the respondents who do not answer are generally not a random selection of the sample but have some biasing characteristics. For example, the elderly are more likely to be ill and unable to respond. The more mobile are less likely to have a current address and thus are less likely to receive the questionnaire. The poorly educated are unable to read the questionnaire and write the answers. Even many highly educated people feel that they can express themselves better through speaking than through writing, or are simply too lazy to write lengthy paragraphs, or feel that their grammar or spelling is not adequate given their educational level, and thus feel embarrassed to tender a written response.

3. *Verbal behavior only.* There is no interviewer present to observe nonverbal behavior or to make personal assessments concerning the respondent's ethnicity, social class, and other pertinent characteristics. An obviously lower-class respondent may pass himself or herself off as upper class in a mailed questionnaire, with no challenge from an interviewer.

4. *No control over environment.* In interview studies the interviewer often takes great pains to ensure that a standardized environment exists for every interview. For example, the interview will be conducted in private, without spouse or other family present to hear answers, and the interviewer will try to make sure that the room is quiet and that the respondent is not rushed or nervous. In a mailed questionnaire study there is no assurance that the respondent will be able to complete the answers in private. A spouse or parent might demand to see the completed questionnaire and censor it. What is worse, some other person might fill out the questionnaire for the respondent if the respondent feels he or she does not qualify or is too busy.

5. *No control over question order.* A masterpiece of question order, devised by the re-

searcher to eliminate response bias, may be ruined by a respondent who reads the entire questionnaire before answering, skips some questions, or does not answer questions in the order in which they are presented. It should be noted, however, that some question-order effects seem more pronounced in interview studies, and may actually be reduced or even eliminated in mailed questionnaire studies (see Ayidiya and McClendon 1990).

6. *Many questions may remain unanswered.* With no supervision while filling in the questionnaire, the respondent may leave some questions unanswered. Thus while 60 percent of all questionnaires may be returned, the researcher might find that only 10 percent of respondents answered a particularly sensitive question.

7. *Cannot record spontaneous answers.* It is difficult to gather spontaneous first opinions, as the respondent has an opportunity to erase a hasty answer that he or she later decides is not diplomatic.

8. *Difficult to separate bad addresses from nonresponses* (Lansing and Morgan 1971, p. 117). Although some questionnaires that fail to reach the respondent are returned to the researcher, many fall into the hands of new tenants who throw them away, while others are forwarded to a second bad address rather than being returned.

9. *No control over date of response.* Lack of control over the time the questionnaire is completed can damage a study greatly. For example, if one is studying natural disasters and a hurricane or earthquake occurs when half the respondents have completed their questionnaires, there would be obvious problems in comparing answers before and after the disaster. However, this is also a problem with interview studies. An interviewer can choose the time he or she arrives at the house, but cannot guarantee that the respondent will be home or will agree to the interview. Further, interviews are so time consuming that they generally cannot all be completed on the same day, while, at least in theory, mailed questionnaires could all arrive the same day.

10. *Cannot use complex questionnaire format.* Not only must the questions on a mailed questionnaire generally be simpler to understand, but a complex format with a lot of contingency questions is also probably too confusing for the average respondent. Highly complex questionnaires can be used in interview studies in many cases only because the interviewer has been given extensive training in understanding the format. Obviously, the respondent in a mailed study cannot receive such training and will generally give up on a questionnaire full of arrows and skips. Further, question wording must be simple enough for the most poorly educated person in the sample to understand. This lowest common denominator may result in such simplistic questions that the more highly educated respondents feel that their intelligence has been insulted.

11. *Possibly biased sample.* Goode and Hatt (1952, p. 174) add another objection: "The questionnaire," they say, "is not an effective research tool for any but a highly select group of respondents . . . because a biased sample is obtained." They base this conclusion on the fact, as discussed above, that responses (and thus also nonresponses) are not a random sample of the entire sample but are generally biased in some fashion. Nonrespondents tend to be more poorly educated and more highly mobile. Also, on a very emotional or controversial issue, the researcher may receive a bimodal response, with those strongly in favor and strongly opposed both responding and neutral persons not responding.

However, several studies have shown that this objection to the mailed questionnaire is either incorrect or overstated. McDonagh and Rosenblum (1965) compared the results of a mailed questionnaire and interviews by studying both persons who responded to the questionnaire and person who failed to respond. They state:

> The principal finding in this study concerning methodology suggests that the data show no statistically significant differences between the mailed questionnaire and the structured interview with respect to identical questions. This study suggests that the mailed questionnaire may reveal representative responses in spite of the partial return from the sample of the universe selected. There were no significant differences between the responses of the mailed questionnaire and those of the interviewed respondents who had not answered the questionnaire. The nonrespondents did not seem to be so selective of some variables as many behavioral scientists assume. The findings of this study imply that researchers should have greater confidence in the questionnaire method as an initial tool of research (McDonagh and Rosenblum 1965, pp. 135–36).

Further, as mentioned above, several studies (Knudsen et al. 1967; Montero 1974) have shown that the mailed survey is superior to the interview for gathering information on sensitive or socially undesirable subjects. Knudsen and associates, who studied women who had been premaritally pregnant, say:

> In the interview situation the respondent was more likely to support the public and restrictive sexual norms that she assumed were adhered to by the interviewer. Through this conforming behavior the respondent wished to avoid the embarrassment caused by revealing deviant norms. The tendency to support public sexual norms was most marked among lower-socio-economic status respondents because they deferred to the norms represented by the higher-status interviewers (Knudsen et al. 1967, p. 296).

The last statement seems to suggest that by increasing the response rate among poorly educated persons, interview studies receive a larger proportion of biased answers. That is, the lower-class respondents are least likely to respond to mailed questionnaires but are the most likely to give biased answers to sensitive or socially undesirable questions if they do respond.

Goyder (1985) has recently argued that there may never have been as much difference in response rates between mailed questionnaires and face-to-face interviews as some researchers seem to think. He says that increasing educational levels and other factors make mailed surveys the "optimal" method for surveying in "post-industrial" society. He concludes (Goyder 1985, p. 248) that mailed questionnaires and telephone surveys are "tailormade for reaching a socially disintegrated citizenry, ensconced in high-rise urban fortresses in which face-to-face contact has been delegitimated.

The Total Design Method

Dillman (1978, p. 1) has said that both mail and telephone surveys have long been considered the "stepchildren" of survey research and not as valuable as interview studies. He has formulated a strategy called the "Total Design Method" (TDM), which he feels can enable mail and telephone surveys to achieve their potential as valuable research tools. The TDM has two basic parts: (1) a theoretical part, which specifies aspects of the research process that affect responses, and (2) a practical part, which simply emphasizes detailed attention to all parts of the survey process.

The first or theoretical portion of the TDM shares our emphasis, as discussed in chapter 8, of viewing social research as a process of social interaction. This is important. I think that it is ironic that social scientists often do not apply social research to their own work. Dillman is to be commended for using social theory to provide insights into ways that mail and telephone surveys can be improved (in chapter 8 we perform a similar task for the interview study).

Dillman (1978, pp. 12–16) uses social exchange theory to explain why respondents respond or fail to respond to surveys. Social exchange theory states that persons' actions are motivated by the return they expect, and usually receive, from other people. Each action entails certain costs and has the potential for certain rewards. The individual is more likely to take the action if the expected rewards exceed the expected costs. At the time at which the action is taken, the actor often has no absolute assurance that the rewards will be forthcoming from the other person that he or she is interacting with but must trust that person to provide the rewards. Thus, the three key concepts in the theoretical portion of the TDM are cost, reward, and trust. Dillman says that these concepts can help us understand why persons either respond or fail to respond to mail surveys.

Rewards are obviously very important in inducing someone to take part in a social interaction. Unfortunately, survey researchers typically do not have money in the budget to pay respondents huge sums for answering questionnaires. Thus, the financial rewards a respondent can expect are rather limited. According to Dillman (1978, p. 13), this may be one reason why response rates for mailed questionnaires are often quite low. Drawing from exchange theory, Dillman suggests that there are still some rewards, albeit largely intangible, that can be offered to potential respondents. One such reward is to show that the researcher has a positive opinion of the respondent. One way to do this is to say that the person is part of a carefully selected sample and thus is very important to the research project. In addition, personalizing the mailed questionnaire, cover letter, and envelope is a way to show positive regard for the respondent, according to Dillman. Further, some persons find it rewarding to be consulted and to know that their opinion is valued. But there are actual rewards that can be given besides. Least expensive, and often quite efficacious, is simply to thank the person in person, perhaps in advance. Also, small monetary rewards or small objects of some sort can be given, and these are also often quite effective at minimal expense.

The important factor in social exchange is not merely the size of the reward or the cost, but rather the ratio of reward to cost. Even a large expected reward may not be sufficient to promote interaction if the expected cost is high. Conversely, in mailed surveys where the reward that can be given to respondents is generally low, it is imperative that costs be kept to a bare minimum. Costs that the respondent will generally incur are time and effort costs and psychological costs. The first two can be minimized by sending a relatively short, clear, well-organized questionnaire that is easy to complete, with a self-addressed, stamped envelope. Psychological costs stem not only from sensitive or embarrassing questions but also from frustration over a poorly worded questionnaire that is difficult to complete (some seem impossible).

The third element of the theoretical portion of the TDM is trust. Regardless of the reward, if the respondent does not trust the researcher, he or she has no expectation that the reward will be forthcoming. Dillman feels that the reason that quite small monetary rewards are sometimes effective in eliciting responses is that they represent a symbol of trust. Sending a self-addressed, stamped envelope may also show the researcher's trust in the respondent and thus elicit the respondent's later trust in the researcher. In my view one of the best ways for a researcher to stimulate trust in potential respondents is to carry out his or her obligations in the researcher's role in the most professional and scrupulous manner possible and to stress his or her legitimacy as a researcher. If you stress that you have the proper credentials for conducting the research in a professional manner and are not misrepresenting yourself or using your position for personal gain (e.g., sales), then trust should be fostered. Sponsorship by a university or government or a corporation also gives the researcher legitimacy and fosters trust. By carrying through your role in a professional manner you will reinforce the trust that your sponsorship provides.

Factors Affecting Mail Surveys

Selltiz et al. (1959) list even variables that can affect the number of questionnaires returned and the adequacy of the data:

1. Sponsorship of the questionnaire
2. Attractiveness of the questionnaire format
3. Length of the questionnaire
4. Nature of the accompanying letter requesting cooperation
5. Ease of filling out the questionnaire and mailing it back
6. Inducements offered to reply
7. Nature of the people to whom the questionnaire is sent

Other factors include:

8. Type of mailing (airmail, business reply)
9. Time of the week, month, or year when the questionnaire is mailed
10. Nature of follow-up

Sponsorship

Sponsorship can affect the respondent's willingness to return a mailed questionnaire by convincing him or her of the study's legitimacy and value and by causing him or her to be afraid not to respond, because of the sponsor's great prestige or power to force a reply. Organizations generally receive a good response rate from their own membership. Sponsorship by legitimate scientific, governmental, university, or well-known nonprofit agencies offers proof of legitimacy. Sponsors who might seem to have an ulterior motive, such as commercial organizations, or organizations that are not well known may have difficulty achieving satisfactory response rates. The second point is highly correlated with the first. The respondent is unlikely to fear sanctions for failure to return the questionnaire if a sponsor is a mail-order firm or some nongovernmental organization of which he or she has never heard. However, he or she may feel that the government has the power to force an answer, and may fear that by not responding to a questionnaire from his or her trade organization, union, or club he or she will risk offending or alienating fellow club members and officers. Further, the respondent may feel that he or she "owes" it to club or country to cooperate.

Scott (1961, pp. 168–69) made an excellent and exhaustive study of mail surveys in England, comparing response rates to questionnaires from governmental, university, and commercial sponsors. He found that after one week only 44.6 percent of respondents had returned the government-sponsored survey, 46.3 percent the commercial questionnaire, and 47.8 percent the university questionnaire. However, after four weeks the government questionnaire had the best response rate (93.3 percent) while the commercial rate was 90.1 percent and the university was 88.7 percent.

Jones found an interaction effect between sponsorship and geographic region, meaning that the effect of sponsorship is different depending upon the particular geographical region surveyed, Jones (1979, p. 110) says: "The results suggest that the benefits of a particular university sponsor may be limited by locale. Also, in the presence of conflicting regional loyalties a specific university sponsor can dramatically decrease response rates."

Fox et al. (1988) conducted a meta-analysis of ten factors thought to affect surveys, including sponsorship. A meta-analysis is a quantitative averaging of findings from individual studies (see the discussion in chapter 16). They found that of all ten factors, sponsorship by a university instead of a private business was the most effective. Unfortunately, this is not generally controllable (except for the rare investigator who is able to switch from business sponsorship to university sponsorship).

Questionnaire Format and Color

Scott (1961, pp. 173–74) also found that the response rate for a printed questionnaire was 95.2 percent and for a duplicated one 94.4 percent. Questionnaires printed on the back of the cover letter brought a higher response rate (95.8 percent) than questionnaires on a separate sheet, probably indicating respondents' preference for a shorter version. Scott also varied the color of the questionnaire, but obtained insufficient evidence to report. Bender (1957) found no difference by color in a survey addressed to U.S. Navy and Air Force personnel, but Dunlap (1950) found that yellow membership-renewal reminders sent to college alumni received the best response, with blue next, and white or cherry last. However, the sample was small and the differences not statistically significant.

Sudman and Bradburn (1982) also say that there is no evidence that color of paper has any effect on response to mailed questionnaires. However, they suggest that dark papers are difficult to read and should not be used. They also suggest that different colors of paper can be used to separate subparts of the questionnaire. For further discussion of questionnaire format (such as the use of type faces and blank space) see Sudman and Bradburn (1982, pp. 229–60). For further discussion of factors such as paper, color, and print, see Alreck and Settle (1985, pp. 193–219).

In their meta-analysis, Fox et al. (1988) also reviewed studies on questionnaire color. They concluded that color can be used to successfully increase response rates. They report (Fox et al. 1988, p. 477) that in eight out of ten studies that they reviewed, the response rate was higher for a green questionnaire than for a white one.

Questionnaire Length

Scott (1961, pp. 173–74) compared a one- and a two-page version of the same questionnaire. The two-page version had a response rate of 94.8 percent, as against 93.6 percent for the one-page version. This suggests that a less cluttered format is preferable even if it requires a longer questionnaire. Also, Heberlein and Baumgartner (1978, p. 452) concluded that "long questionnaires averaged just as high a response as very short instruments." A later study by Goyder (1982) replicated the work of Heberlein and Baumgartner (1978) and generally supported their findings. However, the average length of their questionnaires was seven pages, with 72 questions. There clearly must be some point at which length would begin to make a difference. In a more recent study, Yammarino et al. (1991) conducted a meta-analysis which studied, among other things, the length of the mailed questionnaire. They conclude that response rates can generally be raised by surveys of less than four pages, with longer surveys resulting in lower response rates.

Cover Letter

Virtually all mailed questionnaires are accompanied by a cover letter explaining the nature and purpose of the research project and enlisting the respondent's cooperation. However, letters vary widely in terms of length, nature of appeal, and whether they are on a separate page or reproduced as part of the questionnaire. One of the central controversies in discussions of cover letters is whether it is necessary (or even preferable) for the letter to be personalized, or whether an impersonal letter is sufficient or perhaps even preferable. A personalized letter might be typed rather than reproduced, addressed to the respondent by name, and signed by the researcher. The impersonal letter can be dittoed or mimeographed, with the signature also reproduced, and addressed to "Occupant." Letters sampling an extremely large group generally must be impersonal, as personalizing all letters would be prohibitively expensive. Such letters are often undated, addressed to "Dear Sir or Madam" or "Dear Householder," and facsimile signed.

The personalization of large numbers of letters has been made possible by recent technical advances, such as word-processing equipment, which allows the letter to be typed and stored on tape. Then, merely by punching a button, the typist can produce a freshly typed copy (not a reproduction), personalizing it by adding the individual's address and name and inserting the name in the body of the text (". . . so you see, Mrs. Jones").

Scott (1961) attempted to construct two letters that were the same except for one being formal in style and the other informal. The informal letter contained 22 personal pronouns and the formal letter only 12. The response rate was slightly higher for the impersonal version (91.4 percent versus 89.6 percent), but this difference was not statistically significant. Another way to personalize a cover letter is to add a handwritten postscript urging the respondent to reply. Studies by Frazier and Bird (1958) and by Hoppe (1952) reported a significant increase in response rates (from 25 percent to 31 percent and from 20 percent to 32 percent respectively) through use of the handwritten appeal.

Scott discusses a number of studies that found that (1) a "permissive" letter receives a higher response rate than a "firm" letter; (2) a "short, punchy letter" receives a higher response rate than a longer, more logical appeal; (3) no difference was found among letters addressed variously as "Dear Mr. Smith," "Dear Friend," and "Dear Bulletin-User"; (4) handwriting the address and sender's signature does not seem to increase response rate; and (5) no difference in response rate was found between a true signature and facsimile signature. Scott (1961, p. 173) concludes, "These results may be summed up in the statement that the content of the letter is very much more important than its trappings." As Yammarino et al. (1991) put it, researchers using a cover letter with appeals should definitely be able to increase their response rates (as compared with no appeal).

Ease of Completing and Returning Questionnaires

We have already mentioned that the mailed questionnaire should be easy to complete. Poor questionnaires include those that have no instructions or inadequate instructions for completing questions, have unclear response categories, have too many open-ended questions, and are too long. Most of these matters have been discussed in detail in chapter 6. Another matter that affects response rate is the ease with which the questionnaire can be returned. It is common practice for the researcher to provide explicit mailing instructions and supply a self-addressed and stamped envelope.

Inducements to Reply

The best inducement to reply is simply to convince the respondent that the study is worthwhile and that his or her cooperation is important. Another strategy is to appeal to his or her "good samaritan" instincts, telling him or her that you need his or her help. A professional researcher conducting a survey cannot appeal to respondents' sympathies by telling them that he or she is working his or her way through college, but if the researcher is a student he or she can say that the study is being conducted on a low budget for a class project, that he or she is being graded on it, and that if the respondent does not cooperate the grade might be adversely affected. The respondent may not understand why someone else might not do as well, but, as we have mentioned, he or she can be told that he or she was chosen by a scientific method that does not permit substitutions and that the accuracy of the sample requires his or her cooperation.

One possible means of gaining compliance is the so-called prior commitment (Childers and Skinner, 1979). Prior commitment is a request for cooperation that is made before the questionnaire is mailed rather than after, as is a "follow-up." Childers and Skinner experimented by mailing an advance letter with a commitment postcard to some of the respondents, and not to others. They concluded (Childers and Skinner 1979, p. 561): "In this study the use of a prior commitment postcard did not increase mail survey response or speed of response beyond the results obtained for a control group."

Rewards such as money or prizes are often promised upon return of the questionnaire. The consensus from a number of studies conducted in the 1940s and 1950s, discussed by Scott (1961), was that 25¢ was the optimal amount to be included with the questionnaire for increasing response rates. Less than 25¢ did not work as well; more than 25¢ increased returns very little over the level achieved by 25¢. Hancock (1940) found that a control group with no reward achieved a response rate of only 10 percent, compared with a response rate of 47 percent for a group in which 25¢ was enclosed with the questionnaire and 18 percent for a group in which 25¢ was promised upon return of the questionnaire.

If the money included with the questionnaire is to be interpreted by the respondent as compensation for completion of the questionnaire rather than as a mere gimmick, then $1 would probably be the minimum effective amount today. Most respondents will accept the enclosed dollar but will consider it a goodwill gesture or partial payment for a study with which they probably would cooperate anyway, because they think that the study is worthwhile, or that the researcher needs their help, or out of a sense of loyalty (as when the questionnaire is sponsored by a club to which they belong). The chief problem with offering money, besides the fact that some respondents will take the money and still not respond, is that some respondents (particularly if the amount of money is rather small) will be indignant that the researcher considers the respondent's time to be worth so little and will not respond. Wild (1973), in a study of prepaid pediatric health-care plans, initially included no money. However, the first follow-up letter stressed that as a mother herself she knew that the respondents (who were both students and parents) were short on time, particularly with final exams approaching, so she was including a dime ("all my meager budget will allow") for the respondent's child to play with while the respondent completed the questionnaire. The amount of money was too small to be efficacious as payment for work but served to attract the respondent's attention. It worked quite effectively, although at least one person (who undoubtedly would not have responded in any case) sent the dime back without the questionnaire, saying that his time was more valuable than that.

Other studies reported in Scott (1961) effectively used such inducements as trading stamps, a chance in a lottery for a turkey, and a tie clasp. Some magazines include a miniature pencil in letters to subscribers for the respondent to use in answering the questionnaire. Some researchers enclose a penny, usually with a statement such as "a penny for your thoughts." (Actually, a penny may be preferable to a nickel, dime, or even a quarter. Even the dullest respondent should recognize that a penny is not meant as payment for work done; thus he or she will not feel that the researcher is being insulting by implying that his or her time is not valuable.)

An important question about inducements such as money is how they affect the biases caused by nonresponse, and whether the answers on the questionnaires returned are influenced by the payment. Scott (1961, p. 177) reports that a number of studies have examined this question, and none found evidence that money inducements cause bias. However, Scott feels that none of the studies produced fully satisfactory evidence in support of their claim that no bias exists, and concludes that the matter should be regarded as open.

There have been a number of studies of monetary inducement. Mizes et al. (1984) compared $5 and $1 incentives in terms of their effect on mailed questionnaire return rate. They also experimented with "answer checks" where the questionnaire is actually printed on the back of an inducement check issued to the respondent, and thus is returned to the researcher not by the respondent, but through the banking system. The answer check precludes the possibility of a respondent cashing the inducement check without returning the questionnaire. They found that the $5 incentive was no more effective than the $1 incentive, with both increasing the response rate by 21.1 percent over no monetary incentive, while the $5 answer check resulted in a 19.2 percent increase. Thus, no evidence was found supporting the use of the answer check over a separate check.

Nederhof (1983) studied the effect of including a ballpoint pen (approximate value 35¢) as an incentive in mailed studies in the Netherlands. He found that the gift increased the speed of the initial response rate, but that if follow-ups were used, the final response rates were similar whether or not the incentive was included.

In another study, Tedin and Hoffstetter (1982) compared "importance" incentives (certified mail) with monetary incentives (25¢). They found that certified mail increased responses, but that the effect of the quarter was generally weak. See also Mizes et al. (1984).

In an interesting study, Berry and Kanouse (1987) experimented with the timing of inducements to reply. In studying physicians via a mailed questionnaire, they offered each respondent an incentive in the form of a $20 payment. In a randomly selected half, the respondent received the payment with the original questionnaire. The other half were promised payment after the questionnaire was returned. All in all, the prepayment elicited a significantly greater response than the promised inducement. Berry and Kanouse conclude that a relatively moderate payment to physician respondents can yield mailed questionnaire response rates that are comparable to those from telephone and personal interviewing.

Interestingly, while being efficient and entailing less clerical work, prepayment added little to the cost, as most physicians who failed to respond did not cash the prepayment check (Berry and Kanouse 1987, p. 112). The authors suggest the prepayment inducement for respondents who are difficult to contact (such as lawyers or executives) where the traditional follow-up may be expensive. Another ploy they suggest is a "mixed strategy," which entails first a promise of payment, then a follow-up telephone call, then prepayment with the next questionnaire.

In an even more complex inducement experiment, Hubbard and Little (1988) also compared immediate and promised inducements (against a no-incentive control group). There were two immediate inducements (25¢ and $1) and two promised inducements ($1 contribution to a charity of the respondent's choice, or the opportunity to win a $200 cash prize). The two immediate cash payments and the $200 prize opportunity all yielded significantly greater response rates than the no-incentive control group, but the charity inducement did not.

Fox et al. (1988) conducted a meta-analysis of inducements and nine other factors affecting mail surveys. In discussing the factors affecting response rates, the authors say (Fox et al. 1988, p. 472) that the most frequently analyzed issue in the literature was the cover letter, with the next most frequent being the use of incentives. They say:

> Studies have explored not only the effect of the amount of the incentive, but also the effect of whether the incentive is enclosed or promised. The use of noncash incentives and the promising of gifts to charity have also been examined.

Their overall conclusion is that providing a small cash inducement with the questionnaire has a positive effect on response rate. However, the relationship between increase in response rate and size of the incentive indicates that diminishing returns are quickly experienced (Fox et al. 1988, pp. 485–86). More specifically, they report than an incentive of 25¢ roughly increases response rate by an average of 16 percent, while a $1 inducement produces an average increase of 31 percent.

A study by James and Bolstein (1990) examined the joint and comparative effects of monetary inducements and follow-up mailings. They reported that a *combination* of follow-up mailings and a $1 or $2 incentive produced a significantly higher response rate than mailings without an incentive. For further discussion comparing inducements of 50¢ or less with those of $1 or more see Yammarino et al. (1991).

Scott (1961) also experimented with an "Immediate" slip, written on red paper in black lettering and attached to the first follow-up letter in one experiment and to the second in another. Neither strategy had a detectable effect on response rate. He also used a sticker, printed in red on white paper, which said: "TO SAVE OUR TROUBLING YOU AGAIN WITH REMINDER LETTERS, PLEASE REPLY PROMPTLY." Attached to the initial letter it increased response to 95.8 percent from 94.9 percent with no letter, and to 94.1 percent from 93.0 percent when included on the second reminder letter. These differences are not statistically significant, perhaps because response rates were so high without the sticker that there was little room for improvement. However, the sticker on the initial letter increased from 52.4 percent to 61.1 percent the number of questionnaires returned within the first week.

Another device, perhaps more of a threat than an inducement, is the deadline. Goldstein and Kroll (1957) used a deadline in the cover letter and in all follow-up letters and achieved a very high response rate (98.6 percent). Both Henley (1976) and Roberts et al. (1978) found that in the initial returns (before a follow-up message was sent), a deadline yielded a higher response rate. However, a deadline seemed to make little difference in the final overall response rate (after an initial mailing and two mail follow-ups). The advantage of a deadline is that it may keep the respondent from putting off completion of the questionnaire and thus prevent "unplanned" nonresponse—that is, nonresponse by those who planned initially to respond (and were perhaps even enthusiastic about responding) but who later failed to respond because they became ill or otherwise incapacitated, lost the questionnaire, or discovered it weeks later under a pile of letters and decided that it was too late to reply. This group of nonrespondents probably is fairly representative of the sample. Therefore, the loss of their replies is particularly unfortunate.

However, most people who respond do so quickly. People who did not make the deadline might decide that it was too late to return the questionnaire and throw it away. A person who reserved Saturdays for answering mail and planned to return the questionnaire then might be less likely to respond to a letter with a Friday deadline than to one with no deadline at all. A researcher might compensate for this by setting the deadline a month or so in the future, but this might have the opposite effect, causing people who otherwise would have replied by return mail to wait because "there is no rush." Most studies do not use deadlines, and this is probably safer, particularly if reminder letters are used.

The Nature of Respondents

We can see from the foregoing discussion that response rates of over 90 percent are not unheard of, and so the contention of Goode and Hatt (1952, p. 174) that the mailed questionnaire is effective only for a "highly select group of respondents" seems exaggerated. Furthermore, many mailed questionnaires *are* sent to select groups, such as women, doctors, black professors, alumni, skiers, and airplane owners. Often a researcher needing to study the general population will be able to interview enough respondents in his or her local area. However, a study of, for example, the class of 1949 may find that respondents reside in all 50 states and a number of foreign countries. Sending interviewers to all respondents would entail prohibitive travel expenses, leaving the mailed questionnaire the most viable method. Further, members of special groups are generally good respondents because they tend to be interested, to be loyal to the group, and to feel guilty if they do not respond. They are also usually familiar with the subject and so are able to answer fully and with a minimum of instruction.

In a heterogeneous sample of studies, there is consensus that the most interested persons respond earliest. A person who is apathetic about the subject of the study will, all other things being equal, be the least likely to respond. Thus response will be bimodal, with those for and against the issue responding and those who are indifferent not responding. Greater non-response among the lower educational levels has been found in quite a number of studies discussed by Scott (1961, p. 157). The difference in response rates by sex has been studied by a number of investigators, including Scott, with no significant findings. However, Scott (1961, pp. 154–58) did find that questionnaires are significantly more likely to be passed on to others by married females than by unmarried females, and by persons over 50. Also, persons over 50 tended to return more questionnaires unanswered, but the differences were not statistically significant. Nonresponse was significantly higher for married women than for unmarried women, and for women in households with an "above average" number of women. Scott also found significantly more nonresponse among people whose letter-writing activity was below average. He found no significant differences in response, however, between persons with manual and nonmanual occupations.

Type of Mailing

A number of studies have attempted to determine the effect of such factors as type of postage and type of envelope. It has been found that class of mail affects returns, with the more expensive stamp generally stimulating the highest return. In studies dealing with reminders (follow-up letters), Clausen and Ford (1947) reported returns of 61 percent for airmail and special delivery combined versus 36 percent for regular mail. Gullahorn and Gullahorn (1959) received 62 percent for special delivery versus 35 percent for regular mail, while Sirken et al. (1960) found 80 percent for certified delivery versus 69 percent for regular mail. Of course, at present in the United States all first class mail is sent by air.

On comparisons of the initial cover letter (and presumably the questionnaire also) Gullahorn and Gullahorn (1963a) found a statistically significant difference between the response rate for third-class mail (49 percent) and first-class mail (51 percent). Kephart and Bressler (1958) achieved response rates of 52 percent for first class, 60 percent for airmail, and 66 percent for special delivery. The difference between regular and airmail is not statistically significant, but the difference between regular and special delivery is. For some unknown reason, studies on the return envelope tend to compare type of postage (e.g., business reply or metered versus stamped), while studies on the initial or outgoing letter tend to compare amount or value of postage. In a study comparing type of postage on the initial outgoing cover letter, Bridge (1971) divided his sample randomly into two groups and sent each group a packet containing a two-page questionnaire, a cover letter, and a business reply envelope. For one group the packet bore a U.S. stamp, while for the other group the packet bore postage applied with a postage meter. Bridge's response rates were 37.6 percent for the metered packet and 36.0 percent for the hand-stamped packet.

Research by Dillman and Frey (1974) failed to find a difference in response rate between stamped and metered first class letters. Kahle and Sales (1978) found that bulk rate envelopes received a higher response rate (64 percent) than stamped mail (62 percent) if the bulk rate envelopes were individually addressed. However, address-label bulk rate envelopes (the minimum in personalization) received a significantly lower response rate (52 percent).

Virtually all mail surveys provide a return envelope. The feeling that response rates would be damaged if the respondent were required to supply his or her own envelope is apparently universal, with few researchers bothering to study the matter. One exception is the study by Ferriss (1951) that compared a stamped, self-addressed envelope with no envelope at all, and received a response rate of 66 percent for the envelope and only 12 percent for no envelope.

Scott (1961, p. 170) found that a stamped return envelope that was not preaddressed received a 93.3 percent response rate, while a preaddressed government-franked return label attached to the flap of the return envelope resulted in an 89.2 percent return rate. Robinson and Agisim (1951) found that a hand-stamped, first-class return letter brought a response rate of 73.8 percent while business reply first class brought a response rate of 66.3 percent. Price (1950) found that no postage brought a 17.3 percent response rate compared to 26.3 percent for hand-stamped first class.

A number of reasons have been advanced for expecting a greater response rate from hand-stamped return envelopes than from business-reply envelopes. One is that a stamp tends to attract more attention, especially if it is new, unusual, or commemorative. Another possible advantage of a stamp is that the person will feel guilty if he or she throws it away. Business-reply mail is charged for postage only if it is actually returned, so throwing away a business-reply envelope is not regarded as wasteful. Still another advantage of a postage stamp over business reply is that some respondents may not know that postage will be paid on the latter. Robinson and Agisim (1951) found that business-reply envelopes achieved a low response rate in rural areas, probably because rural people were less familiar with such envelopes.

A further advantage of a stamp over business reply is that the stamp may personalize the letter, signifying that attention has been given to the respondent by taking the time to attach a stamp by hand to his or her envelope. However, as discussed above, there is little evidence that personalization significantly increases response rates. Further, a business-reply printed envelope may seem to indicate a professional, prestigious, long-term organization, while a hand-addressed envelope with a stamp may seem simply amateurish and unprofessional. A printed envelope, especially an official government envelope from someone with franking privileges, seems authoritative, legitimate, formal, and prestigious.

In a more recent study, Fox et al. (1988) analyzed the effects of postage on response rate in their previously mentioned meta-analysis. They concluded that stamped return postage (compared to business reply postage) produced one of the largest increases in response rate in the entire meta-analysis (6.2 percent—after university sponsorship and prenotification by letter). However, contrary to expectations, stamped outgoing postage did not yield significantly higher response rates than metered postage.

In another meta-analysis, this one dealing only with return postage, Armstrong and Lusk (1987) compared business reply with first-class stamps in return postage. They concluded that even though business reply is paid for only if it is used, it is still not cost effective, as first-class postage yields an additional 9 percent response rate. The authors generally recommend use of commemoratives or a set of small denomination stamps on the return envelope. See also Yammarino et al. (1991).

Day, Week, or Month of Mailing

The researcher does not want his or her questionnaires to arrive in the mail the day before a major holiday, when school is beginning, or when the family is on vacation. At such times the respondent will have more important things to do than answer the questionnaire. If it arrives while he or she is on an extended vacation, there is an increased probability that he or she either will not receive it at all or will rationalize that it is "too late" to return it.

Other than the obvious, such as avoiding mailing close to holidays or school openings or closings, there have been few conclusive findings concerning optimum mailing times. Scott (1961) in one study sent questionnaires each week for four weeks, with no noticeable difference in response among the four groups. In another he sent two groups of questionnaires seven weeks apart, with no significant difference in response rates. The effects of such factors as seasonal fluctuation on response rates continue to be investigated. With regard to day of the week, Scott (1961, p. 175) discusses two studies, one of direct mail sent to business firms (mailings early in the week seemed to be better) and another experiment with older women, which found a significantly better response rate when questionnaires were received by the respondent late in the week. Bender (1957) found a rank-order of response rates by months, with February the lowest, April next lowest, and March the highest. The National Education Association (1930) found that questionnaires mailed to school superintendents received the best response in the first month (September), with the response rate declining through time, from 76 percent in September to 61 percent in May.

Follow-up Letters and Telephone Calls

There seems to be consensus that the response rate can be greatly improved through follow-ups, and nearly all mailed studies now use follow-ups as standard operating procedure. Without follow-ups a response rate of 50 or 60 percent is about all that can usually be expected, while with follow-ups one can reasonably expect a response rate of 70 or 80 percent or even more. Donald (1960) studied members of the League of Women Voters. Her questionnaire was 19 pages long, required 198 responses, and took at least an hour to complete. Her response rate, as cited in Lansing and Morgan (1971, pp. 247–48), was as follows:

Responded to:	Percent of Sample
First mailing	46.2
Reminder letter	12.2
Additional letter and questionnaire	8.8
Telephone call	10.1
Total response	77.3
Nonresponse	22.7
TOTAL	100.0

It seems safe to assume that follow-ups (at least one) will receive a response rate approximately 20 percent higher than no follow-up at all, with each succeeding follow-up generally having less effect. However, Clausen and Ford (1947) and Gray (1957) found that while the absolute number of returns was less in later follow-ups, the proportion of returns was about the same, since the potential number to be returned is less with each succeeding follow-up.

Number and Timing of Follow-ups or Reminders

A common procedure, as in Donald's (1960) study, is to send a cover letter with the initial questionnaire, then the first reminder letter by itself, next a second reminder letter accompanied by another copy of the questionnaire, and finally to telephone the respondent. Any follow-ups after three are likely to tax the respondent's patience and may even be viewed as harassment, causing him or her to complain to the organization conducting the survey or even to the police, the post office, or some other governmental agency. Scott (1961, pp. 165–66) reports that most studies in the literature use one or two follow-ups, with the record being held by Toops (1926) who sent six. Scott further notes that only one study reported in the literature (Miller and Enquist 1942) received a negligible increase in response through a follow-up, and that there is almost universal agreement that follow-ups are effective in increasing response rates.

Heberlein and Baumgartner (1981) agree that research has shown the effectiveness of a reminder. However, they say that it is not clear whether a replacement questionnaire included with the reminder letter enhances effectiveness. They concluded from a study of 13 surveys that adding a questionnaire has little influence on response rate in a mailed questionnaire study. However, they found two cases where the questionnaire added 6–9 percent to the response rate, and also concluded that in most cases to send questionnaires added less than $100 to postage costs.

Although some professional survey organizations may have a standard number of follow-ups and individual researchers may have thought in advance about how many follow-ups they would use, many researchers simply "play it by ear" in deciding the number of follow-ups and when each should be done. A researcher might decide after only one follow-up that his or her response rate was already high enough. Or he or she might decide that the follow-ups were antagonizing the respondents unduly and therefore choose to abandon them. On the other hand, he or she might find that each follow-up is effective and that the respondents do not seem to resent them, and so decide to follow up six or more times. The usual pattern is for the bulk of the respondents who will reply to any particular mailing to do so relatively quickly. After a week or so questionnaires will continue to be returned, but at a drastically diminished rate (see figure 7–1, from Wild 1974, p. 53).

Most researchers wait until the response to the initial mailing has nearly ceased (usually one to three weeks) and then send the first reminder. There have been attempts (see, for example, Gray 1957), to infer the proper time for the follow-up from studies of the response curve,

Figure 7–1

Number of Questionnaires Returned: Effect of Follow-up Procedures

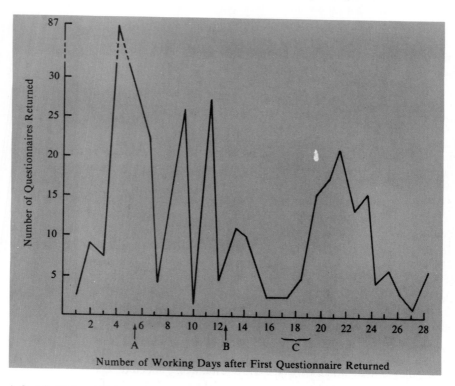

Number of Working Days after First Questionnaire Returned

A. Sent first follow-up letter
B. Sent second follow-up letter with accompanying questionnaire
C. Telephone follow-up for all nonrespondents

SOURCE: From *Sociological Determinants of Utilization of a Prepaid Pediatric Health Care Plan*, by Patricia Breyer Wild, Copyright © 1974 by Patricia Breyer Wild. Unpublished dissertation, Los Angeles: University of California.

but with no definitive results. After the first reminder there will again be an initial upsurge, but generally smaller than the first one. After this response rate has nearly ceased (another week or so) it is time for the second reminder. The overall gain in response achieved by two follow-ups compared to none, and by one follow-up compared to two, are shown in figures 7–2 and 7–3, from Scott (1961, pp. 165–66).

Scott (1961, pp. 164–65) achieved a 74.8 percent response rate with no follow-ups compared to 95.6 percent with two follow-ups. In another study Scott achieved a 93.2 percent response rate with two reminders and an 85.9 percent response rate when the first reminder was dropped but the second retained. Some researchers have tried preview letters sent prior to the questionnaire—sort of a reminder in advance. Kephart and Bressler (1958) found that such preview letters did not increase rates significantly, but Wiasanen (1954) found that a telephone

Figure 7–2

Effect of Two Follow-ups on the Response

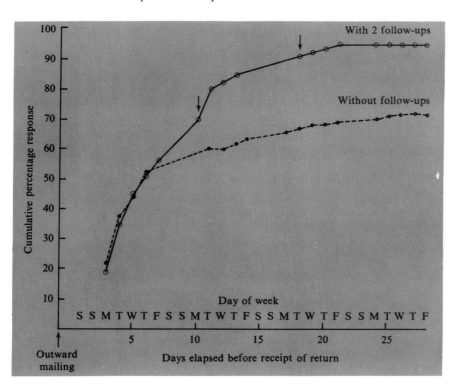

Arrows point to the first day whose returns could have been influenced by each follow-up. Gaps in the sequence of observations are due to weekends and public holidays.

SOURCE: From "Research on Mail Surveys" by Christopher Scott, *Journal of the Royal Statistical Society* 124, Series A: 143–205, 1961. Reprinted by permission of the author and the Royal Statistical Society.

Figure 7–3

Effects of One and Two Follow-ups

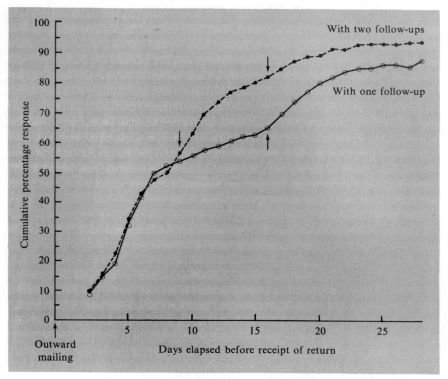

Arrows point to the first day whose returns could have been influenced by each follow-up. Mailing was staggered over five consecutive weekdays, though time *intervals* are comparable for all five groups. The effects of the weekends are lost when the groups are pooled.

SOURCE: From "Research on Mail Surveys" by Christopher Scott, *Journal of the Royal Statistical Society* 124, Series A: 143–205, 1961. Reprinted by permission of the author and the Royal Statistical Society.

call in advance boosted the response rate from 62 percent without the call to 70 percent with it. See Sudman (1982) for a method of estimating (in advance) response to follow-ups in mail surveys.

Content of Reminder Letters.   There is a paucity of literature on the content of reminder letters. My feeling is that a reminder letter should be just that—a reminder and not a threat. The large number of reasons why respondents may not respond, either initially or ever, may be classified into four groups. The first group is composed of respondents whose questionnaire is lost in the mail because of post office error, incorrect address, moving with no forwarding address, and so on. Also in this category are cases in which the completed questionnaire was lost in the return mail. The second group is comprised of respondents who cannot complete the questionnaire because they are physically unable to do so, are in a hospital or other institution, do not speak the language in which the questionnaire is written, are functionally illiterate, or for whom the questionnaire is not applicable (e.g., as when a woman whose first name is Grant receives a mailed questionnaire in a survey of men only). The third group consists of people for whom the questionnaire is applicable and who are capable of filling it out, but who procrastinate, forget it, or misplace it temporarily. These are potential respondents, as are the persons in group one if their next encounter with the mails is more successful. The fourth group consists of out-and-out refusals. These are people who will not answer for various reasons. Some "sophisticated" nonrespondents feel that survey results are invalid, that the sampling techniques are faulty, and that the survey is a waste of time. Others may feel that the survey is an invasion of privacy or is not allowed by their religion. Still others may feel that government-sponsored surveys are a waste of taxpayers' money, or that social scientists are "socialists" or communists. Others may be antiuniversity, antigovernment, or antibusiness (or anti-whatever is sponsoring the survey). Others may be apathetic or feel that the survey is silly, or not understand the reason for it. Last but not least, some have been inundated by surveys and resent having to fill out one more questionnaire.

Reminder letters obviously cannot be effective with the second group, as they are unable to comply. The first and third groups contain people who are willing to cooperate but whose questionnaire was lost in the mail, who have just returned home after a lengthy absence and found the questionnaire waiting, and so on. All that is necessary for these people is a gentle reminder, beginning in this manner: "Dear Respondent, A few weeks ago I mailed you a questionnaire concerning. . . . " The letter then continues with the statement that perhaps the questionnaire was not received or was lost, and includes an offer to send another questionnaire. It is also customary to repeat the original appeal to return the questionnaire (e.g., the study is very important, your compliance important, I need your help, the results will be confidential).

The most difficult group to deal with is the fourth, those who are against all surveys in general or yours in particular. Many of these will not respond to any appeal, but it is important that the reasons for the study be repeated, as respondents may have misunderstood the purpose for the study, the use that is to be made of the data, or the nature of the sponsorship.

Some persons may have begun the questionnaire but become frustrated at their inability to answer a particular question, or may not have understood a question or the directions for answering a question. Each of these occurrences could cause someone to discard the questionnaire. Thus it is good to state in the follow-up letter that if a particular question is bothering you, simply note in the margin that you are unable to answer it and continue with other questions.

It is customary to vary the follow-ups so that the respondent does not grow weary of repetition. The first reminder is often a letter, although it could be a telephone call. Often just a postcard is used. Generally in the first reminder the researcher assumes that the respondent received the questionnaire and still has it and so does not send another copy. A second copy of the questionnaire is often sent with the second reminder letter on the assumption that the first copy was lost or thrown away. The second reminder letter is similar to the first one, although the fact that the questionnaire is enclosed is noted and the appeal to respond may be varied. It is thought that any more than two letters are ineffective, and a telephone call is used for any subsequent reminder. Telephone calls often reveal a sizable number of respondents who are willing to respond but who have not been receiving mail because their address was incorrectly listed, or they have moved, or their spouse picks up their mail and has not given them the questionnaire.

Anonymity and Follow-ups. The degree to which respondents welcome anonymity would seem to be largely dependent upon the nature of the study. Short, inoffensive questionnaires may not require anonymity. Scott (1961) reports that the response rate for a survey in which respondents were asked to sign their names was only 4 or 5 percent lower than response rates on other surveys he conducted, and that only 3.1 percent of the respondents failed to sign their name. However, in studies of more controversial subjects (Scott studied radio and television programs) it may well be that failure to ensure anonymity may greatly increase the number of questionnaires not returned, the number of questions skipped on returned questionnaires, and the number of answers that are false, vague, or exaggerated.

Thus, all other things being equal, it would seem wise to promise the respondent anonymity. By anonymity we do not mean that the researcher knows the respondent's name but pledges not to release it; we mean that the researcher is unable to link the respondent with the questionnaire he or she answered. Ensuring true anonymity is easy enough if no follow-ups are to be conducted, or if everyone is followed-up (respondents as well as nonrespondents). The "no follow-up" alternative is not very attractive because, as we have seen, follow-ups increase the response rate generally by around 20 percent, and studies without any follow-ups can yield response rates as low as 10 percent, which is worthless. Sending a follow-up to everyone, including those who have already responded, is feasible if only one follow-up is planned and if the follow-up says, "If you have already mailed your questionnaire please disregard this notice. We have no means of identifying respondents as all replies are anonymous. Thus we are sending this reminder to all since we have no way of knowing whether or not you have responded already." It is obviously more expensive to mail to everybody rather than just to the nonrespondents. Time and money costs can be reduced somewhat by making two sets of address labels initially instead of one, or perhaps by using a postcard instead of a letter. However, most researchers wish to follow-up more than once, and hesitate to send follow-ups to respondents as well as nonrespondents at the risk of irritating the former. Further, why pay the expense involved in sending follow-ups to 100 percent of the sample when they are applicable to only a small percentage who have not responded? This violates one of the basic survey rules stated in chapter 6, which says that the questionnaire should be relevant to the respondent. There have even been cases in which a respondent completed both the original questionnaire and a follow-up questionnaire (apparently he or she surmised that the first must have been lost in the mail).

Thus most researchers do follow-up, but only to nonrespondents. How can one identify nonrespondents when questionnaires are anonymous? Probably the most common method, at least in studies with a small budget, is not to maintain anonymity but to promise the respondent that only the researcher will know his or her identity and that results will be kept confidential. Usually nonrespondents are identified by assigning each questionnaire an identification number before it is mailed and recording this number by the respective respondent's name. When a respondent receives a questionnaire with no name but only a number (which he or she might not even see, as they are often put on the back of the page), he or she might assume that identification will be impossible.

One method that has been developed for identifying nonrespondents while maintaining anonymity involves mailing a postcard bearing the respondent's name and address with the questionnaire. The respondent is instructed to mail the card when he or she completes the questionnaire, which is mailed separately with no name or identification number. This technique was used successfully by Hill (1957), Bradt (1955), Cahalan (1951), and Larson and Catton (1959). Babbie (1973, p. 169) received a 62 percent response rate using postcards. The only obvious disadvantage with this method, besides the expense and the added work for the respondent in mailing the card, is that respondents can easily return the card but not the questionnaire, and thus be a nonrespondent without fear of further harassment. Other researchers have included identification numbers without the respondent's knowledge, in one case by writing these numbers in invisible ink (Hoppe 1952) and in another by disguising identification numbers as room numbers in the address on the return envelope (Rollins 1940). Such subterfuges may be unethical.

I have mentioned the broad meta-analysis of Fox et al. (1988) several times previously in this chapter. In their study the authors also analyzed the effects of a follow-up postcard on response rate. The postcard follow-up on average yielded an additional response rate of approximately 3.5 percent, which was statistically significant.

Adequate Response Rate

It should be evident from the discussion in this chapter that a large number of factors can affect response rates in mailed questionnaire surveys. Thus it should not be surprising that there has been a tremendous variation in the response rates reported. Goldstein and Kroll (1957) report a phenomenal return rate of 98.6 percent in a study of hospitals conducted for the U.S. Department of Health. Scott (1961) reports that mail surveys conducted by the Central Office of Information in England, for which he works, routinely achieve response rates of over 90 percent. On the other hand, many more studies achieve response rates of 10 to 20 percent than achieve 90 percent rates. There is also some evidence that response rates are declining, probably because of saturation. Given this extreme variation, what constitutes an adequate response rate? This depends on how much time and money one is willing or able to spend on the study. Studies with too low a budget to afford follow-ups cannot expect to achieve the same rate as studies with follow-ups. Some professional researchers are content with rates far lower than 90 percent. Babbie says:

> I feel that a response rate of at least 50 percent is *adequate* for analysis and reporting. A response rate of at least 60 percent is *good*. And a response rate of 70 percent or more is *very good*. The reader should bear in mind, however, that these are only rough guides, they have no statistical basis, and a demonstrated lack of response bias is far more important than a high response rate (Babbie 1973, p. 165).

I would be somewhat more conservative than Babbie. "A "demonstrated lack of response bias" is almost by definition going to be much more difficult to secure with a low response rate, while a very high response rate will permit little response bias. Obviously one should strive for a high return rate and a lack of response bias. However, a casual look at the research literature on mailed questionnaire studies will show that many studies with no follow-up generally do not exceed a 50 to 60 percent response rate. While some will consider this "adequate" and some will not, it is about the most that can realistically be expected except in special cases. The proper use of follow-ups, preferably two reminder letters (with the second accompanied by another copy of the questionnaire) and a telephone call as a third reminder, should achieve a response rate of approximately 75 percent or more. Wild (1974) used this procedure to obtain a rate of 74.6 percent in her study of a prepaid pediatric health-care plan for students, while Donald's (1960) study obtained a 77.3 percent return. Thus with two letter follow-ups and one telephone follow-up, a 50 percent return is not "adequate" but is probably rather poor; a return of over 90 percent is certainly possible if the procedures we have discussed are followed carefully (prestigious sponsor, good cover letter, good instructions, short questionnaire, questions easy to answer, and so on).

As mentioned above, a number of questionnaires will not be delivered to the respondent for various reasons (e.g., the house has been demolished, the address is incorrect, the respondent has moved or has died). Although this category of nonresponse may not be a random selection of the sample, these nonresponses are not refusals and are out of the researcher's control, so some researchers do not include them when computing the response rate, Babbie (1973, p. 165) calls exclusion of undeliverable questionnaires from computation of the response rate the "accepted practice." Thus if a researcher has an initial sample of 110 persons, but 10 questionnaires are returned by the post office undelivered and 80 are ultimately returned by respondents, the response rate is computed by dividing the 80 returned by the *net* sample size of 100, not by the gross or original sample size of 110.

Remember that one disadvantage of the mailed questionnaire is that, without the researcher's knowledge, it can be answered by someone other than the intended respondent. Thus if a researcher has a list of 100 names on his or her sampling frame and receives 90 returned questionnaires, it is possible that only 80 were filled out by the persons in the sample. In one study Scott (1961, p. 152) asked the person completing the questionnaire to sign it, and found that about 10 percent were passed on, usually to the respondent's spouse (usually from wife to husband), and sometimes signed by both husband and wife.

In an interesting study, Jussaume and Yamada (1990) compared response rates of mailed-questionnaire surveys conducted in Seattle, Washington, and Kobe, Japan. The response rates were amazingly similar (55.6 percent in Japan and 57.5 percent in the United States). The authors attribute the similarities in part to the fact that both surveys were based on the Total Design Method discussed earlier in this chapter. For further discussion of the adequacy of response rates for mailed questionnaires see Goyder (1985).

Validity and Reliability

It should be clear from our discussion in chapter 4 of reliability and validity that we generally assess the reliability and validity of each question or group of questions (scale) rather than of the questionnaire as a whole. There may be a great many questions measuring a great many variables on a single mailed questionnaire, some of which may be valid and reliable measures of their respective properties while others are not. After data collection we can take a single question from a mailed questionnaire and subject it to construct-validation procedures. However, our definition of construct validity indicates that it is generally impossible to subject an entire questionnaire to this process, as the construct-validation procedure concerns a single variable, while the questionnaire generally measures many variables. The split-half procedure for assessing reliability entails use of many measures of a single concept, but a questionnaire generally contains measures of many concepts. Therefore it is difficult if not impossible to use split-half procedures to test the reliability of an entire questionnaire.

Nevertheless, it is important to attempt to determine the extent to which the mailed-questionnaire method itself affects the validity and reliability of the questions that comprise the questionnaire. A particular question may be so ambiguous that it will not be valid or reliable whether it is used in the mailed questionnaire, the interview study, or any other data-collection method.

Validity

The validity of mailed-questionnaire data has been assessed by comparing findings from a mailed questionnaire with previously known facts. This is criterion validity, as defined in chapter 4. Individual questions should have face validity before they are included in the questionnaire, and the pretest should detect and remove questions without face validity. We have already indicated that using construct validation for an entire questionnaire is difficult if not impossible, and we know of no studies that have used this procedure for mailed questionnaires. However, one could certainly take individual questions from a mailed survey and compare them in a construct-validation test with questions from an interview study. This is a piece of research that needs to be done, but we are not aware of any existing studies of this type. We know of only two criterion-validity studies of the mailed questionnaire. Scott (1961, p. 179) says the low number is probably due to the fact that researchers who already know the facts are generally reluctant to spend the money necessary to conduct a mailed-questionnaire survey.

Scott (1961, p. 186) compiled a list of 100 persons known to have sent Greetings Letter Telegrams. Their names were taken from the backs of forms filed at post offices. Of 100 mailed questionnaires asking respondents whether they had sent such a telegram, seven questionnaires were undeliverable and were returned by the post office, 78 were completed and returned by respondents,. and 15 were not returned. Of the 78 returned, 69 respondents admitted sending such a telegram and nine denied it. The less-than-perfect correspondence between the forms filed at the post office and the mailed questionnaire shows a lack of complete validity or the existence of measurement error. It is possible that the criterion (the post office records) was incorrect and the questionnaires were correct. It is more likely, however, that the lack of correspondence is due to such reasons as the respondent's faulty memory or the fact that his or her spouse sent the telegram without his or her knowledge. The only other validity study we know of for mailed questionnaires was published by Colley (1945). He found close correspondence between the answers to a mailed questionnaire asking persons what brands of a product they used and the sales figures for the respective brands, indicating the validity of the mailed-questionnaire technique.

Reliability

We have indicated that split-half reliability procedures would be difficult if not impossible to administer for the questionnaire as a whole. Test-retest procedures are feasible, however. Unfortunately, the bulk of studies have not consisted of testing and retesting the same mailed questionnaire but rather of comparing the same questionnaire in mailed versus interview situations. Scott (1961, pp. 180–86) found very close agreement between the mailed questionnaire and the interview on items dealing with sex and marital status, and fairly close agreement on age. There was greater discrepancy on social class. Where a classifiable response was obtained, the mailed questionnaire and the interview were about equally accurate, but the mailed questionnaire received more unclassifiable responses, especially from lower-class respondents. A number of other comparisons of questionnaires and interviews were discussed by Scott (1961). The interview and the mail survey were generally found to be in agreement, showing both to be reliable, with the mailed survey slightly better for studying sensitive questions. With sensitive questions the interview is more likely to get "don't knows" or no answers.

Summary

In chapter 7 we discussed mailed-questionnaire studies. There are a number of advantages of mailed questionnaires compared to interview studies, including a substantial savings of time and money, greater assurance of anonymity, lack of interview bias, accessibility, as well as several other factors. Among the disadvantages of mailed-questionnaire studies are a low response rate, capability of gathering information only on reported behavior (no possibility of observation), lack of control over the research setting, lack of control over question order, and several other problems.

We next discussed a number of factors that may affect response rate, with a view toward maximizing our response rate. Among the factors discussed were sponsorship of the survey, questionnaire length, nature of the cover letter, ease of completing and returning the questionnaire, inducement to reply, nature of respondents, type of mailing, time of mailing, and follow-up letters and telephone calls. The chapter concluded with a discussion of response rates, validity and reliability.

CHAPTER 8

INTERVIEW STUDIES

THE ADVANTAGES AND DISADVANTAGES of interview studies tend to complement those of mailed-questionnaire studies and can be anticipated from our discussion of the latter in chapter 7.

Advantages of Interview Studies

1. *Flexibility.* One major advantage of the interview is its flexibility. Interviewers can probe for more specific answers and can repeat a question when the response indicates that the respondent misunderstood. it may be that different questions are appropriate for different respondents; the interview situation makes it possible for the interviewer to decide what questions are appropriate, rather than writing them all in advance as the researcher must do for the mailed study.

2. *Response rate.* The interview tends to have a better response rate than the mailed questionnaire. Persons who are unable to read and write can still answer questions in an interview, and others who are unwilling to expend the energy to write out their answers may be glad to talk. Many people simply feel more confident of their speaking ability than of their writing ability.

3. *Nonverbal behavior.* The interviewer is present to observe nonverbal behavior and to assess the validity of the respondent's answer.

4. *Control over environment.* An interviewer can standardize the interview environment by making certain that the interview is conducted in privacy, that there is no noise, and so on, in contrast to the mailed study, where the questionnaires may be completed by different people under drastically different conditions.

5. *Question order.* The interviewer has control over question order and can ensure that the respondent does not answer the questions out of order or in any other way thwart the structure of the questionnaire.

6. *Spontaneity.* The interviewer can record spontaneous answers. The respondent does not have the chance to retract his or her first answer and write another, as is possible with a mailed questionnaire. Spontaneous answers may be more informative and less normative than answers about which the respondent has had time to think.

7. *Respondent alone can answer.* The respondent is unable to "cheat" by receiving prompting or answers from others, or by having others complete the entire questionnaire for him or her, as often happens in mailed studies.

8. *Completeness.* The interviewer can ensure that all of the questions are answered.

9. *Time of interview.* The interviewer can record the exact time, date, and place of the interview. Thus if some important event has occurred during the course of the study that may cause changes in the respondent's answers, the researcher has a chance to compare answers before and after the event. In a mailed survey he or she has only postmarks as clues to which questionnaires were answered before the event and which after.

10. *Greater complexity of questionnaire.* A more complex questionnaire can be used in an interview study. A skilled, experienced, and well-trained interviewer can work with a questionnaire so full of skips, charts and graphs, arrows, detailed instructions, and various other contingencies that even a well-educated respondent would feel hopelessly lost or at least intimidated if he or she received it in the mail.

Disadvantages of Interview Studies

1. *Cost.* Interview studies can be extremely costly. The more complex studies require small bureaucracies with a host of administrators, field supervisors, interviewers, and perhaps even public relations personnel. Sampling is often costly. Interview schedules can also be costly to construct and reproduce. In addition, interviewers must be paid not only for the hours that they interview but also for training periods, and they must be reimbursed for travel expenses.

2. *Time.* Interviews are often lengthy and may require the interviewer to travel miles. In addition, the interviewer must arrange the interview for times when the respondent is home; sometimes an interviewer can complete only one or a few interviews each day, even though the actual interviewing time may be relatively brief. Further, it is not uncommon for an interviewer to return to an address three or more times before an interview is finally granted. Interviewing may take as long as six months in studies with a large sample or with respondents who are not geographically centralized. Unfortunately, many events can occur over such a long time period that may affect the answers received.

3. *Interview bias.* The interviewer serves a useful function in making sure that all questions are answered and that the respondent understands the instructions and the questions. However, the interviewer can also cause error. He or she may misunderstand the respondent's answer, may understand it but make a clerical error in recording it, or may simply record an answer even when the respondent failed to reply. In addition, the respondent's answers can be affected by his or her reaction to the interviewer's sex, race, social class, age, dress and physical appearance, or accent.

4. *No opportunity to consult records.* Compared to the mailed questionnaire, the interview generally does not provide the respondent time to conduct research, to check records, to consult family and friends about facts, or to ponder his or her reply.

5. *Inconvenience.* It has been shown repeatedly that a person's reasoning ability is adversely affected by such factors as fatigue, stress, illness, heat, and density. The mailed questionnaire provides the best opportunity for the respondent to answer when the adverse factors are at a minimum, even if it means completing the questionnaire a few questions at a time rather than all at once. In contrast, the respondent may give answers in an interview situation that are less than his or her best effort merely because the interviewer arrived when the baby was crying, the dog was barking, dinner was burning, and the respondent needed to go to the bathroom.

6. *Less anonymity.* The interview offers less assurance of anonymity than the mailed questionnaire study, particularly if the latter includes no follow-up. The interviewer typically knows the respondent's name and address and often his or her telephone number as well. Further, in listing the members of the household, the interviewer often receives the names of the very persons from whom the respondent wishes the information given in the interview withheld. Thus the interviewer poses a potential threat to the respondent, particularly if the information is incriminating, embarrassing, or otherwise sensitive. The respondent can minimize the threat by refusing to respond, or else trust the interviewer not to release the information in any manner that can identify the respondent.

7. *Less standardized question wording.* It may be necessary for the interviewer to probe a great deal, to phrase the same question differently for different respondents, or even to ask

different questions of different respondents. While this flexibility can be an advantage, it can also be a disadvantage if it makes it difficult for the researcher to compare respondents' answers.

8. *Lack of accessibility to respondents.* The fact that respondents live in 12 different states may make little difference to a researcher conducting a mailed questionnaire study, as all can be reached for the price of a stamp. However, travel costs for interviewing in all 12 states may be exorbitant and may prove impossible.

The Interview as Social Interaction

The interview is a special case of social interaction between two persons and as such is subject to some of the same rules and restrictions as other instances of social interaction. Apart from the possible biases and errors that stem from the questionnaire instrument itself or from the sampling design, the social nature of the interview has the potential for all sorts of bias, inconsistencies, and inaccuracies. Many social scientists have been highly critical of the survey in general, and the interview survey in particular, as a data-gathering instrument and have expressed pessimism about the possibility of unbiased data collection via this method. T. R. Williams (1959) said that in certain societies there may be institutionalized patterns of saying one thing but doing another. We all have seen people who believe so strongly in a particular pattern of behavior that they will say (and perhaps sincerely believe) that they adhere to this pattern when, in fact, they deviate from it more often than they conform to it. Many persons who believe that they are not prejudiced or jealous, for example, often exhibit behavior that others consider to be symptomatic of prejudice or jealousy. Williams also argues that responses should be interpreted in context and may not be comparable from one social context to another. To see that this may be true we have only to note that a slang word may have different meanings depending upon the subculture in which it is used, as discussed in chapter 6. The assumption that many words have meanings that are situation-specific is central to ethnomethodology and is discussed at length in chapter 11.

The gist of William's criticism of the survey is that the assumptions on which it is based (equally of word and deed; universally understood and context-free terms) cannot be met in certain populations. A different criticism made by Derek L. Phillips (1971), among others, is that the survey method itself biases the data or can even manufacture data so that the data gathered are not so much a reflection of what actually exists in the population as they are artifacts of the method. Phillips (1971, p. 49) says: "The assumption by many social scientists that they can engage in research without influencing what they obtain in the way of data is preposterous."

Phillips is strongly critical of the survey method, particularly the interview process. There is some basis for the criticisms made by Williams, Phillips, and others. Certainly persons' words often differ from their deeds, and certainly the same word can mean different things to different people or in different situations. The sheer variability in human characteristics or attitudes and the large number of characteristics and attitudes that generally must be studied or controlled for make social research extremely difficult. I doubt, however, that many social researchers go about their studies as naively as Phillips and others would have us believe. By painting the picture of a social researcher who assumes that his or her research methods do not affect his or her data, Phillips is in large part constructing a "straw man" to knock down. Our discussion so far has concerned the pitfalls in research and the problem of assessing and maintaining reliability and validity. Most of chapter 7 dealt with studies analyzing how characteristics of a mailed questionnaire affect the quality of the data received, although Phillips's statements imply that such topics have been almost entirely neglected by survey researchers.

In addition to errors caused by an inadequate sample or an inadequate questionnaire, what are some of the ways in which the interview may adversely affect the data? Errors or bias on the part of the respondent may be caused by (1) deliberate lying, because the respondent does not know the answer, the question is too sensitive, or he or she does not want to give a socially undesirable answer; (2) unconscious mistakes, such as a respondent's believing he or she is giving an accurate account of his or her behavior when he or she is not. This occurs most frequently when the respondent has socially undesirable traits that he or she will not admit even to himself or herself; (3) accidental errors, as when the respondent simply misunderstands or misinterprets the question; and (4) memory failures, when the respondent does his or her best to remember but cannot remember or is not sure.

The first and second errors are most easily affected by the interviewer's physical appearance and manner. An interviewer who seems to be prestigious, of high status, very formal, or otherwise intimidating may arouse the respondent's caution in answering. The third and fourth errors are more likely to be caused by a faulty questionnaire than by the interviewer, although an interviewer who has an accent, does not speak clearly, or speaks very softly can cause errors of the third type if the respondent cannot understand him or her.

There are also at least four types of error that can be made by the interviewer, as listed by Hyman (1954, p. 240): (1) asking errors, or errors that the interviewer makes by altering the questionnaire through omitting certain questions or changing question wording: (2) probing errors, which occur through biased, irrelevant, inadequate, or unnecessary probing: (3) recording errors; and (4) flagrant cheating, or consciously recording a response without even asking the question, or recording a response even when the respondent fails to answer.

Although the literature has given most attention to the possible effects of the interviewer's social and physical characteristics on the respondent's reaction, it should be clear that the interaction goes both ways. The respondent can also bias and intimidate the interviewer, causing him or her to record incorrect or biased answers. Hyman (1954, p. 239) reports a study in which a respondent was "planted" and "instructed to be hostile, uncooperative, and suspicious of the entire situation. He generally required considerable persuasion to answer many of the questions at all and was on the whole quite vicious with the interviewer." All of the nine interviewers involved in this study cheated at least once, generally by recording answers when none were given or when the question was answered in an irrelevant or ambiguous manner (Hyman, 1954, p. 241).

Before we discuss social and physical characteristics of respondents and interviewers that might affect the quality of the data received, it will be helpful to examine the nature of the social interaction involved in the interview situation.

The Interview as a Secondary Relationship

Each of us has not one self, but several different selves. Perhaps the chief evidence is the clear distinction between our private self and our public self. Virtually everyone tends to act some-what differently in public than at a private family gathering. Children who are forced by their mothers to be polite, well-dressed, and well-mannered, and to use impeccable English when at a formal gathering or when company is present may be able to get by with old clothes, slang, and poor manners in the privacy of their own home with just the family present.

The most intimate type of group and the one in which most of us feel most free is the primary group. The concept of a primary group was chiefly developed by Charles H. Cooley in 1909. As described by Martindale:

> Primary groups are characterized by intimate face-to-face association and cooperation. Their chief properties include: (1) face-to-face association, (2) unspecified nature of associations, (3) relative permanence, (4) a small number of persons involved, and (5) relative intimacy of participants. Characteristic examples of the primary group are the family, the old-fashioned neighborhood, the play group of children, the group of elders. In such primary groups, there is an intimate fusion of individuality and group (Martindale 1960, p. 345).

In a primary group such as a family the members know each other intimately and infor-mally. Interaction is often emotional. Furthermore, persons within the primary group react to one another in terms of their whole personality and history, not merely in terms of their appear-ance or their actions at the present time. In a primary group a person's reputation and past actions are important determinants of how he or she is treated and reacted to. Since interaction is long term and intimate, it is difficult if not impossible for a member to deceive others through impression management by "putting up a front" or by lying. Others in the primary group feel that they "know" the person, know what he or she is really like, know his or her real self, know that he or she would never do "that." If a young male grows his hair long, he will still be himself to his primary group, while to the outside world he may be just "a hippie." Social interaction within the primary group may have functional or business purposes, but it may also be for emotional reasons, for conversation, or for enjoyment. The interaction in a primary group is much more emotionally charged when outside of that group, uses more of a person's whole personality, and is much more intimate.

The opposite of the primary relationship is a secondary relationship. A secondary relation-ship is usually functional rather than emotional. The interaction is engaged in for a purpose, often a single purpose. The interaction is likely to be polite and courteous but restrained, and formal rather than intimate. Rather than acting in terms of the whole personality, the two par-ticipants utilize only a single facet of the personality. Since the participants often know little about each other, they tend to depend greatly upon such cues as dress, grooming, hairstyle, skin color, age, sex, tone of voice, and accent. For example, you may go shopping on Saturday and have secondary social interaction with as many as 20 people from whom you buy gasoline, groceries, clothing, and so on. Although the people may be very nice, you learn little about their whole personalities but relate to them primarily in terms of their status (grocer, physician, salesperson) as you perceive it. You know nothing about their religious preferences, financial affairs, or inlaws. You have no way to judge whether the person is acting oddly today, as you would in a primary relationship, and you are vulnerable to deception through impression management.

However, even though you know equally little about each of the persons with whom you have secondary relations, you probably will not deal with each of them in exactly the same way. Whether you realize it or not, you will act differently toward persons of different sexes, age groups, races, and social statuses. Your estimation of the person's social status may be incorrect, as you do not know him or her intimately and have to rely on immediate visual and aural cues.

Most people have been socialized to react differently to persons of different status. Thus, perhaps unconsciously, they tend to use their best grammar when talking to a teacher, refrain from swearing when talking to a clergyman or members of the opposite sex or strangers, refrain from talking about their sexual exploits to members of the opposite sex, and refrain from using racial epithets or telling racial jokes when talking to members of the other racial groups.

Thus the average person has one behavior set for his or her age group that he or she does not consider appropriate for his or her children or for his or her grandparents. He or she has another behavior set for his or her gender group. The wife talking with her friends or the husband "out with the boys" may reveal things, particularly in regard to sexual relations with others, that she or he would not tell a spouse.

The import of this discussion as far as the interview is concerned is that, first, each person has many sets of overlapping behaviors rather than just one. How much he or she is willing to reveal about a particular subject (e.g., sexual activity) is situationally determined, and is largely dependent upon his or her impression of the interviewer. Second, the relationship between interviewer and respondent is virtually always secondary rather than primary. The respondent has little by which to judge the interviewer except his or her appearance and his or her sponsorship, as evidenced by identification and letters of reference. As Goffman (1959) notes, first impressions are very important.

It might seem to the casual observer that the average respondent cannot care much about the sex, age, or race of the interviewer, as he or she will probably never see him or her again anyway. Even if he or she does note the interviewer's status, there might seem to be little reason for the respondent to engage in impression management for the benefit of a mere stranger. However, on closer examination we see that the respondent is not managing his or her appearance for the benefit of the interviewer but for his or her own benefit. That is, he or she cares very much what others, including the interviewer, think about him or her for self-conception is based upon the evaluations of others. This is Charles H. Cooley's famous notion of the "looking-glass self," according to which a person's self-image is formed not in isolation but by adapting to what others think of him or her (or to his or her perception of others' perception of himself or herself). As Cooley (cited in Martindale 1960, p. 345) puts it: "A self-idea of this sort seems to have three principal elements: the imagination of our appearance to the other person; the imagination of his judgment of that appearance; and some sort of self-feeling, such as pride or mortification.

The situation seems hopeless, with so many selves and just one interviewer, and with the respondent's entire conception of himself or herself being dependent upon the interviewer's reaction. Actually, the different selves will yield different behaviors and reactions not to all questions, but only to sensitive ones. Some questions are not much affected by the characteristics of the interviewer, while questions dealing with such sensitive matters as sex, religion, or race relations may be very much affected. The rule of thumb for dealing with sensitive issues is to use an interviewer with roughly the same characteristics as the respondent. The interviewer and respondent will by no means form an instant primary relationship but as we will see below, the interviewer will come closer to obtaining reliable data on sensitive issues.

Effects of Interviewer Characteristics

What happens when the interviewer and respondent differ in their physical or social characteristics? A large number of studies have shown that these differences can have an effect (although not always large or significant) on the quality of the data received.

Race and Ethnicity

Probably the most comprehensive studies on interviewer characteristics were reported by Hyman (1954). In a study with 1,000 black respondents conducted by the National Opinion Research Center in Memphis in 1942, researchers found that white interviewers elicited results significantly different from those obtained by black interviewers. Hyman says:

> On almost all the opinion and attitude questions, the white interviewers obtained significantly higher proportions of what might be called by some people "proper" or "acceptable" answers. Negroes were most reluctant to express to the white interviewers their resentments over discrimination by employers or labor unions, in the army, and in public places; to express any sort of belief in the good intentions or even possibility of victory of Japan or Germany; to reveal to white interviewers sympathy of the CIO (possibly out of fear that the white interviewer might think them too radical). Even on some of the factual questions such as auto ownership, reading of Negro newspapers, and CIO membership, apparently some Negroes reported differently to white interviewers than to Negro interviewers. It must be remembered that the survey was carried out in a southern city where fear of dominant whites is greatest (Hyman 1954, p. 159).

Stouffer et al. (1950), in another study of black respondents conducted during World War II, also found differences between responses obtained by white and black interviewers. For example, the black interviewers found 21 percent more responses indicating racial protest and 16 percent more responses indicating unfair treatment in the army than did white interviewers (cited in Hyman 1954, p. 162).

In a later study J. A. Williams (1964) found that the degree of bias in the data was inversely related to the degree of social distance between respondent and interviewer. He found that white interviewers biased the results more for lower-class black respondents than for upperclass black respondents. In another study Dohrenwend et al. (1968, p. 415) used white interviewers but rated them (after the interview) as to which types of subject they preferred to interview (men, women, poor people, rich people, whites, blacks, old people, young people). They found indications that interviewers who preferred young respondents and rejected old people also rejected poor people and blacks.

In some other research dealing with the interviewer's race, Bradburn and Sudman (1979) studied 372 tape-recorded interviews. In comparing black and white interviewers they found no significant difference in the number of reading errors made by interviewers, although whites made slightly more errors than blacks. Similarly, interviewers (apparently of all races—race of interviewer was not given), made slightly more reading errors when the respondents were white than when they were black.

In a study dealing with Jews and Gentiles, Hyman (1954, p. 162) asked Gentile respondents in New York City: "Do you think that Jewish people in the United States have too much influence in the business world, not enough influence, or about the amount of influence they should have?" When the interviewer was also a Gentile, 50 percent of respondents answered that Jews had too much influence and 38 percent answered that they had the amount they should have. With a Jewish interviewer, only 22 percent answered that Jews had too much influence and 58 percent answered that they had the amount they should have. In another study, Robinson and Rhodes (1946) compared interviewers who were (1) Jewish appearing; (2) non-Jewish appearing; and (3) Jewish appearing who introduced themselves with Jewish names. On the question "Do you think there are too many Jews holding governmental offices and jobs?" the interviewers who were Jewish appearing with a Jewish name received 11.7 percent positive responses, compared to 15.4 percent for those with a Jewish appearance but no Jewish name and 21.2 percent for the non-Jewish appearing. For the question "Do you think the Jews have too much power?" a similar trend emerged. The Jewish-appearing interviewer with a Jewish name received 5.8 percent yes responses, compared to 15.6 percent for Jewish appearance only and 24.3 percent for non-Jewish appearance.

Schaeffer (1980) studied cross-race (black and white) interviewers and respondents for a national-sample survey. She concluded that "race of interviewer effects on items with racial content were large and fairly consistent for both black and white respondents" (p. 417). She added that for most nonracial items, however, "the likelihood of substantial or systematic distortion of findings by race-of-interviewer effects seems low" (p. 417).

Campbell (1981) also found race-of-interviewer effects for Southern blacks and whites, but as Schaeffer noted, those were generally limited to racial questions. He found that the respondent consistently biased the answer in favor of the interviewer's race. Cotter et al. (1982) reached the same conclusion for telephone interviews. Race of interviewer and respondent made no difference for nonracial questions but did result in bias for racial questions, with white respondents being more "pro-black" when interviewed by a black interviewer. See also Bachman and O'Malley (1984).

Weeks and Moore (1981) studied ethnicity of interviewers and respondents in a survey of English-language proficiency of Chicanos, Cubans, Native Americans, and Chinese. They concluded that for nonsensitive questions there was no significant ethnicity-of-interviewer bias.

Reese et al. (1986) tested a theory of deference using a telephone survey of both Anglo and Mexican-American respondents and Anglo and Mexican-American interviewers. Their "general theory of deference" states that respondents try to avoid offending an interviewer, specifically on items which mention the interviewer's race. The deference theory was most strongly supported for Anglo respondents, who were less likely to disagree that they preferred Mexican-American culture (for example), when the interviewer was Mexican-American rather than Anglo. Similar results were not shown for Mexican-American respondents on cultural items. However, ethnicity of interviewer effects were shown for Mexican-American respondents when the questions dealt with education and income. When interviewed by an Anglo, Mexican-Americans reported higher educational attainment and family income than when interviewed by a Mexican-American.

Anderson et al. (1988a) studied black respondents who were interviewed by either white or black interviewers in the National Election Studies (NES) of 1964, 1976, 1978, 1980, and 1984. Black respondents living in predominantly black neighborhoods and interviewed by black interviewers were more likely to report falsely that they voted (and more likely to actually vote) than blacks interviewed by whites.

In a subsequent study, the same authors (Anderson et al. 1988b) extended their analysis to two additional surveys in 1982 and 1986, and focused on the effects of race of interviewer on race-related issues. Blacks interviewed by whites were much more likely to express warmth and closeness toward whites than were blacks interviewed by blacks.

Sex

The sex of the interviewer has also been shown to affect the respondent's reaction. Benney et al. (1956) asked interviewers to rate each respondent on honesty in answering. In a survey of political attitudes, male interviewers said that 68 percent of the male respondents and 56 percent of the female respondents were "completely frank and honest," while corresponding figures for female interviewers were 70 percent for respondents of each sex.

A study reported by Hyman (1954, pp. 164–65) gave each respondent a 50-word summary of a movie and then asked if he or she would like to see the film. The researchers reasoned that if a respondent were undecided, he or she would be tempted to give a response thought to please the interviewer of the other sex. The evidence indicated that such a bias was in fact in effect. For example, for the movie *Helen and Warren* women clearly showed a more favorable response than men when each respondent was interviewed by an interviewer of his or her own sex. Cross-sex interviewing narrowed the gap. That is, women gave fewer favorable responses when interviewed by men and more favorable responses when interviewed by women. In a later study Freeman and Butler (1976) studied variation within the interview (lack of consistency) by sex. They found more variation for males than for females in terms of both interviewer accuracy and the candor of respondents.

In a comprehensive study of interviewer effects in a telephone survey, Groves and Magilavy (1986) studied interviewer effects by gender of interviewer and respondent. They say (Groves and Magilavy 1986, p. 263): "The predominance of female telephone interviewers and their interaction with female and male respondents suggested the possibility of differences in interviewer effects by sex of respondent." However, their study revealed little evidence to support this view. While the overall interviewer effect was slightly higher for female respondents, the specific results were mixed, with some question types showing larger interviewer effects for male respondents, and others for female respondents. In all cases the sex differences were small.

Social Status

Most interviewers are women, and are much more likely to be middle-class, white-collar workers than to be lower-class. On the other hand, lower-class people frequently serve as respondents, and perhaps are even overstudied. Does the class difference between interviewer and respondent have an effect? The classic study on the socioeconomic status (SES) of interviewers was conducted by Katz (1942) in a lower-class area in Pittsburgh. Katz compared a group of 11 interviewers who were blue-collar industrial workers with nine middle-class interviewers, of whom five were experienced members of his staff and four were inexperienced middle-class trainees. The low-income respondents consistently gave more radical answers on labor issues to the lower-class interviewers than to the middle-class interviewers. For example, while the middle-class interviewers reported that 59 percent of union members favored a ban on sitdown strikes, the industrial-worker interviewers found that only 44 percent of their respondents favored such a ban. Katz concluded that lack of rapport between lower-class respondents and middle-class interviewers led to bias in response.

The effect of social distance has also been studied by Dohrenwend et al. (1968), who also found evidence of bias. Hyman (1954, pp. 46–49), while not denying the necessity of good rapport between interviewer and respondent, cautions that too much rapport can also be biasing:

> A certain degree of businesslike formality, of social detachment, may be preferable. When rapport transcends a certain point, the relationship may be too intimate, and the respondent may be eager to defer to the interviewer's sentiments. This would seem especially the case when the respondent has little real involvement in the task. When he is not particularly interested in the issues or has no strong views of his own, he may not mind or even prefer to take over the coloration of a very friendly interviewer (Hyman 1954, p. 48).

Bradburn and Sudman (1979) studied the education of interviewers and found that those with the most education made the fewest errors in question asking. Campbell (1981) found status to interact with race for a small subset of items in his study of race-of-interviewer effects. Status differences produced greater deference to interviewers of the opposite race among low-status respondents.

Groves and Magilavy (1986), in their previously mentioned study of interviewer effects, also examined education. Since they were only studying telephone interviewing, the effects would perhaps not be the same as in the personal interview. However, they speculated that poorly educated respondents would be more easily affected by the behavior and status of the interviewer than more highly educated respondents. In particular, respondents with less education might seek more help in answering from the interviewer, or might use the inflection of the interviewer's voice as a cue for responses to questions they find difficult to answer. However, the authors generally found no evidence for this, as interviewer effects were no greater for respondents with less than 12 years of education, even when analysis was conducted by question type.

Age

Benney et al. (1956) studied the effects of the age of both interviewer and respondent. The expectation was that if the interviewer and respondent were approximately the same age, rapport would be maximal. Interviewers were asked to rank respondents as to whether they were "completely frank and honest" for both a political survey and a mental-health survey. The results were inconclusive. Often respondents of age groups other than the interviewer's were rated equally or more frank and honest than respondents in the interviewer's age group. However, when both age and sex were examined simultaneously, there was a definite tendency for young female interviewers to give young male respondents a higher honesty ranking than they gave older male respondents. For female interviewers under 30, male respondents under 30 received a 64 percent honesty ranking, compared to 56 percent for males ages 30–50 and only 49 percent for males over 50. No such clear trends were evident for older interviewers.

Although not directly related to age, a study by Bradburn and Sudman (1979) found that interviewer experience was inversely related to accuracy in question asking, indicating that interviewers with more experience were the least accurate. This is apparently because more experienced interviewers become more relaxed and perhaps overconfident or bored, or do not take the job as seriously as do neophytes. In one of the few recent studies of interviewer age, Singer et al. (1983) found that age was significantly related to response rates, with older interviewers consistently obtaining better cooperation.

The previously mentioned study of interviewer effects in telephone surveys by Groves and Magilavy (1986) also analyzed age, with respondents categorized into five age groups. The authors expected larger interviewer effects from the oldest age group. They speculated that older respondents might be more suspicious, or tire more easily during the 30-minute telephone interview. Their views were supported in this case, as the oldest respondents did indeed have higher interviewer effects than the younger respondents.

Clothing and Grooming

Although some writers (e.g., Derek Phillips 1971) have speculated on the effect of such "props" as briefcases or umbrellas carried by the interviewer, there have been very few systematic studies of the clothing and grooming of interviewers, and often little or no mention of appropriate dress is made in the interviewer's instruction manual. It should be clear from our discussion so far that rapport between interviewer and respondent is generally found to minimize interview bias, and that such rapport is facilitated by similarity (lack of social distance) between interviewer and respondent. It follows that, all other things being equal, the interviewer should dress similarly to the respondent. Babbie advocates this:

> As a general rule, the interviewer should dress in a fashion fairly similar to that of the people she will be interviewing. A richly dressed interviewer will probably have difficulty getting good cooperation and responses from poorer respondents. And a poorly dressed interviewer will have similar difficulties with richer respondents (Babbie 1973, p. 173).

However, a caveat is in order here. As we said, the interview is a secondary relationship rather than primary. This means that the interviewer is generally a stranger to the respondent, and his or her reason for approaching the respondent is solely to fulfill an obligation to his or her employer—i.e., to gather information. Furthermore, as Goffman (1959) has emphasized, first appearances are very important, as they are the main cues to guide one in responding to the other person in a secondary relationship. In the absence of personal information about a stranger, clothing gives the basic cue to his or her socioeconomic level, role, and function. This is why uniforms are so important in a secondary society such as modern America. All persons whose roles must be understood instantaneously, particularly those dealing with emergencies such as police, firefighters, nurses, and doctors, wear identifying uniforms. Although the interviewer is not dealing with an emergency, his or her dress should fit his or her function and role, so that he or she "looks like an interviewer" to the respondent at first glance. This does not mean that the interviewer should wear a uniform, but it does mean that his or her dress and grooming should be neat and conservative. Even if the interviewer is interviewing members of the counterculture, his or her role is still, according to the expectations of the respondents, that of an "establishment" interviewer. Therefore, the interviewer should dress the way the respondent thinks an interviewer should dress, which may or may not be similar to the respondent's dress and grooming.

The *Interviewer's Manual* of the University of Michigan Survey Research Center says:

> Naturally, the first thing the respondent notices about the interviewer is her appearance. Aim for simplicity and comfort; a simple suit or dress is best. Avoid identification with groups or orders (pins or rings, for instance, of clubs or fraternal orders). The respondent should be led to concentrate on you as a person and the interview you want to take, and not on the way you are dressed. And, of course, always carry your official blue University of Michigan folder (University of Michigan 1969, p. 3-2).

To summarize: (1) dress to look like an interviewer so as to legitimize your role; (2) dress neutrally so as not to bias the respondent's answers; and (3) dress unobtrusively so that the emphasis will be on the interview rather than your appearance.

The Interview

Approaching the Respondent

When first approaching the respondent and introducing himself or herself, the interviewer must perform all the functions that the cover letter performs for the questionnaire. His or her task is perhaps more difficult because he or she is physically present and may be regarded as a potential threat, as compared to a cover letter, which has no potential for bodily harm and can always be thrown away. As listed in the *Interviewer's Manual* (University of Michigan 1969, pp. 3-2–3-3), the introductory tasks of the interviewer are to:

1. Tell the respondent who the interviewer is and whom he or she represents, including showing an identification card.
2. Tell the respondent what the interviewer is doing. This includes telling the respondent what the study is about in such a way as to stimulate his or her interest. It is at this stage

that the interviewer mentions that the respondent's answers are confidential and that neither the individual nor his or her address will be identified.

3. Tell how the respondent was chosen, emphasizing that he or she was not singled out personally for harassment or intimidation but was chosen in an impersonal way merely because a cross section of the population is needed ("We need the views of men and women of different ages in all walks of life.") and his or her address was chosen from a larger sample of city blocks.

4. Use letters and clippings. Interviewers are sometimes given letters that they can send in advance to notify the respondent of the interview. In addition, interviewers may carry newspaper clippings of past survey results and summaries of past findings in order to show the importance of the study and the way the results will be published.

5. Use a positive approach. Assume that the respondent will not be too busy for the interview. Say, "I would like to come in and talk with you about this" rather than, "May I come in?" or "Should I come back later?" or "Do you have time now?" or any other approach that gives the respondent a chance to say no. This first inquiry is usually made on the doorstep. The interviewer, like any good salesperson, should try to keep the doorstep interview brief and get inside the house or apartment, where it is more difficult for the respondent to refuse the interview.

In general, the interviewer must be adaptable, friendly, and responsive. Although he or she should not suggest that the interview be postponed, if the respondent is truly unable to complete the interview and suggests that the interviewer come back another time, he or she should by all means do so. The interviewer should make the respondent feel at ease to say anything he or she wants, even if it is irrelevant. It is much better for the respondent to indulge in unnecessary expansion of his or her answer than to feel that answers must be curt and to the point, providing only the information requested. This latter course can result in stereotyped and socially desirable answers only.

The interviewer may find that the respondent is initially ill at ease and may feel that before proceeding with the interview it would be better to use an ice breaker such as talking about the respondent's home, pets, family, or hobby. However, conversation that is extraneous to the interview or permitting the respondent to give long and rambling answers should occur only when needed to make the respondent feel comfortable. Many respondents, particularly elderly people who are home alone a lot without much chance for conversation, will be very loquacious. If the interviewer permits them to talk as much as they wish, the interview may run for hours.

Dealing with Refusals

There are a number of reasons why respondents may refuse the interview. Among those listed in the *Interviewer's Manual* (University of Michigan 1969, p. 7-2) are the following:

1. Respondent gives flat "no" or "not interested" response, but no reason for refusal.
2. Respondent expresses antigovernment, antiadministration, antibusiness feeling.
3. Respondent expresses feeling that surveys are "silly" or "not worthwhile."

4. Respondent speaks a foreign language, does not understand English well, and views the interviewer's mission with suspicion.
5. Evidence of some antagonism toward the interviewer, with no real reason given for not wanting to give the interview.
6. Respondent reports that he or she is "too busy."
7. Respondent reports that he or she is working and cannot, or does not want to, take time for the interview.
8. Respondent was interviewed by some other survey organization or some sales organization that misrepresented the reason for the visit.

It is the interviewer's job to determine the reason for the refusal and attempt to overcome it. If the interviewer feels that the respondent is nervous and thinks the interviewer is a burglar, salesperson, or bill collector, he or she can show more identification cards and letters of reference. If the interviewer suspects that the respondent does not understand the purpose of the study, thinks the study is not worthwhile, or thinks that the results will not be confidential, the interviewer can show how the results will be published and display magazine or newspaper articles that extoll the value of past studies, or a letter from some influential person stating the value of the present study.

If there is clearly a great deal of social distance between respondent and interviewer because of race, or sex differences, it may be best for the interviewer to withdraw politely and be replaced by another interviewer with characteristics more similar to those of the respondent. If it is simply a matter of the respondent's being willing to cooperate but currently unable to do so, then the interviewer can call back at a more convenient time. It is not unusual for three or more callbacks to be necessary before securing the interview or giving up. When calling back, vary times of day and days of week until you find a time when the respondent is home. It is sometimes helpful to ask neighbors when the respondent is usually at home. You may find that the respondent is on vacation and can save yourself several unnecessary return calls until he or she returns. For further discussion of reluctant respondents and refusals see Fitzgerald and Fuller (1982).

Conducting the Interview

Ask Questions as Worded.   Although there are exceptions, interview studies generally use standardized questionnaires, with every respondent asked the same questions. This allows comparison of answers from all respondents and facilitates the computation of summary statistics, such as the percentage of respondents who answered "yes" to question 5. Thus it is imperative that questions be read exactly as worded for all respondents. If possible, the interviewer's inflection and intonation should be the same for each respondent, so as not to lead the respondent or give him or her a clue as to how the interviewer would answer the question.

Clarification of questions should be avoided since it can lead to subtle changes in question meaning. However, questions should certainly be repeated when the respondent requests repetition or when his or her answer clearly indicates misunderstanding.

The interviewer may have no choice but to clarify a question when the respondent simply cannot understand it or sees two possible meanings to a question and asks the interviewer which one was meant.

Ask Questions in Order.   It should be clear from chapter 6 that attention must be given to proper question order when writing the questionnaire. Therefore, the question order should be retained. (If there are a number of skip or contingency questions, questions must be posed in order, as a particular question might make little or no sense if the appropriate filter question has not already been asked.) If respondent refuses to answer a question, the best procedure is merely to record the lack of response and proceed to the next question. Every question should be asked, even if the respondent has apparently already answered it.

If the questionnaire is well constructed and pretested, there should be no repetitious questions. But in answering an open-ended question the respondent might volunteer a reply that is specifically asked for in a subsequent question. Even if a question has apparently been answered, there is a potential for error, and certainly a potential loss of comparability, unless the interviewer reads it as written and then records the answer. He or she can acknowledge the similarity by prefacing the question with a remark such as, "I know we have already touched upon this, but I have to ask it again."

Do Not Lead Respondents.   Reading the questions as stated will help the interviewer guard against biasing or leading. However, some respondents may feel a need to know the interviewer's opinion on a particular question. It is important to make sure that the respondent does not feel as though he or she is taking an examination or is on trial. Still, some respondents may feel that they must please the interviewer and search for any clue as to the interviewer's feelings. Some interviewers may be very careful to be neutral before asking a particular question so as not to lead the respondent, without realizing that they can also lead respondents by their reaction *after* the question is answered. While this reaction cannot bias the answer already given, it can give the respondent a clue to the interviewer's general ideology and thus influence subsequent answers.

Other respondents feel that the interviewer's job may be contingent upon getting good interviews and thus answer the way they think will be most pleasing to the interviewer's *boss.* Conversely, if the respondent dislikes the interviewer he or she may search for clues to the interviewer's preferences in order to contradict them.

It might be worthwhile for the interviewer to pretest the interview with a respondent in front of a mirror so that he or she can detect any unconscious facial reactions or other body language (such as nods of agreement, frowns, or arching of eyebrows). Even if the interviewer is completely unaware of these cues they may be visible to the respondent. Such cues could give the respondent a basis for (rightly or wrongly) stereotyping the interviewer with some label such as conservative, liberal, religious, or prudish, and cause the respondent to answer in accordance with this label.

Less Structured Interviews

There may be times when the interview will be completely unstructured, with no questions written in advance and the interviewer assigned only a topic. He or she then conducts a free-form interview, composing the questions as it goes along. Much more common, though, is the structured or standardized interview in which *some* of the questions are open-ended.

Open-ended Questions

Closed-end or fixed-alternative questions require only that the interviewer read the question and mark the appropriate answer. Open-ended questions, however, can require the interviewer to transcribe a lengthy statement. In addition, open-ended questions in an interview can require the respondent to dictate an extemporaneous statement on a topic about which he or she may not have thought before.

Probes

You have probably had the experience on an essay examination of making a false start—writing a few lines and then changing your mind and erasing them because you were unsure. Respondents faced with such a situation often respond with a vague or general answer, no answer at all, or a statement that they do not know. Thus a *probe,* or follow-up question, is needed. The chief function of a probe is to lead the respondent to answer more fully and accurately, or at least to provide a minimally acceptable answer. A second function is to structure the respondent's answer and make sure that all topics of interest to the interviewer are covered and the amount of irrelevant information reduced. Probe questions may be written in advance on the questionnaire or developed in the pretest phase if it becomes evident that respondents' incomplete answers fall into several predictable categories. A specific probe may be written for each category. Thus probes are essentially contingency questions to be used only if the respondent answers earlier questions in a certain way.

For the first function—achieving a complete and clear answer—probes may be general and neutral. Rather than being unique to a single question, such probes can be used whenever the respondent hesitates in answering or gives an unclear or incomplete answer. They need not be printed on the interview schedule but can be taught to the interviewer during training. Neutral probes include:

1. *Repeating the question.* This is done whenever the respondent hesitates or appears not to understand the question. With lengthy questions it is often necessary to repeat two or three times before the respondent has it clearly enough in mind to begin concentrating upon an answer.
2. *Repeating the answer.* This type of neutral probe can be used by the interviewer who is not certain that he or she understood the respondent's answer correctly. Repetition of the answer can correct errors and assure both respondent and interviewer that the answer is recorded correctly. Repetition also gives the respondent an opportunity to think about elaborating it further.
3. *Indicating understanding and interest.* The *Interviewer's Manual* (University of Michigan 1969) recommends that the interviewer indicate that he or she has heard the answer and approves of it, thus stimulating the respondent to continue.

4. *Pause.* The *Manual* also recommends that the interviewer pause and say nothing if the response is obviously incomplete. This indicates that the interviewer knows the respondent has begun to answer and is waiting for him or her to finish.
5. *A neutral question or comment.* "How do you mean that?" or "Tell me more" indicates to the respondent that his or her answer is on the right track but that more information is desired.

Examples of Probes.   Consider the question:

18. What do you think are the most important problems that we have in the United States today?
(1) _____
(2) _____
(3) _____
(4) _____
(5) _____

1. Answer: "High taxes." Answer is adequate but incomplete (five problems needed). Probe: Pause, wait for respondent to continue. Or indicate understanding by saying "Yes." Or repeat the question, emphasizing *problems* (plural). If these fail to elicit further responses, a third alternate probe is "More?" or "That's one, I need four more, or five in all."
2. Answer: "Governmental problems." Answer is too vague. Probe. "I'm not quite sure I know what you mean. What kind of governmental problems? Could you be more specific?"
3. Answer: "There are a lot of important problems." Probe: "List the five most important."
4. Answer: "There are more problems than there used to be and there will be even more in the future." Probe: "List the five that are most important right now."
5. Answer: "Things are getting worse all the time." Probe: "List the five things that are the worst at the present time."

Question-specific Probes.   Probes may be specific to a particular question. Consider the question:

20. At different times people have had different ideas about how big a family should be. What would be the right number of children for the average family in the United States to have? _____
A.   IF TWO CHILDREN OR LESS, ASK: Why would it be better to have this size family instead of a larger one? (PROBE FOR ALL REASONS).

A probe such as this one strives to exhaust all possible reasons. After the first reason is given, the interviewer can use the neutral probes, such as pause or assertion of understanding. When the respondent finishes the interviewer can use probes, such as "Okay, and what is the next reason?" or he or she can use this probe after every reason to elicit the subsequent reason. Then he or she can probe with "Are there any more possible reasons that you can think of?"

The Focused Interview and Focus Groups

As an alternative to the structured or standardized interview using a combination of open- and closed-ended questions, one can use a semistructured interview. The most famous semistructured interview is Merton's focused interview. For discussion of the focused interview see Merton, Fiske, and Kendall (1956), Selltiz et al. (1976), and Bernard Phillips (1976). The focused interview uses topics and hypotheses selected in advance. The actual questions, however, are not specified in advance. As described by Merton, Fiske, and Kendall:

> First of all, the persons interviewed are known to have been involved in a *particular situation;* they have seen a film, heard a radio program, read a pamphlet, article or book, taken part in a psychological experiment or in an uncontrolled, but observed, social situation (for example, a political rally, a ritual, or a riot). Secondly, the hypothetically significant elements, patterns, processes and total structure of this situation have been provisionally analyzed by the social scientist. Through this *content* or *situational analysis,* he has arrived at a set of hypotheses concerning the consequences of determinate aspects of the situation for those involved in it. On the basis of this analysis, he takes the third step of developing an *interview guide,* setting forth the major areas of inquiry and the hypotheses which provide criteria of relevance for the data to be obtained in the interview. Fourth and finally, the interview is focused on the subjective experiences of persons exposed to the pre-analyzed situation in an effort to ascertain *their definitions of the situation.* The array of reported responses to the situation helps test hypotheses and, to the extent that it includes unanticipated responses, gives rise to fresh hypotheses for more systematic and rigorous investigation (Merton, Fiske, and Kendall 1956, pp. 3–4).

A crucial element in the focused interview is the structure provided by interviewing people all of whom experienced a particular event such as a race riot, a peace demonstration, or a pornographic movie. The interviewer studies the event itself in advance, decides which aspects of it to probe, and constructs hypotheses. Thus even though question wording is not fixed in advance, question content is. Without the structure provided by these topics and hypotheses, the interviewer might not know which question to ask and the interview could degenerate into a worthless exercise in which questions are asked at random and neither the interviewer nor the respondent knows what the interview is supposed to achieve.

The focused interview goes one stop beyond the open-ended question as used in a structured interview. In the focused interview questions are also open-ended to provide flexibility and allow for unanticipated responses. But in addition the focused interview allows flexibility in terms of the questions asked. Since questions are not written in advance they may be tailored to probe avenues of exploration that seem to be yielding information relevant for the hypothesis or topic being studied. This flexibility can result in questions that are really a long series of probes that can investigate deeply into the subjective areas of the respondent's mind in an attempt to discover his or her real feelings and motives, such as feelings of inadequacy, paranoia, or racial prejudice.

A recent development during the 1980s is the "focus group." The focus group is a direct descendent of the focused interview (see Merton 1987) but takes a somewhat different form (see Morgan and Spanish 1984). Interestingly enough, focus groups have about the same history or growth trajectory as meta-analysis (see chapter 16). Although their roots are quite old, focus groups saw only modest growth in the 1970s, with a rapid rise in the early 1980s, reaching maturity and an almost faddish status in the 1980s and 1990s. In the early 1990s it seemed that almost everyone was conducting focus groups or writing about them. While it is unlikely that this degree of popularity will prove to be permanent, it is nevertheless clear that the method has enduring value and will probably become a staple of social researchers.

The chief difference between the focus group and the original focused interview, as discussed previously, is indicated by the term "group." The original focused interview was generally conducted in a traditional interview setting—meaning that the interviewer asked questions of a single individual in a quiet, private setting conducive to thinking about and answering questions. The focus group, as the name implies, involves a whole group answering questions together. It is still possible for an individual to give his or her own answers, but only in a group context. As Ward et al. (1991, p. 267) say, focus groups are "guided group discussions," designed to provide information on a certain topic from a certain population. The group is generally quite homogeneous, although the design could require the use of different subgroups within a population (one group of men and one group of women, for example). Further:

> The focus group is led by a trained moderator, who is expected to cover a series of questions on a preestablished discussion guide. However, the format of this discussion is spontaneous, and the participants are encouraged to freely discuss their opinions and feelings on these and other topics (Ward et al. 1991, p. 267).

The focus group is generally considered to be a "qualitative" rather than a quantitative method, and generally does not yield results suitable for statistical analysis. Rather, the results are interpreted more subjectively. The data consist of a record of the discussion, and thus may more closely resemble field notes taken in observational field studies (as discussed in chapter 10), rather than rigorous questionnaire data.

As stated above, focus groups are immensely popular and have been used in a wide variety of social-science disciplines, including sociology, marketing, public health, social welfare, education, psychology, and many others. From the late 1970s until the present, focus groups have enjoyed much success in market research, where they are often used to explore (in more depth than a survey can provide) what consumers *really* think about products, whether they will buy them, and why or why not. Although focus groups are often designed to augment larger surveys, they also seem to be enjoying increasing success as a "stand-alone" method (see Ward et al. 1991).

The advantages of focus groups are that (1) they provide data quickly; (2) their cost is relatively low; (3) they provide qualitative data on beliefs, attitudes, and behaviors; (4) they provide more depth of coverage and more detail than is usually possible in a large survey; and (5) they provide more flexibility and opportunity to probe than in a large survey. Among the disadvantages of focus groups are that (1) they do not provide quantitative data, and thus are not suitable for statistical analysis or for meta-analysis (see chapter 16); (2) their results may not be generalizable to a larger population; (3) the number of people interviewed is small; (4) there is generally more nonresponse than in a survey, as not all respondents answer all questions; (5) privacy is lacking, so that respondents may be fearful of answering sensitive questions, may tend to answer normatively, or may be biased by the opinions of others in the group;

and (6) coding and data analysis may be more problematic than in a survey, as focus group data may consist largely of notes somewhat reminiscent of field notes from ethnographic studies (see chapter 10). For further discussion of the advantages and disadvantages of focus groups see Ward et al. (1991).

Focus groups have been compared with mailed-questionnaire studies (Reynolds and Johnson 1978) as well as with personal interview studies (Ward et al. 1991), and have yielded comparable results in most cases. Ward et al. (1991) compared focus groups with surveys in Guatemala, Honduras, and Zaire on opinions toward voluntary sterilization, including tubal ligation. The focus groups yielded results similar to the surveys (personal interviews) in all three cases, leading Ward et al. (1991, p. 269) to conclude, "Thus, in situations where data are needed for the purposes of program development, focus groups may be appropriate as a stand-alone methodology."

The comparability of focus groups and surveys is hampered by the fact that the former yield qualitative data and the latter quantitative data. While surveys yield percentages, focus group results commonly include statements such as "many participants mentioned . . . " (Ward et al. 1991, p. 271). Despite this lack of precision, Ward et al. (1991) took care to compare focus groups and surveys on key variables. The results were judged to be "similar" if both studies would lead to the same conclusions. For example, in regard to the issue of tubal ligation in Guatemala, the focus group and survey were judged to give similar results, since 55 percent of survey respondents mentioned the permanence of tubal ligation, while the focus group participants thought that tubal ligation would eliminate pregnancy worries "for good" (Ward et al. 1991, p. 272). All in all in the three comparisons (three countries), Ward et al. (1991, p. 273), found that for 28 percent of the variables the results were similar; for 42 percent the results were similar but focus groups provided additional detail; for 17 percent the results were similar but the survey provided more detail; and for 12 percent of the variables the results were similar. Thus, the two studies reached similar conclusions for nearly 90 percent of the variables studied (1 percent of the total results were lost due to round-off error).

In summary, what can we say about the efficacy of focus groups? At their worst, focus groups can degenerate into a party, group therapy, or a mere "brainstorming" session, where the person in charge becomes more of a facilitator than a researcher. The data can be difficult to record and analyze, and not all respondents may be equally represented in the results. Also, the number of respondents is generally small, and statistical analysis cannot be used. At their best, focus groups can provide the reasons behind the answers that are given in large (and sometimes superficial) surveys. They thus can complement the survey by telling us in more detail *why* respondents answered the way they did. Further, focus groups can expand the efficacy of a survey. We can use a focus group to probe in more depth about certain survey issues, for example, about what the greatest problems facing our city are, or why a certain contraceptive technique is preferred over others. Further, focus groups can be helpful in the preliminary stages of survey planning by helping us to ask the right questions or to word them in a more understandable manner.

If carefully planned and conducted, focus groups are valuable not only as a complement to a survey or as a check on its reliability, but also as a stand-alone method that is basically intermediate between the sometimes superficial large-scale survey and the long, tedious, time-consuming ethnographic field study (see the discussion in chapter 10). For further discussion of a variety of topics concerning focus groups, including research on sensitive topics, research on minority populations, moderator training, and use of content analysis on focus-group data, please see Morgan (1988; 1993), Krueger (1988), and Stewart and Shamdasani (1990).

The Clinical Interview

The clinical interview, or personal-history interview (see Selltiz et al. 1976, pp. 320–21), is similar to the focused interview. The personal-history interview is often used by professionals such as social case workers, counselors, or prison workers. As in the focused interview, the interviewer chooses certain aspects of the individual's life history about which to question him or her. The interview is flexible and unstructured. For example, a researcher studying gender socialization and gender-identity development among male homosexuals may hypothesize that homosexuality is caused by certain early childhood socialization patterns. Thus, in the life-history interview the interviewer will ask questions about the respondent's childhood, his feelings toward his mother and his father, his relationship with siblings, the number and gender of siblings, and the number and gender of peer-group friends. Accompanied by a lot of probing, such questions should elicit the necessary information, with the possibility that unanticipated factors may emerge as important. The flexibility of the semistructured interview allows these unanticipated factors to be fully explored and probed. The researcher may find that he or she is asking different questions of different respondents, and thus the comparability of the data is impaired. Nevertheless, what is lost in comparability may be gained in serendipitous findings that could result in a breakthrough in the study of homosexuality, a subject as yet not well understood.

The Unstructured Interview

The unstructured or nondirective interview (Rogers 1945) is even less structured than the life-history interview and the focused interview. The chief feature of the nondirective interview is its almost total reliance upon neutral probes that are designed to be as neutral as possible. They are generally very short, such as "Why?" or "Uh, huh" or "That's interesting." The nondirective interview originated in psychotherapy. It is intended to probe the respondent's deepest and most subjective feelings. At its extreme it may elicit repressed feelings that even the respondent did not know he or she had or was not willing to admit even to himself or herself.

Reliability and Validity of Unstructured Interview

Gorden (1969, pp. 48–50) argues that the unstructured interview (he uses the term "unscheduled interview") can sometimes be more valid than the highly structured interview, even though the latter is more commonly used and probably thought to be more valid. The superiority of the unstructured interview, according to Gorden, occurs in several types of interview situations where communication would be impeded by the use of a rigid, highly structured interview schedule with all questions specified in advance.

One situation where the unstructured interview is said to be more valid is where the respondent is experiencing memory failure. Here more valid responses may be received by letting the respondent follow what Gorden (1969, p. 49) calls "the natural paths of free association." Gorden argues that to help the respondent remember facts accurately the interview must be sufficiently unstructured and flexible for the interviewer to be able to return to the same topic several times if necessary to stimulate the memory; he or she must also be free to probe vague portions of the respondent's account. In general, the unstructured interview may be able to provide a relaxed and unhurried atmosphere that is not stressful to the respondent. A respondent who feels hurried by a highly structured interview may not be able to remember things accurately if he or she feels the need to move on to the next question and may be tempted to answer even if unsure of the correctness of the answer so that he or she may remain on schedule. Supposedly the unstructured interview entails less stress for the respondent, and this is conducive to remembering forgotten points.

According to Gorden, the unstructured interview may also be more valid if the *universe of discourse* varies from respondent to respondent so that the interviewer must change the question wording to meet the understanding of the respondent. Another area where the unstructured interview may be superior is for dealing with unconscious experience.

Gorden argues against the idea that the unstructured interview is dangerous because the interviewer is free to bias responses. He says that bias can easily be built into a highly structured interview, for that matter, and that skilled, careful, honest interviewers can conduct unstructured interviews that are relatively free of bias. Gorden cautions that the mere fact that a highly structured interview has a neatly typed questionnaire, is easy to code, and seems to be reliable does not ensure that the information gathered will be superior to that gathered with an unstructured interview. For example, if a department store manager used a structured interview with the question "Do you steal from the company?" he or she could achieve extremely high reliability when questioning employees, as they all would answer "No." Such high reliability is no guarantee of validity, as some of the respondents denying the action would be telling the truth and some would not be.

Projective Methods

In our discussion of various methods for studying children in chapter 17, we discuss doll play, picture interpretation, and sentence completion. These are all examples of projective methods of data gathering. These techniques can be used with both children and adults. Projective methods originated in clinical psychology and psychiatry as a means of eliciting a respondent's inner feelings but are useful whenever direct questioning is inappropriate or whenever the true purpose of the study cannot be revealed. Projective methods are generally regarded as indirect data-gathering procedures, as they avoid direct questions about the topic of interest (that is, they disguise the topic being studied). For example, a researcher might use a projective method to study the respondent's attitudes toward sex if he or she knows that direct questioning would make the respondents nervous and inhibited and affect the quality of the data.

Projective methods are open-ended and unstructured except for a stimulus of some sort (e.g., a picture) that is presented to the respondent. While the interviewer can use specific questions or probes to structure the respondent's answer in part, it is highly unusual for an interviewer to use fixed-alternative categories. Rather, the interviewer presents the stimulus with minimal structure or interpretation so that the response that emerges will be a spontaneous product of the respondent's true feelings—perhaps inner feelings of which he or she was unaware or was afraid to admit.

For example, as Selltiz et al. (1959, p. 287) point out, a respondent who is asked whether he or she first notices a person's race or sex when being introduced may be unable to answer because he or she has never thought about it. By showing the respondent a series of pictures containing people of different races and genders the interviewer can determine whether race or sex is mentioned first.

In addition to doll play, picture interpretation, and sentence and story completion, at least two famous projective tests are commonly used, especially in clinical studies: these are the Rorschach Test and the Thematic Apperception Test (TAT). The Rorschach consists of ten cards containing inkblots that the respondent is asked to interpret. The TAT consists of a series of pictures to be interpreted by the respondent. Some are very ordinary and easy to interpret, while others are more unusual or difficult to interpret.

Another technique that has been found effective is to ask the respondent to describe other persons' motives or attitudes. Many respondents will give a normative or socially desirable response when asked about their own attitudes, either because they really believe they feel this way or because they know that their real feelings are considered undesirable and so are hesitant to respond truthfully. However, such respondents will often attribute their own socially undesirable traits to others, such as neighbors or the "average person." For example, persons who like to watch pornographic movies but are afraid to admit it may indicate their conviction that others, perhaps the majority, enjoy these films.

Another projective technique is to ask the respondent to describe the kind of person who would do a certain thing or buy a certain product—for example, the type of person who would go to Las Vegas to gamble, or the type who would ride a motorcycle to work. For further discussion of projective methods see Selltiz et al. (1976).

The Telephone Interview

We discussed the telephone interview briefly in chapter 7 as a follow-up for a mailed questionnaire, in which instance the telephone is used merely to remind the respondent to return his or her questionnaire. However, the interview itself may be conducted over the telephone. In fact, during the 1990s the telephone interview has matured into a dominant method, rivaling the mailed-questionnaire study and personal interview in popularity. It is certainly no longer the "stepchild" of survey methods as Dillman (1978) once proclaimed it. There are a number of reasons for the popularity of telephone interviewing. For one thing, the telephone has largely replaced letter writing for some respondents. Further, many people are not at home during the day, and hesitate to admit strangers when they are home (especially at night). Further, many interviewers are hesitant to enter strange neighborhoods, especially at night (and this might be the only time that respondents are available). All of these factors, and others have helped the telephone survey to make inroads on the dominance of the face-to-face interview and mailed questionnaire. The telephone shares with the mailed questionnaire the convenience of being nonintrusive, and it is quicker than the mail and less expensive than the face-to-face interview. You cannot use visuals easily with the telephone, but you can probe for more satisfactory answers (which is difficult with the mail), and as with the mail, you eliminate some of the bias which may be caused by the visual characteristics of interviewers. As Goyder (1985) notes, the telephone can be used to reach respondents in their "urban fortresses" even if they cloister themselves from interviewers. Along with these shifts in accessibility and communication patterns are technological advances, such as the development of random digit dialing (RDD) and computer-assisted telephone interviewing (CATI). All of these, along with the increased access to telephones and computer storage of data, have facilitated the rapid growth of telephone interviewing.

Telephone interviewing has become such an integral part of the survey method that most comprehensive books have a section on it. For a general discussion of telephone interviewing see, for example, Sudman and Bradburn (1982) and Alreck and Settle (1985). For a volume solely dedicated to the telephone see Frey (1983). For a special journal issue devoted solely to telephone interviewing see Freeman and Shanks (1983). For an application of telephone interviewing in the health field see Marcus and Crane (1986).

Sudman and Bradburn (1982, p. 263) provide a rather comprehensive checklist for designing questionnaires for telephone surveys. Among the salient points they mention are that numerical scales can be devised for telephone surveys; that if pictures are to be used in the survey they must be mailed in advance; that consultation of other persons or of records is difficult or impossible in telephone interviews; that complex skip questions can be facilitated through CATI systems; and that telephone interviews can be as lengthy as face-to-face interviews, and considerably longer and more complex than mailed-questionnaire studies.

Alreck and Settle (1985, pp. 42–43) disagree with Sudman and Bradburn (1982) on telephone interview length, saying that the telephone interview must usually be shorter than a personal interview, and "considerable resistance or premature termination of the interview by the respondent can result from interviews of more than 15 or 20 minutes." They also note the absence of interviewer bias in the telephone interview through such factors as physical appearance, dress, facial expressions, and gestures. They add that telephone interviewers ordinarily require less training and instruction than face-to-face interviewers and can be monitored more easily if telephoning from a central location.

One chief advantage of the telephone interview is that it is fast. If one is interested in gauging public opinion quickly on some current event, the telephone can be used to get answers to questions before one could even begin to plan a mailed survey or interview study. For example, if a newspaper wishes to survey public reaction to some event such as an assassination or an earthquake or similar natural disaster that has just occurred, it could select a random sample of several hundred households (by using a number of interviewers) on the same day and publish the results in the next day's edition. If a mailed study were conducted it would take approximately a week before an adequate number of returns was received. It might be possible to conduct a number of interviews the same day the event occurred, but probably not with an adequate sample, which often requires interviews in dispersed locations. With a telephone survey or mailed questionnaire the investigator never need leave the office, whereas to interview directly one must take time to travel, almost surely delaying the study too long to make the next edition of the newspaper.

Another advantage of the telephone survey is its lower cost compared to interviewing. Although costs would rise if one were telephoning long distances for long periods of time, they are generally much lower than travel costs for interviewers. Klecka and Tuchfarber (1978, p. 106) estimate that if random digit dialing (RDD) is used, fieldwork and sampling costs for telephone interviewing may be only 20 to 25 percent of costs for personal interviewing.

A third advantage is that a respondent in a telephone interview remains more anonymous than in a personal interview (although perhaps not so anonymous as in a mailed study). In a telephone interview the interviewer can prompt the respondent to answer and can repeat the question or probe if the respondent did not understand or did not respond correctly. Yet the interviewer is not nearly so much of a threat to the respondent as he or she cannot see the respondent's face and so cannot identify him or her to others. Further, since he or she is not in the respondent's home he or she cannot harm the respondent physically, steal anything, or sell anything.

Other advantages of the telephone survey are (Freeman et al. 1982) that the sample need not be geographically clustered but can be dispersed throughout the study area, and the lower costs allow more callbacks to persuade initially reluctant respondents to participate. In addition, telephone surveys make more efficient use of bilingual interviewers, who can undertake interviews throughout the study area and allow greater supervision of interviewers, and hence standardization of practice and higher quality control.

One disadvantage is that respondents are often less motivated over the telephone, probably because the interviewer has no real power to continue the interview, since the respondent can terminate it at any time merely by hanging up. Another disadvantage is that some respondents are distrustful, believing that the interviewer either has some ulterior motive or is playing a prank on them. Another limitation of the telephone interview is that visual materials such as pictures or checklists cannot be used (Lansing and Morgan 1971, p. 112). A further limitation (shared with the mailed questionnaire) is that the interviewer is unable to observe the respondent and thus cannot gather nonverbal data. Finally, since the interviewer is not present in the respondent's home, he or she has minimal control. He or she cannot persuade the respondent to complete the interview, cannot standardize the surroundings in which the interview takes place, and cannot keep the respondent from asking other persons for information.

The value of the contemporary telephone survey can easily be illustrated by examining a study conducted by an undergraduate telephone survey class as Mansfield University of Mansfield, Pennsylvania. These results are published, and constitute a valuable source for the region of the state that their university serves (Largey et al. 1990). The sample is provided by a professional sampling firm, with all telephone interviewing conducted by members of the class. In the study conducted in February and March of 1990, for example, respondents were asked about a variety of salient issues that had been dealt with in the courts or had been prominent in the news media. These included, among others, the perceived quality of education, testing of high school students for drug use, sponsorship of religious clubs in high school, delaying a dropout's driver's license, euthanasia, smoking, and gun control. Their results indicated, for example, that 83 percent of their sample favored random testing of high school students for cocaine use, with 82 percent favoring such testing for marijuana, and 80 percent for alcohol. For further results see Largey et al. (1990).

Random Digit Dialing

Before the increase in telephone accessibility and the advent of RDD, not only did a significant proportion of persons not have access to a telephone, but the ones who did were difficult to sample satisfactorily. One chief reason for this was that many telephone numbers were not listed in a directory, and thus the researcher had no way of sampling them. Also, some numbers were listed more than once, giving them an increased probability of selection in the sample. The basic achievement of RDD is that it avoids listings altogether in most versions, although it can be used in conjunction with listings. RDD is a process for mechanically dialing, in a random fashion, from all possible combinations of the digits in a set of working telephone numbers. For example, the prefix in my university is 825, so that all telephone numbers at the university are 825-XXXX. These can be randomly dialed whether they are listed or not.

This technique clearly has revolutionary potential. It is able to dial all working numbers with equal probability (randomly). Since the researcher does not have to work with telephone directories, there is also no problem with bias stemming from the manner in which names are listed in a directory. Although RDD is a significant advancement, it will not automatically eliminate all bias or all sampling problems. Households with two or more separate telephone numbers will be overrepresented, but this bias can sometimes be corrected by downweighting to compensate for their greater probability of selection. Their number is doubtlessly increasing, especially where one telephone is a business telephone. Further, it is possible that one household member will answer at home and another at a nonresidential (e.g., business) telephone. Groves and Kahn (1979) report that 6 percent of all numbers reached in one study were nonresidential numbers, and there is really no way to eliminate these in the average RDD study, which just seeks to study households.

In fact, one major problem with RDD is that there may often be quite a high "dross rate," meaning that a relatively large number of telephone numbers must be dialed for each working household number. In Groves and Kahn's (1979, p. 46) single-stage sample, only 21.6 percent of the sample numbers were working household numbers. Besides nonresidential numbers, the other 78.4 percent of the numbers included, among others, nonworking numbers (the majority, or 53.3 percent), no results from dialing (6.3 percent), and a ring, but no answer (2.9 percent).

In addition to the dross rate, the use of RDD still poses problems stemming from the now relatively rare number of persons who do not have telephones. Simulation studies (Tull and Albaum 1977; Kviz 1978) have indicated that the households that do have a telephone available are more likely to have white, male heads of a higher average age, income, and educational level and to have the spouse present in the home. RDD thus underrepresents households with no telephone available, and these are most likely to have a head who is black, under 40, not married and living with spouse, low income, low in education, and living in a rural area.

There are a number of technical procedures for random digit dialing. Among those listed by Frey (1983, pp. 68–77) are simple RDD using a directory of numbers and RDD with the aid of a cross-reference (criss-cross) directory, which lists telephone numbers by street and house number. Frey (1983) also discusses RDD by the Sudman and Waksberg designs. The Sudman method yields a sample of numbers proportional to the number of unlisted numbers. The Waksberg design is a two-stage cluster design which reduces the number of unproductive dialings. For further illustration and comparison of various RDD designs see Frey (1983, p. 77).

Another recent development that should be noted is the congruence of RRT (random response technique) and RDD, as discussed by Orwin and Boruch (1982) in "RRT Meets RDD." RRT was discussed in chapter 6 (questionnaire design), and is a randomized technique for sensitive questions such that the interviewer does not know the respondent's answer, thus sparing the respondent embarrassment. The conjunction of RRT and RDD is designed to assure response privacy in telephone surveys.

Computer-assisted Telephone Interviewing (CATI)

Despite the fact that RDD is not perfect, its use, coupled with other advances such as wide-spread usage of WATS lines (Wide Area Telephone Service) and automated dialing equipment has clearly revolutionized the telephone survey. Another advance is the use of computer-assisted telephone interviewing (CATI), in which survey questionnaires are displayed on computer terminals for interviewers, who type respondents' answers directly onto a disk (Shanks, Nichols, and Freeman 1981). In a CATI system, the interviewer not only follows the questions on the computer terminal (which can allow sophisticated use of skips and other techniques), but also codes the respondent's answers directly into the computer. Thus, through programming in advance, a number of processes formerly controlled by the survey interviewer can now be done by the computer. This helps meet a need in telephone interviewing for controlling the interview process and interviewer-respondent interactions (see Shure and Meeker, 1978).

The prototype CATI systems were developed at Chilton Research Services (for commercial usage) and at the University of California, Los Angeles (for academic usage) both in the 1970's (see Frey, 1983, pp. 143–149; Shure and Meeker, 1978; Fink, 1983). CATI systems operate not only with minicomputers (Shure and Meeker, 1978), but also with microcomputers (Palit and Sharp, 1983). Among the advantages of CATI systems outlined by Sudman (1983) are speed, rapid analysis of costs, sampling, record keeping (for example, of sampling procedures), use of complex skip and probing instructions (programmed into the CATI system so they are not part of the interviewer's task), and speedy data processing. Among the disadvantages of CATI (at least for the present) are the need for preplanning and preprogramming, the difficulty in using open-ended questions, and the time required for entering answers into the computer, often requiring pauses in the interview, which must be explained to the respondent.

Groves and Mathiowetz (1984) compared CATI and non-CATI systems in terms of their effects on both interviewers and respondents. In general, they reported only small differences between the two. However, they did find CATI interviews to take slightly longer than non-CATI interviews. They also found less variability and fewer skip-error problems in the CATI interviews.

All in all, there is no doubt that CATI systems have played a large part in the revolution in telephone interviewing. In light of a number of factors, such as continuing rising costs and continuing difficulty in finding respondents at home, Sudman (1983, p. 220) predicts that the trend toward telephone interviewing will continue.

The cost savings through telephone interviewing as opposed to face-to-face interviewing can be dramatic. Klecka and Tuchfarber (1978, p. 106) echo Sudman's sentiment, noting that face-to-face interviewing is becoming more costly because of increasing salary costs for interviewers and increased travel costs resulting from fuel price increases. Further, the increased participation of married women in the labor force has a dual result. It means that fewer females are available to take temporary interviewing jobs and that there is less likely to be a respondent at home to be interviewed during working hours.

Telephone Versus Face-to-Face

One question that has received a substantial amount of attention recently is the adequacy of the telephone interview as compared to the face-to-face interview. There seems to be an overwhelming consensus that the telephone interview is much cheaper and that this accounts for its greatly increased use. However, this may not be sufficient reason to use it if the information received is not adequate.

Most of the studies have shown that the information received by telephone interviewing compares favorably with that received by face-to-face interviewing. There are some differences, however. Groves and Kahn (1979, p. 219) report that the response rate for telephone surveys remains at least five percent lower than that achieved in personal interviewing. Groves and Kahn also report that while very few respondents terminate face-to-face interviews in well-designed studies, approximately five percent of those respondents who begin a telephone interview terminate it. Also, telephone interviews tended to be consistently faster paced than face-to-face interviews in studies made by Groves and Kahn, and this led to quicker and less adequate responses on open-ended questions.

The lowest response rates and the higher rates of termination for telephone interviews would seem to indicate that respondents are not as happy with the telephone interview as with the face-to-face interview. Direct questioning by Groves and Kahn bore this out. Groves and Kahn (1979, p. 222) report that the telephone survey respondents consistently said that they dislike the interaction much more than did the personal interview respondents. Telephone respondents were initially more suspicious, were more likely to ask how long the interview would take, showed less interest in the interview, more often felt that the interview lasted too long, and more often felt uneasy about discussing certain topics. Groves and Kahn conclude that persons using telephone interviewing must strive to increase rapport between interviewer and respondent and must try to develop techniques to establish respondent motivation and trust similar to that achieved in the face-to-face interview.

In spite of these problems, the fact seems to be that telephone interviewing is no longer a "stepchild" of the face-to-face interview, to use Dillman's term, and because of its cost advantages it will be used much more in the future. Further, even though telephone interviewers cannot achieve exactly the same degree of trust and rapport that they could in a face-to-face interview, where they can establish eye contact with the respondent and can communicate nonverbally, there is still evidence that this decrease in rapport is rather slight and does not seem to result in inadequate data for most types of questions. In spite of a few more refusals and terminations on the telephone, Groves and Kahn found telephone answers substantively to be nearly identical to face-to-face answers:

> We found very few such response discrepancies between the two sets of data that were large enough to be considered statistically significant. The differences that did occur included (in addition to the tendency toward more truncated responses to open-ended questions on the

telephone) some suggestion of greater optimism among telephone respondents on consumer sentiment and life satisfaction items, and a greater uneasiness among telephone respondents about discussing some subjects (Groves and Kahn 1979, pp. 221–22).

Jordan, Marcus, and Reeder (1980) also found little difference in the validity of answers on telephone interviews and face-to-face interviews. They reported that the telephone respondents had more missing data on family income, more acquiescence and evasiveness, and somewhat more answers (including more contradictory answers) to checklist items. However, they dismiss these differences as differences in response style rather than in the content of answers.

For example, Sudman and Bradburn (1982, p. 263) say that with "a few exceptions, no differences are observed in the answers given to the same questions asked by mail, phone, or face-to-face." They imply that other criteria such as sampling factors or cost may then be used by administrators in deciding what type of survey to use (telephone or face-to-face).

An interesting study by Herzog and Rodgers (1988) compared the responses of both older (over 60) and younger respondents on both a face-to-face interview study and a telephone interview study. The respondents over age 60 gave a larger amount of DK ("Don't Know") answers, and also required more assistance on the telephone than did younger respondents. However, except for these differences, there was little difference in mode (telephone versus face-to-face) for either the younger or older respondents. Further, while the telephone response rate was somewhat lower for older respondents than for younger respondents, response rates overall were still quite adequate (90 percent for older respondents). Thus, the authors conclude that their findings support the feasibility of using the telephone for reinterviewing older adults.

Aquilino and Lo Sciuto (1990) researched the effect of interview mode (face-to-face versus telephone) on 18–34-year-olds' self-reported tobacco, alcohol, and cocaine use. The telephone survey yielded lower estimates of blacks' alcohol and marijuana use than did the face-to-face interview, and slightly lower estimates of white's alcohol consumption.

Other Issues in Telephone Surveys

As telephone surveys have become more common in the last decade or so, and the telephone survey has matured as a data-collection technique, researchers have had occasion to study a variety of issues concerning telephone surveys. These have dealt with a wide range of topics. Some of the most interesting and important are discussed here. They deal with issues including interviewer voices, confidentiality reminders, RDD versus lists of telephone numbers as the basis for the sample, and optimal times for telephone interviews.

In a study of which interviewers received lower refusal rates (higher response rates) in telephone interviewing, Oskenberg et al. (1986) concluded that certain interviewers were more successful in eliminating refusals. Those interviewers with higher response rates on the telephone generally had higher-pitched voices and greater variation in pitch, and spoke louder and more rapidly. They were also judged as more competent and more positive toward the respondent and the interview.

In a different sort of study involving telephone interviewing, Frey (1986) tested the effect of a confidentiality reminder during a telephone survey. The results showed no significant differences in responses between the group with the confidentiality reminder and the group without it.

Traugott et al. (1987) compared results from telephone surveys in which RDD was used with results from telephone surveys in which lists of telephone numbers were purchased from a commercial firm. The respondents from the lists also received advance letters and household names to establish rapport. The advance letters increased response rates, but the use of names seemed to have little effect on response. In general, the list did increase response rates and interviewer productivity. While lists will probably not be available for more than three-quarters of the population in a given study, the authors suggest combining the list with a RDD sample to produce a dual-frame design that not only increases response rates but also lowers costs.

Weeks et al. (1987) experimented with optimal times for telephone interviews. They found (perhaps not surprisingly) in a national sample of adult males that the chances of obtaining an interview on the first call are much better on weekday evenings and on weekends than during weekday daytime hours, with Sunday receiving the largest response.

One of the factors affecting the telephone survey in the 1990s and beyond is the continuing proliferation of new technologies, such as the fax machine (discussed below). Among the technological developments that may in the future (or already do) affect telephone surveys are automated dialers and redialers, the answering machine, the pager ("beeper"), call waiting, call forwarding, conference calls, caller-number capturing (which informs the answerer of the caller's telephone number), and visual-screen telephones, in which the caller and answerer can see each other.

How all of these developments will affect telephone interviewing is uncertain. Some of them may help and some may hurt. For example, the advent of pagers and fax machines may allow some survey administrators to contact a greater proportion of respondents. On the other hand, they may also find their lists of telephone numbers "contaminated" in an unwanted manner with numbers that appear to be for telephones but are really for fax machines or pagers. Regardless of the ultimate impact of all this new technology, it seems certain that the technological development will necessitate increased supervision of interviewers to ensure standardization and comparability among interviews and to reduce errors. For example, it is common for a group of employees using automated dialing equipment to still be chatting with co-workers when a call is answered, or to lose track of who is being called. Thus, while the use of such automated equipment may speed up the interviewing process, it may require increased supervision to ensure that employees are ready when calls are answered.

Among the questions which new technology poses for telephone interviewing are the pager question ("to beep or not to beep, that is the question"), and the answering-machine question. What if the interviewer calls, asks for John Doe, and the answerer says, "He's not here, but I'll give you his pager number." Should he be paged, even though his environment might not be conducive to an interview (should he be called at the football game)? Answering machines pose another problem. Should the interviewer leave a message? Lavrakas (1987, p. 61) recommends doing so in order to personalize the contact, but says that the message should be brief, polite, and standardized.

All in all, it appears that developing technologies will increase the supervisory role in the future. Lavrakas (1987) discusses this role at length. His work is of help to all persons dealing with telephone surveys, but especially those in a supervisory role.

Regardless of the complications caused by proliferating technologies, telephone surveys remain unsurpassed in their classical role of providing the fastest national surveys. No other mode can compete (including computer surveys, because computers are not as accessible as telephones). Only telephone surveys can deliver results overnight. An example of this occurred when President Clinton delivered an economic address to the nation on February 17, 1993, and survey results were published the next morning, on February 18. The ABC News national telephone survey of 350 people who watched President Clinton's speech on television found that 74 percent approved of its content, and 77 percent thought the Clinton program was fair (Boyd and Hess, 1993).

The Computer or Electronic Survey

In the last decade or so it has become common for survey researchers to use computers not only for analyzing data (which they have done for many years) but also for assisting in the interview. As we have seen in our discussion of computer-assisted telephone interviewing (CATI), the computer can virtually replace the paper questionnaire used by the telephone interviewer. This has many advantages, including flexibility in using a complex questionnaire (for example, the computer can easily skip down to the next relevant question), and ease of storing and analyzing data. In addition to CATI, the computer can also be used (although this is less common) for computer-assisted personal interviewing (CAPI). In both CATI and CAPI the interviewer generally is the only one using the computer, while the respondent simply answers the questions posed by the interviewer, as in traditional surveys that are not computer assisted.

However, in the 1990s and beyond we shall see the rather rapid growth of full-fledged computer surveys (sometimes called electronic surveys—see Kiesler and Sproull 1986). Such computer surveys are quite different from surveys that are merely computer assisted. In a full computer survey, both the respondent and interviewer are working at computers. The interviewer enters the questions into the terminal of one computer, and the respondent enters the answers at the terminal of another computer, which is linked to the interviewer's computer through a computer network or linkage of some sort.

A little reflection suffices to show that while the computer survey seems to be similar to traditional methods in some ways (and probably closest to the telephone interview), it nevertheless differs from all of the previously discussed methods in some ways. The computer survey shares with the face-to-face interview and the telephone interview the fact that the interviewer and respondent are actually interacting. It shares with the mailed-questionnaire method the ability to reach respondents in remote locations (in some cases more easily than the telephone interview). However, like the mailed questionnaire, it has some limitations, including those posed by the reading ability of the respondent, inability to hear characteristics of the interviewer's voice, and so forth.

Advantages

1. *Money savings.* The computer survey reduces processing costs by automating the transformation of raw data into computer-readable form (see Keisler and Sproull 1986).

2. *Time savings.* The computer survey is potentially the fastest method for processing and storing data, as this can be done electronically in a fraction of the time it would take to mail questionnaires back to the office, or even to have an interviewer transport them there, not to mention the time in processing data and entering them into the computer (all can be done almost immediately by the respondent at his or her terminal).

3. *Use of probes and complex questionnaires.* Like face-to-face and telephone interviewing, the computer survey offers the ability to probe or even clarify a question if the respondent appears unable to answer. In addition, having a computer enables the interviewer to use a very complex questionnaire with a lot of skips and contingency questions.

The advantages of interviewing (like use of probes and complex questionnaires) can be combined with some advantages of the mailed-questionnaire study, such as standardization and anonymity.

4. *Anonymity.* While perhaps not as anonymous as a mailed questionnaire, nevertheless the computer survey allows a respondent the advantage of interacting with an interviewer who cannot see the respondent's face or hear his or her voice. Such anonymity may be very helpful in eliciting disclosures from respondents or raising response rates in surveys dealing with sensitive issues.

5. *Ease of completion.* Electronic surveys are ideal for respondents who like to interact with computers and who are accustomed to doing so frequently (for example, responding to electronic mail on a daily basis). Such respondents may judge answering an electronic survey to be as easy as answering their daily computer mail, and may in fact think that it is fun. In fact, while most survey researchers must continually find ways to deal with respondents who refuse to participate, some electronic researchers find the opposite problem—too many people want to be respondents. This is what happened to Walsh et al. (1992) when they designed a computer survey for a sample of 300 oceanographers and found that an additional 104 persons volunteered to participate. Of course, such willingness may dissipate over time when computer surveys cease to be a novelty and computer users become bored with them and find that they have too many to deal with easily.

6. *Remote locations.* Computer surveys may turn out to be the ideal method for studying respondents in remote locations all over the world. They are much faster than mail surveys and may be able to avoid many of the problems engendered by international telephone interviews such as wrong numbers, expense, problems caused by time differences, and so forth. Many computer users seem to much prefer communicating by computer rather than by telephone.

7. *Less evaluation anxiety.* According to Walsh et al. (1992), electronic surveys generally ask for relatively little sensitive social information and so should result in relatively less evaluation anxiety for the respondent.

Disadvantages

Just as computer surveys have a number of advantages resulting from their similarity to methods previously discussed, they also have disadvantages.

1. *Narrow sample.* The most glaring disadvantage of computer surveys in the 1990s is that so many people do not have access to computers or simply are not comfortable using them.

2. *Inability to see nonverbal cues.* The computer survey shares with the mailed question-naire (and the fax questionnaire) the inability to use communication other than written. This means that any information that the interviewer would like to convey via gestures, loudness of voice, and so forth, cannot be used.

3. *No control over environment.* As in the case of the mailed-questionnaire study, the inter-viewer in a computer survey cannot generally control the environment in which the respondent is answering. It may well be the case that the computer is not in a place well suited to answer-ing a questionnaire, as it may be noisy, lack privacy, and so forth.

4. *Possibly biased sample.* Also like the mailed questionnaire, the computer survey may face a biased sample. It is clear at present that accessibility to computers is probably not ran-domly distributed among the American population. Not only is the sample available for a computer survey more likely to favor wealthier and better-educated individuals, it is also likely to preclude older persons, who are less likely to be computer literate.

However, aside from some of these disadvantages that mailed studies and computer studies have in common, the computer study escapes a number of flaws plaguing the mailed surveys. Problems of mailed surveys (see chapter 7) that computer surveys do *not* share include unan-swered questions, inability to record spontaneous answers, no control over question order, and inability to control date of response. While some of these may be minor or occasional prob-lems for computer surveys, the interactive nature of the computer survey eliminates or mini-mizes most of them.

For the present there have been relatively few computer surveys conducted, and relatively few articles written about them. In one of the articles, Keisler and Sproull (1986) define an electronic survey as a survey in which respondents use a text-processing program to self-administer a computer-based questionnaire. Keisler and Sproull list some of the advantages of computer surveys, as we have just done. They then report their study in which they compared responses from an electronic survey with those from a mailed-questionnaire survey. Their ex-perimental data revealed that on closed-ended questions, responses in the electronic survey were less socially desirable (more candid) and more extreme than on the mailed questionnaire. On open-ended questions, the respondents in the electronic survey wrote answers that were long and disclosing.

For now, electronic surveys are most convenient for samples of people linked by a com-puter network. Examples are Kraut's (1984) use of a computer network to conduct research on work behaviors and attitudes in an international computer network, and Sproull's (1986) computer-mail study of organizational communication in a Fortune 500 firm. Because of the advantages listed above, such as flexibility and savings from having the respondent enter data directly into the computer, electronic surveys will surely spread as the number of people who have access to computers and are comfortable with them grows.

In a more recent electronic survey, Walsh et al. (1992) received volunteers from persons not in the sample, as discussed above. The thrust of their study was to compare the responses of the self-selected respondents with those originally in the sample. They note that when they conducted a computer-network survey of 300 oceanographers, 104 additional persons volun-teered. Computer surveys would seem to facilitate volunteering from those who are not in the sample (but are in the network). Should we look these gift horses in the mouth? What are the advantages and disadvantages of including unanticipated volunteers in the analysis?

The disadvantages include a sample that is not representative and not random, so that the assumptions of common statistical procedures are not met, thus severely limiting the analysis. However, the volunteers may not be as unrepresentative as we think, since they are all members of the computer network, and so have that in common with the persons in the sample. In addition, as the authors note, these volunteers are highly motivated, and thus may be more careful and may give more information with fewer errors than would less willing respondents. Further, in some cases such volunteers may be about the only respondents available for electronic surveys.

In comparing the self-selected volunteer respondents with the random sample, Walsh et al. (1992) found that the self-selected respondents gave higher-quality responses, their open-ended responses were large, and they had less missing data.

Regardless of the nuances and complexities of electronic surveys, it is clear that they have a number of distinct advantages for survey research and doubtless will be used increasingly in the future. For further discussion of computer surveys, see Martin and Nagao (1989) and Synodinos and Brennan (1988).

Fax Surveys

The widespread use of facsimile transmission machines, commonly known as fax machines, opens the possibility for yet another variant of survey technology and questionnaire transmission. Although fax machines use telephone lines, surveys conducted via them are not quite a telephone survey, but also not the same as a computer survey. In fact, in some ways they are like a mailed-questionnaire survey, because they have the ability to transmit the entire paper questionnaire document to the respondent. As before, we can briefly list the advantages and disadvantages of fax surveys.

Advantages

1. *Remote locations.* Fax surveys share with mailed-questionnaire surveys and with telephone computer surveys the possibility of reaching respondents in remote locations.

2. *Transmission of questionnaire.* Fax surveys share with the mailed-questionnaire study the ability to transmit the actual questionnaire (though not on the researcher's paper). This means that particular features of the questionnaire such as question placement, length of the questionnaire, and so forth, can be emphasized.

3. *Money savings.* As with the mailed questionnaire, the fax survey saves interviewing costs.

4. *Time savings.* Again, fax surveys allow the relatively simultaneous transmission of questionnaires, saving time over interview studies. However, it may not be possible to fax all questionnaires at exactly the same time.

5–10. *Questionnaire completed at the respondent's convenience, greater assurance of anonymity, standardized wording, no interviewer bias, securing information, and accessibility.* These six advantages are roughly the same as for the mailed questionnaire, and the reader is referred back to chapter 7 for discussion. There are a few differences with fax machines. Fax surveys may not be quite as anonymous as mailed surveys, because there may be only one fax machine in the office, and the operator may be able to see the incoming questionnaire and perhaps the answers, if the results are sent back via fax. By the same token, accessibility may be less with fax machines, as they are not as pervasive as the mail. However, in general fax surveys allow the respondent to answer the questionnaire in private after it is received.

Disadvantages

Again, many of the disadvantages of fax surveys are similar to those of mailed-questionnaire studies, and the reader is referred to chapter 7 for their discussion. They include the following.

1–9. *Lack of flexibility, verbal behavior only, no control over environment, no control over question order, many questions may remain unanswered, cannot record spontaneous answers, no control over date of response, cannot use complex questionnaire format, and possibly biased sample.*

10. *Lack of Accessibility.* Although fax surveys do have the ability to reach remote locations, they are nevertheless limited by the fact that some desired (or even required) respondents simply do not have access to a fax machine.

All in all it is still too early to assess the efficacy of fax surveys. There is as of yet no real literature on their use. Nevertheless, they offer real advantages over the telephone survey in cases where the researcher may want all respondents to receive the same paper copy of the questionnaire (but does not want to wait for the mail). Further, they have the advantage over the telephone survey of not having to call back if the respondent does not answer, as fax machines are generally left on 24 hours a day. This is a particular advantage in international surveys, where there may be a time difference of nine hours or more. They also have the obvious advantage over computer surveys that the respondent does not have to be a computer user, but need only read the paper questionnaire. Thus, it is clear that there are some good reasons for exploring the use of fax surveys, particularly when one desires a quick turnaround time but also wants all respondents to see the same copy of the questionnaire.

Interviewer Training

Occasionally a questionnaire does not require complicated instructions and has few skip questions and probes; in this case the interviewer requires little or no training. At the opposite extreme, many questionnaires used in interview studies are extremely long and complicated, containing a plethora of contingency questions, probes, and complex charts. In addition, there may be instances in which the interviewer cannot ask a question without inserting some information that he or she has collected earlier in the interview. In other cases the questionnaire may require extensive use of auxiliary materials (pictures, charts, lists) to be shown to the respondent when asking a particular question.

In these instances a lengthy set of instructions may be required in addition to those written on the questionnaire itself. The pretest generally uncovers all manner of unanticipated responses, and a major task of interviewer training consists of learning what to do when each of these responses is encountered. A well-trained interviewer must be familiar with all the words in all the questions and must understand all instructions in the instruction book and in the questionnaire. In addition, he or she must be familiar with the general purpose of the study, who is sponsoring it, how the sample was selected, and how the data will be coded, analyzed, and published. However, this familiarity generally does not extend to the exact hypotheses and the findings expected, as this information may tend to bias the results.

Interview training consists of the following stages:

1. *Briefing by study director.* The study director provides a brief survey of the purpose of the study. He or she also indicates approximately how many interviews there will be, how long the average interview should take, how many interviewers will be working, how long the interviewing phase of the study will last, how much travel there will be, and how the interviewers will be reimbursed for expenses. It is essential that aspects of the study that concern the interviewers directly (time, pay) be dealt with at the outset so that the interviewer is free to concentrate on understanding the questionnaire and conducting his or her interviews.

2. *Reading the questionnaire.* After the interviewers have read the questionnaire, instructions, and any additional material the study director may give them, such as discussions of the goals of the study, the study director may discuss the problem areas, such as skip questions, questions in which the interviewer must insert names or other information from earlier in the questionnaire (e.g., "How many times has [Insert answer to q. 1] been sick in the past two weeks?"), and open-ended questions with probes. Then he or she may go over the whole questionnaire to make sure that each interviewer understands each question.

3. *Practice interviews.* When the questionnaire has been thoroughly reviewed, it is time to conduct pretest, or practical interviews. During this phase the interviewer should take notes on any problems, such as unclear or ambiguous questions or unanticipated responses.

4. *Discussion session.* All problems are then reviewed, question by question in a session with the study director and all interviewers, so that they can be discussed and corrected. At this time interviewers are free to ask general questions, such as how to probe or what to do with a respondent who prolongs the interview with a lot of unnecessary conversation.

As an example of the problems for which interviewer training is necessary, consider the following question from a fertility survey: "How many times have you been pregnant?" Normal full-term pregnancies of a single child posed no problems for interviewers. However, some interviewers encountered situations that they did not know how to record. For example, if a woman was currently pregnant, some interviewers counted the current pregnancy while others did not. Some women had given birth to twins, which some interviewers recorded as two pregnancies and others as a single pregnancy. Other women had had a pregnancy terminated by miscarriage or abortion. Some interviewers counted such a situation as pregnancy and others did not, apparently because it was not a full-term pregnancy. In such cases there is a clear need for specific instructions for all interviewers, so that all of these contingencies will be recorded identically. The role of the pretest in discovering unanticipated contingencies is clear.

Entering the Field

Gaining entry to the field may be no easy matter. Some communities, such as exclusive Beverly Hills, California, require a permit for any sort of soliciting activity, and even interviewing cannot be conducted without permission from city officials. Also, since social science research frequently deals with "social problems" and since such problems are more frequently found in lower-class neighborhoods, such neighborhoods tend to be overstudied. This leads to resentment among respondents, who may feel self-conscious and say that the study treats them like "guinea pigs" or animals in a zoo—that is, like something to be stared at and studied as if they were freaks instead of humans beings. Respondents may also object to saturation, saying "This is about the tenth straight study of our neighborhood; why don't you study rich people for a change?" In addition, respondents may have a feeling of alienation or powerlessness at being the objects of a study they had no part in designing and over which they have no control. This effect, common among ethnic minority communities being studied by non-minorities and women being studied by men, is based on the belief that the researcher is hampered in designing the study by the fact that he or she is not a part of the community and by a feeling that if community members had a part in the study design they would greatly improve all aspects of it, including theory, hypotheses, and language used in questionnaire construction.

It is the study director's responsibility to determine what resistance, if any, the study might encounter and to attempt to deal with it in advance. He or she should study the neighborhood carefully in order to learn if there are governmental ordinances regulating surveys, if other surveys have been conducted recently or will be conducted in the near future, if any recent special events in the community might affect response rates (e.g., riots, disputes between citizens and police, strikes of municipal workers). Once the possible resistance has been determined, a number of public-relations approaches may be used to gain entry. Probably the most common is to give a letter of introduction to the interviewer or send it to respondents a few days in advance. An advertisement explaining the goals of the study may be placed in the local newspaper several days before it is scheduled to start. Another strategy is to meet with community leaders to discuss the study and elicit their suggestions and recommendations. Additionally, a field office could be opened in the community to recruit interviewers and other employees.

After the interviewers enter the field they may need to be closely monitored, at least at first, to ensure smooth progress and to correct any unanticipated problems. It is customary to supply interviewers with a telephone number that they can call or even give to a respondent who has a question or complaint about the survey or who wishes to verify the interviewer's identity.

As interviewing proceeds, the field director or study director or an assistant should be available to answer interviewers' questions. Spot-checking of completed questionnaires is also recommended. Spot-checking, especially early in the interview process, can serve the function of an extended pretest. It may reveal problems not caught in the pretest, perhaps because certain situations (e.g., certain respondent characteristics) not encountered there are common in the field. Another purpose of spot-checking is to discover whether any interviewer is obtaining an unusually large number of nonresponses, or unanswered questions, or "don't knows." It may also be possible to discover from spot-checking that a particular interviewer does not understand the directions to one or more questions or is deliberately falsifying data. As part of the supervisory procedure, the director may telephone respondents to make sure the interview was conducted as claimed and may even reinterview a respondent (at least on some questions) to see whether the interviewer is recording responses correctly.

The Panel Study

Surveys are generally conducted at only one point in time, for some very good reasons. Generally the sample surveyed is so large that it would be very costly to repeat it. In addition, the same sampling design may not suffice for more than one survey, as people move away or die. Further, interviewing takes a long time and is very expensive.

However, there are a number of disadvantages in collecting data at only a single point in time. Chance fluctuation in the data may occur only on the day surveyed (analogous to a rare hot day in January), and there would be no way to tell that this was not the normal state of affairs. Also, a cross-sectional survey offers no way to study trends in the data or seasonal variations, and no way to tell whether a relationship found between two variables will remain the same or will change with time. However, the loss of information over time is partly compensated for by the much larger sample that can be used when the study is done at a single point.

If the sample is not too large, sometimes the study can be conducted over time (a longitudinal study). A common longitudinal survey is the panel study, in which exactly the same respondents are reinterviewed at two or more points in time regarding the same problems. Another longitudinal survey is the trend study, which surveys the same number of respondents from the same population each time, but not necessarily the same respondents. The disadvantage of this design is that differences in the data from one survey to the next may not be the result of a trend but merely the reflection of differences in the persons surveyed.

Among the problems of a panel study is that the cost is much greater than a cross-sectional study, since interviews must be conducted two, three, or even more times. In some cases cost can be reduced by drawing a smaller sample. Further, the respondents may be reluctant to participate in repeated interviews, feeling that they have "done their duty" in the first interview. Another problem is what is called "panel mortality." The panel means the original sample of respondents (e.g., 100); each successive interview or stage of the panel survey is called a "wave." Panel mortality means the decrease in the size of the panel from one wave to the next. This decrease may be caused by death but can also result from any event that makes a respondent from an earlier wave unavailable for reinterviewing, including moving to an unknown location or to another state or country where he or she cannot be interviewed because of the expense. A woman's change of name through marriage can cause the interviewer to lose track of her and thus be a source of panel mortality.

For these reasons panel studies are frequently not conducted. There are some cases, though, in which they are greatly needed, if not absolutely necessary. For instance, all studies of trends or changes in opinions require reinterviewing. The researcher studying voting behavior may wish to see at what point before the election most switchovers from one candidate to another occur, or when the undecided voters choose for whom to vote. Another major use of panel studies is in attempting to establish causality. It is very difficult to establish causality in a cross-sectional study because for this purpose we need to see that change in one variable results in change in another. To study change we generally need to study over time.

Some examples of panel studies reported by Glock (1955) include the effect of showing a film on anti-Semitism to a sample of 503 Christians, and the effect of an educational public-health program on knowledge of venereal disease among a sample of 588.

Validity and Reliability

Although few studies have dealt with the reliability of interview surveys, there have been a number of attempts to assess the validity of the interview by comparing its results with data gathered by some other means. There are a number of ways that error can be introduced. A respondent may answer in a socially desirable (but inaccurate) way, or may be ashamed to admit that he or she does not know the answer. Respondents may give accurate answers on questions dealing with recent events but make many errors in replying to questions about events that happened long ago.

Parry and Crossley (1950) compared respondents' answers with known facts for eight classes of information. They found that when asked whether they owned a car, a house, and a telephone, 97 percent of the respondents gave correct responses concerning the car, 96 percent concerning the house, and 98 percent concerning the telephone. However, events occurring some years before were reported considerably less accurately. For example, asked whether or not they had voted in a presidential election held one year before the survey, 96 percent reported accurately, while for an election five years before the survey only 73 percent reported accurately. Most of the error was made by persons who did not vote but reported voting (probably a social-desirability effect).

It should be clear from our discussion of the disadvantages and advantages of the mailed questionnaire in chapter 7 and of the interview in this chapter that the interview tends to be more valid for certain purposes than the mailed questionnaire, but less valid for others. The control one has in an interview study strengthens the quality of the data gathered. An interviewer has the ability to control response rate (or at least more control than in a mailed study). He or she can attempt to ensure that the respondent answers every question adequately, answers in order, and does not pass the questionnaire to someone else to supply the answers.

The quality of the data gathered in interview studies may be weakened by biases or errors introduced by the interviewer by clerical error, interviewer cheating, or by aspects of the interviewer-respondent relationship, such as the social-desirability effect. Further, the respondent cannot consult records as a memory aid, and may not have sufficient time to prepare an adequate answer.

The majority of the studies that have compared the mailed questionnaire and the interview find virtually no difference in the quality of the data gathered on identical questions (Mc-Donagh and Rosenblum 1965, p. 135; Metzner and Mann 1952; Kahn 1962). Those studies that have reported differences (usually fairly minor) have indicated that mailed-questionnaire studies yield better data on sensitive issues about which the respondent is unwilling to talk in the presence of an interviewer (Knudsen et al. 1967; Montero 1974).

Most researchers prefer interviewing to mailing questionnaires, simply because of the higher response rate that is usually achieved through interviewing. The main barriers to interviewing, of course, are the much higher cost and the greater time involved. In general I see no reason to disagree with Maccoby and Maccoby:

It has been widely assumed that the interview is superior to the questionnaire in many ways and should be used when resources permit. Certainly the interview *must* be used at the exploratory stages; for the later stages of research, the meager evidence so far available does not support the superiority of the interview. However, the research done so far is limited in scope and does not permit us to generalize very far. It is entirely possible that the interview is superior for some subject matters, the questionnaire for others (1954, p. 483).

Summary

In chapter 8 we discussed interview studies. Among the advantages of interviews over mailed questionnaires are the generally higher response rate, flexibility, ability to observe nonverbal behavior, control over environment, control over question order, and several other factors. Among the disadvantages are the cost, time spent, interview bias, lack of accessibility to respondents, and several other problems.

We discussed the interview as an instance of social interaction between two people, and as such governed by certain norms regulating social interaction. The success of this interaction, and thus the successful completion of the interview, can hinge upon characteristics and actions of the participants. Factors we discussed that may affect the relationship between respondent and interviewer include the race or ethnicity of each, their sex, their social status, their age, and their clothing and grooming.

Next we discussed ways of approaching the respondent and dealing with potential refusals. We then presented a number of guidelines for conducting the interview, such as asking questions exactly as worded, asking questions in order, and avoiding leading questions.

We then turned to a discussion of less structured interviewing, and techniques of probing. We discussed the focused interview, focus groups, the clinical interview, and the unstructured interview. The latter part of the chapter dealt with projective interviewing techniques, telephone interviewing, computer surveys, fax surveys, interviewer training, and panel studies. We concluded with a discussion of the validity and reliability of interview studies.

PART THREE

NONSURVEY DATA COLLECTION TECHNIQUES

LIVERPOOL
JOHN MOORES UNIVERSITY
I.M. MARSH LIBRARY
BARKHILL ROAD
LIVERPOOL L17 6BD
TEL. 0151 231 5216/5299

LIVERPOOL
JOHN MOORES UNIVERSITY
I.M. MARSH LIBRARY
BARKHILL ROAD
LIVERPOOL L17 6BD
TEL. 0151 231 5216 5298

CHAPTER 9

EXPERIMENTS

THERE ARE TWO APPROACHES to social research concerned with attempting to establish relationships between variables. *Correlational analysis* and *experimentation*. The means by which these two approaches are carried out are quite different. In a correlational study the researcher typically has very little control over the research environment, and in fact often is working with data that have been long since removed from the scene where they were collected and are stored on computer cards or in some other format. In such a case the researcher's control is limited almost entirely to statistical data manipulation. Many statistical techniques allow one only to establish symmetrical relationships between variables and do not attempt to establish causality, while other techniques (so-called causal models) do attempt to establish causality. The use of these statistical techniques is discussed in chapter 16.

Experimentation is somewhat different. The experimenter is present on the scene when the data are collected and exercises considerable control over the experimental environment. This control over the research process allows the experimenter to attempt to establish causation rather than mere correlation, and thus the establishment of causation is the usual goal of the experiment. For a discussion of control and other factors relevant to sociological experiments see Marwell (1992).

As an example of the difference between correlational analysis and experimentation, let us briefly return to the comparison between the Galle et al. (1972) and the Griffit and Veitch (1971) studies discussed in chapter 1. The former is a correlational study and the latter an experiment. In rereading chapter 1, notice that the Galle team was analyzing data that had already been collected and had no control whatsoever over the independent variable (density). There was no way of actually changing the level of density and observing its effects. As an alternative, their analysis sought to show statistically a relationship between density and its effects by essentially comparing areas of varying density in Chicago and attempting to see if the other variables, the so-called social pathologies, also varied.

In contrast, Griffit and Veitch conducted a density experiment inside a laboratory. Griffit and Veitch had at least four forms of direct control. They could control the independent variable of density (and also a second independent variable, temperature). This is extremely important. They could actually vary the heat and density at will, something that Galle et al. were utterly unable to do. (How are you going to change the density of the South Side of Chicago?) Further, they had control over the assignment (by randomization) of persons to groups. They also had control over measuring the dependent variable after persons were assigned to groups. Lastly, they had a relatively high degree of control over extraneous factors, as the research subjects were enclosed in a laboratory during the duration of the experiment. More recent discussions of controlled laboratory experiments in sociology are by Molm (1990) and Bonacich (1990).

Leaving the specific Griffit and Veitch experiment and speaking in general, we can say that the experiment is a highly controlled method of attempting to demonstrate the existence of a causal relationship between one or more independent variables and one or more dependent variables. In the ideal experiment the experimenter has control over the environment in which the experiment is conducted and is able to hold constant or otherwise control any environmental or extraneous factors that might affect it. He or she also can control the composition of the experimental and control groups, generally by assigning subjects to these groups by matching or randomization. In theory, all of these groups initially should be identical in terms of the characteristics of group members. The third type of control in a true experiment is control over the independent or causal variable, often called an *experimental stimulus* (for example, a movie thought to counteract racial prejudice). The investigator ideally has actual physical control over the independent variable and administers this variable to the experimental group but not to the control group. Finally, the experimenter has the ability to measure the values of the dependent variable both before administering the independent variable (the pretest) and after administering it (the posttest). The difference between these scores gives a rough indication of the effect of the causal variable.

Because of practical limitations on social research (including budget and time), the experimenter is often unable to exercise all four forms of control. In the ex post facto experiment, for example, the experimenter cannot control the introduction of the independent variable, but can control the formation of the experimental and control groups, the environment, and the posttest (but generally not the pretest) to a certain extent. In the field experiment the researcher can control virtually nothing, as the analysis is done in the natural environment rather than in the laboratory. However, he or she generally can compare a situation in which the causal variable is present with another in which it is not. For further discussion of general factors in the design of social experiments see Saxe and Fine (1981).

Advantages of Experiments

1. *Establishing causality.* It is debatable whether one can ever actually demonstrate empirically or prove the existence of a causal link between two or more variables. However, the experiment is definitely the best method in social science for establishing causal links. It enables the investigator to measure the value of the dependent variable, introduce the independent variable he or she suspects to be the cause, and observe whether any change ensues in the dependent variable. Thus experimental studies are generally longitudinal, although the time period may be quite short. The survey is inferior to the experiment for establishing causality both because it is usually conducted cross-sectionally rather than over time (the panel study is a salient exception) and because the researcher generally has little control over contaminating factors in the environment. Observational studies are often conducted longitudinally but generally cannot control extraneous factors or provide for precise measurement of change in the dependent variable. Document studies are also often longitudinal but again offer little opportunity for control. Thus if one wishes to study causality the experiment is the obvious method of choice.

2. *Control.* A true experiment offers the ultimate in control. The ability to control has important ramifications for data analysis and hypothesis testing. First, the investigator can probably get by with a smaller sample size than he or she could in a more uncontrolled study, as the experiment offers less chance for error caused by extraneous factors. Second, the greater control in an experiment generally means that the investigator can have more faith in his or her findings.

3. *Longitudinal analysis.* The experiment provides the opportunity for studying change over time. In an experiment the investigator generally observes and collects data over a period of time and measures at more than one interval. Experiments may be of short duration, such as

an hour or less or a few hours, or they may cover months or even years, but even short experiments provide more opportunity to study change than do cross-sectional studies such as surveys.

Disadvantages of Experiments

1. *Artificial environment.* Perhaps the main problem with using experimentation in social science is that sufficient control is impossible in a natural setting. The social behavior of interest must be placed in an artificial environment (laboratory) that affords proper control. Unfortunately, much ongoing social behavior will be drastically altered, or simply will not occur at all, if examined out of its natural habitat. For example, a student of collective behavior who is interested in determining the causes of riots can never expect one to occur in a laboratory. Attempting to create a riot in a laboratory setting would be no solution, because the investigator would know that he or she was the cause and would still not know how riots are generated in a natural setting.

In other instances, ethical considerations or time considerations make it infeasible to study behavior in an artificial setting. Consider the Griffit and Veitch (1971) density experiment discussed in chapter 1. This experiment is adequate as far as it goes and does indicate that density may be a cause of aggression. However, it is entirely possible that density affects aggression only after a long period of time. To yield more definitive results, the subjects would have to be confined much longer in the dense environment. An obvious problem with such an experiment is that confining people in such an environment would be like keeping them in jail and would probably be unconstitutional. Second, if density was shown to cause violent aggression and some subjects were injured, the investigator would doubtless be judged guilty of unethical conduct for putting persons at risk.

2. *Experimenter effect.* The experiment can definitely be a "reactive" method as discussed in chapter 2, in the sense that the experimenter's expectations can affect the results of the experiment (Rosenthal 1966; Rosenthal and Jacobson 1966; Friedman 1967). For example, Rosenthal and Jacobson (1966) identified 20 percent of the children in each of 18 classrooms as high scorers on a test to predict gains in academic achievement. Actually, the children were picked at random but their teachers were led to believe that they were high achievers. Over time these children did in fact show greater achievement than children not identified as high achievers, demonstrating that the teachers' expectations affected their students' behavior. Other studies by Rosenthal (reported in Rosenthal and Jacobson 1966) in more traditional experimental settings have shown similar results. Working with more than one experimenter, Rosenthal found that experimenters who were told what findings were expected had experimental findings more in conformity with the research hypothesis than did experimenters who were not told what to expect.

Why do the experimenter's expectations affect experimental results? Probably one answer is that the experimenter gives cues (perhaps subconsciously) to the research subjects, who then conform to the experimenter's wishes. However, it is also possible that the experimental results are misinterpreted by the experimenter to conform more closely with his or her hypothesis. For example, Rosenthal (1966) had different experimenters experiment with rats. He told some experimenters that their rats were smart and some that their rats were dumb. In reality none were smarter than others, as all groups were randomly assigned, but the experimenters did not know this. The experimenters with the "smart" rats had better results than the experimenters with the "dumb" rats.

One method of counteracting the effect of experimenter expectations is the "double-blind" experimental design. In this design someone other than the experimenter assigns subjects to the control and experimental groups. Thus even the experimenter (as well as the subjects) does not know which group is getting the genuine experimental treatment and which is receiving the placebo, or no treatment. A researcher who cannot determine which group is experimental should not have his or her interpretation of the findings colored as much by expectations as they would be if the identity of the experimental group were known.

3. *Lack of control.* The would-be experimenter in social science is often caught in a dilemma: Placing subjects in a laboratory will alter the very behavior he or she wishes to study, but attempting to conduct the experiment in a natural environment probably will make it impossible to control all of the extraneous variables that could threaten the experiment. It is because of these problems that the experiment is less widely used in social science than in other disciplines, where better control is possible.

4. *Sample size.* By definition, sociology is concerned with the study of groups. The larger the group, the more difficult it is to study it in a laboratory and to control extraneous variables. For example, someone interested in studying the entire population of the United States might be able to conduct a survey but could never conduct an experiment. Thus the experiment is most widely used in psychology, where the focus of interest is generally one person at a time rather than a whole group. In sociology the experiment is most widely used in social psychology or in the study of small groups, which require a fairly small sample.

Closure

The experiment is the major method of data collection in the physical sciences but, for the reasons mentioned, it is less widely used in the social sciences. In effect, what the researcher must do to establish causality is first to specify the cause-and-effect variables, then specify all other variables that might affect the relationship. He or she must then either control all of these variables or assume that the ones he or she cannot control are constants and therefore will not affect the experiment. In other words, the experimenter lists the cause variable, the effect variable, and the variables that need to be controlled, "closes" them off from the remainder of the variables in the world, and assumes the rest of the world away. The extent to which the investigator can control the relevant variables (or the ones assumed to be relevant) is called the degree of "closure."

In a physical-science experiment the researcher typically has a relatively high degree of closure. Often he or she literally closes off the experimental environment from the outside environment and thus creates an artificial environment in which closure is nearly complete. The scientist can construct a laboratory that is completely sealed off from the external environment by thick walls. Inside the experimental chamber only a few variables remain that can affect the experiment and these can be accurately manipulated and controlled. For example, the researcher can control the temperature, humidity, amount of light in the chamber, and amount of oxygen in the air. The environment outside the chamber can be assumed not to affect the experiment. In this situation the experimental method can be used quite successfully to establish causality. After proper controls are applied, the causal variable is changed in value. If subsequent change is noted in the dependent variable, then the independent variable is the cause. If no change is noted in the dependent variable even after change in the independent variable, then it is assumed that the independent variable is not the cause or that its effects on the dependent variable are being canceled out by some other variable that is improperly controlled.

Physical scientists generally study chemicals, minerals, and other inanimate objects having properties such as weight, volume, and temperature, that can easily be manipulated by the scientists with no moral, ethical, or legal ramifications. Social scientists are more likely to deal with human subjects, control over whom is restricted by ethical, moral, and legal considerations. In addition, the researcher cannot change the value of such relevant properties of human subjects as sex, age, socioeconomic status, education, occupation, and income. Although it is physically possible to change a person's sex and perhaps the degree of population density in his or her neighborhood, such changes are generally prevented by legal or ethical considerations, and in any case would involve much time and money. However, even though social scientists generally cannot actually control or change the value of variables in the way that a physical scientist would change the room's heat or humidity, they can achieve a certain amount of "symbolic" control. This can be accomplished not by changing the value of a variable for any individual but by holding the variable constant in value for the subsample. Consider the variable of gender. Imagine that we are going to conduct an experiment in which first we measure the subjects' level of racial prejudice, then show them an antiprejudice film, and then remeasure their prejudice levels to see if they have been lowered. However, we suspect that the film might have different effects on persons of different gender. Thus to separate out the sex effect we need to control for sex, or hold sex constant. We cannot change an individual's sex, but we can conduct the analysis separately for persons of each sex. Thus we can ensure that gender does not cause any observed variation in prejudice level.

The Logic of Experimentation

Ideally the experiment is based upon actual observation of changes in the dependent variable (the effect) as they occur. This is in contrast to methods such as the survey and document study, where the researcher never sees changes in the phenomenon being studied but relies upon the written or spoken statements of eyewitnesses. The basic logic of experimentation is quite simple. The experimenter begins with a causal hypothesis that states that one variable (the independent variable) causes changes in a second variable (the effect or dependent variable). The next steps are to (1) measure the dependent variable (pretest); (2) introduce the independent variable to the situation or change its level if it is already present; and (3) measure the dependent variable (posttest) to see whether there has been resultant change in its value.

As long as closure is complete, any changes in the before and after measures of the dependent variable (computed by subtracting pretest scores from posttest scores) can be attributed to the test stimulus. However, in most cases complete closure cannot be achieved. Even if the test were conducted in a vacuum, administration of the pretest itself may change the scores on the dependent variable. With human subjects, literally thousands of factors may contaminate the experiment.

Suppose, for example, that the experimenter is studying persuasive appeals—and has used his or her theory to produce a series of one-hour-long movies that he or she is convinced will turn antifeminists into feminists if the subjects see one movie a week for three weeks. The only problem is that since the experimenter cannot keep his or her subjects sequestered, their views on feminism might be changed during the three-week period by television programs, newspaper or magazine stories, conversations with friends, school classes, religious teachings, personal experience, and any number of other factors beyond his or her control.

One way to reduce possible contamination is to make the experiment very short so that the subjects can be sequestered for the entire time (e.g., for a few hours). When this is not feasible, the experimenter must simply face the fact that the posttest score will be different from the pretest score even in the absence of the causal variable of interest, and attempt to measure the extraneous change and subtract it from the total change in pretest and posttest scores. The remainder of the change can be attributed to the causal stimulus.

How does one separate the portion of the total change in pretest and posttest scores that is caused by extraneous factors from the portion that is caused by the test stimulus? This cannot be done with a single group of subjects but can be accomplished with two groups if certain assumptions can be made. The first assumption is that the subjects in the two groups are identical in their personal characteristics. The second assumption is that the pretest plus any extraneous factors that affect one group will also affect the second group to the same degree. These assumptions imply that (assumption 1) the average pretest scores should be identical (with some allowance for chance variation) and that (assumption 2) the portion of the difference between pretest and posttest scores that is caused by extraneous factors is the same in each group. If these assumptions hold, one pretests both groups but administers the causal stimulus to only one. The group without the stimulus should show a change in the dependent variable that is attributable only to the extraneous variation, while the dependent variable in the group with the causal stimulus should show a larger change, caused by extraneous variation plus the test stimulus. The group to which the test stimulus is administered is called the *experimental group*. The group that does not receive the test stimulus is called the *control group*. By subtracting the extraneous change (change in the control group) from the total change in the experimental group, one can estimate the amount of change due to the causal stimulus.

One- and Two-group Experimental Designs

Before beginning our experiment we hypothesize that the independent variable is the cause of the dependent variable. The only proof we will have of this is any change that we may observe in the dependent variable following introduction of the independent variable. Suppose we form a single group of subjects, administer a test stimulus, and observe subsequent change in the dependent variable. Does this "prove" that the independent variable is the sole cause of the change in the dependent variable? No it does not, unless we can assume that no other variables are affecting the dependent variable. It may be that our own independent variable is completely unrelated to the dependent, but we observe change in the dependent variable because some other variable is present (and is not sufficiently controlled) and is causing the change. Alternatively, it may be that our independent variable is causing a portion of the change in the dependent variable, but other factors are causing the remainder of the change.

As a hypothetical example, assume that we are working on a medical sociology project on toxic shock syndrome (TSS). Assume that we have an elaborate theory which leads to the hypothesis that TSS is psychosomatic and can be induced in susceptible persons by having them read a written account of TSS.

We then take a group of persons who have not had TSS and have them read a statement about it. Suppose we find that some subjects do develop TSS. Does this prove that a written statement causes TSS? Although an incidence of the disease following closely on the heels of the experimental stimulus fits all of the requirements of causality (see our discussion of causality in chapter 3), most readers would hesitate to answer affirmatively, and they would be wise. This is because the logic of the experiment assumes that we have isolated the cause so that change in it (the statement about TSS) is the *only thing* that can lead to change in the dependent variable (TSS). This is true only when all other variables that could affect TSS have been controlled, and such is not the case in our hypothetical example. There are a number of factors that may have caused the incidences of TSS, including tampon use by women, which is said to be one of the major causes. The best way to deal with this problem is to eschew the single-group design in favor of a two- (or more) group design, including a control group. We shall first present the single-group design, and then move to a discussion of the two-group design.

Before and After Experiment with No Control Group

The simplest experimental design includes a single experimental group and is called a before and after experiment with no control group. Since this design lacks a control group with which to measure extraneous variation, it can be used only when the experimenter can assume that extraneous variation is minimal, so that virtually all recorded change in pre- and posttest scores is caused by the test stimulus. This design includes the following steps:

1. Select subjects
2. Select experimental environment
3. Pretest
4. Administer experimental stimulus (test factor)
5. Posttest

Since total variation in pre- and posttest scores is being attributed to the causal factor, the formula for this cause (with the subscripts indicating the experimental group) is: $Cause_{exp} = Posttest_{exp} - Pretest_{exp}$. If the experimenter's assumption is incorrect (and he or she has no way to tell if the assumption is correct or not) and extraneous factors do cause change in the pre- and posttest scores, then he or she does not know how much of the change in the dependent variable is due to the test stimulus and how much to uncontrolled factors. We can combat this problem by redoing the experiment and adding a control group with the pre- and posttest, but no causal stimulus.

Two-group Design

The control group is most likely to be unnecessary in experiments of short duration in which the subjects are not permitted to leave the experimental laboratory. However, for a number of reasons the experiment is often of longer duration. If the pretest, the test stimulus, and the posttest are all administered in a short period of time, it must be easy for the subjects to guess the purpose of the experiment and thus bias the data. For this reason subjects are often not told the true nature of the experiment. Such deception works to an extent, but the practice is limited by ethical considerations. If the experiment is conducted over a longer period of time, such as a few weeks, months, or even years, with subjects leading normal lives during the interim, any number of extraneous factors can be encountered during the course of everyday living over which the investigator has no control. Even maturational effects can have an effect.

In a case of such extraneous effects, pre- and posttest scores in the control group are likely to be significantly different from zero ($\text{Posttest}_{control} - \text{Pretest}_{control} = \text{Difference}_{control} \neq 0$) and the difference in pre- and posttest scores for the experimental group cannot be attributed entirely to the test stimulus. That is, the experimental difference contains the effect of the causal test stimulus plus the effect of extraneous or uncontrolled factors. Without a control group there is no way to tell how much of the overall effect in the experimental group was true cause and how much was extraneous effect. With both a control and experimental group it is a simple matter to subtract the extraneous effects from the overall experimental group difference; the remainder is assumed to be the true causal effect of the test stimulus. The control difference will equal the experimental difference in cases in which the causal effect of the test stimulus is zero. However, the control difference should not generally exceed the experimental difference, as the latter contains the same difference as the former (extraneous) plus the causal difference. If the experimental difference were smaller than the control difference, that would indicate that the effect of the causal stimulus was negative (or was in the opposite direction of the extraneous effect).

Classical Experimental Design
(One Experimental Group, One Control Group)

Experimental Group	*Control Group*
1. Select subjects	1. Select subjects
2. Select experimental environment	2. Select experimental environment
3. Pretest	3. Pretest
4. Administer experimental stimuli	4. Posttest
5. Posttest	$\text{Posttest}_{control} - \text{Pretest}_{control} = \text{Diff}_{control}$
$\text{Posttest}_{exp} - \text{Pretest}_{exp} = \text{Diff}^{exp}$	

$$\text{Casual effect} = \text{Diff}_{exp} - \text{Diff}_{control}$$

Assignment of Subjects to Control Groups

Experimental designs using two or more groups can effectively show the causal effect of the test stimulus if proper assignment of subjects to groups can be made. The goal is for all groups of subjects to be absolutely identical. This is very difficult as there are so many potential extraneous factors that must be controlled. For example, in the toxic shock example, everything from nutrition to a virus to age to sexual practices could be a possible extraneous factor that could affect the experiments if not controlled in some manner. It is doubtful that the experimenter can even think of all possible extraneous factors, so how can he or she control them?

One obvious way is to have an adequate theory that specifies the correct cause or causes. For example, if the theory specifies that age and sex are important factors in TSS, the investigator can make certain that all groups are identical in their age and sex composition. If these were the only factors to be controlled, the experimenter could match pairs of individuals on age and sex, and then assign one of each pair to the experimental group, and the other (identical) member of the pair to the control group.

But what happens if the factors specified by the theory are not the correct extraneous variables or do not exhaust the list of extraneous factors? This means there may be other factors that can confound the experiment. While technically one need not control factors that do not affect the experiment, the safest procedure, if possible, would be to construct all groups so that they are identical on all factors, whether they affect the experiment or not. There is an emerging consensus that this can be done through randomization, making it the method preferred by most experimenters for assigning subjects to groups. For examples of one-group (single-case) designs in various fields such as psychology and psychopharmacology, as well as an argument for single-case research, see Kazdin and Tuma (1982).

Randomization

Randomization is probably the most popular method of assigning subjects to groups. It does not require a large number of potential subjects from which to select (although a larger number is preferable), and it does not control only on a single factor, but on all factors simultaneously.

Random sampling has been discussed previously in chapter 5. The procedure for random selection of experimental subjects is about the same as for survey sampling, except that a number of groups of subjects are to be selected instead of a single sample. The experimenter first constructs a sampling frame, or list of all eligible subjects, then selects the membership of each group from this sampling frame by means of some random process such as a table of random numbers. As in survey sampling, if the sampling frame can be assumed to be in random order, systematic sampling can be used. For example, the researcher could select every fifth subject from the sampling frame until the experimental group was complete, then continue selecting every fifth person until the control group was complete. As before, any order or systematic bias in the sampling frame could cause grave error in this procedure and result in experimental and control groups of drastically different composition.

The goal of all selection procedures for experimental control groups is to make the groups as similar as possible in terms of the dependent variable, and thus necessarily in terms of all factors affecting it. Therefore, the pretest scores for the experimental and control groups will ideally be identical or similar prior to introduction of the test stimulus in the control group. Randomization does not necessarily ensure that pretest scores for the two groups will be identical. However, it should ensure that whatever differences do remain are random, by which we mean differences due to chance and not to causal factors.

Simple Matching (Precision Control)

The most straightforward way to make an experimental group and a control group equal is to find matching pairs of identical subjects and place one of the pair in the experimental group and the other in the control group. Obviously, it is not sufficient to match the two subjects on a single characteristic. They must be matched on all relevant characteristics simultaneously. Two subjects may be identical in sex and age but very different in some other important characteristic, such as skin color. Unless individuals are matched on all important characteristics the control group and experimental group will not be equal.

The disadvantage of this method is that any subject who does not have a matching partner on all relevant characteristics cannot be assigned to either group, and thus cannot be used in the experiment. Unless the experimenter is able to begin with an extremely large pool of prospective subjects, he or she is likely to find many subjects who differ from all other subjects on at least one characteristic and so cannot be used, but not enough matching subjects to complete the experimental and control groups.

Use of this method becomes more difficult as the number of characteristics considered relevant to the experiment and the number of groups used in the experiment increase. Only characteristics that are correlated with either the independent or the dependent variable will affect the experiment, so only these variables need to be controlled. Fortunately, variables that tend to be correlated with either the independent or dependent variable, and thus relevant for matching, will also tend to be correlated with each other, making them somewhat easier to match. If the groups can be made truly identical in terms of the characteristics being matched, and if these characteristics really are correlated with the dependent variable, then the values of the dependent variable should be roughly the same for each group. Thus the pretest values should be the same for all groups.

Since matching on a large number of variables is difficult, there may be one or more relevant characteristics that cannot be matched. Furthermore, there may be additional characteristics on which the experimenter does not match because he or she does not realize that they are relevant. For this reason it is wise, as Selltiz et al. (1959, p. 104) mention, to supplement matching with randomization. This can be done by first pairing the identical subjects. Once all pairs are constructed, the researcher uses randomization, as described above, to decide to which group each member of the pair should be assigned. In this way any additional uncontrolled factors will be assigned without any pattern and should cancel each other out. That is, with random assignments it is highly unlikely that the two groups will be substantially different in value on a particular variable and thus cause bias.

Frequency Distribution Control

In another common matching technique, called frequency distribution control, the investigator does not attempt to control on all variables simultaneously but concentrates on one variable at a time. He or she makes sure that the two groups are identical (or very similar) in the average value of the variable and the shape of the distribution of values on that variable in the two groups. For example, using precision matching, three pairs of individuals have ages of 20, 25, and 30 years, respectively, and one of each pair is placed in group A and the other in group B. Thus the average age for each group is 25. Frequency distribution also aims for equal average ages in the two groups, but without attempting to match ages for every pair of individuals. Although each group may have an average age of 25, the experimental group may contain persons aged 24, 26, and 25, while the control group has persons aged 22, 25, and 28. Not only the averages but also the distribution of values on the variable should be similar for the two groups. For example, not only should the mean ages be the same in the two groups, but the distribution of age should also have about the same degree of skewness (lopsidedness of the curve) and variance (average deviation from the mean).

The distinct advantage of frequency distribution matching over precision matching is that it requires fewer subjects and does not generate so many residual unusable subjects. The disadvantage of frequency distribution control is that it controls on only one variable at a time. Combinations of variables are not controlled. For example, we might use frequency distribution matching to construct a control group and an experimental group that have equal percentages of blacks and females. However, it may be that in one group all females are black and in the other group all are white, because we did not control on both variables simultaneously as we did with precision matching. Again, randomization should be used in conjunction with frequency distribution control to offset the effects of uncontrolled factors.

Multiple-group Designs

Two Experimental Groups with One Control Group

In the designs discussed so far, the causal variable or test stimulus was a present-absent variable. Since there was only a single experimental group and thus a single application of the causal variable, there was no way to vary the value of the causal variable. For example, if the independent variable were a movie, the only comparison was its presence (experimental group) or lack (control group). There was no way to vary any aspects of the movie such as length, topic covered, and so on.

The two-experimental-group-with-one-control design has the test stimulus present in each of the two experimental groups, but absent in the control group. However, the causal variable differs in value or intensity in the two experimental groups—e.g., if the causal factors were smoking, instead of having merely one experimental group of smokers and one control group of nonsmokers, we would have one experimental group of heavy smokers, one experimental group of light smokers, and a control group of nonsmokers.

Factorial Designs

In addition to presenting different levels or values of the test stimulus or independent variable, it is possible to present more than one independent variable. All of the designs discussed so far have presented only a single independent variable. Presentation of more than one independent variable is going to require an even larger number of experimental groups, and that is a disadvantage of such a design. If only two independent variables are used, each having only two possible values, a minimum of four experimental groups is necessary in order to present all combinations of the two variables. For example, imagine that you are conducting an experiment on the combined effects of liquor and amphetamines, which you think have a substantial interaction effect when ingested simultaneously. One independent variable is the amount of amphetamines taken (high or low), and the other is amount of alcohol consumption (high or low). The four experimental groups have four different test stimuli representing all possible combinations of values of the two variables: (1) high amphetamines, high alcohol; (2) high amphetamines, low alcohol; (3) low amphetamines, high alcohol; and (4) low amphetamines, low alcohol. These experimental groups, as usual, have comparable subjects and the same environmental conditions, pretest, and posttest.

One example of a factorial design is the Griffit and Veitch (1971) study of density and heat, which we discussed in chapter 1 and also earlier in this chapter. Griffit and Veitch used 121 subjects, both males and females. They pretested each on a 24-item attitude questionnaire. Then the subjects were randomly assigned to eight factorial groups. These eight groups were constructed by forming all combinations of temperature (high and low), population density (high and low), and two levels of agreement with the subjects' answers on the attitude scale (.25 agreement or .75 agreement). It was found that although subjects were more hostile to an anonymous same-sex stranger who they were told disagreed with them (.25) than to one who agreed with them (.75), their hostility varied with density and heat. For further discussion of this experiment see chapter 1.

The Griffit and Veitch experiment depended upon a pretest (of the 24-item questionnaire), and without it one could not have formulated the .25 and .75 agreement conditions. In some factorial experiments, however, contemporary experimenters are eschewing the pretest. It is common in social science experimentation to use factorial designs without pretests *if* all groups are constructed via adequate randomization procedures. Campbell and Stanley (1963, p. 25) say that with proper randomization pretesting is not essential to true experimental designs, but they concede: "For psychological reasons it is difficult to give up 'knowing for sure' that the experimental and control groups were 'equal' before the differential experimental treatment."

I share the psychological uneasiness with relinquishing the pretest and would prefer to pretest in most cases. However, there are some reasons for using a factorial design without pretesting, and thus we cannot fault the popularity of this practice. For one thing, random assignment to groups, like random survey sampling, is statistically sound, and there is general consensus on this. Thus, statistically speaking, a pretest is not needed to show that the experimental and control groups are equal. In addition, there may be some instances where a pretest is impossible or unwise. As a possible example, Campbell and Stanley (1963, p. 25) list experiments with presentation of new subject matter in elementary schools and an experiment on the effect of attorneys' briefs on the guilt or innocence verdict of a jury. Further, if one has a great many groups in a factorial design, the use of pretests may be tedious, time-consuming, and costly. Still further, as we shall see in discussing the Solomon designs below, the pretest can itself sometimes be a source of extraneous variation in the dependent variable.

Latin Square Design

An even more parsimonious design, which allows the use of many different independent variables but only one value of each (presence), is the Latin square design. This design presents as many independent variables (experimental conditions) as there are subjects, but the variables are presented in a different and unique order for each subject. For example, the chart below shows the Latin square design for four subjects.

Subject	Variable			
Fred	1	4	2	3
Joe	4	3	1	2
Sue	2	1	3	4
Jill	3	2	4	1

Notice that each of the four experimental conditions (independent variables) appears only once in each row and only once in each column. Notice also that each of the four subjects is exposed to all four independent variables but that the order in which the independent variables are presented is different for each of the four subjects. This design enables the experimenter to detect whether the order in which the variable is presented makes any difference in its effect on the dependent variable. The design is complete, as each independent variable appears in all positions once. For example, treatment 4 appears in the first position for Joe, in the second position for Fred, in the third position for Jill, and in the fourth position for Sue.

Interaction Effect

As mentioned above, the social-scientific experimenter is in a dilemma in deciding on the duration of the experiment. If the experiment covers a long period, such as several weeks, it is often impossible to keep subjects in the experimental laboratory all of the time. However, when subjects are permitted to lead normal lives during the course of a long experiment, extraneous influences are probable. Among those listed by Campbell and Stanley (1953, p. 5) are (1) history, or events occurring between the first and second measurements; (2) the maturation process, including growing older, more tired, and sicker; and (3) experimental mortality, or differential loss of respondents in the experimental and control groups due to death, illness, or moving out of state. The experimenter can avoid these effects to a large extent simply by keeping the experiment to no more than one or two hours in which the subjects are not allowed to leave the laboratory. The disadvantage of this is what Campbell and Stanley (1963, p. 5) refer to as testing effect, or the effect that the test itself (e.g., pretest) can have on the values being tested. The pretest may also have an effect in long-term experiments, but is more likely to be remembered by respondents in experiments of short duration.

Assume that the subjects are not told the goal of the experiment, and thus should not be able to bias the results. Suppose the experiment's purpose is to discover the causal effects of a movie on their level of racial prejudice. The pretest is a questionnaire in which the items forming the prejudice scale are dispersed at random among other items so that the subject does not know that his or her level of racial prejudice is being measured. Nevertheless, the measurement of this variable (prejudice) itself, by presenting questions about race relations, may stimulate the subject's thinking and actually cause a change in his or her level of racial prejudice. Any pretest effect that occurs will be visible as part of the extraneous change (change not caused by the test stimulus) in the control group, as the pretest is also presented to the control group.

After the pretest is administered, the test stimulus (a movie on racial prejudice) is shown, and then the posttest (same questionnaire as the pretest) is given. In all experiments of short duration, even a subject who was unable to guess the goals of the experiment from the pretest alone may be able to figure them out from the combination of the pretest questions on race and the movie on race. Since no one wants to be labeled a bigot, such a person who guesses the purpose of the experiment will probably answer untruthfully so as not to appear prejudiced. Thus, in addition to the effects of the pretest and the causal stimulus, which together (along with effects of uncontrolled variables) make up the total difference between pre- and posttest scores, there is an extra effect, stemming from the respondent's combined knowledge of the pretest and test stimulus, that enabled him or her to alter answers. This extra effect produced by the combination of pretest and stimulus operates in addition to sum of the effect of these two events and is known as an interaction effect.

The idea of an interaction effect is familiar, especially in the area of medicine or illness. As an example, imagine that for a given population of 100 persons, all of the same age and sex, it was found that if all 100 smoked the effect would be a cancer rate of 20 percent. Assume that for an identical group of 100 persons who did not smoke but lived in a smoggy environment such as Los Angeles, 10 percent would get cancer. Now consider a third identical group of 100 persons all of whom smoke and also live in a smoggy environment. The additive effect of both smoking and smog would be 20 percent plus 10 percent, or a total of 30 percent (30 people) having cancer. However, imagine that an actual medical survey of the population shows a cancer rate of 37 percent among persons experiencing both smoking and smog. This extra 7 percent can be computed residually as follows: Interaction effect = total effect − (smog effect + smoking effect) = 37 percent − (20 percent + 10 percent) = 37 percent − 30 percent = 7 percent. Other common examples of interaction effect occur when taking two or more drugs simultaneously. Mixing drugs may have the effect of both added together plus an "extra" effect resulting from the combination of the two. This extra effect is the interaction effect.

Solomon Two/Control/Group Design

Some extended experimental designs are presented by Solomon (1949). The Solomon two/control/group experiment is designed to isolate and estimate the interaction effect that occurs when the subject deduces the desired results from a combination of the pretest and test stimulus. This design is merely the classical one experimental group, one control group design discussed above, with a second control group added. Remember that in the classical design the experimental group has pretest, test stimulus, and posttest while the first control group has only the pretest and posttest (no test stimulus). Thus change in the experimental group can be due both to pretest and test stimulus, but in the control group it can be due only to the pretest. In the two/control/group design the second control group has a test stimulus but no pretest. Thus any change in the dependent variable in this group can be due only to the test stimulus. This gives the following comparison of group effects: experimental group—pretest effect and test-stimulus effect; control group 1—pretest effect only; control group 2—test-stimulus effect only. Total effect in the experimental group = pretest − posttest. In the control groups, total effect = pretest effect (control 1) + test-stimulus effect (control 2) + interaction of pretest and test stimulus. Doing some simple algebra, Interaction effect = (posttest$_{exp}$ − pretest$_{exp}$) − (pretest effect + test-stimulus effect).

The only difficulty that remains is computing the difference between the original value of the dependent variable and the posttest value of the dependent variable in control group 2, since we have no pretest. Since all three groups are equal, we can estimate the pretest value for control group 2 by taking the pretest average of the experimental group and control group 1.

Imagine that a researcher has a prejudice scale of 100 statements. A respondent receives a score of one for each statement with which he or she agrees. The higher the score the higher the prejudice level. Imagine that a group of 30 persons is given the prejudice test and receives an average (mean) score of 80. They are then shown an antiprejudice movie lasting one hour. With a 15-minute refreshment break after the movie, they come back into the experimental room for the posttest (the same prejudice scale as before). Suppose the average on the posttest is a prejudice score of only 40. This means that prejudice levels dropped 40 points in a short time. If the researcher thinks that the pretest had no noticeable effect, that there was no interaction effect caused by the combination of the pretest and test stimulus, and that all relevant variables that might affect the study were held constant or otherwise controlled, he or she could accept the 40-point prejudice drop as the causal effect of the movie.

However, imagine that a critic of the experiment charges that a scale with so many statements enables a substantial number of subjects to guess the nature of the experiment and thus lower their scores on the posttest so as not to appear bigoted. The critic says that the after-only design with no control group is not adequate and that the 40-point reduction in prejudice cannot be attributed solely to the test stimulus; some of the reduction must be attributed to the pretest. Assume that the experiment could be rerun in the classical design, with two groups of 30 persons (one experimental and one control), each exactly like the original group. Again the experimental group shows a 40-point reduction from the pretest to the posttest, but the control group, which has no test stimulus, shows only a 10-point reduction. This difference between the control group and the experimental group cannot be attributed to causal effect, since there is no test stimulus in the control. Subtracting 10 from 40 leaves only a 30-point reduction that may be attributed to the test stimulus alone. The 10-point reduction shown in the control must be attributed to the pretest plus other uncontrolled factors. Notice that the 10-point reduction in control group 1 cannot be due to interaction in that group, because interaction requires both the pretest and test stimulus, and only the former is present in control group 1.

Steps in Solomon Two/Control/Group Design

Experimental Group	Control Group 1	Control Group 2
1. Select subjects	1. Select subjects	1. Select subjects
2. Select experimental environment	2. Select experimental environment	2. Select experimental environment
3. Pretest	3. Pretest	3. No pretest
4. Administer experimental stimulus	4. No experimental stimulus	4. Administer experimental stimulus
5. Posttest	5. Posttest	5. Posttest

However, the possibility still exists that part of the 30-point reduction in the experimental group is due to interaction effect, which is separate from test-stimulus effect, pretest effect, or the effect of uncontrolled factors.

To test for interaction we must utilize the Solomon two/control/group design. Assume that we now have three identical groups of 30 persons each. As in the classical design, we use the pretest and posttest in both the experimental group and control group 1, but administer the test stimulus only in the experimental group. In the second control group we also run the test stimulus and posttest, but no pretest. However, since all three groups are equal, we can use the average of the pretest scores for the first two groups (experimental and control 1) as an estimate of the missing pretest score in control 2. This value is the average of 80, or simply 80. Imagine that the posttest score for control group 2 is 60. Since there is no pretest for this group but only a test stimulus, the difference between 80 and 60, or 20, is equal to the causal effect of the test stimulus alone. By adding the effect of the test stimulus (control 2) to the effect of the pretest (control 1) and subtracting this sum from the total difference (experimental group), we estimate the interaction effect to be $I = (80 - 40) - ([80 - 60] + [80 - 70]) = I = 40 - (20 + 10)$; $I = 40 - 30 = 10$.

Solomon Three/Control/Group Design

Neither the classical design nor the Solomon two/control/group design has enabled us to isolate extraneous uncontrolled factors such as history and maturation. In the first control group the posttest-pretest difference is due to the effect of the pretest plus these extraneous factors (or the pretest alone if extraneous effect can be assumed to be zero). In the second control group the difference is due to test stimulus plus extraneous differences. Only by adding a third control group, which has neither pretest nor test-stimulus effect, can we isolate extraneous effects. As in the two/control/group design, the pretest measure is estimated by using the average of the pretest scores in the experimental group and control group 1. No test stimulus is administered to the third control group. Since there is neither a pretest nor a test stimulus, any change found must be due entirely to extraneous factors. Imagine that in the third control group the posttest score is 77 and the pretest score is estimated to be 80. Thus interaction would be $I = 40 - (30 + 3) = 7$ rather than the 10 estimated by the two/control/group design.

Another method which does not isolate the effect of extraneous or uncontrolled factors but does not run the risk of pretest contamination, is the after-only design with two groups. In this design neither group has a pretest. As usual, the experimental group has the test stimulus and the control group does not. Both groups have the posttest. If both groups are identical in characteristics of subjects and experimental conditions, it can be assumed that their pretest scores should be similar if not identical. Thus the difference between the posttest scores of the two groups will represent the effect of the test stimulus (plus the effects of the uncontrolled extraneous variables).

As Selltiz et al. (1976, p. 140) point out, the Solomon three/control/group method is really two experiments in one. The experimental group and control group 1 represent the classical method, while control groups 2 and 3 represent the after-only two-group design. Thus these two experiments should give similar estimates of causal effect and can be used to check each other.

Further Examples of Laboratory Experiments

We have often alluded to the problems confronting experimentation in social science. These problems can be summarized as follows:

1. A large number of variables that have potential effect upon the experiment and thus must be controlled.
2. The fact that a cause must sometimes be present for a long time before it has any effect (e.g., living in a dense neighborhood for a short period of time may show no causal effects of density, but a long period of residence in a dense neighborhood, such as ten or more years, may show definite causal effects).
3. Inability to control certain variables or introduce certain test stimuli because of potential harmful effects upon subjects.
4. Inability to control all of the necessary variables.
5. The effect that an artificial laboratory environment can have on social behavior.

Thus those social-research projects most successfully conducted in an experimental environment are those which have relatively few variables affecting them, can be conducted quickly, will not harm the subjects, and can be studied in an artificial environment without biasing the results. Research projects that fit these requirements include the effect of seating arrangement, density, or some other independent variable upon problem-solving studies of cooperation, competition, or conformity; and studies of the effect of some stimulus such as a movie, television commercial, or book upon some characteristics of a small group of respondents.

Consider an example of a problem-solving experiment, as discussed by Blau and Scott:

Shaw presented complex puzzles (for example, transporting missionaries and cannibals across a river under specified conditions, or arranging words to complete a poem) to individuals and to groups of four working together. Groups were found to be superior to individuals in solving puzzles (Blau and Scott 1962, p. 118).

One of the most famous social-science experiments is Asch's study of conformity. As described by Morgan:

> Subjects were asked to make judgments concerning the length of lines. Each experimental session typically employed only one actual subject in a group of people who had been coached to express certain opinions. Hence, the real subject often faced a situation in which his eyes told him one thing while the others in the group agreed that something else was correct. Only a minority of the subjects consistently yielded to the erroneous group opinion. Later interviews with those who conformed to the majority opinion suggested that most of these "conformists" thought something was wrong with their eyesight and that the majority was probably correct (Morgan 1961, p. 512).

Another classic experiment is by Sherif, as described by Morgan:

> The subjects were placed in a totally dark room and were asked to judge how far a point source of light seemed to move. Since the walls of the room were not visible, there was no physical frame of reference available to aid in making these judgments. In part of the experiment, individuals were shown the light for the first time in a group situation, and each person expressed his opinion aloud for the others to hear. The group members soon began to influence one another. Their judgments at first did not agree very well, but as they listened to one another's opinions, they seemed to agree that the light moved within a certain range. Each group developed its own range of judgment, i.e., its own way of perceiving this situation (Morgan 1961, p. 511).

While such experiments can be conducted easily, many other topics are not amenable to experimentation. For example, the Griffit and Veitch (1971) density experiment discussed in chapter 1 is ethically acceptable only because the experiment is of short duration, as confining subjects in conditions so hot and crowded as to cause potentially harmful effects would not be tolerated for any length of time. Many other forms of behavior, such as bureaucractic, crowd or riot, and social movements, simply cannot be studied in a laboratory setting without changing the basic nature of the behavior.

Field Experiments

There are some situations in which the study must be conducted in a natural environment rather than in an experimental laboratory, but in which the independent or causal variable is amenable to some control by the experimenter. In some of these cases the experimenter may have a control group utilizing a second natural setting that does not receive the experimental stimuli. Generally, however, he or she will not be able to exert enough control over variables in a natural setting to ensure an acceptable level of equality between the experimental and control groups and thus will not be able to use a control group.

This type of design, in which the experimenter does not control the extraneous variables or the experimental conditions (because the experiment is conducted in a natural setting) but does introduce the test stimulus, is called a *field experiment*. In some cases some manipulation of the field environment is possible.

Swingle (1973) presents approximately two dozen examples of social-psychological field experiments, dealing with such topics as performance and participation, discrimination, helping and honesty, attitude changes, and rumors. One such experiment dealing with helping and honesty is called The Bystander and the Thief, or The Case of the Stolen Beer. In this experiment the robber or robbers (one was used in 48 cases and two in 48 cases) came into a liquor store in which there was a single clerk and either one customer (48 cases) or two customers (48 cases). The robber or robbers asked the clerk, "What is the most expensive imported beer you carry?" The clerk (who was participating in the experiment) would reply that it was Lowenbrau and would then leave the room saying, "I'll go back to check how much we have." After the clerk disappeared, the robber or robbers would pick up a case of beer, saying, "They'll never miss this," carry it out to the car, and drive off (Swingle 1973, p. 68).

Overall, 20 percent of the subjects (customers) reported this theft to the clerk spontaneously when he returned to the room. If such spontaneous reporting did not occur, the clerk prompted it by asking what had happened to the man (or men) who had been in the store. Of the customers who did not report the theft spontaneously, 51 percent responded to the clerk's prompting and reported it. Doubling the number of robbers did not have a significant effect upon reporting, nor did the sex of the customer. However, the number of customers in the store had a substantial effect. When only one customer was present, 65 percent (31 out of 48 instances) reported the theft, either spontaneously or after prompting. The presence of a second customer had a dampening effect upon reporting, with at least one of the two customers reporting the theft in only 56 percent of the cases. Other interesting field experiments deal with education (Slavin and Karweit 1985) and criminal justice (Rossi et al. 1980).

Quasi-experimentation

Experimenters working within an experimental laboratory often aspire to conducting a "pure" experiment, meaning that all of the various forms of experimental control mentioned in this chapter are achieved. However, experimenters in field settings, such as the Swingle studies just discussed, often do not have full control over all sources of variation. This means that they cannot design a "full" or "pure" experiment, with the usual control group, assignment to groups, manipulation of the test stimulus, and pre- and posttests, but must design "partial" experiments lacking one or more of these factors. Such designs are often referred to as "quasi-experimental" designs, or "semi-experimental" designs, to signify that they lack at least some of the control that we expect in a full or pure experiment.

The whole notion of quasi-experimental designs is somewhat controversial. Some experimental purists feel that experimental design is an all or nothing matter and is not a continuum from full experimentation to no experimentation. According to the purist view one either has a proper experiment in a proper laboratory with full control, or one has no experiment at all. To such purists a "quasi-experiment" does not meet all of the criteria of an experiment and thus is not one. Other researchers are less rigid and accept a whole range of designs as legitimate experiments, even though some of them do not allow full experimental control. However, even these adherents recognize that such designs are not "pure" and thus label them as "quasi" rather than merely calling them alternative experiments. While most of these adherents would not condone the use of a quasi-experimental design out of haste or laziness when a pure design is possible, they would recognize that there are instances, most of them in field experimentation, where one uses either a quasi-experimental design or no design at all, as a pure design is not possible. While purists would opt for no design and would abandon the field setting for the laboratory, some researchers feel that field research is valuable and that quasi-experimental designs are thus justified if conducted as optimally as possible.

The position of the quasi-experimentalists was strengthened by the publication of Cook and Campbell's (1979) book, *Quasi-Experimentation: Design and Analysis Issues for Field Settings.* This is a methodologically sophisticated volume which discusses causality in detail and then evaluates various quasi-experimental designs in terms of their efficacy and limitations in establishing causality. For a more recent discussion of quasi-experimental research designs, see Kercher (1992).

A common characteristic of field designs is that random assignment to experimental and control groups is often impossible, and often there is no control group at all. When a control is present, but there has been no random assignment of subjects to groups, Cook and Campbell refer to the groups as "nonequivalent." It is not impossible in such a case for the control and experimental groups to be equivalent, but unfortunately we have no assurance of this and so must assume that they are nonequivalent.

One common quasi-experimental design by Cook and Campbell (1979, pp. 96–98) is the "one-group posttest-only design." This design has no control group at all, and the experimental group lacks a pretest, having only an experimental stimulus (treatment) and a posttest. Researchers may rationalize using this design if they measure many variables at the posttest and if they are so familiar with the field situation that they feel they know what the results would have been without the test stimulus (that is, in a control group). Nevertheless, the lack of a pretest in the experimental group and the complete lack of a control group make this a weak design which generally is not sufficient for establishing causality and must be used with great care.

Another popular quasi-experimental design has an experimental group with a test stimulus and a posttest only (no pretest), and a nonequivalent control group that has only a posttest (no pretest and no test stimulus). Cook and Campbell (1979, p. 98) call this the "posttest-only design with nonequivalent groups." In some cases the experimenter may introduce the test stimulus in the experimental group. However, in one popular version even the test stimulus is beyond the control of the researcher, as the researcher comes upon the scene after the test stimulus has already occurred. This design is often referred to as the *ex post facto* design. For example, suppose you wished to study the psychological effects that earthquakes have on the residents of an area. The earthquake is the test stimulus (independent variable or cause) and any subsequent psychological effect on residents is the dependent variable, which you might measure with some pencil-and-paper test (the posttest). It might be possible in rare cases to pretest before the earthquake. Generally, though, the researcher will have to forgo the pretest and wait until the earthquake occurs. While the researcher will have had no chance to pretest because he or she will not know when or where the earthquake will occur, and will have had no control (obviously) over the test stimulus (the earthquake), he or she can posttest the earthquake victims. The only "control group" possible is to find a group of non-earthquake victims. Obviously, these also cannot be subjected to a pretest but can receive a posttest. The control and experimental groups will be nonequivalent, as subjects were not randomly assigned to either group. While this design is more complete than the "one-group posttest-only design," both the lack of pretests and the lack of control over the test stimulus present problems and make this design generally inadequate for establishing causality.

A third popular design is what Cook and Campbell (1979, p. 99) call the "one-group pre-test-posttest design." This design has a single experimental group and includes a pretest, test stimulus, and posttest, but it lacks a control group. This is the first design presented in this chapter, and its limitations were discussed at length. According to Cook and Campbell this design, like the two just discussed, is generally inadequate for establishing causality. However, users of all three of these designs in certain instances may be able to offer convincing arguments for their validity. Cook and Campbell (1979) discuss a number of more complicated quasi-experimental designs, which, even though they generally have nonequivalent groups, may be adequate for assessing causality. Please refer to their volume for further discussion.

Validity and Reliability

Although much of the discussion in this chapter has focused on attempts to maximize the validity and reliability of experiments (e.g., by control of extraneous variables and by matching subjects in experimental and control groups), we will follow the practice initiated earlier of discussing briefly at the end of each chapter the reliability and validity of the respective method treated therein.

Since experiments differ greatly in design and in the degree of control exercised by the experimenter, they will also vary widely in validity and reliability. In addition, each experiment has several different component parts, each of which displays its own degree of reliability or validity. For example, we can talk of the validity and reliability of the pretest and of the validity and reliability of the test stimulus. It should be pointed out, however, that the experimental designs discussed above generally assume the reliability of the pretest and posttest, even in cases in which the pretest can be shown to have an independent effect (as in the Solomon two/control/group design). The posttest is a repetition of the pretest and thus apparently could constitute a test-retest measure of reliability. However, the causal effects of other factors, such as the test stimulus, generally ensure, at least in the experimental group, that the posttest score will not be the same as the pretest score. Thus these effects prevent us from demonstrating the reliability of the measure. Even in the control group it is assumed that there will be a change between pretest and posttest scores, the lack of a test stimulus notwithstanding. Indeed, if the pretest and posttest difference were not assumed, there would be no need for a control group. Not only is the reliability of the measure of the dependent variable assumed with a particular group, it is also assumed across group boundaries, as long as the groups can be assumed to be identical. Imagine, for example, that our dependent variable is level of prejudice, measured by a prejudice questionnaire consisting of 100 items. Not only do we assume that the pretest and posttest are reliable within the control group, we also assume that the two pretests in the experimental and control groups are reliable. If we cannot make this assumption, we cannot estimate the value of a missing pretest score, as in control groups 2 and 3 of the Solomon two and three/control/group methods.

Since reliability is assumed and generally cannot be tested because of changes in the value of the dependent variable, it is essential that the instrument used in the pretest and posttest be rigorously tested prior to the experiment in order to ensure the truth of the reliability assumption. We said in our discussion of reliability (chapter 4) that if a respondent really changes his or her opinion on an issue, then the instrument or questionnaire, if it is reliable, should register this change. Unreliability is a characteristic of the questionnaire and is caused chiefly by question ambiguity, which makes the respondent unsure of the meaning of the question and thus unsure of the correct answer. An ambiguous questionnaire used in the pre- and posttest will obviously harm the reliability of the experiment.

We can consider an experiment to be valid to the extent that we can determine accurately the causal effect of the independent variable on the dependent variable—i.e., how much change or variation in the scores on the dependent variable are due to the influence of changes in the independent variable. In order to accomplish this we must first have valid pretest and posttest measures of the dependent variable in order to determine the overall amount of change in scores on the dependent variable. (The validity of tests was discussed in detail in chapter 4.) Next, we must be able to separate the portion of the total variation due to the independent variable from the portion due to outside extraneous factors, reactive effects of the pretest, or chance or random factors.

Thus, unless one has some way to measure accurately the validity of all pretests and posttests in the design and to assess the validity of the measurement of extraneous or error variation, it is difficult to assess accurately the validity of a specific experiment. We can only repeat that the controlled experiment is the most valid method of measuring causal effect. Further, in general, the greater the degree of control, the more valid the measurements of causality. Thus rigorous laboratory designs are generally more valid than ex post facto or field designs. For further discussion of experimental design, see Frankfort-Nachmias and Nachmias (1992).

Summary

Chapter 9 dealt with experimentation. The experiment is the premier method for inferring the existence of a causal relationship between one or more independent variables and one or more dependent variables. Other advantages of the experimental method include its greater ability to achieve closure and its use in studying change over time. Disadvantages of experiments in social research include artificiality, experimenter effect, lack of control, and small sample size.

After discussing the basic logic of experimentation, we discussed a number of experimental designs, including the before and after experiment with no control group, the classical experimental design, the Solomon two/control/group design, the Solomon three/control/group design, the factorial design, and the Latin square design. We then discussed a number of techniques for assigning subjects to experimental and control groups, including simple matching, frequency distribution control, and randomizing.

The latter part of the chapter dealt with experiments conducted outside of the traditional artificial laboratory setting. We discussed semi- or quasi-experimental designs (designs lacking either control of the causal stimulus or control over extraneous variables), including the *ex post facto* design, the uncontrolled experiment, and the field experiment. The chapter concluded with a discussion of the validity and reliability of experiments.

CHAPTER 10

OBSERVATION

THE OBSERVATIONAL METHOD is the primary technique for collecting data on nonverbal behavior. Although observation most commonly involves sight or visual data collection, it could also include data collection via the other senses, such as hearing, touch, or smell. Use of the observational method does not preclude simultaneous use of other data-gathering techniques. Observations are often conducted as a preliminary to surveys, and may also be conducted jointly with document study or experimentation.

There are two chief types of observation: participant and nonparticipant. The participant observer is a regular participant in the activities being observed, and his or her dual role is generally not known to the other participants. For example, a researcher studying politically right-wing activist groups such as the John Birch Society would join such a group, attend its meetings, and participate in all other activities. A nonparticipant observer, on the other hand, does not participate in group activities and does not pretend to be a member.

Observation is preferred when one wants to study in detail the behavior that occurs in some particular setting or institution. For example, Kerr (1979) was interested in the use of space by staff members within a hospital. One of her hypotheses was that for a given level of status hospital staff members would maintain greater distance during interaction with other staff members of lower status than with staff members of higher status.

Although everyone maintains interpersonal distance during conversation, for example, many persons do so almost subconsciously and thus are generally unaware of the exact distances they maintain or of changes in the distance maintained. Thus, it is very doubtful that the hypothesis could be adequately tested through a survey. Kerr chose the observational method and studied the day-to-day interactions of 62 subjects over a four-month period. Kerr found some support for this hypothesis. For example, residents (physicians) maintained greater distance in interaction with nurses and ward secretaries than they did with other residents or with senior physicians.

Holdaway (1980) also conducted an observational study of space use, but the setting was a British police station rather than a hospital. Holdaway found that space inside the police station was managed in terms of "public" and "private" areas. In the public areas, such as the foyer where one enters the building, all behavior by the police is within strict legal limits. The police station office represents a border between the public and private areas of the station. The charge room (where charges are filed against arrestees) and cell areas are private areas, and it is here that the practices of interrogation often extend beyond formal legal boundaries.

As in the hospital study, a survey would certainly not have yielded adequate data for this study on the use of space in police stations. Probably many officers use space quite unconsciously and thus could give only superficial answers regarding space use. Further, observation can provide a picture of overall space use by all persons present at a given time rather than the more fragmented and isolated information provided by a survey respondent. Still further, police officers would be unlikely to give answers on questionnaires that detailed their illegal interrogation activities in private areas. Thus, one frequent use of observation is for studying private behavior that individuals might not admit to on surveys, such as homosexual activity in public restrooms (Humphreys 1970). However, observation is certainly not limited to covert activities and is useful any time one desires a comprehensive, in-depth picture of behavior (including nonverbal behavior) in a particular setting over a long period of time. Observational studies are conducted everywhere—in schools, nursing homes, stores, and so forth. For example, recent observational studies in the sociological literature include a study of the training of cooks (Fine, 1985) and a study of a drug treatment center (Peyrot 1985). Recent interest in observational studies has culminated in the publication of a number of interesting and comprehensive books on the subject (see Webb et al. 1981; Burgess 1982; Emerson 1988; Hammersly and Atkinson 1983; Lofland and Lofland 1984; Burgess 1984; Ellen 1984; and Whyte 1984). An example of the maturity of the field is the increasing range of topics being treated in works on observational research. Recent examples of this breadth include work on field methods in cross-cultural research (Lonner and Berry 1986), the politics and ethics of field research (Punch 1986) and reliability and validity in qualitative research (Kirk and Miller 1986).

The maturation of the observational method led in the late 1980s and early 1990s to a series of "how to" books and also a substantial degree of specialization, for example with an entire book devoted to writing field notes (Emerson et al. 1994). That is, rather than write accounts of their own studies, as was the rule previously, many authors were now presenting guidelines for observational research, or critiques of it, sometimes from a "postmodern" perspective, a feminist perspective, or some other perspective (see, for example, M. Wolf, 1992). As Kleinman (1993, p. 12) says, she often gets defensive and tells herself: "These people don't do fieldwork; they only write about it."

This tendency to "write about it" is indeed evident in a significant number of "how to" analyses. Some of these include "grounded theory" procedures (Strauss and Corbin 1990), a "step by step" guide, which gives advice on all stages of observational research, including such things as the needed equipment (Fetterman 1989), a critique of observational research (Hammersly 1992), a careful analysis of observational work (Atkinson 1990), and a book on the politics of field research (Gubrium and Silverman, 1989). For discussion of observational research in urban settings, see Burawoy et al. (1991). For further general discussion see Holstein and Gubrium (1992). Also recommended is the book by Van Maanen (1988).

However, these comments are not meant to imply that *all* 1990s observational research is secondary rather than primary. To the contrary, there is still a lot of interesting research continuing in the field, much of it published in various journals. Among some examples are two studies of lying (Hunt and Manning 1991; Rodriguez and Ryave 1990). The study on police lying (Hunt and Manning 1991) is, along with Van Maanen's (1988) book, evidence of a continuing interest in studying police, as is the work by Holdaway (1980) already mentioned. Among the many other recent observational studies of interest are two on animals by Robins et al. (1991) and Arluke (1991). For many other examples of current observational research see *Qualitative Sociology,* the *Journal of Contemporary Ethnography,* or *Symbolic Interaction.*

Advantages of Observation

1. *Nonverbal behavior.* Observation is decidedly superior to survey research, experimentation, or document study for collecting data on nonverbal behavior. The survey method is superior to observation for discovering a person's opinion on a particular issue. However, a researcher asking the respondent about his or her own behavior will encounter all sorts of difficulties, including deliberate denial of certain behaviors or memory failure. In contrast, an observer on the scene can discern ongoing behavior as it occurs. The observer can make field

notes that record the salient features of the behavior, or may even record behavior in its totality via videotape. In survey research, all data on behavior (except for rare instances when the behavior takes place in the course of the interview) is secondary or secondhand.

While the survey questionnaire is a rather artificial and restrictive instrument limited to a relatively small number of previously chosen questions, the observational method allows in-depth study of the whole individual. Investigators frequently use the observational method in preliminary studies. Many times a researcher plans to conduct a survey but is relatively unfamiliar with his or her respondents and is not sure which questions are appropriate or necessary. By conducting a preliminary observational study the appropriate or necessary. By conducting a preliminary observational study the researcher can discover the appropriate characteristics for study, including some behaviors of which the respondent himself or herself may not be aware. Also, the observational method, especially unstructured observation, is a very flexible technique that allows the observer to concentrate on any variables that prove to be important.

Since the observer often lives with the subjects for an extended period of time, the relationship between them is often more intimate and much more informal than in a survey in which the interviewer sees the respondent for only a few minutes, and on a very formal basis. The relationship between observer and subjects thus is often primary rather than secondary, as in the survey. The primary nature of the relationship provides an opportunity to find out in much more detail what the subject is really like.

However, there is also a danger that the friendship or even love between the observer and his or her subjects may damage the observer's objectivity. The observer may not notice certain things that would seem obvious to an outsider simply because he or she is too close to the subject. Sometimes persons who are very close emotionally to other persons simply refuse to believe certain negative things about them.

2. *Natural environment.* Another major advantage of observation is that behavior takes place in its natural environment. Some proponents of observational technique (e.g., Johnson 1975) feel that observation is less reactive than the other major data-collection techniques. Both the experiment, with its heavy reliance on an artificial environment, and the survey, with reliance on verbal answers to a limited set of questions, can clearly cause bias in the very data they are attempting to study, so that data can be a product of the method rather than merely a measure of an existing empirical reality. Observation is neither as restrictive nor as artificial as either the survey or the experiment. Nevertheless, the presence of a stranger (the observer) and the error involved in human observation and in the recording of data all make bias a real possibility in observation.

3. *Longitudinal analysis.* Unlike the interviewer who must compete with the respondent's everyday activities and obligations for a precious hour of his or her time for the interview, or the experimenter who must constrain his or her subjects for the duration of the experiment in an alien and sometimes hostile or uncomfortable laboratory environment, the observer is able to conduct his or her study in the subject's natural environment, and is thus usually able to study over a much longer time period than with either the survey or experiment. The advantages of this should be obvious. While the survey respondent may have a hazy memory about events that occurred far in the past, the observer is studying events as they occur. He or she is often able to study long enough to observe trends, and to be able to tell the difference between chance occurrences and the accustomed happenings.

Disadvantages of Observation

1. *Lack of control.* The advantages of a natural environment over an artificial laboratory setting have been noted. However, the other side of the coin is that in a natural environment the researcher often has little control over extraneous variables that may affect the data.

2. *Difficulties of quantification.* Measurement in observational studies generally takes the form of the observer's unquantified perceptions rather than the quantitative measures often used in survey research and experimentation. Rather than specifying in advance a characteristic (e.g., prejudice or alienation) and preparing a scale to measure it, the observer is much more likely simply to observe and record events as they occur. Thus at the termination of the study he or she will have records showing, for example, how each person interacted with minority persons, rather than a score for the person on a prejudice scale. Observational data can be quantified to a certain extent, but such quantification is generally limited to frequencies and percentages. For example, the observer can compute the number of times a white subject speaks to blacks, shakes hands with blacks, sits next to blacks in class, and so on.

Because it is a flexible method capable of in-depth coverage of a large range of issues, observation tends to yield massive amounts of data. Such data are often difficult to code or categorize in any systematic fashion, and in this regard are somewhat similar to the answers of open-ended survey questions. In either case a researcher may be faced with perhaps hundreds or even thousands of transcript pages telling in minute detail what happened day after day, but no easy way to synthesize the data sufficiently to reach conclusions pertinent to the hypotheses.

In comparison with survey researchers, observational researchers tend to be nonquantitative types who are seeking a more emotional and humanistic sort of data and a more humanistic relationship with subjects. Many times observers are more interested in subjective analyses of emotion ("He seemed to be in good spirits") than in a quantitative score from some scale that they consider to be dehumanizing and pseudoscienctific. Many researchers feel that instead of reducing human emotions to numbers that can be fed into a computer, it is preferable to observe the person's emotions, make a subjective appraisal of them from the standpoint of an interested and concerned human being, and record such data in writing. Thus the final data will be not numbers but quotes and recollections, as in the following hypothetical example:

> Mary is a charming and sensitive person. She is considerate of others but does not have very many friends as she is a very shy and introverted person. She spends much time alone. Her primary activity is reading. She daydreams a lot.

3. *Small sample size.* It is a safe generalization to say that observational studies tend to use a smaller sample than survey studies but a larger sample than experiments. In theory, observational studies could use thousands or millions of subjects if there were enough observers. However, because observational studies are generally conducted in depth, with data that are often subjective and difficult to quantify, the data gathered by two or more observers may not be readily comparable, and there are no easy checks on reliability in unstructured observations. In addition, the in-depth nature of observational studies generally requires that they be conducted over a much longer period of time than a survey or experiment, each of which is often an hour or so in duration. A lengthy study not only further complicates the problems of reli-

ability when many observers are used, but also means that each observer must be employed for long periods of time, obviously a costly endeavor.

4. *Gaining entry.* Many observational studies are field studies conducted in the natural environment. Such studies might be conducted in a secret society, a government agency, a factory assembly line, or a county welfare organization. Many times the observer has difficulty receiving approval for the study. Some studies can be conducted by clandestine participant observers without the knowledge of anyone in the organization, including the top administrator. The observer must not be seen taking notes during the course of daily activities, as to do so will arouse suspicion. Thus he or she must either trust his or her memory and write field notes at night, or use some secret recording device such as a hidden tape recorder. However, often the observer will have some goal (such as accompanying caseworkers on home visits even though such workers are usually alone) that requires permission of the top administrator. Even if this permission can be secured, the observer is often regarded with suspicion by lower-echelon workers who suspect that he or she is a spy for management.

5. *Lack of anonymity/studying sensitive issues.* Although there seem to be a dearth of studies systematically investigating the reliability of observation for studying sensitive issues, it seems safe to say that the interview is less reliable than the survey because it is difficult to maintain a respondent's anonymity in an observational study. As recently as 30 years ago questions on topics such as sexual practices, abortion, and contraception were considered taboo for survey researchers; now they routinely gather data on such activities. However, it is one thing to admit on an anonymous mailed questionnaire that one masturbates, and quite another to permit oneself to be observed in the act of masturbating. It is possible that many married persons who masturbate would admit this on a questionnaire yet keep the fact secret even from their spouses, and certainly from an outside observer. In the case of sensitive bedroom behavior, when the presence of observers will not be tolerated, we have the choice of accepting a secondary account or obtaining none at all.

Types of Observation

In contrast to experimentation, which is most likely to be conducted in the laboratory, most observation (but by no means all) is conducted in a natural setting. In contrast to survey research, in which questions are standardized, constructed in advance, used as a framework within which to interpret reality, and yield quantitative data, observation tends to use only a minimal framework to structure either the phenomena to be studied or the questions to be asked. Thus there are two types of structure by which we may classify types of observation. The first is the degree of structure of the environment, which can be dichotomized as a natural setting or an artificial or laboratory setting. The other is the degree of structure imposed upon the observational environment by the researcher, which can be dichotomized as structured, such as counting the frequency with which certain behaviors occur or certain things are said, and unstructured, in which the researcher does not look for any particular behaviors but merely observes and records whatever occurs. These two variables can be used to construct a four-cell typology of types of observation (see figure 10–1).

While the distinction between artificial laboratory settings and natural settings may be

Figure 10–1

Types of Observational Study

Degree of Structure Imposed on Setting by the Observer	Degree of Structure of Observational Setting	
	Natural Setting	*Artificial Laboratory*
Unstructured	Type: Completely Unstructured Field Study Examples: Mead 1939; Whyte 1943; Gearing 1970 1	Type: Unstructured Laboratory Analysis Example: Axline 1964 2
Structured	Type: Structured Field Study Example: Sears, Rau, and Alpert 1965 3	Type: Completely Structured Laboratory Observation Example: Bales 1950 4

clear, the line between structured and unstructured observation may be less apparent. Admittedly, these categories are relative. While it is doubtful that any study can be completely unstructured, some may be more structured than others. In theory, at least, each of the four types of observational study could be conducted either as a participant observation study or a nonparticipant observation study. However, a number of other factors intrude to make either participant observation or nonparticipant observation the dominant procedure for each of the four types of observation shown in figure 10–1.

Observation may be either covert, with subjects unaware that they are being observed, or overt, with the observer visible to the subjects and the subjects aware that they are being observed. The major problem with overt observation is that it may be reactive. That is, it may make the subjects ill at ease and cause them to act differently than they would if they were not being observed.

In a natural setting it is difficult for the researcher who wishes to be covert not to act as a participant. If the researcher does not participate, there is little to explain his or her presence, as he or she is very obvious to the actual participants, can affect their behavior, and can, in effect, change a natural setting into an unnatural one. In addition, structured studies generally necessitate the use of some sort of checklist to record frequencies of behavior. Unlike a less-structured study, in which the observer can attempt to remember what occurs during the day while posing as a participant observer and then record these general impressions in privacy at night, structured observation requires counting frequencies. These numbers generally must be recorded immediately, an act difficult to perform during participant observation without arousing suspicion. Thus structured studies in the natural setting tend to be nonparticipant studies. The overall conclusion is that most studies in a natural setting are unstructured participant observations studies (field studies) (cell 1 of figure 10.1) and structured studies in a natural setting generally tend to be nonparticipant studies (cell 3 of figure 10.1), but are much rarer than the field studies.

Much the opposite is true in an artificial environment: Since there is no natural setting, in a sense none of the persons being studied are really participants of long standing, and thus they may accept a nonparticipant observer more easily. Also, in a laboratory setting it is much easier for a nonparticipant observer to remain undetected. For example, it would be difficult for a nonparticipant observer studying the everyday activities of a street gang in its natural setting, to remain undetected by the gang. But many artificial laboratory settings are equipped with one-way mirrors so that a nonparticipant can observe the subjects from the next room without being detected. Such a laboratory setting also enables a nonparticipant observer to use sophisticated equipment such as videotape and tape recordings. Videotape can be used through a one-way mirror without disturbing the subjects. Thus most studies in an artificial laboratory setting will be structured and will be nonparticipant observation studies (cell 4 of figure 10.1), but we will discuss one unstructured laboratory study (cell 2 of figure 10.1) later in this chapter.

The major steps in observation are:

1. Decide upon the goals of the study.
2. Decide upon the group for subjects to be observed.
3. Gain entry to the group (or, in the case of laboratory observation, arrange to have the subjects enter the laboratory).
4. Gain rapport with the subjects being studied.
5. Conduct the study by observing and recording field notes over a period of weeks, months, or even years.
6. Deal with crises that occur, such as confrontations with subjects who think you are some sort of spy.
7. Exit from the observational study.
8. Analyze the data
9. Write a report presenting the findings.

Field Studies

Those studies generally labeled as field studies are among the least structured of the four types of observational study shown in the typology of figure 10–1. They take place in a natural setting, use participant observation (in most cases), and have very little structure imposed upon the setting by the observer. Instead, the observer attempts to become a part of the subculture or culture he or she is studying. The term "field study" is often used almost simultaneously with the term "ethnographic study" or "ethnography."

Ethnography is defined by Spradley and McCurdy (1972, p. 3) as "The task of describing a particular culture." Ethnography is the predominant method used by cultural anthropologists interested in studying relatively primitive cultures, such as Margaret Mead's *Coming of Age in*

Samoa. However, the ethnographic method is also being used increasingly within complex societies such as America to study subcultural groups. One example is Spradley's *You Owe Yourself a Drunk* (1970), an ethnographic study of urban skid-row inhabitants. A number of other examples of urban ethnographies are provided by Spradley and McCurdy (1972), including ethnographies of an urban jewelry store, older people, hitchhiking, a car-theft ring, airline stewardesses, and fire fighters.

Since the purpose of the ethnographic method is simply to describe a particular culture, the ethnographer generally has few hypotheses and no structured questionnaire. Rather than proving any specific hypotheses, his or her goal is a general one: to describe the culture or subculture in as much detail as possible, including language, customs, values, religious ceremonies, and laws. Generally this requires that the observer become, if possible, a participant observer. In fact, the researcher's goal in many ethnographic studies is actually to resocialize himself or herself into the culture that he or she is attempting to describe. The researcher attempts to forget what he or she has been taught about his or her own culture and to become a part of the culture he or she is studying. Obviously, one generally cannot be completely resocialized. Indeed, in many cases the tribe, society, or subculture being studied will ultimately label the researcher an outsider who is not allowed full tribal membership and may not permit him or her even to live in the city or to pitch his or her tent among theirs. Nevertheless, some ethnographers do become resocialized to such an extent that they think like persons of the culture they are studying in the language of that culture, dream in that language, and have severe readjustment problems when returning to their own culture.

Gaining Entry

Nine general steps in field studies were listed above. The first step, deciding the goals of the study, is more or less the same for all field studies: understanding and describing the particular culture as completely as possible, although each observer may have particular interests he or she wishes to emphasize. The second step, deciding which group to study, is purely the decision of the researcher. Groups of theoretical interest, or of particular interest to the researcher for some personal reason, are the obvious choices, as are groups that have not already been overstudied.

Steps three (gaining entry to the group to be studied) and four (achieving rapport with persons studied) require more discussion. In attempting to gain entry, the researcher generally has the same problems of legitimizing himself or herself as does the survey researcher. In some cases, access may be facilitated through friendship with the person to be observed (Hoffman 1980). In general though, the observer will be dealing with strangers. The researcher must have some affiliation (e.g., with a university or research company) that gives him or her a purpose for conducting the study. He or she should have credentials (such as a university degree) that show he or she is capable of conducting such a study. He or she should have a letter of identification that shows he or she is legitimate and has no ulterior motives such as sales or burglary.

Some organizations or subcultures in the field are much more open than others. There are a number of studies one can do either outdoors or in a public place, such as studying the inhabitants of a hobo district, a public park in which soapbox speakers and preachers are heard (e.g., Hyde Park in London) or the regulars at a bus station. In such studies it may not be necessary to get formal permission, although it may be helpful to secure the aid of an informant. Use of informants, or insiders who can explain things to the researcher, introduce him or her to others, and help him or her become socialized into the subculture, is standard practice in ethnographic studies. Many researchers approach informants directly (e.g., they walk up to someone in a park and introduce themselves). However, this is often a difficult way to gain informants, as many persons will reject such advances from a stranger. For this reason it is often preferable, if possible, to secure informants through a middleman. A middleman is some person who knows both the researcher and the potential informant and can introduce the former to the latter. Spradley and McCurdy (1972, p. 48) say that use of a middleman is the best way to find an informant.

Other groups, cultures, or organizations that one might wish to study are much more closed to the public, and permission is necessary before they may be studied. Such organizations again require, as in survey research, that the investigator have an institutional affiliation, letters of identification, and a good reason for conducting the study. In addition, it is helpful if the researcher has had previous experience conducting such studies, or if the present study can be represented (legitimately) as only a portion of a larger study. As in studies of more open situations, it is helpful to have a middleman to make the initial introduction. Johnson (1975), in the field study of county welfare organizations, combined a number of strategies to gain entrance. Since he wished to study a number of different welfare offices, he began with an agency in which he had a contact. After conducting research at this office, he approached another and larger office, also with a contact or middleman, but this time he used the rationale that the study at this office was part of a larger study already "in progress." The fact that other offices have approved the same study takes some of the burden for the decision off the persons in charge. In the first agency an informant personalized the request by "walking it through," meaning that the request was not delivered through regular channels such as mail, messenger, or chain of command, but instead was carried personally to the administrator's desk by the contact or middleman. Another procedure that proved to be effective for Johnson was to gain entry by stages. Originally he requested only a relatively small and short-term study. Then, after he gained entry he was able to make requests that the study be extended. As Johnson puts it:

> In summary, the initial letter of introduction stated the research purposes in general terms and used a minimum request for clearance. After clearance, it was possible to tender other requests for additional clearances and information. The viability of this strategy was noted by the assistant director of the county in which the Metro office was located. She stated that, from her previous experience, rejections of researcher proposals occurred at the point of initial contact with the agency. Subsequent requests were rarely denied when the researcher had already gained an initial clearance, or when research was already in progress (Johnson 1975, p. 66).

The observer must realize that, from the point of view of the administrator, if he or she grants permission to conduct the study he or she may have everything to lose and little to gain. Many times the study will yield few benefits for the administrator. On the other hand, the presence of an outside observer can disrupt or slow the daily routine of work activities and can damage morale if employees think that the observer is a management spy. Further, the observer can hurt the administrator's career by making allegations of waste, inefficiency, discrimination, or scandal within the organization. Lofland (1971) says that it is typical for a known observer to gain entrance through a contact in the organization. He concludes:

> Indeed, I wonder if it is not relatively rare for an observer to go previously unknown to the gatekeepers of a setting and to simply enter as a known observer. It perhaps occurs most often when the persons to be observed are socially defined as less than full persons, as in the case with children and other incarcerated populations (Lofland 1971, p. 95).

Entry can be particularly difficult if one wishes to study a deviant group of some sort (West 1980). In addition, instances where research subjects must be informed of the nature and consequences of the study can play havoc with observational studies as well as questionnaire studies. Many respondents will not return a questionnaire with a long, stern consent form on it. Likewise, participant "covert" observers can hardly display a long consent form to be signed before the observation begins. Fortunately, recent changes in government regulations have limited informed consent in observation studies basically only to those instances involving criminal activity or harmful (or very sensitive) activity. We shall discuss ethics of research, including informed consent, in more detail in chapter 17, on ethics. For further discussion of informed consent in field work see Wax (1980) and Thorne (1980).

Gaining Rapport

Step four, achieving rapport, can be the most difficult and time-consuming task in field research. Indeed, it can be traumatic, but is necessary if valid data are to be obtained. One major problem is that the observer often, at least initially, will not understand fully the language, customs, and habits of the person being studied. Thus it may be easy to commit a severe breach of norms without realizing it. Such a mistake can offend one's hosts and damage the potential success of the study. Violation of local customs is not the only pitfall awaiting the neophyte observer. Persons being studied may also think the observer is a spy for the administration, the police, or some governmental agency.

An example of a field study in which the task of gaining rapport was extremely difficult is Wax's (1971) study in a Japanese relocation camp during World War II. After the Japanese attack on Pearl Harbor, all West Coast Japanese were placed by the United States government in relocation centers. Wax began her fieldwork at the Gila center in Arizona. In addition to the usual problems encountered by field workers, such as loneliness and unfamiliarity with the language and customs, she encountered additional problems. She was in a hostile environment since many of the Japanese in the center were loyal Americans who were bitter about being incarcerated, losing most of their property, and being separated from relatives. Since the camp was run by the United States government, the inhabitants naturally considered Wax to be a government spy. In addition, the camp was in the Arizona desert and she began field work in the summer when the temperature was as high as 120°. Further, she was a beginner at field work.

Wax (1971, p. 71) says, "Week followed week without any noticeable improvement in my 'rapport' or my reports." Finally she became so depressed that she took long walks in the stifling heat and cried. "I ate in a kind of desperation—until the sweat rolled down my face and body. In three months I gained thirty pounds." But Wax persevered, and by a combination of factors, including the arrival of a Japanese anthropologist who could help her, the pursuit of "red herring" studies that were of no interest to her boss but made her appear to be a researcher rather than a spy, and study of the Japanese language, she was able to continue her work until she became sufficiently socialized into the Japanese culture that she was able to develop rapport. Wax says:

> By undergoing this gradual process of instruction and resocialization I had found out things about the Japanese Americans and their situation which made it impossible that I ever again approach or talk to them in the way I had approached and talked to them three or four months before. In this sense I had become a different person, a person who could never go back to being what she had been before (Wax 1971, p. 79).

Wax believes strongly in the development of reciprocal relationships of trust between field worker and hosts as a prerequisite for the proper socialization of the field observer:

> Indeed, the process of involvement is circular and cumulative. The less anxious a fieldworker is, the better he works, and, as he becomes aware that he is doing good work, he becomes less anxious. Usually the essential factor in this transformation is the assistance and support—the reciprocal social response—given him by some of his hosts (Wax, 1971, p. 20).

For further discussion of gaining access, maintaining relationships, and exiting from the study, see Shaffir, Stebbins, and Turowetz (1980). Also, for a comprehensive discussion of the problems of entering the field, as well as the ethics of entry, see Burgess (1984, pp. 31–77).

Observing and Recording

Once rapport is gained, step five consists of observing and recording data. The notes taken by the researcher during the course of ethnographic research are called *field notes* (or *fieldnotes*). Emerson et al. (1994) note the *dual character* of field notes. They say that field notes inevitably must combine two elements: (1) what seems important to those naturally in the field (the people being studied); and (2) what seems important to the researcher himself or herself. Thus, while the field notes are about the people being studied, they also reflect and convey the ethnographer's understanding of these events. Emerson et al. (1994) emphasize that it is only in interaction with others that the ethnographer learns about the culture. Further, the person being studied should be seen not as an isolated entity, but as a person in active relations and exchanges with others. Thus, Emerson et al. (1994) recommend writing field notes in ways that preserve these *sequences of interaction*. This entails giving priority to preserving interactional details, which often means contemporaneous recording of details, or writing field notes as soon and as fully as possible after events have occurred. Lofland (1971, p. 102) recommends that even if one is a known observer, "The general rule of thumb is 'don't jot conspicuously'" when taking field notes. Note taking can make the subjects self-conscious and cause them to act abnormally. An unknown observer may be unable to take any notes at all, and may have to rely on his or her memory. In such a situation the observer may find mnemonics, or memory cues, helpful. Most observers prefer, if possible, to jot down notes during the day and write their full field notes at night. Also, it is sometimes possible to use recording devices during the day and transcribe the tapes later. The jotted notes consist of key words, important quotes, or phrases and memory cues. The events of the day will also remind the observer of earlier, unrecorded occurrences or utterances, and such events should be noted for future recording.

As for the full field notes, Lofland (1971, pp. 104–6) has some suggestions for field workers. He recommends:

1. Record the notes as quickly as possible after observation, since the quantity of information forgotten is very slight over a short time period but accelerates quickly as more time passes.
2. Discipline yourself to write notes quickly and reconcile yourself to the fact that although it may seem ironic, recording of field notes can be expected to take as long as is spent in actual observation.
3. Dictating rather than writing is acceptable if one can afford it, but writing has the advantage of stimulating thought.
4. Typing field notes is vastly preferable to handwriting because it is faster and easier to read, especially when making multiple copies.
5. It is advisable to make at least two copies of field notes and preferable to type on a master for reproduction. One original copy is retained for reference and other copies can be used as rough draft to be cut up, reorganized, and rewritten.

The field notes should contain a day-by-day account of what transpired; that is, what is happening, when it happened, to whom it is happening, what is being said, who is saying it and to whom, and what changes are occurring in the physical surroundings. More specifically, Lofland (1971, pp. 104–6) lists five components of field notes: (1) running description; (2) previously forgotten happenings that are now recalled; (3) analytical ideas and inferences; (4) personal impressions and feelings; and (5) notes for further information. Lofland offers this advice for writing running descriptions:

Be concrete. Rather than summarizing or employing abstract adjectives and adverbs, attempt to be behavioristic and concrete. Attempt to stay at the lowest possible level of inference. Avoid, as much as possible, employing the participants' descriptive and interpretative terms as one's own descriptive and interpretative terms. If person A thought person B was happy, joyous, depressed, or whatever, today, report this as the imputation of person A. Try to capture person B's raw behavioral emissions, leaving aside for that moment any final judgment as to B's "true state" or the "true meaning" of his behavior. The participant's belief as to the "true meaning" of objects, events and people are thus recorded as being just that (Lofland 1971, p. 105).

In addition to information originally regarded as important but simply forgotten due to a hectic schedule, interruptions, or the necessity to record even more important information first, the observer occasionally will conclude that some earlier happening, which at the time seemed

LIVERPOOL JOHN MOORES UNIVERSITY
LEARNING & INFORMATION SERVICES

too unimportant to record, takes on added consequence in the light of new events. For example, a citizen may observe a stranger in the vicinity of his or her apartment building but attach no importance to this observance until he or she learns at a later date that his or her apartment has been burglarized. Similarly, the security guard working at the Watergate on the night of the famous political break-in found a door lock taped open but attached little meaning to it at the time, reasoning that an engineer or maintenance man had probably taped the lock and forgotten to remove the tape at the end of his working day. This single incident did not assume enough importance in his mind for him to report it to police. However, after he removed the tape and later found it replaced, the sequence of tapings increased the significance of the incident in his mind and motivated him to call the police.

Analytic ideas and inferences are the observer's ideas about such details as the theme of the study, the most important things observed, and the organization and classification of the data; in short, any ideas about the analysis of the data that occur to the observer during the course of the study, such as speculation about the causal importance of certain variables or about the way chapters of the final report should be organized, or perhaps even ideas about future observational studies. Lofland (1971) advises including all such thoughts in the field notes, recording them as they occur even if they do not seem very important at the time. He recommends that they be clearly designated as the observer's analytic ideas and inferences, perhaps by separating them from the strictly observational details by means of brackets. Such ideas can greatly facilitate subsequent analysis of the data.

We noted earlier that survey research involves a secondary relationship between interviewer and interviewee that lasts only a short period of time (generally an hour or less) and is primarily a purposeful (secondary) rather than a friendship (primary) relationship. In contrast, participant observation takes place over a longer period of time and generally involves primary relationships between the observer and the persons being observed. Such relationships involve not only emotions such as love and hate on the part of the persons being observed, which are duly recorded in the field notes, but also the emotions of the observer. One of the chief advantages of the observational method is that the observer's emotional involvement can lead him or her to understand the true feelings of the persons observed, and thus allow him or her to analyze and explain their behavior. However, it is also important that the biasing effects of the observer's emotions be kept in mind. Thus the observer should keep a record of his or her own feelings and emotions at all times. As with the analytical ideas, personal emotional notes should be kept separate from the other observational data, either by using brackets or, preferably, by recording them in a private diary.

One reason for the observer to record his or her own feelings is because, as a participant in the events, the observer is not only a researcher but also his or her own research subject. Thus his or her feelings and behavior constitute data in their own right. A second reason is to enable the researcher to analyze his or her own emotions and reactions for possible sources of bias. If the observer sees months later that he or she recorded feelings of love for person A, hate for person B, and envy toward person C, he or she can use these data in analyzing his or her observations of the actions of persons A, B, and C, and can attempt to see whether personal feelings toward these persons biased his or her account of their actions.

The fifth component of the field notes consists simply of jotted notes on things that remain to be done, such as things to look for or other persons to be observed.

Lofland also provides a number of suggestions concerning such details as length of the field notes and style of writing. Since the length of the field notes will obviously depend upon such things as what (and how large a group) is being observed and the written style of the observer, it is difficult to give a general rule concerning length. However, Lofland suggests that:

> One possible rule of thumb is that the notes ought to be full enough adequately to summon up for one again, months later, a reasonably vivid picture of any described event. This probably means that one ought to be writing up, at the very minimum, at least a couple of single-spaced typed pages for every hour of observation (Lofland 1971, p. 107).

Lofland adds that once the observer has written field notes for a while, the procedure often gets to be a habit. Many experienced researchers become compulsive about writing down every detail lest it be lost, since to lose information causes feelings of guilt on the part of the observer. And finally Lofland (1971, p. 108) cautions the neophyte observer not to expect field work to be exciting all of the time, noting that if field notes made interesting and exciting reading they would be published (generally they are not). In fact, it is because field notes often tend to be boring, rambling, and difficult to generalize from that data analysis (of the field notes) becomes necessary. Lofland also cautions that it is often when informants treat the observer as a friend and confidant rather than as a researcher that they will reveal their innermost feelings and make their most intimate and unbiased statements. Unfortunately, since the informant is trusting him or her so completely, the observer may feel a strong sense of guilt about recording a potentially damaging statement in the field notes. For further discussion of the preparation of field notes see Whyte (1984), Lofland and Lofland (1984), and Burgess (1984).

Dealing with Crises

Confrontations between the observer and those being observed are not unusual. As Wax says:

> Even under the best of circumstances, an impartial study of any institution or social system is going to be perceived by its officials or functionaries as a criticism. When these men are in fact engaged in activities of dubious legality or morality, they will be even more hostile to the conduct of independent research. And this is exaggerated when fear is present, especially the fear that those who have been victimized are organizing themselves to challenge their authority (Wax 1971, p. 358).

In addition to fear from those in charge, lower-level employees may confront the observer with the charge that he or she is a management spy. Wax proposes three strategies for dealing with such problems. The first is to appear humble and powerless so that persons in the organization being observed will not perceive you as a threat. This is the strategy Wax used in studying the Japanese relocation center. As a young, single female without much research experience, she probably was not considered much of a threat.

The second strategy that Wax proposes is the opposite of the first; to appear so powerful and prestigious that authorities and others are afraid to challenge you. This can be done by gaining the support of high officials who have a great deal of political power. This is the strategy used by Wax and her husband in their study of the Thrashing Buffalo reservation, which they entered with the endorsement of the Commissioner of Indian Affairs. Wax's third strategy is first to enter the research setting and then align oneself with the most powerful group operating within this setting. But Wax (1971, p. 359) says, "In general, I have found this mode of procedure uncongenial and I cannot honestly discuss its merits."

Data Analysis

Exiting from a field-study setting (step seven) is generally not nearly as difficult as entering: Since it is routine, we need not spend much time discussing it. However, steps eight and nine, analyzing and writing up the data, are important and deserve discussion. Nominal measurement (discussed in chapter 4) consists of constructing mutually exclusive and exhaustive categories. Usually these categories are described by labels, names, or descriptive terms rather than by numbers. For example, colors can be classified nominally as black, red, blue, and so on, or gender can be divided into male and female. The vast majority of field researchers analyze their data by constructing sets of nominal categories rather than by assigning numbers.

Such nominal categories or labels are generally applied to the person being studied in order to delineate meaningful social types. In many cases these labels or categories are constructed by the persons being studied and used to describe themselves. The observer can, of course, invent his or her own terms to classify people in a way meaningful to him or her, or may classify them by means of standard sociological concepts or labels. Spradley, in his study of hoboes, found that the men classified themselves. As he notes (Spradley and McCurdy 1972, pp. 63–65), the public and researchers have a number of names for hoboes, such as bums, vagrants, drunks or homeless men. The men themselves have a set of some 16 categories for distinguishing different types of homeless men. The generic term they use for themselves is not hobo, but tramp. There are eight different types of tramps: ding, boxcar tramp, bindle stiff, working stiff, airedale, home guard tramp, mission stiff, and rubber tramp. These different types are based on several underlying variables, such as method of travel (boxcar tramp versus bindle stiff) and means of subsistence (working stiff versus mission stiff). There is another level of distinction or subtypes; e.g., working stiffs are further divided into five different subtypes—harvest tramp, tramp miner, fruit tramp, construction tramp, and sea tramp—while mission stiffs are further divided into subtypes of nose diver versus professional nose diver. Such sets of categories, based on more than one dimension or variable, are called *taxonomies* or *typologies*. In addition to taxonomies, ethnographic data are often represented in flowcharts that show historical or temporal development.

Thus the chief job of data analysis in field studies consists basically of summarizing the field notes by means of taxonomies or flowcharts. In the case of taxonomies constructed by the persons who are being observed, such as the tramps' taxonomy of themselves, the observer's job becomes one of reporting. In the case of a taxonomy constructed by the researcher, the task of analysis becomes somewhat more difficult, since the researcher must invent names for the various categories and decide what to include and what to leave out.

Examples of various taxonomies from Spradley and McCurdy (1972) include: (1) things for sale in a jewelry store, e.g., rings, costume jewelry, watches, with costume jewelry further divided into hippie junk and mod stuff; (2) things teachers do at school (slam kids' heads down on desks, send kids to office—Davis 1972); (3) people from a Jehovah's Witness perspective (Mann 1972). Examples of flowcharts from Spradley and McCurdy (1972) include stages in witnessing among Jehovah's Witnesses: (1) introduce oneself; (2) witness, give sermon; (3) demonstrate Bible study; (4) invite to meeting; (5) if rejected, offer book (from Mann 1972). Another flowchart by Carlson (1972) show stages in the hitchhiking cycle (getting ready, planning the departure, places to hitch, stopping a vehicle, getting dumped, then either crashing or reaching a destination). Examples of a taxonomy and a flowchart from Spradley and McCurdy (1972) are shown in figures 10–2 and 10–3. For more examples of ways to present the results of the ethnography in written form see Spradley and McCurdy (1972), Hammersly and Atkinson (1983), Burgess (1984), Lofland and Lofland (1984), and Whyte (1984).

Completely Structured Observation

The kind of field study just discussed is completely unstructured. It has no preconstructed hypotheses and no structured measurement instrument. It takes place in a natural setting and does not quantify data. Such a study is an example of cell 1 of our typology of observational studies (figure 10.1). the polar opposite of cell 1 is the completely structured study of cell 4. Completely structured studies take place in a laboratory rather than in the natural environment. Structured observation of this sort is like the survey in that it attempts to test hypotheses, which

Figure 10–2
Taxonomy of Roles of Kids in the Classroom

Roles of Kids in the Classroom	Lunchers	Cold (bag) lunchers Hot lunchers People who go home for lunch
	Officers	President Vice president Secretary Treasurer
	Helpers	Weather Sports News Milk Patrol Door captains Lavatory captains Erasers Messenger

SOURCE: From *The Cultural Experience* by James P. Spradley and David W. McCurdy. Published in 1972 by Science Research Associates, Inc. Reprinted by permission of the authors.

Figure 10–3

Flowchart of Stages of Witnessing among Jehovah's Witnesses

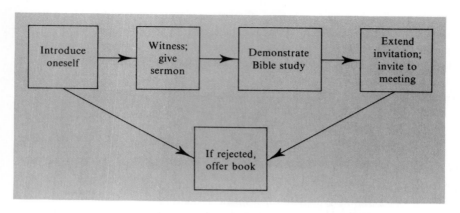

SOURCE: From *The Cultural Experience* by James P. Spradley and David W. McCurdy. Published in 1972 by Science Research Associates, Inc. Reprinted by permission of the authors.

requires a standardized instrument. In completely structured observation the instrument is a checklist of items to be observed rather than a questionnaire.

However, in order for the different groups observed at different times to be comparable in terms of observational categories, it is necessary that these groups be as identical as possible. This is done by standardizing the laboratory so that laboratory conditions are identical at all times. While it may be possible in some observational studies to assign persons randomly to groups, often this is not done. Where assignment is not random, the purposes of the study are usually formulated in such a way that a substantial degree of closure, as defined in chapter 9, can be assumed. That is, the nature of the phenomenon being studied (the dependent variable) is assumed to be unaffected by the artificial environment or by the various characteristics on which some of the persons observed may differ, such as age, sex, and skin color. In other words, all uncontrolled variables are assumed to have no effect on the behavior being studied.

The most famous example of a completely structured study is Bales's method for studying group interaction. On the basis of a large number of preliminary observational studies Bales assumed that groups involved in decision making or problem solving would have common elements in their interaction that are constant enough to be predictable. Bales not only knew from experience what common elements to look for in terms of standard categories, but could also write hypotheses predicting certain behaviors to occur. Bales says:

> One of our basic assumptions is that there are certain conditions which are present to an important degree not only in special kinds of groups doing special kinds of problems, but which are more or less inherent in the nature of the process of interaction of communication itself, whenever or wherever it takes place. . . . We have used averages of large numbers of cases to help us form hypotheses as to what such tendencies of interaction systems might be,

and have then tried to set up conditions in the laboratory, in the form of a certain type of task, of personnel, etc., which will produce actual results like our averages (Bales 1952, p. 146).

All observational subjects involved in Bales's study are asked to imagine themselves as staff members who have been requested by their boss to examine a human-relations case and advise him or her as to why the people in the case are behaving the way they are. A summary of the case is given to each person to read. The subjects are then placed in a special room to decide what they should tell the fictitious boss. The observers watch from an adjacent room through a one-way mirror.

The categories used in observation are shown in figure 10–4 (reproduced from Bales 1952). Each category is one of a pair. There are six problems that each group is expected to encounter, with each pair of observational categories corresponding to one of the six problem areas. For example, categories 6 and 7 refer to problems of orientation, categories 5 and 8 refer to problems of evaluation, categories 4 and 9 refer to problems of control, categories 3 and 10 refer to problems of decision making, categories 2 and 11 refer to problems of tension management, and categories 1 and 12 refer to problems of integration.

Each observer is behind the one-way mirror and so cannot be seen by the subjects. Thus he or she is free to code his or her observations without affecting the behavior being observed. Coding is done on a sheet that lists all 12 categories. Generally there are about five persons in a group. Each is given a number, 1 through 5, with 0 indicating the entire group. Each interaction is coded in one of the 12 categories by noting the number of the person who initiated the interaction (e.g., 2) and the number of the person to whom it was directed (e.g., 5, or 0 if directed toward the entire group). After all interactions are recorded, percentages can be computed as with closed-ended survey questions.

Table 10–1 provides an example of the way data from completely structured observation can be quantified. First the total number of acts recorded is computed. In table 10.1 the total is 719 acts for all 12 categories. Then the number of acts in each of the 12 categories can be divided by the total in order to compute the percentage of the total acts that are in each respective category. For example, table 10.1 shows that almost three-quarters (74 percent) of all recorded acts fall in three categories: agrees, gives opinion, gives orientation. In contrast, the three categories of shows solidarity, asks for suggestion, and shows antagonism account for a total of only 1.5 acts out of every 100 (1.5 percent).

While the survey as we discussed it was basically limited to questions whereas Bales's method is limited to observation, completely structured observation with an instrument such as the Bales category checklist is structurally very similar to survey research with closed-ended questions. Bales's method is probably less reactive or even nonreactive, as the observers are not seen, but both use highly structured instruments that focus the data gathered and prevent the accumulation of superfluous or unimportant data. In both cases the highly structured instrument can also force the data into an unnatural mold. Just as a closed-ended question can force a respondent's answer into a choice of words that he or she would not normally use, it is possible that some of the acts observed in Bales's studies could be more appropriately described in some category other than these 12, but must be forced into one of the 12 because the appropriate category is missing. In Bales's defense it must be pointed out that the categories evolved from long experience and that Bales at one time used more than 50 categories (Selltiz et al. 1959, p. 224).

Figure 10–4

The Bales System of Categories for Recording Group Interaction

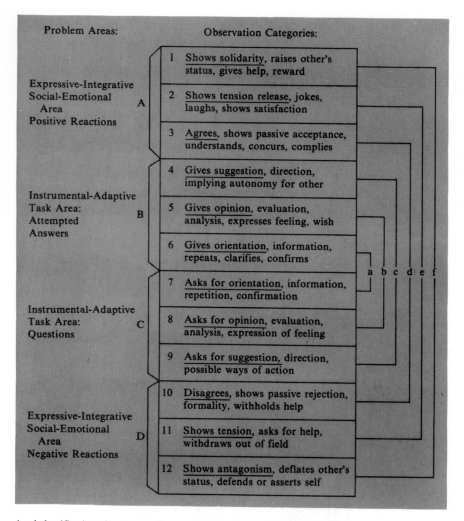

A subclassification of system problems to which each pair of categories is most relevant:

a Problems of orientation   d Problems of decision
b Problems of evaluation   e Problems of tension-management
c Problems of control   f Problems of integration

SOURCE: "Some Uniformities of Behavior in Small Social Systems," by Robert F. Bales, in Guy E. Swanson et al. (eds.), *Readings in Social Psychology*, Revised Edition, New York: Holt, 1952, p. 149. Reprinted with permission.

Table 10–1

Profiles of "Satisfied" Group on Case
Discussion Task (in percent)

Category	Satisfied
1. Shows solidarity	.7
2. Shows tension release	7.9
3. Agrees	24.9
4. Gives suggestion	8.2
5. Gives opinion	26.7
6. Gives orientation	22.4
7. Asks for orientation	1.7
8. Asks for opinion	1.7
9. Asks for suggestion	.5
10. Disagrees	4.0
11. Shows tension	1.0
12. Shows antagonism	.3
Raw score total	719

Source: R. F. Bales (1952) in *Readings in Social Psychology,* rev. ed., edited by G. E. Swanson et al. New York: Holt, Rinehart & Winston. Reprinted with permission.

The completely structured observational study and the survey using closed-ended questions are also similar in that problems of coding data are minimized (in effect, coding is done when the categories of the questionnaire or observation schedule are constructed), quantification of data being thus facilitated. Completely unstructured studies, such as field studies, and survey using open-ended questions are alike in that they are both less likely to force the data into artificial or unnatural categories. However, both methods run the risk of promulgating so much data that summarizing them or presenting them for analysis becomes difficult. Such data are generally qualitative, may be subjective, and may not be consistent enough to facilitate quantification.

While the nine stages of observation already discussed apply to any observational study, including completely structured studies, studies such as Bales's avoid most of the problems arising in field studies (centered around problems of interaction between the observer and those being observed) simply by virtually eliminating communication or interaction of any sort between observer and subjects. The observer in such a study has no problems of achieving rapport or handling confrontations since he or she is behind a one-way mirror and totally unperceived by the subjects. A possible difference in procedure concerns the entry problem. In a completely structured study the entry problem does not entail an observer's entering an organization, but rather involves finding persons willing to participate in such a study. The problems are roughly the same as for survey studies, so a complete discussion is not necessary. Basically, as in a survey, the observer must convince the potential subjects that he or she is legitimate and his or her research is worthwhile. This is generally accomplished by having an affiliation with a university or other research organization, by possessing proper identification, such as a formal letter of identification, and by preparing a statement of the purpose of the study. While it may be impossible to inform subjects of the exact goals of the study without inciting bias, it is important to assure them that the study has no harmful effects. Once the investigator has established his or her credibility, he or she can either use captive audience subjects, such as students, induce persons to cooperate by convincing them of the scientific value of the study, or pay them a nominal wage for participating.

Semistructured Study

A researcher wishing to capture the rigor and ability to quantify that is afforded by the structured study, but not wishing the accompanying artificiality, might conduct a study in a natural setting (as in a field study) using a structured observational instrument (as in Bales's method). Such a semistructured study is an example of cell 3 of our typology. A combination of structured and unstructured studies will have not only the advantage of each (ability to quantify and natural setting) but also the disadvantages of each. Most adherents of completely unstructured studies such as the field study would probably say that their greatest advantage lies in allowing the observer to be immersed in the subject's culture and to see the world through the subject's perspective rather than his or her own. They might argue that use of a set of structured observational categories designed by the research means that the subject's natural social world is seen through the observer's artificial structure rather than through the participant's natural structure, thus destroying the basic advantage of the field method.

On the other hand, adherents of the completely structured observational method might argue that such a semistructured method will encounter problems of reactivity. That is, the presence of the observer will bias the data since there is little opportunity in a natural environment for the observer to be hidden from the subjects, in contrast to the one-way mirror used in the laboratory. Further, with structured observation requiring on-the-spot recording and coding, it is difficult for the observer to maintain secrecy if he or she wishes to operate in disguise. In addition, the natural setting makes control of extraneous variables more difficult and damages comparability from one study to the next, since it is unlikely that any two natural settings will be exactly the same. Some of these disadvantages can often be partially overcome.

The reactivity problems can be dealt with by selecting children as observational subjects. Although children also tend to be self-conscious in the presence of an observer and thus to act unnaturally, generally they forget the presence of the observer, or at least become accustomed to his or her presence, faster than do adults, and thus tend not to remain self-conscious as long as adults. Further, children are more accustomed than are adults to constant observation and supervision from adults.

Another way to decrease the disadvantages of the semistructured method is to use a setting that, while "natural" and definitely not an artificial laboratory, nevertheless provides the observer with some ability to control extraneous variables and some assurance that all persons being observed are subjected to approximately the same environmental influences or stimuli, at least during the time they are being observed. One way to achieve more structure in a natural setting is to observe indoors rather than outdoors. Appropriate indoor settings include school classrooms, club meeting rooms, and offices or work areas. A natural combination of these two ways to improve the semistructured method is to observe children in an indoor setting such as a classroom. Thus it is not surprising that a substantial number of the existing semistructured studies have been conducted in kindergarten or elementary-school classrooms.

One example is a study of nursery-school children by Sears, Rau, and Alpert (1965). Like Bales, Sears and associates developed their structured checklist of behavioral categories through experience, and discarded several categories that did not prove fruitful. The 29 categories retained are classified into five groups: (1) adult role, ten categories (e.g., real adult mannerisms, such as adult tone of voice, and fantasy adult mannerisms, such as dressing up in adult clothes); (2) dependency, five categories (e.g., negative attention getting and reassurance seeking); (3) antisocial aggression, nine categories (e.g., direct verbal or physical aggression); (4) prosocial aggression, three categories (e.g., verbal disapproval of behavior or tattling); and (5) self-stimulation, two categories (e.g., masturbation, such as handling the genital area, or rubbing against an object that provides genital stimulation). In addition to these 29 behavior categories, each observer recorded for each child: (1) its location in the nursery school (45 locations were numbered in advance on a map of the nursery school); (2) whether the child was alone or with others; (3) the object of the behavior category (for the adult role, aggression and dependence categories only); and (4) whether the teacher was present or absent (recorded for the aggression categories only). Sears et al. described the recording procedure as follows:

> Each observer was provided with a clipboard for BUO (Behavior Unit Observations) recordings. At the top of the clipboard was a battery-powered timing device that flashed a small bulb briefly every half-minute. The recording blank consisted of four rows of five boxes each. The observer followed his target child unobtrusively for a ten-minute period, and at each flash of the light made decisions about five matters, as they related to the preceding half-minute, and recorded a symbol for each in a box (Sears et al. 1965, p. 302).

Two types of scores were computed in the BUO study, individual category scores and summary or total scores. The study was conducted for seven weeks using four observers. The individual category scores were computed by first summing for each category the total number of times that category was recorded for a given child during the seven weeks by all four observers, then divided by the number of half-minute periods during which observation took place. This figure, representing the average number of observations per category per observational period, was expressed to three decimal places. Summary scores consisted of the total for each child, of all observations over the total period by all observers in all categories within each major division, divided by the number of half-minute periods.

One source of bias that can occur when an observer is rating the behavior of individuals is the so-called halo effect. Halo effect is the bias resulting from stereotyping the individual on the basis of an earlier rating, and then rating the individual in terms of the stereotype on subsequent behaviors. As Selltiz et al. (1976, p. 408) say, "Thus, if a rater considers a person to be shy and if that same rater believes shy people to be poorly adjusted, he or she is likely to rate the person poorly adjusted as well as shy." Unfortunately, as Kerlinger (1964, p. 517) notes, halo effect is extremely difficult to avoid and is often prevalent among traits that are not clearly defined, not easily observable, or morally important. It is important that the researcher be aware of the possibility of halo effect, and monitor raters periodically to check for its presence.

The general nature of a semistructured method in which a structured observational instrument is used but observation is conducted in a natural environment should now be clear. We shall turn now to the last cell (cell 2 of our typology of observational studies) and discuss semistructured studies in which the observational instrument is unstructured and flexible but the setting is structured (e.g., in a laboratory).

Unstructured Laboratory Study

One of the chief advantages of an observational study in which no structural set of categories is used is that it allows the persons being observed to structure the situation, and allows the observer to learn to view the world through his or her host's eyes. Such unstructured observation, as we have seen, is very useful in a natural setting, but generally requires a relatively long period. If a group of persons is placed in an artificial environment, such as a room with a one-way mirror, they certainly are not likely to carry on day-to-day activities that would give a clue to their culture. Further, they cannot be kept in this confined environment for very long. Thus most studies in an artificial environment are completely structured, such as the Bales (1952) studies in which persons are placed in a laboratory, given a specific task requiring a relatively short period of time, and observed by means of a structured set of observational categories.

However, a few unstructured studies have been conducted in a laboratory setting. One example of such a study is the use of play therapy for the treatment of emotionally disturbed children. In play therapy the child is placed in an artificial environment (a laboratory setting, often with a one-way mirror). In the sense that the room is equipped as a playroom, with a table and chairs, toys, paints, and so on, it may seem to the child to be a "natural" rather than an "artificial" environment. However, it is definitely artificial in the sense that the child is alone and unable to engage in interaction with other humans. Rather, he or she engages in artificial, hypothetical, or fantasy interaction with other persons, generally family members. Frequently a disturbed child has entered that state primarily because of his or her treatment by parents and siblings. The goal of play is basically therapeutic—to improve the emotional health of the patient. Thus the social-science knowledge gained by unstructured observation of the patient is a secondary goal.

A moving account of play therapy, based on the experience of an actual patient but with names changed to protect his identity, is the story of Dibs by Axline (1964). Dibs was unable to adjust in elementary school, either fighting violently or else going limp when time came to return home. He was diagnosed by a pediatrician as probably either psychotic or brain-damaged. However, when placed in play therapy and allowed to act out his aggressive feelings, his mental health improved greatly. The following account by Axline will provide some idea of just what the observer actually observes and hears:

> He walked over to the dollhouse and took out the mother doll. "What have you done to the boy?" he demanded of his doll. "What have you done to him? You are stupid and I have told you the same thing over and over and over again. Aren't you ashamed of yourself?" He carried the mother doll over to the sandbox. "You build me a mountain!" he demanded. "You stay right there and you build it and you do it right. The boy will stand guard to see that you do it right. You better be careful because I am watching you every minute. Oh God! Oh God! Why is he like this? What have I done to deserve it? You build that mountain and don't you tell me you can't do it. I'll show you how. I'll show you again and again and again. And you must do it" (Axline 1964, pp. 184–85).

Since this type of study is a combination of types of studies already discussed, its problems will be a combination of problems noted for the other studies and need not be repeated. Instead we can turn to an analysis of indirect observation.

Indirect Observation

Thus far in this chapter we have been discussing the direct observation of ongoing behavior. The advantages of direct observation are clear: The researcher witnesses the events firsthand as they occur and does not have to rely upon a secondary account of behavior, as in the case of survey research. However, cases sometimes arise in which the researcher is unable to observe persons directly; for example, because the persons are deceased, or are recluses or famous people who will not allow their privacy to be invaded, or because the behavior is discovered by the observer only after it has occurred and he or she had no way to learn the identity of the persons involved. Further, there are many cases in which the researcher does not want to be on the scene to observe or interview, for fear of changing the behavior of the persons he or she is trying to study. Such "reactivity" has been discussed in some detail previously (see chapter 2). The problem of reactivity has led to the development of unobtrusive or nonreactive research methods in which the behavior of the research subject is not changed because he or she does not know that the research is being conducted. Unobtrusive research methods entail a wide variety of techniques, including document analysis and direct observation through a one-way mirror, but most prominent are methods of indirect observation, which are nonreactive chiefly because the researcher is not physically present when the behavior is occurring. Unobtrusive measures are discussed at great length in Webb et al. (1966, 1981).

Unobtrusive measures are often suitable as alternatives for studying a particular phenomenon when the researcher desires to use multiple methods, with one measure serving as a check on the accuracy of another. For example, a researcher may conduct a survey to study racial prejudice, and find upon analyzing the results that all respondents report very low levels of discrimination. He or she might wish to check these results by conducting an unobtrusive study (perhaps by using a hidden camera) to see how the subjects react when approached for conversation by members of an ethnic minority. Some respondents who claim in the survey to be nonprejudiced may exhibit a substantial degree of prejudice in their behavior when they do not know that they are being observed. Some researchers (Webb et al. 1966; Smith 1975) speak of "triangulation," meaning that the correct data are gathered by comparison of the results of two or more methods. This term is derived from the process of triangulation in navigation, in which the correct position of a ship or airplane can be obtained by comparing its position with the position of two known navigational points. For further discussion of multiple measurement, see Lazarsfeld (1959), Webb et al. (1966), and Smith (1975).

Indirect observation as discussed here consists of observing physical traces or clues of past behavior that cannot be observed directly. Such indirect observation is familiar to all of us in the form of police investigations of criminal activity in which the perpetrators obviously work to avoid direct observation. Modern criminologists can re-create a great deal of past behavior by such techniques as chemical analysis of blood and other types of stains or soil analysis to determine a suspect's past whereabouts. Such detective work has also been applied (although relatively infrequently) in social-science research. The most careful social-science treatment of physical-trace research in social science is by Webb et al. (1966). They begin their chapter on physical traces by talking of Sherlock Holmes:

> The fog had probably just cleared. The singular Sherlock Holmes had been reunited with his old friend, Dr. Watson (after one of Watson's marriages), and both walked to Watson's newly acquired office. The practice was located in a duplex of two physician's suites, both of which had been for sale. No doubt sucking on his Calabash, Holmes summarily told Watson that he had made a wise choice in purchasing the practice that he did, rather than the one on the other side of the duplex. The data? The steps were more worn on Watson's side than on his competitor's (Webb et al. 1966, p. 35).

Webb et al. divide physical traces into two categories: erosion measures, in which the degree of selective wear on some material yields the measure (as in Holmes's example), and accretion measures, which are measures of the deposit of some material. In other words, the distinction between materials worn away (erosion) and materials deposited (accretion).

Erosion Measures

Erosion measures mentioned by Webb et al. include studying the wear of the floor around museum exhibits to see which exhibits are the most popular.

> A committee was formed to set up a psychological exhibit at Chicago's Museum of Science and Industry. The committee learned that the vinyl tiles around the exhibit containing live, hatching chicks had to be replaced every six weeks or so; tiles in other areas of the museum went for years without replacement. A comparative study of the rate of tile replacement around the various museum exhibits could give a rough ordering of the popularity of the exhibits (Webb et al. 1966, pp. 36–37).

Other possible studies of natural erosion include the study of wear on library books to see which are the most popular (Webb et al. 1966, p. 37). Controlled erosion studies discussed by Webb et al. include measuring the activity level of children by how quickly they wear out shoes or by having them wear self-winding watches adapted to record amount of movement.

Accretion Measures

Accretion measurement, including not only the measurement and analysis of soil layers but also the mapping and analysis of work sites, garbage dumps, kitchen middens, and so on, is central to the research of disciplines such as archeology and geology. If a researcher in geology can date a certain accretion layer (e.g., a lava flow), he or she can date other objects or layers in relation to it by determining whether they are above or below it. In archeology, much of our knowledge concerning such things as dietary habits of native American Indian cultures of several hundreds or thousands of years ago was obtained by studying accretion. By uncovering and studying layers of garbage we can learn what these people ate. Virtually these same techniques can be used to analyze the dietary habits of contemporary urban Americans by studying the contents of garbage cans.

Among accretion studies mentioned by Webb et al. (1966) are the familiar police methods, such as analysis of soil from shoes and clothing or detection of poisons such as arsenic in hair. Other studies involved the analysis of radio dial settings by garage mechanics to estimate the popularity of radio stations, a comparative observation of cars parked in women's dormitory parking lots with cars parked in men's dormitory parking lots to see whether women or men are more likely to lock their cars (the finding was that a significantly larger proportion of women locked their cars), and a study that estimated the number of people reading a particular printed advertisement by counting the number of different fingerprints on the page. Also noted was the archeological technique of estimating population size by size of floor areas in an excavated dwelling.

Other trace studies include the analysis of liquor bottles in trashcans in order to estimate whiskey consumption or liquor sales in a town in which no sales records are available because there are no liquor stores. Hughes (1958) talks about the analysis of garbage by janitors in Chicago:

> It is by the garbage that the janitor judges, and as it were, gets power over the tenants who high-hat him. Janitors know about hidden love-affairs by bits of torn-up letter paper; of impending financial disaster or of financial four-flushing by the presence of many unopened letters in the waste (Hughes 1958, p. 51).

Even the prestigious Kinsey (Kinsey et al. 1953) study used accretion measures in the form of graffiti on the walls of public toilets.

Other accretion studies measure the popularity of heroes by the volume of confetti used in a parade in their honor, and the popularity of television programs by the drop in water levels for the city during commercials. During very popular programs few people use the toilets between commercials, but during commercials water levels drop precipitously due to the widespread simultaneous flushing. A final accretion study example involves studying the comparative popularity of museum exhibits enclosed in glass by counting the number of nose prints left by children on the glass in front of each exhibit each day. The age of the children can be estimated by measuring the height of the nose prints.

Validity and Reliability

If a researcher is interested in gathering data on human actions, as opposed to beliefs, values, or opinions, direct observation of the act by the researcher would seem to have superior face validity over data collections by questionnaire (either mailed or interviewed) and document study. Both of the latter methods provide only secondary data processed through an intermediary (the questionnaire respondent or the author of the document) who actually witnessed the event and is relating it to the researcher. Events can change much in the telling and retelling, particularly if the occurrence is illegal or sensitive, or if the event occurred long ago and the respondent's memory has faded. Thus I think it safe to generalize that, all other things being equal, observation of an occurrence has greater face validity than a secondhand account gathered either through interviewing or document study as evidenced by the old adage. "Don't believe anything you hear and only half of what you see."

As that adage also indicates, observation is hardly perfect. The known fallibility of eyewitnesses in criminal jury trials will attest to this. There is a long list of possible factors that can damage the validity of direct observation. Most of these factors have been mentioned above, either directly or indirectly, but we can note some of the most important here.

Validity and Direct Observation

Lack of Anonymity.   We noted in chapters 7 and 8 that mailed questionnaire studies were more valid than interview studies for gathering sensitive data because respondents were more assured of anonymity in the former. With the exception of hidden observational studies (e.g., use of one-way mirrors), which have limited application, observation is often a face-to-face process in which the person being observed is careful to conduct himself or herself in an approved (legal) way. Thus, for sensitive data, a mailed questionnaire will probably be more valid than observation, since a person assured of anonymity may admit to behavior that he or she would not allow anyone to observe.

Social Reality as a Construct.   Social reality is partially a mental construct as well as a set of concrete phenomena, and what is observed is partially a picture of what is actually there and partially a picture of the observer's expectations, which are generally based on past observations. Thus, to a certain extent, each observer is not entirely impartial but is biased toward seeing what he or she expects to see (but not necessarily what he or she wants to see). If someone hands me a correct paragraph written in a foreign language unfamiliar to me, and a typewritten copy of that same paragraph that contains a number of typographical errors, I can compare the two copies and detect the discrepancies quite easily. My observational powers are not biased by prior expectations, since I do not know the language and have no idea of what I expect to see. However, if I am then handed a paragraph in English that I myself have written and have rewritten many times, I will have a more difficult time detecting typographical errors even when comparing it with a correct copy, because I know in advance what I am supposed to see and have trouble seeing otherwise.

Lack of Structure in the Observational Instrument.   This factor is closely related to the preceding factor. It is clear that one can easily see what one expects to see even if it is not there, thus causing bias; this is an example of selective perception. However, the opposite—complete lack of expectation of what is to be observed—can also lead to invalidity. Exponents of the field-study method eschew structured sets of categories because they wish to avoid causing the invalidity of the social reality construct by imposing an artificial structure on reality and thus seeing what they expect to see. They find their study more valid if the structure is imposed from within, by the persons being observed, rather than from without by the researcher.

This is a workable strategy, but it implies a considerable period of time for the study to be conducted in order for such an indigenous observational structure to emerge. At the genesis of research an observer without any structured observational categories (at least conscious ones) will see a little of everything but not much of anything. That is, if the observational environment contains a lot to be observed, with many things happening at once, the observer without specific characteristics on which to concentrate will observe an average of random observational sample from the total environment, but will miss specifics he or she might have noticed if he or she had focused upon them.

As an illustration, my wife and I frequently attend the monthly antique swap-meet at the Pasadena Rose Bowl, where hundred of dealers have booths presenting thousands of small antique items, many of them not currently manufactured and not familiar to the average person (especially a young person). Items for sale include everything from cylinders played on an Edison cylinder player (the precursor to the phonograph), to sharp pointed instruments for prying paper tops off milk bottles, to small spoons with a curved handle that were provided by the milkman for dipping cream off the top of milk bottles, to buttonhooks for buttoning button shoes (which could not easily be buttoned with just the fingers). The observer without a specific item to look for will see some of this and some of that. He or she will get an overall picture of the items, but will miss many specific articles that the trained specialist would spot. However, the trained specialist would see these items at the expense of others; that is, he or she will concentrate on seeing one item and look past the others.

Adequacy of Human Sense Organs.   Although the observer will generally prefer to see with his or her own eyes rather than receive someone else's secondhand account, he or she must realize the fallibility of his or her own sense organs. We have been talking throughout this book about the possible effects of our measuring instruments on the phenomenon being measured. However, we must not overlook the fact that the phenomenon being observed can affect the adequacy of our measuring instrument (our senses, especially vision and hearing). For example, when you walk from a darkened movie theater into the bright sunlight, the pupils of your eyes automatically contract so that less sunlight enters. This sort of adjustment to the environment is involuntary. While it can affect the individual's discriminatory powers, he or she generally has little or no control over it. Hearing is also subject to distortion, with one's ability to determine the origin of a sound largely dependent upon the direction in which one was facing when the sound occurred. To see that this is true, merely locate a noise (e.g., an alarm clock) in a fixed position some distance from you, and slowly turn around in a complete circle.

In addition to obvious conditions (such as lighting) that can affect observation, it is well known that a number of other factors such as fatigue, stress, and hunger can affect the quality of sensory perceptions. And, of course, one of the greatest elements is surprise. The reason many witnesses to crime cannot make clear identifications of suspects is that, because of fear coupled with surprise, they simply were not concentrating on the suspect. A former hired killer for organized crime reported that one of his most successful murders was committed in broad daylight at lunchtime in a crowded restaurant. Instead of a silencer, he purposely used a very loud gun. The noise was so unsuspected and frightening that, instead of concentrating on his identification, the witnesses concentrated on diving under tables for their own protection. Over a dozen people provided over a dozen different eyewitness descriptions of the gunman.

Measured Validity

In spite of all these potential pitfalls, observation seems to be the superior method for studying nonverbal behavior. It also seems a valid method, although it is impossible to generalize about validity for all the various types of observational method discussed above. Although the number of attempts to assess the validity of observation empirically has been relatively small, the validity of the method has definitely been demonstrated.

Vidich and Shapiro (1955) assessed the criterion validity of observation by a participant observer's rating of respondent's prestige. The sample consisted of 547 persons between the ages of 20 and 80 chosen at random, one from each household. The rural New York community had a total adult population of about 1,500. In addition to the observer's rating, a survey was conducted in which all respondents were asked five questions concerning prestige, including the person they would choose to represent their part of town at a meeting of the town board, the first three or four people they think of as overall leaders, and what person of the opposite sex they would consider to be a community leader.

The participant observer's ratings comprised 12 categories, from the lowest (deadbeats or nonentities whose existence was frequently not recognized) to the highest in money, prestige, and behind-the-scenes political control. These 12 categories were compared with the scores on the survey questions concerning prestige. Each person in the community received a score from zero to five, depending on how many of the five questions he or she was mentioned on.

Table 10–2 (adapted from Vidich and Shapiro 1955) shows a clear relationship between the observational data (structured observation) and survey data. Summing percentages down the columns, we see that 100 percent of respondents rated by the observer as being in one of the two lowest prestige categories scored in the 0 category on the survey, meaning that nobody listed them as being prestigious on any of the five questions; they failed to score even a single point. In contrast, only 7 percent of persons rated in the highest category by the observer failed to receive at least a point on any of the five survey questions. At the other extreme, 60 percent of respondents placed in the highest category by the observer scored five or more on the survey. The survey and the observational data are essentially in agreement as to who occupies the various prestige categories in the community.

Table 10–2

Correlation Between Participant Observer Classification
and Survey Research Classification of Prestige

Survey Research Ranking	*Participation Observer Ranking (Percentage)*								
	1–2	3	4	5	6	7	8–9	10–11	Not Known
0	100	87	79	63	64	54	36	7	88
1	0	7	15	21	18	14	10	7	4
2–4	0	7	4	8	14	18	21	27	5
5 or more	0	0	2	8	4	14	33	60	2
(N)	(20)	(61)	(53)	(24)	(72)	(56)	(39)	(15)	(207)

Source: A. J. Vidich and G. Shapiro (1955) in *American Sociological Review* 20 (February):31. Reprinted with the permission of the authors and the publisher. © American Sociological Association.

Validity of Indirect Observational Methods

Before turning to our discussion of reliability we might mention the validity of indirect observational methods, such as the erosion and accretion measures discussed above. Two major nonbiasing characteristics of indirect methods stem from their nonreactivity: (1) there is no observer present to bias the persons being observed; and (2) there is no artificial observational structure to bias the data. However, as Webb et al. (1966, p. 50) point out, the possibility of bias for erosion measures remains in the form of possible response sets. For example, a department store might relegate one staircase as the up staircase and another as the down staircase. Greater wear on the up staircase may not be due to greater traffic but simply to people asserting greater pressure on steps when going up than when going down, thus leading to increased wear.

The differential survival ability of different materials can also cause bias in erosion measures. The fact that the stairs to one business are worn more than the stairs to another may not mean that the one with worn stairs has more business, but only that its stairs were made from softer wood, or that the building is older and has been exposed to wear for a longer period of time.

Accretion measures are also generally nonreactive, but they have their potential biases as well. One of the major problems with accretion measures is again the differential survival ability of various materials. This problem is obviously increased with length of time since the event of interest occurred. For example, an urban anthropologist checking upon such things as consumption habits of reading materials by examining the contents of garbage cans placed by the curb can get a good idea of the types and number of magazines and newspapers read by examining those thrown away. However, if the same researcher studies the city dump of a ghost town he or she will find that most contents are at least 50 years old. Thus, while he or she still may study consumption habits of food and drink that were in metal and glass containers, he or she will be foiled in studying reading habits by the failure of paper products to withstand the elements.

The response-set bias noted for erosion measures may also be present in accretion measures. Suppose that an analysis of garbage over a long period of time reveals that neighbor A's garbage regularly contains comic books while neighbor B's garbage regularly contains the *New York Review of Books.* One might conclude that neighbor B's literary tastes are much more sophisticated than those of neighbor A. However, the opposite might be true. Both neighbors might have received gift subscriptions to both comics and literary magazines, but neighbor A values the literary magazines and so saves them and discards the comics, while neighbor B discards the literary magazines and retains the comics.

Reliability

We have noted a number of factors that can affect the accuracy of observational data, such as the inability of the observer to ensure anonymity for persons being observed, the subjective nature of social reality, and the fallibility of the sense organs. Thus it is obvious that if differences occur in such factors, either over time for a particular observer or particular research environment, or between different observers at one point in time, reliability can be adversely affected.

However, as in the case of validity, the extent to which the degree of reliability has been, or can be, assessed depends on the type of observational method used. Field research, much more than the survey or experiment and more than any other method, with the possible exception of document study, is generally an individual effort. Since usually only a single group or culture is studied by a single observer, there is little way to make the comparisons necessary to assess reliability. Further, field research emphasizes the subjective understanding of the researcher. This subjective understanding is generally not quantified and thus does not lend itself to the type of data analysis necessary for the assessment of reliability. It should not be surprising that discussion of reliability is completely lacking in the average report of an ethnographic field study.

The assessment of reliability is much easier in a study that uses a structured observational format, either in a natural or a laboratory setting. For reasons discussed above, assessment of observer reliability is generally emphasized, especially when a substantial number of observers are utilized in a single study. However, test reliability can also be assessed. As with the other methods discussed earlier in this book, attempts to assess reliability of observational studies have often been encouraging. Such assessment shows that if the general guidelines for conducting observational research are carried out, there is no reason why rather high reliabilities (75 percent or higher) cannot be achieved in structured observation.

A study that assesses both observer and test (category) reliability is the study by Sears et al. (1965) discussed above. They compared observers on the last day of the first week of the study, just before beginning formal data collection, the last day of the fifth week, and the last day of the sixth week. There were four observers in all, and each was paired with each of the other three for either three or four ten-minute observation periods in which each pair of observers observed the same child. A total of 63 pairs of ten-minute comparisons were collected, covering 10.5 hours of recorded behavior. Total reliability, as measured by percentage agreement of the two observers being compared, was 81 percent. This is a total for all types of behavior and all time periods. Reliability increased over time, being 72 percent in the first week, 82 percent by the fifth week, and 87 percent in the sixth week.

Comparisons were also made for the various types of behavior. Remember that there were 29 categories in all, comprising four groups. Reliabilities for these four groups were 86 percent for adult role, 78 percent for dependency, 70 percent for antisocial aggression, and 61 percent for prosocial aggression. The overall percentage was as high as it was (81 percent) only because the bulk of all recorded behaviors were in the adult-role group (86 percent reliability) while only 23 cases of the low-reliability prosocial aggression were recorded. There is a clear indication that reliability increases over time and is greater for categories with more recorded instances. This is evidence that experienced observers are more reliable than inexperienced ones. For a critical interpretation of such intercoder reliabilities see the discussion of ethnomethodology in chapter 11. For further discussion of both validity and reliability in observational research see Kirk and Miller (1986), and Feagin et al. (1991).

Summary

Chapter 10 discussed observational methods. After distinguishing between the two chief forms of observation—participant observation and nonparticipant observation—we discussed the advantages and disadvantages of the observational method. The advantages discussed were that observation can be used to gather data on nonverbal behavior, can be conducted in the natural environment rather than an artificial laboratory setting, and can easily be conducted over time. The disadvantages discussed were lack of control over the study setting, difficulties of quantification and coding of data, a sample size that is often small, hampering our ability to generalize our findings to other settings, problems of gaining entry to the setting, and lack of anonymity while studying sensitive issues (this is more of a problem for nonparticipant observers). We also listed nine steps in conducting an observational study.

Observational studies vary depending upon the degree of structure imposed on the setting (for example, a structured laboratory setting versus an unstructured field setting) and the degree of structure in the observational instrument (for example, structured observational categories to look for versus no observational format at all). We discussed both structured and unstructured participant observation studies conducted in a field setting, as this is the type most frequently used in sociological research. We discussed the major problems in field observation, including techniques for gaining entry to the setting, gaining and maintaining rapport with subjects, and writing the field notes.

The latter portion of the chapter we devoted to a discussion of indirect (unobtrusive) observation, or observation in which the observer is not present while the behavior to be studied is occurring. The chief advantage of such indirect observation is that there is no observer to bias the activity being observed (that is, the measure is nonreactive). We discussed both accretion measures, which are studies of accumulated material (such as studies of garbage dumps or graffiti), and erosion measures, which are measures utilizing material that has been worn away (such as determining which pathway is most heavily traveled by observing which exhibits the most wear). We concluded the chapter with a discussion of validity and reliability.

CHAPTER 11

ETHNOMETHODOLOGY

ETHNOMETHODOLOGY IS BASED on the notion that everyday, commonplace, or routine social activities and interactions are made possible through the use of a variety of skills, practices, and assumptions. These skills, practices, and assumptions are what ethnomethodology calls "methods." A chief goal of ethnomethodology is to study how members of society, in the course of ongoing social interaction, make sense of "indexical" expressions. Indexicals are terms whose meaning is not universal but is dependent upon the context (e.g., "he," "she," "they"). Ethnomethodology, which has received greatly increased interest in recent years, is largely the creation of Harold Garfinkel (e.g., Garfinkel 1967; Garfinkel and Sacks 1970), who was inspired by the phenomenological sociology of Schutz (1962; 1964; 1966). Goffman has also had an impact on this school of thought in his many writings (see Goffman 1959; 1962; 1963a; 1963b; 1967; 1969; 1971).

Among vintage ethnomethodological publications are the work of Bittner (1967a; 1967b), Churchill (1963), Moerman (1972), Moerman and Sacks (1974), Zimmerman and Pollner (1970), Sudnow (1972), Sacks (1972; 1974), Sacks and Schegloff (1974), Sacks, Schegloff, and Jefferson (1974), Schegloff (1968; 1972), and Schegloff and Sacks (1973). Later works include Schwartz and Jacobs (1979), Psathas (1979), Leiter (1980), Atkinson and Heritage (1984), Heritage (1984), Maynard (1985), and Molotch and Boden (1985).

After its emergence in the 1960s and 1970s, ethnomethodology went through a rather quiet period during the 1980s. The 1990s seems the decade of a resurgence of ethnomethodological development, although perhaps in a mature and somewhat changed state from the early work. Among the newer ethnomethodological publications are Pollner (1987; 1991), Heritage (1992), Clayman (1993), Boden and Zimmerman (1991), Sacks (1992), and Pollner and Stein (1993). Commenting upon the maturation of ethnomethodology, Pollner (1991, p. 370), says that it is beginning to be accepted:

> To be sure, few want their children to marry an ethnomethodologist, much less to be one—and they rarely hire one. Nevertheless, the discipline recognizes and begins to incorporate the contributions of what was once regarded as a pariah.

A further sign of ethnomethodology's growing acceptance within sociology is the fact that (although it took approximately 20 years) many introductory sociology texts now discuss ethnomethodology (see Farley 1990, p. 71; Robertson 1987, pp. 151–52).

However, Pollner (1991) notes that while ethnomethodology has matured and become increasingly accepted, it has also changed somewhat in its emphases. He particularly laments the decline in emphasis on what he labels as "radical reflexivity." For definitions and further discussion of these changes, see Pollner (1991). Heritage (1992) also notes recent changes in ethnomethodology. Among the significant areas of empirical research in 1990s ethnomethodology that he notes are social structures as normal environments, the creation and maintenance of social institutions and social worlds, and studies of work.

We commented in chapter 1 that professionals in other fields, such as politics and television, are now widely using social science methods such as survey research. Moreover, many if not all members of society conduct their own research every day. Not a day goes by without members of society attempting to explain why Suzie joined a cult, why Bill is on drugs, or why Jane is angry and refuses to speak to us. As Schwartz and Jacobs put it:

If sociology is an inquiry into the nature, causes, and consequences of social action, then this activity is not limited to professionals. Sociological theory can be heard on any radio talk show, sociological data are gathered whenever an employer tries to figure out whom to hire, and sociological analysis is employed by members of a jury as they decide who is guilty and why (Schwartz and Jacobs 1979, p. 209).

Ethnomethodology emphasizes and recognizes the fact that the lay public attempts social explanation, just as social scientists do. Further, the commonsense attempts by members of society to make sense of the social world going on around them are, according to ethnomethodologists, a major way in which social structure is created and perpetuated.

When members of society engage in sociological analysis they are attempting to understand, or make sense of, the ongoing social world. From the viewpoint of ethnomethodology, they are interpreting the social world. As Leiter remarks:

> Ethnomethodology examines the ways in which societal members create a sense of social structure through interpretation. Social reality, along with its sense of being a naturalistic entity independent of perception, is the ongoing accomplishment of the methods people use to observe and describe the society in which they live (Leiter 1980, p. 106).

Ethnomethodology sees social structure as something that is continuously generated by societal members' continual process of interpretation. We never stop trying to make sense of our world and to explain what is happening.

It is my view that ethnomethodology fills a gap that is not filled by other methods such as survey research or observation. Although ethnomethodology is sometimes sharply critical of other methods such as survey research, there is to me a clear complementarity among ethnomethodology and the other methods studied here. One radical difference is that almost all of the other methods used in standard social science treat commonsense knowledge as different from social science knowledge. Standard social science tends to emphasize this difference by contending that "scientific" knowledge is "superior" to commonsense knowledge. Ethnomethodology fills a gap by emphasizing the similarity between social science methods and lay methods. While other methods see commonsense knowledge as inferior knowledge generated by inferior methods, ethnomethodology seeks to understand the way in which members of society use the practices of commonsense reasoning not only to make sense of their world but even to construct and perpetuate the ongoing social world.

Ethnomethodology is primarily concerned with studying the commonsense features of everyday life, with emphasis on those things that "everyone knows." As Zimmerman and Pollner put it:

> In contrast to the perennial argument that sociology belabors the obvious, we propose that sociology has yet to treat the obvious as a phenomenon. We argue that the world of everyday life, while furnishing sociology with its favored topics of inquiry, is seldom a topic in its own right (Zimmerman and Pollner 1970, p. 33).

Ethnomethodologists generally study social interaction as an ongoing process. Many of the studies involve conversational analysis (see especially the work of Sacks, Schegloff, and Jefferson 1974). Other studies involve nonverbal interaction (e.g., Garfinkel 1967) or interaction within a particular organizational system or setting (in Turner 1974 see, for example, the study of juvenile police officers by Cicourel and the study of the convict code in a halfway house by Wieder).

One major data-gathering technique of ethnomethodology is observation. Conversational researchers often study documents in the form of transcripts of recorded conversations. Much work, particularly that of Garfinkel, is often quasi-experimental. Because of the character of the inquiry and the intensive observation required, most ethnomethodological studies are necessarily micro in nature. It would be possible, but probably not practical, to conduct a large-scale ethnomethodological study.

Some ethnomethodologists (for example, Garfinkel) are concerned with the shared meanings that words ("natural language") have for members of a group. The word "member" has special significance inasmuch as it implies a body of knowledge shared by all who are members. One result of ethnomethodological research is the demonstration that much information that is transmitted in a conversation "goes without saying," and is understood but never directly verbalized. Garfinkel (1967, p. 26) reports the following conversation by a student and his wife, with the left-hand column reporting what was actually said and the right-hand column reporting what the two conversants actually understood:

HUSBAND: I got some new shoelaces for my shoes.	As you will remember I broke a shoelace on one of my brown oxfords the other day so I stopped to get some new laces.
WIFE: Your loafers need new heels badly.	Something else you could have gotten that I was thinking of. You could have taken in your black loafers which need heels badly. You'd better get them taken care of pretty soon.

The purpose of Garfinkel's illustration is not simply to demonstrate that some things are understood without being said, but to explore the nature of what we mean by common understanding or "shared agreement" among the parties.

What Garfinkel seems to be saying is that to understand and make sense of what is said, one needs to know how it is said, or the rules that participants follow in the course of social interaction. Further, Garfinkel (1967, p. 29) says, "Then the recognized sense of what a person said consists only and entirely in recognizing the method of his speaking, of *seeing how he spoke.*" A good example concerns the type of speaking or writing that we refer to as sarcasm. We often cannot be sure of a speaker's meaning just by knowing the words that are spoken. Even if all words used are familiar to us and are not ambiguous, we attach a different meaning to them depending on how the person is acting. If he or she is acting a certain way (being sarcastic), the meaning of the words is different than if he or she is acting a different way (not being sarcastic). If we observe the speaker, we may be able to tell from his or her tone of voice, inflections, gestures, and mannerisms, or other forms of nonverbal communication whether or not he or she is sarcastic. If the statement is written, determination of exact meaning can be exceedingly difficult, because we can tell what the author says but not how he or she says it.

For a recent extended discussion of Garfinkel's work see *Garfinkel and Ethnomethodology* by Heritage (1984).

Ethnomethodology Versus Survey Research

I picked survey research as a comparison with ethnomethodology for heuristic purposes, since the two are viewed by ethnomethodologists as having different, and perhaps incompatible, objectives. The experimental method, observation, and document analysis are perhaps more palatable to ethnomethodologists, because these methods are better able to deal with temporal processes and temporal ordering, which are very important concerns for ethnomethodologists.

Process Versus Product

Ethnomethodologists feel that traditional sociological researchers such as survey researchers tend to take for granted the very things that they should treat as phenomena worthy of sociological study. That is, survey researchers (according to ethnomethodologists) take phenomena resulting from social processes as given, or as points for the study to begin. They attempt to find causes or correlates of these phenomena without attempting to explain how these phenomena arose or came to be of interest. According to ethnomethodologists, the problem arises largely because professional sociologists share everyday commonsense practices with laypersons, use the same natural language that laypersons use, and agree with laypersons about which are the proper problems to be studied. These professional sociologists, according to ethnomethodologists, study problems the same way laypersons do, though with more care and with more emphasis on reliability, validity, and so on. The professionals tend to consider lay accounts as faulty and their own as superior, while to ethnomethodologists the two are really quite similar and are both processes that are of interest as phenomena to be studied in their own right.

As Zimmerman and Pollner put it:

> In terms of both the substantive themes brought under examination and the formal properties of the structures examined, professional and lay sociologists are in tacit agreement. For example, the sociologist and the policeman may entertain deeply different theories of how a person comes to be a juvenile delinquent, and they may appeal to disparate criteria and evidence for support of their respective versions. Yet they have no trouble in agreeing that there are persons recognizable as juvenile delinquents and that there are structured ways in which these persons come to be juvenile delinquents. It is in this sense of agreement—agreement as to the fundamental and ordered existence of a phenomenon independent of its having been addressed by *some* method of inquiry—that professional and lay sociologists are mutually oriented to a common factual domain.
>
> The agreement indicates sociology's profound embeddedness in and dependence upon the world of everyday life. Not only does the attitude of everyday life furnish the context of sociological investigation, it also seems to furnish social scientific inquiry with a leading conception of its order of fact and program of research. The factual domain to which socio-

logical investigation is directed is coterminous, with but mild variation, to the factual domain attended by lay inquirees. (Zimmerman and Pollner 1970, p. 34).

Zimmerman and Pollner feel that by accepting the layperson's formulation of the topics to be investigated, sociology becomes part of the very thing it is trying to explain. Thus it is put in the position of the person trying to explain his or her dreams while still asleep and dreaming—it cannot be done. Only by awakening can he or she analyze the dream.

In order to see more clearly the ethnomethodologists' point that sociologists are taking the end result of a process as a given and proceeding from there when they should be studying the prior process, consider the concept of deviancy. The layperson and the professional sociologist may agree or disagree that a certain form of behavior is deviant (some persons today, both lay and professionals, consider homosexuals deviant while others do not). The point is that generally sociologists do not take as their topic of study the process whereby a phenomenon such as homosexuality comes to be labeled by the society as deviant. Rather they take the deviancy as a fact or a given and then seek explanations of it, such as early childhood socialization, relations with mother and father, or parents' social class.

The ethnomethodological position does not treat a social phenomenon (for example, the labeling of a particular behavior such as homosexuality) as a given fact with which to begin the investigation, but rather as a topic of investigation in its own right. Although ethnomethodologists study many topics besides deviance (and researchers who are not ethnomethodologists study the labeling of deviants), those studying deviance are interested in the process whereby a particular form of behavior comes to be labeled as deviant by members of society, and the way that behavior is reacted to by the members once it is so labeled. At the risk of oversimplification, the labeling-theory position contends that deviants are created by being labeled as deviant and then reacted to as if they were deviant, until at last they really become deviant and act deviant. This is more or less the self-fulfilling prophecy at work. If the whole society labels you as "crazy" and treats you accordingly, it will encourage you to believe it yourself and to change your behavior to conform to a deviant role. For a discussion of the ethnomethodological approach to labeling theory see Pollner (1974).

Berger and Luckmann (1967) discuss the "social construction of reality," or the idea that some social phenomena are actually mental constructs. Numerous examples can be given of the construction of social reality through labeling. For example, when a murder case goes to a jury trial, there may be some question of whether the defendent is "legally sane" (knows right from wrong) and thus competent to stand trial for murder, or whether he or she is insane and should be committed to an institution for the criminally insane. Who can determine whether he or she is insane? The obvious answer is that "expert," "professional" psychiatrists will do it. However, the defense is often able to produce professional psychiatrists and psychologists to testify that the defendant is insane, while the prosecutor is able to produce psychiatrists and psychologists to swear that he or she is sane and should stand trail. Ultimately it is up to the jury of laypersons (the defendant's peers) to label him or her as either insane or sane. Regardless of whether he or she is "really and objectively" insane, what subsequently happens to him or her—whether he or she is sent to an institution for the criminally insane or tried for murder and sentenced to prison or executed—depends solely upon the label placed upon him or her by the jury.

Another example of labeling in an attempt to provide the "true meaning" to the situation occurs in evaluating letters of recommendation for faculty positions in universities. The letter is many times not taken at face value. Instead, the reader's personal knowledge of the letter's author is invoked. Many times the author is labeled as either a "strong letter writer" who will write glowing letters for almost anyone, or a "weak letter writer" who has very high standards and is not afraid to criticize the person being evaluated. After the writer is labeled, the letter itself can be labeled as either a "weak letter for that writer" or a "strong letter for that writer." Thus it is entirely possible for job candidate 1 to receive a letter of recommendation from writer 1 that is full of praise, while a somewhat critical letter for candidate 2 from writer 2 can be judged to be a "stronger" letter than that of candidate 1, simply because writer 1 is labeled as always praising persons and writer 2 is labeled as being critical and having higher standards.

To make the point that sociologists should study process rather than accept its effects as given and proceed from there, Garfinkel and Sacks use an analogy:

> If, whenever housewives were let into a room, each one on her own went to some same spot and started to clean it, one might conclude that the spot surely needed cleaning. On the other hand, one might conclude that there is something about the spot and about the housewives that makes the encounter of one by the other an occasion for cleaning, in which case the fact of the cleaning, instead of being evidence of dirt, would be itself a phenomenon (Garfinkel and Sacks 1970, p. 347).

Indexical Expressions

Another way in which the goals of ethnomethodologists differ from the goals of conventional social researchers is in their views toward the study of indexical expressions. Calling traditional researchers' activities "constructive analysis," Garfinkel and Sacks (1970, p. 345) say: "Ethnomethodology's interests, like those of constructive analysis, insistently focus on the formal structures of everyday activities. However, the two understand formal structures differently and in incompatible ways."

Indexicals are situation-specific words and phrases whose meaning may change from situation to situation and may depend on who is uttering the word or to whom the remarks are directed. Among the indexical words listed by Garfinkel and Sacks (1970, p. 347) are: "she, we, he, you, here, there, now, this, that, it, I, then, soon, today, tomorrow." These words are not specific and require clarification or a context. When the Army recruiting poster shows Uncle Sam and says, "Uncle Sam Wants You," obviously "you" varies from situation to situation, depending on who is standing in front of the poster. In fact, in one sense virtually all events, objects, or words are indexical in that their meaning cannot be taken for granted. They must be interpreted by individuals participating in the interaction before their meanings can become clear.

In addition to terms whose referent can change from time to time, other expressions can be formed entirely from objective words but can be indexical in the sense that the meaning of the expression is different depending on who is uttering it. For example, in Wieder's (1974) study of the convict code in a halfway house, he reports that a convict was asked by the program director to organize a baseball team, and replied, "You know I can't organize a baseball team"

(Wieder 1974, p. 161). The basic question in ethnomethodological research (or any social research) regarding this statement is, "What did he mean when he said he could not organize a team?" In this case it was understood to mean that such organization was precluded since it violated the convict code provision that states that prisoners cannot cooperate with officials. Wieder notes that if the same statement had been made by a staff member the meaning would have been different, but would have varied according to which staff member made it, the occasion on which it was made, who heard it, and so on. The remark could have meant that "You know that it is your job, since you are on the recreation committee and I am not." Or, if the speaker was a case-carrying parole agent and the program director was listening, it could have meant. "You know that I am already putting more time into the program than I can afford as it is; I couldn't possibly do more" (Wieder 1974, p. 162).

Leiter (1980, p. 108) provides another example of an indexical expression: "The book is in the pen." Leiter says that when this statement is spoken by one secret agent and directed to another, it might mean that the codebook has been reduced to microfilm and hidden in the fountain pen. But when spoken by the farmer's wife to the farmer, it could mean that she has placed his "filthy" pornographic book in the pig pen where it belongs. We can easily add a third interpretation. The police, wondering how prisoners are able to place bets on horse races, are told by an informant that the bookmaking operation takes place within the very walls of the penitentiary itself.

According to ethnomethodologists, conventional researchers are more concerned with converting indexical expressions into objective nonindexical expressions, or in substituting objective expressions for indexical ones, than they are in studying the rules by which sense is made of indexicals in ongoing everyday conversation. Ethnomethodologists, on the other hand, do not look at indexicals as problems to be remedied by conversion to objective expressions, but rather as phenomena of interest in their own right. As Garfinkel and Sacks put it:

> Their [ethnomethodological] studies have shown in demonstrable specifics (1) that the properties of indexical expressions are ordered properties, and (2) *that* they are ordered properties is an ongoing, practical accomplishment of every actual occasion of commonplace speech and conduct. The results of their studies furnish an alternative to the repair of indexical expressions as a central task of general theory building in professional sociology (Garfinkel and Sacks 1970, p. 341).

The distinction between the two approaches should be clear. Both approaches seek order and the ability to generalize their findings, but they seek them in different ways, or perhaps in different places. The traditional approach takes an ambiguous, situationally or temporally specific indexical expression that is obviously not applicable to all times and all places (and is in this sense not universal or generalizable) and attempts to repair or clarify its meaning until it is generalizable. Ethnomethodology, on the other hand, allows the indexical to remain situationally specific and ungeneralizable and does not attempt to clarify or repair it. That is, ethnomethodology does not seek order in the meaning of the indexical expression. Instead, it seeks order in the way indexicals are handled in everyday ongoing discourse to ensure that the participants in the interaction are able to grasp the meaning of these expressions. While the particular contents of the indexicals do not have order irrespective of the time or place they occur, the rules by which conversationalists deal with indexicals do exhibit a generalizable order that is independent of, or transcends, the particular time, place, or characteristics of the conversationalists.

Conversational Structures

The work of the ethnomethodologists offers ample proof that conversations are not random occurrences, but are quite structured, with members of a society following numerous interactional rules. We may characterize these rules as "norms" that specify which behavior is appropriate for a person of a particular status, in a particular situation or context, and at a particular time. Many times persons adhere quite strictly to these norms without realizing that they are doing so, or indeed without even realizing that the norm exists. An example is the norm regulating the distance one person stands from another person in ordinary conversation. The allowable distance varies among cultures (see Hall 1966), but within a culture the distance is generally quite consistent and adhered to quite rigidly. You can conduct an "ethnomethodological experiment" by standing very close to or unusually far away from a person (even though you raise your voice so he or she can hear) and noting the result. I predict that the person to whom you are standing very close will move back as you move forward in order to maintain the usual distance, if you move unobtrusively and cautiously, he or she may not even realize that he or she is moving away from you (at least the first time). Conversely, the person standing at a distance will move closer to you in order to maintain the correct spatial relationship. There are other norms that one may follow without realizing it, such as raising the voice toward the end of a conversation. The status of the person is also important, as norms dictate different roles depending on such characteristics as one's sex, age, or whether one holds a particular office. Most persons use a higher voice pitch when talking to young children, perhaps without even realizing it.

There are a number of these norms that we take for granted and follow everyday without realizing it. Nonverbal examples are presented by the norms governing choice of seat: (1) in a bus or subway train; (2) on a bus stop bench; (3) at a table in the school cafeteria if no empty tables are available; and (4) at a table in a seminar classroom. Sommer (1969) has done a number of experiments with seating arrangements at tables, and has found seating patterns to be quite predictable.

Any time we do something that others regard as strange behavior in our usual routine of everyday affairs, we are probably violating some norm. The person who laughs and talks to herself or himself is violating a well-understood and widely recognized norm, and the stares, scowls, and finger pointing of other persons serve as punishment or negative sanctions to bring his or her behavior back in line. Once when I was a graduate student I experienced an incident that I am still unsure how to label. I was having lunch at a table in the cafeteria of the student union. I was alone, and had a partially filled glass of water on the table. A young man suddenly appeared through the door from the kitchen area of the cafeteria, grabbed my glass of water, and retreated into the kitchen with it. Since I was aware of ethnomethodological experiments of this sort that had the character of "happenings" but were designed to elicit a reaction on the part of the the victim and record how he reacted, I thought at the time that this was a project for an undergraduate sociology class. I never found out for certain, though, and I also thought it could be the work of a practical joker or of a "crazy" person, as some of the cafeteria workers were from the state mental hospital. It was certainly a puzzling occurrence, and the only way to ascertain what it meant, or to explain it so as to relieve the ambiguity and puzzlement in my mind, was to label it in some form, such as the work of a joker, crazy person, or social researcher.

Garfinkel (1967) reports a variety of experiments he had designed to demonstrate to students the existence of such norms, and to observe and record the behaviors of others when the student violates the norms. In one such experiment Garfinkel required undergraduate students to spend from 15 minutes to an hour viewing the interaction within their homes as if they were boarders or strangers in the household, rather than playing their usual role as familiar family members. Students were instructed only to observe, not actually to act as strangers. Their written reports of what they observed did not take into account any usual "insider's" commonsense knowledge of household history, and references to subjective elements such as imputed motive were omitted. From their vantage point as "boarders," the students were surprised to see the way family members treated one another. The whole atmosphere was one of private rather than public behavior, with little respect for table manners, apparent freedom to criticize others, and a general absence of impression management. The student generally felt that the boarder's account did not represent their "real" home environment (Garfinkel 1967, p. 46).

In the next experiment students spent from 15 minutes to an hour not only assuming they were boarders but actually acting out this assumption. In approximately 80 percent of the cases family members reacted strongly to restore the situation to normal. Family members (who did not know what was happening) were bewildered, anxious, and embarrassed. Students were told by family members that they were being inconsiderate, selfish, and impolite. Students were asked if they were sick, stupid, or mad, or questions such as "What has gotten into you?"

The point to be made by this discussion is that conversation and interaction are closely regulated by orderly rules. Although these rules are often taken for granted as commonplace and are adhered to routinely or even subconsciously, they provide an orderly and generalizable structure of interest to ethnomethodologists. By discovering and cataloging these rules that members take for granted, ethnomethodologists can discover how sense is made out of indexicals; that is, how the meaning of indexicals is made clear through a situationally specific process in which the context may be problematic and differ from place to place or time to time, but the rules by which meaning is explicated remain objective, constant, and nonproblematic.

One way of explicating indexicals in conversation is what Garfinkel and Sacks (1970, p. 350) call "formulating," the process by which one of the conversationalists interprets or explains one part of the conversation. This is done by attempting to state the gist of the conversation, or to translate or summarize it. Formulating often involves showing how the conversation either follows or is a departure from a rule. But essentially formulating is a description of behavior designed to tell what the conversationalists are actually *doing* when they say a certain thing. Garfinkel and Sacks (1970, p. 350) offer the following conversational fragment:

JH: Isn't it nice that there's such a crowd of you in the office?

SM: You're asking us to leave, not telling us to leave, right?

SM's statement is a formulation that explicates JH's statement by telling what JH is really doing when he utters that particular sentence (i.e., telling persons to leave).

In addition to the practice of formulating, ethnomethodologists have studied other ways in which rules are followed to make the conversation meaningful and clear to the participants. Among topics studied are the sequencing of conversations, the manner in which conversations are terminated and the specification of general rules by which conversations are conducted. For example, Sacks, Schegloff, and Jefferson (1974) studied turn-taking in conversations. They found, among other rules, that turn-allocation techniques are used, and that repair mechanisms are available for dealing with turn-taking errors.

The findings most interesting to me resulted from Schegloff and Sacks's (1973) work on ways in which conversations are terminated. They note that conversations normally consist of a series of turn-taking operations in which first one person, then another, speaks. If a speaker wishes to terminate the conversation he or she must somehow break the sequence. That is, he or she must take a turn at speaking, but must not continue to improve on or add additional useful information to the topic being discussed. He or she must terminate discussion of the current topic without initiating a new topic. Thus one must in essence "pass" on one's opportunity to speak by indicating that one has nothing new to say, often by uttering some "preclosing" word or phrase. This phrase will pass the turn to the next speaker, who is not compelled to terminate, but it will provide a clue that the other speaker is ready to terminate. Preclosings noted by Schegloff and Sacks include "well" ("we-ell"), "OK," and "so" ("so-oo"). Another common one is "anyway," which is often preceded by "well" ("well, anyway"), or drawn out with the emphasis on the first syllable ("ANYway"). There are numerous other preclosings, such as "I've got to go now" (but often this too may be preceded by "well" and responded to with "OK") or the familiar "We are costing you too much money" that is often heard on long-distance telephone calls. As with adherence to other rules we have noted in this chapter, the speaker is probably often not aware that he or she is even following a rule in closing.

Before I read the ethnomethodologists' research reports, I was aware that I closed conversations, but not that there was any consistency in the way I did it, or that I said any particular words to occasion such termination. After I read about preclosings I noted that I nearly always closed with "well" or "OK" without thinking about it, and that others did the same.

There has recently been a substantial amount of interest in conversational analysis. Atkinson and Heritage (1984) report a number of studies of conversational analysis, including conversation and body movements, laughter, and audience response to public speaking. Maynard (1985) reported on the function of social conflict among children. He analyzed children's conversations, with emphasis on the manifest functions of conflict. Molotch and Boden (1985) analyzed talk during the Watergate hearings, for example, exchanges between John Dean and Senator Gurney. They show how power is achieved through control of conversation.

Validity and Reliability

Validity

Ethnomethodological studies seem generally to be quite valid, although ethnomethodologists often eschew the process of computing measures of validity or reliability. Defining a valid measure as one that "really measures what we wish to measure," ethnomethodological observation is probably valid simply because ethnomethodologists tend not to follow the traditional practice of proposing an indirect measure for some concept such as alienation or anomia that cannot be seen directly. In a real sense, it can be argued that a person's score on an anomia scale is a causal effect of his or her level of anomia (score is caused by anomia), but is not a direct measure of the always directly unobservable anomie. In contrast to this practice of first mentally constructing a conceptual label such as "alienation" and then attempting to establish its validity by determining whether it corresponds to empirically observed reality, ethnomethodology takes an approach that is closer to the grounded-theory approach discussed in chapter 2. That is, ethnomethodology searches for observable regularities and then labels them. For example, consider the concept of formulating, which describes the way participants explicate a conversational fragment by telling what the speaker is doing when he or she says the fragment. Inasmuch as formulating as a practice is first observed to occur and then labeled after the fact, it has almost perfect face validity, since the practice is the operational definition of the concept. There is no abstract, theoretical, or conceptual definition; the definition of formulation is merely the description of behavior that has been directly observed to occur empirically. Since there is no nonempirical component of the concept, there is no question of error in the fit of the nonempirical to the empirical component, which is what we mean by validity. If all concepts in sociology were amenable to direct observation (if we could see an actual id or attitude) our measurement problems would be considerably less. As Churchill says of his ethnomethodological work:

> The indicator variables do not arise in my research. The categories of immediate response to questions are all that there are. The lack of indicator variables eliminates the whole set of measurement problems involved in how well the indicator represent the theoretical variables (Churchill 1971, p. 188).

Perhaps we can best assess the validity (or at least the reasonableness) of ethnomethodology by contrasting it with a more familiar method—the survey. Ethnomethodologists sometimes doubt the validity of survey research, both interviews and self-reports. We have noted that ethnomethodologists are concerned primarily with the way members of a society communicate by making sense out of unclear, ambiguous, problematic, or indexical words and expressions. They believe that the meaning of these problematic expressions is not predetermined and is not agreed on before the conversation ensues. Rather, the shared agreement or consensus on what is meant arises out of the very interaction. Thus the content (meaning of the conversation) is dependent on the situation in which it is performed, such as the particular place and time, and cannot be generalized. The rules by which the content is made clear, however, are not unique to the situation and can be generalized (though not perfectly). Since survey research has the goal of standardizing content, it is doomed to failure in the view of the ethnomethodologist, who believes that content cannot be generalized. If the survey researcher attempted to use a standardized survey to study the rules that govern conversations, the ethnomethodologist might think this enterprise more valid, since he or she believes that there is regularity in these rules. The problem here is that, as we have pointed out, persons using these rules are often unaware that they are using them, and so would not be able to answer a survey question about them. Thus the rules can be discovered only by observing the regularity of the behavior as the rules are adhered to, and then inferring the existence of the rules.

Further, the person answering the questionnaire, be it respondent or interviewer, will be following rules, and it is these rules that constitute the very phenomena the ethnomethodologist thinks are the most important to study. Any reader who doubts that questionnaires are answered according to formal rules laid down by the survey researcher need only consult chapter 6 for examples. In mailed questionnaires these rules (generally labeled instructions rather than norms or rules) may be kept to a minimum. At the very least they will say "Circle the appropriate answer," "There are no right and wrong answers, only give your opinion," or "Please answer fully." In interview studies, particularly if the interview schedule is long and complicated (e.g., with a lot of skip questions), the separate book of instructions to the interviewer may be very lengthy. Most of these rules (instructions) deal with what to do with exceptional or ambiguous cases that do not fit the structure of the questionnaire.

Churchill (1971, p. 189) gives the example of a question that asks how many years of schooling a respondent's father completed. He asks what should be done if the respondent's father completed eight years of schooling in Sweden, but has been told that eight years in Sweden is the equivalent of twelve years in the United States. In this case it is difficult for the respondent and the coder to know whether eight or twelve is the "correct" answer. The question of father's schooling is an indexical expression whose "correct" answer depends on the context. In the absence of a clarifying instruction to tell him or her the way to answer, the respondent must decide "what the researcher *really* means" (i.e., years of schooling regardless of country, or the United States equivalent). In addition to the formal rules provided by the researcher and printed in the instructions, the respondent and the coder, as members of the system, know (although they may not realize it) the commonsense rules by which they answer questions in everyday life, and they will also rely upon these rules. Thus the phenomenon interesting to the ethnomethodologists is not the answer to the question but the doing of the answering, or the actual search procedure through which the respondent attempts to determine, from studying the questionnaire rules and from his or her own knowledge of everyday life and its rules "what the researcher really wants."

The concern of the ethnomethodologists is that the answers to survey questions will not be an objective measure of independent social reality, but will be more an artifact of the particular set of rules given for completion of the questions and the setting in which the questionnaire is completed. That is, the rules will generate the data artificially, with the survey being a game that the respondent plays according to its printed rules in order to please and to give the researcher what he or she really wants, rather than what the respondent really thinks. As Garfinkel puts it when discussing standard reporting forms:

> If the researcher insists that the reporter furnish the information in the way the form provides, he runs the risk of imposing upon the actual events for study a structure that is derived from the features of the reporting rather than from the events themselves (Garfinkel 1974, p. 117).

Reliability

The reader can guess that ethnomethodologists would also have their doubts about reliability as assessed by survey researchers. If a survey researcher finds a high intercoder reliability coefficient, showing that all coders give consistently identical interpretations to ambiguous cases, an ethnomethodologist may be very impressed. However, he or she will not be impressed with how consistently the objective reality is being measured, but rather with how consistently all coders are able to follow the rules for "doing coding." If all coders interpret an ambiguous situation (such as the father educated in Sweden) incorrectly but consistently, reliability coefficient values will be high but misleading. Such consistency would indicate that some rule was being followed very rigidly, and this would be of interest to the ethnomethodologist.

Another factor damaging reliability in coding is that when coders face ambiguous cases that are not adequately resolved by coding rules, they often resolve them by invoking their own assumptions about and knowledge of the phenomenon being studied. Thus the data ultimately collected are not a pure, objectively collected measure of social reality, but more a reinforcement of, and product of, the researcher's assumptions. However, traditional researchers seem to be damned if they do and damned if they don't on this point. If an outside researcher surveys an organization with which he or she is not familiar, he or she can be accused of not asking the right questions and of imposing an artificial, irrelevant structure on the data through the questionnaire. On the other hand, if the researcher is a member of the organizational system with intimate knowledge of its rules and everyday operations, he or she can be accused of bias and of bending the data to meet his or her own assumptions and prejudices.

Comparison of Positions

In comparing the positions of ethnomethodology and traditional quantitative social researchers with regard of validity, reliability, and measurement in general, several points can be made.

Survey research, as discussed in chapters 6, 7, and 8, is defined primarily as a cross-sectional technique that collects data at a single point in time rather than over time. It is thus efficient for gathering data on the products of social activities but not on the activities themselves. Survey research is efficient for measuring an individual's present income and present level of occupation, but not for measuring the social processes by which he or she attained these products. However, it can be effective in prediction. Polls can predict the vote in a presidential election without explaining the rules by which voters decide for whom to vote. Since study of process by definition requires study over time, a procedure for which survey research is not well suited, for this reason alone survey research is not an efficient method for ethnomethodology. It is, however, an efficient method for those researchers who wish to study product rather than process (we should not forget that ethnomethodologists study documents, such as transcripts of conversations, that are themselves products). Survey research does a good job as long as the questionnaire can be answered routinely, does not have exceptions, and is not ambiguous. Even where ambiguity occurs (as in the Swedish education example), error is often negligible, since only a few respondents have unusual circumstances that render interpretation difficult.

However, when respondents find the question ambiguous and cannot ascertain "what the researcher really wants," then ethnomethodology becomes important, since it helps us understand why the respondent answers the way he or she does. A questionnaire can be successful only if it has few or no indexicals requiring repair through instructions. This is why we emphasized in chapter 6 that questions should not contain ambiguous words. The problem is that while researchers do not include words that are obviously indexicals in a questionnaire, it is difficult to consider all possible situations that might turn a straightforward question into an indexical. A researcher asking how many pregnancies a woman has had, for example, would consider this question to be "clear" and would probably not anticipate that women in certain situations would find the exact meaning of "pregnancy" ambiguous, and thus be uncertain about the correct answer to the question. If the respondents' situations do not vary (e.g., if all who become pregnant have full-term pregnancies resulting in live births), then the term "pregnancy" is not an indexical for this sample. However, how is a woman to answer who has twins or triplets? Are twins the result of one pregnancy or two? What about the woman who is pregnant only a short time and then has either a miscarriage or an abortion? Is such a partial pregnancy to be counted as a fraction of a pregnancy, no pregnancy, or a full pregnancy? If any of these ambiguous situations occur, then the term "pregnancy" becomes an indexical.

Even though Churchill (1971) says that ethnomethodologists use direct rather than indirect measurement, it seems to me that they are interested not only in observing and categorizing behavior that can be directly observed, such as behavior in conversations, but also in inferring the existence of rules that are the cause of these behavioral regularities. Ethnomethodologists certainly seem to be interested in discovering the existence of rules governing behavior. In his definition of shared agreement, Garfinkel (1967) talks of participants recognizing that something was said according to a rule. This definition implies that the existence of rules can be demonstrated. In the view of ethnomethodologists norms are vague and have to be adapted and made clear in each specific situation, but are nevertheless real. Further, Sacks's chain rule (as presented by Churchill 1971) says that "An American to whom a question is addressed should respond with a direct answer and then return the 'floor' to the questioner." It is obvious to me that Sacks never actually saw this "rule" any more than I can see "alienation"; all he saw were its effects (one might say aftereffects). He saw regularized behavior and inferred the existence of a rule that regulates this behavior. Thus the behavior (persons answering a question and then returning the floor to the questioner) is the operational definition, or indirect measure, of the unobservable rule.

Regularity of the observed behavior provides no guarantee that such a rule actually exists. Other explanations for the regularity of the behavior are possible, though they may be unlikely. It is possible that some chemicals affect the central nervous system in such a way that the regularity of behavior results. Perhaps hormonal differences cause differences in male and female behavior. I do not believe this to be true; I believe that a norm probably exists. The point is that there is certainly a possibility that the norm does not exist, and thus the possibility of measurement error, which suggests that ethnomethodologists should join other social researchers in assessing the validity of their measure (the observed behavior) for the concept in question (the rule that cannot be observed).

One might get the impression from reading ethnomethodology that "professional" or "traditional" social researchers deal entirely with effect rather than process. This is not true in regard to measurement, especially so-called operationalism. Bridgman's original definition of the term states:

In general we mean by any concept nothing more than a set of operations: *the concept is synonymous with the corresponding set of operations.* If the concept is physical, as of length, the operations are actual physical operations, namely, those by which length is measured; or if the concept is mental, as of mathematical continuity, the operations are mental operations, namely those by which we determine whether a given aggregate of magnitudes is continuous (Bridgman 1948, pp. 5–6).

What Bridgman seems to be saying is that a concept is not the result of a process but is defined by the process itself. He says that the meaning of the concept is found in operations or behavior, presumably behavior regulated by rules. This seems to me to be nearly identical to the ethnomethodologist's statement that the meaning of a concept is not independent of behavior but is explicated through ongoing behavior that is conducted according to rules.

We have saved the discussion of advantages and disadvantages until the end of the chapter because many readers are not well versed in ethnomethodology, and would not profit from such a discussion until the rudiments of the method had been explicated.

Advantages of Ethnomethodology

1. *Longitudinal.* As a method of ongoing observation, ethnomethodology can record changes as they occur and does not have to rely on the memory of the participants as recorded in a cross-sectional survey.

2. Nonverbal as well as verbal behavior is studied.

3. Ethnomethodology provides an understanding of how respondents make sense of questionnaires, and why they answer the way they do. This approach should prove valuable in analyzing nonresponse in survey studies.

4. Ethnomethodology provides an understanding of how consistency rather than real reliability is sometimes achieved by coders following commonsense rules.

Disadvantages of Ethnomethodology

1. *Products.* Ethnomethodology is not the method of choice if one is interested in studying some social product, as opposed to the process by which that product was derived. That is, if you wish to study attitudes that Americans have in common you would not use ethnomethodology, although you might use it to study the process by which those attitudes are derived.

2. *Large-scale studies.* Larger-scale mass-attitude studies are more appropriate for survey research than for ethnomethodology, both because they study product rather than process and because they cannot be studied effectively with the observational and experimental methods preferred by ethnomethodologists.

Although ethnomethodology often has been omitted from discussions of traditional research methods, we hope the present chapter makes clear that ethnomethodology is not incompatible with traditional methods, but rather fills an important gap left by these methods. Not only does ethnomethodology concentrate on process and on the way that everyday matters are made sense of by participants in social interaction (thus covering a topic neglected by other methods), it also treats other methods themselves as phenomena to be studied, and in so doing provides us with important insights regarding such matters as the clarification of ambiguous survey questions and the reliability of coding survey data.

Summary

Chapter 11 dealt with ethnomethodology. Ethnomethodology studies everyday, common-place, routine social activities. A substantial portion of ethnomethodological research is directed toward the study of how participants in social interaction make sense of the proceedings. In conversations between two people a substantial part of the meaning is shared and understood in advance, rather than being stated literally. For example, if I ask "How was the party?" I am assuming shared knowledge between us of the party I referred to. This sort of shared and unspoken understanding is one thing that often makes interpretation of personal documents such as letters and diaries difficult, as we will note in chapter 12. Ethnomethodologists study how participants in social interaction clarify such shared understandings to ensure that they are communicating properly. They assume that communication begins with some things needing to be clarified, and clarification proceeds in identifiable stages according to distinct rules.

In addition to clarification of shared agreements, there are some words and phrases whose meaning depends partially or solely on the social context in which they are uttered. These are called indexicals. Examples are common terms such as "he," "she," "it," "you," and "they." Ethnomethodologists feel that even though the meaning of these terms can never be generalized to fit all situations, and can never be context free, the rules by which the meaning of such a term is made clear to participants in a conversation are general, and can be studied and learned. In general ethnomethodologists believe that emphasis in social research should be on the process of social interaction through which social reality is constructed and maintained, rather than on the end result or product of such interaction, which they feel is the major research focus of most social researchers. After a discussion of validity and reliability we concluded the chapter with a list of advantages and disadvantages of ethnomethodology.

LIVERPOOL
JOHN MOORES UNIVERSITY
I.M. MARSH LIBRARY
BARKHILL ROAD
LIVERPOOL L17 6BD
TEL. 0151 231 5216/5290

LIVERPOOL
JOHN MOORES UNIVERSITY
I.M. MARSH LRC
BARKHILL RD
LIVERPOOL L17 6BD
TEL. 0151 231 5216/5299

CHAPTER 12

DOCUMENT STUDY

WITH THE EXCEPTION of indirect observation, the data collection methods discussed heretofore have involved deciding which group of people to study and then studying these people directly, either by questionnaire, experiment, or observation. Another major source of data that is in my opinion rather neglected is the analysis of documents, by which we mean any written materials that contain information about the phenomena we wish to study. These documents vary greatly. Some are *primary* documents, or eye-witness accounts written by people who experienced the particular event or behavior. Others are *secondary* documents by people who were not present on the scene but who received the information necessary to compile the document by interviewing eyewitnesses or by reading primary documents. Although there may be some "gray" areas in the primary-secondary distinction, the difference between the two is generally clear. For example, an autobiography is clearly a primary document while a biography is a secondary document.

In addition to the primary-secondary distinction, documents vary widely in terms of degree of structure and of purpose for which they were originally written. Documents are occasionally solicited. For example, a sample of persons of different ethnic groups could be asked to write an account of their childhood. Then the researcher could do a comparative analysis of these materials, perhaps comparing such things as child-parent authority relationships, socialization practices, or peer-group influences. However, solicitation of documents specifically for research purposes is relatively rare, perhaps because if the subject is present it is deemed preferable to conduct a survey, experiment, or observational study.

Thus most documents are written for some purpose other than social research. These purposes vary greatly. Personal, primary documents are generally, almost by definition, written for personal reasons. These include diaries, letters to friends or relatives, suicide notes, autobiographies, and letters of confession (often anonymous). Many nonpersonal documents are written continuously by businesses or organizations to keep a running record of events deemed important but that, because of complexity or quantity, cannot be trusted to memory. Such documents tend to be more structured than personal documents. These include minutes of meetings, interoffice memos, financial records, and files containing various other materials relevant to maintenance of the organization (e.g., employee records or membership lists). Some organizations have special kinds of document source. For example, the Church of Jesus Christ of Latter-Day Saints (Mormon) is famous for its massive genealogical records containing information on relatives of church members. The chief purpose for these records is religious, but access to them has been accorded for social-research purposes, and they provide data that in some cases is unique.

In addition to personal writings and business or organizational records and files, a third major area of documents is the printed mass media, specifically newspapers, magazines, journals and newsletters, and books of fiction or nonfiction.

Advantages of Document Study

1. *Inaccessible subjects.* One of the basic advantages of document studies is that they allow research on subjects to which the researcher does not have physical access, and thus cannot study by any other method. The most obvious group of people who are completely inaccessi-

ble for social research by any means except documents are those who are long dead. For example, Lantz et al. (1968) wished to study marriage and family patterns in America before the Industrial Revolution. Nobody who was alive in the period of interest (the 1700s) is alive today to be interviewed, so the analysis of colonial documents (in this case magazines) offers the only possible data source, in spite of some obvious disadvantages. Since there are no alternative data-collection methods for this study, if one is dissatisfied with the method of document study it is best not to do the study at all.

2. *Nonreactivity.* Document study shares with certain types of observation (e.g., indirect observation or nonparticipant observation through a one-way mirror) the advantage of little or no reactivity, particularly when the document was written for some other purpose. That is, it seems highly unlikely that authors and editors of colonial magazines anticipated being studied by Lantz et al. and thus felt unnatural, self-conscious, or bothered by the "guinea pig" effect. This does not mean that the method is free of bias (it is particularly susceptible to selective survival bias), but the data-collection method itself generally does not change the data being collected, because the method is generally utilized long after the participants in the behavior have died.

3. *Longitudinal analysis.* Like observation and unlike experiments and survey, document study is especially well suited to study over a long period of time. Many times the object of research is a trend. For example, the researcher might realize in 1994 that attitudes of whites toward blacks have changed, and be interested in studying the trend of these changes over the period 1945–1995. He or she cannot go back in time to 1945 to observe, so observational study is out. Since this is a matter of describing what happened empirically and is not an experimental situation, experimentation is eliminated. Survey research could be used to ask older persons about the changes they have seen occur over this 50-year period, but would be subject to much error caused by memory failure and by bias due to a hesitancy to admit the degree of prejudice that used to exist (or still exists). This leaves only document study (if suitable documents can be found) as a method capable of studying the 50-year trend.

4. *Sample size.* In contrast to experimentation and observation, which for reasons discussed in earlier chapters are limited in the size of the sample they can utilize, document study, like survey research, can often use a larger sample. As you remember from our discussion in chapter 5, a large sample means that we can have much more faith in our results, can obtain statistically significant results more easily, and can have more trust in generalizations from our results. As in survey sampling, the size of the population to be studied, and thus the size of the sample that can be drawn from this population, depends upon the persons or groups chosen to be studied. However, if a researcher is studying obituaries or some other portion of a newspaper over a long period of time, there should be no problem in drawing a sample as large as several thousand or more.

5. *Spontaneity.* Document study shares with observation the advantage that spontaneous actions or feelings can be recorded when they occur, rather than at a time specified by the researcher. That is, the particular time when a survey researcher chooses to ask a respondent about his or her feelings may not be the time when the respondent feels like discussing that subject. However, if the respondent is keeping a diary, he or she can record spontaneous feelings about the subject whenever he or she feels inspired to do so.

6. *Confession.* A person may be more likely to confess in a document, particularly one to

be read only after his or her death, than in an interview or mailed questionnaire study. Thus a study of documents such as diaries, posthumously published autobiographies, and suicide notes may be the only way to obtain such information.

7. *Relatively low cost.* Although the cost of documentary analysis can vary widely depending on the type of document analyzed, how widely documents are dispersed, and how far one must travel to gain access to them, documentary analysis can be inexpensive compared to large-scale surveys. Many times documents are gathered together in a centralized location such as a library or newspaper morgue where the analyst can study them for only the cost of travel to the repository.

8. *High quality.* Although documents vary tremendously in quality, many documents, such as newspaper columns, are written by skilled social commentators and may be much more valuable than, for example, poorly written responses to mailed questionnaires.

Disadvantages of Document Study

1. *Bias.* As we noted above, many documents used in social research were not originally intended for research purposes. The various goals and purposes for which documents are written can bias them in various ways. For example, personal documents such as confessional articles or autobiographies are often written by famous people or people who have had some unusual experience, such as having been a witness to the John F. Kennedy assassination or claiming to have been taken for a ride in a spaceship to Mars. While often providing unique and valuable research data, these documents usually are written for the purpose of making money. Thus they tend to exaggerate and even fabricate to make a good story. They also tend to include those events that make the author look good and exclude those that cast him or her in a negative light.

2. *Selective survival.* Since documents are generally written on paper, they do not withstand the elements well unless care is taken to preserve them. Thus while documents written by famous people are likely to be preserved, day-to-day documents such as letters and diaries written by common people tend either to be destroyed or to be placed in storage and thus become inaccessible. It is relatively rare for common documents that are not about some event of immediate interest to researchers (e.g., suicide) and not about some famous occurrence or by some famous person to be gathered together in a public history repository that is accessible to social researchers.

3. *Incompleteness.* Many documents provide an incomplete account to the researcher who has had no prior experience with or knowledge of the events or behavior discussed. A problem with many personal documents such as letters and diaries is that they were not written for research purposes but were designed to be private or even secret. Both of these kinds of documents often assume specific knowledge that researchers unfamiliar with certain events will not possess. Diaries are probably the worst in this respect, since they are usually written to be read only by the author and can consist more of "soul searching" and confession than of description. Letters tend to be a little more complete, since they are addressed to a second person. Still, many letters assume a great amount of prior information on the part of the reader. Consider the following hypothetical account from a personal letter:

On Saturday, Scoot, Skinny, and I went to town. It was the first time we had driven the new car. We really do like it, but it doesn't get very good gas mileage. We went to the same dime store and the same grocery store that you and I used to always go to, but not to our usual drugstore (we went to the drugstore we always referred to as the alternate). Unfortunately, the only boy we saw in town was the creep, you know who, the one we call Linda's boyfriend.

While such a letter builds on the knowledge shared by the two correspondents and provides all the information necessary for satisfactory communication between them, it provides only minimal information for the researcher.

4. *Lack of availability.* In addition to bias, incompleteness, and selective survival of documents, there are many areas of study for which no documents are available. In many cases the information simply was never recorded. In other cases it was recorded, but the documents remain secret or classified, or have been destroyed.

5. *Sampling bias.* Recalling our discussion of sampling in chapter 5, the first task was to construct a sampling frame or complete list of all potential respondents from which the sample could be drawn. One of the problems of bias occurred because persons of lower educational or income levels were less likely to be on available lists (e.g., voter-registration lists) from which sampling frames could be compiled. After the sample was drawn, surveys, particularly mailed surveys, encountered problems posed by the limited ability of poorly educated persons to read the questionnaire and to express themselves in writing. The problem of sampling bias by educational level is even more acute for document study than for survey research. It is a safe generalization that poorly educated people are much less likely than well-educated people to write documents. In addition, poorly educated people read much less frequently than well-educated people. Thus the mass media are not aimed at them, and it is likely that their viewpoints are not well represented in such publications.

6. *Limited to verbal behavior.* By definition, documents provide information only on a respondent's verbal behavior, and provide no direct information on the respondent's nonverbal behavior. The document being analyzed may contain a *description* of nonverbal behavior, either that of the document's author or of another person. However, in direct contrast to the observational method, the experiment, and even the survey, where direct observation by the researcher is common, the document analyst cannot possibly observe the nonverbal behavior of his or her respondents, as they typically are not personally present and he or she has only their written accounts to work with.

7. *Lack of a standard format.* Documents differ quite widely in regard to their standardization of format. Some documents, such as newspapers, appear frequently in a standard format. Large dailies always contain such standard components as the opinion-editorial page, obituaries, comics, sports, and weather report. Such standardization facilitates comparison across time for the same newspaper, and comparison across different newspapers at one point in time. However, many other documents, particularly personal documents, have no standard format. Comparison is difficult or impossible, since valuable information contained in a document at one point in time may be entirely lacking in an earlier or later document.

8. *Coding difficulties.* For a number of reasons, including differences in purpose for which the documents were written, differences in content or subject matter, lack of standardization, and differences in length and format, coding is one of the most difficult tasks facing the docu-

ment analyst. Documents are generally written in words rather than numbers and are quite difficult to quantify. Thus analysis of them is similar to analysis of open-ended survey questions or of observational field notes, as described earlier. However, a method of quantifying documents, called content analysis, is in use and will be discussed below. Content analysis can also be used to analyze open-ended questions and field notes.

9. *Data must be adjusted for comparability over time.* Although one of the advantages of document study is that comparisons may be made over a long period of time, often external events cause changes so drastic that even if a common unit of analysis is used for the entire time period, the value of this unit may have changed so much over time that comparisons are misleading unless corrections are made. A good example is the reduced buying power of the U.S. dollar. Comparisons of average income in 1878 with average income in 1978 would make it appear that contemporary Americans have infinitely more comparative buying power than their counterparts of 1878. An analysis in constant 1920 dollars would show that this is not true.

Further discussion of the advantages and disadvantages of documents as data sources for social research is found in Webb et al. (1981, pp. 162–96). Among the documents that they cite as data sources are film scripts, epitaphs, propaganda pamphlets, airline manifests, and city directories. They also discuss various errors that may impair the adequacy of the documents, and questions about the origins of the documents, which can have bearing on their usefulness in research.

Data Sources

Almost by definition, personal documents tend to be personal and private property, and are often confidential. This fact sometimes makes it difficult to secure possession of even a single particularly interesting (but perhaps personally damaging) document, and exceedingly difficult to accumulate a large sample of such documents. It is probably primarily for this reason that analysts of personal documents, like field observers, are likely to prefer an in-depth intensive case study of one or a few carefully selected documents in lieu of a more superficial study of a large number of them. There may be cases, however, in which a researcher can gain access to a large sample of personal documents in a single source, such as a sample of letters to a politician or newspaper about a particular political issue. Letters of special interest, such as suicide notes, may be gathered in special collections or archives and available to the researcher in quantity. But whether the source of a document is a teenager's personal diary, the collected personal papers of a famous person (such as a past president of the United States), or a newspaper morgue, the procedure for gaining entry is about the same as described for surveys and observational studies: Convince those in charge that you are a legitimate researcher with a legitimate purpose. This is done in ways described earlier, such as letters of introduction on the letterhead of a university or respected private research facility, possession of a government grant, a statement of the research purpose, summaries of past published research, and a promise to share the results of the research if desired. In addition, the usual promises should be made about confidentiality and ethical use of the data.

Within the past few years a number of data archives have been initiated, many with computerized information that is easily retrieved and is readily available to the researcher, often for a fee. An extensive listing of these archives is contained in the book, *Social Science Data Archives: Applications and Potential* (Hofferbert and Clubb 1977). Even more recently, an important resource tool for locating and utilizing data in archives is provided by Kiecolt and Nathan (1985). They provide a comprehensive guide to data archives and provide details on several major files. Also see Stewart (1984). Stewart also discusses information sources, including already published data, and provides information on computerized data bases.

Many archives, such as the Roper Public Opinion Research Center at Williams College, contain only the questions and answers from past surveys. However, a number of them contain documents, generally in the form of biographical information about politicians. For example, the Archive on Political Elites in Eastern Europe, located in the political science department of the University of Pittsburgh, contains biographical information on approximately 12,000 persons who have been leading political figures in Eastern Europe since 1945. Similarly, the UCLA Political Behavior Archives contains biographical data on legislators. The reader is referred to Hofferbert and Clubb 1977 for further information. In addition to a description of the data contained in each archive, the book provides information on how the data are stored (e.g., computer tapes) and procedures to be followed by researchers wishing to use the data.

An increasingly important source of sociological data is the General Social Survey (GSS). It has been conducted since 1972 (except for 1979 and 1981), and some of its questions were asked even earlier. It consists of face-to-face interviews on a national sample of approximately 1,500 respondents, asking a broad range of questions. Thus, the GSS provides an important and continuing source of sociological data. For further discussion see Glenn (1978), Singleton et al. (1988), and Frankfort-Nachmias and Nachmias (1992).

Secondary Analysis

Many researchers use data from the available data archives (either in the form of documents or survey results and codebooks) for *secondary analysis*. Secondary analysis is the analysis of a document or data gathered or authored by another person. The secondary analyst generally has a research goal different from that of the first researcher. For example as a sociologist interested in studying stratification, you might find in a data archive a codebook from a study of voting behavior conducted by a political scientist, and discover upon examination that the study gathered sufficient (as yet unanalyzed) data on social class to enable you to conduct a perfectly adequate stratification study.

Hyman (1972) presents a comprehensive treatment of secondary analysis. Among the benefits of secondary analysis listed by Hyman are: (1) a savings of time and money by use of available data rather than collection of original new data; (2) less invasion of privacy by using existing data rather than collecting new data; and (3) ease in making comparative analyses (for example, comparing different countries through the secondary analysis of data collected in the respective countries). Comparative studies would include trend studies or comparisons over time.

There are also obvious disadvantages to secondary analysis. Perhaps the major disadvantage is that some of the data that the researcher needs may simply not be available. Another is that the original data may contain errors that the secondary researcher is not able to detect.

For example, consider the secondary analysis conducted by Hunt and Hunt (1977). They were interested in the effect that the absence of a father in the household has on the development of children. More specifically, they were interested in the effect that father absence has on the daughter, as most research on father absence has been concerned with sons. Further, they were also interested in the effect of race.

Collection of data for this study obviously would have taken a long time and would have been very expensive. Fortunately, the Hunts were able to use data that had previously been collected for a study of racial esteem by Rosenberg and Simmons (1972). Those data were comprised of interviews from 1,917 Baltimore public school students in grades 3 through 12 in 1968. They included interviews from both blacks and whites and males and females. There was information on father absence, social class, personal esteem, academic activities, dating, and future orientation.

Hunt and Hunt (1977) conclude that father absence does have an effect on a daughter's development and that there are some racial differences. For white daughters, for example, sex role identification and dating are slightly lower when the father is absent, and marriage plans are reduced significantly. The effects of father's absence are not as pronounced for black daughters but are present. A black father's absence leads not only to diminished marriage plans, but also to lower self-esteem.

Another factor to consider in secondary analysis is that even though the original data may be excellent and may contain all the information the researcher needs, the task of working with masses of data may still be considerable. Some researchers think that because the data are already collected and stored, for example on computer cards or a computer tape, they can begin analysis immediately. This is not always the case by any means. Hunt and Hunt (1981, p. 318) reported difficulty in "achieving focus" or moving from the mass of available data to a set of specific questions and their operationalization. Similarly, Watts (1982) studied Jewish fertility, utilizing data from the first National Jewish Population Survey (NJPS) completed in 1971. Although the data were already stored on computer tape, the fertility data were stored separately from other needed data such as social, economic, and religious variables. The goals of Watts's study necessitated combining this information into a single source—a relatively time-consuming task that had to be completed before analysis could begin. For further information on procedures of secondary analysis as well as additional examples, see Hyman (1972) and Kiecolt and Nathan (1985). Kiecolt and Nathan present a very contemporary and helpful analysis of secondary research. They not only provide designs for secondary analysis but also discuss a variety of salient issues, including operationalization, sampling issues, and the analysis of rare populations. For a more recent discussion of secondary analysis, including a discussion of conceptual-substantive, methodological, and economic reasons for conducting it, see Frankfort-Nachmias and Nachmias (1992, pp. 291–318).

Types of Documentary Analysis

In chapter 10 we classified observational studies into four types, depending both on the degree of structure of the observational instrument and whether the setting was natural or an artificial laboratory. In discussing document study we shall limit ourselves to two main types: the relatively unstructured and nonquantitative case-study approach and the structured content-analysis approach that yields quantitative data from verbal documents. Thus we classify documentary methods only on the basis of the structure of our analytical method, and not on the structure of the document itself. This is because, while some documents are more standardized that others, virtually all of them have in common the fact that they were not written for purposes of social research, and are thus generally not organized so as to make them amenable to research. They all pose approximately the same analysis problems for social research, and can all be considered unstructured or natural in this regard. Further, since unstructured methods are more likely to be used on personal documents and structured methods are not likely to be used on nonpersonal documents it is sufficient to limit our discussion to these two chief types: unstructured/personal and structured/nonpersonal.

Since document analysis is basically nonreactive and does not include the problems of rapport, and so on, encountered in the other methods, the list of stages in analysis can be reduced to two major problem areas: (1) gaining access to the documents and (2) coding and analyzing the documents.

Personal Documents

In a way, the study of personal documents is similar to participant observation, while the study of nonpersonal documents is similar to survey research. In studying nonpersonal documents, as in survey research, it is often relatively easy to achieve a rather large sample. For example, a researcher interested in a newspaper study has many newspapers to sample from. The study of personal documents is like observation in that while it has the distinct advantage of the spontaneity of first-person accounts and a depth of intimacy and innermost (even subconscious) feeling not generally available in survey research or nonpersonal document study, it generally does not offer a very large sample size (the Thomas and Znaniecki study discussed below is a prominent exception). Thus many researchers studying personal documents, like ethographers studying alien cultures, generally opt for a small sample or case-study design that can be studied in depth, rather than a large sample that can only be studied in a superficial manner. As in ethnography, the cases to be studied in personal document study are often chosen subjectively by the researcher because of his or her own special interest, rather than being randomly selected.

The case-study approach allows the researcher to select examples that illustrate the points he or she wishes to make. Thus the approach lends itself to qualitative rather than quantitative analysis. Analysis of personal documents will generally consist of the construction of taxonomies, as in the analysis of data from observational field studies. After the taxonomy is discussed, particular examples of personal documents can be chosen to illustrate the different types contained in the taxonomy or to illustrate some theoretical point. That is, rather than constructing a hypothesis about, for example, family structure in peasant communities, and testing it by gathering data from a survey, the personal document analyst is more likely to make a generalization about family structure, then illustrate it with excerpts from personal documents.

A classic study by Thomas and Znaniecki (1918), probably the most famous study of personal documents, used this approach. Their data consisted of a large number of personal letters written by Polish immigrants in America and their relatives in Poland. Thomas and Znaniecki first present a taxonomy of peasant letters. They say that all peasant letters are variations on one fundamental type, the bowing letter:

> The bowing letter is normally written by or to a member of the family who is absent for a certain time. Its function is to manifest the persistence of familial solidarity in spite of the separation. Such an expression became necessary only when members of the family began to leave their native locality; as long as the family stayed in the same community, the solidarity was implicitly and permanently assumed. . . . In accordance with its function, the bowing letter has an exactly determined composition. It begins with the religious greeting: "Praised be Jesus Christus," to which the reader is supposed to answer, "In centuries of centuries. amen." The greeting has both a magical and a moral significance. Magically it averts evil, morally it shows that the writer and the reader are members of the same religious community. . . (Thomas and Znaniecki 1918, vol. I. p. 303).

The letter also expresses that the writer is in good health and wishes good health for the family members. It concludes with "bows" or greetings from all members of the family who are still alive in the same locality. There are five subtypes of bowing letter:

1. Ceremonial letters, which are sent on all occasions normally requiring the presence of all family members, such as weddings and funerals. The ceremonial letter is a substitute for a ceremonial speech.
2. Informing letters, providing detailed information on the life of the absent member if a personal meeting cannot be arranged for some time.
3. Sentimental letters, which have the task of strengthening family solidarity by reviving feelings in the individual, independent of any ceremonial occasion.
4. Literary letters, which substitute for the performance of music and recital of poems during ceremonies by composing the letter in verse.
5. Business letters.

Thomas and Znaniecki (1918 vol. I, p. 311) provide an example of the ceremonial-congratulatory portion of a letter:

Poreby Wolskie, January 30, 1910

Praised be Jesus Christus.

Dearest Children, and particularly you, daughter-in-law:

We write you the third letter and we have no answer from you [Greetings; health; wishes.] We hope that this letter will come to you for February 16, and on February 16 is the day of St. Julianna, patron of our daughter-in-law. Well, we congratulate you, dear daughter-in-law, because it is your name-day. We wish you health and happiness and long life. May you never have any sorrow; may you love one another and live in concord and love; may our Lord God make you happy in human friendship; make you happy and gay; may our Lord God supply all your wants; may you lack nothing; may our Lord God defend you against every evil accident and keep you in his protection and grant you his gifts, the heavenly dew and the earthly fat. May our Lord God give you every sweetness, make you happy, and save you from evil. This your father and mother wish you from their whole heart. . . .

Jan and Ewa Stelmach

Other examples of bowing letters are provided by Thomas and Znaniecki (1918, vol. II, p. 26) from the Kozlowski series, which they used to illustrate primary-group organization of Polish peasants:

July 12, 1907

I, Josef Plata, wish to take your dear mother for my wife. Answer as soon as possible whether you will take her or whether you tell her to marry me. I would give my life for her. I have nothing more to write, only I send a low bow to you all, to the whole family.

Your well-wishing
Josef Plata

The reprinting of these letters constitutes data analysis for Thomas and Znaniecki, with each letter illustrating a theoretical point. This particular letter illustrates the importance of the family rather than the individual in Polish peasant life. As Thomas and Znaniecki say of this letter:

The man simply asks for permission to marry their mother. This indicates once more the degree to which the family is felt as a reality, and the marriage of any member—father or mother, brother or sister, son or daughter—as affecting immediately this reality, is a familial as well as individual matter (Thomas and Znaniecki 1918, vol. II, p. 26).

The Thomas and Znaniecki book is a massive work of two full volumes dealing solely with letters and commentary showing the relevance of the letters for the study of family structure among Polish peasants. The work was quite controversial at the time. As Phillips says of Thomas and Znaniecki's qualitative case-study approach:

Many sociologists felt this method provided an excellent opportunity to convey a thorough account of all phases of life, and, in particular, man's inner mental life. A number of quantitative or statistically oriented sociologists attacked the method on the grounds that the citation of examples does not constitute scientific proof and that the method is highly subjective, especially because the investigator can select life histories to suit his own purposes.

This controversy within sociology has been resolved to some extent, with most sociologists agreeing that both case studies and statistics can contribute to the scientific process (B. Phillips 1971, p. 99).

Plummer (1983) provides a detailed and helpful discussion of various facets of document study. He presents an extensive listing of various types of documents, with emphasis on life-history analysis. His discussion includes the analysis of photographs and films. He then analyzes various studies, including the "Polish Peasant," and also discusses ways of doing life histories.

Content Analysis

Researchers interested in the more traditionally scientific or quantitative sort of hypothesis testing will be uncomfortable with the qualitative sort of description espoused by Thomas and Znaniecki, and will find the highly structured technique of content analysis more to their liking. The basic goal of content analysis is to take a verbal, nonquantitative document and transform it into quantitative data. The results of content analysis can generally be presented in tables containing frequencies or percentages, in the same manner as survey data. How does one perform this marvelous social alchemy that can turn words into number? The answer is often as simple as mere word counting.

Markoff et al. (1974, p. 5) review some of the common definitions of content analysis:

Content analysis is a research technique for the objective, systematic, and quantitative description of the manifest content of communication (Berelson 1954, p. 489).

Content analysis is any research technique for making references by systematically and objectively identifying specified characteristics within text (Stone et al. 1966, p. 5).

In the subsequent discussion, we propose to use the terms "content analysis" and "coding" interchangeably, to refer to the objective, systematic, and quantitative description of any symbolic behavior (Cartwright 1953, p. 424).

For a comprehensive discussion of content analysis see Weber (1985). Weber discusses a variety of content analysis procedures and coding strategies, and also discusses reliability and validity.

Purpose

Content analysis is the equivalent in document study to survey research. It is conducive to the use of formal hypotheses, large scientifically drawn samples, and quantitative data that can be analyzed with computers and modern statistical techniques. Thus the purposes of content analysis cover virtually all areas of specialization encompassed by survey techniques. In addition, content analysis has some special purposes, such as the determination of authorship for documents whose authority is questionable. Holsti (1969, p. 43) lists seven purposes for content analysis in addition to scientific hypothesis testing:

1. To describe trends in communication content
2. To relate known characteristics of sources to messages they produce
3. To audit communication content against standards
4. To analyze techniques of persuasion
5. To analyze style
6. To relate known attributes of the audience to messages produced for them
7. To describe patterns of communication

Content analysis is basically the same process as the structured observation discussed in chapter 10 for both the Bales (1950) and the Sears et al. (1965) studies. In each of those studies the observer looked for a checklist of specific behaviors. The categories in the checklist comprised a nominal classification. That is, they were mutually exclusive, with each behavior listed in only one category, and they were exhaustive, in the sense that all behaviors of interest to the observer were capable of classification in some one (single) category. Content analysis is the same sort of structured analysis applied to documents rather than to observation of non-verbal behavior. In other words, it is a structured document-analysis technique in which the researcher first constructs a set of mutually exclusive and exhaustive categories that can be used to analyze documents, and then records the frequency with which each of these categories is observed in the documents studied. As an example, let us do a content analysis of three short documents: the definitions of content analysis quoted above. Imagine that from our discussion of methods of data collection we have decided that the three chief components of data-collection methods are their degree of structure as classified by whether they are (1) quantitative/qualitative, (2) systematic/nonsystematic, and (3) objective/subjective. We would expect an unstructured method such as the ethnographic observational field study or the Thomas and Znaniecki case-study approach to personal document analysis to be described as basically qualitative, non-systematic, and subjective. In contrast, we would expect a structured method such as content analysis to be described as relatively quantitative, systematic, and objective.

After constructing categories, all that remains is to examine the documents from the view-points of these categories and to classify each document by counting the categories it exhibits. We will code by placing a "1" in each category the document fits. Let us use the following schedule for classification:

Document Number and Name	Category					
	Quantitative	Qualitative	Systematic	Non-systematic	Objective	Subjective
1. Berelson	1		1		1	
2. Stone			1		1	
3. Cartwright	1		1		1	

In percentage terms, the word "quantitative" appeared in 66 percent of the documents, the word "systematic" appeared in 100 percent of the documents, and the word "objective" appeared in 100 percent of the documents. The document that did not mention "quantitative" also did not mention "qualitative," so that the words "qualitative," "nonsystematic," and "subjective" appeared in none of the documents.

Not all content analyses are easily performed as this rudimentary exercise. In general, construction of a structured set of categories for analyzing documents is more difficult than construction of a structured set of categories for analyzing observation (e.g., Bales's 12 categories) because in documents the unit of analysis is generally less clear. For example, in the Sears et al. (1965) structured observational study the unit of analysis was some observable action on the part of the child, such as dressing up like an adult or rubbing the genitals.

There are no individual identifiable and discrete acts in a document. Thus categories used in content analysis will differ not only in content, as they did in observation (e.g, masturbation or adult role), but they are also more likely to differ in the unit of analysis. The unit of analysis can certainly vary in observational analysis but it is less likely to do so. The content analyst also shares with the structured observer the task of developing some coding scheme for converting his or her data into numbers. He or she may use simple frequencies of occurrence, as we did above, or some other scheme. In the order they must be completed (earlier steps are prerequisites for later steps) the five chief tasks facing a content analyst are:

1. Draw the sample of documents.
2. Define the content of categories. The actual content depends upon the purpose of the study.
3. Define the recording unit.
4. Define the context unit.
5. Define the system of enumeration.

Sampling

We have discussed sampling at some length in chapter 5 in conjunction with survey research. Sampling procedures are much the same for content analysis, and need be mentioned only briefly here. The primary step is to compile a sampling frame, or list of units from which the sample is to be drawn. As noted above, this can easily lead to bias, particularly among poorly educated people who are less likely to be the source of documents. For example, a document study that attempted to compare the levels of fatalism among different social class levels (lower class, upper class, and so on) might be severely handicapped by an overabundance of materials representing the upper class and a paucity of materials for the lower class. It might be necessary to gather a disproportionately higher sample for the lower class. Conversely, if we can assume that fatalism levels are lower for the upper class and higher for the lower class, we can predict that a document study that did not note class but merely attempted to estimate the fatalism level for Americans in general would yield an estimate that was too low because of an upper-class bias in the sample.

After a sampling frame is constructed, most of the several sampling methods discussed in chapter 5 can be used. Random sampling is probably the most widely used and least complicated method. However, if the units to be sampled can be assumed to be in random order on the sampling frame, then systematic sampling can be used. Stratified sampling has also been employed, with documents stratified on both circulation and geographical location (Holsti 1969, p. 131). One may also use cluster sampling (e.g., to draw a sample of documents and then to sample words or some other unit within each document). For further discussion of sampling in content analysis see Holsti (1969, pp. 127–35).

Categories

Holsti (1969, p. 95) says that categories should reflect the purposes of the research, and be exhaustive, mutually exclusive, and independent. By "independent" we mean that the value of one category does not determine the value of another category.

The major requirement is that categories be adequate for the purposes of the study. After the researcher has defined the goals of his or her study, then he or she must construct a set of appropriate categories. As with Bales's 12 categories for observation, categories for content analysis are generally not derived from theory or constructed out of thin air, but are constructed by examining the documents to be studied and ascertaining what common elements they contain. Only by letting the categories emerge from the documents to be analyzed can the goals of mutual exclusiveness and exhaustiveness be met. Categories constructed without prior inspection of documents would no doubt exclude many important categories and include many that are superfluous or unnecessary.

Holsti (1969) provides many different examples of category sets that have been used in past content analyses. Some of these, such as Mott's (1942) categories for identifying trends in newspaper content, merely divide the document into various sections according to the content of each section. Mott's 12 categories are (1) foreign news and features; (2) Washington news; (3) columns dealing with public affairs; (4) original editorials; (5) business, financial, marine; (6) sports; (7) society; (8) women's interests; (9) theater, movies, books, art; (10) radio announcements and news; (11) comic strips and singles; and (12) illustration (excluding comics). Many other content analysts have been interested primarily in the values revealed in documents. For example, Berelson and Salter (1946) studied the values displayed in popular fiction. They used the following value categories:

A. *"Heart" goals*
1. Romantic love
2. Settled marriage state
3. Idealism
4. Affection and emotional security
5. Patriotism
6. Adventure
7. Justice
8. Independence

B. *"Head" goals*
1. Solution to immediate concrete problems
2. Self-advancement
3. Money and material goods
4. Economic and social security
5. Power and dominance

Numerous other types of category scheme have been devised. Larson, Gray, and Fortis (1963) studied goals or ends in children's television programs, as well as means to the end. Their seven categories of goals included material success and power and prestige, while means or methods of achieving goals comprised eight categories, including legal and violent.

Still other studies have examined traits of the characters portrayed in documents. Almond (1954) studied the traits of ideal Communists, as portrayed in Communist party literature. His categories included goal traits (esoteric and exoteric) as well as eight tactical qualities or traits (e.g., militance, leadership, dedication). Numerous other category systems have been used. McGranahan and Wayne (1948), in their study of German and American theater, had seven categories for basic themes (love, morality, idealism, power, outcast, career, no agreement) and four for endings (happy, ambiguous, tragic or unhappy, no agreement), as well as other categories for time of action, setting, and patterns of conflict. Other studies have classified propaganda, with categories such as glittering generalities and name calling (Lee 1952), and bias in newspapers, using such categories as number of stories and number of column inches

(Klein and Maccoby 1954). In another study of bias in news magazines, Merrill (1965) used the following categories: (1) attribution bias, (2) adjective bias, (3) adverbial bias, (4) contextual bias, (5) outright opinion, and (6) photographic bias. Obviously there have been as many category systems as there have been different types of document and different purposes for the study.

Recording Unit

Choice of categories does not generally determine the appropriate recording unit (also called the unit of analysis). That is, for a given set of documents and a given set of categories, there is no one single recording unit that must be used. Holsti (1969, pp. 116–19) lists five chief recording units: (1) the single word or symbol, (2) the theme, (3) the character (i.e., a character in a novel, drama, movie, or radio or television show), (4) the sentence or paragraph, and (5) the item.

Single Word.   Although a few studies have used even smaller units, such as letters or syllables, the single word is generally the smallest unit employed. The obvious problem with using a single word as the recording unit is that if one's sample contains a great many lengthy documents there will simply be too many words for the researcher to manage, and he or she will be overwhelmed with data. For this reason the single word has usually been passed over in mass-media content analyses in favor of some larger unit. Holsti (1969, p. 116) says that words or symbols have found widest use as the recording unit in studies dealing with readability, style, psychotherapy, and literary detection. The advantage of using a word or symbol as the recording unit is that a single word is discrete, has clear boundaries, and is relatively easy to identify. This is in direct contrast to some other recording unit such as the theme, which often has no clear and objective nonambiguous boundaries.

The Theme.   Theme refers to the moral purpose, or goal of a document or portion of a document. One theme might be that Russia, or China, or communism in general is a threat to the life and liberty of the American people. Another theme is that without zero population growth the world will be doomed to starvation. The complete elucidation of a theme may take only a few words or part of a sentence, or it may require many paragraphs or even chapters or volumes. The point is that determining the boundaries of a theme may be much more difficult and subjective than determining the boundaries of some other recording unit such as a word. Sub-portions of a document are already clearly bounded by the rules of grammar and writing style. That is, the boundaries of a word are clear because the word is set off by spaces on either side; the boundaries of a sentence are clear because each sentence has double spaces on either side, begins with a capitalized word, and ends with a period or some other mark of final punctuation; and the boundaries of a paragraph are clear because it begins with an indentation and is separated from the following paragraph by another indentation on a new line. Since the theme has no such spatial boundaries, consensus about where the theme begins and ends may be low, leading to low intercoder reliability.

The Character.   The character as recording unit is obviously limited to such documents as novels, plays, television dramas, movie scripts, or any other document that is known to have a cast of characters. The category systems used for characters generally involve such things as socioeconomic status (upper class, middle class) or ethnic status (black, Jewish, Chicano). The recording unit is the particular person, and the number of persons fitting into each of the categories is recorded. The advantage of this type of unit is that an individual person is concrete and unambiguous, thus avoiding the boundary problems involved in coding themes. Further, researchers using the character as a unit will probably not be overwhelmed with numbers. Thus the character is a good unit to use where applicable, but has limited utility and can only be used with a special kind of document.

The Sentence or Paragraph. We have mentioned that grammatical units, including the sentence and paragraph, have the advantage of their boundaries being easily recognized. However, a definite disadvantage of the sentence and paragraph, unlike the word, is that they often contain more than one topic or theme. Thus they are not mutually exclusive and are not very satisfactory recording units. For example, suppose that your categories are Lasswell and Kaplan's (1950) value categories of power, rectitude, respect, affection, wealth, well-being, enlightenment, and skill, and that you are using the sentence as the unit of analysis. Following the rule of mutual exclusiveness, there has to be one, but only one, clear and unique place for each sentence. Now suppose that you encounter the following hypothetical sentence: "While Mr. Jones was treated with great affection in his hometown, he still commanded respect for the covert power that great wealth usually brings." Here a single unit of analysis (the sentence) contains words belonging in four different value categories (affection, respect, power, and wealth), and thus does not fit clearly into any one category. The word or symbol would have been a superior recording unit in this instance.

The Item. Even though it is a unit broad enough to encounter problems with meeting the mutual exclusiveness criterion, the sentence or paragraph is often too small a unit when a large number of documents must be compared. When many documents must be compared, Holsti recommends the item as a unit of analysis:

> The *item* is the recording unit when the entire article, film, book, or radio program is characterized. This unit is too gross for most research, and may present problems when items fall between two categories; e.g., is a war film with a comic theme classified under "war" or "comedy" (Holsti, 1969, p. 117).

Besides its crudeness, a problem with the item as a recording unit is that there is really no clear distinction between an item and a theme, except that the word "item" seems to be used when referring to the entire document, while a "theme" refers to only a small portion of the document.

Context Unit

For any given recording unit (e.g., a word), it may sometimes be difficult or impossible to tell in which category the unit belongs without considering the context in which it is found. That is, suppose that in a study of values the investigator desires to use the word as the recording unit. He or she does not have so many documents that use of a single word is impractical. In addition, he or she feels that any unit larger than a single word will not provide the necessary precision.

For example, imagine that you are interested not only in determining the existence of power but are further interested (as Lantz et al. [1968] were) in whether the husband or wife has the power. The first step is to search for the single word "power," since this is the recording unit and also the name of a value category. However, it may often be impossible to tell from the single word whether the power belongs to the husband or the wife. The word must be read in context, so researchers often choose a context unit, which is a larger unit that includes the recording unit. Thus if the recording unit is the word, the context unit may be a sentence, paragraph, theme, chapter, or the entire volume. With some particular category sets and some types of documents, use of a context unit may not be necessary. However, when it is necessary, it must be chosen subjectively by the researcher, in the same manner as the set of categories and the recording unit.

Systems of Enumeration

After the researcher has decided upon his or her categories, recording unit, and context unit, he or she must decide how to quantify the data. There are four chief ways to enumerate or quantify the data in content analysis: (1) simple binary coding to indicate whether or not the category appears in the document; (2) frequency with which the category appears in the document; (3) amount of space allotted to the category; and (4) strength or intensity with which the category is represented.

Appears or Not.   The type of enumeration that should be used depends at least in part on the purpose of the study. Assume that we wish to conduct a study of sexism or blatant discrimination against females in a sample of newspapers. We have available 50 different newspapers, each covering a span of 75 years, from 1900 to 1975. In addition, we have a number of mutually exclusive and (for our purposes) exhaustive categories about women, including (1) place is in the home; (2) inferior to men; (3) overly emotional; and (4) should not have right to vote. If the purpose of our study is merely to compare the various newspapers to see which are the most sexist, we might be content to note whether any of these categories occurs in a particular newspaper. For example, if the *Star* contains in an editorial the statement that women belong in the home, but the *News* does not contain any of these categories, then we might conclude that the *Star* is more sexist than the *News*. This simple noting of whether a category exists is nothing more than nominal level classification, or what we have been calling qualitative as opposed to quantitative data analysis.

Frequency.   A more informative and more quantitative measure than merely measuring whether or not the category appears is the frequency with which it appears. For example, we might compare the *Tribune* with the *Star* and find that both are sexist in the sense that all of our sexism categories appear in their editorials for a certain year. However, while all categories appear in each of the two newspapers, the frequency of appearance might be much greater in one newspaper. For example, we might ultimately judge the *Tribune* to be much more sexist than the *Star* because the *Star* may have a maximum frequency of five appearances for the year in any one category (e.g., women are inferior, woman's place is in the home), while the *Tribune* may have an average frequency in each category of more than 15, with a high in one category of 30 or more.

Knowing the exact frequency with which a category appears is much more valuable than merely knowing whether or not the category appears at all. All appearance tells us is whether the category has a frequency of zero (does not appear) or of one or more. However, if the frequency is at least one, the category is merely coded as appearing, and we do not know the actual frequency. Frequency measures are probably the most widely used system or method of enumeration and are essential to some types of content analysis. One type of content analysis that relies upon frequency enumeration is the word-frequency study with the goal of determining who authored a certain document. Although determination of authorship may also be accomplished by looking for unique phrases or combinations of words a particular author may have favored, probably the most common way is simply to count the frequency with which a particular word or words appears in a document. This type of content analysis is an assessment of criterion validity (see chapter 4 for a discussion of validity). The basic procedure is first to examine some document that you are sure was written by the author in question, and determine from it the frequency with which certain words are used. You then turn to the document whose authorship is uncertain and compare its word frequencies with those of the known document.

An example of such a word-frequency study is Yule's (1944) study of *The Imitation of Christ*. It was suspected that the author was either Thomas à Kempis or Jean Gerson. Yule compared *The Imitation of Christ* with two other documents, one known to have been authored by Thomas à Kempis and the other known to have been authored by Jean Gerson. Yule made five separate word-frequency comparisons of these three documents. In each of the five instances he counted the frequency of various classes of nouns in each of the three documents. Yule's findings are summarized in table 12–1 (Yule 1944, p. 275).

Table 12–1

Incidence of Special Nouns in *The Imitation of Christ*
and in Known Writings of Thomas à Kempis and Jean Gerson

Test	*The Imitation of Christ*	*Thomas à Kempis*	*Jean Gerson*
1.	671	709	912
2.	376	365	823
3.	59	58	162
4.	6	7	21
5.	0	1	24

Source: G. Udney Yule (1944) in *The Statistical Study of Literary Vocabulary,* Cambridge, Eng.: Cambridge University Press. Reprinted by the permission of the publisher. © Cambridge University Press.

Frequency counting is one of the best methods for determining authorship of questionable ancient documents. However, in many other cases, as in the sexism example above, the researcher is not interested merely in the pattern of words but wishes to infer that the higher the frequency in a certain set of categories, the higher the document scores on a particular scale or dimension. For example, if we had four sexism categories and one document had a frequency of 50 mentions in the four categories, while another document had only 10 mentions, we might say that the former represented a higher value of sexism than the latter. The trouble with this use of frequency measures is that it assumes that all categories are equal and that all mentions of a particular category or recording unit (word, theme, and so on) should be weighted equally. In some cases this is a realistic assumption and in some it is not.

The assumption that each mention is equal does not necessarily hold even for a single word. Some words are ambiguously defined and so mean different things to different people. Also, some words have more than one meaning. Many words have different meanings depending on the context. But even if we can assume that the meaning of a word is identical in every case, we still may not be able to assume that all appearances of that word deserve equal weighting. In some cases the author may use differing adjectives to modify the meaning of the word, or may use modifiers such as "very" or "extremely." The author may also end the sentence with an exclamation point to show emphasis. Consider the following hypothetical quotations:

> I suppose you could say that women are inferior. At least the average woman seems to be inferior to the average man.

> Women are *extremely* inferior, with emphasis on the extremely. They are inferior, period!

> Women are "inferior" to men the way that apples are "inferior" to oranges. They are simply two different dimensions.

If one merely counts the number of times the word "inferior" is used in discussing women, the three passages are equal, since each has a frequency of two. However, regardless of how "objective" such quantification is supposed to be, it does not take a genius to see that the third statement is least sexist, the first statement is next least, or intermediate, and the second statement is most sexist. Mere frequency tabulation does not show this.

In spite of the problems with unequal weighting of units, frequency enumeration has the obvious advantage of simplicity and convenience. Frequency counts (although not necessarily accurate ones) are practically handed to the researcher with a minimum of effort on his or her part in the form of indexes in books and journals. A rough idea of the importance of any particular area of specialization can be achieved by perusing the cumulative index to the *American Sociological Review*. A quick glance will suffice to show the declining interest in rural sociology and the increased interest in urban sociology.

Psychologists use the experimental method more than do sociologists, but sociologists use the survey interview more than do psychologists. Thus one would hypothesize that a cursory inspection of the index of a research-methods text written by sociologists (Goode and Hatt 1952) would yield a higher frequency of entries on interviewing than would a text authored by a psychologist (Kerlinger 1964). The data reveal 46 listings under "interview" for Goode and Hatt and only nine for Kerlinger (23 if one includes entries under "interview schedule").

Amount of Space.   Rather than merely noting whether a category appears in the document, a better measure may be the amount of space devoted to the category. For example, during the week before a major election, a story about both the Democratic and Republican candidates may only appear once. Since both appear in the document, if our only enumeration is whether the candidate's name appears, we might have to conclude that there is no bias in the newspaper toward one candidate or the other. If we change our form of enumeration to amount of space, we may find that the Republican candidate was given two full columns while the Democratic candidate received only a brief mention, covering about one-tenth the space provided the Republican candidate.

Space measures (or time measures in the case of radio or television programs) seem to be most widely used in the analysis of mass media. If the purpose of the study is to compare the emphasis or bias of one newspaper, for example, with either a rival newspaper at the same point in time or the same newspaper at another time, then space analysis seems quite inadequate. The most common measures seem to be number of column inches devoted to a topic or size of headlines used in discussing that topic. The space measure could also be weighted by the position of the article in the newspaper. For example, certain sections of the newspaper, such as the front page or the opinion/editorial page, might be given higher weights. Thus a short article on the front page might be considered as important as a long article buried on the last page of the fifth section of the paper.

However, it should be clear that a very negative article and a very positive article can be of exactly the same length. There is not enough correlation between content and length of article to allow us to predict the former from the latter. Since space measures do not measure content, we have to conclude that they are very crude. In a nonsystematic review of evaluations made by anonymous referees of articles sent to sociology journals for publication, I have noticed some bimodality. That is, very short evaluations (five to seven lines) seem generally to be either unanimously positive or unanimously negative. Longer evaluations (one page or more) tend to be mixed—some good and some bad points of the paper are noted, and the overall evaluation may be negative or positive. Thus it cannot be said that length provides no clue whatever to content, but it does not tell us much. In addition, we might improve the space measure by weighting according to position in the paper, as discussed above. Still, Holsti's (1969, p. 121) conclusion is that space measures are adequate for descriptions of mass media but too crude for analysis of attitudes, values, or style. Space measures also may not prove as useful as word-frequency counts for determining the authorship of documents. Holsti (1969, p. 85) notes that sentence length proved useless in attempting to decide whether James Madison or Alexander Hamilton wrote *The Federalist Papers,* since known writings of Madison average 34.59 (or 34.6) words per sentence, while known writings of Hamilton yielded an insignificantly different average of 34.55 (or 34.6)

Strength or Intensity of the Statement.   With the possible exception of frequency counts, only measures of the strength or intensity of a statement really provide the information in which we are interested: revelation of the content of the document. Space and appearance measures are crude secondary indicators of content. For example, suppose I wished to know who was older, Jim or John. I would need the exact content of the document, i.e., their exact ages. Measures that showed only whether the age of each person appeared in the document, or how much space was devoted to age, or how frequently age was mentioned, would not tell me the exact value of the age variable.

The exact value of the variable or set of categories in question is generally not stated in numerical terms in the document. To derive a number, the researcher must use some scaling procedures, as discussed in chapter 15. One of the simplest kinds of scaling procedure is the summated rating procedure, which can be approximated in frequency counts. In chapter 15 we provide an example of an anomia scale consisting of five items with which the respondent could either agree or disagree. Scoring one for agreement and zero for disagreement, a person's score could range between zero (no anomia) and five (complete anomia). Counting the frequency of sexist statements approximates this simple kind of scaling. To go beyond this, we have to move to simple order scaling in which we can say that one statement represents a higher level of the concept than another statement, so that the higher statement will never be made unless the lower one that serves as a prerequisite is made first.

Consider the following statements:

1. It is all right for an unmarried woman to work outside the home.
2. It is all right for a childless married woman to work outside the home.
3. It is all right for a married woman whose children are grown to work outside the home.
4. It is all right for a married woman to work outside the home regardless of the ages of her children.

If we enumerate in terms of intensity, we would assume that these statements are unequal; that is, they all have different values on a four-point scale measuring attitude toward women working. We would guess that the statements are ordered in terms of intensity, so that persons who would agree with 4 would also agree with 1, 2, and 3. Persons who do not agree with 4 but agree with 3 will also agree with 1 and 2. Persons disagreeing with 3 and 4 but agreeing with 2 will also agree with 1. Persons who disagree with 2, 3, and 4 may still agree with 1, or may disagree with all four.

It is clear that intensity enumeration gives a better idea of content. Under frequency coding, if statement 1 appeared in document A and 4 appeared in document B, we would conclude that both documents represented an equal value on the scale measuring attitude toward working women. With intensity enumeration we would conclude that document A represents the lowest value of agreement on the scale, while document B represents the highest value.

The construction of indexes for intensity enumeration is essentially the construction of scales. Several techniques of scale construction will be discussed in chapter 16 and need not be elaborated here. However, we might mention Thurstone's paired comparison procedure, as this has often been used in content analysis (Holsti 1969, pp. 123–24). It consists of comparing all possible parts of statements to see which rank higher and which lower on any given scale. The four statements above could be ranked to see which showed lower acceptance of women in the labor force and which showed higher acceptance by comparing:

1 versus 2	2 versus 3	3 versus 4
1 versus 3	2 versus 4	
1 versus 4		

If the consensus among several raters is that 1 is lower than 2, 3, or 4 on acceptance of women in the labor force; 2 is lower than either 3 or 4; and 3 is lower than 4, then we have evidence of a scale of attitudes toward women in the labor force.

The major developments in content analysis during the 1990s and beyond will involve computerization. This entails not only the use of computers to conduct the actual content analysis (which began in the 1960s) but also the computerization of the texts (documents) themselves. These are primarily of two forms: (a) documents that were originally printed on paper (the so-called hard copy) and then entered into the computer in machine-readable form, either by being entered through a terminal or scanned by a scanner; and (b) documents that were originally produced in machine-readable form (for example, letters written for electronic mail, or e-mail). Many documents are currently available in computerized form, including the text and abstracts of many periodicals, as well as documents such as the annual "letters to stockholders" of major corporations (see Stone and Weber 1992). Thus, the intriguing possibility arises that researchers can increasingly construct fully computerized content analyses, in which they analyze documents that were originally written on the computer (such as e-mail letters) by using computerized content-analysis programs.

Stone and Weber (1992) list three levels of computerized content analysis programs. The first level consists of relatively simple text-processing programs, generally emphasizing the counting of word frequencies. For example, "key-word in context" (KWIC) programs, which can show how a particular word is used in the text. The next level of computer analyses goes beyond frequencies to utilize statistical procedures such as factor analysis. A third level of computerized content-analysis procedures seeks to classify words into categories. For further discussion of the use of computers in content analysis see Namenwirth and Weber (1987), Weber (1990), and Zuell et al. (1989).

Historical Research

There has been a great deal of recent interest in "oral history," which largely consists of tape-recording and analyzing accounts of elders in the community (or others who possess a bit of history to be recorded). However, apart from oral history, which can be invaluable in capturing the culture of an area (e.g., Appalachia or the Old West), most historical research consists of document analysis. However, the converse is not true, as much documentary research in social science is not historical. Content analysis, which we just discussed, is sometimes historical and sometimes contemporary.

Although there has always been some historical research conducted within sociology, it has been rather limited. There are a number of reasons for this. One reason is a shift in the type of data available to social scientists. Early sociologists such as Karl Marx, Max Weber, and Emile Durkheim all used historical data, even though Marx is widely noted for conducting one of the earliest surveys, and Durkheim used some rather rudimentary statistics (although they were very sophisticated for his time). Since their time surveys and censuses have been widely developed, not to mention statistics and computers. These tools have shifted emphasis from historical research to survey research, which is generally ahistorical and is conducted in a short time span. A related reason is that a scientific or positivistic emphasis has been dominant in some spheres of social science during the twentieth century (see our discussion of positivism in chapter 1). This approach emphasized the discovery of scientific laws. Since scientific laws supposedly hold true at all times and in all places, a historical approach is unnecessary, as a law that was true at some earlier point in history would also be true in the present, and so could be studied with contemporary data. Social scientists generally seek such laws through methods such as survey research or experimentation, and such researchers (rightly or wrongly) seldom feel the need to study history. Further, research is often spawned by theoretical formulations, and some popular theoretical formulations such as functionalism (discussed in chapter 19) have been widely criticized as being ahistorical (Turner and Maryanski 1979). Still another reason for the paucity of historical research is the lack of adequate documents.

Thus, historical research has generally been a relatively small segment of social research (apart from the discipline of history, of course). However, there are obviously advantages to it, when it is feasible. If good data are available, historical research can serve as an effective complement to generalized scientific research by documenting a unique historical event, as in Weber's (1958) *Protestant Ethic and the Spirit of Capitalism*. Further, if one is interested in learning how some contemporary event or institution came into being, a historical approach is indispensable. For example, there is a debate in the literature on the sociology of the family about the role of industrialization in shaping the contemporary nuclear family that is prevalent in America today. There is widespread contention that modern patterns of nuclear family formation, specifically courtship and marriage for romantic reasons rather than economic reasons, are the product of the industrial revolution. This view holds that marriages before the industrial revolution were not made in heaven, but rather were made at home, arranged by parents, and with economics rather than romantic love as the foremost consideration.

This particular research deals specifically with the effect that a particular historical event (the industrial revolution) had on social phenomena, and thus the research by definition must be historical. Lantz et al. (1968) conducted a document study using preindustrial (colonial) magazines published during the period 1741–1794.

There are a number of other historical studies in the sociological literature that either explore social phenomena at an earlier time or explain contemporary phenomena in terms of their historical development. Notable among these studies is Erikson's (1966) study of deviance in colonial America, including the analysis of witch hunts. Another salient study is Piven and Cloward's (1971) historical analysis of the welfare system in the United States since the Depression. Other examples are given by Williamson, Karp, and Dalphin (1977), and by Klegon (1981).

Historical studies tend to be qualitative or humanistic. There has been a tendency for the method to be used by antiquantitative analysts, among them Marxists or socialist scholars interested in "historical/comparative" analysis.

However, not all historical studies are qualitative. The Lantz et al. (1968) study used content analysis. There is also an increasing use of numerical data sources such as censuses, crime reports, and archives by historical sociologists (Lodhi and Tilly 1973). In addition, there is an increase in the use of quantitative analysis in historical studies, but this is still considered controversial. The debate over quantitative analysis in historical research was focused by the publication in the same year (1974) of two historical studies on slavery, one of which (Fogel and Engerman's *Time on the Cross*) used quantitative methodology, while the other (Genovese's *Roll, Jordan, Roll*) did not. The use of quantification generated a great deal of comment (Wilson 1976; Wallerstein 1976), with Wilson (1976, pp. 1190–91) asking rhetorically:

> Is history to remain a humanistic discipline whereby the analysis of data depends upon the historian's sensitivity to subjective experience and his interpretative understanding, or is it to move in the "scientific" direction, relying on data that are quantified, controlled, and manipulated by mathematical techniques?

These questions remain generally unanswered during the 1980s and 1990s. However, it appears that most historical research remains unquantified. Kent (1992, p. 838) implies that history will not move in the "scientific" direction, saying that many of the methodological techniques used in sociology, including surveys, qualitative fieldwork, statistics, and experimentation, "have little if any applicability to historians." Kent (1992) identifies four research areas that he says generate the "most respected" historical research. These areas are: capitalist expansion, the growth of states, collective action, and the sociology of religious development. For further discussion please see Tilly (1981), Abrams (1982), Skocpol (1987), and Schwartz (1987).

Validity and Reliability

Validity

Validity is increased by the fact that documents are often first-person accounts of events or feelings experienced by the author of the document. Thus, as with observation, documents tend to have face validity. Tending to damage validity is that authors often write documents for some purpose other than social research, or have an ulterior motive (such as prestige or money) for making the document exciting or favorable, to themselves. Also, there is often a considerable time lag between the occurrence of the event and the writing of the document, with such a delay leading to memory failures and inaccuracies. Further, due to selective survival, the materials that remain are often a biased sample rather than a random sample, and do not provide an accurate picture of events. In addition, the fact that ancient documents are often valuable and documentation of their authenticity is difficult tempts forgers to produce fakes.

Face Validity. Documents lend themselves to more rigorous checks on face validity than do other data-gathering methods in social research. Not only the content of the document but also word patterns, language, writing style, and composition of paper and ink all can provide checks on the validity or authenticity of a document. If writing style or grammar change within a single document, then the researcher has cause to doubt its authenticity, or reason to believe that it was authored by more than one person. Such checks within a single document are generally referred to as internal checks, as opposed to external checks, which compare the content of the document with some external source. If the document is spurious, this can often be determined by chemical analysis of the ink and paper, unless the forger was able to secure authentic materials from the supposed period of composition. If the materials, language, grammar, writing style, and word usage all seem consistent with a document of the proper period, the researcher can look for clues to face validity in the content of the document. Holsti says:

If the purpose of the research is a purely descriptive one, content [face] validity is normally sufficient. Content validity is usually established through the informed judgement of the investigator. Are the results plausible? Are they consistent with other information about the phenomena being studied? (Holsti 1969, p. 143).

Criterion Validity.   Although Holsti (1969, p. 143) feels that for descriptive studies the establishment of face validity is generally sufficient, I suggest supplementing face validity with the establishment of criterion validity whenever possible. Criterion validity is often difficult to establish. Since many documents were written long ago, it is impossible to compare them with observational studies or to interview people as validity checks. Other documents that may be suitable for comparison often have been destroyed. Also, a study frequently utilizes a whole series of documents covering a considerable time span, and it is difficult to find comparison criteria for all points in time. Nevertheless, it is often possible to make an external check on the validity of a document by comparing the information in the document to have criterion validity. For example, Holsti and North (1966) established criterion validity for their sample of World War I documents even though they conducted the validity check half a century later and did not have access to interviews or observation. They were able to construct quantitative financial indexes (e.g, security prices) as criteria to establish the validity of their measures of the attitude of political leaders, as measured through content analysis of the documents. They found a correlation between the criteria indexes and the attitudes, and thus concluded that their measures had criterion validity.

Construct Validity.   Documents have also been shown to have construct validity. Zinnes (1966), as discussed by Holsti (1969), first tested a set of hypotheses concerning aggressive conduct between nations by studying a set of documents written by high-ranking decision makers immediately prior to the beginning of World War I. He found support for the hypotheses in his content analysis of the documents. He then tested the same hypotheses using as data the messages written by high-school students playing international simulation games (see the discussion of simulation in chapter 13). Since the hypotheses were supported in both contexts, he concluded that the documents had construct validity.

Reliability

As with observation, reliability may be checked either by similar documents at two or more points in time (instrument reliability) or by comparing the results of two or more researchers at the same point in time (analyst reliability). Efforts to determine instrument reliability are hampered by selective survival of documents. In addition, the analysis of documents is often a rather subjective process. Recall that the definitions of content analysis claim that the method is objective and systematic. This would imply that there is little opportunity for subjectivity in content analysis. However, we have seen that the content analysis must construct the categories for analysis and decide the recording unit, the context unit, and the system of enumeration. All of these choices involve subjective decisions on the analyst's part. The subjectivity of content analysis is demonstrated by the failure of content analysis to establish standard categories. Holsti says:

Reasons for the general absence of standard categories are not hard to find. The premium on "originality" and the concomitant reluctance of analysts to adopt the categories of others— tendencies clearly not limited to content analysis research is probably a contributing factor. A more basic reason, however, is that there are few areas of social inquiry in which there is sufficient consensus on theory to inform the selection of categories (Holsti 1969, p. 102).

It seems to me that such alleged lack of consensus is clear evidence of subjectivity, which becomes even more of a problem when a number of different analysts are used in the same study. For this reason there seems to be more attention paid in the literature to assessment of interanalyst reliability than to assessment of interdocument reliability.

Holsti (1969, p. 142) says that there is no single, simple solution for the problem of deciding the proper level of reliability. He declines to suggest an arbitrary level to use as a rule of thumb but says that the analyst must strike a compromise between reliability and relevance of categories, rather than striving for an artificially high level of reliability that can be achieved only through the use of categories that are irrelevant, artificial, or otherwise inadequate.

For a more recent and very comprehensive discussion of research methods in documentary analysis see Scott (1990). Scott uses four criteria (all relevant to the issues of validity and reliability) for assessing documentary evidence: authenticity, credibility (sincerity and accuracy), representativeness (survival and availability), and meaning (literal and interpretive understanding). He also discusses such topics as the State, surveillance, secrecy, and administrative routines. He also includes an interesting discussion of photographs as personal documents.

Summary

In chapter 12 we discussed document study. Among the advantages of document study are accessibility to otherwise inaccessible subjects (for example, deceased subjects), nonreactivity, suitability for longitudinal analysis (in cases where running records are available), and a number of others. Among the disadvantages are bias stemming from the fact that the document was written for some purpose other than social research, selective survival, incompleteness, and a number of other problems. We also distinguished between primary documents—which are authored by eyewitnesses—and secondary documents—whose authors are not eyewitnesses but people who compile the information in the document from interviewing eyewitnesses or reading primary documents.

We discussed both qualitative and quantitative analysis of documents. The method of quantitative analysis we studied is called content analysis. Among the stages of content analysis we discussed were construction of categories, construction of recording units, and selection of an appropriate system of enumeration. We concluded the chapter with a discussion of validity and reliability.

CHAPTER 13

SIMULATIONS AND GAMES

Advantages of Simulation

Disadvantages of Simulation

Types of Games

Two-person Games
N-person Games

Computer Simulation

Validity

Summary

SIMULATIONS AND GAMES are assuming increasing importance in social sciences (mostly since the 1950s), both as heuristic (learning) and as data-gathering devices. Simulations and games are a special kind of model. A model is a representation of a system that specifies not only its parts or components (generally variables in social-science models) but also the relationships among the components. That is, the model demonstrates the structure of the system. A model is a copy, replica, or analogy that differs from the real thing in some way. This difference may be only in size, such as the model ship that is accurate and seaworthy in every detail, except that it is small enough to fit into a bottle. Other models may be full size but may not be complete in every detail, including only those features of the real thing that are necessary for the modeler's purpose.

For example, a department-store mannequin is a model of a human, and a robot is also a model of a human. The latter is much more complete in the sense that it has a number of human features not found in the former, but each has sufficient human features to meet its purpose. Similarly, the goal in social-science models is not necessarily to include all features of the system being modeled, but only those necessary for the research purposes. Many times even some of the important features cannot be adequately modeled because of complexity or lack of information, and the researcher must be content with an incomplete model, a skeletal model, or a model with some of the variables or components represented by unknowns or question marks.

A model as just defined can be a static, cross-sectional (at one point in time) representation of a system. A simulation is a special kind of model—a model in motion, an operating model. It operates over a period of time to show not only the structure of the system (what position each variable or component occupies in the system and the way components are related or connected), but also the way change in one variable or component affects changes in the values of the other variables or components.

Some games are played purely for their own enjoyment and are not models of some system. However, many games that are often played for enjoyment are also true simulations, and these will be our concern in this chapter. For example, chess began as a simulation of medieval warfare (Raser 1969, p. x). As Raser points out, the terms "game" and "simulation" are often used interchangeably. A model is more likely to be called a simulation if it constitutes a very explicit operating model, if all the important variables are formally programmed, and if it seems to be a complete and accurate model of the system it represents (Raser 1969, p. x). A model is also more likely to be called a simulation if it is completely computerized, with no human participants. If the model is made to operate through use of human subjects, then it will generally be called a game. Such a model may also be more informal and tentative than a model that is called a simulation (Raser 1969, p. x).

Advantages of Simulation

Raser (1969, pp. 15–19) lists four chief reasons for simulating: (1) economy, (2) visibility, (3) control (reproducibility), and (4) safety.

1. *Economy.* Operation of a simulation may not only be much cheaper than operation of the real thing, but can also provide dry runs that will help avoid costly mistakes in the real opera-

tion. This feature is probably more of an advantage in physical simulations than in social simulations. Using a variation of Raser's (1969) example, suppose that an engineer wishes to construct a new harbor containing docks, a breakwater or jetty, a deep water ship channel, and so on. By constructing a simulation he or she can study such things as water flow and the resultant accumulation of sand. By operating the model (letting water flow through the simulated harbor) he or she can see what will result: e.g., whether sand will accumulate and clog the channel, or currents will cause pilings under the docks to collapse. It is obviously much less expensive to study the model in the laboratory than to study the actual harbor (which may necessitate use of expensive underwater equipment). Further, if the simulation shows, for example, that construction of a breakwater will cause sanding of the channel, this mistake costs little in the laboratory, but might cost millions and create permanent damage if the real breakwater is constructed without a simulation.

2. *Visibility.* Simulation can heighten the visibility of the phenomenon to be studied by making the phenomenon more accessible to the investigator, and by clarifying the phenomenon by separating the essential components of the system from the irrelevant or less relevant features. The first advantage should be obvious. While it would be difficult to observe simultaneously the international relations among 20 or so nations over a period of years, a game such as the Inter-Nation Simulation (I.N.S.) can be used to simulate such relations (see Raser 1969, p. 57). The INS is described in more detail later in this chapter. Such a game can yield a realistic approximation of the results of relations and interactions among actual nations. In terms of the second advantage, if the researcher attempted to study the actual nations at work, he or she might be overwhelmed by the complexity and mass of detail, and become unsure which features were the most important to study. By examining a simulation such as INS, he or she can get a clear picture of the essential working of relations without being led astray by less crucial features. If there are other variables of interest that are not covered by the simulation, he or she could attempt to study them later in the real system.

3. *Control.* The researcher often has a great deal more control over the simulation of a system than over the actual system itself. While he or she cannot control the actual international relations of twenty nations, he or she can control the INS simulation to a great extent. One of the advantages of his control is reproducibility and ability to replicate. The researcher might have tentative support for a hypothesis but need more evidence. If he or she is forced to deal with the actual social system, one complete cycle of the behavior (e.g., peace negotiations) might take months or even years. Then, if even one more cycle is necessary for further evidence, more years are required. A decade might pass before the researcher feels that the study has been replicated enough times to establish faith in the findings. However, with a simulation the researcher might be able to simulate one year's negotiations in one morning. Thus in the course of a week the researcher may be able to reproduce or replicate the study ten or more times and find support for his or her hypothesis all ten times, thus convincing him or her that the results are valid. Quick reproducibility may also provide sufficient examples of possible outcomes to enable the researcher to compute the probability that a specific outcome will appear under certain conditions.

Another feature of control is the possibility that certain conditions can be manipulated in order to observe the difference in the results of the simulation. In such a case the simulation becomes a quasi-experiment. For example, Raser (1969, p. 17) says that in a simulation of nuclear war we might vary the amount of warning time given a nation. Then we could gauge the amount of destruction with only 15 minutes warning time in comparison to the amount of destruction yielded with 30 minutes warning time. As another example, Raser asks what difference it might make in an international simulation whether the head of a country was paranoid or confident and trusting.

4. *Safety.* A fourth advantage of simulation listed by Raser is safety. In social-science research, simulations have potential use in situations that are theoretically important, but will cause harm, embarrassment, or some other moral and ethical problems if human subjects are used in a natural environment. For example, Kelman (1967) feels that there are ethical problems involved in the deception of experimental subjects. However, experimenters often believe that if they reveal the purpose of the study to the subjects they will bias the results. Kelman thinks that simulations in which subjects know the nature of the study and interact with the experimenter more or less as coinvestigators may yield valid data while at the same time eliminating the need to deceive subjects.

Disadvantages of Simulation

1. *Artificiality.* One of the major disadvantages of a simulation is the fact that it is artificial. By its very definition a simulation is merely an imitation or copy of the real thing. As a working model or substitute there is always the possibility that the simulation is so inaccurate or incomplete that conclusions gained from it are not applicable to the phenomena being modeled, and thus the findings will be invalid. Particularly in social modeling in which the social system may be highly complex, the researcher may have little assurance that all the essential components are included in the model, or that the relationships between components are specified correctly. Alternatively, the researcher may know which components to include but may find that the social system is too complex to model correctly. For example, his or her computer may not be large enough to store all the needed information.

2. *Cost.* Although the possible economic advantages of simulations have been pointed out, it should not be inferred that simulations are necessarily inexpensive. Some simulations, particularly computer simulations, may require a large budget merely for computer time.

3. *Training of participants.* Some games may necessitate the training of a large number of participants. If the rules are complex and a large number of participants or players are needed, training may not only be expensive and time consuming but also difficult to conduct satisfactorily. If participants are unable to learn the rules consistently and accurately, then the validity of the game is placed in doubt.

4. *Quantitative problems.* A complex simulation, particularly a computer simulation, may not only require costly computers or other machines, but may also entail programming (software) costs and complex mathematical problems. If the researcher does not have the ability to solve complex mathematical problems or do sophisticated computer programming, and if he or she is unable to hire someone to solve these problems, then he or she may be unable to complete the simulation.

Types of Games

Many games have been developed for social science, most within the last 25 years. Many of these are sold commercially. We are referring here to games that are not computerized but are designed to be played by human participants, usually in a controlled laboratory setting rather than in a natural or field environment. These games have been developed in several different social-science disciplines (sociology, political science, education, psychology, business administration). They vary widely in terms of complexity and in number of participants required. Rather than attempt an exhaustive review of games, which is beyond the scope of this volume, we shall discuss a selection of a few of the most popular games in social science.

A distinction is often made between zero-sum and nonzero-sum games. In zero-sum games there is a single fixed or constant reward that cannot be increased or decreased during the course of the game, and thus must be divided up among the respective players. This means that one player can gain only to the detriment of other players. The optimum strategy for each player is to maximize his or her reward, thus making the game purely a competitive one. For example, if there is only a given amount of money available for both whites and nonwhites in the United States in a given year, any increase in the income of whites necessitates a like decrease in the income of nonwhites.

In contrast to zero-sum games, the amount of reward in nonzero-sum games is variable. Pursuing the example discussed above, we might find that the total money supply of the United States could be expanded by the U.S. Treasury, making it possible for nonwhite income to increase at the same time that white income was increasing. In a nonzero-sum game the competitive strategy is not necessarily the optimum strategy for a given player. Allowing one's opponent to gain does not necessarily mean that one will lose, and the optimum strategy for all players may be to cooperate, thus maximizing the gain for each. Nonzero-sum games are also called mixed-motive games because a player's motive may be either competition or cooperation. Probably the most famous non-zero-sum game is a two-person game called the Prisoner's Dilemma.

Two-person Games

A number of games for two persons have been developed. The most commonly used is the Prisoner's Dilemma, or P-D game. This game is widely used in research in social science, especially in social psychology. The basic decision a player must make is whether to cooperate or compete with the other player. The name of the game stems from the situation it models—the dilemma of two persons accused as accomplices in a crime and held prisoner by the police. After their arrest they are held in separate rooms and interrogated. Although the police and district attorney feel certain that both prisoners are guilty of the crime, there is not sufficient evidence to convict them without a confession from at least one of them. The district attorney tells each one that if neither confesses he or she will be let off easy and booked on some minor charge such as petty larceny or vagrancy, so that both prisoners will receive a minor sentence. If both cooperate and confess they will be prosecuted, but the district attorney will recommend less than the maximum sentence. However, if one confesses and the other does not, the confessor will receive a lenient sentence while the other will get the maximum penalty. Thus a prisoner fares best if he or she confesses and his or her partner does not; fares next best if neither confesses; fares worse if both confess; and fares worst of all if he or she does not confess and his or her partner does. The dilemma is that the partner has the same odds, and he or she has no way of knowing what his or her partner will choose to do since they are in separate rooms. This can be illustrated in figure 13–1.

The first number in each cell of figure 13.1 is the number of years prisoner 1 would receive in that situation, and the second figure is the sentence that prisoner 2 would receive (prisoner 1, prisoner 2). For example, if prisoner 1 confesses and prisoner 2 does not (cell C), then the sentences are respectively 1 year and 20 years, with prisoner 1 receiving the light sentence and prisoner 2 the heavy sentence. If a prisoner wishes at all costs to avoid the maximum sentence, then he or she will confess. This will assure him or her at the most of an intermediate sentence if the other prisoner confesses, and maybe a very light sentence if the other does not confess. However, if the prisoner thinks his or her partner will not confess, then he or she should not either, thus ensuring a lighter sentence than if both confessed.

A study by Baxter (1973) illustrates how the P-D game can be used in research. Baxter wished to study the effect of race on cooperation, and chose the P-D game as the format for such a study. The subjects were ninety white freshmen females at a southern college. Some were from the North and some from the South, but all were considered "liberal" and were strongly in favor of racial integration. Baxter (1973, p. 132) had four specific research questions. As stated in his own words:

1. Does the race of the other player, [black] or white, affect the extent of a white subject's cooperation? If so, do northern subjects cooperate more with a [black] than do southern subjects?
2. Does the information supplied to the subject concerning the other person's ([black] or white) cooperative or competitive nature affect the extent of the subject's cooperation?

Figure 13–1

Payoff Matrix for Prisoner's Dilemma Game

		Prisoner 2	
		Does not confess	Confesses
Prisoner 1	Does not confess	A 5 yrs, 5 yrs	B 20 yrs, 1 yr
	Confesses	C 1 yr, 20 yrs	D 10 yrs, 10 yrs

3. Is there a relationship between the subject's attitudes (specifically those toward racial segregation and about people in general) and his level of cooperation in the game?
4. Will the subject's evaluations of a [black] other player differ from the ratings given a white other player, and will the ratings taken before the game differ from the same ratings taken after the game?

The experiment was conducted in three soundproof rooms. Subjects were seated in the end rooms, with the experimenter and an accomplice in the middle. Each subject's room contained a table and a chair, speakers on which the experimenter's instructions could be heard, and a control box containing four lights and two switches. The switches were arranged vertically to the left of the lights. The top switch turned on a blue light, the bottom switch a red light. Red and blue horizontal lights indicated to each subject the choice of the other player in the game. The payoff matrix shown in figure 13–2 was on the box, showing the subject's potential risks and rewards (subject's payoff left of comma, other player's payoff right of comma).

None of the subjects ever saw the other player. Instead, each saw an accomplice that she thought was the other player. Half of the subjects saw a white female accomplice and half saw a black female accomplice, both dressed to look like college freshmen. In addition, one group of subjects was given information indicating that the other player was cooperative, another group was given information indicating that the other player was very competitive, and a third group was given no information about the other player.

No support was found for the hypotheses involving region of subject's birth. Northern re-

Figure 13–2
Payoff Matrix

	Blue switch	Red switch
	A	**B**
Blue switch (doesn't confess)	+ 5¢, + 5¢ (neither confesses)	– 4¢, + 6¢ (subject doesn't confess, other does)
	C	**D**
Red switch (confess)	+ 6¢, – 4¢ (subject confesses, other doesn't)	– 3¢, – 3¢ (both confess)

SOURCE: Reprinted from "Prejudiced Liberals? Race and Information Effects in a Two-Person Game," by George W. Baxter, *Journal of Conflict Resolution* 12, no. 3 (March 1973), pp. 131–61, by permission of the author and the publisher, Sage Publications, Inc.

spondents were no more likely than southern respondents to cooperate with a black player, and there was no difference between ratings that northerners and southerners gave the other player on cooperation. However, it was confirmed that white subjects tended to cooperate more with white opponents than with black opponents, especially when the opponent was indicated as cooperative. When the other player was indicated as competitive, the difference between co-operation rates for white and black other players was not statistically significant.

Behr (1981) studied various strategies (e.g., "play well but lose" or "play poorly yet win") for the P-D game, as in any round of the P-D, each player must decide whether-to cooperate or not. He concluded that the P-D is of limited use as a model of political relationships but can yield some helpful inferences in some instances. For further discussion and application of the P-D game, see also Murnighan and Roth (1983), Lindskold et al. (1983), Carment and Alcock (1984), Levy (1985), and Diekmann (1985).

Later studies are Thomas and Feldman (1988), Lichbach (1990), Bendor et al. (1991), and Marinoff (1992). For a more comprehensive discussion see Axelrod (1984). Axelrod's book has had a great impact on Prisoner's dilemma research, as noted by Bendor et al. (1991). Axelrod used a powerful approach—computer tournaments of various strategies for P-D. Iron-ically, one of the simplest strategies in P-D turned out to be the most successful. This strategy is tit-for-tat (TFT), in which a player cooperates on the first move and subsequently does what-ever his or her partner did on the previous move. TFT outperformed the many highly sophisti-cated strategies that have been devised by game theorists who were experts in the P-D game. Axelrod's work clearly shows the power of computerization. This volume is so influential that it will surely continue to influence work on P-D games for years to come.

N-person Games

An N-person game is a game designed for more than two players. N-person games can be divided into two basic groups. One group comprises N-person coalition games, which are used in research. The second group comprises N-person classroom simulation games. The N-person research games are diverse and often complicated and thus are generally beyond the scope of this volume. As one example, Oliver (1980) studied the effectiveness of of-fering incentives to participants in Apex Games. The Apex Game is an N-person game that contains an unequal balance of power. One person, called the Apex, has power equal to N-2 other players, where N-1 is the number of players. All other players (N-1) are called Bases. Each Base has power equal to 1. For example, if there are 20 players, there is one Apex with power equal to 18 (20–2) and 19 Bases, each with power equal to 1. The more players there are, the greater is the power balance between the Apex and each Base. In any case, all N-1 Bases must band together in a coalition if they are to have more power (e.g., 19) than the Apex (e.g., 18).

The Bases may or may not form such a coalition in a given game. Oliver's research studied the effect of negative incentives (negative points or "dings" that could be assigned to Base players) on such coalition formation. She had a control group in which dings were not given, and an experimental game in which they were. The weak players (Bases) were much more likely to form a coalition when they had the ability to "ding" or punish each other (62 percent) than when they did not (as evidenced by only 20 percent coalition formation in the control game).

In another study, Michener, Yuen, and Geisheker (1980) also studied coalition formation in *N*-person games, but they were concerned with sidepayment games. In a sidepayment game, the members of any coalition are able to transfer payoffs among themselves in any manner they choose. A recent debate between Kahan and Rapoport (1981) on the one hand, and Michener and Potter (1981) on the other, has extended analysis of the generalizability of the theory of *N*-person games. Also see the study of *N*-person (three-person) games by Michener and Yuen (1983), Oliver's (1984) study of Apex games, Michener et al. (1989), Ward (1990), McDaniel and Sistrunk (1991), and Michener (1992).

Because of the diversity and complexity of *N*-person coalition research games we shall content ourselves with this admittedly cursory discussion and these brief illustrations and refer the interested reader to additional sources such as the *Journal of Conflict Resolution*. We shall now turn to a more extended discussion of *N*-person classroom simulation games.

Several *N*-person simulation games have been developed for a number of different fields, including business, the military, and various social-science disciplines. Perhaps the most popular *N*-person game in sociology is Gamson's (1969) SIMSOC, or simulated society. SIMSOC is designed primarily as a heuristic tool. Rather than being used for research, it is intended to provide a way for the introductory sociology student to learn how social order is maintained and how the processes of social conflict and social control operate in a society.

There are seven basic groups in SIMSOC:

1. BASIN (basic industry), whose overall objective is to expand its wealth as much as possible.
2. INNOVIN (innovative industry), whose overall objective is again to maximize its wealth.
3. POP (party of the people), whose objective is to mobilize persons sympathetic to the party's programs and to raise money.
4. SOP (society party), whose overall objectives are the same as those of POP.
5. EMPIN (employee interests), whose overall objective is to see that all members of SIMSOC who are not bosses (heads of groups) have a fair share of wealth.
6. MASMED (mass media), whose objective is to keep the society informed about important events.
7. JUDCO (judicial council), whose objective is to clarify and interpret the rules of the society.

In addition to working in one of the seven basic groups as either a boss (group head) or employee, each member of SIMSOC has a private life in which he or she does such things as join a political party, support himself or herself, travel, or even die. All of these activities are governed by rules and are generally accomplished by filling out forms. For example, to subsist, at every session of the game a member must either turn in a subsistence ticket to the instructor or show that he or she owns a permanent subsistence ticket by presenting form D. Such a certificate can be bought from the instructor for $25 (in Simbucks), or subsistence tickets can be purchased from the owner of a subsistence agency at any price that can be agreed on. If a member is unable to achieve subsistence he or she will die. As Gamson says:

A member may die from failing to obtain subsistence in two consecutive sessions or from having his arrest renewed for two consecutive sessions (that is, having had his arrest renewed once, the next renewal is equivalent to execution). A member who dies henceforth cannot participate in the society in any way; he will be asked to observe and assist the instructor (Gamson 1969, p. 15).

The obvious advantage of SIMSOC as a learning experience is that processes of social control that would normally be changing slowly and evolving over the course of an individual's lifetime take place in a much shorter period, so that the interrelationships among various components of society become clearer. Also, the game provides a student with many experiences that he or she would probably never have in real life, such as working for the police force at one session and being arrested at another.

A popular and widely used game in political science is the Inter-Nation Simulation, or INS. As Raser describes it, the INS

> was designed as a generalized model of national and international policies. Human decision-makers or players acting as national leaders operate their nations, worry about consumer-goods levels, national defense, public opinion, elections, revolutions, and democratic values, and at the same time engage in the international politics of trade, negotiation, threat and counter-threat, alliances, war, and other military activities. The internal model of the nations is explicitly formalized in a series of equations, but the relationships among nations are left almost entirely to the players (Raser 1969, p. 57).

The INS has proven useful both as a research tool and as a teaching aid in studying international relations. For further discussion of INS and for discussion of games in other disciplines such as economics, management and business, education, and psychology, see Raser (1969).

For examples of simulations in a number of educational fields such as chemistry, geography, history, and psychology, see Thorson (1979).

Computer Simulation

In addition to simulation games in which players participate, a number of computer simulations (no players, only data fed into the computer) have been developed in social research. One basic advantage of computer simulations is that they allow the logical derivation of a set of assumptions that are too complex to be seen by visual inspection. One famous computer simulation in sociology is Gullahorn and Gullahorn's (1963b) HOMUNCULUS, which is a computer simulation of George Homans's social theory. Computer simulations in political science include Benson's "Simple Diplomatic Game," de Sola Pool's "Simulatics," and Pool and Kessler's "Crisiscom" (see Raser 1969 for further discussion).

Computer simulations are generally too complex to discuss adequately here. However, perhaps Markley's (1967) presentation is succinct enough to provide an illustration, yet complex enough to show clearly what simulation is all about. Markley's goal was to construct a computer simulation of Caplow's (1964) model of organizational behavior. Specifically, he wished to see whether the system as proposed by Caplow would reach stable equilibrium as Caplow assumed.

Caplow's model consisted of four interrelated variables: *SIVA. S* refers to the *strength* of the parties (a pair of individuals) in the organization; *I* is a measure of their degree of mutual *influence; V* is a measure of the *volitional* component of the situation; and the *A* variable measures the result of the joint *action* of the parties. The four *SIVA* variables are interrelated, so that if an outside force were to change the value of one of these variables, values of others in the system would also have to change. For example, if someone other than the two individuals involved were somehow to change the degree of mutual influence (*I*) of these two individuals, then necessarily the values of *S, A,* and *V* would change.

To test the model one need only start with some arbitrary values (Markley chose a value of zero for each variable), then iteratively compute the equations interrelating the variables and observe the values that the *SIVA* variables take on. By "iteration" we mean the procedure of computing values progressively for the equations by plugging in the old values of the variables from a prior computational sequence to compute new values of other variables in a new computational sequence. Markley reasoned that by iterating the system of equations sufficiently the system would finally either: (1) establish stable equilibrium (as Caplow assumed); (2) go into "stable oscillation," with the values recurring cyclically; or (3) "blow up," with all values continuing to increase or decrease continuously with no end in sight.

Markley found that after eleven iterations (from time 0 through time 10) the *SIVA* model apparently "blows up," with values continuing to increase indefinitely. Thus Caplow's contention that the model reaches stable equilibrium is shown to be erroneous.

After a number of sociological computer simulations in the 1960s, activity in this field slowed down. Why was this? Ronald Anderson (1992, p. 285) says others followed in the footsteps of the first researchers, "but the excitement of the pioneers was lost, and few simulations or formal computer models were developed in the 1970s." However, in the 1980s and 1990s there has been renewed interest, due in part to the emergence of new approaches such as artificial intelligence and expert systems. For further discussion of these developments, see R. Anderson (1992), Hanneman (1988), Brent and Anderson (1990), Garson (1990), and Ragin and Becker (1989).

Validity

Raser (1969, p. 144) lists four validation criteria that he has distilled from various discussions of validation procedure in the simulation and gaming literature:

1. An all-man or man-machine game used as a complex environment laboratory should provide an environment that seems realistic to the subjects (players).
2. A game is valid to the degree that its structure (the theory and assumptions on which it is built) can be shown to be isomorphic to that of the reference system.
3. It is valid to the degree that the processes observed in the game are isomorphic to those observed in the reference system.
4. It is valid to the degree that it can reproduce historical outcomes or predict the future.

The game whose validity has probably been most rigorously assessed is the Inter-Nation Simulation (INS). Raser (1969) says that in attempting to validate any game in terms of his first criterion, persons who have never been a player in a social-simulation game might doubt that such a game could ever seem very realistic to the players. However, Raser argues convincingly that not only do players become very involved in such games and take them seriously, but also that persons in "real-life" international situations such as those that the INS simulates often tend to isolate themselves from reality and be even less involved in real events than are players in the simulation. Raser says:

> Anyone who has conducted complex games can testify to the intense involvement of most players. I have witnessed fisticuffs among theological seminary students; Navy recruits who wept in the presence of their peers after losing office in a game; a participant who suffered temporary blindness and paralysis when his "country" was under attack; I know of a four-star general who broke into a barracks in the middle of the night to spy out the secrets of an opponent team; and on one occasion I had to break up a knife fight. . . . In contrast there is some evidence that high level governmental decision-makers tend to be insulated from the actual consequences and ramifications of their decisions. They sit in offices surrounded by papers and advisors; they move in a tight circle of their peers who pride themselves on their unemotional professionalism; and they usually develop a neutral and highly abstract terminology with which to discuss their work. (For example, the military euphemisms of "floorspace" and "population response" refer to amount of property totally destroyed and number of people killed by a nuclear blast . . .) (Raser 1969, pp. 146–47).

Raser goes on to say that, using realism as a criterion of validity (criterion 1), the INS game has also been found to be realistic in the sense that the players show strong national loyalties and ethnocentric attitudes, their behavior changes during crises in the game, and in general they react just as would actual decision-makers involved in actual international relations.

Raser's second criterion stipulates that, to be valid, the structure of the simulation (its theory and assumptions) must be isomorphic to the structure of the reference system (the system being modeled). The INS has been studied fairly intensively to see whether its assumptions reflect actual facts about the "real world." Raser (1969, pp. 148–49) reports that comparison of 75 assumptions about basic elements or relationships among basic elements of INS with recently collected data about the actual world of international relations revealed that a number of the INS assumptions were questionable, and perhaps not completely accurate representations of real-world occurrences. Interestingly, however, this analysis also led researchers to question a number of "facts" gathered about the real world. Overall, INS has been shown to provide quite a bit of similarity to the real world with two-thirds of 55 comparisons in one study being similar (Raser 1969, p. 149).

Raser's third criterion for establishing validity asks whether the processes involved in the game are isomorphic to those in the system being modeled. Raser answers this question as follows:

> In the majority of social science games, the answer often is a qualified "yes." Most people who have observed these games in operation are struck by the extent to which the players seem to assume the behavior characteristics of real life decision-makers in language, development of attitudes, and responses to the possession of power. In a simulation such as the INS, office charges, cabinet crises, resource allocation, and other processes based on player

choice rather than on pre-programming all seem to occur in appropriate manners; wars, bargaining, trading, diplomatic meetings, alliance formation and dissolution, and so forth, all happen much as they do in the particular international situation being modeled. Furthermore, the relationships among these processes appear to conform with recognized patterns, (Raser 1969, p. 150).

Raser's fourth criterion is whether the game can reconstruct past events or predict future events. On this point Raser (1969, p. 151) says: "The record of social science games is not impressive." Summarizing findings on validity of simulation, Raser says:

> What do these assessments of game and simulation validity for research yield? I suggest that as realistic laboratories, games appear to rate very well, certainly better than the available alternatives. Their structural isomorphism with the reference system is difficult to ascertain, and where ascertainable, not very impressive, particularly when first designed; but this is an aspect that can be changed as theory and data improve. The process isomorphism of games is perhaps better, though in this respect it is often difficult to compare their validity with that of other research techniques, for almost no techniques generate comparable processes. Finally, in post-dictive and predictive power, games are no worse than other methods, but whether they are better is uncertain; the experimental results are too ambiguous and contradictory. These comments all apply to the validity of games as experimental research tools, a form of validity that implies excellence as an experimental laboratory, at least to some degree of structure and process isomorphism with the reference-system, and some pre- and post-dictive power (Raser 1969, p. 153).

For further discussion of the reliability and validity of simulations see Inbar and Stoll (1972, pp. 278–86).

Summary

Chapter 13 dealt with simulations and games. We defined a model as a representation of a system showing not only the system's components, but also the relationships among these components. We defined a simulation as a model that operates over time, and shows how change in one component of the model affects changes in others. Simulations may be completely computerized, or may use human participants. Simulations having human participants are generally called games rather than simulations, although the terms "simulation" and "game" are often used interchangeably.

The advantages of simulation that we discussed are economy, visibility, control, and safety. The disadvantages are artificiality, cost, difficulty in training participants, and computational problems.

We next turned to a discussion of types of games, including zero-sum and nonzero-sum games, a popular two-person game (the Prisoner's Dilemma), and two N-person games—one developed in sociology (SIMSOC) and another developed in political science (INS). We then briefly discussed computer simulation, before concluding the chapter with a discussion of validity and reliability.

PART FOUR

DATA REDUCTION, ANALYSIS, INTERPRETATION, AND APPLICATION

CHAPTER 14

CODING AND DATA REDUCTION

THE SOCIAL RESEARCHER, particularly the neophyte, is often at somewhat of a loss as to what to do with data after they have been collected. The quantity of the data may be so great that the researcher cannot report all of it in the research report. The mass of data must be reduced and then analyzed, so that a succinct set of conclusions or findings can be reported to a scientific audience. We shall refer to the process of reducing the data to some form suitable for analysis as *data reduction*. Data reduction generally consists of *coding* the data, often to make them suitable for computer analysis. *Data analysis* consists of running various statistical procedures and tests on the data.

Computer data must be stored on some physical carrier in such a form that they can be read into the machine, processed and stored in the machine, and later retrieved in a proper form to be utilized by the researcher. For approximately the first three decades of widespread computer use (the 1950s, 1960s, and 1970s), most data entry into computers was via paper computer-punch cards, paper cards containing 80 columns on which data could be punched directly from a codebook or questionnaire and then entered into the computer. After entry into the computer, data could then be stored on some other format such as a tape, and later a disc. Through the 1970s, the main task of data reduction was to code data and transmit them physically from questionnaires to computer cards. Paper computer-punch cards are now generally obsolete in their intermediate role as transmitters of data from questionnaire to computer. They still remain valuable for certain storage purposes.

However, while data are no longer punched on computer cards, these cards have left a legacy in the form of standardized computer coding. The computer cards utilized 80 columns, and it is still customary to code in lines of 80 columns each. Thus, each respondent is assigned one or more 80-column "cards" as needed. Sometimes the data are entered directly from the questionnaire into the computer. Other times they are first coded onto a separate sheet of paper. This sheet contains 80 columns per line and is known as a computer-coding sheet or data transfer sheet (see Frankfort-Nachmias and Nachmias 1992, p. 330). After data from the questionnaires are transferred to the computer-coding sheets, these sheets are then used for entering the data into the computer. This is done by entering data into the keyboard of the computer, and viewing it on the screen of the terminal. Terminals also generally have 80 columns per line. The data are stored on a computer tape or diskette and are called a *computer file* or *data file*. Each row of information (generally representing one 80-column "card") is called a *record*. For further discussion see Singleton et al. (1988, pp. 385–86).

The fact that data are entered not onto cards but directly into computer terminals affords a great advantage. Not only does it eliminate the need to carry the cards physically to a card reader for entry into the terminal, it allows easy correction of entry errors. While mispunches on cards could not be corrected without punching a new card, errors on terminals are generally rather easily rectified. Of course, the primary disadvantages of the terminal are its cost and the subsequent access problems that some researchers, particularly those on a low budget, may face. After the data are entered into the terminal, they can be stored in a variety of ways, including computer tapes and discs. The latter include both "hard" and "soft" ("floppy") discs. Each has certain advantages and disadvantages. The type that one uses can depend on preference but often depends primarily upon the equipment available (for example, whether one is using a large, centrally located "mainframe" computer or a "personal," "mini," or "micro" computer).

338

Data Reduction

The main task of data reduction is coding. Coding for computer analysis generally consists of assigning a code number to each answer category (for a particular survey question, for example) so that the answers may be stored in the computer. It is much easier to store and retrieve numbers than it is letters or words, thus the necessity to change categories from word or sentence responses to numbers. That is, rather than punch a "yes" or a "no" response into the computer (which can be done), it is much simpler and takes less space to assign each answer a number (e.g., yes equals 1 and no equals 2) and simply punch the appropriate number into the computer.

Response categories are provided in the case of closed-ended questions. For open-ended questions, however, codes that paraphrase the meaning of the verbal responses are typically constructed after the data are acquired. By representing those response phrases or paraphrases by distinct numbers, the meaning or informational content of the data set is preserved. Suppose there are *n* respondents who are asked *r* questions. By representing the answer to every question by a distinct measurement number (including a number indicating "no response" and "not applicable"), the information can be represented by a *data file,* which is a rectangular matrix in which the rows are sample elements (e.g., persons responding to the questionnaire) and the columns represent the questions answered.

The responses to the items are most conveniently analyzed if they are numbers rather than letters, words, or other character strings. Response categories that contain alphabetical as well as numerical characters, such as "X22," "SMITH," "Y," and "23SL," are called string variables. String variables can be useful in the initial stage of coding, where the use of letters can be better remembered by interviewers. But such letters must be changed to numbers by a process called *re*coding.

It is standard procedure to assign each respondent, or sample element, a distinct identification or "ID" number. It is typical in social research, especially in surveys, that a great many variables are coded. When data cards were the basic technology for storing and analyzing information, the number of columns was restricted to 80. Given that many variables require fields of more than one column, this means that several "cards" were used for each case. Ordinarily, the first three to five columns were reserved for "ID" numbers (e.g., 001, 002, 003, and so on), and some other column represented the card number for the case. Now that data cards, keypunch machines, and other such equipment have become obsolescent, data files are now typically entered directly onto a disc or diskette via computer terminals. Lines of data for each case, or respondent, are still called "cards."

Precoding

Numerical coding can be conducted either when the questionnaire itself is being written (precoding) or after the questionnaire has been administered and the questions answered (postcoding). Precoding is necessarily limited chiefly to questions whose answer categories are known in advance. These are primarily closed-ended questions (e.g., yes/no/don't know) or questions whose answer is already a number and thus does not need to be converted (e.g., age or number of children). In open-ended questions the researcher is often not sure exactly what answers or how many different answer categories will be given, and so he or she often cannot establish codes until he or she has analyzed the data.

Coding, whether pre- or post-, is a two-part procedure involving: (1) choice of a different number for each and every possible answer category; and (2) choice of the appropriate column or columns on the computer card that are to contain the code numbers for that variable. As an example consider question 40 of Wild's (1973) study of pediatric health care among college students:

```
40. I believe in trying out different doctors to find which one I think will
    give me the best care. (CIRCLE ONE)
                        Strongly agree............1          71/
                        Agree..................2
                        Disagree...............3
                        Strongly disagree........4
```

Notice that each respondent circles only one answer to this question, and that each respondent has his or her own computer card. The number in the right-hand margin indicates the column of the computer card in which the code for question 40 is to be punched. Answers to closed-ended questions should be mutually exclusive and exhaustive. Thus having two or more answers to a single question should be avoided. When multiple answers are unavoidable they pose special coding problems and cannot be coded into a single column. If necessary, one or more separate columns must be allowed for every potential answer in order to avoid multiple punches in the same column.

If the code for a particular variable must run larger than 9, then it is impossible to place the next number (10) in a single column, and letters can be used, or two columns can be used to code one variable. Two columns suffice up to 99; if 100 is required as a possible code, three columns must be used; and so on. For example, imagine that after coding question 40 in column 71 (as shown above) the next question was age of father. Since most college-aged fathers will be in their 20s or 30s, a single column will not suffice, and at least two columns will be necessary. However, three columns will not be necessary unless we expect a father to be 100 years old or more. Since this is extremely unlikely (our sample consists only of parents of young children), we decide that two columns will suffice. Thus we could write the question and predetermine the columns as follows:

```
41. Father's age at last birthday _____          72-73/
```

Imagine that the respondent enters 43 as father's age. This needs no further coding since it is already in numerical form. All the keypuncher must do is punch 4 in column 72 and 3 in column 73.

If it turns out that not enough columns have been allotted but that extra columns are needed for relatively few cases, the researcher may decide either to discard these (treat them as non-responses) or lump them into the highest allowable category as a residual category. For example, if age was allotted two columns but one respondent was 100 years old and another was 108 years old, both could be coded into the highest allowable two-column category (99) and treated as 99+.

Open-ended questions are extremely difficult to precode because the complete range and number of potential answers may not be known, making it very difficult to know how many columns to allow for the variable. For example, Wild's (1973) question 58 asked "whether most of your friends have children." Answers that indicated friends with children directed the respondent to answer question 58A, which asked:

```
If so, to your knowledge, where do they take their children for medical
care?                                                            29-32/
```

The edge coding of columns 29,30,31 and 32 allows for one variable to be coded with up to 1,000 different responses (four columns), or for four different single-value variables to be coded. If it turns out that all four columns are not needed, then one or more columns can be left blank without any harmful effects. However, if more columns are needed than have been allotted, then the data file can be enlarged appropriately.

Multiple answers pose special problems. Consider Wild's (1973) question 62:

```
62. Which of the following University facilities, if any, do you often use?
    (CIRCLE ALL THAT APPLY)
    Student Health services ......................................... 1    61/
    Recreation Center ............................................... 2    62/
    University library system ....................................... 3    63/
    Student Union for dining ........................................ 4    64/
    UCLA Book Store ................................................. 5    65/
    Housing services ................................................ 6    66/
    Financial Aid office ............................................ 7    67/
    UCLA Child Care Center .......................................... 8    68/
    Other ........................................................... 9    69/
```

A respondent is instructed to circle as many responses as he or she wishes but, as mentioned above, only one can be punched in a single column. The only viable alternative is to code as Wild did and allot a separate column for each response. Such coding really amounts to transforming one variable containing nine different response categories into nine variables. Now each of the variables is binary, or dichotomous—that is, it is coded only as present or absent. For example, suppose that the respondent circles only Student Union for dining (4) and Book Store (5). Then the researcher will enter a 4 in column 64 of the data file and a 5 in column 65, and nothing in columns 61,62,63,66,67,68, or 69. Since we are coding the question as nine categories of a single variable, it is really not necessary to code with nine different numbers. We could use a 1 for each of the responses and enter it as such in the appropriate column for each category that is circled. However, using the same response number for all the choices could confuse the respondents.

Although multiple answers may be coded by dividing one variable into many, such coding is not without disadvantages. It takes up valuable space on a computer card and may necessitate using several more cards per person than would otherwise be necessary. Also, since each column for which a response is not circled remains blank, it may appear to be a nonresponse (although it is not). Nonresponses pose particularly vexing problems in data reduction and analysis. They will be discussed in some detail in subsequent passages.

Precoding has two distinct advantages. First, it saves a tremendous amount of labor because the respondent can indicate a numerical code at the time he or she is answering the question, obviating the need for a coder to read all questionnaires and mark a code for each answer. Second, with precoding the actual questionnaire can serve as a code book that defines the meaning of each code number, making a separate code book (usually used with postcoding) unnecessary. However, as seen above, precoding is impractical if the researcher is unable to predict which answer categories will be given or how many categories will exist for a particular question. Underestimation of the number of answer categories may necessitate renumbering columns for all subsequent variables on the computer card.

Postcoding

Postcoding refers to coding of responses after the questionnaires have been answered by the respondents. Postcoding is unnecessary and disadvantageous for simple questions for which precoding can easily be done. For example, consider a question asking the respondent's gender. To precode this question we would write it as follows:

```
1. Circle one: Female 1.
              Male    2.
```

To postcode it we would write the following question:

```
1. Sex _____
```

Since we cannot assume that the coder will memorize the appropriate codes for every question, the question that is not precoded would require that we go through every questionnaire and enter the appropriate number (either 1 or 2). This separate step requiring tedious paper handling and a chance of clerical error is made unnecessary through precoding.

The chief advantage of postcoding over precoding is that postcoding allows the coder to ascertain which answers are actually given by respondents before beginning coding. This can lead to great simplification. For example, if a question has ten possible answers, an examination of the returned questionnaires may reveal that only three of the answer categories were used by the respondents. Thus only three codes are necessary, and only one column is required instead of two.

Remember that the researcher does not provide answer categories for open-ended questions, but leaves determination of the categories to the respondent. The usual way to code such answers is to read all respondents' answers to that particular question. Each time a new answer is encountered it is recorded, as is the frequency of each answer category. After all answer categories and their frequencies of occurrence are known, postcoding is as straightforward as precoding. One merely decided how many columns are needed and assigns the numbers. Possible responses that were not given by any respondents need not be coded.

Postcoding also allows the researcher to code multiple answers to a single variable by writing a different code number for each combination of answers given. For example, if the respondent is instructed to select two answers from a total of five, there would be 2^5 or 32 possible different combinations (a and b, b and c, c and d, and so on). The 32 different combinations of responses could be assigned 32 different code numbers and coded in two columns. However, if the respondent is instructed to select all applicable answers from a substantial list of alternatives, as in Wild's question 62, the number of potential combinations is very great. In such a case the researcher can code combinations by counting all combinations that occur and deciding whether coding combinations is feasible.

Code-Book Construction

The purposes of the code book are to define the meaning of the numerical code and to tell the location of the variable on the computer card. If a questionnaire can be completely precoded, with a numerical code for each answer category for every question and an edge-code to indicate the location of the variable on the data file, then a separate code book is unnecessary, and a blank copy of the questionnaire can be used as a code book. However, particularly for postcoding, and for open-ended questions that receive many answers, there is not sufficient room on the questionnaire to identify all codes. In this case a separate code book is compiled. Figure 14–1 shows a page of a code book from a fertility study (Sabagh et al. 1973), covering columns 21–26 (the other columns are covered by pages not shown here).

Coding Nonresponses

Some nonresponses (simple failure to provide any answer at all for a question) are inevitable in any questionnaire. In writing the questionnaire the researcher should do everything possible to prevent nonresponses, as they present many problems. However, if nonresponses are received, the researcher must devise some scheme for coding them, preferably a standard scheme so that the same code can be used for nonresponse regardless of the particular question.

Some researchers indicate lack of response simply by leaving the column or columns blank. However, as Babbie (1973, p. 194) cautions, blanks should be avoided because different computer systems handle blanks in different ways, some merely coding them as zeroes and others attaching special significance to them, and because a researcher seeing a blank column cannot tell whether it represents nonresponse or is merely an error caused by failure to punch the correct code. Babbie strongly recommends assigning a numerical code for nonresponse.

The numbers used most often for nonresponse are 9 or 0. For variables requiring more than one column the number is merely repeated for each column (e.g., 99 or 999). Any numerical code is satisfactory for nonresponse as long as it is not a number that could occur as a legitimate response. For example, if you were asking the respondent to list the number of children

Figure 14–1

Excerpt from a Code Book

		CARD 21 PAGE 2
COLUMN	QUESTION AND DESCRIPTION	CODES
	Q77. When you (first) married?	
20-21	MONTH R married	01-January etc. 12-December
		99-NA
22-23	YEAR R married	Precoded.
		99-NA
24-25	Q78. How old were you when you married your (present) husband?	Precoded. 99-NA
26	Q79. Where was that?	See List 10

SOURCE: G. Sabagh et al. (1973) in *Codebook: Growth of the Mexican-American Family* (University of California at Los Angeles. Study funded by contract HD-12215 of the National Institute of Health). Reprinted by permission.

in his or her family, you should not use 9 for nonresponse because you could not distinguish a nonresponse from a family of nine children.

Using Wild's (1973) questionnaire as an illustration, most questions have answer categories of strongly agree/agree/disagree/strongly disagree, which are coded 1,2,3, and 4, respectively. Thus for most questions either 9 or 0 will suffice as a code for no answer. Zero is preferable for Wild's questionnaire because the few questions for which 9 is a legitimate code begin with 1, and thus allow 0 to be used for nonresponse. For the few questions for which both 0 and 9 are possible answers (for example, number of children in family), some other code must be devised for nonresponse. This must be some number that will never appear empirically (such as 99 for number of children). It may be necessary to add an additional column to the code in order to write such a number.

In addition to nonresponse items, codes may also need to be assigned for DK (don't know) responses and for INAPP (inapplicable) responses, where the question does not apply to a particular respondent. "Don't know" responses are often coded as 8 or 88, while "inapplicable" responses are often coded as 0 or 00.

After coding is completed the next step is to enter the coded information into a file, which can be stored on a disc, diskette, or tape. If questionnaires are precoded, including edge coding to signify the proper columns in the date file for each variable, the codes can be extracted directly from the questionnaires. This is advisable if possible since it saves clerical work, which not only costs time and money but also provides the potential for additional error. However, if the questionnaire has been postcoded and if the codes are complicated, requiring a lengthy code book, it will be difficult or impossible to work directly from the questionnaires. The effort involved in looking up each code in the code book could lead to numerous errors. In such a case the standard procedure is to split the task of constructing the data file into two separate operations: (1) reading the questionnaires and code book and transferring the correct numerical codes for each question onto a sheet of computer paper and (2) entering the data into the computer through a computer terminal.

Data Entry

Entering data into the memory of a computer requires a clear code number for each variable on the questionnaire, as well as the column and line "card" in which the code is to be punched. This information can be presented either on a precoded copy of the questionnaire or on separate computer code sheets, as discussed above. In some cases the data can even be directly entered by the interviewer from the questionnaire into the computer, by various means to be discussed shortly. In other cases the data must be entered into the computer by persons using the computer code sheets. In either case, the questionnaires and code sheets should first be edited.

Editing

Editing consists of searching for problems, just as you would edit a paper or article. The editor simply begins by looking over each completed questionnaire, searching for incomplete answers, cases where questions were misunderstood, answers that could not possibly be correct, answers that conflict with answers from other questions, and so forth. For example, a questionnaire which shows a respondent's date of birth as 1840 probably indicates a simple entry error on the part of the interviewer, who wrote 1840 instead of 1940. Other cases might reveal that a respondent gave a correct response, but it was simply recorded in the wrong place. In this case the computer would list it as the answer for another question, as it would be stored in the wrong column. Obviously, the better the editing the better the final product, as all errors at this stage of the research project will cumulate throughout the coding and data entry and analysis phases.

Direct Entry: Scanning

In some cases, optical scanners can be used to input the questionnaire data directly into the computer. This is facilitated by precoding. It can also be facilitated by scanning sheets (like those used on examinations) for marking answers in columns with a pencil. Such "machine-readable" sheets can be directly scanned into the computer. For example, with the question,

"Are you married?" the respondent will fill in column 1 for "Yes" and column 2 for "No." Then no further coding is necessary, although editing may still be needed.

Direct Entry: Interviewer Computer Entry

Recently developed computer techniques have made it efficacious for interviewers who use terminals during the interview to enter information directly into the computer during the course of the interview. We discussed both CATI (Computer Assisted Telephone Interviewing) and CAPI (Computer Assisted Personal Interviewing), as well as computer surveys, in chapter 8. All of these methods enable the interviewer to view the questionnaire on the screen of the computer terminal. The codes are either precoded or coded by the interviewer. Once an answer is given, the interviewer types its code directly into the computer. In the case of direct online computer surveys (for example on networks), it may even be possible for the respondent to view the questions on the terminal screen and directly enter codes into the computer without the interviewer having to do it. In either case, this is obviously a great advantage over the traditional practice of writing the answer on a paper questionnaire page, then turning it over to another person for coding, cleaning, and data entry into the computer.

Data Cleaning

If one has a very large sample and a lengthy questionnaire requiring several lines of data, or "cards" per person, there may not be time to proofread every number. A listing or printout of the entire data file can be studied. While such proofreading is certainly advisable, many researchers do not do it, but instead compromise with a crude method of checking for clerical errors that is often called *data cleaning*. Then by comparing each column or set of columns with the code book, the researcher can tell at a glance whether there are any "illegal" or erroneous entries.

Suppose that the code book shows that Wild's (1973) question 19 ("The personnel where I take my children act like too many patients come for nonexistent illnesses") is coded in column 26, and that the only allowable response codes are 1,2,3, or 4 (strongly agree/agree/disagree/strongly disagree). By drawing two vertical lines down all the sheets of computer paper, one line on the left side of column 26 and one on the right, the researcher can glance down the column and note the entry for column 26 on all data in the file. If he or she sees any entry besides 1, 2, 3, or 4, it is an error. He or she may see a blank that he or she knows is an illegal entry (as long as a blank is not used to code a nonresponse), and will surmise that the column was inadvertently skipped over in the data-entry process. It is a simple matter to look up and enter the proper number. If the researcher sees some other number, such as 8 or 9, he or she knows that a typing error was made, or the code for some other column was mistakenly put in column 26. If the latter is the case, it may indicate that the answers to a number of questions have been entered in the wrong columns (e.g., they may all have been entered one column too far to the left, so that the code for column 27 appears in column 26, the code for 26 in 25, and so on).

An easier way to conduct possible-entry cleaning is through the use of computer programs.

Most computer systems in operation at major universities have a simple program that will print out each symbol contained in a particular column (or columns) and the frequency with which it occurs. For example, if Wild's question 19 is coded in column 26 for a sample size of 100 respondents with only the 1,2,3, and 4 allowable, the computer program might reveal that 1 has a frequency of 23; 2 has a frequency of 36; 3 has a frequency of 25; 4 has a frequency of 12; 6 has a frequency of 3; and 8 has a frequency of 1. Since 6 and 8 are illegal entries they are obviously errors and need to be corrected. Suppose that we next examined question 20, coded in column 27, and found 1 with a frequency of 30; 2 with a frequency of 23; 3 with a frequency of 17; and 4 with a frequency of 30. This would indicate that there are no blatantly illegal codes and it would not be necessary to proofread the printout for all lines of data.

The great timesaving feature of such computer possible-entry cleaning is that one can see very quickly if a variable contains any illegal values. For variables with no illegal values the researcher need not proofread, in contrast with noncomputer cleaning in which every single line of data must be read to make sure there are no errors. Only when a variable with errors is found, as in question 19, does it become necessary to proofread all of the lines to find the errors. For question 19 the researcher knows that the entire set of cards contains only four cards with errors for column 26 (three lines with 6 in column 26 and one line with 8 in column 26), but the computer program gives no clue to the position of these incorrect codes.

One should be aware that possible-entry data cleaning is only a compromise measure that is no substitute for complete verifying and proofreading. The only errors that can be detected by possible-entry data cleaning are those involving illegal punches. All typographical errors involving legal punches are undetectable, and thus uncorrectable.

Contingency Cleaning

In addition to possible-entry cleaning, Babbie (1973, p. 201) discusses what he calls *contingency cleaning*. As you recall from our discussion of questionnaire construction in chapter 6, contingency questions are questions that are not answered by all respondents. Whether or not a respondent is supposed to answer the question is contingent upon his or her answer to an earlier question. Contingency cleaning entails checking to see that such a question was actually answered only by those respondents who qualified to answer it by means of an earlier response. This type of cleaning is much more difficult than possible-entry cleaning if done without a computer program, since it involves proofreading two or more variables at a time. Contingency cleaning is generally also less important than possible-entry cleaning but may be easily done with computer programs that cross-tabulate two or more variables, so that permissible codes for one variable can be studied for differing codes for one or more other variables. Errors can generally be avoided by data processing. For example, if the researcher believed that there were errors in the data because of childless respondents answering questions on child rearing, but did not have the time or money to do a complete job of contingency cleaning, he or she could avoid the problem by recording the variable "number of children" in two categories, "zero" and "one or more," and then, for example, looking at questions intended for "one or more," to see that they are not coded "inapplicable" and looking at "none" to see that they are all coded "inapplicable."

Summary

Chapter 14 discussed coding and data reduction. We first discussed the task of coding data so that they can be entered into the computer. We discussed both precoding (coding of each answer on the questionnaire before data are gathered) and postcoding (coding of answers after all data have been gathered). We also discussed codebook construction, and alternative strategies for coding nonresponse.

We next turned to a discussion of data entry and a discussion of ways of cleaning the data (detecting and correcting errors) after the data have been entered into the computer. The data-entry topics we discussed are editing, direct entry through scanning, and direct entry by the interviewer through a computer terminal. The methods of data cleaning we discussed are possible-entry cleaning and contingency cleaning.

CHAPTER 15

SCALING

THE BASIC RATIONALE for measurement and scaling was discussed at some length in chapter 4. This chapter presents some of the technical scaling techniques that are commonly used in social research. We shall discuss scaling methods separately for the three major levels of measurement: nominal, ordinal, and interval-ratio.

Scaling is the process of assigning numbers or symbols to the various levels of a particular concept that we wish to measure. Most of the time we will assign numbers, but occasionally we may designate different values of a concept by symbols such as group A or group B, particularly at the nominal level. In general, though, we will assign numbers. The concept to be scaled will thus be assigned a range of possible values that it can assume. In addition, each person to whom the finished scale is administered will have a value or scale score on that particular scale. In a sense, any test that you take in school is a type of scale. For example, your teacher could construct a mathematics test with a range of possible scores from zero to 153. This is a scale of mathematical ability. After the scale is constructed, it can be administered to persons. Each person who takes the test then achieves a given test or scale score between zero and 153, which is his or her supposed level of mathematical ability. A great many scales have been constructed in social science. Delbert Miller (1991) lists a large number. These include scales of social status, social participation, morale, job satisfaction, alienation, and marriage-adjustment. In addition to Miller's general handbook of measures, a number of more specialized handbooks are available, giving scales for specific areas of interest. These include Beere (1979) for scales on women, Brodsky and Smitherman (1983) for measures of crime and delinquency, and Touliatos et al. (1990) for measures of family issues. For further general discussion see Borgatta (1992) and Straus and Wauchope (1992).

Nominal Scaling

Scaling at the nominal level is basically a matter of creating mutually exclusive and exhaustive groups that are as homogeneous as possible. Since researchers are generally interested in at least ordinal-level measurement, or preferably interval-level, relatively little attention has been paid to the development of sophisticated methods for nominal scaling. For example, if you are a married woman and your husband is asking you about your love for him, he will not be concerned with love as a nominal qualitive variable (what kind of love do you have for me, type A or type B?) but as a quantitative ordinal or interval-level variable (how much do you love me on a scale of 10?).

Construction of a nominal scale consisting of only one variable or dimension is really nothing more than the coding of a closed-ended (forced-choice) question. For example, if we ask the respondent to list his or her gender (male/female), we are constructing a nominal scale of gender. However, nominal scaling can be much more difficult if we wish to construct a multidimensional set of categories (e.g., to code simultaneously on age, gender, and race instead of merely on gender). Such multidimensional nominal scaling will be discussed at the end of this chapter when we consider multidimensional scaling.

Ordinal Scaling

Scales, particularly attitude scales, as used in social research serve three main functions: (1) measurement; (2) to aid in defining the concept by providing an operational definition (intelligence is what the intelligence test measures; see the discussion of operationalism in chapter 3); and (3) to prevent bias by covertly measuring a sensitive topic so that the respondent does not even realize, for example, that his or her level of prejudice is being measured, and so cannot manipulate his or her answer.

Summated Rating

The first objective can perhaps be met by scaling with a single question. For example:

```
Rate your spouse's physical attractiveness on a scale of 1 to 10 (circle one)
                     1 2 3 4 5 6 7 8 9 10
```

To meet the other two objectives, it is generally necessary (or at least traditional) to construct the scale from a whole series of questions, even though only a single variable or dimension is being measured. Since there are a substantial number of questions, a person's score can vary, depending on how many questions he or she either agrees with or answers correctly. A higher score represents a higher level of the concept being measured. This type of scale is called a *summated ratings scale,* because a person's score is computed by summing up the number of questions he or she answers a certain way. Often questions for an attitude scale are coded either 0 (for disagree) or 1 (for agree). A person who agrees with all questions makes a maximum score on the scale, and a person who disagrees with all questions makes a score of 0.

Suppose that we are interested in studying attitudes toward natality (birth) in America over a long period of time. We know that the birthrate has been dropping for a number of years and is now quite low (2.1 children on the average per family). However, we want to see whether attitudes toward number of children will change over time in the future, and whether the recent decline in birthrate is due to a constant attitude toward births but increased effectiveness of birth control, or whether attitudes toward birth itself are changing. Let us construct a 10-item natality scale, with agreement coded as 1 and disagreement coded as 0:

	Bailey Natality Scale	Agree	Disagree
1.	One of the major reasons for getting married is to have children.	1	0
2.	It is wrong to have only one child, as an only child grows up lonely and sad for himself or herself because he or she has no brothers or sisters.	1	0
3.	Giving birth to a baby is one of the most profound experiences a woman can have.	1	0
4.	It is better to have at least one child of each sex than to only have children of one sex	1	0
5.	A woman who does not have children can never feel completely fulfilled	1	0

6. A man is not a "real man" until he has proven himself by fathering a child.	1	0
7. Sexual activity that cannot result in conception (because of birth control, sterilization, or advanced age) is morally wrong.	1	0
8. A man who is not married, or a married man with no children, is probably a homosexual	1	0
9. A woman's first role obligation is motherhood, and it is all right for her to have a career only if that career does not interfere with her mothering role.	1	0
10 A married couple without children should be pitied.	1	0

We would say that a respondent scoring 10 on this scale would feel a strong obligation to have children if at all possible, while a respondent with a score of 0 would feel no obligation to have children. A major difficulty with this type of scale is that we have no assurance that all questions are measuring exactly the same thing—attitude toward giving birth. We do know that all of the questions seem to be fairly relevant to the topic being measured, and thus have face validity. For example, as question 11 we could ask:

	Agree	Disagree
11. It is better to eat fish on Friday than to eat meat.	1	0

This question might actually be a good indicator of attitude toward giving birth, since it measures degree of adherence to Catholic principles, which are strongly pronatal. However, it does not have face validity because it apparently has nothing to do with giving birth, so we would not use it in the scale. Even when all of the questions have face validity, there is still no assurance that they are all measuring the same thing, and thus that the scale is a unidimensional and linear measure of a single attitude.

One major difficulty with such a scale is that there is more than one way for a respondent to make a single score. There is only one way to make a score of 10 (by agreeing with all 10 questions) and only one way to make a score of 0 (by disagreeing with all 10 questions). However, there are many different ways to make a score of 2 by agreeing with any two questions. For example, suppose that Ms. Smith agrees with questions 5 and 9 but disagrees with all others; Mr. Jones agrees with questions 6 and 8 but disagrees with all others; Ms. Barnes agrees with questions 1 and 10 but disagrees with all others; and Mr. Johnson agrees with questions 2 and 4 but disagrees with all others. If our scale is valid, unidimensional, and linear as designed, then all of these people are exhibiting exactly the same (low) degree of pronatalism. However, a critic might well argue that, rather than indicating the same level of agreement on a single variable, these various scores of 2 actually are measuring four different and distinct concepts. The critic might say that Ms. Smith's answers measure her attitude toward female roles; Mr. Jones's answers measure his attitude toward male roles; Ms. Barnes's answers measure her attitude toward marriage as an institution; and Mr. Johnson's answers measure his attitude toward child socialization. Instead of measuring a single attitude (toward childbearing), we are measuring at least four additional attitudes.

Likert Scaling

If there were only one way to make each score, or if there were many ways to make a score but we knew for certain that each question measured the same concept, then we would have confidence in the scale. However, the major problem with summated rating scales is that, as in our example above, we cannot be sure that all questions measure the same concept. Likert (1932) has developed a technique for helping to eliminate questionable items from the scale. The essence of the Likert technique is to increase the variation in the possible scores, by coding from "strongly agree" to "strongly disagree" instead of merely "agree or disagree." A scale score is computed for each respondent. If person A makes a very high score and person B a very low score, their answers to all questions can be compared to see if there is any single question that the person with the two very different scores answered identically. Such a question obviously does not discriminate well between discrepant scores on the concept, and so would be eliminated from the scale. For example, if person A had a score of 55 and person B a score of 3, but both had identical answers on question 7, then 7 would be dropped from the scale.

The basic procedure for Likert scaling is as follows:

1. Write a large number of questions thought to measure the dimension to be scaled.
2. Select a sample of respondents representative of the population on which the scale will be used.
3. Code all responses so that a higher score on a particular item indicates a stronger agreement with the attitude being scaled (code 5 for either strong agreement with a positive statement or strong disagreement with a negative one, and code 1 for strong disagreement with a positive statement or strong agreement with a negative one); compute a scale for each person by summing her or his scores on all questions.
4. Analyze responses and select for the scale the items most clearly differentiating between the highest and lowest scores.

The researcher can divide the respondents into quartiles and compute the median score on each item for the highest 25 percent and the lowest 25 percent of scales scores. If any question has the same median score for both the high and low groups it can be eliminated from the scale. Only questions that reveal widely different median scores for the highest and lowest groups will be retained. Also, each item can be correlated with the total score or with other items that discriminate well between the highest and lowest quartiles of scores. Items that do not correlate highly can be eliminated from the scale.

Guttman Scaling

Louis Guttman (1944) has devised a method of scaling called *scalogram analysis* that is designed to ensure that there is only one (unique) combination of responses for each different scale score. That is, while there may be ten or more different ways to make a score of 2 with Likert scaling, there is only one way to make a score of 2 on a Guttman scale. Thus a Guttman scale is more likely than a Likert scale to be unidimensional. If some combination of scores other than the desired combination forms a particular scale score, it is considered an error. If there are many scaling errors, or exceptions to the desired pattern, the scale is inadequate.

Guttman's scalogram analysis is cumulative in the sense that the combination of responses required to make a particular score includes the responses to all questions required to make the next lower score, plus the response to one additional question, in a stepwise fashion. For example, suppose that we wish to walk up a stairway containing 10 steps. We number all steps from 1 to 10 beginning at the bottom. Now imagine that we have all of our respondents walk up as many steps as they wish, and stop. They may not skip any steps (step up more than one step at a time). We will give them 1 point each for each step they traverse. It should be clear that there is only one way to make each score. To make a score of 3 a person must walk up steps 1, 2, 3 only. To make a score of 8 he or she must walk up steps 1, 2, 3, 4, 5, 6, 7, 8 only. We say the scale is cumulative because a score of 4 is made by walking up 3 steps for a score of 3, plus the fourth step; a score of 8 is made by walking up the first 7 steps (for a score of 7) plus the eighth step. Since each score represents a unique set of responses, we know from a person's score exactly which steps he or she walked up (or exactly with which items he or she agreed).

The Guttman scaling procedure begins about the same way as the summated ratings or Likert procedure. The researcher selects a group of items that he or she thinks should form a unidimensional scale of whatever concept he or she wishes to scale. These items should all have face validity (they should all at least *appear* to measure the concept in question). They may be derived either from theory or from past empirical investigation, and some of them may have previously been found to be highly intercorrelated. In the simplest forms of scalogram analysis, only two responses are allowed for each question. These can be coded with any binary coding system (1 or 0 is probably the most common, but other possibilities include + or − and a or b). It is also better to have many more cases (respondents) than questions to be scaled, because use of only a few respondents increases the possibility of forming an error-free scale by chance.

We will illustrate the Guttman scaling method with an example from Udy's (1958) study of bureaucratic characteristics in 25 nonindustrial production organizations. In this case the respondents or cases were not individual persons but primitive societies. The concept to be scaled was bureaucracy, based on Max Weber's conception of bureaucracy. For bureaucracy to fit the cumulative Guttman pattern, the least bureaucratic or completely unbureaucratic society would have none of the items or characteristics, the next least bureaucratic would have one item, the next would have that item plus one more, the next would have those two items plus one more, and so on, with the most bureaucratic having all items. The four characteristics to be scaled are whether each organization exhibits: (1) compensatory rewards (compensation from higher to lower authority); (2) specialization (three or more operations performed simultaneously); (3) performance emphasis (reward proportional to work done); and (4) segmental participation (explicit contractual agreement). The question here is not whether the respondents agree or disagree with an item, but simply whether or not they possess it.

Table 15–1 shows the 25 societies and the number of characteristics each possesses. Notice that the Samoan fishing society is an "error" in the accumulative pattern, since it possesses characteristic 2 without characteristic 1. All 24 other societies fit the Guttman pattern perfectly. If they have only one characteristic it will be number 1; if they have two they will have 1 and 2; if they have three they will have only 1, 2, and 3. Simply by knowing a society's score (with the exception of Samoa) one can tell exactly which characteristics the society possesses. The characteristics will not necessarily be in the proper order at the beginning of the scale-construction process, but the proper order can be determined empirically.

Coefficient of Reproducibility.   If we did not have one error (Samoa), we could reproduce every society's pattern of characteristics perfectly simply by knowing its score. If we had a large number of errors, we would not have much ability to reproduce a particular pattern of responses from the scale score, and would not have much confidence that the set of items actually forms a unidimensional scale. Guttman invented the *coefficient of reproducibility* as a measure of our ability to reproduce scores. The higher the value of the measure, the higher the proportion of scores we can reproduce accurately. The coefficient is computed by subtracting the proportion of responses that are errors from 100 percent (all responses). We can compute the proportion of responses that are errors very easily. We need only know the number of errors (1 in the present example), and divide it by the total number of responses. The total number of responses is simply the number of items times the number of respondents that can answer each item, or in this case 4 items times 25 societies, or 100. In equation form, $CR = 1.00 - \#errors/[(\#respondents)(\#items)]$. For our particular example:

$$CR = 1.00 - (1)/[(25)(4)]$$
$$= 1.00 - 1/100$$
$$= 1.00 - .01$$
$$= 0.99$$

Any coefficient of reproducibility over .90 is supposedly adequate to indicate scalability and the ability to reproduce responses to the various items from knowledge of the total score. However, as Edwards (1957, p. 191) notes, a *CR* of .90 is not a *sufficient* condition for the scalability of a set of statements. This is, as Edwards says,

> for the simple reason that the reproducibility of any single statement can never be less than the frequency present in the modal category. For example, if we had a statement with only two categories of response and found that .90 of the 100 subjects fell in one of the categories, this statement would have as its minimum reproducibility 90 percent. Thus, it might be possible to have a set of 10 statements, each with just two categories of response, and each with a very high modal frequency, and these statements would yield—would have to yield—a very high coefficient of reproducibility (Edwards 1957, pp. 191–92).

Minimal Marginal Reproducibility.   Edwards goes on to point out that if each item contained only two categories and every item had exactly 50 percent of all responses in each category, then only two scale scores would be possible. Thus, since the coefficient of reproducibility is affected by the proportion of responses in the modal category (the category with the most responses), an artificially high but relatively meaningless coefficient of reproducibility can be achieved for even an unsatisfactory scale. That is, a high coefficient of reproducibility with an

Table 15–1

Bureaucratic Characteristics Possessed by Each of Udy's (1958)
25 Nonindustrial Production Organizations*

Number	Organization	Variables			
		(1) Compensatory Rewards	(2) Special- ization	(3) Performance Emphasis	(4) Segmental Participation
1.	Navaho Hunting I	1	1	1	1
2.	Navaho Hunting II	1	1	1	1
3.	Paiute Hunting	1	1	1	1
4.	Sanpoil Hunting	1	1	1	1
5.	Lobi Construction I	1	1	1	1
6.	Kaybles Construction I	1	1	1	0
7.	Betsileo Agriculture	1	1	0	0
8.	Haitians Agriculture	1	1	0	0
9.	Lobi Hunting	1	1	0	0
10.	Kaybles Construction II	1	1	0	0
11.	Solomon Islanders Construction	1	1	0	0
12.	Bantu (Southeast) Agriculture I	1	0	0	0
13.	Bemba Agriculture I	1	0	0	0

uneven distribution of responses may be misleading, just as a percentage gain of 100 percent would be labeled misleading when it was discovered that the gain was from 1 to 2. Just as percentages are misleading with small frequencies, a high coefficient of reproducibility is misleading with high modal frequencies. To interpret the coefficient of reproducibility properly, one needs some idea of how low it is free to go, given the particular distribution of responses received. This can be determined by computing the minimal marginal reproducibility.

$$MMR = \sum_{i=1}^{N} \frac{(\% \text{ responses in modal category})}{N}$$

where N = number of items.

Let us compute *MMR* for table 15–1. There are only two possible categories (1 or 0) for each of the four items in the table. For characteristic 1 the modal category is 1, since 21 of the 25 responses are in that category. Thus proportion of responses in the modal category is 21/25.

Table 15–1

Continued

		Variables			
Number	Organization	(1) Compensatory Rewards	(2) Special- ization	(3) Performance Emphasis	(4) Segmental Participation
14.	Bemba Agriculture II	1	0	0	0
15.	Dahomey Agriculture	1	0	0	0
16.	Hopi Agriculture	1	0	0	0
17.	Iroquois Agriculture	1	0	0	0
18.	Muong Fishing	1	0	0	0
19.	Crow Construction	1	0	0	0
20.	Kikuyu Construction	1	0	0	0
21.	Lobi Construction II	1	0	0	0
22.	Bantu (Southeast) Agriculture II	0	0	0	0
23.	Tibetans Agriculture	0	0	0	0
24.	Basuto Hunting	0	0	0	0
25.	Samoans Fishing	0	1	0	0

*Presence of the variable is indicated by 1 and absence of the variable is indicated by 0.

Source: S. Udy, Jr. (1958) in *American Sociological Review* 23 (August): 417. Reprinted with the permission of the author and the publisher, © American Sociological Association

For characteristic 2 the modal category is 0, giving a proportion of 13/24. For characteristic 3 there are 19 zeros, giving a proportion of 19/25. The 20 zeros in characteristic 4 yield a proportion of 20/25. Thus, for table 15–1:

$$MMR = \frac{(21/25 + 13/25 + 19/25 + 20/25)}{4}$$
$$= \frac{2.92}{4}$$
$$= .73$$

Since $CR = .99$ while $MMR = .73$, it is clear that the CR is not high solely because of the modal frequencies, and that in fact it could be considerably lower. Thus the CR we found signifies considerable improvement in reproducibility over the minimum level of .73, and indicates the adequacy of our scale.

Cornell Versus Goodenough Technique.   There are two different basic methods of determining the number of errors. As McConaghy explains it:

> The original Cornell method counts as error the least number of response changes necessary to produce a correct response pattern . . . The Goodenough method counts each incorrectly predicted item response as an error (McConaghy 1975, p. 345).

When computing *CR* for table 15–1 we used the Cornell method. The only error is for Samoa, which should be "0000" instead of "0100." By either method, since Samoa possesses one characteristic, it must possess characteristic 1 to be correct. By the Cornell method Samoa has only one error, since simply by moving the 1 from characteristic 2 to characteristic 1 we can achieve the correct response. However, by the Goodenough technique Samoa contains two errors, since there is a 0 instead of a 1 for characteristic 1 (one error) and a 1 instead of a 0 for characteristic 2 (a second error).

According to McConaghy (1975), the *MMR* gives a misleading low value with the Cornell scoring method and a misleading high value with the Goodenough scoring method. McConaghy has devised a minimum-error formula based on marginal frequencies that will provide an accurate *MMR* level with Cornell scoring. McConaghy's formula is rather complex, and is beyond the scope of this book. For further discussion see McConaghy (1975).

Advantages and Disadvantages of Guttman Scaling.   Construction of a Guttman scale is more difficult than construction of summated ratings scales in the sense that the former requires all items to be responded to in a certain cumulative order while the latter does not. As a result, Guttman scaling ensures that each scale score can be made in only one way, while the summated rating technique does not. The summated rating technique allows ties, in the sense that two or more separate sets of responses can yield an equal value of the scale. This property of separate but equal scores, or more than one way to make a score of a certain rank on an ordinal scale, is sometimes called partial order (B. Phillips 1976, p. 146). Guttman scaling does not allow two different and separate combinations of responses to tie for the same rank score. This is known as simple order (B. Phillips 1976, p. 146). However, simple order does not ensure unidimensionality. Thus for Guttman scaling to be proven superior to Likert scaling we must show that it is more likely to lead to unidimensionality.

Interval-ratio Scaling

Summated rating, Likert scaling, and Guttman scalogram analysis techniques all construct scales that are at most ordinal rather than interval. Even with a Guttman scale such as the bureaucracy scale of table 15.1 there is no claim that the scale is interval. For example, perusal of table 15.1 reveals that the Paiute Hunting organization has a score of 4 on the bureaucracy Guttman scale, while Kaybles Construction 1 has a score of 3 and Lobi Hunting has a score of 2. If the scale were interval, there would be the same degree of bureaucratization between a score of 4 (Paiute) and 3 (Kaybles) as between 3 (Kaybles) and 2 (Lobi). We cannot make this claim for the Guttman scale. It may be, for example, that organizations with a score of 3 are much more similar (in terms of bureaucracy) to organizations with a score of 2 than they are to organizations with a score of 4.

There are at least two good reasons for attempting to construct an interval scale: (1) the added information available from the knowledge that the intervals between any two adjacent points on the scale are equal; and (2) the requirement of many statistical techniques (e.g., multiple regression) for interval data. One technique designed to construct an interval scale is Thurstone's method of equal-appearing intervals (Edwards 1957, pp. 83–117).

The Thurstone technique is similar to the common practice mentioned at the beginning of this chapter of asking someone to rank a person on a scale of beauty ranging from 1 to 10. However, the Thurstone technique uses a scale of 11, with the middle category neutral. Generally the categories are labeled A through K rather than 1 through 11, so that the middle category is F. Also, instead of ranking persons on the scale, the judges whose rankings create the scale rank statements. The 11 categories are arranged from A on the left to K on the right, with A representing the most unfavorable attitude, F neutral, and K the most favorable. The judges are given a set of items supposedly all measuring the attribute to be scaled. Then each judge places each item in on the 11 categories to represent her or his judgment of how favorably or unfavorably it represents the attribute to be scaled. In the original study, Thurstone and Chave (1929) told their judges only what the two end and middle categories represented (extremely unfavorable, extremely favorable, and neutral). The remaining cards were not defined but were supposed to represent equal-appearing intervals, or equal degrees of favorableness and unfavorableness. The scaling procedure can be summarized as follows:

1. After the attitude to be scaled is selected (e.g., alienation, authoritarianism, prejudice), a large number of items believed to measure this concept are chosen.

2. A sample of judges is chosen to rank each item according to the 11-point scale of favorableness-unfavorableness. In the original study Thurstone and Chave used 300 judges to rank 130 statements, and found that each judge required on the average 45 minutes to rank the 130 statements.

3. There is a possibility that some judges will perform incorrectly, for example, rating statements according to their personal opinion rather than on how the statement measures the attitude to be scaled. Rankings by judges felt to have done a poor job are eliminated. Specifically, Thurstone and Chave eliminated those judges who placed 30 or more statements (out of 130) in one of the 11 categories. In the original study 41 out of 341 judges were eliminated on this basis. Also, those statements on which the judges cannot reach a consensus on ranking are eliminated.

4. The median value of each statement is taken as its scale value. For example, if half the judges rate item 99 above 7 and half rate it below 7, then 7 is the median value, and thus becomes the scale value for that item.

5. Approximately 22 items (or twice the number of original categories) are chosen to form the final scale. These items are chosen on the basis of their scale scores. It is hoped that the 22 items will be about equally spaced along the whole continuum, from unfavorable through neutral to favorable. Thus the scale value, called the S value (see Edwards 1957), is the primary criterion for selecting the final set of items. If it is necessary to choose between items with about the same scale score or S value, the one with the lowest Q value is chosen. Q measures the interquartile range, or the difference between the score for the seventy-fifth and the twenty-fifth centile. Q is thus the middle score, or the middle 50 percent of all scores. The smaller is Q, the more agreement there is on the appropriate ranking of the item, and thus the less ambiguous the item. Thus for two items with the same S score, the least ambiguous is the one with

the lowest Q score, and this is the one that should be chosen. In general the item with the smallest variance in scores, or smallest range of scores, should be chosen. This will usually be the item listed in the smallest number of the 11 categories.

6. After the 22 items are selected, they form the scale. It must be stressed that at this point the original 11 categories have done their job and are discarded. They are not presented to the respondents and serve no part in determining the final scale scores. The job of scale construction is now complete. The next step is to administer the scale to the respondents. These respondents are not judges, but are persons whose score on the scale you wish to determine. The 22 statements are worded so the respondent can agree or disagree, and are arranged in random order (so there will be no response set). The respondent's score is determined by computing the mean or median value of the scale scores of those items agreed with (items not agreed with are not counted, so that if no items are agreed with the respondent's score would be 0).

Work in scaling by Andrich (1985) has focused upon extending Guttman scaling statistically through elaboration of the Rasch model. This article also provides some discussion of Thurstone scaling and other scaling methods. An analysis by McIver and Carmines (1981) presents a contemporary discussion of Thurstone scaling, Likert scaling, and a variety of issues in Guttman scaling, such as what to do with too many respondents or too many items. The reader is referred to these original sources for further discussion.

Factor Scaling

Factor analysis is a statistical technique for synthesizing a large amount of data. It lends itself well to scale construction but requires a large amount of computation, and before the development of computers was generally impractical for the average researcher to compute. However, the accessibility of computers and "canned" computer programs have made factor analysis and factor scaling generally available even to the neophyte. All that is necessary is that the researcher be able to construct the control cards to set up the computer program properly and that he or she understand the basic assumptions and procedures of factor analysis.

Factor analysis generally uses as input data a table containing correlation coefficients (r) showing the correlations among all pairs of variables to be analyzed. Thus in factor scaling one would first decide which items were to be included in the scale, and would then compute the correlation between each pair of variables. As we shall see when we discuss correlation in chapter 16, r assumes all variables to be intervally measured. Computer programs are readily available for computing all correlations among all combinations of variables, and presenting them in one correlation matrix.

One example of factor analysis is provided by Wagenaar's (1981b) analysis of teacher morale questions. Wagenaar found that the 13 items shown in figure 15–1 were highly correlated with three underlying dimensions. Items, 1, 6, 7, and 12 are all highly correlated with Factor 1. Items 2, 4, 8, 9, and 13 are all highly correlated with Factor 2. The remaining three items, numbers 3, 5, and 11, are all highly correlated with Factor 3. Notice that these three factors tap different underlying dimensions. All of the items mentioned for Factor 1 relate to interaction with the principal, all items mentioned for Factor 2 relate to interaction with teaching colleagues, and all mentioned for Factor 3 deal with teaching as a career.

Figure 15–1

Factor Analysis of Selected Teacher Morale Items* (N = 280)

Item	Factor 1	Factor 2	Factor 3
1. My work is appreciated by my principal	.73	.13	.16
2. Little arguing occurs among teachers	.19	.76	−.04
3. Teaching gives me personal satisfaction	.18	.03	.75
4. Teachers cooperate in our school	.17	.78	.11
5. I love to teach	.16	−.01	.81
6. My principal makes my work easier/more pleasant	.83	.17	.09
7. My principal recognizes good teaching procedures	.77	.19	.14
8. Our teaching staff is congenial to work with	.25	.79	.01
9. My colleagues are well prepared	.20	.64	.01
10. I discuss problems with my principal	.80	.07	.14
11. If I could choose over, I would choose teaching	.10	.10	.74
12. My principal is interested in me	.85	.11	.11
13. Teachers in this school work well together	.25	.87	.01

*Contains only a subset of the complete list of 42 items.
SOURCE: Theodore C. Wagenaar (1981) in *Readings for Social Research* (Belmont, Calif.: Wadsworth).

As a detailed example of factor scaling consider the 20 items developed by Armor and Couch (1972) in the *Data-Text Primer*. These items measure attitude toward the Vietnam War (administered in June 1971 to 152 respondents). The correlation of each item with each of the 19 other items is shown in figure 15–2 (from Armor and Couch 1972, p. 73).

With factor scaling it is not necessary to assume that all 20 items will form a single unidimensional scale. Rather, essentially we assume that there are a number of underlying dimensions and that a substitute of items will correlate highly with each of these dimensions, forming a scale. For example, notice in figure 15–2 that variable 5 (no choice but to continue Vietnam War) correlates highly with variable 7 (Vietnam War necessary, $r = .651$), 14 (Vietnam win necessary, $r = .460$), and 18 (U.S. will win war, $r = .612$). Variable 10 (U.S. cannot gain a political victory) is also highly correlated with variable 5, but inversely ($r = −.554$). Since the rule we have been following in scaling is that all items must run in the same direction, item 10 can be used in the scale if it is reversed (U.S. will gain a political victory). The factor-analysis program is able to reverse such items.

The results of a factor analysis on these 20 items are shown in figure 15–3 (Armor and Couch 1972, p. 89), which contains three factors. Each factor can be thought of as a hypothetical variable, or underlying dimension, that is correlated with some of the 20 variables. That is,

Figure 15–2

Intercorrelation of Items on Attitudes Toward Vietnam War

VARIABLE DESCRIPTION	NAME	ITEM (1)	ITEM (2)	ITEM (3)	ITEM (4)	ITEM (5)	ITEM (6)	ITEM (7)	ITEM (8)	ITEM (9)	ITEM (10)
WAR IS UNJUSTIFIABLE	ITEM(1)	1.000	0.195*	0.242**	-0.005	-0.351***	0.059	-0.358***	0.035	-0.002	0.264**
VIETCONG WILL WIN WAR	ITEM(2)	0.195*	1.000	-0.082	-0.057	-0.394***	0.017	-0.419***	0.050	-0.113	0.359***
GIVE UNIONS VOICE	ITEM(3)	0.242**	-0.082	1.000	-0.009	-0.047	0.288***	-0.128	0.293***	0.161	0.038
DEMOCRACY SUPERIOR	ITEM(4)	-0.005	-0.057	-0.009	1.000	0.078	0.002	0.055	0.263**	0.080	-0.101
NO CHOICE BUT CONT. WAR	ITEM(5)	-0.351***	-0.394***	-0.047	0.078	1.000	-0.146	0.651***	-0.210*	0.218*	-0.554***
SOCIAL. MEDICINE GOOD	ITEM(6)	0.059	0.017	0.288***	0.002	-0.146	1.000	-0.309***	0.388***	0.118	0.201*
VIETNAM WAR IS NECESSARY	ITEM(7)	-0.358***	-0.419***	-0.128	0.055	0.651***	-0.309***	1.000	-0.294***	0.217*	-0.521***
GOVT SHOULD INSURE JOBS	ITEM(8)	0.035	0.050	0.293***	0.263**	-0.210*	0.388***	-0.294***	1.000	-0.180*	0.126
RAPID CHANGE IS UNWISE	ITEM(9)	-0.002	-0.113	0.161	0.080	0.218*	0.118	0.217*	-0.180*	1.000	0.020
US NOT GAIN POL. VICTORY	ITEM(10)	0.264**	0.359***	0.038	-0.101	-0.554***	0.201*	-0.521***	0.126	0.020	1.000
MUST NOT LOSE POWER	ITEM(11)	-0.238**	0.015	-0.153	-0.087	0.218*	-0.064	0.214*	0.148	0.325***	-0.048
WAR SOMETIMES NECESSARY	ITEM(12)	-0.695***	-0.198*	-0.125	0.036	0.306***	-0.087	0.278**	0.047	-0.070	-0.248**
VIETNAM WIN NECESSARY	ITEM(13)	0.421***	0.160	-0.007	0.022	-0.309***	0.286**	-0.316***	0.124	-0.239**	0.187*
BETTER RED THAN DEAD	ITEM(14)	-0.273**	-0.262**	0.050	0.013	0.460***	-0.142	0.567***	-0.131	0.099	-0.335***
MOST MEN WOULD NOT WORK	ITEM(15)	-0.112	-0.052	-0.281**	0.050	-0.175*	0.196*	-0.340***	0.124	0.300***	-0.073
WAR IS ALWAYS AVOIDABLE	ITEM(16)	0.552***	0.257**	0.024	0.054	-0.131	-0.356***	-0.382***	0.052	0.101	0.307***
NATIONALIZATION BAD	ITEM(17)	-0.139	-0.183*	-0.247**	0.037	0.204*	-0.356***	0.283***	-0.427***	0.275**	-0.104
US WILL WIN WAR	ITEM(18)	-0.278***	-0.403***	-0.086	-0.007	-0.356***	-0.240**	0.623***	-0.176*	0.216*	-0.692***
NATIONALIZATION GOOD	ITEM(19)	0.222**	0.076	0.335***	-0.002	-0.273**	0.351***	-0.194*	0.285***	-0.193*	0.102
VIETNAM WAR UNNECESSARY	ITEM(20)	0.124	0.245**	-0.019	-0.035	-0.492***	0.150	-0.703***	0.204*	-0.062	0.451***

VARIABLE DESCRIPTION	NAME	ITEM (11)	ITEM (12)	ITEM (13)	ITEM (14)	ITEM (15)	ITEM (16)	ITEM (17)	ITEM (18)	ITEM (19)	ITEM (20)
WAR IS UNJUSTIFIABLE	ITEM(1)	-0.238**	-0.695***	0.421***	-0.273**	-0.112	0.552***	-0.139	-0.278***	0.222**	0.124
VIETCONG WILL WIN WAR	ITEM(2)	0.015	-0.198*	0.160	-0.262**	-0.052	0.257**	-0.183*	-0.403***	0.076	0.245**
GIVE UNIONS VOICE	ITEM(3)	-0.153	-0.125	-0.007	0.050	-0.281**	0.024	-0.247**	-0.086	0.335***	-0.019
DEMOCRACY SUPERIOR	ITEM(4)	-0.087	0.036	0.022	0.013	0.050	0.054	0.037	-0.007	-0.002	-0.035
NO CHOICE BUT CONT. WAR	ITEM(5)	0.218*	0.306***	-0.309***	0.460***	-0.175*	-0.131	0.204*	-0.356***	-0.273**	-0.492***
SOCIAL. MEDICINE GOOD	ITEM(6)	-0.064	-0.087	0.286**	-0.142	0.196*	-0.356***	-0.356***	-0.240**	0.351***	0.150
VIETNAM WAR IS NECESSARY	ITEM(7)	0.214*	0.278**	-0.316***	0.567***	-0.340***	-0.382***	0.283***	0.623***	-0.194*	-0.703***
GOVT SHOULD INSURE JOBS	ITEM(8)	0.148	0.047	0.124	-0.131	0.124	0.052	-0.427***	-0.176*	0.285***	0.204*
RAPID CHANGE IS UNWISE	ITEM(9)	0.325***	-0.070	-0.239**	0.099	0.300***	0.101	0.275**	0.216*	-0.193*	-0.062
US NOT GAIN POL. VICTORY	ITEM(10)	-0.048	-0.248**	0.187*	-0.335***	-0.073	0.307***	-0.104	-0.692***	0.102	0.451***
MUST NOT LOSE POWER	ITEM(11)	1.000	0.167	-0.252**	0.391***	0.179*	0.252**	-0.186*	0.230**	-0.112	-0.007
WAR SOMETIMES NECESSARY	ITEM(12)	0.167	1.000	-0.288***	0.189*	0.123	-0.052	0.210*	0.318***	-0.190*	-0.050
VIETNAM WIN NECESSARY	ITEM(13)	-0.252**	-0.288***	1.000	-0.311***	-0.153	0.333***	-0.300***	-0.320***	0.337***	0.139
BETTER RED THAN DEAD	ITEM(14)	0.391***	0.189*	-0.311***	1.000	0.213*	-0.070	0.210*	0.130	-0.095	-0.487***
MOST MEN WOULD NOT WORK	ITEM(15)	0.179*	0.123	-0.153	0.213*	1.000	-0.070	0.405***	0.130	-0.286**	-0.078
WAR IS ALWAYS AVOIDABLE	ITEM(16)	0.252**	-0.052	0.333***	-0.070	-0.070	1.000	-0.300***	-0.319***	0.139	0.320***
NATIONALIZATION BAD	ITEM(17)	-0.186*	0.210*	-0.300***	0.210*	0.405***	-0.300***	1.000	0.236**	-0.525***	-0.155
US WILL WIN WAR	ITEM(18)	0.230**	0.318***	-0.320***	0.130	0.130	-0.319***	0.236**	1.000	-0.149	-0.402***
NATIONALIZATION GOOD	ITEM(19)	-0.112	-0.190*	0.337***	-0.095	-0.286**	0.139	-0.525***	-0.149	1.000	0.099
VIETNAM WAR UNNECESSARY	ITEM(20)	-0.007	-0.050	0.139	-0.487***	-0.078	0.320***	-0.155	-0.402***	0.099	1.000

SOURCE: D. J. Armor and A. S. Couch (1972) in *Data-Text Primer* (New York: The Free Press). Reprinted by the permission of the authors and the publisher. © David J. Armor and Arthur S. Couch.

Figure 15–3

Factor Loadings of Vietnam War Attitude Items

```
VIETNAM ATTITUDE STUDY

                                              ROTATED FACTOR LOADINGS

     VARIABLE DESCRIPTION      NAME          1        2        3          COMMUNALITY

     WAR IS UNJUSTIFIABLE      ITEM(1)     -0.148    0.103    0.860         0.772
     VIETCONG WILL WIN WAR     ITEM(2)     -0.551   -0.016   -0.132        0.328
     GIVE UNIONS VOICE         ITEM(3)      0.165    0.562   -0.211        0.387
     DEMOCRACY SUPERIOR        ITEM(4)      0.102   -0.073   -0.020        0.016
     NO CHOICE BUT CONT. WAR   ITEM(5)      0.727   -0.207    0.251        0.635
     SOCIAL. MEDICINE GOOD     ITEM(6)     -0.148    0.551   -0.051        0.328
     VIETNAM WAR IS NECESSARY  ITEM(7)      0.792   -0.273    0.185        0.736
     GOVT SHOULD INSURE JOBS   ITEM(8)     -0.149    0.650    0.120        0.459
     RAPID CHANGE IS UNWISE    ITEM(9)      0.126   -0.504   -0.129        0.287
     US NOT GAIN POL. VICTORY  ITEM(10)    -0.723    0.021   -0.179        0.555
     MUST NOT LOSE POWER       ITEM(11)     0.087   -0.375    0.231        0.202
     WAR SOMETIMES NECESSARY   ITEM(12)     0.128   -0.001    0.849        0.738
     BETTER RED THAN DEAD      ITEM(13)    -0.183    0.310   -0.476        0.356
     VIETNAM WIN NECESSARY     ITEM(14)     0.622   -0.182    0.175        0.451
     MOST MEN WOULD NOT WORK   ITEM(15)     0.044    0.598    0.061        0.360
     WAR IS ALWAYS AVOIDABLE   ITEM(16)    -0.331   -0.045   -0.680        0.574
     NATIONALIZATION BAD       ITEM(17)     0.132    0.736    0.010        0.556
     US WILL WIN WAR           ITEM(18)     0.744   -0.195    0.222        0.642
     NATIONALIZATION GOOD      ITEM(19)    -0.001    0.646   -0.248        0.479
     VIETNAM WAR UNNECESSARY   ITEM(20)    -0.751    0.083    0.056        0.574

                  SUM SQUARES             3.800    3.058    2.577          9.435
```

Source: D. J. Armor and A. S. Couch (1972) in *Data-Text Primer* (New York: The Free Press). Reprinted by the permission of the authors and the publisher. © David Armor and Arthur S. Couch.

if each of these 20 items measured some different concept, then 20 different one-item scales would be represented in the data, and use of more than one item at a time in construction of a unidimensional scale would be impossible.

However, if a number of variables have some variance in common, so that they correlate highly with some underlying dimension, then this dimension will appear as a factor and can be considered a scale. Notice, though, that rather than naming beforehand the concept to be scaled (e.g., alienation), as we did with Likert, Guttman, and Thurstone scaling, with factor scaling we draw the scale directly from the data (rather than from a prior theory) and do not name it until after it is constructed. The factor scale is usually given a name derived from the variable that correlates most highly with it.

The numbers given in figure 15–3 are called *factor loadings,* but can be considered the correlation between a variable and each respective factor. The variance of each variable is divided up so that the variable can load on (be correlated with) more than one factor at a time, but generally it will be considered only to be a part of the factor scale with which it has its highest loading. The *Data-Text Primer* considers a factor loading with an absolute value of .4 or more to load highly enough to be considered part of the scale. Items that qualify on each of the three factors are circled in figure 15.3. The factor-analysis program derives the three factors so that they are uncorrelated with each other (independent of each other). Thus we have three separate and distinct scales rather than one three-part scale. Scale 1 consists of items 2, 5, 7, 10, 14, 18, and 20. Scale 2 consists of items 3, 6, 8, 15, 17, 19. Scale 3 consists of items 1, 12, and 16. Items 4, 9, 11, and 13 are not included in any of these three scales, meaning that they load highly on additional factors not shown here (the factor-analysis program extracted five factors, only three of which are shown here; for the others see Armor and Couch 1972, p. 90).

It is up to the researcher to name the various scales. This can often be done quite easily by examining the variables forming each scale. For example, from a perusal of the items forming scale 1 it seems evident that they all measure attitude toward U.S. involvement in and commitment to the Vietnam War specifically (rather than war in general). Scale 2 measures attitude toward socialism. Scale 3 measures attitude toward war in general, and whether it is justifiable. Thus we could name the scales; scale 1—"Scale of Attitude Toward U.S. Involvement in Vietnam War"; scale 2—"Scale of Belief in Socialism"; and scale 3—"Scale of Belief in Justifiability of War."

After the scales are constructed, the next step is to compute a particular respondent's score on a particular scale. In the present example each question was coded from 1 (strongly disagree) to 5 (strongly agree). We need all items coded in the same direction. A negative item is permissible, but must be coded in the opposite direction. That is, a "strongly agree" response on the item "The Vietcong will probably win a military victory" will receive a code of 5, so a "strongly disagree" response to the reverse statement, "The Vietcong will probably *not* win a military victory," should also receive a code of 5, since the two are equivalent. However, in the original coding all "strongly disagree" were given a code of 1 and all "strongly agree" a code of 5. This means that when we encounter a reversed item (any item that correlated negatively with a particular scale) we must reverse its score in order to achieve a proper scale score. For example, on scale 1, item 2 (Vietcong will win war) is inversely correlated. A positive score on this item as originally coded, such as a "strongly agree" (coded 5), will be a negative score on scale 1 due to the inverse or negative correlation. This can be corrected, as the *Data-Text Primer* points out, by subtracting each such reversed-item score from 6. Subtracting 5 from 6 will give us a correct score of 1, because strongly agreeing on a reversed item is the same as strongly disagreeing on a positive item.

To compute an individual respondent's total score on a particular scale, simply take his or her score on each item in the scale (scored from 1 to 5 and corrected for negative items), weight it by the factor loading for the respective item on that particular scale, and sum. For example, if a respondent (after reversing scores for negative items) scored, for scale 3, 3 on item 1, 2 on item 12, and 4 on item 16, his or her scale score for scale 3 would be $.860(3) + .849(2) + .680(4) = 2.580 + 1.698 + 2.720 = 6.998$.

A note of clarification is in order here. Some discussions of factor scaling speak of factor score coefficients instead of factor loadings. The example used above discusses a form of factor analysis known as principal components factor analysis. This is the most common form of factor analysis in use today. As long as principal components is used, factor loadings are equal to factor score coefficients. If some other type of factor analysis is used, many researchers prefer to use factor score coefficients instead of factor loadings. Unfortunately, these are difficult to derive and must be estimated. The "canned" computer package SPSS (Nie et al. 1975) includes a program for such estimation. This topic is beyond the scope of this chapter, but the interested reader can refer to Nie et al. (1975), and Alwin (1992) for further discussion.

Advantages of Factor Scaling

Factor scaling is rapidly becoming the standard method of developing scales in survey-research analysis. There are several distinct advantages of factor scaling that account for its popularity.

1. *Computational ease.* Although factor analysis in general, and factor scaling in particular, requires a great deal of computation, the fact that factor-analysis programs are commonly

included in statistical programming packages makes this technique fairly easy to use, because the computer does all the work. Before computerization, factor scaling took a great deal more time to compute than did other techniques such as Likert scaling and Thurstone scaling, which are computationally much simpler.

2. *Unidimensionality.* Factor scaling more or less ensures unidimensionality. That is, the goal of factor analysis is to discover the independent underlying dimensions that may be present in the set of correlations, and to provide an estimate (factor loading) of how strongly each item or variable is correlated with each dimension. Most factor-analysis programs rotate factors so that they are orthogonal (uncorrelated). This allows us to assume not only that each factor scale is unidimensional, but also that it is completely uncorrelated with, and independent of, the other factor scales that are constructed simultaneously.

3. *Weighting of items.* Perhaps the most distinctive feature of factor scaling, and the greatest difference between this scaling technique and the ones discussed heretofore, is that factor scaling does not assume each item to be of equal value in determining a person's scale score. Instead, factor scaling weights each item according to its correlation with the factor. For purposes of illustration, let us assume that the natality scale discussed earlier in this chapter is interval instead of ordinal, and thus can be used in factor analysis. Consider items 1 (major reason for getting married is to have children) and 3 (giving birth is one of the most profound experiences a woman can have). With traditional scaling techniques such as Likert scaling, the item is either used or eliminated, but all items that are ultimately chosen are scored the same way (5 if strongly agree, down to 1 for strongly disagree). Thus if both items 1 and 3 were used in the scale and a person strongly agreed with both, they would count 10 points toward his or her total scale score. If these items were used to construct a factor scale, we might find, for example, that item 3 had a factor loading (correlation with the factor) of .90, but item 1 had a factor loading of only .60. These loadings would be used as weights in determining the person's final scale score. Thus, his or her scale score on just these two items, if he or she answered "strongly agree" (coded 5) on both, would be .90(5) + .60(5), for a total of 7.5.

The fact that item 1 loads only .60 on the natality factor indicates that it also contributes to some scale other than natality, and is not a pure measure of natality. For example, although it measures attitude toward natality to a certain degree, it also measures a different attitude—attitude toward marriage. Factor analysis does not require that we count an item either 100 percent or 0 percent, as do the other methods of scaling we discussed, but allows us to weight the item according to the actual contribution it makes to this particular scale.

4. *Continuous scores.* Even though the items may be scored discretely (e.g., 5, 4, 3, 2, or 1), the final scale score is continuous, since the factor loadings that serve as weights and are multiplied by the person's score on each item are continuously measured. For example, a score of 5 is a discrete score, but when multiplied by a factor loading of .83 the final scale score for this item is a continuous score of 4.15.

Disadvantages of Factor Scaling

1. *Difficulty of computation by hand.* Without a computer, calculation of a factor scale can require perhaps literally hundreds of hours to compute. Thus it is not recommended for persons who do not have access to a computer.

2. *Ad hoc nature.* One potential difficulty with factor scaling is that it is susceptible to

"data-dredging" procedures whereby a researcher simply takes a large number of items, correlates them, and factors them to see what sort of scale may emerge. If a factor is found with high loadings, the researcher can name it and claim that he or she has constructed a new scale. The only problem with this procedure is that it is purely descriptive, and a scale derived in this way may have little theoretical value.

The Semantic Differential

We stated above that one of the functions of a scale was to provide an indirect or underlying measure of a concept. This function might be important if we wished to measure a sensitive concept without biasing the subject's answers by questioning him or her directly about it, or if we wished to measure the underlying, perhaps even subconscious, feelings of a subject about a particular concept or word. The semantic differential (S.D.) method was developed by Osgood, Suci, and Tannenbaum (1957). Osgood et al. say that for "highly intelligent and verbally fluent subjects" direct questioning about the meaning of a concept is valid:

> Less fluent subjects, however, find it very difficult to encode meanings spontaneously (in a taste test of brands of ice cream, one of the authors found that most subjects could produce "creamy," "tasty," and a few other terms, but little more, yet given a form of the semantic differential these same individuals quickly and confidently indicated a large number of judgments) (Osgood et al. 1957, p. 19).

The response categories for the semantic differential consist of seven categories ranging from one extreme to the other, with the middle category representing neutral. This is similar to the Likert scaling categories ranging from strongly disagree to strongly agree, except that in the SD only the two end categories have names. The middle categories simply have a blank space, or sometimes a number. Also, the two end categories are not strongly agree—strongly disagree, but rather a pair of opposite adjectives thought to express the subject's feelings about the concept. For example, for the concept of abortion the adjective pair forming the opposite ends of the seven categories might be bad-good. The format for the response categories generally places the concept to be judged centered on one line, with the rating categories centered below it. For example:

ABORTION
Good _____ Bad

A large number of respondent categories could be placed under a single concept. For example, under abortion we could also have nice—awful and pleasant—unpleasant.

Responses from a great many SD studies have been factor analyzed in order to determine whether any underlying identifiable dimensions (scales, in fact) can be found. It appears that three basic dimensions are being measured—evaluation, potency, and activity. These findings have been replicated (see Osgood et al. 1957; Heise 1970). In other words, people tend to react to various concepts largely (but not entirely) in terms of these three dimensions. As Heise says:

> Evaluation is associated with the adjective contrasts: nice-awful, good-bad, sweet-sour, and helpful-unhelpful. Some concepts which lie on the positive (good) side of this dimension are:

DOCTOR, FAMILY, GOD, CHURCH, HAPPY, PEACE, SUCCESS, TRUTH, BEAUTY, and MUSIC. Some concepts which lie toward the negative (bad) pole are: ABORTION, DEVIL, DISCORDANT, HATE, DISEASE, SIN, WAR, ENEMY, and FAILURE.

Some scales which define the Potency dimension are big-little, powerful-powerless, strong-weak, and deep-shallow. Concepts which lie toward the positive (powerful) pole are: WAR, ARMY, BRAVE, COP, MOUNTAIN, ENGINE, BUILDING, DUTY, LAW, STEEL, POWER, and SCIENCE. Concepts which lie toward the negative (powerless) pole are: GIRL, BABY, WIFE, FEATHER, KITTEN, KISS, LOVE, and ART.

Activity scales are fast-slow, alive-dead, noisy-quiet, and young-old. Some concepts high in Activity are: DANGER, ANGER, ATTACK, CITY, ENGINE, FIRE, SWORD, TORNADO, WAR, WIN, CHILD, and PARTY. Among the concepts which lie toward the negative pole on the Activity dimensions are: CALM, SNAIL, DEATH, EGG, REST, STONE, and SLEEP (Heise 1970, p. 237).

For further examples consult Heise (1965), "Semantic Differential Profiles for 1,000 Most Frequent English Words."

Question Format

Presentation of Concepts. As Heise (1970, p. 240) points out, one can present either: (1) one concept followed by all adjective-pair scales; (2) one concept followed by only one adjective-pair scale; or (3) one adjective-pair scale and all concepts to be rated on it.

Ordering of Concepts. Heise (1970, p. 240) says that when the first format is used (one concept followed by all of its scales), the ordering of concepts is immaterial and does not affect the results. Sommer (1965, cited in Heise 1970) found that, for example, POLITICIAN was rated the same whether preceded by JANITOR, GARBAGE COLLECTOR, FARMER, or STATESMAN, SCHOLAR, and SCIENTIST.

Ordering of Potency, Evaluation, and Activity Scales. Heise (1970, p. 240) recommends mixing up these three types of scale as much as possible to disguise the nature of the SD test and to prevent response sets.

Adverbial Quantifiers. A study by Wells and Smith (1960, pp. 393–97) justified use of adverbial quantifiers such as "extremely," "quite," and "slightly" to describe the categories between the polar adjectives. They found in a sample of 400 housewives that when these labels were omitted there was less variation in the responses, with many more ratings in the end points of the scales than when the labels were used. Further, respondents understood the labeled scales better and were more cooperative, yielding a higher response rate.

Administration of the SD

Instructions. Heise (1970, p. 241) recommends that the subject be instructed not to "figure out the right answer," but to put down his or her first impressions. Instruction should state that the purpose of the SD is "to find out how people feel about things and so the respondent should rate the way he or she feels." Also, the instructions should include an example that is non-ambiguous and easy to answer, such as TORNADO. Heise notes that while Osgood et al. (1957) suggested that subjects be instructed to work rapidly, it has been found that even if they are instructed to work slowly, subjects soon begin working rapidly, achieving about the same results as if they were originally instructed to work rapidly.

Number of Questions.   Osgood et al. (1957, p. 80) suggest use of 400 ratings (e.g., 80 concepts on 5 scales each or 25 concepts on 16 scales each). Heise (1970) says that even more can be used with a sample of college students, but that for subjects unused to taking tests this number may be too large. He suggests a maximum number of 50 ratings for noncollege survey respondents.

Interpreting the Results

The results of the SD analysis can be used to compare each concept on each of the three dimensions of evaluation, potency, and activity. For example, Osgood et al. (1957) compared the concepts TAFT, U.S. POLICY ON CHINA, SOCIALISM, STALIN, TRUMAN, ATOM BOMB, UNITED NATIONS, and EISENHOWER, as rated by a sample of Republicans. The study was conducted shortly before the 1952 presidential election. The evaluation dimension was character-ized as fair-unfair, the potency dimension as strong-weak, and the activity dimension as active-pas-sive. The results show how the subjects rated each of the eight concepts on each of the three dimen-sions. Concepts that rated high on all three dimensions (fair, strong, and active) are Taft, Atom bomb, and Eisenhower. The only concept that was ranked low on all three dimensions (unfair, weak, and passive) was U.S. policy on China. The other concepts had a mixture of high and low rankings on the three dimensions. For example, Stalin was rated unfair, but strong and active, while the United Nations was regarded as fair, but weak and not as active as Stalin. These results can also be presented in the form of a three-dimensional graph (see Osgood et al. 1957).

Multidimensional Measurement

Many concepts that we wish to measure are really multiple concepts composed of a particular combination of the values of several component variables, or subconcepts. We call such con-cepts or variables, constructed by combining two or more variables, *multidimensional con-cepts.* As can be imagined, the measurement of multidimensional concepts is considerably more difficult than the measurement of single-dimension or unidimensional concepts. An ex-ample of a multidimensional variable is the cosmopolitan-local distinction. The three dimen-sions involved are: (1) the individual's loyalty to the employing organizations, measured as high or low; (2) reference-group orientation (outer or inner); and (3) commitment to special-ized skills (high or low). Cosmopolitans are low on loyalty to the employing organization, high on commitment to specialized skills, and have an outer reference-group orientation, while locals are high on loyalty to the employing organization, low on commitment to specialized skills, and likely to have an inner reference-group orientation.

Typology Construction

These three dichotomized variables, when combined, form an eight-celled classification. Such a multidimensional classification, formed by combining all possible categories of two or more variables, is called a *typology*. Each cell is called a type. A full typology constructed from these three variables is shown in figure 15–4. Notice that this particular typology combines two ordinal variables (loyalty to organization and commitment to skills) with one nominal variable (reference-group orientation). Of the eight possible cells, only two were named, with the six remaining left unnamed. In other words, the contrasting multidimensional concepts of local and cosmopolitan represent a partial typology. Such partial typologies are often generated through observation. This is similar to the process of deriving grounded theory (see chapter 3). Through observation the researcher notes that certain configurations of values (such as low on loyalty, high on commitment and outer reference-group orientation) tend to "hang together" to such an extent that they can be observed repeatedly in different times and places, while other combinations may never be found. Cells in which no cases are ever found are called null (empty) cells. However, it may also be true that many other configurations are observed during the course of fieldwork, but are simply not of theoretical interest to the observer. For example, a person who is low on loyalty, low on commitment, and with an inner orientation (cell 8) may simply be a withdrawn and apathetic individual who is of theoretical interest to personality theorists but not to formal organization theorists, who are much more interested in the person with great professional commitment but little local loyalty (the cosmopolitan).

When partial typologies are employed, generally at least two contrasting types are used for comparison purposes. When only a single type is used, it is usually extreme on all dimensions. The most famous example of such a single type is Weber's ideal type which is rarely itself found empirically but is used as a criterion for comparing empirical cases.

Figure 15–4

Local-cosmopolitan Typology

	LOYALTY TO ORGANIZATION			
	HIGH Commitment to Skills		LOW Commitment to Skills	
Reference Group Orientation	*High*	*Low*	*High*	*Low*
Outer	1	2	Cosmopolitan 3	4
Inner	5	Local 6	7	8

Most of the variables used in typologies are discrete, either nominal or ordinal. If interval or continuous variables are used they must be arbitrarily divided. If relatively few variables are used and if each variable has only a few categories, typologies can be kept manageable. However, if each variable has many categories, or if many variables are used, the number of cells quickly becomes prohibitive. For example, a typology of only seven variables with two categories each contains 2^7 or 128 cells. If partial typologies are generated through observation, however, the researcher may be able to construct one or a few types consisting of specific observable recurrable configurations on as many as ten or more variables, and simply forget the other possible cells in the typology. For further discussion of typologies see Bailey (1989a; 1992; 1994b).

Substruction and Reduction

Occasionally a researcher will encounter a single type concept (e.g., cosmopolitan) in the literature and wish to know the potential comparison types. He or she can discover related types first by ascertaining the underlying dimensions comprising the type (loyalty, orientation, and commitment, in the case of the cosmopolitan type) and then by extending these dimensions to form the full typology. The result will be similar to the typology shown in figure 15–4 Lazarsfeld (1937) calls this process of constructing the full typology from a single type *substruction*. Lazarsfeld calls the full typology formed by extending all dimensions through substruction a *property space*. The property space is often presented graphically as a set of coordinate axes rather than as a typology.

The opposite of substruction is *reduction*, which consists of reducing the full typology or property space down to one or a few types that are theoretically most meaningful and easier to work with. Many times it is simply impossible to work with the full typology because it contains too many cells (some of which may not be theoretically meaningful). The three types of reduction discussed by Lazarsfeld are pragmatic, functional, and arbitrary numerical. Pragmatic reduction is accomplished by combining several contiguous types into a single (but more heterogeneous) type. Functional reduction is accomplished by discarding types that are null or that have only a small cell frequency. Arbitrary numerical reduction consists of weighting one of the dimensions more heavily than others. As Lazarsfeld (1937, p. 128) says, in determining housing conditions one could rate a house with central heat, a refrigerator, but no plumbing equal to a house with plumbing but without the other two. This reduces the typology by making two types equal to each other in value on the housing attractiveness scale.

Cluster Analysis

Typologies can be constructed verbally by deriving the dimensions from theory without analyzing any data. They can also be derived empirically from the data through a method of statistical analysis called *cluster analysis.* Such empirical construction of typologies is similar to the grounded-theory approach to theory construction discussed in chapter 3. (For further discussion of the various approaches to typology construction see Bailey 1973).

There are many different methods of cluster analysis. For a review of various methods see Bailey (1974), Jardine and Sibson (1971), Sokal and Sneath (1963), Sneath and Sokal (1973).

Virtually all methods begin with some sort of table of coefficients indicating the similarity or difference among the objects or variables to be clustered. Table 15–2 shows correlation coefficients for all pairs of persons. To illustrate cluster analysis, consider one of the simplest methods, McQuitty's elementary linkage analysis. The method begins by underlining the largest coefficient in each column. All the underlined coefficients are then perused to find the largest coefficient in the matrix. This is the nucleus for the first cluster (the nucleus in table 15–2 is the pair A and B, with a correlation of .95). A and B are diagramed with a double-headed arrow in figure 15–5 to indicate that they are both more highly correlated with each other than with any other object in the matrix.

The next step is to read across the rows of the matrix for all individuals in the cluster and to identify any underlined coefficients in these rows. There is one such coefficient (linking C with A) in A's row. This means that C joins the cluster, and so in the next step we will examine its row to see if it has any underlined coefficient linking other objects to the cluster through C. Clustering proceeds in this fashion until no further underlined coefficients can be found for any of the objects in the first cluster. It is then necessary to examine all objects not in the cluster, identify the largest coefficient to serve as the nucleus for a new cluster, and proceed as in the first cluster. The data in table 15–2 yield the two additional clusters shown in figure 15–5. See if you can derive these same clusters. If not, see Bailey (1972) for additional discussion of this method.

There has been a surge of interest in cluster analysis and multidimensional scaling procedures in social science in the 1980s. For example, Hudson (1982) presents a number of theoretical analyses of clustering, as well as applications in areas as diverse as geography and used

Table 15–2

Hypothetical Correlation Matrix for 10 Individuals on 40 Variables

Individual	A	B	C	D	E	F	G	H	I	J
A	1.00	*0.95*	*0.90*	0.79	0.20	0.55	0.15	0.30	0.01	0.65
B	*0.95*	1.00	0.79	*0.90*	0.09	0.05	0.40	0.51	0.22	0.49
C	0.90	0.79	1.00	0.77	0.68	0.32	0.62	0.13	0.29	0.01
D	0.79	0.90	0.77	1.00	0.50	0.19	0.07	0.33	0.11	0.21
E	0.20	0.09	0.68	0.50	1.00	0.40	0.49	*0.85*	0.68	0.51
F	0.55	0.05	0.32	0.19	0.40	1.00	*0.80*	0.69	0.13	0.31
G	0.15	0.40	0.62	0.07	0.49	*0.80*	1.00	0.25	0.27	0.29
H	0.30	0.51	0.13	0.33	*0.85*	0.69	0.25	1.00	*0.80*	0.60
I	0.01	0.22	0.29	0.11	0.68	0.13	0.27	0.80	1.00	*0.75*
J	0.65	0.49	0.01	0.21	0.51	0.31	0.29	0.60	0.75	1.00

SOURCE: K. D. Bailey (1972) in *Sociological Methodology,* edited by H. L. Costner, San Francisco: Jossey-Bass. Reprinted by permission of the publisher, © Jossey-Bass.

Figure 15–5

Clusters Formed from Table 15–2 by McQuitry's Elementary Linkage
Analysis

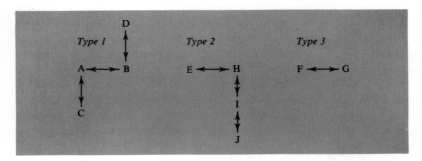

SOURCE: K. D. Bailey (1972) in "Polythetic Reduction of Monothetic Property Space" in *Sociological Methodology,* edited by H. L. Costner (San Francisco: Jossey-Bass). Reprinted by
the permission of the publisher. © Jossey-Bass.

cars. See also Lorr (1983), Bailey (1982; 1983; 1985; 1993), Aldenderfer and Blashfield
(1984), Schiffman et al. (1981), Janssen et al. (1983), and Hulin et al. (1983).

Smallest Space Analysis

Smallest space analysis (SSA) is a close cousin to cluster analysis, and can, roughly speaking, be
considered a form of multidimensional scaling. Although the method does not yield clusters, it
provides a graph showing the objects or variables plotted in a property space in such a fashion that
clusters can often be drawn merely by identifying groups of points and drawing boundaries around
them. SSA was invented by Guttman (1968). Its basic goal is to find the smallest number of dimensions that can be used to graph all of the objects or variables satisfactorily. Thus each object has a
score on each of the several dimensions presented. For further discussion of SSA and other multidimensional scaling methods see Bailey (1972), Guttman (1968), and Bailey (1974).

Properties of Groups

In addition to measuring such characteristics of individuals as intelligence or prejudice, social
scientists occasionally wish to measure properties of groups. Lazarsfeld (1958) has classified
group properties into analytical, global, and structural.

Analytical

Analytical group properties are computed by aggregating properties of the individuals comprising the group. For example, median income in the United States for 1980 is an analytical

property of the collective (United States) and is computed by averaging properties of individuals (U.S. residents).

Global

Global properties are properties of groups or collectives that require no information about the properties of individuals in the groups. Lazarsfeld provides some examples of global properties:

> The cultural level of a city might be measured by the presence or absence of certain "cultural" institutions (theatres, libraries, etc.) or by the proportion of its buildings which are used for cultural purposes.

> Having a city manager form of government is a global property of a city. The insistence on specified initiation rites as a prerequisite to membership is a global property of a religious cult or a college fraternity (Lazarsfeld 1958, pp. 112–13).

Structural (Sociometric Measures)

Structural properties are defined by Lazarsfield (1958, p. 112) as "properties of collectives which are obtained by performing some operation on data about the relations of each member to some or all of the others." For example, cliquishness would be a structural property of a classroom, indicating the degree to which the students were divided up into recognizable cliques. A closely related property is a property of an individual that Lazarsfeld labels "relational." Relational properties, like structural properties of groups, are computed from information about the relations among members of a group. An example is a measure of an individual's popularity computed by adding the number of choices as "most popular" that he or she receives from the other members of the group.

Both structural and relational measures belong to the class of measures known as *sociometric* measures. Sociometric measures are generally constructed by administering to all members of the group a questionnaire asking each about his or her relations with the other members of the group. One could ask each member with whom he or she would rather play, study, eat, and so on. Or one could ask "Who is your best friend?" or "Who is the most popular?" Alternatively, if one did not wish to use a questionnaire, sociometric data could be derived by observing who each person sits besides, talks to the most, and so on.

One way to present and analyze sociometric data is in the form of the *sociometric matrix*. A sociometric matrix lists the persons' names in both the rows and columns, and uses some code (usually 1 if chosen, 0 if not chosen) to indicate which person is chosen by the subject in response to the question. For example, consider table 15–3, containing hypothetical data for Sue, Judy, Jane, Jill, and Wanda based on the question "Whom do you admire most in your class?"

We can understand table 15–3 best by reading across each person's row. Each person has one choice only for most popular of her fellow classmates, and the numeral "1" indicates the person chosen. By reading down the column for each person we can see how popular she is by summing the number of 1s she received. We see that Wanda is the most popular, since she was

Table 15–3

Sociometric Matrix

	Sue	*Judy*	*Jane*	*Jill*	*Wanda*
Sue	0	0	0	0	1
Judy	0	0	0	0	1
Jane	0	0	0	1	0
Jill	0	0	1	0	0
Wanda	0	1	0	0	0
Total	0	1	1	1	2

chosen by two classmates (Sue and Judy). We see further than Sue is least popular because no one chose her. Judy, Jane, and Jill all tied for intermediate popularity with one vote each. Examination of table 15–3 will also show us all symmetrical pairs, that is, instances in which two people chose each other as most popular. The table reveals two such pairs of mutual admirers: Wanda-Judy and Jill-Jane.

In addition to matrixes, sociometric data can also be presented in the form of various indexes and in graphs. Simply by summing the number of choices each person received in each column, we have already constructed a rough index of popularity. If we divide this sum by n-1 (because a person cannot choose himself or herself) we have a measure of average popularity called the *choice status*. For further discussion of this measure and others see Kerlinger (1964, pp. 558–60). To make a graph we merely use arrows to show which person chose whom, with a single-headed arrow indicating that the person the arrow is pointing from chose the person the arrow is pointing toward (but not vice versa). A double-headed arrow shows that the choice was mutual, with each person in the pair choosing the other. The information shown in table 15–3 is provided in graphical form in figure 15–6. For further discussion of sociometry see Kerlinger (1964, pp. 554–63), Lin (1976, pp. 329–49), and Lindzey and Borgatta (1954). Much work in the area of sociometric relationships is now conducted under the rubric of "network analysis." For further discussion of network analysis see Marsden (1992).

Figure 15–6

Graph of Relations in Table 15–3

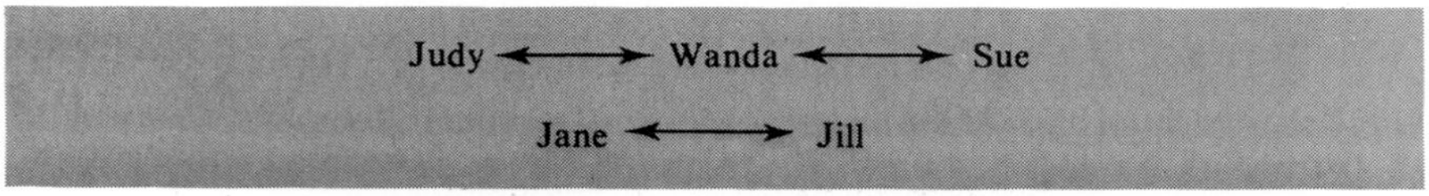

Judy ◄─────► Wanda ◄─────► Sue

Jane ◄─────► Jill

Summary

Chapter 15 discussed the construction of scales for measuring social concepts (for example, we could construct an alienation scale or an authoritarianism scale). After a brief treatment of nominal scaling, we went on to treat ordinal scaling in more depth, discussing summated ratings scales, Likert scaling, and Guttman scaling. We next turned to interval-ratio scaling, discussing Thurstone's scaling, factor scaling, and the Semantic Differential (SD). In the latter part of the chapter we discussed multidimensional measurement, including typology construction, cluster analysis, and smallest space analysis. We concluded the chapter with a brief discussion of sociometric measurement and the measurement of group properties.

LIVERPOOL
JOHN MOORES UNIVERSITY
I.M. MARSH LIBRARY
BARKHILL ROAD
LIVERPOOL L17 6BD
TEL. 0151 231 5216/5290

LIVERPOOL
JOHN MOORES UNIVERSITY
I.M. MARSH LIBRARY
BARKHILL ROAD
LIVERPOOL L17 6BD
TEL. 0151 231 5216/5299

CHAPTER 16

ANALYSIS, PRESENTATION, AND INTERPRETATION OF DATA

STATISTICAL DATA ANALYSIS is the culmination of the long process of hypothesis formulation, instrument construction, and data collection. We would hope that the goals and tasks discussed in previous chapters have been successfully carried out—for example, if we conducted a mailed survey, that our hypotheses were properly constructed (chapter 3), our sampling was adequate (chapter 5), our questionnaire was properly constructed (chapter 7), and the data were properly entered into the computer (chapter 14). Unfortunately, all of this good work has little impact if the data merely reside in columns in a computer. To culminate our study properly it is necessary to analyze the data so that (1) we can properly test our hypotheses or otherwise answer our research questions, and (2) we can present the results of the study to our readers in an understandable and convincing form. As we have seen in earlier chapters, our data may be interpreted and presented in entirely verbal terms, particularly in observational studies, document analysis, and ethnomethodology. However, when we are dealing with numerical data, as in most surveys and experiments, and often in other types of studies as well, we will often wish to conduct statistical analyses.

As in all other aspects of social research we have studied, our goal in statistical analysis is to further our overall goal of understanding social phenomena. At the risk of oversimplification, we can say that this is achieved during statistical analysis through the processes of description, explanation, and prediction. Description, generally the easiest of the three tasks, consists primarily of simply telling what the data "look like"—for example, how many cases were analyzed, what the range of scores was, what the mean or median score was, and so forth. This is often conducted for one variable at a time (univariate analysis), but it can be conducted for two or more variables, either simultaneously or serially.

Explanation and prediction are generally more complicated than description and require more computation as well as more interpretation. Often the assumptions and requirements for the use of explanatory and predictive statistics are quite restrictive. Explanatory statistical analysis can take a number of forms but generally consists of the analysis of a relationship (as discussed in chapter 3) between two or more variables. The first task is often to use the laws of probability to see whether we can say with confidence that a relationship (that is, a nonzero relationship) even exists between the two variables. This is often accomplished through the computation of so-called statistical tests of significance. If a relationship is found to exist, we can utilize various statistics, generally coefficients of correlation, to assess the strength of relationship between variables. By strength of relationship we simply mean how much one variable affects the other, for example how much change we can see in one variable when the other variable changes. If we either suspect or have shown that a relatively strong relationship exists between variables, we can use a statistical technique that enables us to predict the score of one variable from knowledge of the other variable. The most popular statistical method for prediction is regression analysis. Regression analysis also forms the basis for most so-called causal models, which attempt to show causal relationships rather than mere correlations among variables.

A brief comment is in order on the number of statistical techniques discussed in this chapter and on the length of the discussion of each. The research methods course is generally accompanied by a full course in statistics. There are so many statistical techniques currently available (with the number growing all the time) that they cannot all be covered in a single chapter, and in fact not in a single book. Professional social researchers often take several statistics courses and even then do not necessarily master all of the useful techniques, especially the newer ones. Thus, the role of this chapter cannot be to substitute for the study of statistics. Rather, it must be merely to present statistical analysis as a crucial step in the overall pattern of social research and to discuss some of the major statistics used in research. I made the decision to discuss more than just a few techniques, even at the cost of drastically limiting the discussion of some of them. Thus, while the discussion of some techniques is brief, it does provide the minimum understanding for using the technique. A cursory discussion at least allows one to understand the relationship of the technique to other techniques. Further, formulas are often presented in this chapter even though much statistical computation is now done on the computer. One reason for presenting formulas is that a formula is a parsimonious and exact representation of the statistic (a shorthand account, if you will) that conveys as much information as a long verbal discussion. Further, inclusion of a formula may aid the researcher who is using this volume as a guide to social research and who wishes to make a few simple computations (perhaps in the field) that do not require or justify the use of a computer.

Table Presentations

Statistical analysis is generally presented either in equation form or in a table or graph of some sort. We will first discuss tabular presentations. We can present a table containing a single variable (univariate presentation) or can combine two or more variables in a single table (bivariate or polyvariate presentation). Since tables are limited to the two-dimensional space of the page on which they are written, and since a large number of variables means a large number of cells in the table, two-variable tables are most popular and three variables are about the maximum commonly presented in a single table. The popularity of two-variable tables stems not only from their simplicity but also from the fact that most hypotheses contain two variables, making a bivariate table sufficient to test a hypothesis.

Univariate Presentation

In a descriptive study, especially an exploratory one, the researcher may be more concerned with describing the extent of occurrence of a phenomenon than with studying its correlates. In such a case a univariate presentation is in order. For example, as a first step in a fertility study we may wish to present the distribution of fertility levels before attempting an analysis of causes of fertility differences. Although it may be impossible to present all fertility scores, it is feasible to present several types of information about the distribution of scores. One useful and easy presentation is the *range* of scores, which is defined as the highest score minus the lowest score, or range $= H - L$. For example, the range of ages may be 93, from a low of 6 to a high of 99.

In addition to the range, the researcher can present averages or measures of central tendency such as the mean, median, and mode. The mode is the score or value of the variable that occurs most often. For example, if the variable were number of children in the family, the mode would probably be either 2 or 3. The median is the middle value, or the score for which half of the respondents have a higher value and half a lower value. The mean is simply the sum of all scores divided by the number of scores. If the distribution of scores is the normal distribution, which is the familiar symmetrical bell-shaped curve (discussed below), then the mean and median will be identical. In addition to the mean it is helpful to compute a measure of dispersion such as the variance. The variance is

$$\sigma^2 = \frac{\Sigma\,(X_i - \bar{X})^2}{N - 1}$$

where X is the mean, X_i is the individual score for the ith person, and N is the number of persons in the sample. The variance is basically the average amount of squared deviation from the mean. If all persons in the sample scored the same as the mean, then the variance would be 0. For example, if all persons in the sample had two children exactly, then the mean number of children would be 2, but the variance would be

$$\frac{\Sigma\,(2 - 2)^2}{N - 1} = 0$$

Other succinct measures that can be given without presenting all scores are the frequency distribution and grouped data. The frequency distribution is a listing of the frequency with which each score occurs. For example, for the number of children, the frequency distribution might be as follows:

Score	Frequency	Score	Frequency	Score	Frequency
0	12	4	30	9	1
1	26	5	16	10	2
2	48	6	4	11	0
3	43	7	4	12	1
		8	0		

For an interval variable with many possible scores, such as income, even presentation of a frequency distribution may not be feasible. In this case the researcher may wish to group the data into categories and present the frequency of scores within each category. Such a grouped frequency distribution is obviously a compromise. It provides frequencies of each group of scores from low to high, but provides no information on ranges or variations of scores within each group. For example, instead of giving the frequency with which each single year of age appears, we would give frequencies for age groups, such as ages 1–4, 5–9, 10–14, 15–19. One has to compromise by providing few enough groups so that the data are manageable without making each group too broad.

Percentages

Much of the time data are presented in percentage form, whether in the univariate, bivariate, or polyvariate case. For example, if one had 100 respondents, one could compute the percentage female and the percentage male. The computation of percentages is generally straightforward and consists merely of dividing the number in each category by the total number. One question, as discussed by Babbie (1973, p. 240), is what to do about nonresponses. As discussed in chapter 14, nonresponses should be coded with some numerical code so that they are easily identifiable. They can be handled two ways when computing percentages. One way is to subtract the number of nonresponses from the total sample size and use this smaller figure as the base for the percentages (i.e., eliminate nonresponses completely from the analysis). For example, if one had a total sample size of 100 but only 90 listed their gender, then the 10 nonresponses would be omitted and 90 rather than 100 would be the base for computing the male and female percentages. The alternative is to use the total sample size (e.g., 100) as the base and include the nonresponses as a percentage. Assume that out of a sample of 100, 45 were female, 45 were male, and 10 were nonresponses. By the first method (using 90 as the base) we would say that we had 50 percent females and 50 percent males. By the second method (100 as the base) we would have 45 percent females, 45 percent males, and 10 percent nonresponses.

The chief advantage of including nonresponses as part of the analysis is that the base number stays constant from one analysis to the next. That is, one can always use the sample size as the base for percentages regardless of the magnitude of nonresponse. A good reason for excluding nonresponse is that it is not a meaningful substantive category of the variable being analyzed, but is more or less a residual or error category.

Bivariate Presentation

Bivariate presentation places two variables together in a single table in such a manner that their interrelations can be examined. Such tables are called contingency tables or cross-tabulations (cross-tabs). In contingency tables all combinations of categories of all variables are presented. This is quite complex if there are a large number of categories in each variable. We will limit our current discussion to two variables, each of which is dichotomous (contains two categories only). Two dichotomous variables form a table with four cells, often called a fourfold table.

By tradition and convention, one variable, called the *column variable,* is usually labeled across the top so that its categories form columns vertically down the page. The second variable, or *row variable,* is labeled on the left margin, with its categories forming rows horizontally across the page. The intersections of the categories of the two variables form the interior cells of the table. By convention in sociology the independent variable (if one can be identified) is usually the column variable and the dependent variable is the row variable.

Probably the easiest way to begin table construction is to list the total frequencies in each category for each variable. Assume that we wish to construct a table (figure 16–1) from the dichotomous variables of gender (male and female) and race (black and white). In this case neither can be said to be the independent or dependent variable since neither precedes the other or is the cause of the other. Let us arbitrarily pose sex as the column variable and race as the row variable.

Assume that we have 100 respondents in all. Since each respondent has both a gender and a race, the total race should be 100 and the total for gender should be 100. Assume that we

Figure 16–1

Race by Gender

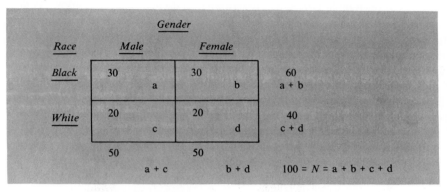

have 50 males and 50 females and 60 blacks and 40 whites. Without knowing how many blacks are males or females or how many whites are males or females, we can outline the outside of the table as shown in figure 16–1.

The numbers on the outside margins are generally referred to as *marginals*. For example, 60 and 40 are the row marginals (sum of the interior cells in each row) and 50 and 50 are the column marginals (sum of the interior cells in each column). Notice that the row marginals (for race) are merely the frequency distribution for race and provide no information on sex. Similarly, the column marginals are the frequency distribution for sex and provide no information on race. Information on the combinations of race and sex is provided only in the interior cells (cells, a, b, c, d). Notice also that the number at the lower right-hand corner of the table is *N*, or the total sample size. This number is the sum of the frequencies in all four cells a, b, c, d, or the sum of either the row or column marginals, which are themselves the sums of all interior cells (either horizontally or vertically).

Cell frequencies, or absolute numbers, are the preferred entries when the researcher is planning to conduct a statistical analysis of the table (to be discussed below). However, for presentation without statistical analysis the researcher will often prefer to present percentages rather than raw numbers in the cells. One could use *N* as the base for computing percentages, and find, for example, that 30 percent of the respondents are both male and black (cell a). However, instead of finding what percentage of the total sample is in a particular cell of the table, the researcher is usually interested in finding the correlation between two variables. In other words, he or she wishes to know to what extent having a particular value on one variable (e.g., race) affects a person's score on a second variable. For such purposes it is more useful to use the marginals for the base when computing percentages. Generally one uses either the row marginals (percentaging across) or the column marginals (percentaging down) as the base, but not both. However, I have seen tables with four entries in each cell—absolute frequency, row percentage, column percentage, and total percentage. Such tables are valuable but very difficult to read, as it is easy to confuse the various figures.

Figure 16–2

Opinion on Abortion by Gender

Opinion on Abortion	Gender		
	Male	*Female*	
Yes	12	36	48
No	18	24	42
	30	60	90

Whether we percentage rows or columns depends upon which variable is chosen to be the column variable and which is the row variable. It is generally advisable to percentage along the independent variable, so we will generally percentage the columns. As an example, imagine that we are analyzing a survey question that asks, "Do you approve of abortion (yes/no)." We find from preliminary analysis that gender is an important variable in determining response to this question, and decide to construct a bivariate table containing these two variables. Obviously a person's opinion cannot affect his or her sex, but his or her sex can affect opinion. Thus we know that sex is the independent variable and opinion on abortion is the dependent variable. Let us first set up a hypothetical table containing frequencies (figure 16–2) so that we can decide how to percentage.

By percentaging the independent variable we can see whether change in the independent variable (e.g., from male to female) results in a different distribution of yes/no scores on the dependent variable. If we percentaged along the dependent variable we would see whether a difference in the value of the opinion variable results in a different distribution of sexes—not a valid research question, since change in a dependent variable does not cause change in an independent variable, and opinion does not affect gender.

To illustrate this point let us construct two tables (figures 16–3 and 16–4), percentaging down in the first and across in the second. Figure 16–4 treats the opinion question as the prior variable in that the table tells us what percentages of all those people who answered "yes" on the question are male (25 percent) and female (75 percent). Similarly, of all those who answered "no," 43 percent are male and 57 percent female. Thus if we are most interested in how an answer to the question affects the sex ratio, we should percentage across, as in figure 16–4. However, many researchers will be most interested in how the sex ratio affects opinion on abortion, and should percentage down, as in figure 16–3. We see from figure 16–3 that a higher percentage of females than males answered "yes" on abortion, and thus a lower percentage of females than males disapproved of abortion.

Figure 16–3

Percentaging Down

Opinion on Abortion	Gender	
	Male	Female
Yes	40%	60%
No	60%	40%
	100% (N = 30)	100% (N = 60)

Table Format

Notice the difference in the format of figures 16–2, 16–3, and 16–4. Figure 16–2 is the standard format for statistical analysis. It contains frequencies rather than percentages in all interior cells and presents all marginals as well as the total sample size. Figures 16–3 and 16–4 both present the standard style for presentation of percentages. This format usually presents either the column or row percentages, but not both. It does not present the total sample size (N = 100), but this can be computed by summing the marginals. It presents only the marginal frequencies (either row or column) to supplant the marginal percentages, but this enables the reader to compute interior cell frequencies if desired. For example, in figure 16–3, if the reader knows that the column marginal is 30 and the per-

Figure 16–4

Percentaging Across

Opinion on Abortion	Gender		
	Male	Female	
Yes	25%	75%	100% (N = 48)
No	43%	57%	100% (N = 42)

centage in the first cell (male, yes) is 40 percent, then he or she can compute the cell frequency of .40 × 30, or 12. Tables of this second format (figures 16–3 and 16–4) are widely used for presenting results from survey research (often without lines delineating the cells).

There are other variants of these two standard formats. Whatever the format, the researcher should be sure that the title of the table indicates adequately the information contained therein, including the variable names, and tells whether cell entries are frequencies of percentages. For example, a heading for figure 16–3 might be, "Percentage of Each Sex Approving or Disapproving of Abortion." This heading tells not only each of the variables involved but also that the figures are percentages.

Bivariate tables of more than two categories each are constructed in the same manner as fourfold tables, but simply take more space. The decisions regarding choice of row and column variables and whether to percentage across or down are generally the same for an $N \times N$ table as for a 2×2 (fourfold) table.

Trivariate Tables

As previously mentioned, three variables are generally the maximum found in social-science publications, since tables with four or more variables are very difficult to construct in the two-dimensional space of a printed page. The most common three-variable table is the simplest: the $2 \times 2 \times 2$ table containing three dichotomous variables.

Look back at figure 16–2, which shows opinion on abortion by gender. We can extend this 2×2 table to a $2 \times 2 \times 2$ table simply by adding another variable. However, doing this will change the cell frequencies currently in figure 16–2. Suppose that we have survey data on the respondent's race and feel that race (black or white) may affect the relationship between gender and attitude on abortion. That is, the effect of gender on abortion attitude may be different for whites than for blacks. A standard $2 \times 2 \times 2$ table is generally constructed by using two column variables and one row variable, so that a separate 2×2 table is constructed for each of the two values of the third variable (race) as shown in figure 16–5.

Cell a shows the number of black males who approve abortion, cell h shows the number of white females who disapprove of abortion. In this instance race is called a *control* variable. Figure 16–2 showed the relationship between gender and abortion attitude when race was not known. If the researcher feels that the relationship between gender and abortion attitude will be the same regardless of a person's race, then there is no need to construct figure 16–5, since both parts of the table will yield identical results. However, if the researcher feels that race will have an effect on the relationship between gender and abortion attitude, then he or she is basically predicting that the interior cell frequencies in two halves of figure 16–5 will be different. That is, cell a ≠ cell e; cell b ≠ cell f, and so on. This effect, in which the relationship between two variables is dependent upon the value of a third variable, is called *statistical interaction effect*. If the researcher feels that race will have such an effect, then the relationship shown in figure 16–2 is inadequate and mislead-

Figure 16–5

Abortion Attitude by Sex and Race

Race

Black

	Gender	
Opinion on Abortion	*Male*	*Female*
Yes	a	b
No	c	d

White

	Gender	
Opinion on Abortion	*Male*	*Female*
Yes	e	f
No	g	h

ing, and needs to be recomputed controlling for race. We say that race is controlled for because within each cell of figure 16–5 race is a constant (all black or all white) and thus cannot affect the results.

Three-variable 2 × 2 Table

Heretofore in this chapter we have been discussing only tables constructed from variables containing discrete categories (either nominal variables such as gender or race or ordinal variables such as education levels), as opposed to intervally measured variables such as age. If an intervally measured variable is to be used in such a table it must be collapsed into discrete categories (e.g., above retirement age or below retirement age). Also, all tables discussed heretofore contain as cell entries either frequencies or percentages computed from such frequencies.

The reader of social-research reports will sometimes encounter a somewhat different type of three-variable table. This type of table combines two categorical variables of the type we have been discussing to form a 2 × 2 table very similar, for example, to figure 16–2. However, instead of containing frequencies of occurrence (number of cases), as does figure 16–3, this new type of table contains summary data (usually the arithmetic mean) of a third, intervally measured variable. This type of table is widely used in reporting experimental research and for computing statistical analysis of variance (discussed below).

For an example of such a 2 × 2 three-variable table, imagine that for each respondent we gathered information on race (black or white) and gender (female or male), both of which are nominal variables, and IQ, an intervally measured variable. We could then construct figure 16–6 (data are hypothetical).

The cell entries in figure 16–6 are not frequencies of occurrence as before but are average (mean or median) values of IQ. For example, if figure 16–6 were only a two-variable table

Figure 16–6

Mean IQ Score by Race and Gender

	Sex	
Race	Male	Female
Black	110.8 a	112.1 b
White	109.6 c	110.3 d

showing race and sex, the figure in cell a would be the number of black male respondents. In the three-variable table the figure (110.8) is the average IQ score of all the black male respondents, but we cannot tell from this table how many black male respondents there are. Such a 2×2 three-variable table is very parsimonious and also facilitates use of statistical techniques, such as analysis of variance, that utilize a combination of categorical and continuous variables.

Constructing Categories for Tables and Collapsing Tables

If one wishes to construct tables from intervally measured variables it is necessary to collapse the total range of possible values into manageable categories. For example, if you wished to construct a bivariate table containing sex and age, the table might be 2×100, covering two genders but 100 different age groups. Rather than construct a table with 200 cells we would collapse age into a smaller number of categories.

There are three basic collapsing strategies, one theoretical and two empirical. In the theoretical strategy the researcher's theory or research goal provides clues about where to split the variable. For example, in a geriatric study the researcher may be interested only in whether the persons are above or below retirement age. In a study of young children he or she may be interested only in knowing whether the children are preschool age or in elementary school. In a fertility study the crucial question is whether women are currently in the childbearing ages (roughly 15–49), below 15, or above 49.

One of the empirical strategies is to look for gaps in the empirical distribution of cases along the range of possible values of the variable. The second is uniform or proportionate collapsing. The basic goal of the former strategy is to avoid borderline cases, which violate the by-now familiar criterion of mutual exclusiveness, since a borderline case is essentially in both categories. A common example of this is grading. Professors often decide where to split an A from a B, for example by looking for a gap in the distribution of scores. Consider the following hypothetical examination scores (in percentages):

Examination Score (%)	Number of Students Making Score
93	2
92	5
91	3
90	1
89	2
88	0
87	7
86	3
.	.
.	.
.	.

Since no person scored 88, we let 89 and above be an A. This eliminates any borderline cases.

In proportionate or uniform collapsing the researcher collapses either so as to have a certain proportion of cases in each cell or so that each cell contains a certain proportion of the possible range of values. For example, suppose that a particular survey question contained eight possible values, scored from 1 through 8. The researcher might collapse this variable into two groups of equal potential numbers of values, e.g., group 1 consisting of scores 1 through 4 and group 2 consisting of scores 5 through 8. Alternatively, the researcher might examine the range of scores and find that 50 percent of all respondents answered 1 or 2, while the remaining 50 percent answered 3 through 8. He or she could then collapse 1 and 2 into one group and 3 through 8 into another so that the two groups are unequal (not uniform) in terms of number of answer categories contained, but equal in terms of proportion of respondents in each.

Collapsing is often necessary to make tables manageable. Unfortunately, it not only results in loss of information but can also be used unscrupulously to manipulate results. As an extreme hypothetical example of possible information loss through collapsing, suppose that, of 20 respondents in your sample, 12 were 49 years old and 8 were 51. If you dichotomized age so that 50 and over was considered old and below 50 was labeled young, then the table would merely show that 12 respondents were young and 8 were old. The information that all respondents were actually about the same age would be lost. Most researchers would not collapse categories so poorly, but this example does illustrate the possible information loss inherent in collapsing. The fewer the number of categories (and thus the larger each category), the greater the danger of information loss, since all persons within a given category appear to have the same value. For example, if "young" covered the age range 1 through 49, there would be no way to differentiate the person aged 1 from the person aged 40. A second problem is that sometimes statistical measures (discussed below) are somewhat sensitive to collapsing and their values can be affected by what is basically "gerrymandering" of group boundaries. Thus some researchers employ the highly dubious practice (definitely not recommended here) of playing with different alternative groupings to see which one yields the most statistically significant test or the strongest relationship between the variables. For an excellent and comprehensive discussion of tabular analysis see Kim (1992).

Hypothesis Testing

Statistics that are used to infer the truth or falsity of a hypothesis are called *inferential statistics,* in contrast to *descriptive statistics,* which do not seek to make an inference but merely provide a description of the sample data. We noted that such statistics as the mean, mode, and range could be used to provide a description of the data when it was impossible to present the entire distribution of values. In this chapter we will be concerned primarily with hypothesis testing and thus will be discussing inferential statistics.

The general inference to be tested is that some phenomenon that is true for a sample is also true for the population from which the sample was drawn. For example, the phenomenon may be a statistic (e.g., a mean), and we may test the inference that the mean value computed for the sample could have come from a population with a hypothesized mean value (with the hypothesized value to be set by the researcher depending upon the research objectives). The usual case is that our ultimate goal is to gain information of some sort about the population, but unfortunately we have information only about the sample from which the population is drawn rather than from the population itself. However, inferential statistics allow us to make accurate inferences about the population itself on the basis of our sample data.

Another distinction often made is between *parametric* and *nonparametric* statistics. Nonparametric statistics are those used when the variables being analyzed are either nominal or ordinal, and interval measurement may not be assumed. Thus nonparametric statistics are also called *order* statistics (Hays 1963, p. 615). The name "nonparametric" stems from the fact that these statistics are not based on assumptions about the parameters of the distribution (the normal or bell-shaped distribution is not assumed, for example). However, this does not mean that no assumptions are necessary for using nonparametric statistics. All the reader need remember for now is that nonparametric statistics are those that are used for the kinds of tables discussed above in which the variables are considered to be ordinal or nominal. Parametric statistics are used when interval measurement can be assumed.

Much statistical analysis consists of hypothesis testing. We may test the hypothesis that means from two different samples are significantly different, for example, or that a sample mean is significantly different from a particular population mean. In this chapter we will be concerned with testing hypotheses that a relationship between two variables is significantly different from zero. That is, if the relationship between two is zero, then there is no relationship, and a condition of statistical independence is said to exist. By testing that the relationship is significantly different from zero (independent) we assure ourselves that there really is a relationship between the two variables in the population and that the relationship we have found in the sample is thus not just a fluke or the result of sampling error.

Our goal is to hypothesize a relationship between two variables and then to show through statistical analysis of our data that such a relationship actually exists. Although we can never prove our hypothesis "beyond the shadow of a doubt," the statistical theory of probability does allow us to prove the hypothesis within a specified margin of error. We can determine our probability of error either by rejecting our hypothesis or failing to reject it if we know the distribution of scores of a particular statistic. As an example, consider the correlation coefficient r, (discussed below). If both of the variables we are correlating are intervally measured and if we have a sufficiently large random sample (at least 30 but hopefully much larger), we can assume that our sample rs are normally distributed around the population r, as in figure 16–7. We symbolize the population r with ρ (rho) to distinguish it from the sample r. The normal distribution is the familiar bell-shaped curve. The *empirical rule* for normal distributions tells us that 68 percent of the sample rs will occur within one standard deviation on each side of the population r; 95 percent within two standard deviations; and 99.7 percent within three standard deviations. This knowledge enables us to determine what percentage of the time we would make an error by concluding that a certain sample r value did not come from a normal distribution with a certain population r value.

Statistically, it is much easier to estimate our error of incorrectly rejecting a true hypothesis than to estimate our error of incorrectly accepting a false one. To see why this is so consider figure 16–8. The error made by rejecting a true hypothesis is called *Type I* error, the error made by accepting a false hypothesis is called *Type II* error. To test whether there is a statistically significant relationship between two variables, we first compute the value of the sample correlation coefficient, labeled r in figure 16–8. Most of the time r will not be exactly zero, indicating that there is some degree of relationship between the variables. However, to see if this relationship is *statistically significant* we must conduct a hypothesis test. Specifically, we wish to estimate the chance that our non-zero sample r could be obtained from an actual condition of independence or no relationship (i.e., a population r of zero). If the sample r is large and the sample is large, the chance is very small that such a sample r came from a population in which r was really

Figure 16–7

The Normal Distribution of Samples rs Around the Population r

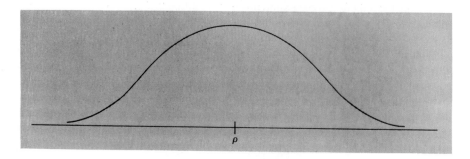

Figure 16–8

Two Normal Distributions Around Two Different Population *r*s

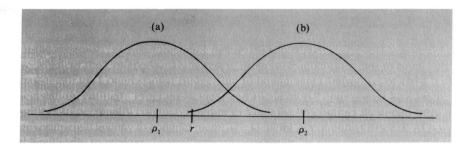

zero; if the sample *r* is small, or if the sample size is small, it is more likely that the sample could have come from a population in which *r* was zero. In general, the larger the sample size, the smaller *r* can be and remain statistically significant.

We must write two hypotheses. The first is called the null hypothesis, or hypothesis of no difference, and specifies independence ($\rho = 0$). As noted above, statistical independence means that there is no relationship between the variables. The second hypothesis is called the alternative hypothesis and is the research hypothesis we have proposed (i.e., $\rho \neq 0$). The null hypothesis is symbolized by H_o and the alternative by H_a:

$$H_o : \rho = 0$$
$$H_a : \rho \neq 0$$

The reason it is easier to compute a Type I error (rejecting a true null hypothesis) than a Type II error (accepting a false null hypothesis) is that Type II error occurs only when the sample *r* is actually from a different population distribution (figure 16–8b) than from the one we hypothesized (figure 16–8a). We have no way of actually knowing the true value of ρ in figure 16–8b, only that it is not equal to zero.

Thus it is customary to attempt to fail to reject H_a rather than test H_a directly, even though H_a is the hypothesis we wish to confirm. to reject H_a is tantamount to accepting H_a (the only alternative), with a known degree of Type I error. It is conventional to set our acceptable level of Type I error at either .05 (so that if we reject H_o we are in error 5 times out of 100) or .01. The level chosen (.05 or.01) is called the *significance level,* and is often symbolized by ρ, representing probability (of Type I error). Such a test for independence at a given level of error is called a *test of significance.* It must be emphasized that we are speaking of statistical significance only. When we say a relationship is statistically significant, this simply means that we can be sure, within a statistical margin of error, that the relationship exists. It does *not* mean that the relationship is necessarily significant or important in a theoretical or sociological sense. For further discussion of hypothesis testing see any introductory statistics text, such as Blalock (1972).

Figure 16–9
The Chi-square Distribution

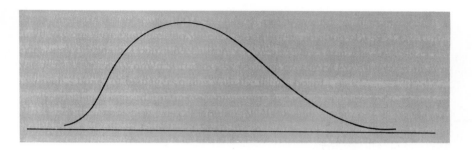

Chi-square (χ^2)

The most commonly used test of significance for independence for tables containing nominal and ordinal variables is χ^2. Chi-square, like the normal curve, is simply the name of a distribution. However, chi-square is not a symmetrical bell-shaped distribution but is skewed to the right (larger on the right than the left). The chi-square distribution is shown in figure 16–9.

Imagine that we conducted a survey to ask about education and income and received the hypothetical data shown in figure 16–10. To support our hypothesis we have to show that a person's education makes a difference when predicting his or her income. It is clear from a glance at figure 16–10 that education and income are not independent but are related. Eighty percent (40 out of 50) of people with high education also have high income while only 20 percent of those with low education also have high income. Thus we would guess that the relationship is nonzero. The question is whether it is statistically significantly different from

Figure 16–10
Hypothetical Data Relating Education and Income

Income	Education		
	High (College)	Low (High School or Less)	
High	40 a	10 b	50
Low	10 c	40 d	50
	50	50	100

non-zero. A good way to approach the problem is to determine what independence, or a zero relationship, would look like in figure 16–10 and to compare our data with independence to see how much the two tables differ. In chapter 3 we said that if there is no relationship, knowledge of the value of the independent variable (education) for a person will not help us in predicting his or her value on the dependent variable (income). Remember that the marginals of a table tell us the values of a variable when we have no knowledge of any other variables. This means that if the proportions in the interior cells of a table (which are determined not simply by the values of one variable, but by both variables) are the same as the marginals (which are determined by only one variable), then there is no relationship between the variables. In other words, the row marginals in figure 16–10 show that, not considering educational level, 50 percent of our sample have high income and 50 percent have low income. Thus it is logical that, if education does not affect income, 50 percent of high education people should have high income and 50 percent low income, and the same should hold true for the low-education people. This state of independence is shown in figure 16–11.

The values in figure 16–11 are known as *expected values,* since they are the ones we would expect in the case of independence (no relationship). In a sense these values are only hypothetical in that they are computed but not found in the data collected. They merely serve as a criterion for comparing the data actually collected during research. The values actually collected are shown in figure 16–10 and are known as *observed values.* To see whether the results we found (figure 16–10) are significantly different from independence (figure 16–11), we compare the observed data with the expected data. The distribution of the difference between observed and expected values has been found to approximate the χ^2 distribution, as indicated by the formula:

$$\chi^2 = \sum_{\text{all cells}} \frac{(O - E)^2}{E}$$

Figure 16–11
No Relationship (Independence) Between Education and Income

Income	Education		
	High	Low	
High	25	25	50
Low	25	25	50
	50	50	100

where O indicates the observed value and E the expected value. The larger the summed difference between observed and expected values as a ratio of expected values, the larger the value of chi-square and the greater the likelihood that the relationship is statistically different from zero. To see whether our relationship is significant we need only compare each respective cell of figure 16–10 with 16–11 as follows:

$$\chi^2 = \frac{(40-25)^2}{25} + \frac{(10-25)^2}{25} + \frac{(10-25)^2}{25} + \frac{(40-25)^2}{25}$$

$$= \frac{15^2}{25} + \frac{(-15)^2}{25} + \frac{(-15)^2}{25} + \frac{(15)^2}{25}$$

$$= \frac{225}{25} + \frac{225}{25} + \frac{255}{25} = \frac{225}{25}$$

$$= \frac{900}{25} = 36$$

Most statistics texts provide a table of χ^2 values that allow us to determine whether our value is statistically significant. We have mentioned that the larger the sample size, the more faith we have in our results. Since χ^2 is basically only a probability measure of the faith we can have that our relationship is nonzero, it, too, is affected by sample size. The table requires us to know the number of *degrees of freedom,* which means the number of cell entries we are free to vary without also determining the value in additional cells. For example, in a fourfold table, since we know the marginal values, we only have one degree of freedom and are free to vary the value of only one cell. After this cell value is determined (regardless of which cell it is) all other cell values can be computed, and are not free to vary. For example, suppose that in figure 16–2 we know the row and column marginals are 48,42 and 30,60 respectively, but all interior cells (a,b,c,d) are empty. After filling in only one cell we can subtract from the marginals to fill in all others. For example, if we put 12 in cell a, then b must be 38 to make a row marginal of 50. If b is 38, d must be 12 to make a column marginal of 50 and, similarly, c must be 38. The general formula for computing degrees of freedom (d.f.) for contingency tables is $(R-1) \times (C=1)$, where $R =$ number of rows in the table and $C =$ number of columns. In the 2×2 case, d.f. $= (2-1)(2-1)$, or 1. A χ^2 table tells us that for 1 d.f., a χ^2 value of 7.88 is significant at the .005 level, meaning that if we reject the null hypothesis of independence we will be wrong only 5 times out of 1,000 (Type I error). Our value of 36 is far above 7.88, so we reject the hypothesis and conclude that the relationship between education and income in figure 16–2 is statistically significant at the $\rho = .005$ level.

Fisher's Exact Test

The probabilities (ρ values) yielded by χ^2 are not exact possibilities, but approximations or estimates yielded by the distribution. However, the distribution of differences between the expected and observed values only approximates the χ^2 distribution if the cell frequencies (expected values) are large enough. Specifically, unless all expected values are at least 5, one cannot assume the distribution to be χ^2. In such a case the probability that the relationship is statistically significantly different from independence can still be computed, and can be computed exactly, by means of Fisher's exact test. The computations are quite laborious, but fortunately this statistic appears in many social-science statistical computer program packages. One merely plugs in the data and the computer performs the computations. Even if one does not have access to a computer program, there are tables that provide the probabilities (e.g., Pearson and Hartley, 1954; Siegel 1956) so that it is not necessary to perform the computations. However, for your reference the formula is:

$$\text{Fisher's exact test probability} = \frac{(a+b)\,!\,(c+d)\,!\,(a+c)\,!\,(b+d)\,!}{N\,!\,a\,!\,b\,!\,c\,!\,d\,!}$$

Measures of Association

The concept of a relationship between two (or more) variables was discussed at length in chapter 3 and was mentioned briefly at the beginning of this chapter. Basically a relationship is said to exist between two variables X and Y when a change in the scores of one of the variables is accompanied by changes in the scores of the other variable. We can speak in terms of the strength of relationship, or the degree of correspondence between the variation in scores of one variable and the variation in scores of the second variable. At one extreme, the scores of one variable could vary drastically while the other variable remained constant in value. This represents no relationship between the variables (the strength of relationship is a minimum), and is often referred to as statistical independence. In quantitative terms, we can say that independence represents a zero relationship. Any measure of the strength of relationship should indicate a zero value for such a relationship (there may be exceptions to this but they are rare). At the other extreme, change in the scores of one variable is always accompanied by corresponding and predictable changes in the value of the other variable. This is called a perfect or pure relationship and is indicated by the highest possible score on a measure of strength of relationship. This perfect score is generally fixed at 1.00 (or 100 percent) for most measures of strength of relationship, but for some measures the maximum score is different from 1.0. A perfect relationship between variables does not require that the two variables have the same values but only that a given degree of change in the scores of one variable is always accompanied by a certain fixed degree of change in the other variable. Statistical measures of strength of relationship are called either coefficients of association or correlation coefficients. The former term is generally used when the variables are nominally measured and displayed in a contingency table. The latter term is generally used for intervally measured variables. For example, if we compute phi (discussed below) for the two nominal variables of sex (male or female) and skin color (black or white), then we call phi a coefficient of association. If we compute r (discussed below) for the interval variables of age and IQ, we call r a correlation coefficient. However, the two terms are often used interchangeably.

The notion of a relationship is very important for social explanation and prediction. A zero relationship (independence) essentially means that knowledge of one variable tells us absolutely nothing about the score of the other variable. Thus, if we say that there is a zero relationship between the number of radishes in Russia and the length of university students' hair, knowing hair length will not help us predict the number of radishes, and vice versa. However, if we say that there is a perfect relationship between radishes and hair length, then knowing the score on one variable will allow us to predict the score on the other variable with 100 percent accuracy. Obviously the goal of social research is to find perfect relationships, thus achieving perfect explanation and prediction. However, we generally are not completely successful. Often we are able to find relationships between variables that are stronger than zero but substantially short of perfection. In such an intermediate case, knowing the score on one variable will enable us to predict the score on the other more accurately than if we did not know the score on the first, but not with complete accuracy. In other words, knowing the score on the first variable is helpful and is better than nothing but does not allow perfect prediction of the second variable. Some error in prediction remains, but not as much as if there were no relationship at all (independence).

Costner (1965) has elaborated a framework for the interpretation of measures of strength of relationship. This framework interprets a given statistic in terms of the proportional reduction in error (PRE). PRE indicates how much error the knowledge of a relationship eliminates in predicting the score of one variable from the score of another. For example, if there is no relationship between two variables, then knowing X will not help us predict Y, and our best estimate for Y is simply the mean of all Y scores. For example, if age and weight are uncorrelated, then if I know the average age of persons in your research methods class, this is of no help whatsoever in predicting the weight of individuals in your class, and my best estimate of the weight of any individual in your class is simply the class average or mean. However, if there is some relationship between variables, the stronger the relationship, the greater the proportional reduction in error (PRE). Thus, a statistical technique with a PRE interpretation can be directly read as indicating that the higher the value of the statistic, the larger is the proportional reduction in error. This is a very valuable tool for interpreting and comparing statistical techniques. Unfortunately, not all techniques have an easy PRE interpretation, but some of the most widely used ones do. Two important statistical techniques that have PRE interpretations and are discussed in this chapter are Pearson's r and gamma.

If we find a statistically significant relationship between two variables, the next step is to measure the strength of this relationship, since the significance test only tells us that the relationship exists. Coefficients that measure the strength of the relationship are generally called *measures of association or correlation*. The most popular measures of association include the phi coefficient (also called the fourfold point coefficient) for two nominal variables of two categories each; gamma and its fourfold equivalent, Q, for ordinal variables; rho for ranked ordinal variables; and Pearson's product moment correlation coefficient (r) for interval variables. For further discussion of measures of association, see Costner (1992).

Phi-coefficient

Except for Q (discussed below), probably the most popular coefficient of association for 2×2 tables is the phi coefficient, also called the fourfold point coefficient. The formula is:

$$phi = \frac{(bc - ad)}{\sqrt{(a + b) \, (c + d) \, (a + c) \, (b + d)}}$$

This measure is directly related to χ^2. In fact, $\chi^2 = N \text{ phi}^2$, or

$$\text{phi} = \sqrt{\frac{\chi^2}{N}}$$

where N = sample size. Computing phi for figure 16–2, we get

$$\text{phi} = \frac{(10 \times 10 - 40 \times 40)}{\sqrt{(50)(50)(50)(50)}} = \frac{-1500}{\sqrt{(6,250,000)}} = \frac{-1500}{2500} = \frac{3}{5} = -.600$$

The phi coefficient is the 2×2 contingency table form of the Pearson product moment correlation coefficient (r), which is the most popular coefficient for use with two interval variables. Like r, it varies from 0 (no association) to + 1.00 (perfect positive association) and − 1.00 (perfect negative association).

Gamma

Perhaps the most commonly used measure of association for contingency tables is called gamma. Gamma is used on ordinal tables larger than 2×2 (sometimes referred to as $R \times C$ tables, where R = row and C = column). The fourfold form of gamma is called Yule's Q. The formula is

$$Q = \frac{(ad) - (bc)}{(bc) + (ad)}$$

where a,b,c,d, are the four cells of the table.

	+	−
+	a	b
−	c	d

Notice that if the two variables in the table are each coded + and, −, then a and d are the consistent cells (+ + and − −) and b and c are the inconsistent cells (+ − and − +). Notice also that a and d form one diagonal of the table and b and c form another. The products (a)(d) and (b)(c) are also called cross-products.

Yule's Q varies from − 1 (perfect negative association) through 0 (independence or no association) to + 1 (perfect positive association). It should be clear that Yule's Q can be 0 only if ad = bc, so that bc − ad yields 0 in the numerator. Since we said that independence is defined as a zero relationship, and that the expected values in figure 16–3 indicate independence, the Q value for figure 16–3 should be 0. To see if this is true,

$$Q = \frac{(25 \times 25) - (25 \times 25)}{(25 \times 25) + (25 \times 25)} = \frac{(625 - 625)}{(625 + 625)} = \frac{0}{1250} = 0$$

By plugging various values into a fourfold table the reader can verify that, given a constant set of marginals and sample size, there cannot be four 0 cells unless the sample size N is 0; there cannot be three 0 cells unless one of the marginals is 0; that as one cross-product increases in size the other will get smaller until one of the cross-products reaches 0. If b × c is 0, then $Q =$ (ad/ad) = 1. If ad = 0, then $Q = -$ bc/bc $= -$ 1. Notice that for ad to be 0, either a or d or both must be 0, and for bc to be 0, b or c or both must be 0, but in each case only one cell in the pair need be 0 to insure a 0 cross-product. This means that if any cell of the four is 0, the coefficient will be perfect, either $\pm$ 1. If the cell is not 0, but is near 0, the value of Q will be close to 1.

Figure 16–10 exhibits a strong positive relationship because when education is high income is high, and when education is low income is low. We can compute Q for figure 16–10:

$$Q = \frac{(40 \times 40) - (10 \times 10)}{(10 \times 10) + (40 \times 40)} = .882$$

When the table has more than four cells, the Q coefficient is called gamma instead of Q. Unfortunately, the formula for gamma is different for every different-sized table. That is, each change in the number of rows or number of columns in the table changes the computing formula. However, this is not a severe problem in most cases because the formula is easily computerized. Most researchers do not compute gamma or any other commonly used statistics by hand, but rely upon so-called canned or packaged computer programs, such as Statistical Package for the Social Sciences (S.P.S.S.). Such programs require only that the researcher have a clean computerized data file, and that he or she enter a few salient details into the computer, such as the statistic to be used, the columns that the variables are in, and the number of cases. After the results are received, the researcher need only know how to interpret the statistics. Gamma has the same interpretation as Q, with 0 representing independence, $-$ 1 representing perfect negative correlation, and 1 representing perfect positive correlation.

Additional Measures of Association for Contingency Tables

In addition to phi, Q, and gamma, there are a number of less commonly used coefficients of association for use with contingency tables, such as the contingency coefficient and lambda. These are sometimes available on computerized statistical programs, and the researcher interested in knowing their assumptions and interpretations can consult a statistics text such as Hays (1963).

Rho

Rho, also called Spearman's coefficient of rank-order correlation (r_s), is like gamma, an ordinal measure of association. To compute (r_s), the two variables are each rank-ordered, with ties being given the arithmetic mean of the ranks that would have been received. For example, if what would have been the fifth and sixth scores are tied, each will be scored 5.5. Thus each person (or case) has two ranks, one on each variable. The difference between the pairs of ranks for each person is symbolized by D_i. For example, if John ranked 6 on variable 1 and 10 on variable 2, his D score would be 4. The formula for r_s is

$$r_s = 1 - \frac{6 \sum\limits_{i=1}^{N} D_i^2}{N(N^2 - 1)}$$

The value of r_s varies among $+1$ when all pairs of ranks are identical (so that $\Sigma D_i^2 = 0$); -1 when no pairs are identical; and 0 when there is no relationship between the two variables (no pattern to the pairs of ranks). When there are too many ties a correction factor is needed. For further discussion and an example see Blalock (1972, pp. 416–18).

Interval Data

Pearson's r

When both variables are intervally measured (e.g., age and height), the most commonly used measure of strength of relationship is the Pearson product moment correlation coefficient (r). This measure can also be used as a test of significance by testing the null hypothesis that the value of r in the population is 0. If the sample r is substantially different from 0, then the null hypothesis can be rejected and we can be satisfied that the two variables are not independent, but are related at a statistically significant level. For example, if we have a relatively large sample and find a high sample value of r (e.g., .90), then we can safely reject the null hypothesis that this sample came from a population whose true r value was 0, as we could not have gotten such a high sample value purely by chance if the true population value were 0.

As is true for gamma, r varies from -1 (perfect negative relationship), through 0 (no relationship, or independence), to $+1$ (perfect positive relationship). Recalling the distinction between linear and curvilinear relationships in chapter 3, r is a measure of linear relationship. To see examples of extremely different values of r, suppose that we took two different samples of 10 persons each and asked each person his or her education and income, with the hypothetical results shown in figure 16–12 (income in thousands of dollars).

We are interested in knowing a person's score on income. If income and education are unrelated, then our best prediction of a person's income is simply the average income, or mean. If education and income are related, then by knowing a person's level of education we can make a prediction of his or her income that is closer to his or her true income than is the mean of all incomes. We make this prediction by means of a straight line (called a best-fit line) drawn through the set of points. Rarely will we be able to draw a single straight line that will touch all points, as in figures 16–12a and b. The usual case is more like figure 16–13. It is obviously impossible to draw a single straight line that connects all points in this figure. For example, for any given level of education, the line represents only a single point on the income dimension. Since in figure 16–13 a single level of education may be shared by persons with varying incomes, not all of these points will fit on a single line. The objective is to draw the one line that will come closest to all points on the graph. The most commonly used criterion is least-squares. The least-squares regression line is drawn so that the sum of the squared distances between each actual value and its corresponding estimate on the regression line is minimized. In other words, the least-squares criterion is to estimate a and b in the linear regression line $y' = a + bX$ so as to minimize $(y_i - y'_i)^2$, where y_i is the actual value or variable y for person i, and y'_i is the value predicted by the regression line.

The coefficient r is a measure of scatter around the regression line. Every point in the graph that is not directly on the regression line represents error when attempting to predict a person's score on the dependent variable (e.g., income) from knowing his or her score on the independent variable (e.g., education). Figure 16–12a shows perfect positive correlation ($r = 1.0$), since every point is on the line and score on education goes up as score on income goes up.

Figure 16–12

Illustrations of Perfect Positive (a) and Negative (b) Relationships

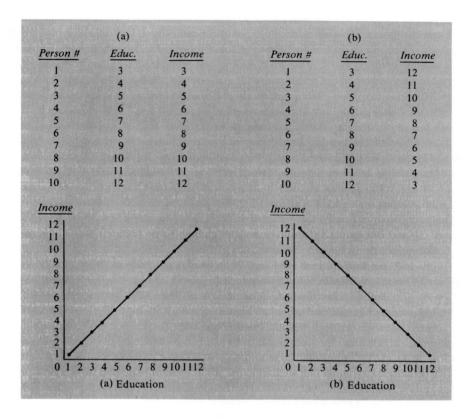

Figure 16–12b shows a perfect negative correlation ($r = 1.0$)—all points are on the regression line, but when education goes up, income goes down.

Figure 16–13 represents no correlation ($r = 0.0$), because there is maximum scatter around the regression line. The points are so widely dispersed that there is no possible way to draw a single straight line through all or even most of the points. In fact, very few of the points fall on even the best-fit line (the line that hits the maximum possible number of points). In this case knowing a person's education does not help in predicting his or her level of income, since several income levels for every educational level are represented in the sample.

Sometimes there is a strong relationship between two variables, but the relationship is curvilinear rather than linear. That is, the points in the graph fall on a curve rather than a straight line. Since r is a measure of linear relationship, even a strong curvilinear relationship may yield only a weak value of r, because r measures only the linear portion of the relationship. For example, consider the relationship between income level and number of children. Poor people tend to have more children than middle-class people. Poor people feel that children are all they

Figure 16–13

An Illustration of No Relationship (Independence)

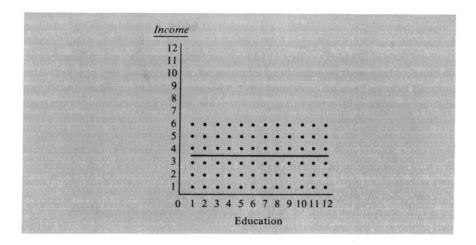

can hope for in life, so they do not think of them as an expense, while rich people can afford large families. It is primarily the middle classes who delay gratification and have only the few children whom they can educate properly. Thus the relationship between income and number of children might be curvilinear, as in figure 16–14. If one's sample contained only people

Figure 16–14

Curvilinear Relationship Between Fertility and Social Class

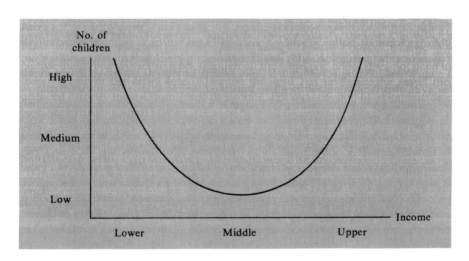

ranging from low to middle class, then one would find a strong negative correlation, for as class increases, number of children decreases. If the sample contained only respondents ranging from middle to upper class, r would be strongly positive since, for that range of class, number of children increases as income increases. However, if the researcher has a properly large sample, he or she should have respondents of all classes, and thus r would be near 0, since the positive and negative curves would cancel each other out. Thus if one receives an r of 0, it does not necessarily mean there is no relationship, but only that there is no linear relationship. If a low r is found but it is suspected that a curvilinear relationship exists, then the correlation ratio, or eta, should be computed. Eta is a measure of curvilinear correlation. For its assumptions and interpretation consult any standard social-statistics text such as Blalock (1972), Champion (1970), or Hays (1963).

Computing r.   A commonly used formula for computing r for variables X and Y is

$$r = \frac{N\Sigma XY - (\Sigma X)(\Sigma Y)}{\sqrt{[N\Sigma X^2 - (\Sigma X)^2][N\Sigma Y^2 - (\Sigma Y)^2]}}$$

The five sums used in this formula (ΣX, ΣY, ΣX^2, ΣY^2, ΣXY) are also used in the formula for computing the regression coefficient b and the Y-intercept a, to be discussed below.

Testing for Statistical Significance of r.   If the r value as computed from the sample is very low (e.g., less than .10), then it probably will not be either empirically or statistically significant, and the researcher will discontinue the analysis. If the r is quite high (e.g., .75 or higher), then it will be empirically significant and probably statistically significant (however, it could fail to be statistically significant if the sample size were very small). If the r is of intermediate value (e.g., from .10 to .75, a range encompassing most rs found in sociology), then the researcher may wish to test for statistical significance. With the null hypothesis that the population $r = 0$, he or she is testing the probability that a sample r of the size he or she found (e.g., .25) could occur by chance when the sample was drawn from a population in which p is really 0. Obviously, the larger the sample, the less likely are the results to have occurred by chance. Thus for a larger sample we do not need as large an r value to be statistically significant. We discussed this testing procedure earlier in this chapter and the reader is referred to that discussion. Table 16–1 (from Johnson 1976, p. 103) shows for a given r and a given sample size whether the sample r is statistically significant at the .05 level.

Assumptions of r.   We referred earlier to statistical measures for contingency tables as "nonparametric," or assumption free. Although such measures are not truly free of assumptions, they do require fewer assumptions than measures such as r, which utilize intervally measured variables. Specifically, use of r assumes:

1. Both variables are intervally measured.
2. The two variables are distributed in a bivariate normal distribution.
3. The relationship is linear.
4. The sample is of adequate sample size to assume normality. The law of large numbers generally sets the minimum sample size at about 30 (see Champion 1970, p. 89).

These assumptions can be treated as additional hypotheses to the research hypotheses. For example, assume that our major research hypothesis is that educational level and income are

Table 16–1

Minimum Level of *r* Required to Be Significant
at *p* = .05 for a Sample of Size *N*

N	r	N	r	N	r
5	0.878	15	0.514	30	0.361
6	0.811	16	0.497	40	0.312
7	0.754	17	0.482	50	0.279
8	0.707	18	0.468	60	0.254
9	0.666	19	0.456	80	0.220
10	0.632	20	0.444	100	0.196
11	0.602	22	0.423		
12	0.576	24	0.406		
13	0.553	26	0.388		
14	0.532	28	0.374		

Source: R. R. Johnson (1978) in *Elementary Statistics,* 2nd ed. Belmont, CA: Wadsworth.
Reprinted by permission of original publisher, Duxbury Press, © Duxbury Press.

related (call this hypothesis 1) and that we know our sample is of adequate size. Suppose we find an *r* between education and income of only .05, which is not statistically significant, meaning that this sample *r* could be drawn by chance from a population in which education and income are uncorrelated. We may be surprised by the findings, because we were sure education and income were related. It may turn out that education and income really are linearly related, but that the assumptions were not met.

Interpretation of r.   There are two chief interpretations of *r*:

1. r^2 = amount of variance explained. We defined variance earlier as the average squared deviation of all scores from the mean value. If we compute *r* and square it, this value gives us the proportion of variance in the dependent variable that is explained by the independent variable, or more correctly, since *r* is symmetrical, the proportion of variance in one variable explained by the other variable.
2. *r* measures the degree of scatter around the regression line. That is, it tells us how accurately we can predict with the regression line (discussed below).

The first interpretation is the one most commonly used by researchers. It is routine in research reports to report the value of *r* and also to report r^2, interpreted as the percentage of all possible variance that is explained by the relationship. Recall our hypothesis, stated at the beginning of this chapter, that the higher the education, the higher the income. Since the hypothesized relationship is positive, it can range between 0.00 and 1.00. If r is 0.00, then $r^2 =$ 0.00, signifying that no variance is explained (this is to be expected since the two variables are independent, or completely unrelated). When $r = 1.00$ (perfect correlation), then $r^2 = 1.00$. Stating this figure as a percentage, an r^2 of 1.00 means that 100 percent of the correlation is explained. Virtually all r values found empirically are neither exactly 0 nor exactly 1.00 but in between. Since an r value of one decimal place becomes two decimal places when squared (from tenths to hundredths), generally it becomes smaller, and quite a large r is required to yield a respectable-looking r^2. For example, an r of .5 yields an r^2 of only .25 (25 percent of the variance explained). To explain one-half of the variance requires an r value beyond .7 (.7^2 = 49 percent variance explained). The plain unsquared r value could be interpreted as the proportion of the standard deviation explained, but this interpretation is not common in the literature.

Least-squares Regression Line

The correlation coefficient r tells us how strongly two variables are related, but does not enable us to predict a person's value or score on one variable from knowledge of his or her score on the second variable. The regression line enables us to make such a prediction. Examine figure 16–15. As you remember from high school mathematics, any two points are sufficient to determine a straight line, and the generic (general) formula for a straight line is $Y' = a + bX$, where Y' = the person's predicted score on the dependent variable (e.g., income), X = the person's score on the independent variable (e.g., education). The constant a is called the Y-intercept, since it is the value of Y' where the regression line passes through the Y-axis (that is, a is the value of Y' when X is 0). If r is very small, indicating little relationship between the two variables, there is really no reason to try to predict the value of one variable from the other.

Figure 16–15

The Least-squares Regression Line

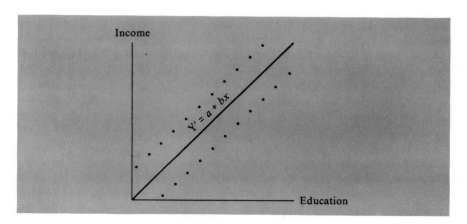

However, if r is large, indicating a substantial relationship, then it may be possible to predict the value of the dependent variable quite accurately from the regression line. The coefficient b is called the regression coefficient. It tells how much change there is in the value of Y' for each unit's change in X. The coefficient b also is the slope of the line. That is, it determines the angle at which the line rises (or declines in the case of negative correlation). For example, if X is education, Y' is income, and b has a value of .5, then we know that for each one unit's change in education (horizontal movement on the graph) there is b X or .5 × 1 unit's change in income (vertical change). Thus the line rises at a 45° angle, since it rises vertically only half as fast as it moves horizontally.

The computing formulas for b and a, using the same five sums we used previously in the computation of r, are

$$b = \frac{N\Sigma XY - (\Sigma X)(\Sigma Y)}{N\Sigma X^2 - (\Sigma X)^2}$$

$$a = \frac{\Sigma Y - b\Sigma X}{N}$$

Multiple Correlation, Partial Correlation, and Multiple Partial Regression

It is generally the case in social science that there is no single cause of a given phenomenon. Thus a single independent variable will not explain all the variance. If a dependent variable Y is correlated with a single independent variable X_1 and a correlation of $r_{x1y} = .50$ is found, this means that r^2 is .25 and that X_1 explains only one-fourth of the variance in Y. In order to explain the remaining 75 percent of the variance we must add additional independent variables to the analysis. For example, if education explains only 25 percent of the variance in income, we can add the variables of age, gender, and race to the analysis, and label these respectively X_2, X_3, and X_4. These additional variables can be added to the original regression equation, resulting in the following multiple partial regression equation:

$$Y' = a + b_1X_1 + b_2X_2 + b_3X_3 + b_4X_4$$

Such a regression equation is called multiple whenever it includes more than one independent variable. It is called multiple *partial* regression because each of the regression coefficients (b_1, b_2, b_3, b_4,) indicates only the effect of its respective independent variable on the dependent variable, with the effects of all other independent variables in the equation controlled for. Thus the equation is an additive one, with each regression coefficient indicating an independent or unique effect not shared by other variables in the equation. These separate effects may be added together to find the total effect on the independent variable. For example, b_3 will indicate only the unique effect of gender on income. But suppose that occupation were added as independent variable five (X_5). Education and occupation are clearly highly correlated. Thus occupation could be correlated with income (without considering the other independent variables) and show a high correlation. Similarly, if only education were correlated with income it would show a high correlation. But part of the correlation with income is held in common (shared) by both occupation and education, because these two independent variables are highly correlated with each other. If education and occupation are both placed in the same equation, multiple regression computes the correlation of occupation for only the part of income not already explained by education. Multiple regression assumes that independent variables will not be highly intercorrelated.

Multiple Correlation. The multiple correlation coefficient is symbolized by a capital R, and shows the correlation among more than two variables. As with r^2, R^2 indicates the proportion of variance explained by all variables. R^2 is commonly reported along with a multiple regression equation to show how much variance the regression explains, R is usually written with subscripts to indicate the variables being correlated, with a decimal after the dependent variable. For example, if variables 1 through 4 were being correlated and variable 1 were the dependent variable and the other three were independent variables, the multiple correlation coefficient would be written $R_{1.234}$.

Partial Correlation. Earlier in this chapter we showed how to construct a three-variable ($2 \times 2 \times 2$) contingency table, and showed that the correlation between variables 1 and 2 might be different for different values of variable 3. That is, the correlation between two variables (zero-order correlation) can be affected by a third variable that is correlated with one or both of them. An apparently high and statistically significant correlation between two variables can actually be spurious (no relationship) if both variables are effects caused by a third variable. When the effect of an additional variable is suspected, a partial correlation coefficient should be used.

Recalling the Galle et al. (1972) study discussed in chapter 1, you will remember that while Calhoun (1962) found in his study of rats that density (D) caused social pathologies (SP) (diagrammed $D \rightarrow SP$), the authors felt that for humans the relationship could be drastically affected by class, or social structure (SS). If SS is correlated with density, people at different class levels of the social system will be subjected to different levels of density. If SS is correlated with pathology, persons at different class levels will be subjected to different levels of pathology.

It is reasonable to assume that SS is inversely correlated with density, since poorer people live in more dense environments than do richer people. It is also reasonable to assume an inverse correlation between SS and pathology (as defined by Calhoun 1962; see chapter 1), since poor people have higher infant-mortality rates (for example) than richer people. If we considered people only at a single level of SS (e.g., only upper-class people), then we could determine the relationship between density and pathology with class held constant. Since all persons were of the same class, class could not affect the relationship. This is basically what we do when we use partial correlation, although the statistical technique does not actually hold the third variable constant, but simply controls for it by removing its correlation with one or both of the variables.

If the third variable is highly correlated with both D and SP, then the correlation between these two variables may disappear when the third variable is partialed out. This may occur either with SS as a cause of both D and SP, or with SS intervening between D and SP. In the former case the relationship between D and SP is apparent, but not real, because the real cause of both is SS. This is called a spurious relationship, and is shown in figure 16–16a. Figure 16–16b shows SS as an intervening variable, appearing between D and SP That is, D causes SS which in turn causes SP. In either case the apparent relationship between D and SP can result completely from SS. Thus even a perfect correlation of 1.0 between D and SP ($r_{D.SP} = 1.0$) can

Figure 16–16

Illustration of Spurious Relationship (*a*) and Intervening Relationship (*b*)

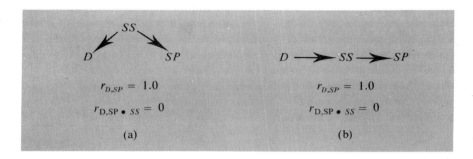

(a)

$r_{D,SP} = 1.0$

$r_{D,SP \bullet SS} = 0$

(b)

$r_{D,SP} = 1.0$

$r_{D,SP \bullet SS} = 0$

disappear when *SS* is held constant ($r_{D.SP \cdot SS} = 0.0$). $r_{D.SP \cdot SS}$ is called the partial correlation coefficient, and $r_{D.SP}$ is called the zero-order correlation coefficient.

Analysis of Variance

Occasionally one will wish to compute statistical tests with a combination of categorical (nominal) and interval variables. Analysis of variance is such a technique and is used frequently in experimental work. In experimentation the before and after groups represent the two categories of the categorical variable. The interval variable is represented by a mean score that is presented in each of the categories. Two different hypothetical experiments are shown in figure 16–17. In each case the mean score tells the average score for the group on a prejudice

Figure 16–17

Illustration of Analysis of Variance

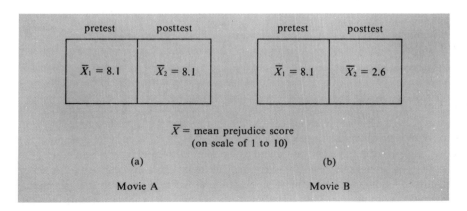

pretest	posttest
$\bar{X}_1 = 8.1$	$\bar{X}_2 = 8.1$

pretest	posttest
$\bar{X}_1 = 8.1$	$\bar{X}_2 = 2.6$

$\bar{X}$ = mean prejudice score
(on scale of 1 to 10)

(a)

Movie A

(b)

Movie B

scale of 1 to 10. In (a) the test stimulus is movie A, which is designed to reduce prejudice. In each case the pretest group has not seen the movie and the posttest group has (see chapter 9 for discussion of experimental design).

Notice that in experiment (a) both the pre- and posttest prejudice score are the same, showing that the movie had no effect and caused no change in prejudice level. However, in experiment (b) there was a great decrease from the pre- to the posttest, which is attributable to movie B. In order for the test stimulus (movie) to have a causal effect, it is necessary that the value of the dependent variable (prejudice) be different in the two groups, as in experiment (b). Analysis of variance divides the variance between groups by the variance within each group. In experiment (a), since 8.1 is merely an average score there is probably variation within each group. However, there is no variation between groups, making the F ratio (ratio of between-variance to within-variance) 0. In experiment (b), assuming that each group is fairly homogeneous in prejudice values, the ratio is quite a bit above 1. The greater the ratio, the more likely that group membership affects prejudice score and thus indicates a causal effect to the test stimulus. Tables of significant F values (the appropriate number of degrees of freedom must be known) are available in most statistics texts.

A useful extension of analysis of variance is analysis of covariance. Analysis of covariance uses one categorical variable and one or more interval variables. The idea is similar to partialing—to see how much the correlation between the two interval variables is affected by the category or group of the third variable. Analysis of covariance is beyond the scope of this book. For further discussion see a statistics text such as Hays (1963), Blalock (1972), Bohrnstedt and Knoke (1982), Devore and Peck (1986), or Freedman et al. (1991).

Path Analysis

The technique of path analysis has enjoyed great popularity in sociology in recent years after being introduced and popularized by Duncan (1966). In its simplest form, path analysis consists of a series of regression equations, with each variable in the model (except usually the last one or two) taking its place respectively as the dependent variable. Most of the variables in the model will be a dependent variable in one equation and an independent variable in one or more different equations. Figure 16–18 (from Duncan 1966, p. 4) shows a five-variable path model. The arrows represent a causal effect of one variable on another. The equations for this model are:

$$(1)\ \ X_3 = p_{32}X_2 + p_{31}X_1 + p_{3u}R_u$$
$$(2)\ \ X_4 = p_{43}X_3 + p_{42}X_2 + p_{41} + p_{4v}R_v$$
$$(3)\ \ X_5 = p_{54}X_4 + p_{53}X_3 + p_{52}X_2 + p_{51}X_1 + p_{5w}R_w$$

In each equation p represents the path coefficient, X is the variable, and R is the residual or unexplained variance (the variance not accounted for by the model). If the Rs are assumed to be uncorrelated with each other, the three equations can be thought of as conventional multiple-regression equations, and the ps can be computed as the regression coefficients in a regression program on any standard computer statistical routine for the social sciences such as SPSS or Data-Text (discussed below). Although beyond the scope of this volume, path analysis is useful in allowing one to compute not only the direct effect of an independent variable on a de-

Figure 16–18

A Recursive Path Model

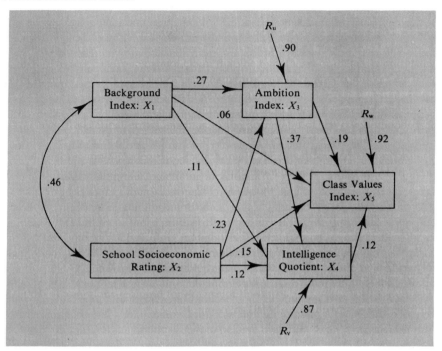

pendent variable, but also the indirect effect of that variable through another variable. For example, in figure 16–18 school socioeconomic rating (X_2) not only has a direct effect of .15 on class values index (X_5) but also has an indirect effect through its effect on both ambition index (X_3) and intelligence quotient (X_4), each of which have an effect on class values index.

Path analysis also appeals to many researchers because of its succinct graphic presentation that shows relationships among all variables in the model simultaneously. Notice that all causal arrows in this model point in one direction (toward the right), with no feedback loops (for example, arrows from X_5 toward the other variables). Such a one-way model is called a *recursive model*. Recursive models are mathematically much simpler than nonrecursive models, and are much more common in the social-science literature. For further discussion of path analysis see Duncan (1966), Land (1969), Heise (1969), Blalock (1971), Bohrnstedt and Knoke (1982), and Blalock (1992).

Nonresponse

We discussed means of dealing with nonresponses in contingency tables. With interval data we can also eliminate all nonresponses from the data analysis. This is probably the most common strategy and perhaps the best. The major limitation is that sample size may be severely decreased. In dealing with interval data we should not code nonresponse with a number (e.g., 9) unless we plan to eliminate nonresponse from the analysis. If such numbers are used in computing statistical measures such as the correlation coefficient, the results will be misleading, since nonresponse is not a legitimate substantive value and should not be treated as one.

Another technique is to substitute a substantively meaningful value for the nonresponse. Probably the most frequent substitution is the mean value. By computing the mean of the responses and substituting this value for each nonresponse, one is able to maintain the full sample size without changing the value of statistics such as the correlation coefficient. For a discussion of other strategies for dealing with missing data, see Cohen and Cohen (1975).

Meta-analysis

A new technique called meta-analysis emerged in the 1970s, grew to prominence in the 1980s, and reached maturity in the 1990s. Although precursors of this technique have been in existence since the 1930s, it was not until the 1980s that this technique achieved widespread use, with a great many meta-analyses being conducted.

Simply stated, meta-analysis is a statistical technique for synthesizing quantitative results from existing studies. One generally uses it to compare and/or combine statistical findings from two or more previously published studies (see Rosenthal 1984). The term "meta" essentially means "second-order." Thus, meta-analysis is "analysis of analysis." However, we must distinguish between meta-analysis and ordinary secondary analysis, as discussed in chapter 12. As an example, if we conduct a survey and analyze its data, this is called *primary* analysis. If someone else reanalyzes our data from the survey, or uses some of the survey data that we had not analyzed, this is called *secondary analysis.* However, if a statistical technique is used in order to compare or combine our research findings with the findings of other similar studies, such an integrative study is called *meta-analysis* (see Wolf 1986, p. 11).

The basic rationale underlying meta-analysis is that of finding some way accurately to synthesize research findings in the existing literature. The traditional method is nonquantitative. It consists of the researcher's simply reading a great many studies and conducting a "review of the literature" in a subjective or qualitative fashion, with no (or few) guiding rules. The author simply decides what studies to include and what overall conclusions best represent all the studies. In some cases this may be relatively easy, when all of the studies are similar in design and the results reach a consensus.

However, many times this is not the case. When the studies being reviewed are diverse both conceptually and in terms of their designs, and when their results conflict, the author's conclusions may be dubious at best, and are often unreliable. As Wolf (1986, p. 10) says, "These studies not only use disparate definitions, variables, procedures, samples, and so on, but their conclusions are often at odds with each other." There is thus a great need for some rigorous, quantitative mechanism for synthesizing the statistical results of a number of studies. Meta-analysis fills this need.

In one experiment conducted by Rosenthal (1984, pp. 17–18), seven studies supported the hypothesis that females showed greater task persistence. These studies were reviewed both by researchers using old-fashioned, qualitative literature review methods (which were unsystematic), and researchers using quantitative meta-analytic techniques. Seventy-three percent of the traditional reviewers *failed* to detect the support that existed for the relationship (only 27 percent were successful), while only 32 percent of the meta-analytic reviewers failed (68 percent were successful).

Why is meta-analysis superior to more traditional methods of literature review? Because often there is variation in the results of the studies being analyzed, or even conflicting results. The traditional reviewer has no systematic means for resolving discrepancies. However, meta-analysis statistically looks for patterns underlying the surface discrepancies. It results in a tool that allows the researcher effectively to accumulate the results of an entire literature consisting of a large number of studies.

Recalling our discussion in chapter 7, we were interested in determining which of the many factors (independent variables) that had been studied (such as sponsorship, type of postage, color of questionnaire paper) affected response rates of mailed questionnaires (the dependent variable). The meta-analytic studies allowed these questions to be answered not just for a single study or a number of studies reviewed consecutively, but for a synthesis of all of the studies.

However, meta-analysis should not be considered a panacea of "miracle method." It is not some kind of statistical alchemy that can turn bad studies into good ones. Still, it does offer an effective means of combining a number of studies. Wolf (1986, pp. 10–17) lists five advantages of meta-analysis (as compared to traditional literature reviews), and four criticisms of it. Compared to traditional, qualitative literature reviews, meta-analysis has advantages in: selection of studies for analysis; weighting of studies; interpretation of findings; finding explanations of disparate or inconsistent results; and examining moderating variables.

The criticisms of meta-analysis are: conclusions cannot be reached in some cases because the original studies are too dissimilar; results may be uninterpretable because poorly designed studies are included with well-designed studies; published research has a bias toward significant findings, because editors will reject studies with nonsignificant findings; multiple results from a single study may not be independent and, if used, may make the findings seem more reliable than they really are.

We can summarize both the advantages and weaknesses simply by saying that while meta-analysis is clearly more rigorous and accurate or reliable than traditional, more subjective techniques, it is in a sense no stronger than the studies it is analyzing. Meta-analysis simply cannot be successful if there are too many problems inherent in the original studies, but then, neither can any other technique. This seems to make meta-analysis the best technique currently available for quantitatively synthesizing existing studies from the literature. To say it another way, if the original studies were all well designed, then the subsequent meta-analysis has the greatest chance of success.

The logic of meta-analysis is really quite simple. Although there are many types and applications of meta-analysis, for our purposes we are most interested in the relationship between an independent variable X and a dependent variable Y. In the discussion in chapter 7 concerning mailed questionnaires, the dependent variable Y is the response rate, and the various independent variables (Xs) are the factors affecting response rate, such as sponsorship, type of mailing, color of paper, and so forth. A key concept in meta-analysis is "effect size," or "size of effect" (Rosenthal 1984). This refers to the effect of the independent variable on the dependent variable. For example, if sponsorship were found to be completely uncorrelated with response rate, then effect size would be zero. In reality, it does generally have an effect size well above zero, as discussed in chapter 7.

In addition to effect size, meta-analysis also frequently uses tests of significance, such as F, discussed previously in this chapter. The general relationship is that the test of significance equals effect size times the size of the study (see Rosenthal 1984, pp. 20–21). The complexity and difficulty of performing a meta-analysis can vary widely depending upon the number of studies being utilized, their design, the measures they used, and the goals of the meta-analysis.

For a simple study where all the measures are correlation coefficients (r), it may be sufficient to compute the effect size by simply averaging the rs (see Wolf, 1986, p. 29, for the formula). However, in most cases the analysis is more complicated, and may involve a variety of measures, such as correlation coefficients, regression coefficients, or measures of association. Here some transformation to a standardized effect size such as z or some other measure will generally be needed. Further technical discussion is beyond the scope of this volume. For such discussion the reader is referred to Rosenthal (1984) and Wolf (1986).

In order to illustrate the manner in which meta-analysis can be applied, let us revisit the discussion of mailed-questionnaires in chapter 7 for a familiar example. A number of meta-analyses have been conducted in order to determine the effect that various factors have on response rates in mailed questionnaire studies. The meta-analyses discussed in chapter 7 are by Armstrong and Lusk (1987), Fox et al. (1988), and Yammarino et al. (1991). All three studies provide valuable examples of how meta-analysis can be applied in social research, including discussions of effect size, coefficients, and tests of significance. The reader should refer to the original studies for further discussion of technical aspects. Also, the study by Yammarino et al. (1991) is helpful, as it compares past meta-analyses and other sorts of quantitative comparisons in terms of the variables studied.

It may be helpful to summarize briefly the procedure used by Fox et al. (1988). The authors began searching for relevant literature with the selection of three "seed" journals known to have published many articles on the topic of response rates in mailed-questionnaire studies. They took all issues of each journal for the last 25 years and conducted a computerized keyword literature search. The authors concentrated on experimental studies. Thus, each study reviewed had both a control group containing a "zero" level of the treatment (for example, no incentive to reply), and an experimental group containing the treatment (independent variable). They then measured effect size as the difference between the experimental-group response rate and the control-group response rate. They then further computed a chi-square statistic as a test of significance (see Fox et al. 1988, p. 478).

It is clear from the applications in these three studies of response rates that meta-analysis is a valuable and effective tool for enhancing literature-review procedures. The use of modern meta-analysis techniques takes us closer to our goal of achieving a true accumulation of research findings in social science. Of course, we have to remember that meta-analysis can be used to combine only studies with quantitative results. However, when such studies exist, as in the case of response rates, meta-analysis can be truly effective.

Statistical Computer Packages for the Social Sciences

Adequate understanding of the statistical measures discussed in this chapter can be achieved only through a much more comprehensive treatment than we are able to provide in a book concerned primarily with data-collection methods rather than with statistical analysis. Fortunately, there are currently a number of computer packages available that relieve the researcher of the necessity of doing tedious computations. It is often sufficient for the student to learn only the basic goals and assumptions of a particular statistical measure, because the computer can do the computation, and even some of the interpretation.

Probably the three best-known computerized statistical packages for social scientists are SPSS (and the newer version, SPSS-X, which is particularly useful in sociology), Data-Text, SAS, and BMD. Each of these packages consists of a substantial number of "canned" (already written) computer programs, which are stored on the computer. This relieves the researcher of the necessity of writing his or her own program. The programs are written to be as flexible as possible in terms of the kinds of data that can be used, the minimum or maximum sample size, the number of variables allowed, and so on. Generally all the programming the researcher has to do is to enter into the computer some control commands specifying such information as the number of variables he or she wishes to analyze, their location in the data file, and the number of cases (sample size). Many university social-science departments have a computer programmer on the staff to aid faculty and students with their computer runs. For further discussion see the manuals for SPSS, Data-Text, SAS, or BMD. For discussion of SPSS-X see Norusis (1983, 1985), and Babbie (1986).

Summary

In chapter 16 we discussed the analysis, presentation, and interpretation of data. We began by discussing the presentation of results in tabular form. We discussed one, two and three variable tabular presentations, and also discussed strategies for collapsing the categories of a table. We next turned to a discussion of statistical hypothesis testing. We discussed tests of significance, defined a null hypothesis, and discussed Type I and Type II error. The χ^2 test of significance and Fisher's Exact Test were also presented.

We next turned to measure of association (measures of strength of relationship). The measures we discussed are the phi coefficient, Gamma, Q, rho, and Pearson's r. We also discussed multiple regression, multiple correlation, partial correlation, analysis of variance, meta-analysis, and path analysis. We concluded the chapter with a brief discussion of statistical computer-program packages for the social sciences.

CHAPTER 17

INCLUSIONARY RESEARCH METHODS

WHETHER THEY ARE SO INTENDED or not, research methods are sometimes exclusionary, either leaving out certain groups or including them in ways that they or others find unsatisfactory. This chapter is about groups that are excluded from research and how they can be included in ways that are satisfactory both to them and to the researcher conducting the study.

Theoretically, if we always had the perfect study with the perfect sample, we would not have to worry much about problems of inclusion, as they would be minimal. A very large random sample should adequately represent all of the persons in the population, assuming that we did not deliberately seek to exclude any groups, nor did any groups avoid our study. In reality, many persons are excluded. Sometimes this is merely inadvertent, and other times it perhaps cannot be avoided. However, sometimes the researcher deliberately excludes or neglects certain groups. There are also cases where persons in certain groups do not wish to be studied for a variety of reasons.

In this chapter we shall be unable to discuss in detail all of the excluded groups and the reasons for their exclusion. However, we can generally discuss some of the types of groups that are excluded and some of the general reasons for their exclusion. We can then focus in more detail on examples of a few groups.

What groups are generally excluded? Perhaps the easiest way to answer this is to say that in the United States, for example, mature white males of European descent serve as the research standard, with the bulk of research being conducted by, on, and perhaps for this group. Even when other groups are studied, they are often compared (either explicitly or implicitly) with white males. All other groups may be excluded at one time or another. The excluded groups include women; members of various racial and ethnic groups; religious groups; young persons; elderly persons; ill persons; blind, deaf, and disabled persons; foreign-born persons; illiterates; prisoners; and mentally ill persons. All of these persons may be excluded either by design or simply because there is no emphasis placed on ensuring that they are included. Since their inclusion may require extra time, effort, and perhaps expense, they simply do not get studied.

Other groups may also be excluded. This is partly because they, like the groups above, are not in the "mainstream," but also because they may resist inclusion or may be difficult to identify or locate. These include a variety of groups, including so-called deviant persons, stigmatized persons, traumatized persons, or simply persons who may be ashamed about their behavior or about what happened to them. Among this group are former mental patients, rape victims, families of murder victims, families of suicide victims, concentration camp survivors, war survivors, homosexuals, bisexuals, criminals sought by authorities, ex- convicts, alcoholics, drug addicts, and many others.

Like the groups listed previously, these groups may tend to be neglected simply because they are "out of sight and out of mind" or because they are not like the researcher. In fact, the researcher may have little direct knowledge of these groups and may not even realize that they have been excluded. In addition, some persons may avoid being studied for fear of punishment, incarceration, or discrimination. Others may simply be traumatized and feel that recalling their experiences for an interviewer is simply too painful, especially if the researcher does not seem to be knowledgeable or sensitive. Sometimes traumatized persons such as rape victims or concentration camp survivors may begin the interview but find that certain questions trigger memories so painful that they are unable to continue. Still others may simply be impossible to locate. Even when located, some persons may not agree that they fit the requirements of the study, as in the case of alcoholics who are in denial and cannot admit (even to themselves) that they are alcoholics.

Even these brief remarks should suffice to show that there are sometimes problems involved in inclusionary research. Inclusionary research is not always easy; it may require extra planning, effort, time, and expense. Further, it should be obvious that not every study can include every group. However, it is clear that in diverse societies, attention to the matter of inclusion is very important and should not be taken lightly. Inclusionary research generally justifies the extra time, effort, and expense that it may entail, and its importance should not be ignored.

Our basic goal in this chapter is to increase our sensitivity to the groups we study. One good way to begin might be to take the "other" test. It is common on questionnaires (see chapters 6, 7, 8) to include an "other" category in an open-ended question. Does anybody really like to be an "other"? Yet how many researchers would classify themselves as "other" on even one question in their own questionnaire?

Although we have no way to answer this question, I would guess that the number is small. To illustrate this point, let us devise some nonstandard questions with "other" categories. Consider the following three questions.

1. What is your religious affiliation?
   a. Buddhist
   b. Hindu
   c. Muslim
   d. Other.

2. What is your sexual orientation?
   a. Gay
   b. Lesbian
   c. Bisexual
   d. Other.

3. What is your racial designation?
   a. African-American
   b. Mexican-American
   c. American Indian
   d. Other.

Are these response categories customary on the questionnaires that you have seen? If not, why not? They are all common categories in the United States, especially in large cities. Nevertheless, if they answer these questions, it is likely that many readers will find themselves to be an "other" on at least one.

How does it feel to be an "Other American" or a "Residual-American"? If it feels a little strange to you, you have started to realize why some people feel uncomfortable in social research. They feel "marginalized," "left out," "invisible," "different," or "made to feel like an outsider." Although we obviously cannot have a separate open-ended response category for every single ethnic, religious, or racial group in America (there are hundreds), we can nevertheless use our heightened awareness to increase our sensitivity to this issue and can "think twice" before constructing a study that may diminish some person's identity.

Insiders and Outsiders

The goal of inclusionary research is to bring "inside" our realm of understanding those people who feel "outside," such as those who answer "other" on questionnaires. At times it almost seems that the whole world is divided into insiders and outsiders, and research methods reflect this polarization. It is common to hear someone (from the group in power) ask, "What do *they* want?" "Won't you people ever be satisfied?" Unfortunately, the question is the answer. Many times, all "they" want is not to be referred to as "they." They merely want to be part of "us" or "we," rather than "they," "them," "those people," or "you people."

Often insiders bolster their antipathy for "them" with feelings that "they" are "abnormal." This can depend greatly upon one's vantage point. Consider any excluded groups, such as alcoholics or homosexuals. Assume that any large population contains approximately X percent alcoholics and Y percent homosexuals (see the discussion later in this chapter). From the standpoint of a given individual "insider," each of these is an "abnormality," as the majority of respondents in a study would not identify themselves as either alcoholics or homosexuals. However, from the standpoint of the population as a whole, these conditions are all "normal" in the sense that they are statistically expected. Thus, a population without any cases of alcoholism or homosexuality would be the "abnormal" one, and I know of no large population for which this is true.

Who are the insiders? Insiders are people with the power to control others' actions. They are the people who control jobs and money. Outsiders are the people lacking this power. We can easily stereotype both insiders and outsiders. If I ask you to describe the person who is an insider such as a high-ranking government official, Supreme Court Justice, or chief executive officer (CEO) of a major corporation, you will be most likely to describe an older, wealthy, white male (although the situation is changing somewhat). Conversely, if I ask you to describe an outsider such as a gang member, you will likely describe a young male member of a racial minority group.

In reality, though, the status of outsider is very multidimensional. There are many dimensions on which one can have diminished status or relative powerlessness, and thus be an outsider of sorts. These dimensions include not only age and race, but also gender, ethnicity, sexual orientation, physical condition, and so forth. Outsiders include women, the elderly, the ill, the obese, alcoholics, drug addicts, the very short or very tall, the mentally retarded, the physically disabled, the blind, deaf, and many others. Often persons can become stigmatized because of their behavior, such as convicted felons, whose outsider status becomes legally defined and sanctioned, and who lose their voting rights. Other stigmatized outsiders include family members of suicide or murder victims. Your outsider status may result not from your own actions, but from the actions of others, as in the case of a person who becomes a paraplegic because of a drunk driver. We can also be forced into outsider status by conditions beyond our control, as in the case of cancer victims. Probably all of us either is an outsider in one or more ways, or has a family member or friend who is. That is, returning to our earlier example of the "other" category, I could make virtually anyone an outsider, "other", or "Residual-American" if I asked enough questions.

The insider/outsider distinction has been applied to the study of research methods by Merton (1972). Here "insider" was defined differently, as one with "inside knowledge," not necessarily as one with power. Thus, for the study of black people, a black researcher would be an insider, and a white researcher an outsider. The issue was whether only blacks can legitimately study blacks. Merton concluded that black people should be studied by both blacks and whites, as should white people. In this usage, the insider/outsider distinction is basically a horizontal one (although Merton did recognize power issues as well).

More recently, Williams and Sjoberg (1993) have defined insider/outsider in terms of power, as we have. The distinction then ceases to be merely a horizontal one as in Merton's usage, but becomes a vertical or hierarchical distinction, with the "insider" being dominant and ranking higher in the hierarchy than the subordinate "outsider" (see also Collins 1986; 1990). In this formulation a black researcher is first an outsider (as a black person) but becomes an insider as a social scientist, thus being, in Collins's (1986) terms, "the outsider within." Not only are black women sociologists who penetrate the "old boys' network" also "outsiders within," but, as Williams and Sjoberg put it:

> In effect, if we conceive of insiders and outsiders in hierarchical rather than horizontal terms, we discover that Merton's insiders (black scholars) are really outsiders with respect to power and privilege, while his outsiders are insiders. In a sense, the black scholars were "outsider insiders," rather than, as Collins puts it, "outsiders within." In effect, Merton and his supporters were insiders with respect to power, outsiders with respect to the black cultural heritage (Williams and Sjoberg 1993, p. 162).

Williams and Sjoberg emphasize that the privileged, powerful researchers are at the top of the hierarchy (insiders), with underprivileged women and minorities at the bottom (outsiders). They contend that too much research has been initiated "from the top down" (that is, imposed on the underprivileged from the researcher's perspective), rather than "from the bottom up" (that is, initiated from the perspective of the powerless people being studied). They also say:

> Merton, reflecting the views of most social scientists, seems unaware of the role of privileged researchers in justifying, directly or indirectly, the existing power arrangements. In effect, oppressed ethnic minorities fail to receive a fair hearing within the social science community and the broader society. Given Merton's framework, he cannot come to terms with the fact that the interests, knowledge, and activities of the privileged often diverge markedly from, or are at odds, with, those of the nonprivileged (Williams and Sjoberg 1993, p. 191).

They say further (p. 162), "Taking the role of divergent Others becomes exceedingly difficult in situations where persons of power seek to understand those who are essentially powerless." It should be clear that many of the groups that are often excluded from social research are relatively powerless, although some have more wealth and power than others.

Social Research and Excluded Groups

Given that some groups are relatively powerless and have often been excluded from research, we should ask what groups want (or need) from research. That is, what are the advantages to these groups of being included in research, and what disadvantages can research have for them?

Disadvantages of Research for "Outsiders"

1. *Exclusion.* One of the worst things that research can do to powerless persons is to simply fail to recognize them. If they are not included in studies, they will not be represented in the published literature. Thus, a student of this literature would not only fail to appreciate the culture and accomplishments of this group, but might literally never know that they existed. Thus, the group might as well have died, or never have been born. This is a cruel fate indeed.

2. *Reinforcement and perpetuation of stereotypes.* Another possible disadvantage of research for powerless groups is that false or misleading stereotypes or rumors about them can be perpetuated, or even legitimized, by "scientific research." This can be done by exclusion, for if no research is done, there is no effective way to counter stereotypes. It can also be done by prejudiced or ineffective researchers. For example, a faulty sample that overrepresents respondents holding stereotyped views, or survey questions that are prone to normative answers, could result in a study that merely reinforces stereotypes instead of countering them (see chapters 5, 6, 7, and 8).

3. *Failure to acknowledge internal group diversity.* One of the pernicious aspects of stereotyping is that it can often lead to the erroneous conclusion that "they are all alike." When one says of a group that "they" are lazy, or childlike or unintelligent, or _____ (you fill in the blank), the implication is not only that the group possesses a negative trait, but that *all* members of that group have the trait, with little or no diversity. Members of such groups often find it quite galling that other people cannot recognize the diversity within the group. In reality, for women and for most ethnic and racial groups, there is quite a range of diversity within the group. Not all members of a minority group like the same foods, or the same sports, or the same colors, or have the same intelligence, and so forth. By failing to recognize diversity, research not only paints a false picture of the group but also eliminates or renders invisible the individuality of group members. One factor that contributes to the elimination of diversity is the tendency in statistics to emphasize measures of central tendency such as the mean or median, rather than measures of diversity, such as variance (see chapter 16). One advantage of entropy measures (Bailey 1990) is that they provide a clear picture of the diversity of scores within a group.

4. *Exaggeration of differences between powerful (insider) and powerless (outsider or excluded) groups.* If all people were perceived to be the same, then there would be no insiders or outsiders, no majority and minority. One way that groups are designated as powerless, outsider, or minority, is to exaggerate the differences between them and the powerful group. By the combination of exaggerating differences between two groups, and diminishing differences within the exploited group, the dominant group can create the illusion not only that "they" are

very different from "us," but also that "they are all alike." For example, it may be that members of the dominant group have a diverse array of musical interests, as do members of the subordinate group. One step toward inclusion of the subordinate group would be for members of the dominant group to acknowledge that, "like us, they have a wide variety of musical interests." In contrast, the exclusionary tactic is to portray the subordinate group by saying that "they like a different kind of music than we do."

5. *Bias.* A number of studies have shown that a researcher's expectations of his or her research subjects can affect the research results (see Rosenthal 1966). If a researcher is prejudiced toward a group or is simply unenthusiastic about the research, or does not expect to find significant results, the study can be affected. It is common in universities to find resistance toward the establishment of ethnic research centers on the grounds that such research is unnecessary, unimportant, or not academic.

6. *Poor study design.* Powerful researchers attempting to study excluded groups may simply lack sufficient knowledge of the group to design an adequate study. If a group has been sorely neglected, there may be nobody among the group of elitist researchers who knows what hypotheses to formulate, what characteristics the potential respondents in the sample should have, or what concepts or variables should be emphasized.

7. *Poor study execution.* Poor study design or inadequate advance planning can easily lead to a poorly executed study. Even if the study is well designed, lack of familiarity with a previously excluded group could lead a researcher astray, resulting in various procedural errors. For example, a powerful male researcher studying a group of powerless minority women might be at the right place at the right time, but may simply not realize the significance of certain statements or events. Such a researcher doing an observational study might record statements or events that turn out later to be irrelevant for the study, while failing to record facts that would have proved invaluable for understanding these groups. In fact, Williams and Sjoberg (1993) imply that it might be virtually impossible for a privileged researcher to succeed in taking the role of an underprivileged person.

This discussion of these seven disadvantages illustrates that it is not sufficient simply to decide to include previously excluded groups in research. The very fact that these groups have been excluded might indicate that they are so unknown and inaccessible to powerful "insider" researchers that studies of these "outsider" groups, no matter how well meaning, might be very difficult. This is especially true of the initial studies. After a literature has developed, researchers can use previously published studies as models for their research. We can now turn to a discussion of the advantages of social-science research in previously excluded groups. It is easy to see that some of these advantages are simply the converse of some of the disadvantages just discussed.

Advantages of Research for "Outsiders"

1. *Inclusion.* Choosing a group for research signifies that persons with sufficient power and resources to conduct studies consider this group to be worthy of knowing something about. To this extent the group then becomes one of "us" who have been studied, as opposed to "they" who have not been studied. The mere fact of inclusion for study is thus socially significant,

even if the results of the study prove disappointing. This may be doubly true if the study is large and expensive, and has respected sponsorship such as the government.

2. *Rejection of stereotypes.* A research study, particularly a large one with prestigious sponsorship, can do a great deal toward dispelling myths and disproving stereotypes. In fact, if pernicious rumors and stereotypes abound regarding a particular group, there may be virtually nothing that can combat them effectively, short of a very authoritative "scientific" study conducted by prestigious researchers under government sponsorship. It also helps if research results are disseminated widely in the mass media, such as newspapers and television.

3. *Documentation of internal group diversity.* The same people who accept group stereotypes may also readily believe that "they are all alike." Research results may be more effective in dispelling the latter than the former. It is safe to say that virtually no large group, be it women, a racial group, religious group, or so forth, exhibits complete unanimity of opinion. I have read the results of a great many studies, and I do not recall ever seeing one where every member of a certain group had the same opinion. Obviously, if one had an extremely small sample, there might be complete consensus, but because of the small sample the results could not be considered statistically significant. It would be a rare case indeed where a large group did not exhibit any internal diversity on attitudes (although behavior might be more constrained if norms were strongly internalized and rigorously enforced).

4. *Diminution of differences among groups.* Research studies are also effective in demonstrating that perceived differences among groups are often more apparent than real. While it is not uncommon to see differences on a particular variable between two groups, often these differences disappear or are diminished when some other variable is controlled for. For example, assume that 50 percent of the respondents in Group A agree with question 1, while only 25 percent of the respondents in Group B do so. While this appears to be a substantial difference, it may turn out that this difference is largely due to differences in educational level, for example, between the two groups. Thus, when educational level is held constant, there is little difference in the responses to question 1 between the two groups. There are certainly many cases where real differences exist between groups, and research should establish these. However, it should not exaggerate these differences, and should expose spurious differences.

5. *Reduction of bias.* One would hope that social researchers are less biased than the general public, due to their generally higher educational levels. While it may be naive to hope that all bias can be removed from social research, it might be reasonable to assume that trained social researchers are at least less biased (or no more so) than the general public. In some case they should be much more sophisticated and less biased than the general public, who may not have had access to social science information.

6. *Sophisticated study design.* Again one would hope that trained social researchers would at least be able to design a study better than the generally unorganized and *ad hoc* methods used by untrained observers to obtain their data.

7. *Sophisticated study execution.* Similarly, while trained researchers may still have flaws, their study execution is generally superior to that exhibited in the methods of untrained researchers or the general public.

The discussion to this point has shown that contemporary social science has limits in its study of outsiders. We have also shown that merely including a previously excluded group may not be sufficient (and may be even more harmful), unless done in a sensitive and sophisticated fashion. A poorly done or insincere study may do more harm than good if it leads to erroneous conclusions.

However, despite the problems, it is clear that social science has unique opportunities, and perhaps obligations, to include the previously excluded. In the absence of precedents, models, and a cumulative literature, it may be too much to expect perfect studies at first, but we can expect sincere efforts. In this spirit we now turn to the analysis of research challenges in specific groups. Despite our abhorence of the dreaded "other" category, it is simply impossible to include all groups in a single chapter, as the reader surely recognizes.

Further, there is more literature on researching some excluded groups than on others. In fact, it seems safe to say that there is *no* comprehensive literature on including previously excluded groups, and so this chapter is relatively unique, at least in terms of its generality. As such, we do not have the luxury of drawing upon an established literature but have to explore some uncharted ground.

However, when I say that there is no *comprehensive* or general literature on inclusionary research, this should not be construed as saying that there is *no* relevant literature. There is a scattering of helpful works, many of them on women. Examples of helpful literature are Eichler's (1988) *Nonsexist Research Methods,* Warren's (1988) *Gender Issues in Field Research,* Marin and Marin's (1991) *Research with Hispanic Populations,* Nielsen's (1990) *Feminist Research Methods,* and Renzetti and Lee's (1993) *Researching Sensitive Topics.* I have searched for comparable publications regarding other groups (such as racial and ethnic groups), and have concluded that they simply do not exist. Because women are undoubtedly the world's largest excluded group, and because they also have the largest relevant literature, it seems fitting to begin our more specialized analysis with them.

Including Women in Research

There may be some who doubt that women are really excluded from social research. After all, many universities have Women's Studies programs and research centers, which conduct a great deal of research on women. Further, there are highly respected journals such as *Signs* devoted primarily to gender research. Recently a female sociologist noted that women are studied so much in demography that she was concentrating on the study of male age at marriage, which had received less attention.

Such discussion notwithstanding, it takes only casual perusal of the literature to see that women are often underrepresented in research and publications. There are many aspects of this underrepresentation. One, of course, is the number of women in the sample. To their credit, many contemporary studies do include a representative number of women in their sample. However, merely including women with men in a sample does not guarantee full inclusion, as there are many ways in which research methods can be sexist (see Eichler 1988).

The reality is that women are still excluded from social research quite frequently or are included only partially or in inappropriate ways. To see why this is so, let us first review some reasons for exclusion. We shall then turn to an examination of inadequacies in studies even when women are included.

Why Women Are Excluded

1. *Bias.* One obvious reason that women are excluded from research is because they are outsiders, relatively powerless compared with the male insiders. To be sure, sexism is not so blatant in the 1990s as it was 100 years ago. Then, men rarely allowed women to make important decisions. For example, the World Columbian Exposition of 1893 (The Chicago World's Fair), was originally controlled entirely by men. Then Susan B. Anthony, President of the National American Women Suffrage Association, pressured exposition promoters to organize a women's board of managers along with the men's board.

The women proposed minting a commemorative silver quarter, and Congress approved the idea. Since the exposition was celebrating the 400th anniversary of Columbus' voyage (a year late), and since Queen Isabella of Spain financed the voyage, the "Isabella" quarter featured the queen's portrait. That was the first United States coin to feature a woman. The only other coin with a woman's likeness, and the only circulating coin, is the Susan B. Anthony dollar. The women's board commissioned an artist named Caroline Peddle to design the coin (there was no female engraver at the U. S. Mint), but her designs were overruled by the Mint. The board's idea of a women's building was rejected (Giedroye 1993).

Ultimately, the women had the last laugh, as their Isabella quarter today sells for much higher prices than the half-dollar issued by the men. The Susan B. Anthony dollar has suffered a crueler fate; it is easily confused with a quarter, and thus is unpopular and generally fails to circulate.

While sexism in social research is today seldom as blatant as in our example of more than a century ago, it is still clear that bias may be a factor in causing women to be excluded for studies. Many men running studies probably still live in a largely male world and do not strongly consider efforts to include women. Sometimes failure to include women is rationalized by claiming that study results can be generalized to all people, including both men and women. This is similar to using the "generic he" to refer to both sexes. Other times, the decision to exclude women may be more blatant, as when a researcher in one department on my campus admitted excluding women from experiments on the grounds that changes due to their menstrual cycles made them too inconsistent or unreliable to be satisfactory experimental subjects.

While we need not always expect bias in social research, neither should we be surprised by it, as it is endemic in the larger society. Also, we should not be surprised when women enforce bias against women, because they have been socialized just as the men have in many cases. I have almost had to fight with women in the new accounts section of the bank to have my wife's name listed first on our checks instead of mine, because that is the way they always have done it. The larger society also continues such practices as charging more to have women's shirts dry-cleaned than men's shirts. When a class action suit was threatened, the cleaners replied that women's shirts cost more to dry-clean (even though they are often smaller) because "they do not fit on the standard equipment." Did they ever stop to think the "standard" does not have to be men's clothes? The point is that everyday life is full of exclusionary practices toward women, and men, women, and children often follow along with many of them, probably many times without even realizing it. Thus, we should not be surprised when bias is encountered.

2. *Lack of precedents ("inertia").* One chief source of inspiration for new research studies

is the published literature. Researchers often draw upon the published literature (as in our discussion of meta-analysis in chapter 16) to replicate past studies, modify them, or compare them in literature reviews. If the past literature reveals no or few studies of women, then replications are impossible, and there is no precedent for new studies of women and no chance to conduct a literature review on studies of women.

3. *Model simplification.* Some social science models can be very complex. Mathematical models may contain a great many variables and equations, rendering them very difficult to solve, even on a computer. It is thus common in quantitative social science for researchers to make simplifying assumptions, which make the model less complex and easier to use successfully in research. For example, it is common to simplify models by studying at one point in time, rather than over time. This is commonly done in regression analysis (see chapter 16). Also, it is common when analyzing a life table in demography to focus on death rates and to make the assumption that no in-migration or out-migration exists—merely for model simplification.

Model simplification has also been cited as a reason for omitting women from a study. For example, Yamaguchi, in a study of intergenerational mobility, says "In this paper, I limit my analysis to non-black men to simplify the model" (Yamaguchi 1983, p. 218). Although as a mathematical sociologist, Yamaguchi may be accustomed to searching for ways to simplify models, as a Japanese-American he should be sensitive to the exclusion implied in this action. Furthermore, models can be simplified without excluding women (excluding men by limiting the model to the study of women only would simplify it just as well).

4. *Sample and subsample deficiencies.* We say in chapter 5 that thanks to the efficiency of modern survey sampling techniques, even national samples may be only a few thousand cases, or as small as 500. Of course, local samples may be even smaller. Random samples of this size might get a fair sampling of women, but perhaps not of racial minorities. However, the initial sample size is only a part of the problem. Often in research we wish to control one or more variables in addition to the main variables in the hypotheses. By the time we do this, our subsample size may be too small for statistically significant analysis (see chapter 16).

As an illustration, suppose we conduct a study in a small town and assume that a random sample of 100 people is sufficient. We might very well have 50 women in the sample. Suppose our hypothesis relates occupation and income. We decide that sex must be controlled for. Then we decide that race must be controlled for, then education, then age. By this time we find that one cell in our table designates elderly, black, college-educated women. Much to our dismay we find that there are none in the sample, or are too few to ensure statistical significance. This can be avoided through a stratified sampling procedure (see chapter 5), but that might take a resolve to attempt to include excluded groups, which means a great deal of advance planning and extra effort.

5. *Distributional problems.* A related problem is that women and other excluded groups are not only excluded from research but are also excluded from many other domains (such as management positions) in the larger society. Thus they may be distributed geographically or socially in such a manner that routine sampling tends to miss them. For example, a random sample of university full professors or electrical engineers will yield few women, simply because there are as of yet relatively few women in these positions. Conversely, random samples of occupations such as elementary school teachers or nurses will yield many women. Thus, if

a researcher truly wanted to avoid studying women, but without appearing to have blatant bias, the best strategy would be to concentrate on survey studies of occupations with few women.

6. *Focus on variables, not persons.* While observational field studies (see chapter 10) often do a good job of describing the whole individual and her or his chief characteristics, this is often not the case for either verbal theories (particularly macro or large-scale theories, which tend to be very abstract) or statistical studies. Often the latter never really focus on the individual as a holistic entity. Rather, the process begins in hypothesis formulation with statements of relationships between two variables (see chapters 3 and 4) and ends with a statistical analysis assessing the degree of relationship between the two variables. Thus, rather than focus on whole persons (real persons), studies tend to focus on abstractions. This means that even a study which ostensibly focuses on gender may in reality be an abstract theory or an obtuse statistical analysis, concerning two variables such as X (gender) and Y (income), which really provides little insight into women's lives. Not only is that true of statistical analyses, but it can also be true of the typologies used in ethnography if they contain labels in the cells rather than real persons (see chapter 10). The main place where "real people" are found in many surveys are in descriptions of the sample.

This issue of a focus on variables is a little more complex than some of the other issues, and thus requires more extensive discussion. For one thing, a focus on variables excludes not just women, but *all* humans, including men as well. That is, the focus is on variables abstracted from the whole, rather than on the person. This can leave out men as well as women, and can be quite dehumanizing.

As we saw in chapter 16, what is entered into the computer is not a person, but simply a line of data, or 80 columns representing a number of variables coded for each person. Many people of a humanistic bent see this as dehumanizing. Another aspect of the focus on variables is that by deciding which variables to study (particularly the dependent variable), the researcher may be indirectly dictating which persons or groups will be studied. As an example, say that a person studies to be a demographer, with a special interest in fertility. In order to learn about fertility, it is necessary to study women in the childbearing ages (15–49). This should not be interpreted necessarily as the result of a desire to learn more about women or indicative of a sensitivity toward women's issues. The study of women as a group is merely dictated by the desire to study fertility.

Thus, the researcher who studies women may be somewhat reluctant, or even inadvertent. He could in fact be a man who adheres to the old "keep them barefoot and pregnant" view, rather than a feminist or someone sympathetic to women's issues. He might be a person that would be studying men if only he could find some way for them to become pregnant. We might label this as an example of "inadvertent inclusion of women," necessitated by an interest in a particular variable (in this case, fertility).

Conversely, we can also identify "inadvertent exclusion." An example would be where a researcher studies men exclusively, not out of bias or from lack of sensitivity towards women's issues, but simply because the variable of interest (for example, percentage with vasectomies), can be studied only for a group of males. We also must acknowledge that the relationship between a particular characteristic and the group possessing it can be a "chicken or egg" problem, where we do not know which came first. For example, when we see a study of abortion, it may be difficult to ascertain whether the researcher was first motivated by an interest in abortion, and was thus led to study a sample of women, or was in fact first interested in women's issues, and only secondarily focused on abortion as a field of study. Still further, the researcher could be interested in both the variable and the group simultaneously.

7. *Popular statistical models not suited to the analysis of nominal variables.* Another major problem in contemporary sociology is that it depends heavily upon statistical models such as multiple regression (see chapter 16). Regression requires dependent and independent variables that are continuous—ideally ration variables, but at least interval variables (see chapter 4). However, some of the most central and theoretically important variables in social science are *not* interval level or even continuous, but are discrete, categorical, or nominal level variables such as gender (or sex), race, religion, political affiliation, region of birth, and so forth. These variables are basically unsuitable for regression analysis, as they do not meet its requirements. Thus, the tendency is to exclude them. Often, the best that can be done with sex is to enter it as a "dummy variable," for example, coding the independent variable as "1" for male and "0" for female (for an example, see Arnold and Hagen 1992). In Arnold and Hagen's study sex was included by coding male = 1. However, 94.5 percent of the sample were male (less than six percent were female), and sex had an effect of only −.009.

Why were women virtually excluded from Arnold and Hagen's study? Apparently for two reasons just discussed: emphasis on variables, and distributional problems. They studied misconduct among lawyers in Canada. The distributional problem arises because they studied only lawyers, and men predominate in this profession. As for emphasis on a particular variable, they were interested in misconduct, and perhaps to their credit, women were less charged with misconduct than men. Whatever the reasons for the virtual exclusion of women, it is debatable statistically as to whether it is even wise to include sex as an independent variable when for all practical purposes almost the entire sample is male. Thus, one is almost in the position of using a constant (95 percent male) as an independent variable. It is sad but true that as long as quantitative social science has such heavy reliance on statistical models requiring interval data, variables such as sex will simply be excluded, or at best will be included in a strained and often inadequate or misleading manner.

This discussion has revealed a number of reasons why women can be excluded from social research. It should not be assumed that they are always excluded. Despite tradition, bias, distributional problems, the desire for model simplification, and all the other reasons, women are definitely included in many studies. However, even when they are included, the results of the studies are often criticized. Some of the criticisms (such as reinforcement of stereotypes and exaggeration of differences between groups) have been listed in our general discussion above.

Critiques of Quantitative Studies

Williams (1991) offers four critiques of quantitative studies.

1. *Collapsing the sex/gender distinction.* Sex refers to biological and anatomical features of males and females, while gender refers to their learned behavior. The genital differences

between babies are sexual differences. The extremely prevalent practices of dressing infant girls in pink and boys in blue are learned differences, or gender differences. We can refer to the sexes as male and female, while referring to the meanings, beliefs, and practices associated with gender as masculine and feminine (see Williams 1991, p. 226). Williams notes that the distinction between sex and gender (or between male-female and masculinity-femininity) is often collapsed (conflated). In commenting on one published study, she says, "The implication is that biological sex actually *causes* changes or differences in the dependent variables under examination: change the respondent's genitals, and their behavior changes" (Williams 1991, p. 226, emphasis in the original). She notes that the behavioral changes are learned or gender changes, not changes due to sex. This can be seen as "biological reductionism," where focus is on the biological aspects of sex rather than on the sociological aspects of the learned behavior (gender).

2. *Exaggerating minor differences.* Williams's second criticism of quantitative studies is that they often exaggerate minor differences. We have already discussed this in general terms above. However, we have not discussed the statistical implications. For example, Williams (1991, p. 227) notes that we are told that "women are more Democratic than men," when in reality there is only an eight percent difference in voting behavior, and the majority of women and men vote for the same candidate.

There are at least two related factors that contribute to this emphasis on differences: tests of significance and the "file drawer problem." We saw in chapter 16 that statisticians generally begin with a null hypothesis, a hypothesis of "no difference." An example, would be the hypothesis that women's mathematics scores are no different from men's. It is only if this hypothesis can be rejected that the results are declared "statistically significant." Findings in which women's and men's scores are about equal are not statistically significant. While it is often emphasized that lack of statistical significance does not imply lack of theoretical significance, in reality the statistical criterion generally prevails, and studies that lack statistical significance are not valued.

This leads to the "file drawer problem" (see Fox et al. 1988) that we noted in our discussion of meta-analysis in chapter 16 (although we did not use this term). It refers to the fact that findings that are not statistically significant are much more likely to be rejected by journal editors. They thus remain unpublished, languishing in "file drawers." The problem is that conceivably one hundred studies could be conducted with only ten showing statistically significant differences in women's and men's scores, with the other 90 not being significant. However, the ten "significant" studies (which are really the exceptions) would be published, and the majority finding, as represented by the vast majority of studies (90), would be rejected. The cumulative result is that the published literature thus "conclusively" shows that men's scores are higher than women's, and these results are further disseminated through secondary studies, meta-analyses, literature reviews, newspaper and television coverage, and so forth.

In reality, there is often overlap between groups, for example, with many women scoring higher than men on mathematics tests. By exaggerating differences, researchers disguise this overlap, making the two groups appear to be nonoverlapping "sexual dichotomies" (Eichler 1988).

3. *Reifying existing stereotypes.* Williams's third criticism of quantitative studies is that

they often reify existing stereotypes. While we have discussed this in a general way, Williams (1991, p. 228) gives examples for women. She cites the case of the Bem Sex Role Inventory, which lists the following characteristics (among others) as "masculine": ambitious, analytical, assertive, has leadership abilities, strong personality. In contrast the "feminine" characteristics are much less flattering, including: childlike, gullible, shy, yielding.

Reification means treating an abstract theoretical construct as if it were an empirical, concrete reality. What do you think? Does a high score on the feminism scale indicate a person who is "really" high on femininity, or rather a person who is merely high on the stereotype of femininity?

4. *Decontextualizing gender.* Williams's (1991) fourth criticism of quantitative studies is that they tend to take gender out of context, thus hiding the variation that exists in different groups and contexts. This is similar to our point about decreasing internal differences as discussed previously, but is not quite the same. Williams (1991, p. 229) notes that looking at aggregate characteristics of all women and men makes gender seem consistent and universally understood and perceived, while in reality *masculinity* and *femininity* probably mean different things to different people, depending upon the particular context. When one talks about relationships among women and men, there is no realization that these relationships might be very different for women and men of different races (black, white, Chinese, American Indian) or religions (Hindu, Buddhist, Methodist, and so forth).

Critiques of Qualitative Studies

Williams prefers qualitative to quantitative methods for gender research. She notes, however, that qualitative research is not without flaws.

1. *Questions about central tendency.* Williams says that since most sociologists are trained in statistics, this carries over into their qualitative research, where they try to answer questions about averages, such as "What does the average person think?" Such questions are better answered with quantitative surveys than with qualitative ethnographic studies.

2. *Quantitative findings from nonrandom samples.* Another flaw that Williams notes is for qualitative researchers to cite results in quantitative terms, such as saying that "30 percent of the sample said so-and-so." The problem here is that the qualitative group of subjects is not a randomly selected sample (see chapter 5 and chapter 10), and so the rules of statistics cannot be used to generalize the results. In fact, both of these criticisms stem from researchers' attempt to use ethnographic field studies to do the work of surveys, which they cannot do.

3. *Research/subject gender differences.* In Chapter 8 we discussed the effect of gender differences in interviewing, as for example, when the interviewer was a man and the respondent a woman. The problem may be even more acute in qualitative fieldwork. In survey research, it is possible for the interviewer to be quite remote from the respondent. This possibility is increasing with technological developments. For example, while gender may be a factor in telephone interviewing (see chapter 8), the respondent and interviewer can judge each other's gender only from their voices. With mailed questionnaires and computer surveys, it may be virtually impossible to determine the sex of the interviewer and subject, and so the

effect is minimized or even eliminated. Even in experimentation, experimenters are now using technology to remove themselves form the experimental setting by running experiments on video terminals (see Williams 1991, p. 240).

Such removal from the scene is virtually impossible in fieldwork. Here, all of the gender problems and prejudices found in everyday life may be present, or in some cases even compounded. Female researchers might find a distinct lack of respect from male subjects, for whom the researcher's gender counts for more than her status as a professional social scientist (see Warren 1988, p. 17). Also, female researchers might find themselves erroneously labeled with cultural stereotypes by their subjects. This happened to one female ethnographer who was branded a prostitute because she unknowingly checked into a hotel frequented by prostitutes and wore a type of shoe worn locally only by prostitutes (see Warren 1988, p. 30).

4. *Accessibility.* As discussed in chapter 10, accessibility is a crucial factor in fieldwork. The problem here may be a distributional one, as discussed earlier. It is often necessary to obtain permission to enter a setting (such as a factory) from high-ranking executives, who are likely to be men. Thus, at this level, the researcher may be dealing almost entirely with men, with women being excluded from the process. Since the person determining who is to be studied is male, it is likely that the ethnographer will be steered to the study of other males, rather than to the study of women (although this is not necessarily so). The issue is just that of having to deal with a male "gatekeeper" in order to study women in the organization.

Further, there are still some places restricted to females, where male researchers are not allowed to enter, and some places restricted to males, where female researchers are not allowed to enter. Although these may be holy places, or even clubs, more and more such restrictions are being dropped, so that the primary restrictions will be on places associated with nudity (such as bathhouses), or sexual activity. Warren discovered in her research on homosexual males that she was given full access to some activities but denied access to others. In her words:

> I was able to do fieldwork in those parts of the setting dedicated to sociability and leisure—bars, parties, family gatherings. I was not, however, able to observe in those parts of the setting dedicated to sexuality . . . Thus my portrait of the gay community is only a partial one, bounded by the social roles assigned to females within the male homosexual world (Warren 1988, p. 18).

Warren (1988, p. 18) notes also that a researcher may sometimes find that initial entree is not restricted by gender, but that internal access is. She studied a drug rehabilitation center open to both males and females. While the males even allowed her access to areas where persons who were not residents of the facility were not normally permitted to go, the females were much more restrictive and uncooperative with her.

However, accessibility has another side. There is some evidence in the literature that women sometimes have superior access to fieldwork settings. As Warren says:

> Although women may sometimes be prevented from entering male worlds, they may nevertheless encounter more willingness on the part of both males and females to allow access to inner worlds of feeling and thought. Female fieldworkers seem at once less threatening and more open to emotional communication than men (Warren 1988, p. 44).

Techniques for Including Women in Research

Now that we have written at length about difficulties involved in including women in social research, the premier question remains, "How can women be included?" Fortunately, Eichler (1988) has written a "practical guide" to nonsexist research methods, which gives explicit suggestions for including women in research. Eichler begins by presenting a discussion of seven sexist problems in research. These include four primary problems (androcentricity, overgeneralization, gender insensitivity, and double standards), as well as three "derived" or secondary problems (sex appropriateness, familism, and sexual dichotomism). The last three can all be seen as special cases of the first four.

Eichler (1988, p. 5) defines androcentricity as a view of the world from a male perspective. Two extreme forms of this are gynopia (suggests female invisibility) and misogyny (hatred of women). Overgeneralization consists of studying one sex, but acting as though the study were applicable to both sexes. Its converse is overspecificity, which consists of reporting a study in such a manner that one cannot determine whether it applies to one or both sexes. As an example of overgeneralization, Eichler cites using a sample of male workers only for a study of social class. As an example of overspecificity, she cites the use of single sex terms where both sexes are involved, such as "man is a mammal." The latter is also sometimes known under the rubric of the "generic he."

Gender insensitivity consists simply of ignoring sex as an important research variable. Double standards exist when different measures or standards are used to judge the two sexes. Eichler says that double standards are likely to be inspired (or lead to) androcentricity.

Sex appropriateness is a specific instance of the double standard. As example is when behavior is considered appropriate for one gender but not the other. For example, it is appropriate for women to cry in public, but not for men. Familism is a specific case of gender insensitivity. It consists of using the family as the smallest unit of analysis, thus ignoring the actions of individuals within the family. Sexual dichotomism is another specific instance (like sex appropriateness) of the double standard. This is Eichler's term for what we and Williams earlier called exaggeration of differences between sexes. It means that one fails to recognize overlapping abilities between men and women, but rather acts as though they were two separate and discrete categories. For many examples of this see Eichler (1988).

Eichler provides guidelines that researchers can use in attempting to ensure that their research is nonsexist. Her basic strategy is for the researcher to examine the various components of the study (the sample, the questionnaire items, the data analysis) and to ask questions about them in terms of her seven categories. It is a strategy that any researcher can pursue, and it is certainly worth the time and effort if it results in a more gender-sensitive and inclusionary study. Study the following examples presented by Eichler, and then you can see how to utilize this strategy yourself. For example, with regard to gender insensitivity in reporting on your sample, Eichler (1988, p. 155) proposes that you ask yourself the following question: "Is the sex composition of the sample adequately reported?" If you answered "no," then change your reporting.

Eichler (1988, p. 156) also provides guides for determining whether a questionnaire question is biased in a sexist fashion. To do so, ask yourself the following three questions: "Does the question use generic terms for sex-specific purposes, or sex-specific terms for generic purposes?" "Does the question take one sex as the norm for the other, thus restricting the range of possible answers?" "Is the question premised on some notion that particular behaviors are appropriate for one sex but not for the other, either explicitly or implicitly, by failing to ask equivalent questions of the other sex?" If you answered "yes" to any of these questions, change your questionnaire items so that you answer negatively to all three questions. In order to guard against using double standards in coding procedures, Eichler (1988, p. 158) suggests asking yourself the following question: "Are identical coding procedures used for males and females?" If not, change your coding process.

Eichler also offers guidelines for data interpretation. One common error is overgeneralization, where researchers only include one sex in the sample, but try to generalize their findings to all people. You can test for this by asking yourself the following questions (Eichler 1988, p. 160): "Is only one sex considered? If so, are conclusions drawn in general terms?" If you answered "yes" to both questions, as is commonly the case, then the study should be revised in one of two alternate ways. Either change the sample to include both sexes (preferable, but probably impossible in later stages of the study), or restrict the conclusions to the sex that was studied.

As an example, consider Shively's (1992) analysis of Western movies. Her respondents were 20 American Indian males and 20 Anglo males living in a town on an Indian reservation. Shively (1992, p. 726) justifies the decision to limit the sample to one sex by stating that "Because the Western genre is primarily about males, only males were included in the sample." However, in a footnote (Shively 1992, p. 727) she says that her data show the Western genre to be popular among women, but that she "controlled for gender" because the major focus was on racial differences, and because she had a limited budget.

Let us apply Eichler's questions to Shively's study. For this study we answer "yes" to question number one. There is no problem to this point. The problem arises in the interpretation. In the "Findings" section, Shively says, "I began my research with the assumption that *people* understood movies based on their own cultural backgrounds . . . My most striking finding, however, is an overall similarity in the ways Indians and Anglos experienced *The Searchers*" (Shively 1992, p. 727, emphasis added). The problem is that "people" refers to both sexes, while only males were studied. This could be remedied either by including females in the sample (preferable), or by altering the interpretation to read, " . . . the assumption that males understand movies. . . . My most striking finding . . . in the ways Indian males and Anglo males experienced *The Searchers*." Do these findings also apply to Indian females and Anglo females, or are they restricted only to males? We cannot reach a conclusion from the study as it is currently designed and reported. Another slight problem is the use of the term "males" rather than "men." To some readers, "males and "females" connote sex, while "men" and "women" connote gender. Quite obviously Shively is studying the effects of gender, rather than of sex. Further, if she refers to "males," we have to refer to "females" (rather than "women", which would be preferred), in order to maintain parallelism in the terminology (see the following discussion).

Shively's study is a good example of the complexities, some of them quite subtle, that are involved in gender inclusion. Her explanation that she "controlled for gender" is somewhat euphemistic from a methodological standpoint. The reality is that women were excluded. This does control for gender by assuring that only males were in the analysis. However, it is misleading to assume that to control for gender one *must* exclude women. The standard way to control for gender is to include both women and men in the sample, but then to separate them for the analysis. This is definitely preferable, as it allows the researcher either to compare the sexes or to combine them in an aggregate sample, if desired.

Shively's explanation that women were excluded because of "a limited budget" is also troubling. This implies that it is more important to study men than women, so if we have only enough money for one gender, the women have to be excluded; or else, study men first, and then, if you can afford it, include the women also. Doubtless there is more to this decision than meets the eye. She probably focused on men's reactions because most of the characters in the Western movies are men. Thus, the exclusion of women is an example of what we called above inadvertent exclusion because of the variables being studied, or because of distributional problems, with women simply not being well represented in the occupations being studied. However, then the question becomes, given that Western movies are often androcentric, do androcentric movies (or other forms of popular culture) justify androcentric research about them? Another point to remember is that Shively's article was published in the most prestigious journal in American sociology (the *American Sociological Review*), and she was one of only five women authors or co-authors (along with 17 men) in this issue. It is entirely possible that the reviewers (we do not know their gender, but based on past experience they were probably predominantly male) would not have looked as favorably on the article if it had been written in a more gender-neutral fashion, and it might never have been published.

Clearly the issue is complex. What do you think, through the value of hindsight and the discussion in this chapter? Would you have handled preparation of this article any differently given a limited budget, or would you have proceeded the same way Shively did?

Shively also apparently contradicts two other of Eichler's guidelines. Under the heading of "Sexism in Titles," Eichler (1988, p. 135) says, "Making titles appropriately reflect the content of a study will not solve all problems of sexism in research, but it will help make sexism visible." As an example, she says that an article entitled "The Elderly Sick Role" deals with males only, and so could be changed to something like, "The Male Elderly Sick Role". Similarly, Shively's article is entitled "Perceptions of Western Films Among American Indians and Anglos," giving the perception that it is gender inclusive when it is not. A more accurate title would be "Perceptions of Western Films Among American Indian and Anglo Males [Men]."

Another problem that Eichler examines is the very common practice of using nonparallel terms for the genders (Eichler 1988, p. 86). Examples of parallel terms are; female/male, woman/man, feminine/masculine, wife/husband, gentlemen/ladies, gals/guys, and girls/boys (if these seem "backward" to you, it is because you are accustomed to seeing the masculine term listed first (except in the case of "ladies and gentlemen"). Parallelism also exists in names and professional titles. It is very common to see women and men addressed in nonparallel ways, such as addressing Professor Betty Jones and Professor Richard Smith as "Smith and Betty" or "Professor Smith and Betty" or "Professor Smith and Ms. Jones," or saying, "The Professor came to visit, and he brought a girl with him." Not only are women's earned titles and courtesy titles often stripped from them, but also the parallel terms for women and men are mixed, as in "man and wife" (have you ever seen "woman and husband," or "the men and the girls," or "males and women," or "the men and ladies." "Man and wife" is particularly objectionable (but very common), because it emphasizes marital status for the woman but not for the man. Also a problem, as discussed previously, is the term "lady." It is widely used, although its parallel term, "gentleman," is not. Further, of all the parallel gender terms used in English, "ladies and gentleman" is virtually unique in being about the only pair where the feminine term precedes the male. In all other cases the masculine term is first (as in "husband and wife" or "guys and gals").

An example of nonparallel terms is found in Shively's (1992, p. 727) article, when she says that the Western genre is popular among "women" but she looked at "males" only. Parallel terms would be "women and men," or "females and males." An example of the correct usage of parallel terms is Williams's (1991, p. 235) use of the terms "female marines and male nurses."

Obviously Eichler's guidelines and strategy of asking ourselves questions about our research are very effective in helping us include women in our research. We are not able here to pursue Eichler's work in any more detail. Having shown its efficacy, the reader is now directed to Eichler (1988) for further discussion and many more valuable examples.

The Politics of Gender

Before turning to an analysis of other groups, it may be helpful to consider briefly the politics of gender research. Our goal in this chapter is to help readers to be sensitive to gender issues. This is an intermediate position. We certainly do not want to be insensitive, but neither need we be oversensitive, or paranoid, lest someone criticize us as "sexist." No matter how rich you become, it always seems that someone is richer. Similarly, no matter how "nonsexist" you become, there is always someone who is more "nonsexist" than you. Even people who study gender issues are not immune from sexist technicalities. Although the generic "he" is avoided in this book in favor of "he and she," there are those who would advocate alternating the term which appears first (such as "she or he"; then "he or she"), or randomizing terms (see Eichler 1988). Others would advocate using coined terms such as "s/he" (not in the dictionary), or using the generic "she."

Williams (1991, p. 226) warns against collapsing the sex-gender distinction. Yet how can we really do this without constantly referring to "masculine persons" and "feminine persons"? Williams (1991, pp. 226–27) does not do this, but refers to "men and women" and "females and males." The question I am raising is, how can a writer clearly convey to readers that *gender* rather than sex is being discussed, short of constantly using the terms "masculine" and "feminine"? Does reference to females and males always connote sex (rather than gender), and is the use of "men and women" sufficiently different from "males and females" to connote gender? These are difficult questions and they need not be answered definitively. Another possible complication is age of the persons referred to, as "men" and "women" connote maturity, while "males" and "females" do not. In the rather infrequent instances where children are the research subjects (see the discussion later in this chapter), males and females may be the more appropriate terms for them, rather than men and women. Rather, the goal should be to be sufficiently sensitive to issues of sex and gender, but to not let "political correctness" drive you to absurd or nonefficacious positions or practices.

Racial Groups: Including the "Hyphenated-Americans"

Modern society is filled with a variety of identifiable racial and ethnic groups, and these will be the next focus of our discussion. Some persons think that a country such as America should be a "melting pot," where immigrants become homogenized into a common culture with a common language, and with similar beliefs and behaviors. Others favor a pluralistic society, where various groups can peacefully coexist while each group retains its original language and culture. Regardless of your views on this, it is clear that many identifiable groups exist in contemporary society, and researchers must be sensitive to the need to include groups not only on the basis of gender but also according to race and ethnicity.

We discussed gender first because women are often excluded from research, and because women are members of every racial group. Elsewhere (Bailey 1990, 1994a) I have identified sex and race, along with age (date of birth) as "immutable" characteristics. This means that, relatively speaking, they are unchangeable, in comparison to "mutable" characteristics of individuals, such as education, occupation, or residence. In reality, all groups exhibit some mutable and immutable features. Sex can be changed (through surgery), and race can be socially constructed (as when an individual decides his or her racial self-identification). Further, different racial groups certainly have different "mutable" cultures.

For the vast majority of persons, however, sex (and gender), race, and age are immutable. We can cross-dress, color our hair (or even our skin), wear wigs, and dress "younger" or "older," but for the most part we will die with the same sex (gender), race, and birth date that we were born with. Thus, for all practical purposes, these are immutables. These can be contrasted with mutables such as our religion, political affiliation, or occupation, which many of us will change (perhaps several times).

Returning to our distinction of insider/outsider, remember that we are defining insiders as the group in power (predominantly older, white men). Immutable characteristics are crucial in power relations, because power-holders can use them to identify outsiders (such as women and blacks) quickly, and to exclude them or discriminate against them. The excluded then have little recourse, because they are ultimately unable to alter their immutable characteristics in such a way as to avoid exclusion or to make themselves into "insiders."

Our task here is to figure out how the traditionally excluded racial and ethnic groups, such as blacks, American Indians, Hispanics, Asian-Americans, and others, can be included appropriately in social science research. Unfortunately, while there has been a great deal published about various racial and ethnic groups, there has been very little (almost nothing) published about our particular topic—including these groups in research studies. Bear in mind that in our discussion of women we were not discussing how to study women alone, but how to *include* them in nonsexist studies that analyze both men and women together.

Similarly, here, for example, we are not discussing the literature on black studies (which is large), but the literature on how blacks may be best included, along with other groups, in a nonracist research study (such literature is virtually nonexistent). Unfortunately, in discussing this matter with scholars who study various racial groups, I have not encountered *any* resource publications for large groups such as African-Americans, American Indians, or Asian-Americans. The only source that I have seen is for Hispanics, Marin and Marin's (1991) *Research with Hispanic Populations*.

The paucity of literature on the process of including ethnic and racial groups in social science research, though a handicap, need not deter us. We have posed our list of disadvantages of research for outsiders in such a way that these seven disadvantages can be used as a checklist of things to avoid in research on any group, including ethnic and racial groups, and including those groups that we will be unable to discuss in this chapter. We shall apply these seven factors to the study of racial and ethnic groups, and will then see how our study of including women can be generalized to racial and ethnic groups as well.

1. *Exclusion.* As with women, racial groups are often excluded from social research. There are a variety of reasons. As with women, these groups may be the object of bias on the part of researchers or may be simply invisible or underrepresented in the published literature. Thus, researchers searching the published literature for inspiration on needed research will not have a precedent of research on the group to guide them. One difference from women, though, is that ethnic or racial groups may be invisible because they are newly arrived in this country.

2. *Perpetuation of stereotypes.* Racial groups may be even more prone to stereotyping than are women. The researcher must be careful to ensure that all concepts, hypotheses, and variables referring to the outsider group are indeed derived from legitimate research concerns and not from stereotypes. This may be a particular problem if the group has such a history of exclusion that there is little or no research on it.

3. *Failure to acknowledge internal group diversity.* Like women, racial and ethnic group members come in all sizes, shapes, and ages, and with a diversity of beliefs, interests, skills, and behaviors. The researcher should be careful not to diminish these internal differences, either through theoretical formulation or statistical analysis.

4. *Exaggeration of insider-outsider differences.* If you are a researcher, it makes no difference that your grandparents are convinced that "those people are different—they are not like us." You have an obligation as a social researcher to ensure that your research measures differences between groups as accurately as possible. These differences should not be exaggerated or diminished. Again, in order to ensure this, you will probably have to make a concentrated effort in all phases of the research project, from hypothesis formulation and coding through data analysis.

5. *Bias.* As a product of her or his culture, the researcher can be expected to have racial biases along with everyone else (see the discussion of "value-free" and "value-full" sociology in chapter 2). Again, however, the researcher has an obligation to do whatever she or he can to diminish the influence of these biases. One technique is to follow Eichler's strategy of asking yourself questions about your own questionnaire. After you write your questionnaire, for example, you can choose a question and rewrite it, substituting another group for the original group. If the revised question is now untrue, ask yourself whether this is due to real differences in the two groups or to your bias. If you have deeply ingrained, repressed, or subconscious biases, you probably will not be able to evaluate them reliably yourself. In this case it will be helpful to have colleagues and members of the group to be studied review the questions in advance and tell you if they think bias is present.

One of the biggest problems of bias that confronts us is the domination of social science by "dead, white European males." To put it another way, you have probably heard many times about the "founding fathers" of sociology such as Durkheim, Weber, or Marx. But how many "founding mothers" of sociology have you ever heard of? Not only was classical sociology dominated by men, but this remains so today, with few women or minorities represented either among the theorists who formulate hypotheses for studies or the methodologists who design and execute studies and analyze the data.

6–7. *Poor study design and poor study execution.* As noted earlier, if a group has been long neglected and excluded, with no prior studies to use as models, a researcher may simply not be able to design and execute a satisfactory study. As noble as the goal of inclusion is, in such a case it may be better simply to abort the study. In some cases perhaps a knowledgeable researcher or member of the excluded group can save the study. If no such person is available, no study at all will be better than a study whose results are damaging to the group being studied.

Generalizing from Nonsexist to Nonracist Studies

There are some clear points of overlap between procedures for achieving both nonsexist and nonracist studies. Let us briefly review the guidelines provided by Eichler (1988) for nonsexist methods to see how we can generalize from these to racial groups. One thing we learned from Eichler is that general titles are often used for research dealing with only one gender. Similarly, general titles are often used for research on a single race. An example is Connell's (1992) article entitled "A Very Straight Gay: Masculinity, Homosexual Experience, and the Dynamics of Gender." Since the title implies that only males are studied, it is not necessary to specify sex. But what about race? Perusal of the article shows that the results are based on a study of eight men in Sydney, Australia. No mention is given of their race, so I presume all are white. A more accurate title might be, "A Very Straight Gay: Masculinity, Homosexual Experience, and the Dynamics of Gender Among White Australians."

We also learned from Eichler that sexual terms are often used in a nonparallel fashion. This is common for racial and ethnic terms as well. It is even common to use gender terms in a racist manner, such as referring to dominant males as "men" and racially subordinate males as "boys." Common parallel racial names are Negro/Caucasian, black/white, and African-American/Anglo-American. Another curious form of nonparallel terminology is seen in Williams's (1991, p. 230) article where she refers to "white men and white women" but capitalizes "black," referring to "Black men and white women, or between white men and Black women." This may be "politically correct," but it is not stylistically correct.

We also saw earlier that male dominance (androcentricity) was a major problem in the study of gender. If we specify "old, white, European males," this is a problem for the study of racial and ethnic groups as well. As long as the white male European viewpoint is dominant, other groups will continue to be "outsiders."

Discontinuities Between Race and Gender

Clearly, much of what we learned about including women can be applied to including ethnic and racial groups as well. However, there are some distinct differences between studying gender and studying racial and ethnic groups that must be noted here.

1. *Physical and social distance.* Although the world may be male-dominated, females and males interact frequently. It is the rare man who does not have frequent contact with women.

Thus, the male researcher, even if he is a confirmed sexist, is probably accustomed to dealing with women.

This may not be the case for research on racial and ethnic groups. Many researchers, although they profess to be "liberal," may have had little experience dealing with members of excluded groups. This can lead to the problems of poor study design and execution noted above.

2. *Language.* We have noted the role that language plays in including women in research. A male researcher may find his study compromised if he addresses his female subjects by the wrong term, or even if he uses nonparallel language forms. Further, there may be some "women's language" that he does not know. However, language problems are usually minimal when the task is to include women in research.

This may not be the case when attempting to include racial and ethnic groups. Here the researcher may encounter foreign languages or dialects and slang. This can be a severe impediment, necessitating translation of questionnaires, for example.

Research with Hispanic Populations

We shall now turn to the analysis of the particular group for which there is some literature, the Hispanic population. Fortunately, the book by Marin and Marin (1991) serves us as a guide, much in the same manner that Eichler's (1988) book does for women. Although the authors deal with a number of issues, focus is on the two points just discussed: translating languages and learning the culture.

Identification of research subjects can be a major problem, even for a Hispanic research, as there is so much diversity in this population. Although Marin and Marin (1991) use the term "Hispanic," they note that there is not total agreement on this word within the community. In general, we are talking about the Spanish-speaking community in the United States, who primarily come from Mexico, Cuba, Puerto Rico, or Central and South America. However, some Mexican-Americans no longer speak Spanish, some Spanish-speaking people come from Europe (Spain), and some from Central and South America may speak English (Belize) or Portuguese (Brazil).

"Hispanic" is a term coined by the United States Office of Management and Budget in 1978 to operationalize the label as "a person of Mexican, Puerto Rican, Cuban, Central or South American or other Spanish culture of origin, regardless of race" (Marin and Marin, 1991, p. 20). As noted by them (pp. 21–23), many persons prefer the terms "Latino," Chicano," or "Raza." A particular problem with the first two is that the "o" ending denotes masculinity in Spanish, so we are back to a sexist designation that once again renders the feminine gender invisible, unless we write the terms as "Latino or Latina," "Chicano/a," or something of the sort. The tendency is to do as Marin and Marin (1991, pp. 21–22) do, and speak only of Latino, thus making women invisible. We must be careful not to exclude one group (women) in the process of including another (Hispanics). In other words, we must include all Hispanics, not just Hispanic men.

Even when the problems of identification are solved, non-Hispanic researchers may have difficulty gaining access to the Hispanic community. Marin and Marin (1991, pp. 42–65) note that Hispanics could be expected to be more wary of researchers from other groups for a variety of reasons (such as fear of being turned over to immigration authorities if they are in the country illegally). See Marin and Marin for suggestions on various aspects of access to the Hispanic community, including becoming familiar with the community, establishing legitimacy, obtaining community sponsorship, and informing the community about the study (also see chapters 5–8 of this volume).

Marin and Marin (1991, p. 60) provide the following five suggestions for a successful study of Hispanics (which in many cases can be generalized to other ethnic and racial groups as well: (1) Ethnic minority respondents should be able to choose the language in which the study is to be conducted; (2) researchers and subjects should be of the same ethnicity (see the discussion in chapter 8); (3) minority research participants should be compensated; (4) complex scales or questions should be carefully pretested and explained to respondents; and (5) the usual survey approaches seem equally useful and appropriate for Hispanics. Telephone surveys are economical and may be better for sensitive or personal topics.

Marin and Marin (1991, pp. 87–88) also provide detailed instructions for researchers needing to translate their questionnaires from English to Spanish (or some other language). Among their recommendations are: Use simple (approximately third-grade level) English; words with Latin roots are easier to translate (for example, use "abundant" rather than "plentiful"; use nouns rather than pronouns; avoid metaphors and colloquialisms (such as "awesome"); use specific rather than general terms ("ducks" rather than "fowl"); use short and simple sentences (fewer than 16 words); use the active rather than the passive; avoid possessive forms, the subjunctive, adverbs and prepositions telling where and when; and avoid sentences with two different verbs.

In addition to these guidelines, there are variations in how the actual translation is done. The four chief forms discussed by Marin and Marin (1991, pp. 88–95) are one-way translation, translation by committee, double (two-way) translation, and decentering. The one-way is the simplest form, with a single translator translating the questionnaire from English to Spanish, for example. This technique is not recommended, as errors are frequent. The committee technique (also one-way) entails having two or more persons translate independently, and then checking the results. The preferred technique is double translation, where one person translates from English into Spanish, and then a different person translates back from Spanish into English. This is basically a form of replication. If the final result is not the same as the original questionnaire, then errors have been made, and the Spanish version must be corrected.

Decentering is a form of double translation in which corrections are made not only to the Spanish version, but also to the original English version (a form of pretesting). That is, if you write an original question in English that does not translate well into Spanish, you may decide that the Spanish version is better and change your English question to match the Spanish question, rather than vice versa. After the translation is completed, its accuracy can be tested by a number of translation probes. These probes include field pretests, checks by bilingual persons, and performance checks, where respondents are asked to perform some behavior (for further discussion, see Marin and Marin 1991).

Marin and Marin also discuss problems in data interpretation. One problem is extreme response sets (see chapters 6–8), with Hispanics (and also African-Americans) said to choose extreme responses more often than non-Hispanic whites (see Marin and Marin 1991, pp. 101–3). As the authors say, in four large data sets that they studied,

... Hispanics consistently preferred extreme responses to a greater extent than did non-Hispanic whites. Hispanics chose extreme responses to as many as 72% of the questions in one of the data sets (Marin and Marin 1991, p. 102).

The authors report some evidence that this is a culture- specific response pattern, as the more acculturated Hispanics show less tendency to extreme responses than the less acculturated.

Related issues are acquiescence response sets (*yea-saying,* or agreeing with everything), giving socially desirable responses, inaccurate reporting of behaviors (such as underreporting negative behaviors), incomplete answers, and unwillingness for self-disclosure. There is some evidence that Hispanics may have higher rates than non-Hispanic whites on all of these. However, data are limited, and there may be variability with education and acculturation. For further discussion on how to deal with these problems, and for other aspects of studying Hispanic populations, please see Marin and Marin (1991).

Including "Deviant" Groups: Mutable or Immutable?

We are now ready to discuss means of including groups whose very identity is much more controversial and concealed. In the cases of sex/gender and race and ethnicity just discussed, there may be quibbling over the proper term to be used (women versus females or Hispanic versus Latina/Latino), but for the vast majority of group members, their basic identity is accepted by both insiders and outsiders.

This is not the case for some other groups. These groups are often considered to be "deviant," and there is great disagreement over what causes the condition for group membership, how to define it, and whether it is immutable ("nature") or behavioral and social ("mutable"). We can focus on two common examples of this type, alcoholics and homosexuals. While there have been many studies of both groups, they are often excluded from "mainstream" research, and indeed from society as a whole. Further, their behavior is generally considered to be "deviant" by sociologists. As an example, Connell's (1992) study of gay men, already discussed, was published in the *American Sociological Review* under the heading "Three Studies of Deviant Careers." The other two studies dealt with criminality and misconduct. Should we infer that gay men are also guilty of misconduct?

A basic problem in including both alcoholics and homosexuals in mainstream research studies is that we have no census of either. Neither is considered a group in the United States Census. The customary procedure is to estimate the population of each group as a percentage of the American population. Thus, homosexuals are said to approximate 10 percent of the population, and alcoholics about six or seven percent. These figures, based on survey data, are very tentative.

The 10 percent figure for homosexuality was widely accepted for some 45 years, after being presented by the Kinsey (1948) report in 1948. It was challenged in 1993 by a federally funded survey conducted by the Alan Guttmacher Institute (Rensberger 1993). The newer findings showed that only 2.3 percent of American men respondents in their twenties and thirties admitted having sex with another man, while only 1.1 percent reported being exclusively homosexual. In contrast, the median number of female sex partners reported was 7.3, with 20 percent of men saying that they had 20 or more partners and only 4.6 percent saying they had never had vaginal intercourse.

It does not take a sociological genius to determine that the normative or "socially desirable" way for a young man to answer such questions is to underreport homosexual experience (or remain "in the closet") while overreporting heterosexual experience. Thus the best guess is that the estimates of homosexuality are somewhat too low, while the responses concerning heterosexual experience are too high.

We also have no census to tell us how many alcoholics exist and must depend on estimates from surveys. Many alcoholics that have stopped drinking belong to Alcoholics Anonymous. This group estimated its worldwide membership at over 1,000,000 in 1988 (Alcoholics Anonymous, 1976, 31st printing, 1988, p. xxii) including more than 73,000 groups in more than 114 countries, with almost one-third being women and about one-fifth being 30 or under. However, AA keeps no formal membership lists. Further, these figures exclude all the alcoholics who are still drinking (the "practicing alcoholics").

Notice that the fact that we do not know how many alcoholics or homosexuals there are makes them quite different from the other groups we have studied. Further, it is often difficult to identify members of these groups. But one of the biggest problems in studying these two groups (and others such as drug addicts) is the controversy over whether the conditions of alcoholism and homosexuality are immutable (meaning that members cannot control their identity and/or behavior), or mutable, meaning that the alcoholic or homosexual is defined behaviorally, and that this is subject to individual control and will. It is interesting that there is controversy among alcoholics and homosexuals themselves, as well as between their critics and their supporters who are nonalcoholic and nonhomosexual, over this point.

Many (but not all) alcoholics seem to believe that they "were born alcoholic," while many (but not all) homosexuals seem to believe that they were "born homosexual." While there are many nonalcoholics and heterosexuals who agree that alcoholics and/or homosexuals were "born that way," both groups have strong foes, often the religious "right wing" of politically conservative persons who believe that alcoholism and/or homosexuality is largely behavioral. They believe that this behavior is chosen by the individual (just like smoking) and is sinful. They believe that such behavior often shows the individual to be "weak-willed," although foes also may think that alcoholism and homosexuality are learned behaviors, which are taught by people who "recruit" other people to their "cause," just as they might be recruited into a cult.

There are a number of fascinating parallels between these two groups which are not generally recognized: (1) as noted above, members of both groups often think they were born that way; (2) both groups have been characterized in terms of "disease"; (3) members of both groups are often characterized as "practicing" or not (as in "practicing alcoholic" or "practicing homosexual"); (4) both groups (at least the "practicing" members) are seen as engaging in behavior that is wicked, sinful, deviant, or perverted (and in fact may be illegal); (5) both groups are often discriminated against, even to the extent that physical violence against them may be accepted, as in the practices of "rolling drunks" or "bashing queers": and (6) members of both groups may deny their characteristics not only to others but to themselves as well.

Despite the similarities between the two groups, there are at least two major differences between alcoholics and homosexuals that affect a researcher's ability to include them in research: (1) Alcoholics (particularly members of Alcoholics Anonymous) are likely to endorse the notion that alcoholism is a disease, while homosexuals are more likely to dispute the notion that homosexuality is a disease; and (2) homosexuals are politically organized in a "gay rights movement," while there is no real "alcoholic rights movement," and in fact Alcoholics Anonymous is steadfastly nonpolitical.

Alcoholics

While it is relatively simple to conduct a small study such as an experiment on a few alcoholics, large-scale studies of alcoholics such as national samples are not only nonexistent but in some ways nearly impossible. One of the chief difficulties in surveying alcoholics is the extremely high level of denial, not only among alcoholics themselves but among their families as well. Another problem is that members of AA believe that they are "bodily and mentally different" from nonalcoholics (Alcoholics Anonymous 1976). This means that many alcoholics have little faith that nonalcoholic researchers can ever "really understand" what it is like to be alcoholic.

The result of denial is that if an interviewer asks a practicing alcoholic respondent if he or she is an alcoholic, the answer will often be "no." Sometimes this is a normative or socially desirable answer, with the person knowing that he or she is alcoholic but not wanting to admit it to the interviewer. Often, however, the alcoholic has not yet admitted to himself or herself that he or she is an alcoholic. Many people came to AA not believing that they are really alcoholics. As it says in the book, "Most of us have been unwilling to admit we were real alcoholics. No person likes to think he is bodily and mentally different from his fellows" (Alcoholics Anonymous 1976, p. 30).

This denial means that only a relatively few practicing alcoholics may be self-identified. This means that the only way for a researcher to identify the population of alcoholics (for example, for purposes of constructing a sampling frame—see chapter 5), is to search for people who have been labeled as alcoholics by the medical or legal profession. This is quite unsatisfactory.

If a researcher wants alcoholics who are not in denial, the place to go is AA. Members of this "twelve step" program will usually admit that they are alcoholics, because the first step entails such an admission. The irony is that these people generally are not drinking. Thus, the people who are drinking alcoholically say they are not alcoholics, while sober people who never drink say they are. This means that the people whom many nonalcoholics see as alcoholic say in surveys that they are not, while the people whom nonalcoholics see as "former alcoholics" say in surveys that they are alcoholics. Members of AA see alcoholism as a lifelong ailment, with a reprieve based on their spiritual condition. To put it another way, there can be a clear dichotomy here between identity and behavior, with many who have an alcoholic identity not practicing the drinking behavior, and those without the identity drinking alcoholically. This is truly a challenge for survey researchers. Ethnographers may find the study of alcoholism a little easier, as they may be able to observe the drinking behavior.

Suffice it to say that alcoholics are difficult to identify and may be difficult for a nonalcoholic researcher to understand. Further, identification is confounded by the fact that many people who drink are not alcoholics, and there seems to be a fine line between "heavy social drinkers" and alcoholics. Further, members of Alcoholics Anonymous are generally reluctant to label anyone else as an alcoholic, feeling that self-identification is vital to an alcoholic's recovery. Besides, today many people are "dually addicted" to both drugs and alcohol, and sometimes a respondent may identify as an alcoholic when in reality he or she uses drugs much more than alcohol. For all these reasons, the study of alcoholism (especially in large surveys) has lagged. It is definitely a worthy topic for study, but researchers should be aware of the problems involved and should seek input from alcoholics and from experts in alcoholism.

Homosexuals

Probably the majority of homosexuals today resist the disease label. Many admit to having emotional difficulties but often attribute them to discrimination and homophobia. As with alcoholics, many homosexuals remain in denial (both to themselves and to others) for years, and some for a lifetime. American homosexuals are not allowed to marry each other and thus are denied legal property rights, such as spousal inheritance. Further, they are often attacked physically or verbally and may suffer job or housing discrimination. There have been ballot measures in several states to restrict their rights (see chapter 1). They may also be blamed for spreading Acquired Immune Deficiency Syndrome (AIDS).

In view of all of these factors, it is not surprising that homosexuals may be reluctant to identify themselves as such in face-to-face interviews. According to Rensberger (1993), commenting on the Guttmacher survey:

> Robert Bray, a spokesman for the National Gay and Lesbian Task Force, said nobody really knows how many homosexuals there are, but he challenged the study's figures as too low. Bray said many gay men are reluctant to identify themselves as homosexual to interviewers.

The true number of homosexuals is an issue not only for researchers but also of political interest. Conservative opponents of gay rights can seize upon a low estimate of the number of homosexuals to bolster their argument that a very small number of individuals are seeking disproportionate rights and privileges. An assumption that the number of homosexuals is relatively small, along with the fact that many remain "in the closet," allows homophobic persons to continue their "presumption of heterosexuality," whereby sometimes even flagrantly homosexual persons are assumed to be heterosexual (that is, the whole world is assumed to be heterosexual). Estimates of a large homosexual population, along with organized marches such as the 1993 march in Washington, D.C., make it difficult for homophobic people to maintain the illusion that almost everyone is heterosexual. As an example, commenting on the reaction to the 1993 gay rights march, Boxall (1993) says:

> "I'm scared," admitted a woman from Baltimore as she stood with her husband watching chanting, smiling gays and lesbians stream by hour after hour. "I didn't realize there were so many. It scares me to see so many of them . . . It's unbelievable to see how much they've organized."

There are a number of reasons why homosexuals may be reluctant to self-identify in face-to-face interviews: (1) Some probably deny to themselves that they are homosexual. Just as not

all who drink are alcoholics, not all who have had homosexual experiences consider themselves to have a homosexual identity (in the Guttmacher study discussed above, note that 2.3
percent of respondents admitted sex with another man, but only 1.1 percent reported being
exclusively homosexual—the remaining 1.2 percent might identify themselves as heterosexual or bisexual); (2) some respondents may feel guilt about being homosexual and are ashamed
to admit it to an interviewer; and (3) some fear retaliation, loss of privacy, physical violence,
loss of job or home, and so forth.

Some of these nonresponse problems can surely be alleviated with mailed questionnaires,
telephone interviews, or computer surveys. However, beyond the problems of personal interviews, there are characteristics of specific studies which may greatly affect the percentage of
respondents admitting homosexual acts or identifying themselves as homosexuals. A potential
problem with the Guttmacher study is that the respondents are so young (in their twenties and
thirties) that a large proportion of their sexually active life was lived during the years of AIDS.
This is a time when persons in the heterosexual community, but especially in the homosexual
community, were warned to be celibate, curtail sexual activity, and practice "safe sex." An
unknown number of persons probably heeded these warnings and reduced their homosexual
activity. Others are undoubtedly more reluctant to identify themselves as homosexuals for fear
of being blamed for spreading AIDS. That may be especially true for bisexuals, who are vulnerable to accusations that they spread AIDS from the homosexual to the heterosexual communities. Still another acute problem with self-identification of homosexuality in surveys is
the matter of question wording. Some respondents may identify as "gay," others as "homosexual," others as "bisexual." Failure to provide the label that the respondent identifies with could
further lower the number identified as homosexual. The Kinsey study was very thorough and
allowed for a number of intermediate categories (a continuum) of homosexuality. It appears to
remain the best estimate of the number of homosexuals, although the number may well be
somewhere between the 10 percent reported by Kinsey and the 2 to 3 percent reported in other
studies.

Lesbians and Gay Men

I have been writing about homosexuality in as generic a fashion as possible (although the
survey data discussed above were from a sample of males only). Thus, most of the discussion
so far applies equally well to males, females, and bisexuals. However, it is helpful to focus
briefly on each of these. Let us first consider the problems of studying lesbians. Lesbians, like
heterosexual women, face the problem of sexism. But for lesbians, this can occur both inside
and outside the homosexual community. Although Lesbians and homosexual men in general
cooperate quite well in the political rights movement, there is sometimes friction in terms of
charges of sexism or emphasis on male priorities. Further, researchers wishing to follow
Eichler's (1988) suggestions strictly and to use parallel gender terms will find challenges in
studying the homosexual community.

The biggest problem in maintaining parallel gender language is that there seems to be no
parallel male term that is the equivalent of the term "lesbian." If homosexual men had a term
of their own, it could be used in parallel with lesbian, as in lesbians and XXXXXXs. Since

there seems to be no parallel term for lesbian, we are stuck with only two parallel gender pairs: homosexual women and homosexual men; and gay women and gay men. Both seem generally acceptable, with the latter (gay) probably being generally preferred as a self-identification to the more clinical and formal "homosexual." The biggest problem here is that standardization of these terms would deprive women of the self-determination evident in the term "lesbian" and so would be widely opposed for that reason.

Another problem with "gay" is that many writers do not seem to know whether it is a noun or an adjective. It is commonly seen both ways. In the quote recently cited (Rensberger 1993), Bray spoke of "gay men," using the term as an adjective. But in Boxall's (1993) article, the term is used quite differently, as a noun, and in parallel with "lesbian," as in "gay and lesbian goals." Which is correct? According to *Webster's Dictionary*, "gay" means "homosexual," whereas "lesbian" is a noun meaning "a female homosexual." Thus, I suppose as in "the gays" (meaning either or both males and females), that one could use "gay" as a gender-neutral noun, or as an adjective, as in "gay women and gay men." However, Webster's definition would seem to preclude using it as a noun meaning "male homosexual," so it should not be used in parallel with "lesbian," as in "gay and lesbian." To clarify, "gay men and lesbians" would be correct in terms of meaning (but not parallel), while "gays and lesbians" would be incorrect, leaving both "gay women and gay men" and "homosexual women and homosexual men" as correct and parallel (but omitting the gender-specific term "lesbian"). Also, both "homosexuals" and "gays" would seem to be correct as gender-neutral (or gender-nonspecific) terms referring to women or men or both. I would guess that most women would prefer in this case to sacrifice the parallel language and to stick with "lesbians and gay men."

Although united in their homosexuality, the lesbian and gay men's communities are obviously very distinct in terms of their sexual practices. The ramifications of this fact are that some common statements about the homosexual community can often be seen not only as homophobic but as sexist (androcentric) as well. A case in point is the common statement that homosexuality is a sin, and AIDS is punishment for this sin. That is supposedly based on the assumption that rates of AIDS are higher in the "homosexual community" than in the heterosexual community. In fact, this is *not* true for all homosexuals. Male homosexuals have a higher rate of AIDS than the heterosexual community, but female homosexuals have distinctly *lower* rates (excluding intravenous drug users) than do heterosexual women or men. Logic would dictate that if gay men are being punished with AIDS for their behavior, lesbians are being rewarded for their homosexual activity with lower rates of AIDS (probably not the conclusion that homophobic persons would like to publicize).

Bisexuals

Even many researchers who feel that they are sensitive to the need for inclusionary research probably exclude some groups in their own relationships. Lesbians and heterosexual men exclude men as lovers, while gay men and heterosexual women exclude women. It is only the bisexuals (both women and men) who are truly inclusionary, viewing both women and men as lovers. However, I think it would be safe to argue that bisexuals are the largest "invisible" group in America. As with alcoholics and homosexuals, probably no one knows how many bisexuals there are.

Politically, bisexuals are in a problematic position. While lesbians and gay men can "come out of the closet," bisexuals (when I use this term I shall refer to both women and men) often feel caught in a "double closet," where they must "come out" to both the homosexual and the heterosexual communities. Many bisexuals feel that heterosexuals identify them as homosexual, while homosexuals identify them as heterosexual, homosexual, or "undecided." Claiming to be bisexual is often viewed in the homosexual community (and also among some heterosexuals and psychologists as well) as being an excuse for homosexuals in "partial denial" who are too fearful to admit their homosexuality fully, so admit it "halfway" by claiming to be bisexual. For this reason, some bisexuals misrepresent their identity as homosexual to avoid being labeled as "politically incorrect."

Because of their invisibility, bisexuals pose the ultimate challenge for researchers, especially survey researchers attempting to determine the number of bisexuals that exist. While ethnographers can easily study bisexuals in small numbers, and samples of them can be constructed through snowball sampling techniques (see chapter 5), researchers desiring to get a census of bisexuals or simply to sample them in large numbers will probably be frustrated.

Including Persons with Disabilities

Another group of persons that may be excluded from research includes persons who are physically or mentally ill or impaired in some fashion. This includes the blind, deaf, mentally retarded, autistic, people confined to wheelchairs, cancer and heart disease patients, AIDS patients, crime victims, and many others. In some cases, including such people may be very straightforward and may only involve adapting to their disabilities. In other cases, it may require extreme expense and effort. Though ill people may not be explicitly labeled as deviant, they often will be stigmatized. Doubtless some ill people feel abused and frustrated, if for no other reason than that they, like the groups already discussed, are often excluded and made to feel invisible.

Common sense will tell the researcher what to do in many cases. Blind people, for example, could even be included in mailed-questionnaire studies through the use of braille questionnaires. In most cases it would be preferable, however, to reach them through personal interviews or telephone interviews. While deaf people cannot be reached through regular telephone equipment, they can be interviewed with special equipment or with mailed-questionnaires.

How can a researcher find persons in these excluded groups? It may be possible to identify persons with disabilities the same way as other groups. It is possible that lists of persons obtained through hospitals, charities, or self-help groups can be used to construct sampling frames.

Once an interview is obtained, the interviewer may sometimes need to show special sensitivity to the needs of the respondents. Attention spans may be short, special explanation or illustrative materials may be required, or the interview may have to be interrupted because the respondent is experiencing stress or pain or needs to take medication, or for some other reason. Robin (1993) recalls her experience in interviewing patients in a cardiac unit in the course of her research on pain. While she was interviewing, her respondent noticed that his heart monitor had "flat-lined," indicating, in effect, that he had died. This understandably caused him some stress and was distracting, leading to some interruption of the interview. It turned out that the wire to the monitor had simply become unplugged, and the interview was resumed in due course.

As with the other groups studied in this chapter, the researcher must be sensitive to the terms used to label group members. Fortunately, here the terminology does not seem to present the gender confusion that we encountered in attempting to include ethnic and racial groups and homosexuals. Here the chief problem is that, as with other excluded groups, there is some sensitivity about the proper label to be applied. There are a variety of extant terms including disabled, invalid, handicapped, visually impaired, blind, hearing-impaired, deaf, mentally impaired, physically impaired, crippled, and so forth. Group members may object to some of these terms (for example, they may feel that "handicapped" is too negative, as they simply have a physical problem to deal with, but are not otherwise "handicapped" in competing with other people). Since there are such a wide variety of conditions and applicable terms, it probably behooves the researcher to conduct a careful preliminary study in order to determine which terms the respondents will accept. It may prove beneficial to eschew general terms such as "handicapped" or "disabled" for specific terms applicable to the group you are studying, such as "persons in wheelchairs."

Including Children in Research

Interviewing Children

There are a number of interesting research areas (e.g., early childhood socialization, development of racial awareness and prejudice) in which it is necessary or at least helpful to gather data from children. However, there are at least three basic problems that must be dealt with by the researcher wishing to interview young children: (1) the child's limited vocabulary and ability to understand abstract concepts; (2) the child-adult role relationship; and (3) the child's lack of understanding of the interview situation and short attention span.

Language Skills

There has been general reluctance to use direct interviewing with preschool children (under six years old), based presumably on the assumption that children of this age possess insufficient language skills to understand and respond adequately. However, those studies that have been done indicate that direct interviewing (obviously with a somewhat limited vocabulary) can be accomplished successfully with four-year olds (Yarrow 1960, p. 564). Two- and three-year-olds can often be successfully interviewed by using props such as pictures they can point to or dolls that they can play with and answer questions about. Interviewing children under two years of age is very difficult (unless they are intellectually gifted), as the average total vocabulary of a two-year-old is 200 words (Yarrow 1960, p. 563). Furthermore, these 200 words do not include abstractions or multidimensional concepts that the social scientist might wish to study.

In part because of the paucity of language skills, there is often a high refusal rate among very young children (56 percent among two-year-olds versus only 10 percent among five-year-olds in a study by Ammons [1950]). Another problem is that about 30 percent of the responses by two-year-olds are incomprehensible, while by age three and one-half virtually all responses are comprehensible (Yarrow 1960). A researcher wishing to ensure that the words he or she uses are understood by young children should begin by consulting educators and a standard list of words for preschool and school-age children, such as the International Kindergarten Union (1928) list or *A Combined Word List* (Buckingham and Dolch 1936).

The Child-Adult Relationship

We have discussed the formal nature of the social relationship between interviewer and respondent. When interviewing children (unless children are used as interviewers, which is uncommon and generally not feasible), the nature of the role relationship between interviewer and respondent can be of even greater importance than when both respondent and interviewer are adults. The child, especially if he or she is very young, may perceive all adults as parent or teacher figures and may not understand the interviewer's role as clearly as most adults would. Further, the child might consider it strange that an adult would come to him or her for information, as he or she may feel that all adults know far more than any child. He or she may believe the interviewer is trying to trick or test him or her by asking questions to which every adult already knows the answers.

There is often considerable testing out of adults among children of three to five years old. They may tease, delay their answers, refuse to answer, or deliberately give incorrect answers. Preschool children can be particularly sensitive and shy with strangers and may require a good deal of attention from the interviewer. The interviewer must be able to provide that attention, yet at the same time attempt to retain the role of neutral investigator and not suggest an answer, for young children may be much more suggestible than adults. Many young children have wild imaginations. They have imaginary siblings or friends whose exploits they report, and may also tell outrageous stories about animals or objects. The interviewer must be careful not to allow a child's imagination to run wild (or at least to discern when this is happening).

While preschool children often think aloud but have trouble communicating, children of about seven years old have good verbal skills but often are reluctant to reveal their attitudes and feelings to adults. This is considered by clinicians to be a normal developmental phenomenon (Yarrow 1960, p. 156). Another possible problem in interviewing children in middle childhood (approximately seven up to twelve years old) is that boys of this age may profess a dislike for girls. There is no adequate documentation of a similarly widespread pattern for girls of this age. Such dislike of the opposite sex may indicate that interviewers of the same sex as the respondent will be more successful (especially if the respondent is male), but the findings on this issue are contradictory. In some cases female interviewers have done as well as male interviewers in interviewing young boys; in other cases female interviewers have had less success than males.

The Interview Situation

One reason the very young child often sees all adults as either parents or teachers is that, with the exception of family friends and relatives, he or she may have had no contact with adults in any other role. Similarly, a child who has never encountered adult strangers in a setting other than school, day-care centers (which are schools to him or her), or the doctor's office will generally not understand the interview situation. He or she often will not comprehend the nature of the surroundings or why he or she was placed in the situation, will not understand the interviewer's role, and will not know what behavior is expected of him or her.

If the respondent were an adult, the interviewer would explain the purpose of the study and ask for the respondent's cooperation. Preschool children probably cannot understand such an appeal, although a limited appeal stated in simple terms might be partially successful. Generally the interviewer makes no attempt to explain the purpose of the study in any detail but simply invites the child to play a game. Not only does this define the situation for the child and explain why he or she is placed in this environment (play is reason enough for a child), but it also puts him or her in a good mood. A child engrossed in a game becomes less self-conscious and gives better answers.

Interviewers using toys as ice breakers should be careful that the toy or game is not so interesting that the child forgets about the interviewer and the relationship he or she is trying to establish, or refuses to stop playing to participate in the interview. Any game used should not be too difficult for the child to master, as a frustrating experience does not facilitate interviewing. In general, there should be a relatively short time limit on play activity so that the interview may proceed.

Rather than playing a game prior to the interview, another tactic is to call the interview itself a game. This can be accomplished by using props such as pictures or dolls to ask questions. The interview may proceed by talking through toy telephones or through dolls or puppets.

Doll Play.   Doll play has been used extensively, both in therapy and in data-gathering interviews. For example, the investigator studying sibling rivalry can set up a scene containing a mother doll breast-feeding a baby doll, with another doll of the same gender as the respondent looking on. Then the investigator asks the child what he or she thinks the child doll will say and do when he or she encounters the mother and baby (Yarrow 1960, p. 584). Dolls have also been used extensively in studies of racial prejudice. For example, the researcher might produce a black doll and a white doll and ask the child which one he or she would rather play with, which is better, or which is smarter. Or, rather than asking questions, the researcher can simply observe which doll the child chooses to play with.

Pictures.   Instead of using dolls or puppets, many researchers present pictures to the child and ask questions about the pictures. In racial-prejudice studies one could present pictures of black and white children and ask which one the child would rather play with. Another technique is to present a series of alternate pictures and let the child choose the appropriate one.

Story or Sentence Completion.   For school-age children with fairly good language skills, story or sentence completion may be superior to doll play. Such completion may be entirely verbal or may be combined with dolls or pictures. One simply tells a story, leaving off the ending and asking the child to finish it. For discussion of observational research with children see Fine and Sandstrom (1988).

Including Persons with Combinations of Characteristics

Although we have discussed various groups separately and sequentially, in reality many people belong to more than one group simultaneously, as in the case of homosexual alcoholics. For example, a blind, black lesbian belongs to four excluded groups (blind people, black people, homosexuals, and women). Williams and Sjoberg (1993) in studying women of color refer to their dual status as "double jeopardy." In some cases people who are such "multiple minorities" will feel discrimination mostly from the most salient characteristic, while others will feel like minorities within minorities. We must be careful in attempting to include groups that we do not inadvertently exclude one group while including another. For example, in including blacks and homosexuals in research, researchers must be careful not to exclude women within these groups, by concentrating only upon male leaders.

The Politics of Inclusion

I should not close this chapter without some discussion of "backlash" from conservative groups who oppose the inclusion of previously excluded groups, and will actively work to keep them excluded. These opponents may particularly fight social science research that they view as attempting to "validate" or legitimate the position of the excluded groups that they oppose. I discussed deconstructionism and value-free and value-full sociology in chapter 2. Deconstructionism entails the view that dominance by white, male (often dead) Europeans must be dismantled or "deconstructed" and replaced with more inclusionary views. Deconstruction is a major tenet of postmodernism, which has been very popular and is influencing curriculum in the humanities and social sciences of many universities. Curriculum revision often entails changing courses to include more references to women, racial and ethnic groups, and (less frequently) homosexuals.

Not surprisingly, conservatives have reacted. The editors of *Executive Intelligence Review* (1993) cite the "insanity" of postmodernism and decry "political correctness." They criticize politically correct actions at Stanford University and quote Lyndon La Rouche, who objects to "banning the requirement that students study the words of 'dead, white European males.'" They quote La Rouche as also saying that "most of what we know on this planet . . . certainly depends upon the contributions (admittedly there were other contributions from other sources) of dead white European males." Another article is entitled "Without 'Dead White European Males' There Would Be No Civilization" (Klenetsky 1993).

While changes in curriculum may involve a lot of rhetoric and bickering between liberals and conservatives, inclusionary research methods can probably be pursued with a minimum of rhetoric. In many cases all they entail are common sense and a little sensitivity.

It may be that some readers have found the discussion in this chapter somewhat overwhelming or intimidating. I do not intend that a single researcher or research group can (or should) include *everyone* in a given research project. The main goal of this chapter is to show the reader what sources are available to include groups in research and to stimulate thinking about how this can be done. In some cases (as with bisexuals) researchers probably will not be able to include a group satisfactorily until it becomes more visible in the society at large. In the meantime, a sensitive and knowledgeable approach to research will suffice to minimize the number of "invisible" groups.

Assessment

How can we now evaluate the state of inclusionary research? It is clearly a mixed bag of success and failure, encouragement and discouragement. It must be acknowledged that there is currently no comprehensive or general field of inclusionary social research (although there is a related literature on curriculum revision—see M. Anderson 1988). In fact, in searching for a title for this chapter I was forced to coin the term "inclusionary research methods." Thus, there is no general literature to draw upon.

However, there is some specialized literature. As we have seen, this literature deals mostly with women (see, for example, Harding 1986, 1987; Nielsen 1990; Eichler 1988; C. Williams 1991; Williams and Sjoberg 1993), but some deals with racial and ethnic groups (see Marin and Marin 1991). Still other related literature deals with research on sensitive topics (Renzetti and Lee 1993). There are encouraging signs that women and some racial and ethnic groups are beginning to be included. Among the discouraging signs is the scant literature on ways to include racial and ethnic groups, and virtually nothing for homosexuals, alcoholics, people with disabilities, and the other groups mentioned.

Anderson (1988) presents five phases of curriculum integration. We can adapt these for social research. In phase one, social research is by, for, and about healthy, "nondeviant" (non-alcoholic and heterosexual) white males. In phase two, women nonwhites, homosexuals, drug addicts, and others are added. In phase three, such outsiders are treated as anomalies that do not fit existing theories. In phase four these previously excluded groups begin to be studied on their own terms. Phase five is fully integrated research, reflecting all of the diversity represented in this chapter, as well as the groups that could not be represented because of space limitations. Obviously in phase five a single chapter will not suffice, but rather whole volumes on inclusionary research methods will be needed.

Clearly, inclusionary research has proceeded past phase one but is nowhere near phase five. However, the most invisible groups, such as bisexuals and alcoholics, cannot be fully included in social research until the larger society at least deems them worthy of being counted, in a literal sense, so that we know how many there are.

Summary

This chapter deals with means of including previously excluded groups in research. Part of the problem is that the excluded groups, including women, racial and ethnic groups, homosexuals, alcoholics, and others, are often seen as "outsiders," while those in charge of the research process are generally "insiders." We next discussed seven disadvantages that social research can have for these outsider groups (if poorly executed), and seven corresponding advantages (if properly executed).

Discussion then turned to means of including women in research, including a discussion of seven reasons why women are often excluded, followed by eight criticisms of published research that does include women. This section ended with a discussion of specific techniques for including women.

We next turned to the inclusion of racial and ethnic groups. We saw that some of the general problems of including these groups were the same as for women, while some (such as language problems and unfamiliarity) were different. Techniques for including Hispanics were discussed in detail.

Discussion then turned to the particular problems of including so-called deviant groups, such as alcoholics and homosexuals. Part of the problem here is in simply identifying the members of these groups.

The last groups discussed were people with disabilities and children. The chapter ended with discussion of the politics of inclusion and an assessment of where we now stand.

CHAPTER 18

ETHICS IN SOCIAL RESEARCH

LIVERPOOL
JOHN MOORES UNIVERSITY
I.M. MARSH LIBRARY
BARKHILL ROAD
LIVERPOOL L17 6BD
TEL. 0151 231 5216/5299

ACCORDING TO A DICTIONARY DEFINITION (*Webster's* 1981), to be ethical is to conform to accepted professional practices. Although these minimal practices to which social researchers should conform have long been known and passed on by word of mouth, only within the last 25 years has a general attempt been made to codify and clarify these standards in print. There is general agreement about ethical principles in research, but some disagreement about the way to word codes of ethics, and what to do in a situation in which there is conflict of interest, such as between the right of the majority to know and the right to privacy of the minority.

It is generally agreed that it is unethical for researchers to harm anyone in the course of research especially if it is without the person's knowledge and permission. This includes deceiving a respondent about the true purpose of a study, asking a respondent questions that cause him or her extreme embarrassment, causing emotional turmoil by reminding him or her of an unpleasant experience, causing guilt, or invading his or her privacy. Respondents may also be injured by being studied without their knowledge, or by violation of a promise of confidentiality. Researchers can also act unethically when analyzing data, e.g., by revealing only part of the facts, presenting facts out of context, falsifying findings, or offering misleading presentation, such as "lying" with statistics.

In general, researchers want and have every reason to be ethical. Any researcher who has a reputation for unethical conduct will soon find himself or herself unable to find a sponsor for his or her research, and unable to convince respondents that they should cooperate in the study. Occasionally a researcher might be tempted to equivocate a bit on his or her findings if the findings do not support the hypothesis but he or she is convinced that the hypothesis is correct and that this deception will only be temporary. This is somewhat like the gambler who embezzles money, fully intending to pay it back when he or she wins. When such falsification is discovered, professional and public reaction is often quite severe. Several cases of data falsification by physical scientists have recently been uncovered and received a great deal of news coverage, resulting in dismissal of the researchers.

But if we can see why a desperate researcher might falsify data, why would a researcher conduct research harmful to his or her respondents? An ironic feature of social research (or applied physical or medical research, for that matter) is that the most critical practical issues are often negative things, or problems we wish to ameliorate. Researchers are interested in discovering, for example, what causes cancer or suicide, or drug or alcohol addiction, or the negative effects of excessive population density. Persons not afflicted with such maladies are presumably happier and less likely to be studied. We do not do a study to see why someone is healthy (or why he or she does not commit suicide). We tend to be most interested in finding causes of harmful effects. Herein lies the dilemma: We are interested in these effects precisely because they are harmful and we wish to ameliorate them, but precisely because they are harmful we feel it is unethical to inflict them on healthy persons. If we think we know a cure for some malady, it may be ethical to try it on an afflicted person. But generally, in order to find a cure we first have to find a cause. When a cause is suspected we need to demonstrate its existence, but to do so means that we might harm our subjects quite severely. For example, we can hypothesize that density and overcrowding have negative effects on persons (see chapter 1), but may feel it is unethical to test this hypothesis by actually harming people. For further discussion of ethical research as a dilemma see Reynolds (1979).

Before discussing how to avoid ethical dilemmas, we should briefly discuss why they occur, and how to predict them. Research in the 1990s reveals two avenues toward analysis of ethical dilemmas, one contextual and the other theoretical. I have pursued the contextual analysis in three research articles (Bailey 1988a; 1988b; 1989b). In this research I show that there are some predictable contexts or situations in which ethical problems arise. I rely on an exchange perspective similar to the one by Dillman (1978) discussed in chapter 7. As we saw in chapter 7, the ratio of benefit/cost is important in social research. For example, in utilizing mailed questionnaires the researcher might be subjecting the respondent to some cost, such as time expended or psychological costs in terms of invasion of privacy, while the researcher has little of benefit to give to the respondent (see chapter 7 for further discussion of monetary or other rewards to respondents). Thus, the researcher may be in an ethical dilemma if he or she exacts costs from the respondent without giving the respondent equal benefit, thus shortchanging the respondent in the exchange relationship.

The full model identifies five groups of actors or "publics" involved in the research process. These are: the (1) research subjects; (2) researchers; (3) sponsors (who fund the research); (4) media; and (5) general public. The interdependencies among these five groups constitute the context for exchange relationships among them. Given this model, it is possible now to summarize characteristics which are predictive of ethical dilemmas in social problems research. These are:

1. Negative benefit/cost ratios for research subjects (1)
2. Positive benefit/cost ratios for researchers (2)
3. Positive benefit/cost ratios for research sponsors (3)
4. High status configurations (both ascribed and achieved) for researchers (2)
5. High status configurations (both ascribed and achieved) for sponsors (3)
6. Low status configurations (both ascribed and achieved) for research subjects (1)

When *all* of these contingencies appear simultaneously, the success of the research project is immediately jeopardized, because of potential harm to the respondent (1) (usually the most vulnerable person in the project, although others, particularly researchers (2), can also be harmed). There are a number of potential responses, most of them ethical. These are:

1. To simply terminate the project, at the initiation of the research subjects (1), researchers (2), sponsors (3), or others. It may be possible to reschedule it later when conditions are more favorable.
2. To increase benefits to research subjects, perhaps through better information about the nature of the study and its benefits, or through increased remuneration brought about by increased funding from sponsors, etc.
3. To decrease costs to research subjects, perhaps through improved efforts to guarantee privacy and confidentiality, or changes in study design to lessen potential harm
4. To advise the research subjects of the potential cost, persuade them to cooperate (perhaps for the public good) while absolving the researchers and sponsors of culpability through signed informed consent

If the study is not terminated (response 1) and if the three other responses above (responses 2, 3, 4) are not successful, the researcher may be tempted to engage in unethical behavior. This often takes the form of "norm abeyance," where powerful or high-status researchers simply revoke the norms applying to research or change the rules. Researchers may rescind rules that normally serve to protect the research subject and may consider it their prerogative to do so "in the name of science" or "for the good of the nation."

But how can researchers rationalize such behavior? Work on the theoretical presuppositions of social research by Sjoberg and Vaughan (1993) reveals that there are certain philosophical foundations of research that may lead researchers into ethical dilemmas. In addition to questioning the reality of "value-free sociology" (see chapter 2), Sjoberg and Vaughan discuss three ethical principles they say underline American sociology: ethical relativism, ethical commitment to a social system, and utilitarianism.

Ethical relativism consists of tolerance for other ethical or cultural practices, even if they clash with our values (for example, understanding how people of other cultures can eat dogs even if we would not). In the notion of ethical commitment to a social system (such as an organization or nation), emphasis is on the good of a whole community rather than what is good for a single individual. In utilitarianism, there is an assumption that "the greatest good for the greatest number emerges from the individual's pursuit of his or her own self-interest" (Sjoberg and Vaughan 1993, p. 125). For further discussion of utilitarianism and other ethical issues see Sjoberg and Vaughan (1993) and Greenwald (1992).

All these ethical principles may help researchers to justify engaging in norm abeyance or other research practices that may prove harmful to research subjects or others. However well-meaning some of these researchers might be, there would seem to be limits on all these views. For example, while the notion of cultural or ethical relativism might be helpful in making us realize that there are other points of view, does that mean we should endorse *everything* another culture does or advocates? It would seem not. As Sjoberg and Vaughan (1993, p. 118) say, "The rise of Nazism and the resultant Holocaust undermined faith in ethical relativism."

As for ethical commitment to a community or group, how can we blindly champion this, when there are so many diverse communities in the world, or even in one large city? Similarly, how can we blindly endorse utilitarianism by claiming that actions taken in our own self-interest will aid everyone, if we clearly see that this is false? The problem is that researchers and others are taught to have these various ethical views and to base their actions on them. As a solution, Sjoberg and Vaughan suggest that researchers instead adopt a "human rights" view, in which all persons can claim their rights simply by virtue of the fact that they are human beings, without having to believe a certain way, belong to a certain group, or have a certain level of wealth or status. Clearly this work on ethics by Sjoberg and Vaughan is important and should be continued by them and others. For further discussion see Sjoberg and Vaughan (1993).

How to Remain Ethical

If we have a scientific interest in demonstrating the way harmful effects on people are caused, but an ethical interest in avoiding such harm, how can we solve the dilemma by serving both goals and demonstrating harmful effects empirically without actually harming people? There are a number of approaches to this problem, but most of them have some sort of disadvantage. Among the approaches are:

1. Animal studies
2. Computer simulation
3. Finding a condition in which the negative effects already exist so that the researcher is not responsible for producing them
4. Application of only a very low level of cause, or for only a short period of time, so that the effects, though negative, are very mild
5. Informing respondents of the possible negative effects and securing their permission (informed consent)
6. Rationalization on the part of the researcher that the study is not unethical because the harm inflicted on the subject is justified either because it is a lesser evil than the harm the investigator is attempting to cure, or because the researcher considers the subject evil and feels justified in harming him or her
7. Use of samples rather than complete populations so that fewer persons are harmed
8. Maintenance of privacy through publication of aggregate data only

Animal Studies

Research utilizing animals in lieu of human subjects is common in the physical and medical sciences. Administration of a drug to an animal can, for example, disclose its harmful side effects. Social-science research using animals as surrogates for humans is much rarer. An example is Calhoun's (1962) study of the effect of density on rats, as discussed in chapter 1. The obvious reason that animals are of limited use as substitutes for humans in social research is that animals lack the very social factors (e.g., religion, education, income) that social scientists most often study. However, recently there has been increased interest in the study of animals, with one notable discovery being that chimpanzees can communicate with humans in sign language. Discovery of advanced communication or other cultural features in animals might make them more suitable for social-science research that is aimed at humans. On the other hand, discovery of such cultural factors would make it more difficult for humans to claim superiority over animals, and thus more difficult for scientists to rationalize their practice of using animals in harmful research in lieu of humans. There are many people who feel that research harmful to animals is unethical and should be banned.

Computer Simulation

This topic is treated in detail in chapter 13. By simulating social interaction and gaining response from the computer instead of the individual, it may be possible to reduce greatly the number of subjects required in the experiment, and thus the number that can be harmed by the research.

Already Existing Negative Effects

This strategy involves finding instances of negative effects or of the hypothesized harmful cause already existing in natural surroundings, so that the researcher will not feel responsible for any harm done to subjects. An example is Galle et al.'s (1972) study of density in which they compared dense areas of Chicago with less dense areas in order to see if there were negative effects of density. Since they did not create the dense populations studied, they were not responsible for the harmful effects of these populations. The problem with such naturally occurring studies is that it is difficult to find the desired value of the independent variable (e.g., the proper degree of density). Also, the researcher has a minimal amount of experimental control over extraneous variables.

Even if the researcher is not responsible for introducing the negative effect, ethical problems can still arise if the researcher observes the negative occurrence and fails to attempt to prevent it. Thus, when Luckenbill (1981) studied police reports of murders which had already occurred, he avoided ethical problems. However, he felt that if it had been possible to use observation to study murders, "To have sacrificed the victim's life by my nonintervention would have been unethical" (Luckenbill 1981, p. 145). Thus, Luckenbill decided against observation and used document study instead.

Small Cause or Short Time

This technique is often used in experimental studies. One example is the experimental density study by Griffit and Veitch (1971) reported in chapter 1. Subjects were subjected to a relatively high degree of density created by the experimenters, but only for a short time. The obvious problem is that this strategy affords no opportunity for ethical study of the effects of long-term density.

Informed Consent

This is probably the most common method in medical and social research. Informed consent essentially entails making the subject fully aware of the purpose of the study, its possible dangers, and the credentials of the researchers. The reader will recall that these are some of the basic elements of information contained in the covering letter or introductory statement accompanying a questionnaire. It has been traditional in survey research to give the potential respondent this information in order to induce him or her to participate in the study. However, if the respondent does participate he or she does so voluntarily and is not asked to sign a release, whereas in medical studies it is customary not only to inform the respondent but also to secure his or her written permission to conduct the study or operation. In the future social researchers will probably move in the direction of signed informed-consent statements, and will undoubtedly pay more attention to informing the respondent adequately.

For example, any university receiving federal funds now has a committee on human subject policy that oversees all grant proposals prepared by university faculty. Any study that is considered to place human beings "at risk" must be reviewed by this committee. These include not only hazardous medical experiments but also any social research that might involve such things as discomfort, anxiety, harassment, invasion of privacy, or demeaning or dehumanizing procedures. In cases where informed consent is judged necessary by the committee, the researcher is required to construct and administer an "Informed Consent Form" containing the following elements among others (University of California, Los Angeles, Human Subject Policy Committee 1979):

1. A fair explanation of the purpose(s) of the study and the procedure(s) to be followed, including an identification of those which are experimental (In complex experimental designs, a simple flow chart may be helpful.)
2. An identification of the individuals performing the procedures and their degrees (e.g., M.D., Ph.D., etc.; the word "Doctor" should not be used exclusively)
3. A description of the possible immediate and long-term discomforts, hazards and risks, and their potential consequences (if none, so state); patients as subjects should be advised that their condition may become worse despite participation and that they may derive no specific benefit
4. A description of the potential benefits to the subject and/or humanity
5. An offer to answer any inquiries concerning the study at any time (principal investigators should list their office address and telephone number[s])
6. An instruction that the subjects are free to withdraw their consent and to discontinue participation in the project or activity at any time without prejudice
7. An assurance that any information derived from the research project which personally identifies the subject will not be voluntarily released or disclosed without the subject's separate consent, *except as specifically required by law*
8. An assurance to subjects that if the study design or the use of the collected information is to be changed, they will be so informed and their consent reobtained (New consent forms must be approved by the review committee.)
9. A paragraph stating: "I understand that if I am injured as a direct result of research procedures not done primarily for my own benefit, I will receive medical treatment at no cost. The University of California does not provide any other form of compensation for injury." (revised statement, January 1986)

The trend in recent years has been for the requirements of informed consent to become more and more technical and bureaucratic. In addition to the points listed above, there are a host of special circumstances regarding minors, persons who speak foreign languages, and so forth. While every researcher desires to protect research subjects (and it is to his or her advantage to do so), several of these provisions can cause real difficulty for researchers in certain studies. To begin with, a long and cumbersome consent form attached to a mailed questionnaire may be just the straw that breaks the camel's back. Merely reading it increases the time the respondent must spend on the study, and its rather formal, bureaucratic, legalistic, and even ominous tone (even though the form is supposed to be written in lay language) may easily intimidate respondents. Further, the promise that subjects may withdraw from the study at any time (6) can hardly increase responses. Still further, technically the researcher must obtain consent all over again if any changes are made in the study (8).

While we would expect informed consent to have greater effect on a mailed-questionnaire study, it can affect an interview study as well. Singer (1979) experiments with informed consent in an interview study. Some respondents were asked to sign the informed consent form before the interview and some after the interview (which of course violates a basic premise of informed consent— that consent must be given *before* the study is done). A control group did not sign any form at all. The questions were sensitive ones for which we could assume a high refusal rate. They were on issues such as drinking, marijuana use, and sexual behavior (the questions were basically the same as in the Sudman and Bradburn [1974] study discussed in chapter 6). Interviews were granted for 71 percent of the group that was not asked to sign a form. A request for informed consent lowered the percentage willing to be interviewed to 64 percent when the signature was requested before the interview and 65 percent when the signature was requested after the interview. Thus, while informed consent lowered response rates significantly, the timing of the signature did not cause a significant difference.

Informed consent can cause problems for researchers in observational research as well. Such problems (among others) prompted the journal *Social Problems* to devote its entire February 1980 issue to "Ethical Problems of Fieldwork" (Cassell and Wax 1980). *The American Sociologist* (August 1978) also devoted an entire issue to ethics in social research. The obvious problem in ethnographic research is that covert participant observation is almost wholly precluded by the requirement of informed consent. One cannot maintain secrecy in observation if one is required to present an informed consent form to each subject being observed. Duster et al. (1979, p. 140) say that while most researchers must identify themselves before they can obtain permission to conduct an observational study, "there are, however, instances in which that is not possible for valid data collection."

Thorne (1980, p. 285) has complained that federal regulations regarding informed consent are based on a "biomedical model" of research, which may not be suitable for observational field research. This is because the risks in fieldwork are less dramatic than in medicine, and the fieldworker has less control over the research situation. She adds:

> The requirement that one obtain signed consent forms from everyone one studies may violate anonymity and actually increase risks for some groups of subjects. In the end the procedures may result in meaningless ritual rather than improving the ethics of field research (Thorne 1980, p. 285).

But while noting the problems with bureaucratically imposed informed consent procedures, Thorne does agree that the principle of informed consent is relevant to fieldwork ethics. However, the questions still remain of "how much information" and "how much consent" constitute "informed consent," and these still have not been fully resolved.

On January 26, 1981, new regulations were issued by the U.S. Department of Health and Human Services (HHS), which was formerly known as the Department of Health, Education, and Welfare (HEW). The new regulations (46 Federal Regulations 8366–8391) permit social-science research to be treated differently from biomedical research with regard to human subjects. Specifically, no Institutional Review Board (IRB) approval is needed for survey research and observation as long as the subjects are not identified and are not exposed to criminal or employment risks, and as long as the behavior being studied is not sensitive (e.g., sex or alcohol). For further discussion of ethics in social science, including informed consent, see Bulmer (1982), Capron (1982), Beauchamp et al. (1982), Sieber (1982), Hamnett et al. (1984), Greenwald (1992), and Sjoberg and Vaughan (1993).

Harm of Subject Is Justified

Earlier in this chapter we discussed situations that might lead researchers to justify their harm of subjects, and the ethical principles that might aid them in these rationalizations. Also, in chapter 2 we cited Bierstedt's (1957) description of sociology as value-free. Bierstedt said that "Sociology is silent about questions of value. Sociology cannot decide the direction in which society ought to go." Until recently this seemed to be the predominant view in sociology, and the one shaping most codes of ethics for social researchers. A researcher adhering to this principle would not invoke his or her own values to label any potential respondent as "bad" and the goals of the research as "good" in order to justify any potential harm that might come to the "bad" subject because of the study. However, some researchers have departed from the value-free stance, particularly when they feel that they have uncovered wrongdoing on the part of public officials or political groups with whom they disagree. Galliher says:

> While all people may be worthy of the same respect as human beings, it does not necessarily follow that their activities merit the same degree of protection and respect. . . . It is questionable whether the files of the American Nazi Party are deserving of the same respect as any other data source; must one secure the active cooperation of the Ku Klux Klan, or for that matter of the Pentagon, before doing research in their organizations or with their personnel? While doing research in South Africa, van dèn Berghe [1967, p. 185] concluded: "From the outset, I decided that I should have no scruples in deceiving the government. . . . The question is, how much honor is proper for the sociologist in studying the membership and organization of what he considers an essentially dishonorable, morally outrageous, and destructive enterprise?" (Galliher 1973, p. 96).

Some researchers feel that the elite such as governmental and business leaders should be studied even if such research is antagonistic. This partially stems from a view that middle-class social scientists have too long studied poor people ("studying down") and now should study leaders ("studying up").

Because of his feelings, Galliher (1973, p. 98) recommends changing rule 4 of the Code of Ethics of the American Sociological Association:

FROM: All research should avoid causing personal harm to subjects used in research.

TO: All research should avoid causing personal harm to subjects used in research unless it is evident that the gain by society and/or science is such that it offsets the probable magnitude of the individual discomfort. The revelation of wrongdoing in positions of public trust shall not be deemed to cause "personal harm" within the meaning of this rule.

I find this proposal dubious at best. Not only does it set the sociologist up as somehow superior and able to judge both the gain by society and the harm to the individual, but it also brings the sociologist directly into the political realm.

Interestingly, Galliher has mellowed in recent years. He still argues that rule 4 should be changed (Galliher 1980, pp. 298–99), but he concedes that his 1973 statement was overstated:

> However, I was a little melodramatic in discussing clandestine methods. . . . It is not just that government should be monitored, but I implied that it is the people's enemy (1980, p. 301).

He further admits:

> In interviewing state government officials, civil servants and business leaders ... I have found few refusals and little hostility in studies of the origins of criminal laws, even when the details of such interviews are discrediting to respondents. In beginning each study, I was quite willing—even eager—to use duplicity, but it never was necessary (Galliher 1980, p. 302).

However, these statements do not mean that Galliher now thinks that all governmental officials are righteous: "Powerful people seem so convinced of their own righteousness and so sure of their power that they usually talk freely" (Galliher 1980, p. 303).

Wax (1980, p. 278) also presents a moderate view of antagonistic research:

> Those who advocate the antagonistic mode of "studying up" prefer to portray the chosen subjects of their inquiries as if they were similar to inhuman monsters. Yet, in fact, many persons (biographers, journalists) who have known these subjects intimately have portrayed them as persons who considered themselves guided by severe ethical standards.

Sampling

Although the basic purpose of sampling is to represent adequately the views of an entire universe or population without actually interviewing everyone in the population, sampling has an added benefit when invasion of privacy is an issue. For example, suppose that one is interviewing all 10,000 members of a national organization. If there are three questions that many respondents in the pretest felt were an invasion of their privacy, the researcher would probably find it advantageous to draw a random subsample (stratified, if necessary) from his or her full sample for these three questions only, so that persons not in the subsample will receive a questionnaire that omits these three sensitive questions. Persons in the subsample will get the identical questionnaire, with the addition of the sensitive questions.

Publishing Aggregate Data

If the researcher gathers information that the respondent considers an invasion of privacy, the researcher can placate the respondent by refraining from identifying him or her in print. One way to do this is to use pseudonyms; another is to publish aggregate data only. For example, instead of publishing the respondent's individual income the researcher publishes only the average income for the whole state, so that a given individual's income cannot be identified.

Invasion of Privacy

The charge of invasion of privacy is most commonly made against survey research, but may also arise with observational studies, document studies, or experiments. What constitutes invasion of privacy is obviously very subjective. In general, any question that arouses feelings of anxiety or guilt in a respondent is an invasion of privacy. For example, a person in a very strict religious environment may have masturbated, but may have felt extremely guilty about it and never admitted it to another living soul, even when questioned about it. He or she will feel quite understandably that his or her privacy is being invaded if asked whether or not he or she masturbates. Consider the words of a female respondent who was in a university class that was asked to answer questions on sexual practices, including masturbation: "I very much resented the questionnaire. What right did she have to ask me whether or not I have masturbated? She better have a very good reason for asking such questions."

This quote underscores the importance of telling the respondent the purpose of the study. If the respondent thinks that the information to be gathered is important enough, he or she may be willing to be embarrassed and have his or her privacy invaded, but he or she will not cooperate if the study seems to be a trivial matter with no good purpose but to harass the respondent. The volume of questionnaires that pass across some persons' desks these days is so great that the potential respondent is likely to consider all questionnaires of minor importance unless the researcher can convince him or her otherwise. For further discussion of invasion of privacy in social research, including multiple definitions of privacy, and justifications for invasion of privacy, see Kelman (1982) and Pinkard (1982).

Deception

Ethical Questions

There are a number of ways that research subjects may be deceived. One way is simply to study them without informing them of the fact securing their permission, as in the case of a participant observer who joins an organization merely to study the members. Many subjects might consider such behavior unethical. Some persons might feel that such observation without permission is tantamount to spying. Others simply dislike being the objects of research, especially experiments. Some people apparently associate experimentation with laboratory animals such as rats or monkeys, and find experiments degrading or dehumanizing, as if they reduce persons to the level of laboratory animals. One of Garfinkel's students conducted an ethnomethodological experiment on his family without advance warning and with no explanation until the experiment was complete. A sister, speaking for the family of four, said, "Please, no more of these experiments. We're not rats, you know" (Garfinkel 1967, p. 49).

A more common form of deception involves informing the subject that he or she is part of a study but deceiving him or her about its true nature. For example, mailed-questionnaire studies to determine the effects of such questionnaire features as length or type of postage have been labeled deceptive because the respondent thought the purpose of the study was purely informational, and did not know that he or she was involved in a study to compare different types of questionnaires.

In general, however, deception is not needed in survey studies, and is rare. Deception is much more common in psychological and social psychological experiments, but its use varies greatly with the subject matter of the experiment. Stricker (1967) studied four psychology journals for 1964 and found that out of 457 studies described in 390 articles, 88 or 19.3 percent used deception. The percentage using deception varied greatly by subject matter. Studies of opinions, attitudes, and values (survey research) as well as studies on hypnosis, response styles, and birth order had no deception at all, while conformity studies had 81.2 percent deception (13 out of 16), cognitive-dissonance and balance-theory studies had 72.2 percent deception (13 out of 18), and decision-making studies had 50 percent deception (3 out of 6).

Apparently deception is more necessary for research in some substantive areas than in others. For example, in a conformity study there might be only one actual experimental subject, with all the other supposed subjects actually confederates. The confederates may all agree that the shortest line is really the longest, and see if the subject will conform to their answer when he or she knows it is obviously incorrect. A researcher might argue that conformity experiments cannot be conducted effectively without deception.

But Kelman (1967, p. 2) thinks that some instances of deception are unnecessary. He says that "deception has been turned into a game, often played with great virtuosity and skill." Most of the studies using deception are probably not dangerous to the subject and are of short duration, so they should not have permanent effects. Still, no one likes to be deceived, made a fool of, or laughed at. Further, some experiments have been quite traumatic for the deceived subjects, and may well have caused permanent scars. For example, in one study cited by Kelman (1967, pp. 4–5) subjects were given a drug that temporarily interrupted their breathing. Though not permanent or painful, subjects reported that to be temporarily unable to breathe was a "horrific" experience, and that "all the subjects in the standard series thought they were dying" (Kelman 1967, p. 4). In another study designed to produce stress (Kelman 1967, p. 5), a group of army recruits flying on an airplane were told that the plane was malfunctioning and would have to crash land.

How can researchers get away with such potentially harmful deception? Their main justification seems to be that scientific investigation is governed by a different set of norms from those that govern everyday human interaction. As Kelman says:

> In our other interhuman relationships, most of us would never think of doing the kinds of things that we do to our subjects—exposing others to lies and tricks, deliberately misleading them about the purpose of the interaction or withholding pertinent information, making promises or giving information that we intend to disregard (Kelman 1967, p. 5).

The fact that behavior considered appropriate under a certain carefully controlled and regulated set of conditions is not allowed or is considered inappropriate otherwise is hardly unusual. Traveling at a high rate of speed in an automobile is against the law on a city street, but considered perfectly acceptable under controlled conditions at the racetrack (even though such activity is highly dangerous for the driver, and even spectators near the track run the risk of injury or death). Fist-fighting is another activity that is allowed under the strict supervision of officials and according to strict rules in the boxing ring, but not allowed among the general public on the street.

Scientific research is really no different from these activities and many others. Potentially dangerous behavior is allowed in the experiment, but only on the assumption that all activities are carefully regulated and controlled by competent supervisors. Among the assumptions governing the experiment are the following:

1. The researcher is qualified to conduct the research. Usually he or she must have a doctoral degree of some sort (M.D. or Ph.D.) or some other professional degree or license, and must have some institutional affiliation (such as university, government,

or corporation). The institution not only regulates the research by making him or her follow its rules, but also makes sure that he or she has the proper laboratory facilities to perform the research adequately.

2. The potential public good from the study will outweigh the potential harm to the individual.
3. The potential harm to the subject is relatively minor and of short duration (not permanent).
4. The subject knows he or she is participating in an experiment, has been informed of the possible danger, and has agreed to participate.

If any of these conditions are violated—if the researcher is incompetent to perform the research or has an ulterior motive, if the experiment is of no scientific value, or if the subject has not been informed of the danger—the researcher is not justified in treating the subject less courteously than he or she would in normal everyday interaction. Furthermore, some critics feel that there is a greater tendency for abuses to occur when the subjects are relatively powerless or of low status (in the study in which breathing was stopped all subjects were male alcoholic volunteers). For further discussions of ethical problems of deception in social research see Kelman (1982) and Elms (1982).

Methodological Implications

In addition to the ethical questions it raises, deception also has methodological implications. The major reason for deceiving a subject about the real purpose of a study is a feeling that if the subject knows the purpose, it will be more difficult to fulfill the goals of the study. This may be because the subject's subconscious biases are aroused, or because he or she consciously manipulates the data for such reasons as to make himself or herself appear intelligent, to please the researcher, or perhaps to make the researcher appear incompetent. It was pointed out in chapter 9 in our discussion of experiments that even if the subject is deceived about the real purpose of the experiment he or she may deduce the real objective from a combined knowledge of the pretest and the test stimuli. The Solomon two/control/group experimental design was formulated on the belief that even with deception the subject might deduce the purpose from the interaction of pretest and stimuli. This design provides a means of estimating the magnitude of such an interaction effect.

Obviously it is easiest to keep the nature of the experiment unknown if subjects are naive and are not aware that the practice of deception is widespread among social researchers. Experienced subjects who expect to be deceived will assume that the stated purpose of the study is fallacious (even if it is not) and will attempt to discern the "real" purpose from clues such as the pretest or test stimuli. The problem is that there are increasingly fewer naive subjects, especially among college students who traditionally have been used as "captive audiences" by researchers who were also their teachers.

Kelman (1967, p. 6) cites one college student subject as saying "Psychologists always lie." Bonacich (1970, p. 45) reports that almost all of his subjects have been lied to by previous experimenters, and that this greatly damages his chances for a successful experiment. In his experiments studying solidarity, cohesion, and social control, Bonacich found that when he informed the group of subjects that one of them had betrayed the others, without telling which one it was, there was a strong tendency for subjects to believe that none of them had really given in to temptations offered by the researcher, but rather that the experimenter had lied to them. Bonacich reports that this invalidates the experiment for his purposes because the social-control processes he wishes to study cease to exist.

The difficulty of securing naive subjects from the college-student population undoubtedly is caused in part by the recruitment practices typically used by experimenters. Rather than choosing a random sample from the entire student body, as do survey researchers, experimenters are more likely to let subjects select themselves. A common procedure is to post notices on a bulletin board or in the school newspaper asking for volunteers to participate in an experiment for money. Undoubtedly many persons answering such advertisements are "professional," sophisticated subjects who supplement their income by participating in experiments. Many are probably students who plan a research career and who take part in experiments as a learning process or to secure experience. If the experimenter would select subjects randomly and then attempt to secure permission from those drawn in the sample, he or she would stand a much better chance of securing unsophisticated student subjects.

Kelman (1967, p. 7) says that deception (1) may cause the subject to dismiss the stated purpose of the study and search for alternative interpretations of his or her own; (2) gives the social researcher a reputation as someone who cannot be believed; (3) causes the subject to attempt to outsmart the researcher and beat him or her at his or her own game; (4) deprives the subject of necessary information that would be helpful in enabling him or her to follow the instructions for the experiment; and (5) causes the subject to receive contradictory messages from the researcher, inasmuch as there is a contradiction between the researcher's statements about the purposes of the study and the information the subject receives from the experimental conditions themselves and from covert cues given off by the experimenter.

As an overall result, different subjects may each have their own different definitions of the situation, and be adhering to different rules or strategies. This is somewhat analogous to survey respondents having various understandings of an ambiguous question, so that in a real sense different respondents are answering different questions while all are ostensibly answering the same question. Kelman feels that by involving subjects in role-playing simulation games, researchers and subjects can cooperate in the experiment without deception (see the discussion of simulation and gaming in chapter 13).

Sponsored Research

We have been discussing the ethical problems involved in researchers' treatment of their respondents or subjects. Questions of ethics may also arise concerning the nature of the relationship between a researcher and the sponsor of the research. It is well known that many social-research projects may be exceedingly expensive. Expenses are incurred, for example, because of the need to draw a large sample, to train a large number of interviewers, to pay a lot of postage and spend a lot of money on paper, printing, and supplies, and to analyze the data on a computer. Thousands or even hundreds of thousands of dollars may be required just for sample design, or interviewer training, or buying computer time. Because of such expenses, individual researchers generally cannot afford to pay for the study out of their own pocket and must seek a sponsor willing to provide the funds. In most cases the funds are provided by some public agency, such as the government, or a charitable foundation whose only goal is (ostensibly) advancement of knowledge, and who will thus let the researcher be his or her own master with no strings attached. Occasionally, however, the nature of the relationship between researcher and funding sponsor will raise questions of ethics. Earlier in this chapter we presented a model to help us predict when ethical problems might occur in research. This model included the role of research sponsors. We will now discuss more specifically some of the ethical problems that can arise with sponsored research.

1. *Sponsor informs researcher of the findings it expects or tells him or her how to conduct study.* The sponsor may have a vested interest in certain results and may not wish to fund the study unless these results will be found. For example, I was once approached by a representative of a company operating "singles" apartments in which only unmarried adults were allowed. The apartments encountered a substantial degree of hostility from neighbors, who complained that the unmarried persons in the singles apartments were often "perverts," or engaged in sinful sexual activities, or were in some way undesirable as neighbors. The representative wanted a study conducted that would show that the singles were not like that at all, but were as respectable as anyone else, and were in fact desirable neighbors. The question that arises here is, what would happen if the study were conducted but the singles were indeed found to be on the average more undesirable than, for example, married couples? Would the sponsor feel that the researcher had some special obligation, since he or she was receiving money from the sponsor? If a special obligation were claimed, what result would it have?

2. *Suppression of findings.* Outright falsification of findings to bring them in line with the desired results would be one option, but would obviously be unethical. The sponsor might be more likely to suggest that the researcher withhold the most injurious of the findings, or cite them out of context, or somehow "lie with statistics" in order to give a false impression. Any such tactic that gave an erroneous impression of the findings would obviously be unethical.

3. *Concealing true sponsor of study, or concealing true purpose for study.* Studies sponsored by agencies of the government of one country, but with research to be conducted on foreign soil, are especially susceptible to charges of concealment. One charge might be that the study, while legitimate is not being sponsored by a neutral party, but is actually being conducted by the government so that the results can be used against other countries. Another charge is that the study, whether or not it is of scientific interest, is being used to conceal an undercover spying operation. For example, it has been charged that research programs sponsored by the United States Agency for International Development (AID) are sometimes a cover for CIA activities. The AID program gives the United States a reason for being in the country, and although the researchers are legitimate, their facilities can be used as headquarters from which agencies such as the CIA can conduct surveillance activities.

The most infamous example of this type is Project Camelot. Project Camelot was originated in the Office of the Chief of Research and Development, Department of the Army (United States), and subsequently conducted by the Special Operations Research Office (SORO) of American University, Washington, D.C. SORO does contract research for the army in the social- and behavioral-science fields "in support of the army's mission" (Sjoberg 1967, p. 142). The study was funded for $6 million. Its purpose was to study the causes of civil vio-

LIVERPOOL JOHN MOORES UNIVERSITY
LEARNING & INFORMATION SERVICES

lence, specifically to gather data on problems of counterinsurgency that would enable the army to cope more effectively with internal revolutions in foreign nations.

Surveys and field studies were to be conducted in various countries, first in Latin America and later in other parts of the world. A number of well-known social scientists served as consultants on the project.

The project director was appointed in December 1964 and by June 8, 1965, the project was canceled by Secretary of Defense Robert McNamara before any actual fieldwork had been carried out. A Norwegian anthropologist then in Chile allegedly found out about the project and brought it to the attention of the Chilean intellectuals. Ultimately word of it reached members of the Chilean Senate and various left-wing groups. The Chilean left denounced the project and criticized American researchers and the United States, leading the American ambassador to Chile to call for the project's cancelation. According to Sjoberg (1967, p. 143), the project caused long-standing tensions concerning research to surface between the Defense Department (which sponsored the study) and the Department of State (whose ambassador to Chile was apparently not informed of it). As a result of the incident, a presidential communication gave the Department of State authority to review all federally financed research projects involving research activities in other nations and potentially affecting foreign policy (Sjoberg 1967, p. 143).

Project Camelot is quite controversial, with a number of social scientists condemning it, but others supporting it. At least two questions arise. First, was Project Camelot basically an "objective" attempt to secure important social-science knowledge, or merely a way for the army to gain entry to a country so that they could learn about the causes of counterrevolution in that country and take steps to counteract it, perhaps illegally interfering in the affairs of a sovereign nation? Second, if the project was a legitimate one, were the eminent social researchers connected with it being duped to believe that their findings were the primary purpose of the study, while they were really serving as "window dressing" or a "cover" for undercover spying activities in that country?

For further discussion of Project Camelot see Horowitz (1965) and Sjoberg (1967). Other social-research projects with government involvement mentioned by Sjoberg (1967, p. 156) are those that CIA has supported in other countries. One that, according to Sjoberg, has achieved much publicity is Michigan State University's research and action program in South Vietnam, which was partially staffed by CIA personnel. Also, the Center for International Studies at Massachusetts Institute of Technology was partially financed for a time by CIA funds, according to Sjoberg (1967, p. 156). One point raised by Sjoberg is whether CIA support of American social-science research projects might undermine the legitimacy of American social research in foreign countries, and cause foreign citizens to question the goals of all American social researchers (Sjoberg 1967, p. 156).

Professional Codes of Ethics

Concerns with the types of ethical issue discussed in this chapter have resulted in drafting of codes of ethics by social-scientific professional societies. The codes of the American Sociological Association and the American Association for Public Opinion Research are printed in full in the Appendixes. It is not surprising that codes of ethics were drafted, only that they were so late in coming. The public opinion code was published in 1960 and the ASA code not until 1968. The ASA code of 1989 is also reprinted, but the 1968 code is retained for comparison purposes so that we may see how much change there has been in the sociological code of ethics and the direction of this change. I can only speculate on reasons for the failure to publish codes of ethics at an earlier date. Undoubtedly among the reasons are the following:

1. Until fairly recently social research was conducted on a much smaller scale, so questions of ethics did not arise in nearly the same magnitude as they do now. The membership of social-science professional societies was much smaller, and there was much less funding for social research.

2. The codes of ethics probably always existed, but were passed by textbook and word of mouth rather than being formally written and labeled. For example, a number of characteristics contained in Bierstedt's (1967) description of a sociological researcher (discussed in chapter 2 of this book, represent components of present-day codes of ethics (e.g., a researcher is ethically neutral, value-free, objective, does not make policy, and does not tell what should be, only describes what is).

3. Not all sociologists agreed with the description supplied by Bierstedt. The ones who did agree were those sociologists who thought that sociology should be "scientific." The ones who disagreed often identified themselves as humanistic sociologists. These humanists were less likely to do any type of empirical research using human subjects, but were more inclined to write essays based upon personal experience or beliefs about "human nature." Since such humanists did not deal much with human subjects they had little need to develop a written code of ethics. Persons who did not identify with either the scientific position (which had a fairly formal if largely unwritten code) or the humanistic view (which had little need for a code) were often applied sociologists who were likely to identify closely with social welfare, a profession that has a rather highly developed bureaucracy to regulate it.

The need for a written code of ethics has developed within the last ten to fifteen years probably chiefly for two reasons. First, many more studies are now being conducted, and sample size per study is probably much larger than in the past. Thus many more persons are being used as subjects in social research. Further, the development of computers for storing large banks of data raises new questions about the researcher's ability to ensure confidentiality and anonymity for his or her subjects. Second, radical social scientists have rejected the unwritten "scientific" rules that social researchers must, when doing research, be apolitical, value-free, and objective, and refrain from making policy statements about the way things should be. Radical sociologists tend to see apolitical research as an impossibility; they feel that any researcher has values, both conscious and unconscious, that will color his or her perceptions and affect his or her analysis of the data. Further, such radical sociologists often reject Bierstedt's contention that sociology must be a "pure" or theoretical, rather than an applied, science. Bierstedt agreed that sociological findings could be applied, for example, in formulating government policy, but he contended that this was the job of planners or policy-makers, not sociological researchers.

Some radical sociologists reject the whole notion that theory should be (or even could be) divorced from action. They seem to feel that the major role of a social scientist is to identify problem areas in society and to attempt to ameliorate these problems. The social change they advocate is often not directed solely or even at all to such traditional "social problems" as crime and delinquency, but rather to the form of government. In fact, they may feel that if the form of government is changed, the other problems, being merely a function or reflection of the form of government, will also disappear.

It seems likely that the traditional, more conservative researchers within social science were reacting at least in part to this radical departure from the traditional image of the social researcher when they drafted codes of ethics, which in general emphasize the traditional approach and do not reflect the radical position. In other words, as long as the traditional role of the researcher was generally accepted, there was little need to formalize it in writing. However, when this role came under attack from the radicals, the traditional group retaliated by formalizing their position as a code by which all members of the association should abide.

Some sociologists have proposed revisions of the ASA code of ethics that would bring the code more in line with the radical position (Galliher 1973). Others have advocated "conflict methodology," including such tactics as lawsuits with the power of subpoena being used to gather data from unwilling respondents (See Young 1971)—quite a departure from the traditional stance that research subjects must comply voluntarily, and that any persons who wish to refuse are free to do so. Although such radical spokespersons have had their statements published in sociological journals, they have not yet succeeded in achieving a formal objective, such as revision of the published code of ethics.

A quick perusal of the two codes reprinted in the Appendix shows that most of the issues discussed in this chapter are included. One other matter that has not been directly discussed concerns a breach of confidentiality or misrepresentation of data, not by the researcher or respondent but by some third party, such as the press. In response to such issues, the following amendment was added to the AAPOR Code in 1970:

> We shall maintain the right to approve the release of our findings, whether or not ascribed to us. When misinterpretation appears, we shall publicly disclose what is required to correct it, notwithstanding our obligation for client confidentiality in all other respects.

We should comment briefly on the changes in the American Sociologist Association's Code of Ethics between 1968 and 1989. The earlier code focused almost entirely upon ethics in research conducted by sociologists. The emphasis was upon the ethical and objective behavior of the researcher and the treatment of research subjects. The later code includes virtually all of the earlier provisions but is greatly expanded. The 1989 code also deals with sociologists working in nonacademic settings, with publication and the review process, with teaching and relationships with students, and with relationships among professional colleagues. Thus, the trend in recent years has been to codify ethics not only for research but for all facets of the professional sociologist's role. A recent example of this is the proposal by Epstein (1986) for a code of ethics governing faculty employment search committees, so that candidates for faculty positions are not subjected to unethical treatment such as being interviewed when there is no intention to hire the candidate or asking whether statements in the resumé are "lies."

The foregoing discussion should make it clear that while most researchers are concerned about the welfare of their subjects and have no desire to harm anyone, they may feel that sometimes the interest of science or the larger public can only be served through studies that might prove injurious to a few subjects. There is disagreement over how one can determine when the public good from a study is high enough to outweigh the private injury. Researchers also disagree over proper tactics and proper subjects for research. While there is a consensus that a code of ethics is needed, but disagreement over whether certain instances are unethical, there will surely be increased formal attention paid to ethical questions in the future by all parties to the controversies, and by subjects, politicians, and the general public, as well as researchers themselves. Future ethical questions of research may well be decided by the courts rather than being chiefly an academic issue, as is now the case. For example, there have already been court rulings that even though researchers have promised their respondents confidentiality, they have no legal right to keep such information confidential, and must divulge it when so ordered by a court of law, as in a lawsuit.

Ethics in Observational Research

Earlier in this chapter we discussed ethnography to some degree, especially in regard to informed consent. And of course, all of chapter 10 is devoted to observation. However, it behooves us here to discuss observation in greater detail, simply because the special circumstances of ethnographic research can lead to particular ethical problems. Specifically, the close proximity between researcher and subject, and the frequent covert nature of the research, often make it difficult for the researcher to avoid joining the subjects in unethical or illegal behavior, as to do so would lead to discovery of his or her research role.

Fetterman (1989) offers a very comprehensive analysis of ethical factors for ethnographers. He distinguishes between the ethical challenges of academic and applied ethnographers, further dividing the latter into administrative ethnographers, "action" ethnographers (who only conduct research and remove themselves from a power role), and advocate ("activist") ethnographers. He also breaks the ethnographic research process into a "research life cycle" and analyzes ethical considerations for each stage in this life cycle. These stages are the inception (the problem), birth (proposals), childhood (field preparation), adulthood (fieldwork), and retirement.

Among the challenges for the adult (fieldwork) stage that he discusses are the use of pseudonyms, "guilty knowledge" (knowledge of illegal activities), and "dirty hands" (where the ethnographer cannot remain innocent of wrongdoing. For further discussion see Fetterman (1989), pp. 120–38). For a related and valuable discussion see Kimmel's (1988) analysis of ethics and values in applied social research.

Neglected Aspects of Research Ethics

Discussion of ethics generally focus (as we have done) upon the degree of harm that the subject is subjected to and ways in which this can be alleviated. Two other facets of the research process are often neglected: the degree of harm to the researcher and the beneficial aspects of the research for the research subject. Even though the researcher instigates the study, he or she should not overlook the personal consequences of the project. Miller and Humphreys (1980) studied homosexual persons whom they described as "socially oppressed individuals" who in many cases suffered from acute depression and desperately needed a neutral listener. They said:

> Both authors found it impossible to do more than two interviews per day and, in nearly every instance, reacted to interviews with emotional and physical exhaustion. A major part of this postinterview reaction was an awareness of ethical and intellectual responsibilities of dealing fairly and objectively with respondents who were often emotionally fragile (p. 221).

In addition to the impact of research on the researcher, another neglected ethical aspect that Miller and Humphreys (1980) point out is the possibility of a positive effect of the research project on the research subject. Miller and Humphreys kept in touch with subjects for years after the initial research. A number of their homosexual subjects reported subsequent positive effects of the research. One subject whose low self-concept had been raised by participation in the study (Miller and Humphreys 1980, p. 220) said, "You know, that research really changed my life." Others reported that being interviewed helped decrease their isolation and gave them an increased awareness of their identity. Clearly, not all research will have a similar beneficial effect on the subjects. Similarly, it may be years before any beneficial effects are seen. Thus, harm of subjects should not be rationalized by saying that the study may help them in some other way. On the other hand, it is reasonable for a researcher who is contemplating a study to think not only of possible negative effects but also of possible beneficial effects to the subjects.

Summary

Chapter 18 discussed ethics in social research. In order to conduct research on social problems we often must expose our subjects to the harmful effects we are attempting to eliminate. We discussed a number of ways to ethically conduct such potentially harmful research, including animal research, computer simulation, study of existing conditions, exposure of subjects for only a short duration, informing subjects of danger, rationalizing the harm to subjects is justified by the greater scientific good, use of samples rather than complete populations so that fewer subjects are harmed, and maintenance of privacy through publication of aggregate data. We next turned to a discussion of the ethical problems involved in using deception in experiments (deception is often resorted to so that subjects will not guess the purpose of the experiment and bias the data). Following that we discussed ethical problems that may arise in sponsored research, such as a sponsor requesting that the researcher suppress findings. We concluded the chapter with a discussion of professional codes of ethics, ethics in observational research, and neglected aspects of research ethics.

CHAPTER 19

APPLICATIONS

IN THIS CHAPTER we shall be concerned with applications of social research. We have touched on applications briefly several times in this book. In chapter 2 we discussed the distinction between pure and applied research, and our discussion of values and objectivity in chapter 3 has relevance for the present discussion, as does the chapter on ethics (chapter 18). Social research has not been applied as often or as successfully as some people think it should have been for such purposes as solving pressing social problems or deciding matters of public policy. In this chapter we will discuss some possible reasons for the relative paucity of applications, and indicate the diversity of applications that do exist. Then we will present some of the more celebrated and controversial applications. Finally, we will analyze these controversial studies to determine what makes them controversial, and to attempt to determine what their ultimate impact on society may be.

Factors Limiting Applications of Social Research

There are a number of reasons why we do not see more applications of social research: (1) mistrust of social science by the public; (2) inability to conduct needed research because of expense, ethical considerations, or other reasons; (3) inability to apply the knowledge gained from studies because of expense, ethical considerations, or other reasons; (4) disagreement concerning the worth of a study among those holding conflicting value orientations.

Mistrust of Social Science

There are still persons, both in and out of academia, who do not believe that social science has much to offer or that its findings are sound. Social science is younger, generally less quantitative (although this is rapidly changing), and in some sense less mature then the physical and life sciences, medicine and engineering. For these reasons, some persons in the latter fields characterize their endeavors as "hard science" and label social sciences as "soft science." Outside of academia, social scientists face not only publicity-seeking senators who label their grant proposals as a waste of the taxpayers' money (such people often attack physical-science research for the same reason), but the lay public and journalists who are fond of attacking sociologists for using jargon and belaboring the obvious.

Consider the words of one newspaper columnist, as quoted by Lowry:

> Sociology, as we all know, is a scholarly discipline which elevates the obvious to the esoteric. A sociologist will devote several years to a study which eventually will disclose that most men and women like sex, in one form or another. A sociologist will pontificate on the inequitable distribution of wealth in language neither the rich nor the poor will understand. These savants who relentlessly pursue things everyone-knew-in- the-first-place often exceed their own seemingly infinite capacity for revealing revealed truths (Lowry 1974, p. 3).

Such charges have some basis in fact, are easy to make, sound clever, and attract attention. The facts are, though, that many social-science findings and theories are not obvious simply because they are complex and not normally contemplated by the lay public. Such topics as status inconsistency, women's fear of success, the labeling theory of deviance, and the theory of

474

middleman minorities, all discussed in chapter 2, are examples of nonobvious social science. Other research cannot be considered obvious simply because findings are inconclusive. Consider the effects of density on humans, as discussed in chapter 1. Even though it may appear "obvious" to one person that density is harmful, and equally "obvious" to another that it is not, the facts are that we do not know whether or not it is harmful.

There are still other findings that are not inconclusive, but are the opposite of what critics "obviously" expect. Rose answers one such criticism of social-science testimony in a court case as follows:

> According to Cahn, these social scientists provided weak or unreliable evidence to support what everyone knows unequivocally by intuition; or to use a cliché, they "proved the obvious." Regarding the school segregation issue, he states that "one speaks in terms of the most familiar and universally accepted standards of right and wrong when one remarks (1) that racial segregation under government auspices inevitability inflicts humiliation, and (2) that official humiliation of innocent, law-abiding citizens is psychologically injurious and morally evil." In stating this, Cahn points up the distinction between the lawyer's approach and the social scientist's empirical approach based on tests, attitude surveys, and systematic observation. It is obvious that Cahn is not aware that the overwhelming majority of white Americans in 1896 believed that segregation was right and just and that practically all the relevant literature also took this position (Rose 1967, p. 111).

The year 1896 is significant because it is the date of the Supreme Court's historic decision in *Plessy* vs. *Ferguson,* which condoned segregation with "separate but equal" facilities.

A somewhat more sophisticated charge that may be made against social scientists is one that should be familiar to readers of this book—that long and close study of social phenomena biases the researcher by making him or her more sympathetic to the problems of the research subject. Rose counters this charge rather effectively, advising attorneys and judges thusly:

> Don't accuse the social scientist of being biased *because* he has studied a matter for a long time; this argument can readily be turned against a conscientious lawyer or judge and seems to make a plea for ignorance (Rose 1967, p. 114).

The most legitimate charge against social science is that it is an infant discipline, and as such the reliability and validity of its findings are as yet unproven. I would agree with this statement and consider it a fair criticism. I am much less willing to accept stereotypical charges of bias and belaboring the obvious, and I think that a critic who makes such charges is doing not only social science but himself or herself and the general public a disservice unless he or she has evidence to support these claims.

Inability to Conduct Research

This point should be clear to readers of this volume. We have seen numerous instances in which needed research is hindered by such factors as lack of access to data, great complexity necessitating large expenditures of time and money, or situations in which conduct of the research would cause ethical or moral problems.

Inability to Implement Research Findings

Even when the research necessary to gather vital information for solving a social problem can be conducted, the suggestions stemming from these findings often cannot be implemented. One of the major problems with implementing research findings is the elaborate bureaucracy that often must be dealt with. Systems analysts have commented that their models can be implemented fairly easily within a more-or-less total environment such as an individual corporation or a military unit, where the authority structure is such that one person is able to give a command and see that it is carried out. Such models are much more difficult to implement in dealing with urban social problems. The researcher seeking to implement his or her social policy in the urban milieu will often find not only layers of bureaucracy with their attendant paperwork, red tape, and buck-passing inefficiency, he or she will also encounter many cases of overlapping jurisdiction, with no one agency possessing sufficient responsibility to implement needed policies.

Disagreement over the Worth of Findings

One reason research findings are so hard to apply in a complex modern urban society is because in a pluralistic society there are so many competing interest groups that it is difficult to secure agreement on a single policy. Even if your research findings are reliable and valid, you may not be able to implement the policy these findings dictate if it conflicts with someone's values or self interest. Consider the presidential committee on population. For many years politicians shied away from the whole field of population policy making because it was a sensitive area not only involving sexual activity in the bedroom and the future family structure, but also influenced at least in part by religious concerns. When a commission was finally appointed that took its mission seriously and advocated that the United States adopt the policy of striving toward a maximum birthrate of two children per family, President Nixon quickly rejected this policy decision, not on the grounds that the research finding was "obvious," biased, or unreliable, but because he said it would endanger the future of the nuclear family in America. We have here a question of values with a president rejecting a policy recommendation based on solid research because it conflicts with his personal values. Similarly, since he was opposed to legalization of marijuana, President Nixon announced that he would not support its legalization regardless of the findings of the national commission on marijuana. One may easily wonder why we should even perform social-science research for the purpose of making policy recommendations in areas where the politicians are going to set policy solely on the basis of values, even if the policy is opposite to that implied by the research findings. Of course, if the policy recommended on the basis of sound social research is identical with the policy that the politicians and their constituencies favor because of their particular value orientation, then everybody is happy.

Range of Applications of Social-science Data

When we say that applications have been *relatively* few, this should not be interpreted as meaning that there have been no social-science applications, only that there have been relatively few compared to the large number of physical-science applications. Some people feel that if we can send people to the moon we should be able to solve urban problems, for example. Such people often suggest putting space scientists to work on urban ills, in the belief that such scientists are more capable than social scientists. The fact is that the social sciences get only a fraction of the government financial support received by the physical scientists. Perhaps if social scientists obtained more financial support they could achieve more spectacular results. The most likely outcome of putting space scientists to work on social problems would be that, even if they were able to make valid policy recommendations, they, like the social scientists, would find their recommendations rejected either because they conflict with the value system of some politician or his or her constituents, they are opposed by some powerful interest group, they become ensnarled in red tape or in inefficient bureaucracies, or simply cost too much. Consider the space program, for example. While many American citizens were proud of it, others considered it a distortion of priorities and would rather have seen the money spent for such social causes as elimination of slum housing. Even though the program faced some opposition, the government was able to carry it through, since it was relatively removed from the daily lives of the rank-and-file citizenry. A social program that faced equal opposition but had to be implemented in an urban neighborhood rather than in outer space might easily incite mass rioting.

Rose (1967) provides examples of social-science testimony by expert witnesses in court cases. Rose says that of all social sciences, only economics seems to have been used extensively in court cases. He cites an example in which economists testified concerning the monopoly power of a patient. Rose also provides illustrations of three cases involving racial matters in which he personally testified as a qualified expert witness. In addition to courtroom testimony, social science has been applied in a great number of fields. Various federal, state, and local governments employ a substantial number of social scientists such as economists, sociologists, and psychologists. Social scientists were active in such "Great Society" social programs as the Job Corps and the Head Start program.

For a look at a wide range of social-science applications see Lazarsfeld et al. (1967) and Horowitz (1971). For example, in the Lazarsfeld volume Gans notes that the Mobilization for Youth program was based on the "opportunity theory" of Richard Cloward and Lloyd Ohlin, "which argued that much delinquency was a reaction to the lack of opportunities in achieving normal American working class and middle-class goals" (Lazarsfeld et al. 1967, p. 452). Also in that volume, Kahn says that "Albert Cohen's book *Delinquent Boys* marked a turning point for workers in the field of delinquency, as it may have for sociological theory in this field" (Lazarsfeld et al. 1967, p. 482). Other chapters in this large volume deal with such areas as education, law, medicine, management, the military, law enforcement, consumer affairs, desegregation, and aging. The Horowitz volume includes chapters on such topics as "Policy Scientists and Nuclear Weapons" and "Policy Initiation in the American Political System."

When we think of research applications in social science we generally think of the application of substantive research findings in various subject matters of interest to the society at large. For example, courts or government agencies interested in school desegregation or the general planning of educational systems may seek to apply social science research findings from the areas of race relations or education. However, in addition to applying substantive findings, it is also possible to apply the actual *methods* of social research rather than merely the findings that these methods yield. One salient example of this is the widespread use by the media of survey research, particularly in political forecasting. After years of success, political forecasters generally failed quite badly in predicting the outcome of the 1980 U.S. presidential election, as discussed in chapter 1, thus generating new controversy for surveying, and prompting a special issue of *Public Opinion Quarterly* (Winter 1980) on this topic. This controversy is a continuing one (see chapter 1), because even though public opinion polls were more accurate during the U. S. presidential elections of 1984, 1988, and 1992, there is still Congressional concern that early "calling" of the election by the media, based on polling results, will negatively affect the election process in areas where the election is still in progress (see Milvasky 1985; Swift 1985).

The courts also began to utilize social science research methods to a greater degree than ever before in the 1980s. A book by Vinson and Anthony (1985) entitled *Social Science Research Methods for Litigation* contains discussion of various legal issues to which social science research can be applied, such as the use of survey research in jury selection. In addition the book discusses a wide variety of social science methods, including data collection, survey research, sampling, experimental design, and various types of statistical analysis. The increasing application of social science methods in the legal system is also signaled in a special issue of *Sociological Methods and Research* on "Social Research and the Courts" (Hawkins 1983). Among the topics discussed are statistical evidence in employment discrimination cases, methods of presenting evidence in school desegregation cases, methodological issues in pre-trial release decisions, and jurors' use of judges' instructions. In addition to political surveys and use in the courts, social research methods are also being increasingly applied in evaluation research and program evaluation, discussed later in this chapter.

Controversial Social-science Applications

Brown Versus Board of Education

In 1986 in the case of *Plessy* vs. *Ferguson,* the U. S. Supreme Court ruled that "separate but equal" facilities in intrastate transportation did not violate the constitutional rights of black persons. State and federal courts used this precedent to rule that separate but equal school facilities were not unconstitutional. The *Plessy* doctrine held more or less until 1954. Before 1954 there were two significant segregation cases (*Sweatt* vs. *University of Texas* and *Mc-Laurin* vs. *University of Oklahoma*), both of which involved disputes between black students and state-supported law schools. The basis for the suit in *Sweatt* was that the state-supported facilities provided for blacks were not equal, and could not realistically be made equal because of the inordinate expense involved. McLaurin had already been admitted to the University of Oklahoma Law School, but brought suit because even though he had the same teachers, curriculum, and classroom, he was seated apart form the white students. The Supreme Court ruled as follows:

> We concluded that the conditions under which this appellant is required to receive his education deprive him of his personal and present right to the equal protection of the laws. . . . We

hold that under these circumstances the 14th amendment precludes differences in treatment by the state based upon race . . . (quoted in Clark 1953, p. 6).

In both of these cases the Court decided in favor of the black student. According to Clark:

> The Sweatt case was the first of these cases in which expert social-science testimony was presented and became a part of the argument and legal record. Robert Redfield, anthropologist of the University of Chicago, testified that: "given a similar learning situation a [black] student tended to react the same as any other student and that there were no racial characteristics which had any bearing whatsoever to the subject of public education." This testimony was relevant to the argument that the segregation of students on the basis of race was an arbitrary and unreasonable classification (Clark 1953, p. 6).

These cases moved the courts past the *Plessy* doctrine of "separate but equal" and paved the way for the argument that racial segregation per se was a violation of the black student's constitutional rights. In January 1953, five segregation cases using this new approach were brought to the Supreme Court, with their resolution leading ultimately to the historic *Brown* case. (In the *Brown* decision the Supreme Court ruled that separate racially segregated education could not be equal, and ordered the desegregation of public schools.) Social scientists were used as qualified expert witnesses in all of these cases. According to Clark (1953, p. 7), the testimony covered the following points:

1. That racial classification for the purposes of education segregation was arbitrary and irrelevant since the available scientific evidence indicates that there are no innate racial differences in intelligence or other psychological characteristics. . . . This line of testimony was consistently unchallenged by the attorneys for the states.
2. That contemporary social-science interpretations of the nature of racial segregation indicates that it blocks communication and increases mutual hostility and suspicion; it reinforces prejudices and facilitates rather than inhibits outbreaks of racial violence.
3. That segregation has detrimental personality effects upon Negro children which impair their ability to profit from the available educational facilities. Segregation also has certain complex detrimental effects upon the personality and moral development of white children.
4. That the consequences of desegregation are in the direction of the improvement of interracial relations and an increase in social stability rather than an increase in violence or chaos.
5. That, if nonsegregation can work on the graduate and professional level, it can work equally well on the elementary and high school level, since children at this stage of development are more flexible in their attitudes and behavior.

Although it is not known how much this social-science testimony influenced the Court in making its 1954 decision, the Court did refer to this testimony in a footnote of the written decision, and it did ask for additional information on the effects of different forms of desegregation (Rose 1967, p. 110).

The Moynihan Report

The *Brown* decision did not generate much controversy among the academic community of social scientists, many of whom held liberal values and approved of school desegregation, although court-ordered desegregation created disturbances in many public school districts (such as Little Rock, where National Guard troops were brought in). The Moynihan report, on the other hand, was widely publicized by the mass media and created quite a stir, drawing heavy criticism from civil-rights supporters and liberal academicians. The report was published in March 1965 by Daniel Patrick Moynihan as a report of the Office of Policy Planning and Research, United States Department of Labor. At the time Moynihan was an assistant secretary of labor, and director of the Office of Policy Planning and Research. His report, entitled "The Negro Family: The Case for National Action," is reprinted in full in Rainwater and Yancey (1967, pp. 38–124).

The report met with much criticism, probably more than it would have encountered had its author not been in a high government policymaking position. What did Moynihan say that was so controversial? Consider the following quote from the preface:

> The fundamental problem, in which this is most clearly the case, is that of family structure. The evidence—not final, but powerfully persuasive—is that the Negro family in the urban ghetto is crumbling . . . for vast numbers of the unskilled poorly educated working class the fabric of conventional social relationships has all but disintegrated. . . .

> A national effort is required that will give a unity of purpose to the many activities of the Federal government in this area, directed to a new kind of national goal: the establishment of a stable Negro family structure (p. 43).

Moynihan implies not only that black family structure is disintegrating, but that this has disastrous effects on youth from such families, resulting in such things as higher delinquency rates. Moynihan begins by discussing recent demands by blacks for racial equality. He then discusses black family structure, saying, among other things, that:

> the white family has achieved a high degree of stability and is maintaining that stability. By contrast, the family structure of lower-class Negroes is highly unstable, and in many urban centers is approaching breakdown. . . . Nearly one-quarter of urban Negro marriages are dissolved. . . . Nearly one-quarter of Negro births are now illegitimate. . . . Almost one-quarter of Negro families are headed by females. . . . The breakdown of the Negro family has led to a startling increase in welfare dependency . . . (pp. 51, 52, 54, 55, and 58).

In his third chapter Moynihan discusses the possible causes of alleged breakdown in family structure, including slavery, reconstruction, urbanization, unemployment and poverty, and the wage system. He says that reconstruction was very destructive to the black male's personality, and gave black women the dominant role in the family. In other words, "Keeping the Negro 'in his place' can be translated as keeping the Negro male in his place: the female was not a threat to anyone" (p. 62). In chapter 4, entitled "The Tangle of Pathology," Moynihan attempts to document the negative effects of the breakdown of the black family by comparing black and white attainment, mostly by analyzing data either from the United States Census or from other government agencies such as the Bureau of Labor Statistics. He has tables by race, on years of school completed, percent of youth one or more grades below the mode for their age, average IQ ("By the 8th grade, Central Harlem Pupils' average IQ was 87.7 compared to the national norm of 100" [p. 81]), juvenile delinquency, attainment on military tests ("Almost four times as many Negroes as whites fail the Armed Forces Mental Test" [p. 87]), and rates of narcotics use.

The Coleman Report

Section 402 of the Civil Rights Act of 1964 says:

> Sec. 402. The Commissioner shall conduct a survey and make a report to the President and the Congress, within two years of the enactment of this title, concerning the lack of availability of equal educational opportunities for individuals by reason of race, color, religion, or national origin in public educational institutions at all levels in the United States, its territories and possessions, and the District of columbia.

The results of the first such survey were published in 1966 by the Office of Education of the United States Department of Health, Education, and Welfare. This report was authored by James S. Coleman and six other researchers. It is entitled *Equality of Educational Opportunity,* but is commonly known as the Coleman report.

Among the findings of the Coleman report were the following:

1. That if social class (SES) of the student's home is controlled for, "Schools are remarkably similar in the way they relate to the achievement of their pupils" (Coleman et al. 1966, p. 21). However, the school attended seems to affect the achievement of minority students more than the achievement of white students. For example, for southern students, the school attended accounts for 20 percent of the variation in the achievement of black students, but only 10 percent of the achievement of white students. Some proponents of integration are upset by this finding because it implies that busing can have relatively little ultimate effect (10–20 percent) on the student's achievement, while other factors account for the remaining 80–90 percent.

2. The rather small effect that schools do have is not chiefly the result of their curricula or facilities, but stems mainly from the quality of their teachers, as measured both by the level of education of the teacher and his or her parents, and the teacher's score on a verbal skills test. The level of teachers who teach minority students was found to be lower on both of these measures in the schools studied (Coleman et al. 1966, p. 22).

3. There is a strong positive correlation between the student's achievement and the educational aspirations and background of his or her student peers, as measured by the proportion of students with encyclopedias in the home and the proportion planning to go to college. Again the relationship is stronger for black students than for whites (Coleman et al. 1966, p. 22).

4. The analysis of school factors indicates that integration should have, in the long run, a positive effect on the achievement of black students. Further, "An analysis was carried out to seek such effects on achievement which might appear in the short run. This analysis of the test

performance of Negro children in integrated schools indicates positive effects of integration, though rather small ones" (Coleman et al. 1966, p. 29).

The Jencks Study

The data in the Coleman report were reanalyzed by Jencks and his associates and published in 1972. Jencks argues that equalizing schooling for all American students will have only minimal effect in narrowing income gaps (and thus erasing poverty) among adult Americans. Jencks says:

> There seem to be three reasons why school reform cannot make adults more equal. First, children seem to be far more influenced by what happens at home than by what happens in school. . . . Second, reformers have very little control over those aspects of school life that affect children. . . . Third, even when a school exerts an unusual influence on children, the resulting changes are not likely to persist into adulthood. It takes a huge change in elementary school test scores, for example, to alter adult income by a significant amount (Jencks et al. 1972, p. 255).

Jencks admits to having no answers as to how to equalize income, saying "These conclusions do not tell us much about the actual causes of economic inequality, much less about the best way to reduce it" (p. 263). Jencks says that some income inequality among American adults is due to genetic influences, adding that "if all the nongenetic causes of inequality were eliminated, and if America still placed the same value it now places on various kinds of skills, the income gap between the top and the bottom fifth of all male workers would fall from around 7 to 1 to around 1.4 to 1" (p. 262). Jencks concludes that genetic differences and their environmental "consequences' (environmental conditions stemming from genetic factors) "explain" 50 to 60 percent of the variance in IQ scores, while purely environmental factors explain about 20 to 30 percent.

The Jensen Study

Perhaps the most vigorously attacked of all the social research discussed in this chapter is the work of Arthur R. Jensen (1969; 1973). Jensen has been criticized by civil-rights activists, political liberals, and persons who believe that social environment is a major determinant of intelligence. Jensen's research deals with the relationship between IQ and social and genetic factors, including racial differences in intelligence. The publication that attracted the most attention (and criticism) was entitled "How Much Can We Boost IQ and Scholastic Achievement?" (1969). In this article Jensen states that "Negroes test about 1 standard deviation (15 IQ points) below the average of the white population in IQ. . . . This magnitude of difference gives a median overlap of 15 percent, meaning that 15 percent of the Negro population exceeds the white average" (Jensen 1969, p. 81).

Jensen uses as a subheading for one paragraph of his paper, "Failure to Equate Negroes and Whites in IQ and Scholastic Ability," saying "No one has yet produced any evidence based on a properly controlled study to show that representative samples of Negro and white children can be equalized in intellectual ability through statistical control of environment and education" (Jensen 1969, pp. 82–83). Jensen criticizes purely environmental explanations of racial differences in intelligence and achievement. For example, he says that while some social scientists would explain lower achievement among blacks by the fact that blacks have a higher proportion of fatherless homes (remember Moynihan?), the two largest studies he has seen indicate no such effect (he cites the Coleman report on this point). Citing studies of identical (monozygotic) twins raised apart, and unrelated children raised together, Jensen (1969, pp. 50–51) estimates that approximately 75 percent of the variance in IQ is accounted for by heredity, with 25 percent due to environment.

Jensen says that a unidimensional concept of intelligence is inadequate. He distinguishes between "Level I" learning, which he describes as associative learning, including rote memory learning of digits, and "Level II" learning, which includes abstract problem solving and conceptual learning. Jensen says that even lower-class children with IQs as low as 60 can often score quite high on Level I learning and basic memory, but cannot master the abstract thinking required by Level II learning. He says that this explains why teachers often feel that a disadvantaged child who appears bright in nonscholastic ways, such as memorizing the names of classmates, but is unable to perform well conceptually is performing below his or her level of ability.

Analysis

We have said that the studies selected for discussion in this chapter (*Brown,* Moynihan report, Coleman report, Jensen's study) were among the most controversial social-science studies, but we have not indicated reasons for the controversy. We can now specify that the controversies are largely generated by four factors. One source of dispute is the media, which often has a salient role in fanning controversies over research applications. The other three factors involve issues of whether the research can ever have the desired effect (determinism), whether the research is biased, and whether researchers are unethical. All of these studies attracted attention because they were all relevant for policymaking decisions in the area of school desegregation and busing.

The Media

Because this is a salient public issue, and is thus newsworthy, the press was quick to pick up and disseminate these studies, often with little background research or little effort to check for accuracy, something that is especially important with statements taken out of context. The end result was that often only one side of an issue was given publicity, and this was often, in the view of the researcher, "blown out of proportion" and popularized before the social-scientific community of the researcher's peers had an opportunity to read and evaluate the study. For example, Rainwater and Yancey say:

> Therefore, in July 1965, we read the first news article about the Moynihan report with great interest. . . . The tone of the article suggested some kind of direct intervention into family life.

. . . Early in the fall of 1965, when we were able to read Moynihan's report, *The Negro Family: The Case for National Action,* however, we did not find in it any such suggestion of distraction from the basic institutional sources of Negro disadvantage. Instead, we were impressed with the "fit" between Moynihan's summary of previous research and current statistics on the situation of lower-class Negro families and our own intensive participant observation and interview data from our St. Louis research . . . (Rainwater and Yancey 1967, p. x).

Social scientists appreciate the media when they publicize important research that would otherwise be lost forever in the ivory tower. However, there is reason for concern if the media rush to popularize a controversial piece of research in an oversimplified manner.

In addition to the manner in which the media treat the research, whether or not it is controversial (and thus how well it is accepted and applied) center around three major issues: (1) determinism (the nature-nurture controversy, for example); (2) values; and (3) ethics.

Determinism

A common issue in several of the studies discussed is whether or not it is even possible for social policy to have the desired effect, or whether the end result (e.g., low achievement in school) is predetermined. Both the Jensen and the Jencks studies emphasize that heredity has a far greater effect on IQ than do social factors, implying that there is really little the society can do in the way of school improvement that will increase the scholastic achievement of minority students. Jencks goes still further, emphasizing the point that even if achievement is raised in early life (e.g., in elementary school), this will have relatively little effect on income in late adulthood, and thus will do relatively little to eliminate poverty in this country, which was a major goal of President Johnson's War on Poverty as it was fought in his "Great Society" administration in the 1960s. Similarly, the Coleman report said that the type of school would have relatively little effect on improving achievement, and the Moynihan report implied that neither the type of school nor any other institution or measure could make much difference in the achievement of black youths as long as black family structure remained unchanged. However, at least the Coleman and the Moynihan reports dealt with alternative social factors rather than genetic factors, and thus were not nearly as threatening to social scientists as the Jensen report, which argued that inheritance was the key, with social factors (and thus social scientists) of rather minor importance. In any event, all of these studies were frustrating and annoying to civil-rights leaders and liberal social scientists and liberal politicians, all of whom were trying to achieve equality between blacks and whites in America by making changes in the social structure, particularly in the schools.

Values

We talked at some length in chapter 2 about the role of value bias in research and the possibility of holding one's values in abeyance in the interest of value-free sociology. While most researchers wish to remain objective and unbiased, analysis of the controversies surrounding the studies discussed in this chapter reveals that most of the conflict is due to a difference in values: those who favor school desegregation and busing versus those who do not. Often one side will accuse the other of bias, or of taking an "ideological" stance rather than an objective, "scientific" position. For example, writing in the Rainwater and Yancey (1967, p. 467) volume, Carter characterizes the Moynihan report as follows: "With the publication of this document a sociological theory which borders on an ideology has become a political weapon which we all are obliged to examine." Of course, as we mentioned above, the Moynihan report doubtlessly appeared even more political and ideological, since its author had a high government policymaking position at the time.

Ethics

Many among the lay public, social scientists, and politicians fail even to raise a question of ethics as long as the research findings are consistent with their values, but are quick to call a researcher "unethical" if the findings lead to policy implications incongruent with their personal values. As an example, consider the aftermath of the Coleman report. Although, as we have seen, the Coleman report recommended busing as having some effect in boosting minority achievement. Coleman's subsequent public statements switched from advocacy of forced busing to advocacy of voluntary busing, thus angering some sociologists who favored busing. Writing in *Footnotes,* the newspaper of the American Sociological Association, the outgoing president of the ASA, Alfred McClung Lee, says, "In my estimation, Coleman's contentions require serious consideration both by the committee on Professional Ethics and the ASA council" (Lee 1976, p. 9). Coleman is a mathematical sociologist who is empirically oriented and quantitative (the Coleman report was replete with sophisticated statistical analysis), while Lee comes from the "softer" humanistic tradition in sociology that often eschews rigorous statistical analysis for more subjective observation and interpretation. Yet Lee charges, "In his presentations in opposition to court-ordered busing before various tribunals, Coleman has given a great many social scientists, lawyers, and newspaper people the impression that he is a casemaker with slim regard for evidence" (Lee 1976, p. 9).

In the "Letters" section of that same issue of *Footnotes,* August 1976, p. 7, several sociologists commented on the controversy. William Foote Whyte wrote, "I wonder if Coleman's interpretations of his new data are any weaker than his interpretations of the earlier data. I am suggesting the possibility that we liberal sociologists were not much concerned about the quality of the original data because we were happy with interpretations Coleman gave those data, and we are now inclined to be much more critical because we are upset by the seeming anti-integration interpretations now being attached to Coleman's statements." Jackson Toby says that Lee suggests "That Lee's pro-busing position is the only one that a sociologist with ethical integrity can hold." Herbert Hamilton comments, "One's first reactions to this episode include the ironic role reversal seemingly involved in the actions of the principal protagonists." Lee, a leading spokesman for humanistic sociology and one of the social scientists testifying as an expert witness (in favor of desegregation) in the court cases leading to the *Brown* decision, is stressing the ethical responsibility of sociologists to adhere to strict standards of scientific evidence, while Coleman, a well-honored leader of behavioral science sociology, is being asked to answer the charge that he has been making policy recommendations with inadequate scientific evidence to support these recommendations.

Evaluation Research and the Development of Social Indicators

In recent years there has been a substantial expansion of interest in two separate but related efforts; (1) systematic evaluation of the effect of social-science applications (such as the Head Start and other War on Poverty Programs of the 1960s) and (2) development of indicators of the quality of social life similar to the indicators of economic level (for example, the gross national product) that have existed for some time.

Evaluation Research

There was a tremendous increase in interest in evaluation research and program evaluation in the 1970s. While this continues in the 1990s and would seem to be a permanent phenomenon, it is nevertheless clear that the field has matured somewhat. According to Freeman:

> Evaluation research is no longer the growth industry it was in the 1960s and 1970s. . . . Rather, it is an accepted component of social program development and implementation and is undertaken as part of both established and innovative human service activities (Freeman 1992, p. 595).

Policymakers, funding organizations, planners, and program staffs need answers to a number of questions:

1. Is the intervention reaching the appropriate target population?
2. Is it being implemented in the ways specified?
3. Is it effective?
4. How much does it cost?
5. What are its costs relative to its effectiveness?

Providing the answers to these questions is at the heart of evaluation research (Rossi, Freeman, and Wright 1979, p. 20). As defined by Smith (1981, p. 241): "Evaluation research is now commonly understood to mean the assessment of the effectiveness of social programs that were designed as tentative solutions to existing problems." Clearly evaluation research should not be limited only to new programs but can be applied to existing programs as well. However, there is clearly more pressure from the government or elsewhere to evaluate new programs, especially if they are controversial or particularly costly (or both, as in the 1960s Head Start programs).

Although government intervention in program evaluation has not yet reached the levels seen in informed consent, for example, the trend of increased evaluation requirements for social programs, particularly new ones, is clear. A special issue of *Evaluation and Change* (formerly *Evaluation*) (1978) discusses the federal politics of evaluation research. On October 6 and 27, 1977, the Senate Committee on Human Resources, under the chairmanship of Senator Harrison A. Williams, held the first Congressional hearings on program evaluation in human services. According to Senator Williams, the key issues in the hearings were:

> "Do human resource programs work?" "If so, how?" and "What evaluation tools will provide a good track record of a program's strengths and weaknesses, thereby enabling Congress to

know better whether to extend, modify, or eliminate the programs?" (*Evaluation and Change* 1978, p. 24).

In the course of the hearings a number of expert witnesses agreed on the increasing importance of evaluation in government programs but concluded that, "as yet, it is too undeveloped scientifically to use as an exclusive instrument for determining the ultimate worth or effectiveness of the programs" (*Evaluation and Change* 1978, p. 10).

Much of the Congressional interest in program evaluation seems to be an outgrowth of the passage of the Congressional Budget and Impoundment Control Act of 1974. Title VII of this legislation, entitled "Program Review and Evaluation," empowered all Congressional committees to personally conduct program evaluations, to contract them out, or to request some governmental agency to conduct them. The General Accounting Office (GAO) was also given the authority to evaluate federal programs, either on its own initiative or at the request of the House or Senate or a Congressional committee. Within the GAO, the priority issue of "evaluation guidelines, techniques, and methodology" has been assigned to the Program Analysis Division (PAD).

It seems clear from this brief review that there will be increasing governmental intervention in evaluation in the future, as even a cursory historical analysis of bureaucracies shows that once they begin to grow it is difficult to stop them. For the time being, however, these regulations will generally be applied only to large programs and not to relatively small-scale social science projects. Still, there is clearly a trend not only to evaluate but to evaluate by external sources. The 1980s will see evaluation procedures increasingly built into new government programs. For example, the Program Evaluation Act of 1977 proposed an automatic termination data on all federally funded programs. Such a concept is popularly knows as a "sunset" clause, as it causes the sun to set on a program in a relatively short time, and the program cannot be renewed without governmental evaluation, probably every five years.

Evaluation research differs from other social research basically in terms of its focus on the assessment of social programs. As Smith says:

> Strictly speaking, there are no formal methodological differences between basic research and evaluation research. The methods, techniques, and research designs discussed in other chapter of this book may be used in either research realm (Smith 1981, p. 247).

However, this does not imply that all methods are equally useful in evaluation research, but only that evaluation research in general does not employ unique methods. The methods most amenable to the study of change, such as experimental designs, are particularly useful, as one generally wishes to assess the changes accomplished during the time period form before program implementation until the time the evaluation is conducted.

As outlined by Weiss (1972), evaluation research consists of determining the purposes of the evaluation and the groups to be served by it, formulating the program goals and selecting proper measures, designing the evaluation and utilizing and disseminating evaluation results. In a larger context, Freeman (1992) says that evaluators are involved in the following four sets of tasks: (1) diagnosing human and social problems that require communal action: (2) planning, refining, and revising intervention programs; (3) monitoring program implementation; and (4) assessing program efficacy and efficiency. The research designs used in evaluation research, as presented by Weiss (1972, pp. 60–88), are familiar experimental, quasi-experimental, and nonexperimental designs. Thus, with the exception of such techniques as cost-benefit analysis (in which the evaluator compares the potential benefits of a program with its potential costs), the researcher familiar with the techniques of this or a similar book should be relatively well equipped to understand and conduct evaluation research in its present stage of development. For example, as discussed by Weiss (1972, p. 61), a researcher using an experimental design would randomly select two groups, one to receive the program to be evaluated (and thus to be the experimental group) and the other to be a control group that does not receive the program. Then both the experimental and control groups would be measured before the program to be evaluated is begun and after it is finished. If the experimental group shows greater change in the intended direction than does the control group, the program is judged to be a success (Weiss 1972, p. 61).

A very comprehensive and current survey of all the major facets of evaluation research is found in Rossi and Freeman (1985). Rossi and Freeman discuss the general problem of strategies for impact assessment and provide a detailed analysis of various research designs, including a comparison of randomized and nonrandomized designs. Their analysis encompasses a "catalogue" of nine different impact designs, including randomized, quasi-experimental, regression, before-and-after, retrospective, panels, time-series, cross-sectional, and judgmental (Rossi and Freeman 1985, pp. 210–19). For further discussion of these and other designs see Rossi and Freeman (1985; 1993), and Babbie (1986).

One problem in evaluation research is that there are often conflicting interest groups involved in the program, each with different vested interests and different program goals. The problem is acute if a zero-sum situation develops in which one group's gain is another group's loss. For further discussion of interest groups in evaluation research see Coleman (1972).

Another basic problem is the measurement of the program's progress. There are often a number of facets that could be chosen as indicators of program efficacy such as cost, impact on the public, and attainment of goals as originally stated. Sometimes it is a relatively simple matter to measure success, and sometimes it is exceedingly difficult. The first decision is the selection of appropriate measures.

One convenient measure of whether the program is meeting its goals is the number of persons served. Often there is some "target" population, or a set of persons eligible for the program. The program is meeting its goals if it delivers 100 percent of planned services to 100 percent of the target population. Often program goals are not fully met, especially early in the program. One often used measure of program success is program "shortfall," or the difference between the number of people targeted for human services programs and the number actually served. For example, as cited in *Evaluation and Change* (1978, p. 27), approximately 499,000 seasonal and full-time farm workers receive health services provided by the Migrant Health Act of 1962. However, an estimated 700,000 full-time workers plus two million seasonal workers make up the eligible population. Thus, the "shortfall" is 2,700,000 − 499,000 or 2,201,000 target persons that are not being served by the program. Expressed as a percentage, roughly 20 percent of eligible persons are being served, leaving a shortfall of 80 percent. As another example, Head Start programs serve 365,000 (plus 26,000 in the summer) out of 1.7 million eligible preschoolers, resulting in a 78 percent shortfall with approximately 22 percent being served. Obviously, shortfall statistics are only a rudimentary measure of program effectiveness. Even if a target individual is served, he or she may not receive full funding. Further, even if the person receives the full quantity of target services, the quality of these services may still vary greatly, and thus require evaluation in addition to the shortfall statistics.

In addition to shortfall, programs are often assessed in terms of some quantitative measure of services provided during some particular time period. For example, there are a number of possible measures for the evaluation of hospitals (Cromwell 1976). One way to measure hospital productivity is by the number and types of illnesses treated. A measure used more often is the amount of patient time spent in the hospital. Obviously the measure of productivity chosen is a crucial research decision. In a program having many departments and/or many different services, it may be necessary to select several different measures of program efficacy. For further discussion of evaluation objectives see Moursund (1973), Rossi and Freeman (1985; 1993), and Freeman (1992).

Fortunately, not all programs are as large and as difficult to evaluate as are government Head Start programs or hospitals. Many evaluation studies deal with smaller and simpler programs. Among the program evaluations reported in *Evaluation Review* (formerly *Evaluation Quarterly*) in 1980 were contraceptive delivery programs, a water conservation campaign, energy conservation in university buildings, volunteer assistance to parolees, parent training, and a program for decreasing dog litter. In the litter study the independent variable was a program by a community group in Chicago to encourage dog owners to pick up after their pets. The measurement of the dependent variable was rather direct (the number and weight of dog droppings in the target area). The study (Jason et al. 1980) illustrates that the measurement of program efficacy is not always as complicated as the examples cited above. Another comparatively small study is the assessment of the impact of the abandonment of a railroad in Montana (Brock et al. 1985). Among other more recent studies of interest are those dealing with the environment (Gerlach 1991) and crime (Berecochea and Gibbs 1991).

Despite the various problems inherent in evaluation research, the interest in evaluation undoubtedly will continue with increased application of social research. Campbell and Converse (1972) write of future research designs with built-in evaluative procedures. For further discussions of evaluation research see Campbell and Converse (1972); Coleman (1972); Weiss (1972); Glazer (1973); Suchman (1967); Rossi, Freeman, and Wright (1979); Smith (1981); Wagenaar (1981a), Rossi and Freeman (1985), and Babbie (1986). For discussion of ethics in evaluation research, see the special issue of *Evaluation and Program Planning* (Smith 1985).

Social Indicators

The social-indicator movement began in the mid-1960s. Among the reasons advanced for developing indicators are: (1) to use indicators as measurement instruments in evaluation research; (2) to establish a system of regular measurement of the quality of social life analogous to regular measurement of economic progress; and (3) to establish social goals and set social policy (Land 1975, p. 5). Among the content areas to be measured by social indicators are population, labor force and employment, income, knowledge and technology, education, health, leisure, public safety and legal justice, housing, transportation, physical environment, social mobility and stratification, family, religion, politics, voluntary associations, alienation, use of time, consumption behavior, and aspiration, satisfaction, acceptance, and morale (Land 1975, pp. 21–22). Recent social indicator studies have dealt with the military in American society (Evans, Felson, and Land 1980), and with indicators of property crime rates (Cohen, Felson, and Land 1980). Further, the journal *Social Indicators Research* has published in the 1980s a number of studies of the quality of life in different geographical areas, such as the Caribbean (Young 1980), Belgium (Bellen and Van Herbrugger 1980), Hungary (Andorka 1980), Australia (Headey et al. 1985), Canada (Kennedy and Mehra 1985), Thailand (Leela-kulthanit and Day 1992), and Finland (Toivonen 1992).

Land (Land and Felson 1976) distinguishes between "welfare indicators" (also called "goal-output indicators") and "indicators of social change." Indicators of the first type are concerned with measuring a certain phenomenon (e.g., welfare) so that social policy can be designed to optimize the public's satisfaction in this area. In contrast, indicators of social change are used to measure and verify a historical pattern of change (for example, change in female unemployment rates). These two types of indicators represent two major areas of inter-est in social indicator research but may not be mutually exclusive. If a variable that is studied as a change indicator is also the object of social policy, it is considered to be both a welfare indicator and a social change indicator. As an illustration, as long as the employment rates of women are not the object of social policy (affirmative action), indicators of these rates are merely social change indicators. As soon as such rates become the object of affirmative action policies the indicator remains a change indicator but becomes a welfare indicator as well. Thus, we really have three types—welfare indicators only, social change indicators only, and dual welfare/change indicators. For further discussion and examples of social indicators see Land and Spilerman (1975), Bauer (1966), Sheldon and Moore (1968), Cohen et al. (1980), Connerly and Marans (1985), Ferriss (1990), Land (1992), and Markides (1992).

Summary

Chapter 19 dealt with the application of findings form social-research studies to social policymaking. We noted a number of factors limiting applications of social research, including mistrust or ignorance of social science by the public, inability to conduct necessary research due to expense, ethical considerations or other reasons, and disagreement over the worth of a particular research project. Although these factors have limited the number of applications in social science compared to the large number of physical-science applications, a number of notable applications, some of them controversial, exist. Those that we discussed are: social-science testimony in the *Brown* versus *Board of Education* United States Supreme Court case; the Moynihan report; the Coleman report; the Jencks study; and the Jensen study. We noted that these applications were controversial, and pointed out reasons for these controversies, including the role of the media in reporting social research, a controversy over determinism, differing values, and a dispute over ethics. We concluded the chapter with a discussion of evaluation research and social indicators.

CHAPTER 20

CONSTRUCTING AND REVISING COMPLEX THEORIES

THIS CHAPTER DISCUSSES the construction of complex social science theory. The construction of social theory obviously plays an important role in the social research process. Unfortunately, however, in its present state of development, theory construction is still exceedingly complex and fraught with controversies and uncertainties. Such material is important but may be too complex for a general discussion of social research methods. We dealt with the problem by avoiding most of the complexity in chapter 3, discussing only the rudiments of theory construction necessary for the subsequent discussion. This chapter provides advanced study of theory construction for those who desire it. In addition this chapter illustrates the circularity of the research process as discussed in chapter 1. In this final chapter we have completed our discussion of the various stages in the endless circle of social research and are ready to return again to the beginning—construction and revision (on the basis of our findings) of social theory.

Explanations

There are many concepts that are so familiar that "everybody knows what they mean" but that are difficult to define precisely, or in all of their ramifications. Brown says:

> The verb "explain" is such a general term that in the sense of "making matters plain or intelligible" it is often used as an inclusive synonym for a number of more specific terms. A Christian minister may be said to explain a chapter in the Bible; alternatively, he may be said to *clarify* or *elucidate* its obscurities by the way in which he *expounds* the dogma and brings out the meaning of the passages with his sympathetic *interpretation*. In clarifying a point, expounding a view, interpreting a character, he is often, according to common speech, giving an explanation. And when two lovers adjust their differences this may be the result of one having managed to "explain away" what troubled the other. Explaining away, then, is the removing of an impediment, an impediment either to someone's relationships with other people or to his intellectual understanding. All explanations are attempts to explain away impediments of some kind. They are efforts to deprive puzzles, mysteries, and blockages of their force, and hence existence (Brown 1963, p. 41).

Brown (1963) lists seven chief types of explanation in social research: (1) genetic explanation, (2) intentional explanation, (3) dispositional explanation, (4) explanation through reasons, (5) functional explanation, (6) explanation through empirical generalizations, and (7) formal theory. Although Brown reserves the label of "theory" for only one type, I would call any statement of these seven types a theory as long as it is testable. Only the last three types—functionalism, empirical generalizations (inductively derived), and formal or axiomatic theory—have widespread usage in social research. Thus we will devote the major portion of this chapter to these three forms, but will first discuss briefly the other four forms.

A genetic explanation consists of explaining why a phenomenon exists in its present form by tracing its historical development from an earlier form. For example, the use of certain words and phrases in present-day black American English could be explained by tracing the development of black English from the time blacks were brought to this country as slaves. Similarly, the present-day liturgy and practices in the Catholic church in America (including use of English in services) could be explained by tracing the development of the Catholic church in this country, and the present-day nuclear family form could be explained by tracing changes in the family that occurred before, during, and after the Industrial Revolution. Obviously this type of explanation is most useful in historical research.

Intentional analysis is usually applied to single individuals, and is simply the everyday practice of explaining a person's actions by explaining his or her intentions. If another person performs an action that is puzzling to us and requires explanation, we may explain this action by learning his or her goal or intention.

Broadly speaking, a disposition as Brown (1963, p. 43) defines it is simply a tendency of a person to act in a certain way. Some persons might be disposed to be loquacious or rowdy, while others have wanderlust or are introverted. Still others have a tendency to use tobacco, alcohol, or drugs. Such tendencies may be learned or acquired, or may be "innate drives" said to be ascribed rather than achieved, and thus part of "basic human nature," such as the sex drive, hunger, or thirst. As with intentional explanation, dispositional analysis is generally applied to explaining actions on the part of a particular individual that puzzle us. For example, a person's failure to share a portion of his or her resources with a needy person might be explained by pointing out that the person, though rich and well able to afford helping others, is basically greedy and selfish.

As with intentional explanation and dispositional explanation, explanation by reason is yet another type of analysis, similar to the other two, for explaining puzzling actions of individuals. This type of explanation is familiar to all of us in everyday life. If we are mystified at the action of a person we will ask him or her "what earthly reason" he or she had for acting the way he or she did.

With the possible exception of genetic explanation, these four forms of explanation suffice as explanations of unique events or specific individual acts, but are not well suited for explaining general social problems with which we are often concerned in social research. For example, in delinquency research we might select one individual male juvenile offender for study, and might seek genetic, intentional, dispositional, and reason explanations for his behavior. As a genetic explanation, one might study the boy's early childhood and find that he grew up in an impoverished fatherless home, without a stable male role model and without proper food. An intentional explanation might find that the boy's main intention (goal) was somehow to become economically secure, and for him the goal was far more important than the means, so that he would not hesitate to commit a crime if necessary, or to destroy the property of rich people whom he hates and envies. A dispositional explanation might show that the boy is violence prone and vicious, with a particular hatred of older people. A reason explanation might find, upon questioning the boy, that his reason for committing vandalism, robbery, or other delinquent acts was to "get even with society" for the rough time he had had in life.

Generally, however, in social research we are not content to understand only a single case, but wish to generalize so that we can explain all cases of juvenile delinquency. Thus we eschew individualistic forms of explanation such as the genetic, dispositional, intentional, and reason, in favor of some form of explanation that can utilize a large sample size, or even a whole society, as the basic unit of analysis. Three such forms of explanation are functionalism, formal (deductive) theory, and inductively derived empirical generalizations, with the two latter forms often used in combination. For further discussion of explanation and its relation to prediction, see Willer and Heckathorn (1980).

Formal Theory

Formal deductive theory, with its emphasis on the establishment of laws (often expressed in quantitative form), is the archetypal theory of the physical sciences. Social researchers have been much less successful in using formal theory than have physical scientists, leading to charges that social science is not "real science." As Brown says:

> Now the notion of explanation is at the center of almost all controversies about the success or failure of the social sciences. For they are commonly attacked on the ground that they do not give us knowledge of laws and theories as do the physical sciences. From this deficiency the conclusion is often drawn that knowledge of laws and theories is not obtainable about the social behavior of human beings—that explanations of human conduct cannot be offered in terms of laws but must take some other form (Brown 1963, p. 40).

Brown offers the following definition of formal theory:

> A deductive system or theory in the *natural* sciences—a formal theory—is couched in words or other symbols, at least one of which describe or refer to a subject matter. The system consists of: (1) a set of axioms which have these properties: their truth is assumed; their truth can be tested only by the testing of some of their logical consequences; they cannot be deducted from other statements within the system; (2) those statements (theorems) that are entailed by the axioms or by the axioms in conjunction with theorems and definitions; such theorems may be either theoretical laws, and so open to testing only by means of certain of their logical consequences, or they may be empirical generalizations and thus open to direct testing; (3) a set of definitions of some of the descriptive (nonlogical) terms that appear in the axioms; other definitions may be introduced in the course of proving the theorems, but those will be based upon the earlier ones (Brown 1963, p. 174).

Notice that Brown distinguishes between two types of statement in the formal theory: (1) axioms (often called postulates), which are treated as givens and thus assumed to be true and never subjected to test; and (2) theorems, which are not originally stated but can be logically derived (deduced) from the set of axioms. While the axioms are not subject to test, some or all of the theorems must be tested in order for the theory to be proven or disproven. It is ironic that, while the term "theory" is often used in conversation to mean untested and perhaps untestable statements, in research it is generally felt that a theory that cannot be tested is worthless, since it provides no indication of whether we were right or wrong and gives no basis for revision. In a sense the axiomatic theory gives us the best of all possible worlds. It allows us to include axioms that contain abstract or unmeasurable concepts, thus making the axiom untestable. However, we can use such axioms only if we are ultimately able to deduce from them some empirically testable theorems.

Generally each proposition in the axiomatic theory designates a specific relationship between two variables. For example, the statements may be "if—then" statements such as "If A, then B," which may be read "If condition A occurs, then condition B occurs." Thus a simple axiomatic theory would be:

THEORY 20.1

AXIOM 1: If *A*, then *B*
AXIOM 2: If *B*, then *C*
Therefore:
THEOREM 1: If *A*, then *C*

Both axiom 1 and axiom 2 are true by definition or assumption, and need not be tested or proven true. The truth of theorem 1 is dependent upon the truth of the two axioms. That is, IF axioms 1 and 2 are true as assumed, THEN theorem 1 logically follows and is true by implication. Thus the process of deduction itself follows the "if—then" format. Notice that "If *A*, then *C*" is not stated as an axiom, simply because this statement follows logically from the other two axioms, and to state it would be redundant. Also, we would not include any axiom in the theory that contradicted any other axiom. For example, if we say "If *A*, then *B*" (axiom 1), it would not make sense to include as another axiom the statement "If *A*, then not *B*." If we included these two contradictory axioms, we would have a contradictory deduction ("If *A*, then *B*, but also not *B*").

The variables *A*, *B*, and *C* in the above theory are essentially stated in dichotomous or binary form: Each either exists or does not exist. We can also state variables in interval or ratio measurement form. For such variables we can state axioms in various forms of precision. For example, we could write:

THEORY 20.2

AXIOM 1: $A = f(B)$
AXIOM 2: $B = f(C)$
Therefore:
THEOREM 1: $A = f(C)$

This simply says that each variable is a function of its partner in the proposition, and is thus quite imprecise language. To be more specific we could write:

THEORY 20.3

AXIOM 1: $A = 2.33B$
AXIOM 2: $B = 3C$
Therefore:
THEOREM 1: $A = 6.99C$

Generally in social science we are not able to write propositions in such precise language. Axiomatic theories in social science are often written in language such as "The greater the *A*, the greater the *B*," or "The higher the *A*, the lower the *B*," or "*A* varies inversely with *B*," or "*A* varies directly with *B*."

As an example of an axiomatic theory in social research, let us construct a theory by selecting some propositions from the list of propositions presented by Hage (1972, p. 53) in his theory of organizations. The name in parentheses indicates the social theorist who first presented that particular proposition.

THEORY 20.4

AXIOM 1: The higher the centralization, the higher the formalization (Weber).
AXIOM: 2: The higher the formalization, the higher the efficiency (Weber).

These two axioms enable us to deduce a theorem about the relationship between centralization and efficiency that is not stated explicitly above, but is implied. That is, if axioms 1 and 2 are indeed true (and that is our assumption), then it must be true that:

THEOREM 1: The higher the centralization, the higher the efficiency.

We can construct an even more involved theory by adding another of Hage's propositions to the top of the theory, and labeling it as axiom 1, with our old axiom 1 now beginning axiom 2.

THEORY 20.5

AXIOM 1: The higher the complexity, the lower the centralization (Thompson).
AXIOM 2: The higher the centralization, the higher the formalization (Weber).
AXIOM 3: The higher the formalization, the higher the efficiency (Weber).

This provides us with sufficient information to deduce a relationship between the first variable in the theory (complexity) and the last variable in the theory (efficiency), if this is indeed what we wish to do. We can deduce this theorem, called the grand theorem, as follows:

Therefore:
GRAND THEOREM: The higher the complexity, the lower the efficiency.

If the reader cannot see how we deduced this theorem, or why we call it the grand theorem, it is probably because we have left out some steps that we must explain. In the first place, for each N axiom in a theory, it is possible to deduce $N(N-1)/2$ different theorems. In this case $N = 3$, so we can deduce $3(2)/2 = 3$ different theorems. Thus the grand theorem is only one of three that can be deduced. Further, since the grand theorem links both the first and last variable in the entire theory, it is the last theorem that can be deduced. That is, it cannot be deduced until all the other theorems are deduced.

Such deduction in which only the grand theorem connecting the first and last variables in the chain of propositions is explicitly deduced, with all other theorems remaining implicit, is called the chain pattern of deduction, or deduction by the chain rule (Zetterberg 1965, pp. 90–92). In all cases it will be possible to deduce a relationship between the first and last variables in the chain. However, one might question how the theorist can determine the sign of the relationship in the grand theorem (whether the relationship is inverse or direct) without deducing all of the intermediate theorems and observing their signs. This can be done by following the sign rule (Costner and Leik 1964; Bailey 1970). The sign rule states that "The sign of the deduced relationship is the algebraic product of the signs of the postulated relationships" (Costner and Leik 1964, p. 820). This rule refers only to the product of the signs of relationships in the original postulates, not in the deduced intermediate theorems. That is, the sign of the grand theorem can be inferred from this rule merely by examining the signs of the original postulates. For example, a minus times a minus (a deduction from two minus or inverse relationships) is a plus (a positive relationship in the theorem), while a minus times a plus (a deduction from one inverse relationship and one direct relationship) is a minus (an inverse relationship in the theorem). An even simpler application of the sign rule is simply to count the number of minus signs in the original set of postulates: An even number of minus signs indicates a positive relationship in the grand theorem (the negative relationships cancel each other out), while an odd number of minus signs indicates a negative relationship in the grand theorem.

By applying the chain rule and sign rule of theory 20.5 we can deduce the grand theorem and specify its sign without deducing any intermediate theorems. We know from the chain rule that the grand theorem will specify a relationship between complexity and efficiency. We could state the grand theorem as follows: "There is a relationship between complexity and efficiency." However, we can also specify the sign of the deduced relationship merely by following the sign rule. In examining the signs of the three axioms we see that the relationship in axiom 1 is inverse (higher complexity leads to lower centralization) but that the relationships in axioms 1 and 2 are both positive. Thus, according to the sign rule, minus times plus times plus yields a minus, and the relationship between complexity and efficiency as stated in the grand theorem is inverse.

In order to make explicit the implicit theorems we have avoided through use of the sign rule and chain rule, let us rewrite theory 20.5, this time deducing all intermediate theorems.

THEORY 20.6

AXIOM 1: The higher the complexity, the lower the centralization.
AXIOM 2: The higher the centralization, the higher the formalization.
THEOREM 1: The higher the complexity, the lower the formalization.
AXIOM 3: The higher the formalization, the higher the efficiency.
THEOREM 2: The higher the centralization, the higher the efficiency.
THEOREM 3 (grand theorem): The higher the complexity, the lower the efficiency.

Notice that if one wishes to work through all the steps one really does not need to apply either the sign rule or the chain rule. After the theorem 2 is deduced, the grand theorem can be deduced directly from axiom 1 and theorem 2. For a discussion of axiomatic theory in sociology, see Freese and Sell (1980).

Synthetic and Explanatory Deductive Theories

We have said that the axioms or postulates in a formal theory are assumed to be true and need not be tested. An unanswered question is how we can find propositions that we can assume are true. One way is to use only those propositions that have previously been tested as hypotheses and have been proven true. Such empirical generalizations can then be used to deduce theorems. Coleman (1964, p. 9) calls this type of theory synthetic theory, while Northrop (1947, p.

109) calls it abstractively deductively formulated theory. Propositions that have been proven true and are used to deduce theorems are, technically speaking, called "postulates," while the term "axiom" is used for those propositions that have not been demonstrated to be true but are merely assumed or defined to be true. "Axiom" also has a mathematical connotation. In actual practice, though, the terms "axiom" and "postulate" are used interchangeably.

Synthetic Theory

As an example of a synthetic deductive theory, assume that the following two propositions have been replicated many times in social research projects and have been proved true every time:

THEORY 20.7

POSTULATE 1: The higher the educational level, the more politically liberal a person is.
POSTULATE 2: The more politically liberal a person is, the less racially prejudiced he or she is.

The problem with combining two such propositions and calling them a synthetic theory is that this process often yields minimal results. What can one learn from such a theory that one did not already know simply by studying the two empirical generalizations separately? About all that one can learn from these two postulates in combination is the information in the theorem that can be deduced from them:

THEOREM 1: The higher a person's education level, the less racially prejudiced he or she is.

If one has a great many postulates, he or she may not be able to see all of the possible theorems without doing the formal deductions. However, if he or she has only a few postulates, as in the example above, he or she can probably visualize all of the combinations of relationships without going through the construction of an axiomatic theory.

Explanatory Theory

Many times the set of axioms is not tested because some or all of the individual axioms cannot be tested, only the theorems derived from the axioms can possibly be tested. This type of axiomatic theory is called explanatory theory (Coleman 1964, p. 9) or hypothetically inferred deductively formulated theory (Northrop 1947, p. 109). The axioms in an explanatory theory cannot be tested directly primarily because some of the variables in the axioms cannot be measured satisfactorily. Frequently such variables cannot be measured because they are abstract entities such as mathematical definitions, rather than empirically based variables. Other variables are based on concepts that cannot be directly observed (such as the id, ego, and superego). Still other variables are perhaps observable and not overly abstract, but cannot be measured because of cost or other reasons.

There are two subtypes of explanatory deductive theory. In one subtype the theorist begins with the set of axioms, as in synthetic deductive theory, then deduces the theorem or theorems. Since the axioms are of theoretical interest (and actually serve as the explanation—they solve the puzzle) but cannot be tested, the theorist's objective is to deduce theorems that can be tested.

One example of such an explanatory theory is Gibbs and Martin's (1964) chain-rule theory of status integration and suicide. Building upon Durkheim's (1951) theory of suicide, Gibbs and Martin postulated that the suicide rate of a population varies inversely with the stability and durability of social relationships within a population. This one proposition might suffice as a reasonably complete and elucidating explanation of suicide. However, the variable "stability and durability of social relationships" is rather vague, imprecise, and difficult to measure. One alternative is to attempt to construct some satisfactory measure of the "stability and durability of social relationships." Another alternative is to deduce a relationship linking the first variable (suicide rate) with some testable variable. This suggests a chain rule of deduction, with deduction continuing until a suitable relationship is reached. The theory-construction process is then terminated, making this last deduced theorem the grand theorem. This is the alternative that Gibbs and Martin chose. Their theory is as follows:

THEORY 20.8

POSTULATE 1: The suicide rate of a population varies inversely with the stability and durability of social relationships within that population.

POSTULATE 2: The stability and durability of social relationships within a population vary directly with the extent to which individuals in that population conform to the patterned and socially sanctioned demands and expectations placed upon them by others.

POSTULATE 3: The extent to which individuals in a population conform to patterned and socially sanctioned demands and expectations placed upon them by others varies inversely with the extent to which individuals in that population are confronted with role conflicts.

POSTULATE 4: The extent to which individuals in a population are confronted with role conflicts varies directly with the extent to which individuals occupy incompatible statuses in that population.

POSTULATE 5: The extent to which individuals occupy incompatible statuses in a population varies inversely with the degree of status integration in that population.

Since there are five main postulates, we know that (N) $(N-1)/2$ or $5(4)/2 = 10$ theorems can be derived. However, it happens that Gibbs and Martin know how to measure the last variable in postulate 5 (degree of status integration) but cannot measure the intermediate variables (such as extent to which individuals occupy incompatible status). Thus we are interested only in relating suicide rate (which can be measured) to degree of status integration (which can also be measured), which means that we need deduce only the grand theorem. This can easily be done by applying the chain rule and the sign rule.

By the chain rule we know that suicide rate (the first variable in the chain theory) is related to degree of status integration (the last variable in the chain theory). To find the sign of this relationship we simply apply the sign rule, which in its simplest application merely means counting the number of minus signs or inverse relationships. A quick perusal of the five postulates reveals inverse relationships in postulates 1, 3, and 5, with direct relationships in postulates 2 and 4. The total of three inverse relationships is an odd number and so, according to the sign rule, the sign of the grand theorem will be negative. Thus the grand theorem is:

> **GRAND THEOREM:** The suicide rate of a population varies inversely with the degree of status integration in that population.

In the second form of explanatory deductive theory (type 2 explanatory theory), the goal is somewhat different. In this form one starts with an empirical generalization that assumes the role of a theorem rather than a postulate. With this type of theory one generally has established the empirical generalization to be true, but does not quite know why. One then develops a set of higher-level postulates that cannot be directly tested themselves, but that explain why the empirical generalization is true. Notice that this type of explanatory theory reverses the normal procedure of first writing a set of postulates, then deducing testable theorems. In this latest form the testability has already been achieved, but we require some logical explanation for why the relationship holds.

As an example of type 2 explanatory theory, imagine that Gibbs and Martin had tested the hypothesis stated in the grand theorem, that suicide rate of a population varies inversely with the degree of status integration in that population. Imagine, however, that they had no theory to explain why the relationship was true, but had discovered it by accident, perhaps by correlating a large number of different variables with suicide rate. They feel that the finding is an interesting one, but for it to have maximum value they must be able to explain why the relationship exists. One way would be to write a series of postulates that perhaps themselves cannot be directly proved but that, if true, would explain why the relationship holds. Then they could write a set such as the five postulates in theory 20.8 that would offer such an explanation.

Strength and Form of Relationship

We have repeated in this chapter that postulates and axioms are "true," but we have not said exactly what constitutes a true proposition. Strictly speaking, a true relationship means that the statement is completely true and holds 100 percent of the time. For example, suppose we are seeking to relate variables that are dichotomously coded as present (exist) or absent (do not exist). If we code smoking and cancer in this way, and postulate "If smoking, then cancer," we will be implying that if a person smokes, he or she will always have cancer. That is, if smoking exists, cancer exists. In this example smoking is a sufficient but not necessary cause of cancer. The statement of relationship says nothing about whether or not cancer will be present in the absence of smoking and leaves open the possibility that there are other causes of cancer besides smoking. If we say "If and only if smoking, then cancer," this statement implies that smoking is the only cause of cancer and that if smoking is absent then cancer will be absent. Notice that each of these postulates holds regardless of the effects of other variables. In effect we are assuming a *ceteris paribus* clause, that is, "all other things are equal."

The problem with axiomatic theory construction in sociology is that many times we do not have statements of relationship that are completely true 100 percent of the time. Also, many of our variables are not present or absent variables, but intervally measured or ordinally measured variables. We may use correlation coefficients to measure the degree or strength of the relationship, with + 1 indicating a perfect direct relationship − 1 indicating a perfect inverse relationship, and 0 indicating no relationship, or independence. If the correlation coefficient is 1.0 or very close to it (e.g., .99 or .98), we have no problem. If the correlation coefficient is 0 or very low, we also have no problem, because it is clear that such a statement of relationship is too weak ever to be considered "true," and thus cannot be used as a postulate in an axiomatic theory.

The real problem comes in deciding whether intermediate-size correlations are high enough for the postulate to be considered "true." This problem arises only in synthetic theories, for in explanatory theories the axioms are never tested and are merely assumed to be true. If the theorem deduced from them is found to be true, then this constitutes some evidence that the postulates are true. If the theorem cannot be substantiated, then this constitutes evidence that the postulates from which it was deduced may be false.

Some unfortunate articles in the sociological literature of the 1960s presented synthetic theories with low correlation coefficients. It was pointed out quite correctly by Duncan (1963) that in order for the sign rule to be valid, every postulate must have a correlation coefficient of at least $\sqrt{.75}$. With lower correlations it is not even possible to deduce with any degree of certainty whether the sign of the theorem will be positive or negative.

Costner and Leik (1964, p. 820) say that valid use of the sign rule is possible even with very small correlations as long as theorists meet the following requirements:

1. State all postulates in asymmetrical causal form.
2. Make deductions only from postulates in which the common variable is prior to one or both of the other two variables included in two postulates.
3. Assume a "closed system," that is, assume that there is no connection (casual or spurious) between the variables in the postulates except those stated or implied in the postulates.

Functionalism

In addition to formal axiomatic theory, the other major form of explanation that is widely used in social research is functionalism. Like axiomatic theory, functionalism is also a multivariate form of explanation. Although functionalism is sometimes viewed in a substantive context as a conservative alternative to approaches such as conflict theory, here we are concerned with its logical structure as one of the forms of explanation listed above. Functionalism assumes that the particular variable or phenomenon to be explained is a part of a larger system. Rather than looking for causes of the phenomenon and saying that it is explained when its cause can be found, functionalism explains the existence of a phenomenon by discovering what function it has for the larger system of which it is a part. The basic tenet of functionalism is that phenomena exist in the system only because, and only so long as, they are needed and perform a useful function. Phenomena that are dysfunctional, or impair the system, will either disappear or be altered until they become functional. In its most extreme form functional theory speaks of functional prerequisites that are necessary for survival of the system. In most social systems, however, one can find phenomena that clearly perform a useful function but are not necessary for survival of the system (if the particular phenomenon were removed the society might suffer a bit and be altered in form, but would probably survive). A distinction can also be made between manifest functions, which are overt and obvious, and latent functions, which might not be visible to a casual observer. Thus a phenomenon that had no apparent function in a system, and was perhaps even dysfunctional, might not seem to be susceptible to a functional explanation. However, it could still be explained by functionalism if it were found to have a latent positive function.

Generally speaking, functional theory is best suited to explaining the existence of a phenomenon. It is not well suited to explaining changes in phenomena, except in the sense that if a phenomenon provides a particular function for a society, and subsequently the required function changes so that the phenomenon no longer adequately fulfills it, then the functional model would predict that the phenomenon would alter its form until the required function were again fulfilled.

As a classic example of a functional explanation, consider the Davis and Moore (1945) functional theory of stratification. The problem to be explained is why virtually all societies throughout history have had at least a rudimentary stratification system containing a hierarchy of occupational classes, with occupations higher in the hierarchy paying greater salaries and commanding more prestige than positions lower in the class structure.

One need not seek a functional explanation. It would be difficult to establish a dispositional, intentional, or reason explanation when the unit of analysis is an entire society instead of a single individual. A genetic explanation might be feasible. However, as stated in the discussion above, the genetic explanation, like the reason, intentional, or dispositional explanation, is best suited for explaining unique or puzzling cases. This is to say that if a society differs in some way from most other societies, we might expect a genetic explanation to tell us why it differs. In this case, however, our question is not why one society is different in one respect, but why *all* societies are the *same* in one respect. A formal theory may also explain this, probably by means of one or more statements written in causal or "if—then" form. For example, form of government might be thought to be directly responsible for form of stratification system. However, if virtually all societies, including those with very different forms of government, can be shown to possess stratification systems, then the hypothesis that form of government determines stratification system will not be substantiated.

A functional explanation for the fact that all societies have stratification systems is that societies cannot function or survive (at least in their present form) without such a system. Let us now explore Davis and Moore's argument, considering our basic problem as "Why do all societies pay more money and prestige for some occupational positions than for others?" The chief argument is that differential reward and prestige is functional for the society. Why is it better for some people to be paid more for their work than other people? Because some jobs are both more important to society and harder to qualify for, usually because they require more training than other jobs. Put another way, if a job does not provide an important function for the society, then it really is not very important that this job be filled, and thus the pay for it need not be high. Alternatively, if a job performs an extremely important function for society but takes only a small skill level, so that virtually anyone can fulfill its requirements, then again it is unnecessary to allocate a high monetary reward and great prestige to this job.

The Davis and Moore theory argues that a minimum number of extremely important jobs serving vital functions for society will always exist, and that only relatively few people have the talent and ability to make them trainable for the position. Since such jobs are crucial to the survival of society but only a few persons can perform them, it is necessary to ensure that these jobs pay very high salaries and have a great deal of prestige, in order that the talented persons can be induced to secure the necessary (often long, arduous, and expensive) training and to perform the job diligently.

Thus, according to the Davis and Moore functional theory of stratification, differential reward, with some persons securing more pay and prestige from their jobs than other persons, is not a flaw in society, but is in fact necessary and functional for society. As Tumin (1953, p. 388) says in speaking of the Davis-Moore theory, "Therefore, social inequality among different strata in the amounts of scarce and desired goods, and the amounts of prestige and esteem which they receive, is both positively functional and inevitable in any society."

Critics of functionalism have charged that functionalism is a conservative theory, and it is easy to see from the Davis-Moore theory of stratification why this is so. For example, suppose that you were a rich person and were approached by poor people who said that you should be heavily taxed until all wealth in the society were redistributed equally, and that from that time on all jobs should receive that same monetary reward and prestige regardless of inherent stress or danger or amount and difficulty of training required. You could rebut their argument by invoking the Davis-Moore theory and arguing that if rewards were equalized, then the most dangerous and difficult jobs would not get filled, even if they were necessary for societal survival, because a given individual would have no incentive to fill a difficult job when he or she was equally rewarded for an easy one. Critics of functionalism would call this argument clearly conservative, since it can be used by the power structure to maintain the status quo and is not a theoretical formulation that tends to stimulate social change.

However, the apparent conservative nature of functionalism only exists inasmuch as the function fulfilled by the phenomenon being explained is a constant. If the function changes, then the phenomenon must change. Thus, if functional requirements change rapidly in a society, functionalism must be a "liberal" theory that dictates social change in societal institutions, rather than a conservative theory that supports the status quo. For example, the police force is a necessary institution with a vital function as long as no way can be found to eliminate crime. If social researchers were ever able to eliminate crime completely, then functional theory would predict that the police force would be eliminated, since it would no longer serve a useful function.

In addition to being criticized as essentially conservative and ahistorical, the functional mode of explanation has also been criticized as being vulnerable to illegitimate teleology and tautology (Turner and Maryanski 1979, pp. 118–26). For an example of the latter, if institution *A* is said to be a functional prerequisite for the survival of society *X,* it is easy to lapse into circular reasoning, and to say that *X* survives because *A* is functioning and that we can tell that *A* is functioning because *X* survives.

Functional analysis is also susceptible to illegitimate teleology. Teleological explanation consists of explaining something in terms of its subsequent purpose or function. Such reasoning is generally not considered illegitimate unless one says that the reason the thing (an institution, for example) came into being was to "serve" that purpose. A teleological explanation in this form may take on a mystical or divine nature that is not considered a suitable explanation by some. However, if one can show how the institution came into being, then a teleological explanation of its continued existence may be acceptable. Turner and Maryanski (1979) conclude that while functional analysis is vulnerable to illegitimate teleology and tautology, the careful theorist can avoid these flaws. For further discussion see Turner (1991) and Bailey (1990; 1994a).

Evaluating Social Theory

The different forms of theory (attempts at explanation) discussed in this chapter have quite different applications. The genetic, dispositional, intentional, and reason are more appropriate for explaining unusual events, while empirical generalizations, formal theory, and functional theory are more useful for explaining events common to many cases, and generally require a relatively large sample and/or large unit of analysis, that is, a macro unit of analysis, such as a society. Functionalism and formal theory are the most widely used theoretical forms in social science, and both have their devoted adherents and severe critics. However, it seems clear that it is not the type of theory but the specific theory and its application that must be evaluated. Both formal theories and functional theories can be used successfully in social research. Conversely, any given functional theory or formal theory can be a disaster in the hands of an incompetent theorist. Thus, rather than provide a list of advantages and disadvantages for the different forms of theory, it seems preferable to list some criteria that can be used for evaluating individual theories (regardless of the type) and for deciding which of two alternative theories is superior for the purposes at hand.

1. *Testability.* Perhaps the primary and ultimate criterion of a good theory is that it be testable. The worst theory is one that is so complex and vague that the reader cannot determine a suitable test for it, and thus has no way to tell whether a specific datum supports the theory or contradicts it. On the other hand, a theory can be perfectly clear, and explain a phenomenon beautifully, and yet cannot be tested immediately because of expense or technical or bureaucratic problems. Such a theory can be very valuable. The main requirement is not that one be able immediately and easily to test the theory, but simply that the theory be written so as to be ultimately testable. The theory must be written so that one can tell how to measure the crucial variables, and whether or not a specific piece of information supports the theory.

2. *Clear and unambiguous language.* If one is evaluating comparatively two competing theories of the same phenomenon, the one written in the most precise, unambiguous, and simple language is to be preferred. A theorist has little to gain by using unnecessarily complicated language. Use of such language may damage the theory's testability, make the theory more difficult for laypersons to understand, and generally discourage use of the theory.

3. *Parsimony.* If two theories each explain the same phenomenon equally well, but one is shorter and more parsimonious than the other, this theory is generally considered superior. Indeed, one sign of progress in theory construction is that complex, overly wordy, and difficult theories can be replaced by simple and elegant theories that explain the same puzzle more clearly and simply or in fewer words.

Revising Social Theory

What is the social theorist to do if a theory is tested and not supported by the data (as is often the case)? There are a number of possibilities: (1) the hypothesis is incorrect as stated; (2) one or more assumptions underlying the hypothesis or the statistical tests used are incorrect; (3) the sample is in error; (4) an inappropriate statistical test was used; or (5) simple clerical errors occurred. In any case, one cannot claim that the hypothesis or theory is correct as long as any of these situations occur. It is not convincing to say that failure to support the hypothesis must be due to statistical error, unless such error can be demonstrated.

If the researcher feels that the hypothesis is true in spite of negative evidence, the first step is to check for clerical errors, such as in the arithmetic of the computation of the statistical measure, or an error in transcribing results. If no clerical errors are found, the next check should be for sampling adequacy. If the sample appears to be nonrandom or not a probability sample, or if the sample size is low, it might behoove the researcher to redo the analysis with a larger and more adequate sample, because it is possible that the hypothesis was true in the total population from which the sample was drawn, but was not true in the sample (which means that by definition the sample was inadequate, because it was not an accurate representation of the population).

If the sample seems adequate, the next thing to check is the statistical test. By consulting a statistics textbook the researcher can usually determine for himself or herself whether the statistical test used was appropriate for his or her purposes, and whether his or her data appear to meet the assumptions required for the use of this test.

If a check of possibilities 2, 3, 4, and 5, as listed above, reveal a source of error, the best procedure is to rectify the deficiency and rerun the analysis. If errors cannot be found, then the researcher must accept the fact that his or her hypothesis is erroneous, at least in part. He or she then must revise his or her hypothesis in the direction indicated by the data, and test it again. Having gone full circle, as discussed in chapter 1, it is time to begin again with a revised or new hypothesis. Even if the hypothesis is fully supported, it is desirable for the same researcher or some other researcher to complete the circle again in order to replicate the study. Only through such replication can we be truly sure that our results are valid.

A recent trend is the analysis of the relationship of theory to other aspects of research such as data collection or statistical analysis. Bailey (1984b) analyzed in detail the similarities and differences of theory and method, while Collins (1984) studied the relationship between theory and statistical analysis in sociology. Also, Bailey (1986; 1990; 1994a), analyzed the philosophical foundations of concept formation, measurement, and theory.

Summary

Chapter 20 discussed construction and revision of complex social theories. We listed seven types of explanation in social research: genetic; intentional; dispositional; reasons; functional; empirical generalizations; and formal theory. We devoted most of our discussion to the last three, as these are the most widely used. Formal or axiomatic theory was clarified in the greatest depth, and distinguished between the explanatory and synthetic forms of axiomatic theory. We followed our discussion of axiomatic theory with a fairly detailed treatment of functional theory. We next discussed some criteria for the evaluation of social theory. The criteria we discussed were testability, clarity, and parsimony. The chapter concluded by discussing the revision of social theory.

GLOSSARY

Accretion measure   An unobtrusive measure utilizing deposited physical material.

Analytical measure   A measure of some characteristic of a group computed by aggregating characteristics of individual members of the group (for example, the median income of all group members).

Applied research   Research whose findings can be applied to solve social problems of immediate concern.

Asymmetrical relationship   A relationship in which a change in one variable results in a change in the other variable, but not vice versa.

Axiom   A statement of relationship assumed to be true and not tested. The set of axioms is used in an axiomatic or deductive theory to derive theorems, at least some of which are testable.

Axiomatic theory   A deductive theory in which a set of axioms or postulates is assumed to be true and is used to derive theorems, some of which (but not all) must be testable.

Bales category system   A set of 12 categories used to code interaction in groups; the Bales technique is highly structured for an observational technique, using both structured observational categories and a structured laboratory setting.

Bivariate   Two variable; a bivariate relationship is a statement of a relationship between two variables.

Case study   An in-depth study (usually longitudinal) of one or a few cases, in contrast to a more superficial cross-sectional study of a larger sample; usually, but not always, an observational study.

Categorical variable   A noncontinuous variable consisting of two or more discrete nonoverlapping categories (for example, male and female).

Central Limit Theorem   A theorem that states that with repeated samples of the same size from the same population, the sample means will be normally distributed (bell-shaped curve) around the population mean; this means that the majority of the sample means will be similar in value to the population mean.

Chi square   A measure of statistical significance for a contingency table.

Clinical interview   A completely unstructured interview in which the interviewer lets the respondent talk in depth about some topic of concern to the respondent; most widely used in psychotherapy.

Closed-ended questions   Also called forced-choice or fixed-response questions; questions that force the respondent to answer in one of the response categories provided.

Closing (or pre-closing)   In conversational analysis, a verbal cue used by one of the parties in a conversation to indicate that the party wishes to terminate the conversation; common closings are "well" and "OK."

Closure   The condition in which the variables in an experiment are closed off or isolated from extraneous factors that could negatively effect the experiment; an ideal example would be an experiment conducted in a sealed vacuum chamber. In social science the experimenter generally cannot physically seal out extraneous variables, but must simply attempt to control them as much as possible.

Cluster analysis   A numerical technique for grouping objects or variables on the basis of similarity.

Cluster sampling   Sampling conducted in several stages. In the first stage a cluster of cases is sampled; then from these initial clusters, the actual sample of cases is selected (for example, if a sample of households is needed, the researcher might initially randomly sample blocks for efficiency, then within the blocks chosen, sample again for households).

Codebook   A book compiled by the survey analyst that tells the meaning of each code from each question on a questionnaire. For example, the codebook might reveal that for question #3, male is coded as 1, and female as 2.

Coding Assigning codes in the form of symbols (usually numbers) for each category of each answer or variable in a study (usually a survey study).

Coefficient of reproducibility A measure that indicates how accurately a score on a Guttman scale (scalogram analysis) can be used to reproduce the scores on the individual items used to construct the scale; the greater the number of errors in predicted item scores, the lower the coefficient of reproducibility.

Computer assisted personal interviewing (CAPI) A method of personal (face-to-face) interviewing in which survey questionnaires are displayed on computer terminals for interviewers, who type responses directly onto disk.

Computer assisted telephone interviewing (CATI) A method of telephone interviewing in which survey questionnaires are displayed on computer terminals for interviewers, who type responses directly onto disk.

Computer survey Also called an electronic survey. A survey in which both the interviewer and respondent are working at computer terminals linked by a network of some sort.

Concept A mental image or perception.

Concurrent validation Same as criterion validation (see criterion validation).

Construct validation A procedure for validating a new measure by substituting it for an older measure in the test of a theory; the new measure is validated if the test of the theory yields the same results with the new measure as with the old measure.

Content analysis A method of analyzing documents by using a quantitative coding scheme; the method attempts to be objective and systematic.

Contingency question A survey question asked only of some respondents; respondent's eligibility to answer the question depends upon his or her answer to a previous (filter) question (for example, a filter question might ask the person's sex. If male, skip question #3. If female, answer #3, "Have you ever had an abortion." Question #3 in this case is a contingency question).

Contingency table Also called a cross tabulation (see cross tabulation).

Control group In an experiment, a group selected to be identical to the experimental group and does not receive the experimental stimulus (receives nothing or receives a placebo).

Control variable A third variable that is controlled for or held constant in order to see whether it affects the relationship between two variables.

Convenience sample   A nonprobability sample in which the most convenient (most readily available) cases are chosen for the study.

Cover letter   The letter that accompanies a mailed questionnaire; the cover letter should minimally identify the sponsor of the study, tell why the study is important, and in general encourage response.

Criterion validation   A technique for assessing the validity of a new measure or scale by comparing the score on the new measure with the score on an old measure thought to be valid, and thus chosen to be the criterion.

Cross-sectional study   A study (usually a survey) conducted at a single point in time with a sample thought to be a representative cross-section of the population in terms of relevant variables (age, sex, education, etc.).

Cross tabulation (cross tab)   A tabulation or table showing the relationship between two or more variables by presenting all combinations of categories of variables (also called a contingency table).

Curvilinear (nonlinear) relationship   A relationship between two or more variables that when graphed forms a curved line rather than a straight line as a linear relationship does.

Data (plural)   The information gathered and analyzed in a study.

Data cleaning   The process of checking for errors after the data have been entered into the computer.

Data file   The complete set of data for all persons or cases in the sample, as stored on a computer diskette in 80-column "cards."

Data reduction   The process of reducing data from questionnaires to some form suitable for computer analysis, generally through coding and computer entry.

Decentering   A form of double translation in which changes are made not only to the second-language questionnaire, but to the first-language questionnaire as well.

Deconstruction   The process, associated with postmodernism, of dismantling white, male, European-centered perspectives so that they can be modified or replaced with more diverse and inclusionary perspectives which take into account the views of women, ethnic and racial groups, and others.

Dependent variable   A variable in an asymmetrical relationship that is affected by the independent variable, but cannot in turn affect it.

Descriptive statistics   Statistical analysis that merely describes a sample (for example, by computing the mean) rather than making inferences as to how accurately the sample data represents the population, as one does in inferential statistics.

Dimensional sampling   A multidimensional nonprobability sampling method in which the researcher specifies all the conceptual dimensions on which sampling is desired, then selects a quota of cases for all combinations of dimensions.

Direct entry   The process of entering data directly from the questionnaire into the computer without an intermediate coding step. This can be accomplished either through scanning, or by having the interviewer enter the respondent's answers into a computer terminal.

Direct relationship   A positive relationship; a relationship in which an increase in the value of one variable is accompanied by an increase in the value of the other variable, and a decrease by a decrease.

Discrete variable   A noncontinuous variable containing discrete categories with clear boundaries between categories (for example, male and female).

Distorter variable   A third variable that distorts the real relationship between two variables, so that the observed relationship is not the real one (see also control variable, suppressor variable, and spurious relationship).

Double-barrelled question   A survey question that is really two distinct questions disguised as one.

Double translation   Two-way translation, in which a questionnaire is translated into a second language, and then back into the first language, to check its accuracy.

Empirical   Amenable to the senses; empirical phenomena are phenomena that can be measured directly by the senses such as sight (observation), hearing, touch, smell, etc.

Empirical generalization   An inductively derived generalization about empirical occurrences.

Erosion measure   An unobtrusive measure based on the wearing away of physical materials.

Eta   A nonlinear correlation coefficient (to be computed in place of Pearson's *r* when one expects that the relationship is curvilinear).

Ethical neutrality   The perspective that a researcher should remain neutral and not take positions dictated by moral issues or values (see value-free sociology).

Ethnography   Literally, the study of culture; a term traditionally used for anthropological observation of primitive cultures, now applied to observation in general.

Ethnomethodology   The study of the methods used in everyday, commonplace, routine social activity.

Evaluation research   Research that seeks to determine how successful applied social programs have been (for example, antipoverty programs).

Exit poll   A survey of voters as they leave voting areas, to determine how they voted, and thus predict the outcome of the election.

Experimental group   In an experiment, the group to which the experimental stimulus is given, in contrast to the control group, which is an identical group but receives nothing (or a placebo).

***Ex post facto* experiment**   A quasi-experimental design conducted after the experimental stimulus has occurred; thus, the experimenter cannot introduce the test stimulus, but can control (but often only statistically) extraneous factors.

External validity   The degree to which a measure is valid when generalized to other populations.

Face sheet   A part of a questionnaire containing items to be answered by the interviewer, such as household census tract number and attempts to contact a respondent.

Face validation   Validation of a measure by simply determining whether the measure appears to be valid, or is valid "on the face of it."

Factor analysis   A statistical technique for determining the existence of a set of latent dimensions underlying a set of intercorrelations.

Factorial experimental design   A complex experimental design that allows the use of multiple independent variables.

Factor scaling   Construction of a scale through factor analysis.

Fax survey   A survey conducted via fax machines, which can be seen as a hybrid form between a telephone survey and a mailed-questionnaire survey.

Field study   A study conducted in the "field" or the natural habitat of the subjects being studied, as opposed to an artificial experimental laboratory.

Focused interview   A form of semistructured interview in which questions are not specified in advance, but the interviewer focuses on a particular event or topic.

Focus group   A qualitative method of gathering data consisting of a guided group discussion, led by a trained moderator, and designed to provide information on a certain topic from a certain population. It is often, but not always, used in conjunction with survey.

Frequency distribution control   A matching technique used by experimenters in selecting persons for experimental and control groups so that each group has the same average value on each variable (for example, age).

Funnel technique   A technique in questionnaire construction that entails beginning with general questions to put the respondent at ease, and then "funneling down" to more specific questions.

Gamma   A nonparametric measure of association (relationship) for ordinal variables in a contingency table.

Global property   A group property that does not use any characteristics of individuals in the group; for example, measuring the religiosity of a city by the number of churches within the city limits.

Grand theorem   In an axiomatic theory, the final theorem derived from a chain of axioms and prior theorems.

Grounded theory   Theory derived inductively from intense prior study of the actual empirical data the theory attempts to explain (in contrast to theory formulated in "an ivory tower").

Guttman scaling (scalogram analysis).   A popular scaling method for creating an ordinal scale, usually an attitude scale, having the property of simple order (there is only one way—one combination of answers—to make each scale score).

Halo effect   A rating error in which the general impression of the respondent (perhaps as gained from the respondent's answer on a previous question) leads the rater to give a biased rating.

Hawthorne effect   A reactive effect in which subjects' performances are altered by the knowledge that they are the objects of research; for example, subjects who know that they are in an experiment at work may have increased morale due to their new "importance" and subsequently perform better at their jobs.

Hypothesis   A testable statement; hypotheses are generally either derived from a theory, or from direct observation of data (see grounded theory). Hypotheses are often bivariate (for example, the higher the education, the higher the income).

Immutable characteristic   A characteristic which is generally unchangeable or very difficult to change, such as sex, race, or age.

Inclusionary research methods   Methods designed to include groups which have often been excluded from research, such as women, racial and ethnic groups, and others.

Independent variable   In an asymmetrical relationship, the variable that can affect changes in the other variable (the dependent variable), but cannot itself be affected by changes in the dependent variable.

Indexical   In ethnomethodology, a word or expression whose meaning depends upon the context, such as who is speaking and who is being spoken to (for example, he, she, it, you).

Inferential statistics   Statistical analysis in which sample data is used to make an inference concerning the population from which the sample was drawn.

Insider   A person who has the power to control research, as opposed to an outsider, who lacks power and is often excluded from research. A second meaning of insider is a person who has special knowledge by virtue of being a group member.

Interval measurement   Level of measurement that indicates not only rank order, but also the amount of distance between each rank on the variable being measured.

Intervening variable   A variable intermediate between an independent variable *A* and a dependent variable *C*, so that *A* affects *C* only through *B*.

Interview schedule   A list of questions read by an interviewer to a respondent, with the interviewer then writing down the respondent's answers on the schedule; this is in contrast to a questionnaire that is self-administered by the respondent (although in this book we use the term *questionnaire* as a generic term to cover all lists of survey questions whether they are interviewed or self-administered).

Inverse relationship (negative relationship)   A relationship in which the value of one variable increases when the value of the second variable decreases, and decreases when the value of the other variable increases.

Item   A question in an attitude scale.

Labeling theory   The theory of deviance (can also be applied in some other areas besides deviance) that says that persons who are labeled and reacted to by others as deviant in fact begin to act in a deviant fashion, so as to meet the other's expectations.

Latin-square design   A complex experimental design using as many independent variables (experimental conditions) as there are subjects.

Likert scaling   A type of summated rating scale designed to aid elimination of questionable items from the scale.

Linear relationship   A relationship between variables that, when graphed, appears to be a straight line.

Longitudinal study   A study conducted over time, in contrast to a cross-sectional study conducted at one point in time; although there are exceptions, observational studies tend to be longitudinal, while surveys tend to be cross-sectional.

Macro analysis   Large-scale analysis; a macro study is one in which the unit of analysis is a large aggregate (such as a nation) as contrasted with a micro study in which the unit of analysis is a single individual or a small group.

Marginal   The sum of all frequencies in a given row or column of a contingency table.

Mean   The sum of all values, divided by the number of cases; along with the mode and median, a standard measure of the average or central tendency.

Median   The mid point of the sample; the value on a variable for which half of a sample or population have lower values and half have higher. Along with the mode and the mean, a standard measure of the average or central tendency.

Meta-analysis   A statistical technique for synthesizing quantitative results from existing studies.

Micro analysis   Small-scale analysis; analysis that uses a single individual or a small group as the unit of analysis (as in psychology) in contrast with macro analysis, which uses a large aggregate such as a nation as the unit of analysis.

Mixed motive game   In game theory, a game in which either a competitive or cooperative strategy may be optimal for a given player depending on the actions of the other player or players.

Mode   The most frequent value in the sample or population; along with the mean and median, a standard measure of the average or central tendency.

Model   A representation of a system that differs from the actual system in some way, but is accurate enough to provide information on the system; for example, a computerized mathematical model of a formal organization can show the interrelationships within the organization, and provide helpful information about it.

Mutable characteristic   A characteristic which is generally changeable, such as education or occupation.

Negative relationship (inverse relationship)   See inverse relationship.

Nominal measurement   The simplest sort of measurement in which one has only discrete categories but no ranking of categories; the categories are generally assigned names rather than numbers (quarterback, halfback, etc.).

Nonparametric statistics   Statistics that do not assume a normal distribution of the variables in the population. Most nonparametric statistics are used in analyzing data presented in the form of contingency tables.

Nonprobability sample   A sample in which the probability of selection of each case is not known.

Nonresponse bias   Bias that occurs because persons who fail to respond to a survey (generally a mailed questionnaire) are not representative of the total sample to whom questionnaires were administered.

Normal curve   The familiar bell-shaped distribution of scores; parametric statistics assume the normal distribution.

Open-ended question   A survey question in which no answer categories are provided; the respondent is merely given space to respond to the question.

Operational definition   The empirical measurement of a verbal concept; for example, the operational definition of intelligence in the IQ test.

Ordinal measurement   Measurement where one can specify not only discrete categories as in nominal measurement, but can also rank order the categories.

Panel mortality   Attrition of respondents in a panel study due to death, migration, or inability or refusal to be reinterviewed.

Panel study   A longitudinal survey study in which the same respondents are reinterviewed at several points in time.

Paradigm A research perspective or view (a school of thought) that holds views about what research goals and methods are appropriate (how research should be conducted) and has its own values and assumptions.

Participant observation Observation in which the researcher is a member of the organization or group being studied and participants in all organizational activities, generally (but not always) other group members, are unaware that the observer is conducting research.

Path analysis A statistical technique for analyzing the direct and indirect relationships between a number of intervally measured variables, and representing them graphically in a path diagram.

Pearson Product Moment Correlation Coefficient (Pearson's *r* or just *r*) A common measure of strength of relationship between two intervally measured variables.

Phi coefficient A measure of strength of relationship for two dichotomized nominal variables presented in a two-by-two contingency table.

Population (universe) The total group to be studied; if the total population cannot be studied, it is the group from which the sample is taken; one hopes the sample is representative of the entire population.

Positive relationship (direct relationship) See direct relationship.

Positivism The application of the logic and methods of physical science to uncover the laws which govern social phenomena.

Postmodernism The general perspective (which has several variants) that white, male, European-centered thought (and especially science) must be modified or deconstructed (see deconstruction).

Posttest In an experiment, a test to measure the values of the dependent variable after applying the experimental stimulus.

Postulate This term is sometimes used interchangeably with the term *axiom* when referring to a proposition in an axiomatic deductive theory. A postulate is a statement assumed to be true and not tested; a set of postulates is used in an axiomatic theory to deduce theorems, some of which must be testable.

Pragmatic validation (criterion validation) See criterion validation.

Pretest In a survey, preliminary administration of a questionnaire to a small sample in order to identify and correct problematic items. In an experiment, a test to measure the values of the dependent variables before applying the experimental stimulus.

Probability sample   A sample in which the probability of selection of each case is known.

Proportional reduction in error (PRE)   The proportion of error that is eliminated in predicting the value of one variable when the value of another variable is known.

Proposition   The generic name for any statement of relationship between two or more variables; as used in this book, hypotheses, axioms, postulates, and theorems are all types of propositions.

Pure research   Research designed to advance knowledge that may not have clear immediate or future applications.

Purposive sample   A nonprobability sampling procedure in which the researcher uses his or her judgment to select those respondents that best meet the needs of the study (see chapter 5).

Qualitative analysis   Nonnumerical analysis; generally, analysis limited to nominal variables (for example, race, sex, religion) rather than ordinal variables or interval variables, or observational data analysis of a nonstatistical nature (interpretation of field notes).

Quantitative analysis   Analysis of numerically coded data, specifically ordinal, interval and ratio data, and often involving computation of statistical measures and tests of significance.

Quasi-experimental design   An experimental design that does not meet all of the ideal standards of the pure experiment; specifically, an experimental design in which the experimenter has only partial control (control over the experimental stimulus or control over extraneous factors, but not both).

Questionnaire   A list of questions to be answered by the survey respondent; often the term *questionnaire* is restricted to a self-administered instrument as opposed to an interview, but in this book we use the term *questionnaire* generally to refer to any list of survey questions, whether self-administered by the respondent or read to the respondent by an interviewer.

Quota sampling   The nonprobability sampling equivalent of stratified sampling; nonprobability sampling in which one first selects necessary strata, then gathers a specific quota of cases in each strata (see chapter 5).

Random digit dialing   A telephone survey sampling method in which a probability sample of all dialable telephone numbers is selected from a study area's working exchanges.

Randomization   A probabilistic method of selecting subjects for a sample or assigning subjects to experimental and control groups in which each subject has an equal probability of selection.

Random sample   A probabilistic sample in which each element has an equal probability of being selected.

Ratio measurement   A level of measurement that shows not only rank order as in ordinal measurement, and distance between ranks as in interval measurement, but also has a unique (absolute) zero point.

Recording unit (also called unit of analysis)   In content analysis, the unit (single word, theme, paragraph, etc.) used as a basis for recording data (see chapter 12).

Recursive model   An asymmetrical causal statistical model such as a path model in which all causation proceeds in one direction (no feedback loops or symmetrical causation).

Reduction   In typology construction, the act of reducing the number of cells in a typology into a fewer number of types; the opposite of substruction.

Reliability   The consistency of a measure.

Replication   Exact repetition of a study to determine whether or not identical results may be obtained as in the previous research.

Respondent   The person who answers questions in a survey.

Response set   In a questionnaire, a tendency for the respondent to reply to questions in a certain way, regardless of the appropriate answer; response set may result from such factors as social desirability bias, poor question order or acquiescence (desire to agree rather than disagree)—see chapter 6.

Sample   A selection, hopefully representative, of the total population or universe that one desires to study.

Sampling distribution   The distribution of values of a sample statistic (for example, the mean) obtained by taking repeated samples of the same size from the population.

Sampling element   The case, or ultimate object, to be selected in the sample; for example, male Protestants between the ages of 21 and 50.

Sampling unit   Either a single sampling element or, as in cluster sampling, a collection of sampling elements.

Scale   An item or set of items (generally more than one) for measuring some characteristic or property, such as an attitude. The property is generally considered to be unidimensional, and a quantitative score is usually derived (for example, an IQ score or an alienation score).

Secondary analysis   Literally second-hand analysis; analysis of data gathered by some other researcher or for some other purpose (generally both).

Semantic differential   A seven-point scale for measuring the underlying or covert meaning of a verbal concept to the respondent.

Semistructured interview   An interview in which the topic is decided in advance, but the interviewer has some leeway in deciding which questions to ask and what sort of answer categories to use.

Serial order preference   In a questionnaire, a tendency for an individual to choose the response listed first in a series of questions with identical response categories.

Simple matching   In experimentation, selecting subjects for control and experimental groups by finding pairs of individuals that are identically matched on all relevant variables, and assigning one to the experimental group and the other to the control group.

Simulation   The process of operating a model over time to show how variables in the system respond to changes in other variables in the system.

Smallest space analysis   A statistical technique for visually (graphically) representing all of the variables or objects in a property space of the fewest adequate dimensions.

Snowball sampling   A nonprobabilistic form of sampling in which persons initially chosen for the sample are used as informants to locate other persons having necessary characteristics making them eligible for the sample (see chapter 5).

Social construction of reality   The idea that some sociological concepts (for example, deviance) are mentally constructed or defined rather than existing as concrete empirical entities.

Social indicator   A social variable (usually macro) which can be used to measure the level of living of a given society at a given point in time; for example, median educational level of the population could serve as a social indicator.

Sociometric measure   A measure of social relationships (for example, popularity or best friends) among the members of a group.

Split-half reliability   A method of assessing reliability of a measure at a single point in time by dividing the items comprising the measuring instrument into two identical halves, administering both, and comparing scores on the two halves; if the two scores are identical or similar, the measure is said to be reliable.

SPSS (Statistical Package for the Social Sciences)   A set of "canned" or preprogrammed statistical techniques.

Spurious relationship An apparent relationship between two variables A and B that is found to be false (does not exist) because both are caused by a third variable C. When C is properly controlled for or held constant, the apparent relationship between A and B disappears (see control variable, suppressor variable, distorter variable).

Statistical significance A term used to indicate that a particular value of a statistical measure would not be likely to occur by chance.

Stratified random sample A probability sampling procedure in which the population is first divided into strata (for example, freshman, sophomore, junior, senior), then sampling is conducted within each strata.

Strength of relationship The degree to which the value of one variable in a relationship changes when the value of the other variable changes.

Substruction In typology construction, the opposite of reduction; the process of identifying the underlying dimensions of one or a few types, and then extending them to form the full typology or property space.

Summated ratings scale A scaling method for constructing an ordinal scale by summing up an individual's scores on a set of agree-disagree items.

Suppressor variable A third variable related to each of two variables in a relationship that suppresses the observed relationship between two variables (that is, makes the relationship appear weaker than it actually is); see also control variable, distorter variable, and spurious relationship.

Survey A data collection technique that asks questions of a sample of respondents generally at a single point in time, either with a self-administered questionnaire or an interviewer.

Symmetrical relationship A relationship in which change in either variable A or variable B will result in change in the other variable, in contrast to an asymmetrical relationship in which the independent variable can affect the dependent variable but not vice versa (see asymmetrical relationship).

Systematic sample A sample in which every kth case is selected (usually with a random start), where k is any constant.

Test-retest reliability A procedure for assessing the reliability of a measure by comparing results of the measure at two or more points in time.

Theorem In an axiomatic theory, the proposition that is deduced from the set of axioms or postulates.

Theory   A proposition or set of interrelated propositions that purports to explain a given social phenomenon.

Thurstone scaling   An attitude scaling procedure in which judges rank proposed scale items in attempt to construct an interval scale.

Type I error   In hypothesis testing in inferential statistics, the error made by rejecting a true null hypothesis.

Type II error   In hypothesis testing in inferential statistics, the error made by failing to reject a false null hypothesis (see chapter 16).

Typology   A multidimensional classification.

Uncontrolled experiment   An experiment (generally a field experiment, or experiment in the natural social habitat) in which the experimenter can control neither the experimental stimulus nor extraneous factors.

Unit of analysis   The basic unit whose properties the researcher chooses to measure and analyze; in sociology, generally the individual person, or some aggregate of individuals such as a group, club, city, county, nation, etc.

Univariate   One variable, as in univariate analysis, a univariate hypothesis, or a univariate table.

Unstructured interview   An interview in which the interviewer specifies only the topic in advance, but specifies no particular questions or fixed-answer categories in advance.

Value-free sociology   The perspective or school of thought that sociological research can (and should be) conducted with the values of the researcher held in abeyance so that they cannot bias research (see ethical neutrality).

Value-full sociology   The perspective that rather than attempt to remain value-free, researchers should consciously espouse political values chosen from the full range available.

Variable   A concept, often but not always quantitatively measured, that contains two or more values or categories that can vary over time or over a given sample (for example, age), in contrast to a constant, the value of which remains fixed and never varies.

Verstehen   Understanding; the notion inspired largely by Weber that one can understand human behavior through empathy, or through having personally experienced it. Some adherents feel that verstehen then supplements deductive theory, experimentation, and the whole scientific method, taking up where the latter leaves off.

Wave   A reinterview of respondents in a panel study.

Weighted sample   A sample (generally a cluster or stratified sample) in which some clusters or strata of the population are sampled disproportionately in order to ensure that they are adequately represented in the final sample. When subsamples from the various strata are combined in the final sample, they must be weighted so that all cases have an equal probability of selection, or else the sample will not be random.

Working Hypothesis   A tentative hypothesis used in the initial stages of research and subject to revision after preliminary data analysis.

Yule's Q   A measure of association (relationship) for two dichotomous ordinal variables represented in a contingency table; the two-by-two version of gamma.

Zero-sum game   In mathematical game theory, a game in which only a given finite amount of reward exists, so that all gains made by one player are made at the expense of the other player; thus, the game is almost by definition competitive rather than cooperative.

[library stamp, illegible]

LIVERPOOL
JOHN MOORES UNIVERSITY
I.M. MARSH LIBRARY
BARKHILL ROAD
LIVERPOOL L17 6BD
TEL. 0151 231 5216/5299

APPENDIXES

A. Table of Random Digits

B. Code of Ethics of the American Sociological Association
Revised ASA Code of Ethics

C. Code of Professional Ethics and Practices of the
American Association for Public Opinion Research

LIVERPOOL
JOHN MOORES UNIVERSITY
I.M. MARSH LIBRARY
BARKHILL ROAD
LIVERPOOL L17 6BD
TEL. 0151 231 5216/5299

APPENDIX A

Table of Random Digits

The RAND Corporation, *A Million Random Digits* (New York: The Free Press, 1955), pp. 1–3. Reprinted with the permission of the publisher and the RAND Corporation.

Table of Random Digits

00000	10097	32533	76520	13586	34673	54876	80959	09117	39292	74945
00001	37542	04805	64894	74296	24805	24037	20636	10402	00822	91665
00002	08422	68953	19645	09303	23209	02560	15953	34764	35080	33606
00003	99019	02529	09376	70715	38311	31165	88676	74397	04436	27659
00004	12807	99970	80157	36147	64032	36653	98951	16877	12171	76833
00005	66065	74717	34072	76850	36697	36170	65813	39885	11199	29170
00006	31060	10805	45571	82406	35303	42614	86799	07439	23403	09732
00007	85269	77602	02051	65692	68665	74818	73053	85247	18623	88579
00008	63573	32135	05325	47048	90553	57548	28468	28709	83491	25624
00009	73796	45753	03529	64778	35808	34282	60935	20344	35273	88435
00010	98520	17767	14905	68607	22109	40558	60970	93433	50500	73998
00011	11805	05431	39808	27732	50725	68248	29405	24201	52775	67851
00012	83452	99634	06288	98083	13746	70078	18475	40610	68711	77817
00013	88685	40200	86507	58401	36766	67951	90364	76493	29609	11062
00014	99594	67348	87517	64969	91826	08928	93785	61368	23478	34113
00015	65481	17674	17468	50950	58047	76974	73039	57186	40218	16544
00016	80124	35635	17727	08015	45318	22374	21115	78253	14385	53763
00017	74350	99817	77402	77214	43236	00210	45521	64237	96286	02655
00018	69916	26803	66252	29148	36936	87203	76621	13990	94400	56418
00019	09893	20505	14225	68514	46427	56788	96297	78822	54382	14598
00020	91499	14523	68479	27686	46162	83554	94750	89923	37089	20048
00021	80336	94598	26940	36858	70297	34135	53140	33340	42050	82341
00022	44104	81949	85157	47954	32979	26575	57600	40881	22222	06413
00023	12550	73742	11100	02040	12860	74697	96644	89439	28707	25815
00024	63606	49329	16505	34484	40219	52563	43651	77082	07207	31790
00025	61196	90446	26457	47774	51924	33729	65394	59593	42582	60527
00026	15474	45266	95270	79953	59367	83848	82396	10118	33211	59466
00027	94557	28573	67897	54387	54622	44431	91190	42592	92927	45973
00028	42481	16213	97344	08721	16868	48767	03071	12059	25701	46670
00029	23523	78317	73208	89837	68935	91416	26252	29663	05522	82562
00030	04493	52494	75246	33824	45862	51025	61962	79335	65337	12472
00031	00549	97654	64051	88159	96119	63896	54692	82391	23287	29529
00032	35963	15307	26898	09354	33351	35462	77974	50024	90103	39333
00033	59808	08391	45427	26842	83609	49700	13021	24892	78565	20106
00034	46058	85236	01390	92286	77281	44077	93910	83647	70617	42941
00035	32179	00597	87379	25241	05567	07007	86743	17157	85394	11838
00036	69234	61406	20117	45204	15956	60000	18743	92423	97118	96338
00037	19565	41430	01758	75379	40419	21585	66674	36806	84962	85207
00038	45155	14938	19476	07246	43667	94543	59047	90033	20826	69541
00039	94864	31994	36168	10851	34888	81553	01540	35456	05014	51176
00040	98086	24826	45240	28404	44999	08896	39094	73407	35441	31880
00041	33185	16232	41941	50949	89435	18581	88695	41994	37548	73043
00042	80951	00406	96382	70774	20151	23387	25016	25298	94624	61171
00043	79752	49140	71961	28296	69861	02591	74852	20539	00387	59579
00044	18633	32537	98145	06571	31010	24674	05455	61427	77938	91936
00045	74029	43902	77557	32270	97790	17119	52527	58021	80814	51748
00046	54178	45611	80993	37143	05335	12969	56127	19255	36040	90324
00047	11664	49883	52079	84827	59381	71539	09973	33440	88461	23356
00048	48324	77928	31249	64710	02295	36870	32307	57546	15020	09994
00049	69074	94138	87637	91976	35584	04401	10518	21615	01848	76938

00050	09188	20097	32825	39527	04220	86304	83389	87374	64278	58044
00051	90045	85497	51981	50654	94938	81997	91870	76150	68476	64659
00052	73189	50207	47677	26269	62290	64464	27124	67018	41361	82760
00053	75768	76490	20971	87749	90429	12272	95375	05871	93823	43178
00054	54016	44056	66281	31003	00682	27398	20714	53295	07706	17813
00055	08358	69910	78542	42785	13661	58873	04618	97553	31223	08420
00056	28306	03264	81333	10591	40510	07893	32604	60475	94119	01840
00057	53840	86233	81594	13628	51215	90290	28466	68795	77762	20791
00058	91757	53741	61613	62269	50263	90212	55781	76514	83483	47055
00059	89415	92694	00397	58391	12607	17646	48949	72306	94541	37408
00060	77513	03820	86864	29901	68414	82774	51908	13980	72893	55507
00061	19502	37174	69979	20288	55210	29773	74287	75251	65344	67415
00062	21818	59313	93278	81757	05686	73156	07082	85046	31853	38452
00063	51474	66499	68107	23621	94049	91345	42836	09191	08007	45449
00064	99559	68331	62535	24170	69777	12830	74819	78142	43860	72834
00065	33713	48007	93584	72869	51926	64721	58303	29822	93174	93972
00066	85274	86893	11303	22970	28834	34137	73515	90400	71148	43643
00067	84133	89640	44035	52166	73852	70091	61222	60561	62327	18423
00068	56732	16234	17395	96131	10123	91622	85496	57560	81604	18880
00069	65138	56806	87648	85261	34313	65861	45875	21069	85644	47277
00070	38001	02176	81719	11711	71602	92937	74219	64049	65584	49698
00071	37402	96397	01304	77586	56271	10086	47324	62605	40030	37438
00072	97125	40348	87083	31417	21815	39250	75237	62047	15501	29578
00073	21826	41134	47143	34072	64638	85902	49139	06441	03856	54552
00074	73135	42742	95719	09035	85794	74296	08789	88156	64691	19202
00075	07638	77929	03061	18072	96207	44156	23821	99538	04713	66994
00076	60528	83441	07954	19814	59175	20695	05533	52139	61212	06455
00077	83596	35655	06958	92983	05128	09719	77433	53783	92301	50498
00078	10850	62746	99599	10507	13499	06319	53075	71839	06410	19362
00079	39820	98952	43622	63147	64421	80814	43800	09351	31024	73167
00080	59580	06478	75569	78800	88835	54486	23768	06156	04111	08408
00081	38508	07341	23793	48763	90822	97022	17719	04207	95954	49953
00082	30692	70668	94688	16127	56196	80091	82067	63400	05462	69200
00083	65443	95659	18288	27437	49632	24041	08337	65676	96299	90836
00084	27267	50264	13192	72294	07477	44606	17985	48911	97341	30358
00085	91307	06991	19072	24210	36699	53728	28825	35793	28976	66252
00086	68434	94688	84473	13622	62126	98408	12843	82590	09815	93146
00087	48908	15877	54745	24591	35700	04754	83824	52692	54130	55160
00088	06913	45197	42672	78601	11883	09528	63011	98901	14974	40344
00089	10455	16019	14210	33712	91342	37821	88325	80851	43667	70883
00090	12883	97343	65027	61184	04285	01392	17974	15077	90712	26769
00091	21778	30976	38807	36961	31649	42096	63281	02023	08816	47449
00092	19523	59515	65122	59659	86283	68258	69572	13798	16435	91529
00093	67245	52670	35583	16563	79246	86686	76463	34222	26655	90802
00094	60584	47377	07500	37992	45134	26529	26760	83637	41326	44344
00095	53853	41377	36066	94850	58838	73859	49364	73331	96240	43642
00096	24637	38736	74384	89342	52623	07992	12369	18601	03742	83873
00097	83080	12451	38992	22815	07759	51777	97377	27585	51972	37867
00098	16444	24334	36151	99073	27493	70939	85130	32552	54846	54759
00099	60790	18157	57178	65762	11161	78576	45819	52979	65130	04860

Table of Random Digits (*continued*)

00100	03991	10461	93716	16894	66083	24653	84609	58232	88616	19161
00101	38555	95554	32886	59780	08355	60860	29735	47762	71299	23853
00102	17546	73704	92052	46215	55121	29281	59076	07936	27954	58909
00103	32643	52861	95819	06831	00911	98936	76355	93779	80863	00514
00104	69572	68777	39510	35905	14060	40619	29549	69616	33564	60780
00105	24122	66591	27699	06494	14845	46672	61958	77100	90899	75754
00106	61196	30231	92962	61773	41839	55382	17267	70943	78038	70267
00107	30532	21704	10274	12202	39685	23309	10061	68829	55986	66485
00108	03788	97599	75867	20717	74416	53166	35208	33374	87539	08823
00109	48228	63379	85783	47619	53152	67433	35663	52972	16818	60311
00110	60365	94653	35075	33949	42614	29297	01918	28316	98953	73231
00111	83799	42402	56623	34442	34994	41374	70071	14736	09958	18065
00112	32960	07405	36409	83232	99385	41600	11133	07586	15917	06253
00113	19322	53845	57620	52606	66497	68646	78138	66559	19640	99413
00114	11220	94747	07399	37408	48509	23929	27482	45476	85244	35159
00115	31751	57260	68980	05339	15470	48355	88651	22596	03152	19121
00116	88492	99382	14454	04504	20094	98977	74843	93413	22109	78508
00117	30934	47744	07481	83828	73788	06533	28597	20405	94205	20380
00118	22888	48893	27499	98748	60530	45128	74022	84617	82037	10268
00119	78212	16993	35902	91386	44372	15486	65741	14014	87481	37220
00120	41849	84547	46850	52326	34677	58300	74910	64345	19325	81549
00121	46352	33049	69248	93460	45305	07521	61318	31855	14413	70951
00122	11087	96294	14013	31792	59747	67277	76503	34513	39663	77544
00123	52701	08337	56303	87315	16520	69676	11654	99893	02181	68161
00124	57275	36898	81304	48585	68652	27376	92852	55866	88448	03584
00125	20857	73156	70284	24326	79375	95220	01159	63267	10622	48391
00126	15633	84924	90415	93614	33521	26665	55823	47641	86225	31704
00127	92694	48297	39904	02115	59589	49067	66821	41575	49767	04037
00128	77613	19019	88152	00080	20554	91409	96277	48257	50816	97616
00129	38688	32486	45134	63545	59404	72059	43947	51680	43852	59693
00130	25163	01889	70014	15021	41290	67312	71857	15957	68971	11403
00131	65251	07629	37239	33295	05870	01119	92784	26340	18477	65622
00132	36815	43625	18637	37509	82444	99005	04921	73701	14707	93997
00133	64397	11692	05327	82162	20247	81759	45197	25332	83745	22567
00134	04515	25624	95096	67946	48460	85558	15191	18782	16930	33361
00135	83761	60873	43253	84145	60833	25983	01291	41349	20368	07126
00136	14387	06345	80854	09279	43529	06318	38384	74761	41196	37480
00137	51321	92246	80088	77074	88722	56736	66164	49431	66919	31678
00138	72472	00008	80890	18002	94813	31900	54155	83436	35352	54131
00139	05466	55306	93128	18464	74457	90561	72848	11834	79982	68416
00140	39528	72484	82474	25593	48545	35247	18619	13674	18611	19241
00141	81616	18711	53342	44276	75122	11724	74627	73707	58319	15997
00142	07586	16120	82641	22820	92904	13141	32392	19763	61199	67940
00143	90767	04235	13574	17200	69902	63742	78464	22501	18627	90872
00144	40188	28193	29593	88627	94972	11598	62095	36787	00441	58997
00145	34414	82157	86887	55087	19152	00023	12302	80783	32624	68691
00146	63439	75363	44989	16822	36024	00867	76378	41605	65961	73488
00147	67049	09070	93399	45547	94458	74284	05041	49807	20288	34060
00148	79495	04146	52162	90286	54158	34243	46978	35482	59362	95938
00149	91704	30552	04737	21031	75051	93029	47665	64382	99782	93478

APPENDIX B

Codes of Ethics of the American Sociological Association

1. *Objectivity in Research.* In his research the sociologist must maintain scientific objectivity.

2. *Integrity in Research.* The sociologist should recognize his own limitations and, when appropriate, seek more expert assistance or decline to undertake research beyond his competence. He must not misrepresent his own abilities, or the competence of his staff to conduct a particular research project.

3. *Respect of the Research Subject's Rights to Privacy and Dignity.* Every person is entitled to the right of privacy and dignity of treatment. The sociologist must respect these rights.

4. *Protection of Subjects from Personal Harm.* All research should avoid causing personal harm to subjects used in research.

5. *Preservation of Confidentiality of Research Data.* Confidential information provided by a research subject must be treated as such by the sociologist. Even though research information is not a privileged communication under the law, the sociologist must, as far as possible, protect subjects, and informants. Any promises made to such persons must be honored. However, provided that he respects the assurances he has given his subjects, the sociologist has no obligation to withhold information of misconduct of individuals or organizations.

Excerpted from "Toward a Code of Ethics for Sociologists," *The American Sociologist* 3 (November 1968):318. Reprinted with the permission of the American Sociological Association.

If an informant or other subject should wish, however, he can formally release the researcher of a promise of confidentiality. The provisions of this selection apply to all members of research organizations (i.e., interviewers, coders, clerical staff, etc.), and it is the responsibility of the chief investigators to see that they are instructed in the necessity and importance of maintaining the confidentiality of the data. The obligation of the sociologist includes the use and storage of original data to which a subject's name is attached. When requested, the identity of an organization or subject must be adequately disguised in publication.

6. *Presentation of Research Findings.* The sociologist must present his findings honestly and without distortion. There should be no omission of data from a research report which might significantly modify the interpretation of findings.

7. *Misuse of Research Role.* The sociologist must not use his role as a cover to obtain information for other than professional purposes.

8. *Acknowledgement of Research Collaboration and Assistance.* The sociologist must acknowledge the professional contributions or assistance of all persons who collaborated in the research.

9. *Disclosure of the Sources of Financial Support.* The sociologist must report fully all sources of financial support in his research publications and any special relations to the sponsor that might affect the interpretation of the findings.

10. *Distortion of Findings by Sponsor.* The sociologist is obliged to clarify publicly any distortion by a sponsor or client of the findings of a research project in which he has participated.

11. *Disassociation from Unethical Research Arrangements.* The sociologist must not accept such grants, contracts, or research assignments as appear likely to require violation of the principles above, and must publicly terminate the work or formally disassociate himself from the research if he discovers such a violation and is unable to achieve its correction.

12. *Interpretation of Ethical Principles.* When the meaning and application of these principles are unclear, the sociologist should seek the judgment of the relevant agency or committee designated by the American Sociological Association. Such consultation, however, does not free the sociologist from his individual responsibility for decisions or from his accountability to the profession.

13. *Applicability of Principles.* In the conduct of research the principles enunciated above should apply to research in any area either within or outside the United States of America.

Revised ASA Code of Ethics

PREAMBLE

Sociologists recognize that the discovery, creation, transmission, and accumulation of knowledge and the practice of sociology are social processes involving ethical considerations and behavior at every stage. Careful attention to the ethical dimensions of sociological practice, teaching, and scholarship contributes to the broader project of finding ways to maximize the beneficial effects that sociology may bring to humankind and to minimize the harm that might be a consequence of sociological work. The strength of the Code, its binding force, rests ultimately on the continuing active discussion, reflection, and use by members of the profession.

Sociologists subscribe to the general tenets of science and scholarship. Sociologists are especially sensitive to the potential for harm to individuals, groups, organizations, communities and societies that may arise out of the incompetent or unscrupulous use of sociological work and knowledge.

Sociology shares with other disciplines the commitment to the free and open access to knowledge and service, and to the public disclosure of findings. Sociologists are committed to the pursuit of accurate and precise knowledge and to self-regulation through peer review and appraisal, without personal and methodological prejudice and without ideological malice. Because sociology necessarily entails study of individuals, groups, organizations and societies, these principles of access and disclosure may occasionally conflict with more general ethical concerns for the rights of clients and respondents to privacy and for the treatment of clients and

Source: Code of Ethics, American Sociological Association, 1722 N Street, NW, Washington, DC 20036, August 14, 1989. Reprinted with the permission of the American Sociological Association.

respondents with due regard for their integrity, dignity, and autonomy. This potential conflict provides one of the reasons for a Code of Ethics.

The styles of sociological work are diverse and changing. So also are the contexts within which sociologists find employment. These diversities of procedures and context have led to ambiguities concerning appropriate professional behavior. The clarification of ethical behavior in diverse contexts provides a second reason for this Code.

Finally, this Code also attempts to meet the expressed needs of sociologists who have asked for guidance in how best to proceed in a variety of situations involving relations with respondents, students, colleagues, employers, clients and public authorities.

This Code establishes feasible requirements for ethical behavior. These requirements cover many—but not all—of the potential sources of ethical conflict that may arise in research, teaching and practice. Most represent *prima facie* obligations that may admit of exceptions but which should generally stand as principles for guiding conduct. The Code states the Association's consensus about ethical behavior upon which the Committee on Professional Ethics will base its judgments when it must decide whether individual members of the Association have acted unethically in specific instances. More than this, however, the Code is meant to sensitize all sociologists to the ethical issues that may arise in their work, and to encourage sociologists to educate themselves and their colleagues to behave ethically.

To fulfill these purposes, we, the members of the American Sociological Association, affirm and support the following Code of Ethics. Members accept responsibility for cooperating with the duly constituted committees of the American Sociological Association by responding to inquiries promptly and completely. Persons who bring complaints in good faith under this Code should not be penalized by members of the Association for exercising this right.

I. THE PRACTICE OF SOCIOLOGY

A. *Objectivity and Integrity*

Sociologists should strive to maintain objectivity and integrity in the conduct of sociological research and practice.

1. Sociologists should adhere to the highest possible technical standards in their research, teaching and practice.

2. Since individual sociologists vary in their research modes, skills, and experience, sociologists should always set forth *ex ante* the limits of their knowledge and the disciplinary and personal limitations that condition the validity of findings which affect whether or not a research project can be successfully completed.

3. In practice or other situations in which sociologists are requested to render a professional judgment, they should accurately and fairly represent their areas and degrees of expertise.

4. In presenting their work, sociologists are obligated to report their findings fully and should not misrepresent the findings of their research. When work is presented, they are obligated to report their findings fully and without omission of significant data. To the best of their ability, sociologists should also disclose details of their theories, methods and research designs that might bear upon interpretations of research findings.

5. Sociologists must report fully all sources of financial support in their publications and must note any special relations to any sponsor.

6. Sociologists should not make any guarantees to respondents, individuals, groups or organizations—unless there is full intention and ability to honor such commitments. All such guarantees, once made, must be honored.

7. Consistent with the spirit of full disclosure of method and analysis, sociologists, after they have completed their own analyses, should cooperate in efforts to make raw data and pertinent documentation collected and prepared at public expense available to other social scientists, at reasonable costs, except in cases where confidentiality, the client's rights to proprietary information and privacy, or the claims of a fieldworker to the privacy of personal notes necessarily would be violated. The timeliness of this cooperation is especially critical.

8. Sociologists should provide adequate information and citations concerning scales and other measures used in their research.

9. Sociologists must not accept grants, contracts or research assignments that appear likely to require violation of the principles enunciated in this Code, and should dissociate themselves from research when they discover a violation and are unable to achieve its correction.

10. When financial support for a project has been accepted, sociologists must make every reasonable effort to complete the proposed work on schedule, including reports to the funding source.

11. When several sociologists, including students, are involved in joint projects, there should be mutually accepted explicit agreements at the outset with respect to division of work, compensation, access to data, rights of authorship, and other rights and responsibilities. Such agreements may need to be modified as the project evolves and such modifications must be agreed upon jointly.

12. Sociologists should take particular care to state all significant qualifications on the findings and interpretations of their research.

13. Sociologists have the obligation to disseminate research findings, except those likely to cause harm to clients, collaborators and participants, or those which are proprietary under a formal or informal agreement.

14. In their roles as practitioners, researchers, teachers, and administrators, sociologists have an important social responsibility because their recommendations, decision, and actions may alter the lives of others. They should be aware of the situations and pressures that might lead to the misuse of their influence and authority. In these various roles, sociologists should also recognize that professional problems and conflicts may interfere with professional effectiveness. Sociologists should take steps to insure that these conflicts do not produce deleterious results for clients, research participants, colleagues, students and employees.

B. *Disclosure and Respect for the Rights of Research Populations*

Disparities in wealth, power, and social status between the sociologist and respondents and clients may reflect and create problems of equity in research collaboration. Conflict of interest for the sociologist may occur in research and practice. Also to follow the precepts of the scientific method—such as those requiring full disclosure—may entail adverse consequences or personal risks for individuals and groups. Finally, irresponsible actions by a single researcher or research team can eliminate or reduce future access to a category of respondents by the entire profession and its allied fields.

1. Sociologists should not misuse their positions as professional social scientists for fraudulent purposes or as a pretext for gathering intelligence for any organization or government. Sociologists should not mislead respondents involved in a research project as to the purpose for which that research is being conducted.

2. Subjects of research are entitled to rights of biographical anonymity.

3. Information about subjects obtained from records that are opened to public scrutiny cannot be protected by guarantees of privacy or confidentiality.

4. The process of conducting sociological research must not expose respondents to substantial risk of personal harm. Informed consent must be obtained when the risks of research are greater than the risks of everyday life. Where modest risk or harm is anticipated, informed consent must be obtained.

5. Sociologists should take culturally appropriate steps to secure informed consent and to avoid invasions of privacy. Special actions may be necessary where the individuals studied are illiterate, have very low social status, or are unfamiliar with social research.

6. To the extent possible in a given study sociologists should anticipate potential threats to confidentiality. Such means as the removal of identifiers, the use of randomized responses and other statistical solutions to problems of privacy should be used where appropriate.

7. Confidential information provided by research participants must be treated as such by sociologists, even when this information enjoys no legal protection or privilege and legal force is applied. The obligation to respect confidentiality also applies to members of research organizations (interviewers, coders, clerical staff, etc.) who have access to the information. It is the responsibility of administrators and chief investigators to instruct staff members on this point and to make every effort to insure that access to confidential information is restricted.

8. While generally adhering to the norm of acknowledging the contributions of all collaborators, sociologists should be sensitive to harm that may arise from disclosure and respect a collaborator's wish or need for anonymity. Full disclosure may be made later if circumstances permit.

9. Study design and information gathering techniques should conform to regulations protecting the rights of human subject, irrespective of source of funding, as outlined by the American Association of University Professors (AAUP) in "Regulations Governing Research On Human Subjects: Academic Freedom and the Institutional Review Board," *Academe,* December 1981:358–370.

10. Sociologists should comply with appropriate federal and institutional requirements pertaining to the conduct of research. These requirements might include but are not necessarily limited to failure to obtain proper review and approval for research that involves human subjects and failure to follow recommendations made by responsible committees concerning research subjects, materials, and procedures.

II. PUBLICATIONS AND REVIEW PROCESS

A. *Questions of Authorship and Acknowledgment*

1. Sociologists must acknowledge all persons who contribute to their research and to their copyrighted publications. Claims and ordering of authorship and acknowledgments must accurately reflect the contributions of all main participants in the research and writing process, including students, except in those cases where such ordering or acknowledgment is determined by an official protocol.

2. Data and material taken verbatim from another person's published or unpublished written work must be explicitly identified and referenced to its author. Citations to ideas developed in the written work of others, even if not quoted verbatim, should not be knowingly omitted.

B. *Authors, Editors and Referees have Interdependent Professional Responsibilities in the Publication Process*

1. Editors should continually review the fair application of standards without personal or ideological malice.

2. Journal editors must provide prompt decisions to authors of submitted manuscripts. They must monitor the work of associate editors and other referees so that delays are few and reviews are conscientious.

3. An editor's commitment to publish an essay must be binding on the journal. Once accepted for publication, a manuscript should be published expeditiously.

4. Editors receiving reviews of manuscripts from persons who have previously reviewed those manuscripts for another journal should ordinarily seek additional reviews.

5. Submission of a manuscript to a professional journal clearly grants that journal first claim to publish. Except where journal policies explicitly allow multiple submissions, a paper submitted to one English language journal may not be submitted to another journal published in English until after an official decision has been received for the first journal. Of course, the article can be withdrawn from all consideration to publish at any time.

C. *Participation in Review Processes*

Sociologists are frequently asked to provide evaluations of manuscripts, research proposals, or other work of professional colleagues. In such work, sociologists should hold themselves to high standards of performance in several specific ways:

1. Sociologists should decline requests for reviews of work of others where strong conflicts of interest are involved, such as may occur when a person is asked to review work by teachers, friends, or colleagues for whom he or she feels an overriding sense of personal obligation, competition, or enmity, or when such requests cannot be fulfilled on time.

2. Materials sent for review should be read in their entirety and considered carefully and confidentially. Evaluations should be justified with explicit reasons.

3. Sociologists who are asked to review manuscripts and books they have previously reviewed should make this fact known to the editor requesting review.

III. TEACHING AND SUPERVISION

The routine conduct of faculty responsibilities is treated at length in the faculty codes and AAUP rules accepted as governing procedures by the various institutions of higher learning. Sociologists in teaching roles should be familiar with the content of the codes in force at their institutions and should perform their responsibilities within such guidelines. Sociologists who supervise teaching assistants should take steps to insure that they adhere to these principles.

A. *Sociologists are obligated to protect the rights of students to fair treatment.*
1. Sociology departments should ensure that instructors are qualified to teach the courses to which they are assigned. Instructors so assigned should conscientiously perform their teaching responsibilities.
2. Sociologists should provide students with a fair and honest statement of the scope and perspective of their courses, clear expectations for student performance, and fair, timely, and easily accessible evaluations of their work.
3. Departments of Sociology must provide graduate students with explicit policies and criteria about conditions for admission into the graduate program, financial assistance, employment, funding, evaluation and possible dismissal.
4. Sociology departments should help students in their efforts to locate professional employment in academic and practice settings.
5. Sociology departments should work to insure the equal and fair treatment of all students, by adhering both in spirit and content to established affirmative action guidelines, laws, and policies.
6. Sociologists must refrain from disclosure of personal information concerning students where such information is not directly relevant to issues of professional competence.
7. Sociologists should make all decisions concerning textbooks, course content, course requirements, and grading solely on the basis of professional criteria without regard for financial or other incentives.

B. *Sociologists must refrain from exploiting students.*
1. Sociologists must not coerce or deceive students into serving as research subjects.
2. Sociologists must not represent the work of students as their own.
3. Sociologists have an explicit responsibility to acknowledge the contributions of students and to act on their behalf in setting forth agreements regarding authorship and other recognition.

C. *Sociologists must not coerce personal or sexual favors or economic or professional advantages from any person, including respondents, clients, patients, students, research assistants, clerical staff or colleagues.*

D. *Sociologists must not permit personal animosities or intellectual differences vis-a-vis colleagues to foreclose student access to those colleagues.*

IV. ETHICAL OBLIGATIONS OF EMPLOYERS, EMPLOYEES, AND SPONSORS

No sociologists should discriminate in hiring, firing, promotions, salary, treatment, or any other conditions of employment or career development on the basis of sex, sexual preference, age, race, religion, national origin, handicap, or political orientation. Sociologists should adhere to fair employment practices in hiring, promotion, benefits, and review processes. The guidelines outlined below highlight some, but not all, ethical obligations in employment practices. Clear specification of the requirements governing practices of fair and equal treatment are stated in the guidelines of the U.S. Equal Employment Opportunity Commission and the AAUP. Employers, employees, and sponsors should abide by these guidelines and consult them when a more complete description of fair employment practices is needed.

A. *Employment Practices and Adherence to Guidelines*
1. When acting as employers, sociologists should specify the requirements for hiring, promotion, and tenure and communicate these requirements thoroughly to employees and prospective employees. Voting on tenure and promotion should be based solely on professional criteria.
2. When acting as employers, sociologists should make every effort to ensure equal opportunity and fair treatment to all persons at all levels of employment.
3. When acting as employers, sociologists have the responsibility to be informed of fair employment codes, to help to create an atmosphere upholding fair employment practices, and to attempt to change any existing unfair practices within the organization or university.
4. All employees, including part-time employees, at all levels of employment, should be afforded the protection of due process through clear grievance procedures. It is the obligation of sociologists when acting as employers, to communicate these procedures and to protect the rights of employees who initiate complaints. They should also communicate standards of employment, and provide benefits, and compensation.

B. *Responsibility of Employees*
1. When seeking employment sociologists should provide prospective employers with accurate information on their relevant professional qualifications and experiences.
2. Sociologists accepting employment in academic and practice settings should become aware of possible constraints on research and publication in those settings and should negotiate clear understandings about such conditions accompanying their research and scholarly activity. In satisfying their obligations to employers, sociologists in such settings must make every effort to adhere to the professional obligations contained in this Code.
3. When planning to resign a post, sociologists should provide their employers with adequate notice of intention to leave.

C. *Sponsor's Participation Employment Processes*
1. In helping to secure employment for students and trainees, sociologists should make every attempt to avoid conflicts of interest. When a conflict of interest does arise, full disclosure of potential biases should be made to job seekers.

V. POLICIES AND PROCEDURES

The Committee on Professional Ethics (COPE) appointed by the Council of the American Sociological Association, shall have responsibility for: interpreting and publicizing this Code, promoting ethical conduct among sociologists, receiving inquiries about violations of the Code investigating complaints concerning the ethical conduct of members of the American Sociological Association, mediating disputes to assist the parties in resolving their grievances, holding hearings on formal charges of misconduct, and recommending actions to the Council of the American Sociological Association.

A. The Committee shall:

1. At any time, not necessarily in the context of the investigation of a particular case, advise the Council of the Association of its views of general ethical questions, which the Council may elect to publish in appropriate publications of the Association;

2. Receive complaints of violations of the Code of Ethics, and endeavor to resolve them by mediation, and if mediation is unsuccessful, proceed to a hearing. If, after a hearing, the Committee determines that an ethical violation occurred, it should so notify the parties and prepare a report for Council, which may or may not recommend one of the following actions:

a. Apply no sanctions

b. Suspend the membership and attendant privileges of a member (e.g., participation in the Annual Meeting for a period to be recommended by the Committee;

c. Request the resignation of a member or,

d. Terminate the membership of a member.

B. The Council of the Association shall receive case reports and recommendations from the Committee, and from the Review Board hereinafter provided, and take appropriate action.

C. The following are the rules and procedures under which the Committee operates:

1. Except as hereinafter provided, all formal actions of the Committee shall be adopted at a meeting at which a quorum is present, by a majority vote of the members present and voting. A quorum shall consist of a majority of members of the Committee. Members of the Committee with conflicts of interest as outlined in "COPE's Guidelines for Committee Conduct" will be excluded from Committee deliberations and will not be included in determining a quorum.

2. All inquiries about violations of the Code of Ethics should be directed to the Executive Officer of the Association, who shall determine whether the alleged violator is a member of the Association. A person making an inquiry should be sent a copy of the Code and requested to specify in writing the Section(s) of the Code that is (are) believed to have been violated. After receipt of this formal and specific complaint, the Executive Officer shall notify the Chair of the Committee of the inquiry. The Chair, in conjunction with the Executive Officer, shall determine whether or not the complaint is in fact covered by the Code. If so determined, the complainant will be notified of the acceptance by the Committee of the Complaint. The Executive Officer shall then communicate the entire complaint to the person or persons accused, together with a copy of the Code and an explanation of the composition and purpose of the Committee (by registered mail with return receipt requested) and request a response within 90 days.

a. The Committee shall consider complaints received from both members and nonmembers of the Association against members of the Association.

b. In order to be considered by the Committee, complaints must be received within eighteen months of the alleged violation or, if received later, must be certified for Committee consideration by the ASA Council.

c. The Executive Officer shall acknowledge receipt of the complaint, shall send a copy of the Code, and, where necessary, advise the complainant that a formal complaint must include specification of the time, place, persons, and events constituting the alleged violation and cite the paragraph(s) of the Code alleged to be violated.

3. In cases in which negotiation between the parties is deemed proper, the Chair of COPE will designate members of the Committee to cooperate with the Executive Officer in trying to find an informal and satisfactory solution to the problem.

4. The Executive Officer shall send copies of the complaint, responses and supporting documents to all members of the Committee and to the complainant and the alleged violator. After deliberation, the Committee shall decide by majority vote whether (1) the case should not be pursued further, (2) further information is needed, (3) mediation should be attempted, or (4) the case should not come to a hearing.

a. If the Committee decides there should be no further pursuit of the case, the Chair shall communicate the decision and the reasons therefore to the Executive Officer, who should notify all parties.

b. If the Committee decides that further investigation of the case is necessary, it may direct inquiries through the Executive Officer to either the complainant or the alleged violator, with copies of the request and responses thereto in every instance to the other party.

c. If the Committee decides to attempt mediation, it shall appoint a mediator from among members of the Association, acceptable to both parties. The mediator shall in due course notify the Committee that the matter has been resolved by written agreement of the parties, or if no such resolution has been achieved, the mediator may (1) recommend that the matter be dropped, or (2) recommend that the case proceed to a hearing.

d. If the Committee decides that a hearing is appropriate, either upon the recommendation of a mediator, or upon its own initiative, it shall advise the complainant and the alleged violator that a hearing will be conducted, giving at least 90 days notice of time and place. The alleged violator, as well as the complainant, should be advised of their rights to introduce witnesses and evidence in their behalf, to cross-examine witnesses, and to have the assistance of professional or other counsel at the hearing. All documentary evidence to be introduced by the complainant, and the names of all witnesses to be offered in support of the charges shall be supplied to the alleged violator at least 80 days prior to the hearing. If either complainant or alleged violator refuses to participate in the hearing, the Committee may elect to continue without their participation.

e. At the hearing, the evidence in support of the complaint shall be presented by the complainant, by complainant's lawyer or by a representative of the ASA Council, and the alleged violator shall have full opportunity to answer the charges. The Committee may introduce its own witnesses in order to answer factual questions.

f. The Committee shall record the proceedings of the hearing. The alleged violator shall have the right to be present either in person or, with the consent of all parties, through a conference telephone hook-up at all evidential sessions of the hearing and to have a transcript at cost. Every attempt will be made to conduct hearings at one time and place so as to reduce travel costs of the parties involved in the dispute.

g. Unless the alleged violator requests and the Committee grants a public hearing, the hearing of the complaint shall be private. All persons except those necessary for the conduct of the hearing shall be excluded.

h. At the conclusion of the introduction of all evidence, the alleged violator, counsel for the alleged violator, or both shall be permitted to argue against or in mitigation of the complaint.

i. Thereafter, the Committee shall conduct its further discussion in private.

j. If the Committee finds that no ethical violation has occurred, the parties, organizations and individuals contacted during the investigation shall be so notified by the Executive Officer and the case closed.

k. If the Committee finds that an ethical violation has clearly occurred, it shall prepare a report of the case summarizing its findings and recommendations. A copy of that report shall be sent to the alleged violator and complainant who shall have an opportunity to prepare written comments within 30 days as part of the appeals process.

l. When the Committee has followed the procedure set forth in paragraph "k", the findings shall be automatically appealed to a Review Board composed of three past Presidents of the Association appointed by the current President. The Review Board shall consider the written record alone, and by majority vote shall recommend to the Council that the findings of the Committee be upheld, reversed or modified. Copies of the recommendations of the Review Board shall be sent to the complainant, the alleged violator, and the Committee on Professional Ethics, all of whom shall have 30 days to comment in writing before the recommendation is forwarded to Council.

m. The Council, after examination of the Committee's and the Review Board's recommendations and comments thereto, shall make a final determination of the case on behalf of the Association, and either dismiss the case or take appropriate action.

D. The effective date of these procedures is August 14, 1989.

APPENDIX C

Code of Professional Ethics and Practices of the American Association for Public Opinion Research

We, the members of the American Association for Public Opinion Research, subscribe to the principles expressed in the following code. Our goal is to support sound practice in the profession of public opinion research. (By public opinion research we mean studies in which the principal source of information about individual beliefs, preferences, and behavior is a report given by the individual himself.)

We pledge ourselves to maintain high standards of scientific competence and integrity in our work, and in our relations both with our clients and with the general public. We further pledge ourselves to reject all tasks or assignments which would be inconsistent with the principles of this code.

THE CODE

I. PRINCIPLES OF PROFESSIONAL PRACTICE IN THE CONDUCT OF OUR WORK

    A. We shall exercise due care in gathering and processing data, taking all reasonable steps to assure the accuracy of results.

Reprinted with the permission of the American Association for Public Opinion Research, 420 Lexington Ave., Suite 1733, New York 10017.

B. We shall exercise due care in the development of research designs and in the analysis of data.
  1. We shall employ only research tools and methods of analysis which, in our professional judgment, are well suited to the research problem at hand.
  2. We shall not select research tools and methods of analysis because of their special capacity to yield a desired conclusion.
  3. We shall not knowingly make interpretations of research results, nor shall we tacitly permit interpretations, which are inconsistent with the data available.
  4. We shall not knowingly imply that interpretations should be accorded greater confidence than the data actually warrant.
C. We shall describe our findings and methods accurately and in appropriate detail in all research reports.

II. PRINCIPLES OF PROFESSIONAL RESPONSIBILITY IN OUR DEALINGS WITH PEOPLE

A. The Public:
  1. We shall cooperate with legally authorized representatives of the public by describing the methods used in our studies.
  2. We shall maintain the right to approve the release of our findings, whether or not ascribed to us. When misinterpretation appears, we shall publicly disclose what is required to correct it, notwithstanding our obligation for client confidentiality in all other respects.
B. Clients or Sponsors:
  1. We shall hold confidential all information obtained about the client's general business affairs and about the findings of research conducted for the client, except when the dissemination of such information is expressly authorized.
  2. We shall be mindful of the limitations of our techniques and facilities and shall accept only those research assignments which can be accomplished within these limitations.
C. The Profession:
  1. We shall not cite our membership in the Association as evidence of professional competence, since the Association does not so certify any persons or organizations.
  2. We recognize our responsibility to contribute to the science of public opinion research and to disseminate as freely as possible the ideas and findings which emerge from our research.
D. The Respondent:
  1. We shall not lie to survey respondents or use practices and methods which abuse, coerce, or humiliate them.
  2. We shall protect the anonymity of every respondent, unless the respondent waives such anonymity for specified uses. In addition, we shall hold as privileged and confidential all information which tends to identify the respondent.

STANDARDS FOR REPORTING PUBLIC OPINION POLLS

Good professional practice imposes the obligation upon all survey research organizations:

1. to include, in any public release, essential information about how the survey was conducted; and
2. to inform their private clients in detail as to the elements of the research design and how it was implemented.

A proper concern for the public interest imposes the obligation upon the news media to inform themselves as to the credentials of any poll results that come to their attention and to report them in the light of such information.

Minimal Disclosure

The following minimum essential for a professional assessment of how a survey was conducted should be incorporated in the text of any releases:

1. Identity of *who sponsored* the survey.
2. The *exact wording* of question asked.
3. A *definition of the population* actually sampled.
4. *Size of sample.* For mail surveys, this should include the number of questionnaires mailed out *and* the number returned.
5. An indication of what allowance should be made for *sampling error.*
6. *Which results are based on parts of the sample,* rather than the total sample. (For example: likely voters only, those aware of an event, those who answered other questions in a certain way.)
7. Whether *interviewing* was done personally, by telephone, or mail; at home or on street corners.
8. *Timing* of the interviewing in relation to relevant events.

We strongly urge the news media to ask for and to include ALL the above information when preparing final copy for publication or broadcast. This should apply not only to polls conducted for publication but also to "private polls" whose results are publicized.

We strongly urge survey organizations that conduct polls for the news media to prepare standard descriptions of their methods for public distribution.

We recommend that survey organizations use professional journals and meetings to inform their colleagues in detail of their activities and methods.

We encourage the news media, and the professional staffs of political parties, who use these professional sources of information to become aware of what is accepted research practice.

We wholeheartedly endorse the practice now adhered to by many survey organizations of making their surveys available to scholars for further analysis, and recommend its extension to confidential polls whenever possible.

REFERENCES

ABRAMS, PHILIP. 1982. *Historical Sociology.* Shepton Mallet, Eng.: Open House.

ADLER, FRANZ. 1947. "Operational Definitions in Sociology." *American Journal of Sociology* 52(March):438–44.

Alcoholics Anonymous. 1976. *Alcoholics Anonymous.* New York: Alcoholics Anonymous World Services, Inc.

ALDENDERFER, MARK S., and BLASHFIELD, ROGER K. 1984. *Cluster Analysis.* Beverly Hills, CA: Sage.

ALMOND G. A. 1954. *The Appeals of Communism.* Princeton, NJ: Princeton University Press.

ALRECK, PAMELA L., and SETTLE, ROBERT B. 1985. *The Survey Research Handbook.* Homewood, IL: Richard D. Irwin.

ALWIN, D. R. 1992. "Factor Analysis." In Borgatta and Borgatta (1992) 2:621–38.

ALWIN, DUANE R., and KROSNICK, JON A. 1985. "The Measurement of Values in Surveys: A Comparison of Ratings and Rankings." *Public Opinion Quarterly* 49:535–52.

The American Sociologist. 1978. Vol. 13, No. 3 (August).

AMMONS, R. B. 1950. "Reactions in a Projective Doll-play Interview of White Males Two to Six Years of Age to Differences in Skin Color and Facial Features." *Journal of Genetic Psychology* 76:323–41.

ANDERSON, BARBARA A.; SILVER, BRIAN D.; and ABRAMSON, PAUL R. 1988a. "The Effects of Race of the Interviewer on Measures of Electoral Participation by Blacks in SRC National Election Studies." *Public Opinion Quarterly* 52: 53–83.

———. 1988b. "The Effects of the Race of the Interviewer on Race-Related Attitudes of Black Respondents in SRC/CPS National Election Studies." *Public Opinion Quarterly* 52: 289–324.

ANDERSON, MARGARET L. 1988. "Moving Our Minds: Studying Women of Color and Reconstructing Sociology." *Teaching Sociology* 16: 123–32.

ANDERSON, RONALD E. 1992. "Computer Applications to Social Research." In Borgatta and Borgatta (1992) 1: 282–88.

ANDORKA, RUDOLF. 1980. "Long-Term Development of Hungary, Measured by Social Indicators." *Social Indicators Research* 8 (March): 1–13.

ANDRICH, DAVID. 1985. "An Elaboration of Guttman Scaling with Rasch Models for Measurement." In *Sociological Methodology 1985.* Edited by Nancy Brandon Tuma. San Francisco: Jossey-Bass. Pp. 33–80.

AQUILINO, WILLIAM S., and LO SCIUTO, LENOARD A. 1990. "Effects of Interview Mode on Self-Reported Drug Use." *Public Opinion Quarterly* 54: 362–95.

ARLUKE, ARNOLD. 1991. "Going into the Closet with Science: Information Control Among Animal Experimenters." *Journal of Contemporary Ethnography* 20: 306–30.

ARMOR, DAVID J., and COUCH ARTHUR S. 1972. *Data-Text Primer: An Introduction to Computerized Social Data Analysis.* New York: The Free Press.

ARMSTRONG, J. SCOTT, and LUSK, EDWARD J. 1987. "Return Postage in Mail Surveys: A Meta-analysis." *Public Opinion Quarterly* 52: 223–30.

ARNOLD, BRUCE L., and HAGAN, JOHN. 1992. "Careers of Misconduct: Prosecuted Professional Deviance Among Lawyers." *American Sociological Review* 57: 771–80.

ARNOLD, DAVID O. 1970. "Dimensional Sampling: An Approach for Studying a Small Number of Cases." *American Sociologist* 5 (May): 147–50.

ATKINSON, J. MAXWELL, and HERITAGE, JOHN, eds. 1984. *Structures of Social Action: Studies in Conversational Analysis.* Cambridge, Eng.: Cambridge University Press.

ATKINSON, PAUL. 1990. *The Ethnographic Imagination: Textual Constructions of Reality.* London: Routledge.

AXELROD R. 1984. *The Evolution of Cooperation.* New York: Basic Books.

AXLINE, VIRGINIA M. 1964. *Dibs: In Search of Self.* New York: Ballantine.

AYIDIYA, STEPHEN A., and MCCLENDON, MCKEE J. 1990. "Response Effects in Mail Surveys." *Public Opinion Quarterly* 54: 229–47.

BABBIE, EARL R. 1973. *Survey Research Methods.* Belmont, CA: Wadsworth.

———. 1986. *The Practice of Social Research.* Fourth ed. Belmont, CA: Wadsworth.

BACHMAN, JERALD G., and O'MALLEY, PATRICK M. 1984. "Yea-Saying, Nay-Saying, and Going to Extremes: Black-White Differences in Response Styles." *Public Opinion Quarterly* 48: 491–501.

BAILEY, KENNETH D. 1970. "Evaluating Axiomatic Theories." In *Sociological Methodology 1970.* Edited by Edgar F. Borgatta. San Francisco: Jossey-Bass.

———. 1972. "Polythetic Reduction of Monothetic Property Space." In *Sociological Methodology 1972.* Edited by Herbert L. Costner. San Francisco: Jossey-Bass.

———. 1973. "Monothetic and Polythetic Typologies and Their Relation to Conceptualization, Measurement, and Scaling." *American Sociological Review* 38 (February): 18–33.

———. 1974. "Cluster Analysis." In *Sociological Methodology 1975.* Edited by David R. Heise. San Francisco: Jossey-Bass.

———. 1982. "Clusters as Systems." *The Classification Society Bulletin 5:* 18–35.

———. 1983. "Sociological Classification and Cluster Analysis." *Quality and Quantity* 17: 251–68.

———. 1984a. "A Three Level Measurement Model." *Quality and Quantity* 18: 225–45.

———. 1984b. "On Integrating Theory and Method." In *Current Perspectives in Social Theory.* 5 Vols. Edited by Scott G. McNall. 5: 21–44.

———. 1985. "Systems as Clusters." *Behavioral Science* 30: 98–107.

———. 1986. "Philosophical Foundation of Sociological Measurement: A Note on the Three Level Model." *Quality and Quantity* 20.

———. 1987. "Replication as a Holistic Process: An Application of the Three Level Model." *Contemporary Social Psychology* 12: 73–81.

———. 1988a. "Ethical Dilemmas in Social Problems Research." *The American Sociologist* 19: 121–37.

———. 1988b. "Ethical Dilemmas in Systems Research." *Systems Research* 5: 323–32.

———. 1988c. "The Conceptualization of Validity: Current Perspectives." *Social Science Research* 17: 117–36.

———. 1989a. "Taxonomy and Disaster: Prospects and Problems." *International Journal of Mass Emergencies and Disasters* 7: 419–31.

———. 1989b. "Etika Druzboslovnega Raziskovanja." ("The Ethics of Social Research"). *Teorija in Praksa* (Ljubljana, Slovenia) 26: 659–68.

———. 1990. *Social Entropy Theory.* Albany: State University of New York Press.

———. 1992. "Typologies." Borgatta and Borgatta (1992). 4: 2188–94.

———. 1993. "Strategies of Nucleus Formation in Agglomerative Clustering Techniques." *Bulletin de Methodologie Sociologique,* no. 38, pp. 38–51.

———. 1994a. *Sociology and the New Systems Theory: Toward a Theoretical Synthesis.* Albany: State University of New York Press.

———. 1994b. *Typologies and Taxonomies.* Newbury Park, CA: Sage.

BALES, R.F. 1950. *Interaction Process Analysis.* Reading, MA: Addison-Wesley.

———. 1952. "Some Uniformities of Behavior in Small Social Systems." In *Readings in Social Psychology,* Revised ed. Edited by Guy E. Swanson, Theodore M. Newcomb, and Eugene E. Hartley. New York: Holt.

BAUER, R. A., ed. 1966. *Social Indicators.* Cambridge: MIT Press.

BAXTER, GEORGE W., JR. 1973. "Prejudiced Liberals? Race and Information Effects in a Two-person Game." *Journal of Conflict Resolution* 17 (March): 131–61.

BEAUCHAMP, TOM L.; FADEN, RUTH R.; WALLACE, R. JAY, JR,; and WALTERS, LEROY, eds. 1982. *Ethical Issues in Social Science Research.* Baltimore: Johns Hopkins Press.

BECKER, HOWARD S. 1963. *Outsiders: Studies in the Sociology of Deviance.* New York: The Free Press.

BEERE, CAROLE, A. 1979. *Women and Women's Issues: A Handbook of Tests and Measures.* San Francisco: Jossey-Bass.

BEHR, ROY L. 1981. "Nice Guys Finish Last—Sometimes." *Journal of Conflict Resolution* 25:289–300.

BELLEN, H., and VAN HERBRUGGER, C. 1980. "Evaluating the Quality of Life in Belgium." *Social Indicators Research* 8 (September): 311–26.

BENDER, D.H. 1957. "Colored Stationery in Direct-mail Advertising." *Journal of Applied Psychology* 41: 161–64.

BENDOR, JONATHAN; KRAMER, RODERICK M.; and STOUT, SUZANNE. 1991. "When in Doubt . . . : Cooperation in a Noisy Prisoner's Dilemma." *Journal of Conflict Resolution* 35: 691–719.

BENNEY, MARK; RIESMAN, DAVID; and STAR, SHIRLEY. 1956. "Age and Sex in the Interview." *American Journal of Sociology* 62: 143–52.

BENTON, J. EDWIN, and DALY, JOHN L. 1991. "A Question Order Effect in a Local Government Survey." *Public Opinion Quarterly* 55: 640–42.

BERECOCHEA, JOHN E., and GIBBS, JOEL B. 1991. "Inmate Classification: A Correctional Program That Works?" *Evaluation Review* 15: 333–63.

BERELSON, BERNARD, 1954. "Content Analysis." In *Handbook of Social Psychology.* Edited by Gardner Lindzey. Cambridge, MA: Addison-Wesley.

BERELSON, BERNARD, and SALTER, PATRICIA. 1946. "Majority and Minority Americans: An Analysis of Magazine Fiction." *Public Opinion Quarterly* 10: 168–90.

BERGER, JOSEPH; NORMAN, ROBERT A.; BALKWELL, JAMES; and SMITH, ROY F. 1992. "Status Inconsistency in Task Situations: A Test of Four Status Processing Principles." *American Sociological Review* 57: 843–55.

BERGER, PETER L., and LUCKMAN, THOMAS. 1967. *The Social Construction of Reality.* New York: Doubleday-Anchor Books.

BERRY, SANDRA H., and KANOUSE, DAVID E. 1987. "Physician Response to a Mailed Survey: An Experiment in Timing of Payment." *Public Opinion Quarterly* 51: 102–14.

BIERNACKI, PATRICK, and WALDORF, DAN. 1981. "Snowball Sampling: Problems and Techniques of Chain Referral Sampling." *Sociological Methods and Research* 10: 141–63.

BIERSTEDT, ROBERT. 1957. *The Social Order.* New York: McGraw-Hill.

BISHOP, GEORGE F. 1987. "Experiments with the Middle Response Alternative in Survey Questions." *Public Opinion Quarterly* 51: 220–32.

BITTNER, EGON. 1967a. "Police Discretion in Emergency Apprehension of Mentally Ill Persons." *Social Problems* 14 (Winter): 278–92.

———. 1967b. "The Police on Skid-row: A Study of Peace Keeping." *American Sociological Review* 32 (October): 699–715.

BLALOCK, HUBERT M., JR. 1967. *Toward a Theory of Minority-group Relations.* New York: Wiley.

———. 1968. "The Measurement Problem: A Gap Between the Languages of Theory and Research." In *Methodology in Social Research.* Edited by Hubert M. Blalock, Jr., and Ann B. Blalock, New York: McGraw-Hill.

———. 1971. *Causal Models in the Social Sciences.* Chicago: Aldine-Atherton.

———. 1972. *Social Statistics,* Second ed. New York: McGraw-Hill.

———. 1982. *Conceptualization and Measurement in the Social Sciences.* Beverly Hills, CA: Sage.

———. 1992. "Causal Inference Models." In Borgatta and Borgatta (1992). 1–177–88.

BLAU, PETER M., and SCOTT, W. RICHARD. 1962. *Formal Organizations: A Comparative Approach.* San Francisco: Chandler.

BODEN, DEIRDRE, and ZIMMERMAN, DON, 1991. *Talk and Social Structure.* Cambridge, MA: Polity Press.

BOHRNSTEDT, GEORGE W., and KNOKE, DAVID. 1982. *Statistics for Social Data Analysis.* Itaska, IL: Peacock.

BONACICH, EDNA. 1973. "A Theory of Middleman Minorities." *American Sociological Review* 38 (October): 583–94.

BONACICH, PHILIP, 1970. "Deceiving Subjects: The Pollution of Our Environment." *American Sociologist* 5 (February): 45.

———. 1990. "Communication Dilemmas in Social Networks: An Experimental Study." *American Sociological Review* 55: 448–59.

BORGATTA, EDGAR F. 1992. "Measurement." In Borgatta and Borgatta (1992), 3: 1226–36.

BORGATTA, EDGAR, F. and BORGATTA, MARIE L., eds. 1992. *Encyclopedia of Sociology,* 4 vols. New York: Macmillan.

BOXALL, BETTINA. 1993. "Gathering Seen as Both Defining and Two-edged." *Los Angeles Times,* Monday, April 26, pp. A1, A18.

BOYD, ROBERT S., And HESS, DAVID. 1993. "Clinton's Cure: $500 Billion in Spending Cuts, New Taxes." Los Angeles *Daily News,* February 18, pp. 1, 20.

BRADBURN, NORMAN M., and SUDMAN, SEYMOUR. 1979. *Improving Interview Method and Questionnaire Design.* San Francisco: Jossey-Bass.

———. 1988. *Polls and Surveys: Understanding What They Tell Us.* San Francisco: Jossey-Bass.

BRADT, K. 1955. "The Usefulness of a Postcard Technique in a Mail Questionnaire Study." *Public Opinion Quarterly* 19: 218–22.

BRENT, EDWARD, and ANDERSON, RONALD E. 1990. *Computer Applications in the Social Sciences.* New York: McGraw-Hill.

BRIDGE, R. GARY. 1971. "Alternative Postage Methods in Mail Surveys." Occasional Paper no. 7101. Los Angeles: University of California Survey Research Center.

BRIDGMAN, PERCY W. 1948. *The Logic of Modern Physics.* New York: Macmillan.

BRINBERG, DAVID, and MCGRATH, JOSEPH E. 1985. *Validity and the Research Process.* Beverly Hills, CA: Sage.

BROCK, JAMES; SCHWALLER, RICHARD; and SWINTH, ROBERT L. 1985. "The Social and Local Government Impacts of the Abandonment of the Milwaukee Railroad in Montana." *Evaluation Review* 9: 127–43.

BRODSKY, STANLEY L., and SMITHERMAN, H. O'NEAL. 1983. *Handbook of Scales for Research in Crime and Delinquency.* New York: Plenum.

BROWN, ROBERT. 1963. *Explanation in Social Science.* Chicago: Aldine.

BUCKINGHAM, B. R., and DOLCH, E. W. 1936. *A Combined Word List.* Boston: Ginn.

BULMER, MARTIN, ed. 1982. *Social Research Ethics.* London: Macmillan.

BURAWOY, MICHAEL; BURTON, ALICE; FERGUSON, ANN ARNETT; FOX; KATHRYN J.; GAMSON, JOSHUA; GARTRELL, NADINE; HURST, LESLIE; KURZMAN, CHARLES; SALZINGER, LESLIE; SCHIFFMAN, JOSEPHA; and UI, SHIORI. 1991. *Ethnography Unbound: Power and Resistance in the Modern Metropolis.* Berkeley: University of California Press.

BURAWOY, MICHAEL, and KROTOV, PAVEL. 1992. "The Soviet Transition From Socialism to Capitalism." *American Sociological Review* 57:16–38.

BURGESS, ROBERT G., ed. 1982. *Field Research: A Sourcebook and Field Manual.* London: George Allen & Unwin.

———. 1984. *In the Field: An Introduction to Field Research.* London: George Allen & Unwin.

CAHALAN, D. 1951. "Effectiveness of a Mail Questionnaire Technique in the Army." *Public Opinion Quarterly* 15: 575–78.

———. 1989. "The Digest Poll Rides Again." *Public Opinion Quarterly* 53: 129–33.

CALHOUN, JOHN B. 1962. "Population Density and Social Pathology." *Scientific American* 132 (February): 139– 48.

CAMPBELL, ANGUS, and CONVERSE, PHILIP E. 1972. *The Human Meaning of Social Change,* New York: Russell Sage Foundation.

CAMPBELL, BRUCE A. 1981. "Race-of-Interviewer Effects Among Southern Adolescents." *Public Opinion Quarterly* 45: 231–44.

CAMPBELL, DONALD T., and STANLEY, JULIAN C. 1963. *Experimental and Quasi-experimental Designs for Research.* Chicago: Rand McNally.

CAPLOW, THEODORE. 1964. *Principles of Organization.* New York: Harcourt Brace Jovanovich.

CAPRON, ALEXANDER MORGAN. 1982. "Is Consent Always Necessary in Social Science Research?" In Beauchamp et al. (1982). Pp. 211–31.

CARLSON, DONNA. 1972. "Thumbs Out: Ethnography of Hitchhiking." In Spradley and McCurdy (1972).

CARMENT, D. W., and ALCOCK, J.E. 1984. "Indian and Canadian Behavior in Two-Person Power Games." *Journal of Conflict Resolution* 28: 507–21.

CARMINES, EDWARD G., and ZELLER, RICHARD A. 1979. *Reliability and Validity Assessment.* Beverly Hills, CA: Sage.

CARP, FRANCES M. 1974. "Position Effects on Interview Responses." *Journal of Gerontology* 29: 581–87.

CARTWRIGHT, D. P. 1953. "Analysis of Qualitative Material." In *Research Methods in the Behavioral Sciences.* Edited by L. Festinger and D. Katz. New York: Holt, Rinehart & Winston.

CASSELL, JOAN, and WAX, MURRAY L., eds. 1980. "Ethical Problems of Fieldwork." *Social Problems* 27 (February).

CHAMPION, DEAN J. 1970. *Basic Statistics for Social Research.* Scranton, PA: Chandler.

CHILDERS, T., and SKINNER, S. 1979. "Gaining Respondent Cooperation in Mail Surveys Through Prior Commitment." *Public Opinion Quarterly* 43: 558–61.

CHURCHILL, LINDSEY. 1963. "Types of Formalization in Small-group Research." *Sociometry* 26 (September): 373–90.

———. 1971. "Ethnomethodology and Measurement." *Social Forces* 50 (December): 182–91.

CLARK, KENNETH B. 1953. "The Social Scientist as an Expert Witness in Civil Rights Litigation." *Social Problems* 1 (June): 5–10.

CLAUSEN, J. A., and FORD, R. N. 1947. "Controlling Bias in Mail Questionnaires." *Journal of the American Statistical Association* 42: 497–511.

CLAYMAN, STEVEN E. 1993. "Booing: The Anatomy of a Disaffiliative Response." *American Sociological Review* 58: 110–30.

CLYMER, ADAM. 1989. "Election Day Shows What the Polls Can't Do." *New York Times,* November 12, "Week in Review," p. 1.

COHEN, JACOB, and COHEN, PATRICIA. 1975. *Applied Multiple Regression/Correlation Analysis for the Behavioral Sciences.* Hillsdale, NJ: Lawrence Erlbaum.

COHEN, LAWRENCE E.; FELSON, MARCUS; and LAND, KENNETH C. 1980. "Property Crime Rates in the United States: A Macrodynamic Analysis, 1947–1977, with Ex Ante Forecasts for the Mid-1980's." *American Journal of Sociology* 86: 90–118.

COHN, WERNER. 1984. "What's in a Name: On Himmelfarb, Loar, and Mott." *Public Opinion Quarterly* 48: 660–64.

COLEMAN, JAMES S. 1964. *Introduction to Mathematical Sociology.* New York: The Free Press.

———. 1972. *Policy Research in Social Science.* Morristown, NJ: General Learning Press.

COLEMAN, JAMES S., et al. 1966. *Equality of Educational Opportunity.* Washington, DC: U.S. Government Printing Office.

COLLEY, R. H. 1945. "Don't Look Down Your Nose at Mail Questionnaires." *Printers' Ink,* March 16, pp. 21–108.

COLLINS, PATRICIA HILL. 1986. "Learning from the Outsider Within: The Sociological Significance of Black Feminist Thought." *Social Problems* 33: 14–32.

———. 1990. *Black Feminist Thought.* Cambridge, MA: Unwin Hyman.

COLLINS, RANDALL. 1984. "Statistics Versus Words." In *Sociological Theory 1984.* Edited by Randall Collins. San Francisco: Jossey-Bass. Pp. 329–62.

CONNELL, R. W. 1992. "A Very Straight Gay: Masculinity, Homosexual Experience, and Gender." *American Sociological Review* 57: 735–51.

CONNERLY, CHARLES E., and MARANS, ROBERT W. 1985. "Comparing Two Global Measures of Perceived Neighborhood Quality." *Social Indicators Research* 17: 28–47.

CONVERSE, JEAN M. 1987. *Survey Research in the United States: Roots and Emergence 1890–1960.* Berkeley: University of California Press.

CONVERSE, JEAN M., and PRESSER, STANLEY. 1986. *Survey Questions: Handcrafting the Standardized Questionnaire.* Newbury Park, CA: Sage.

COOK, THOMAS D., and CAMPBELL, DONALD T. 1979. *Quasi-experimentation: Design and Analysis Issues for Field Settings.* Chicago: Rand McNally.

COOLEY CHARLES HORTON. 1922. *Human Nature and the Social Order.* Revised ed. New York: Scribner's.

COSTNER, HERBERT L. 1965. "Criteria for Measures of Association." *American Sociological Review* 30: 341–53.

———. 1992. "Measures of Association." In Borgatta and Borgatta (1992). 3: 1940–43.

COSTNER, HERBERT L., and LEIK, ROBERT K. 1964. "Deductions from Axiomatic Theory." *American Sociological Review* 29 (December): 819–35.

COTTER, PATRICK R.; COHEN, JEFFREY; and COULTER, PHILIP B. 1982. "Race-of-Interviewer Effects in Telephone Interviews." *Public Opinion Quarterly* 46: 278–84.

CROMWELL, JERRY. 1976. "Hospital Productivity Trends in Short-term General Non-teaching Hospitals." In *The Evaluation of Social Problems.* Edited by Clark C. Abt. Beverly Hills, CA: Sage Publications.

DALTON, MELVILLE. 1959. *Men Who Manage: Fusions of Feeling and Theory in Administration,* New York: Wiley.

DAVIDSON, MARK. 1989. "Wilder Says He's Happy with Margin: Many Didn't Tell the Truth in Exit Polls." *Hampton Roads Morning Newspaper,* November 8.

DAVIS, FRED. 1959. "The Cabdriver and His Fare: Facets of a Fleeting Relationship." *American Journal of Sociology* 65 (September): 158–65.

DAVIS, JANET. 1972. "Teachers, Kids, and Conflict: Ethnography of a Junior High School." In Spradley and McCurdy (1972).

DAVIS, KINGSLEY, and MOORE, WILBERT E. 1945. "Some Principles of Stratification." *American Sociological Review* 10 (April): 242–49.

DEVORE, JAY, AND PECK, ROXY. 1986. *Statistics.* St. Paul: West.

DIEKMANN, ANDREAS. 1985. "Volunteer's Dilemma." *Journal of Conflict Resolution* 29: 605–10.

DILLMAN, DON A. 1978. *Mail and Telephone Surveys: The Total Design Method.* New York: Wiley.

DILLMAN, DON A., and FREY, JAMES H. 1974. "Contribution of Personalization to Mail Questionnaire Response as an Element of a Previously Tested Method." *Journal of Applied Psychology* 59: 297–301.

DOHRENWEND, BARBARA SNELL; COLOMBOTOS, JOHN; and DOHRENWEND, BRUCE P. 1968. "Social Distance and Interview Effects." *Public Opinion Quarterly* 32: 410–22.

DONALD, MARJORIE N. 1960. "Implications of Nonresponse for the Interpretation of Mail Questionnaire Data." *Public Opinion Quarterly* 24 (Spring): 99–114.

DUNCAN, OTIS DUDLEY. 1963. "Axioms or Correlations." *American Sociological Review* 28 (June): 1–16.

———. 1966. "Path Analysis: Sociological Examples." *American Journal of Sociology* 72: 1–16.

DUNHAM, H. WARREN. 1937. "The Ecology of the Functional Psychoses in Chicago." *American Sociological Review* (August): 467–79.

DUNLAP, J. W. 1950. "The Effect of Color in Direct Mail Advertising." *Journal of Applied Psychology* 34: 280–81.

DURKHEIM, EMILE. 1951. *Suicide: A Study in Sociology.* Translated by John A. Spaulding and George Simpson. New York: The Free Press.

DUSTER, TROY; MATZA, DAVID; and WELLMAN, DAVID. 1979. "Fieldwork and the Protection of Human Subjects." *The American Sociologist* 14: 136–42.

EDGELL, STEPHEN E.; HIMMELFARB, SAMUEL; and DUCHAN, KAREN L. 1982. "Validity of Forced Responses in a Randomized Response Model." *Sociological Methods and Research* 11: 89–100.

EDITORS, *EIR.* 1993. "Gulliver Travels to 'Politically Correct' Stanford University." *Executive Intelligence Review* 20: 20–22.

EDWARDS, ALLEN L. 1957. *Techniques of Attitude Scale Construction.* New York: Appleton-Century-Crofts.

EICHLER, MARGRIT. 1988. *Nonsexist Research Methods: A Practical Guide.* Boston: Unwin Hyman.

ELLEN, R. F., ed. 1984. *Ethnographic Research: A Guide to General Conduct.* London: Academic Press.

ELMS, ALAN C. 1982. "Keeping Deception Honest: Justifying Conditions for Social Scientific Research Strategems." In Beauchamp et al. (1982). Pp. 232–45.

EMERSON, ROBERT M., ed. 1988. *Contemporary Field Research: a Collection of Readings.* Prospect Heights, IL: Waveland Press.

EMERSON, ROBERT M.; FRETZ, RACHEL I.; and SHAW, LINDA L. 1994. *Writing Fieldnotes.* Chicago: University of Chicago Press.

EPSTEIN, STEWART. 1986. "Search Committee Ethics: A Critique and Proposal." *SSSP Newsletter* 17: 19–21.

ERIKSON, KAI. 1966. *Wayward Puritans: A Study in the Sociology of Deviance.* New York: Wiley.

Evaluation and Change. 1978. Special issue.

Evaluation Review. 1980. No. 4.

EVANS, M. D.; FELSON, MARCUS; and LAND, KENNETH C. 1980. "Developing Social Indicator Research on the Military in American Society." *Social Indicators Research* 8: 81–102.

FARLEY, JOHN E. 1990. *Sociology*. Englewood Cliffs, NJ: Prentice Hall.

FEAGIN, JOE R.; ORUM, ANTHONY M.; and SJOBERG, GIDEON, eds. 1991. *A Case for the Case Study*. Chapel Hill: University of North Carolina Press.

FERRISS, A. L. 1951. "A Note on Stimulating Responses to Questionnaires." *American Sociological Review* 16: 247–49.

———. 1990. "The Quality of Life in the United States." *SINET: Social Indicators Network News* 21: 1–18.

FETTERMAN, DAVID M. 1989. *Ethnography Step by Step*. Newbury Park, CA: Sage.

FINE, GARY ALAN. 1985. "Occupational Aesthetics: How Trade School Students Learn to Cook." *Urban Life* 14: 3–31.

FINE, GARY ALAN, and SANDSTROM, KENT. 1988. *Knowing Children: Participant Observation Among Minors*. Newbury Park, CA: Sage.

FINK, JAMES C. 1983. "CATI's First Decade: The Chilton Experience." *Sociological Methods and Research* 12: 153–68.

FITZGERALD, ROBERT, and FULLER, LINDA. 1982. "I Hear You Knocking but You Can't Come In: The Effects of Reluctant Respondents and Refusers on Sample Survey Estimates." *Public Opinion Quarterly* 11: 3–32.

FOGEL, RICHARD, and ENGERMAN, STANLEY. 1974. *Time on the Cross: Evidence and Methods*. Boston: Little, Brown.

FOWLER, FLOYD JACKSON, JR. 1992. "How Unclear Terms Affect Survey Data." *Public Opinion Quarterly* 56: 218–31.

FOX, RICHARD J.; CRASK, MELVIN R.; and KIM, JONGHOON. 1988. "Mail Survey Response Rate: A Meta-analysis of Selected Techniques for Inducing Response." *Public Opinion Quarterly* 52: 467–91.

FRANKEL, MARTIN R., and FRANKEL, LESTER R. 1987. "Fifty Years of Survey Sampling in the United States." *Public Opinion Quarterly* 51: S127–S138.

FRANKFORT-NACHMIAS, CHAVA, and NACHMIAS, DAVID. 1992. *Research Methods in the Social Sciences*. 4th ed. New York: St. Martin's.

FRAZIER, G., and BIRD, K. 1958. "Increasing the Response to a Mail Questionnaire." *Journal of Marketing 23: 186–87*.

FREEDMAN, DAVID; PISANI, ROBERT; PURVES, ROGER; and ADHIKARI, ANI. 1991. *Statistics*. 2d ed. New York: Norton.

FREEDMAN, J. 1971. "The Crowd: Maybe Not So Maddening After All." *Psychology Today* 5:58–61.

FREEMAN, HOWARD E. 1992. "Evaluation Research." In Borgatta and Borgatta (1992). 2: 594–98.

FREEMAN, HOWARD E.; KIECOLT, J. JILL; NICHOLLS, WILLIAM L. II; and SHANKS, MERRILL J. 1982. "Telephone Sampling Bias in Surveying Disability." *Public Opinion Quarterly* 46: 392–407.

FREEMAN, HOWARD E., and SHANKS, J. MERRILL, eds. 1983. "The Emergence of Computer-Assisted Survey Research." *Sociological Methods and Research* 12: 115–230.

FREEMAN, JOHN, and BUTLER, EDGAR W. 1976. "Some Sources of Interviewer Variance in Surveys." *Public Opinion Quaterly* 40: 79–91.

FREESE, LEE, and SELL, JANE. 1980. "Constructing Axiomatic Theories in Sociology." *Theoretical Methods in Sociology: Seven Essays*. Edited by Lee Freese. Pittsburgh: University of Pittsburgh Press, Pp. 263–368.

FREY, JAMES H. 1983. *Survey Research by Telephone*. Beverly Hills, CA: Sage.

———. 1986. "An Experiment with a Confidentiality Reminder in a Telephone Survey." *Public Opinion Quarterly* 50: 267–69.

FRIEDMAN, N. 1967. *The Social Nature of Psychological Research*. New York: Basic Books.

FRIEDRICHS, ROBERT. 1970. *A Sociology of Sociology*. New York: The Free Press.

GALLE, OMAR R.; GOVE, WALTER R.; and McPHERSON, J. MILLER. 1972. "Population Density and Pathology: What Are the Relations for Man?" *Science* 176: 23–30.

GALLIHER, JOHN F. 1973. "The Protection of Human Subjects: A Reexamination of the Professional Code of Ethics." *American Sociologist* 8 (August): 93–100.

————. 1980. "Social Scientists' Ethical Responsibilities to Subordinates: Looking Up Meekly." *Social Problems* 27: 298–308.

GAMSON, WILLIAM A. 1969. *SIMSOC: Participants' Manual.* New York: The Free Press.

GARFINKEL, ALAN. 1981. *Forms of Explanation.* New Haven, CT: Yale University Press.

GARFINKEL, HAROLD. 1967. *Studies in Ethnomethodology.* Englewood Cliffs, NJ: Prentice-Hall.

————. 1974. " 'Good' Organizational Reasons for 'Bad' Clinic Records." In *Ethnomethodology.* Edited by Roy Turner. Harmondsworth, England: Penguin.

GARFINKEL, HAROLD, and SACKS, HARVEY. 1970. "On Formal Structures of Practical Actions." In *Theoretical Sociology: Perspectives and Developments.* Edited by John C. McKinney and Edward A. Tiryakian. New York: Appleton-Century-Crofts.

GARSON, D. DAVID. 1990. "Expert Systems: An Overview for Social Scientists." *Social Science Computer Review* 8: 387–410.

GEARING, FREDERICK O. 1970. *The Face of the Fox.* Chicago: Aldine.

GEER, JOHN G. 1988. "What Do Open-ended Questions Measure?" *Public Opinion Quarterly* 52: 365–71.

————. 1991. "Do Open-ended Questions Measure 'Salient' Issues?" *Public Opinion Quarterly* 55: 360–70.

GENOVESE, EUGENE D. 1974. *Roll, Jordan, Roll: The World the Slaves Made.* New York: Pantheon Books.

GERLACH, LUTHER P. 1991. "Global Thinking, Local Acting: Movements to Save the Planet." *Evaluation Review* 15: 120–48.

GIALLOMBARDO, ROSE. 1966. "Social Roles in a Prison for Women." *Social Problems* 13 (Winter): 268–88.

GIBBS, JACK P., and MARTIN, WALTER T. 1964. *Status Integration and Suicide.* Eugene: University of Oregon Press.

GIEDROYE, RICHARD. 1993. "1893 Isabella Quarter Marks Centennial: Tangible Evidence of Women's Emerging Public Profile." *Coin World,* Monday, April 19, p. 10.

GLASER, BARNEY G., and STRAUSS, ANSELM L. 1965. *Awareness of Dying.* Chicago: Aldine.

————. 1967. *The Discovery of Grounded Theory: Strategies for Qualitative Research.* Chicago: Aldine.

GLAZER, D. 1973. *Routinizing Evaluations: Getting Feedback on Effectiveness of Crime and Delinquency Programs.* Washington, DC: U.S. Government Printing Office.

GLENN, NORVAL D. 1978. "The General Social Surveys: Editorial Introduction to a Symposium." *Contemporary Sociology* 7: 532–34.

GLOCK, CHARLES Y. 1955. "Some Applications of the Panel Method to the Study of Change." In *The Language of Social Research.* Edited by Paul F. Lazarsfeld and Morris Rosenberg. New York: The Free Press.

GOFFMAN, ERVING. 1959. *The Presentation of Self in Everyday Life.* Garden City, NY: Doubleday-Anchor Books.

————. 1962. *Asylums: Essays on the Social Situation of Mental Patients and Other Inmates.* Chicago: Aldine.

————. 1963a. *Behavior in Public Places: Notes on the Social Organization of Gatherings.* New York: The Free Press.

————. 1963b. *Stigma: Notes on the Management of Spoiled Identity.* Englewood Cliffs, NJ: Prentice-Hall.

————. 1967. *Interaction Ritual: Essays on Face-to-Face Behavior.* Chicago: Aldine.

————. 1969. *Strategic Interaction.* Philadelphia: University of Pennsylvania Press.

————. 1971. *Relations in Public: Microstrudies of the Public Order.* New York: Basic Books.

GOLDSTEIN, H., and KROLL, B. H. 1957. "Methods of Increasing Mail Response." *Journal of Marketing* 22: 55–57.

GOLLIN, ALBERT E., ed. 1980. "Polling and the News Media: A Symposium." *Public Opinion Quarterly* 44 (Winter).

GOODE, WILLIAM J., and HATT, PAUL K. 1952. *Methods in Social Research.* New York: McGraw-Hill.

GORDEN, RAYMOND L. 1969. *Interviewing: Strategy, Techniques, and Tactics.* Homewood, IL: Dorsey.

GOULDNER, ALVIN W. 1957. "Cosmopolitans and Locals: Toward an Analysis of Latent Social Roles—1." *Administrative Science Quarterly* 2 (December): 281–306.

———. 1962. "Anti-Minotaur: The Myth of a Value-free Sociology." *Social Problems* 9 (Winter): 199–213.

GOYDER, JOHN C. 1982. "Further Evidence on Factors Affecting Response Rates to Mailed Questionnaires." *American Sociological Review* 47: 550–53.

———. 1985. "Face-to-Face Interviews and Mailed Questionnaires: The Net Difference in Response Rate." *Public Opinion Quarterly* 49: 234–52.

GRADUATE COUNCIL, UCLA. 1974. "Graduate Student Questionnaire." Los Angeles: University of California.

GRAY, P. G. 1957. "A Sample Survey with Both a Postal and an Interview Stage." *Applied Statistics* 6: 139–53.

GREENWALD, HOWARD P. 1992. "Ethics in Social Research." In Borgatta and Borgatta (1992). 2: 584–88.

GRIFFIT, WILLIAM, and VEITCH, RUSSELL. 1971. "Hot and Crowded: Influences of Population Density and Temperature on Interpersonal Affective Behavior." *Journal of Personality and Social Psychology* 17: 92–98.

GROVES, ROBERT M., and KAHN, ROBERT L. 1979. *Surveys by Telephone: A National Comparison with Personal Interviews.* New York: Academic Press.

GROVES, ROBERT M., and MAGILAVY, LOU J. 1986. "Measuring and Explaining Interviewer Effects in Centralized Telephone Surveys." *Public Opinion Quarterly* 50: 251–66.

GROVES, ROBERT M., and MATHIOWETZ, NANCY. 1984. "Computer Assisted Telephone Interviewing: Effects on Interviewers and Respondents." *Public Opinion Quarterly* 48: 356–69.

GUBRIUM, JABER F., and SILVERMAN, DAVID, eds. 1989. *The Politics of Field Research.* London: Sage.

GULLAHORN, JOHN T., and GULLAHORN, JEANNE E. 1959. "Increasing Returns from Nonrespondents." *Public Opinion Quarterly* 23: 119–21.

———. 1963a. "An Investigation of the Effects of Three Factors on Response to Mail Questionnaires." *Public Opinion Quarterly* 27: 294–96.

———. 1963b. "A Computer Model of Elementary Social Behavior." *Behavioral Science* 8, no. 4: 354–62.

GUTTMAN, LOUIS. 1944. "A Basis for Scaling Qualitative Data." *American Sociological Review* 9: 139–50.

———. 1968. "A General Nonmetric Technique for Finding the Smallest Coordinate Space for a Configuration of Points." *Psychometrika* 33 (December): 469–506.

HAGE, JERALD. 1972. *Techniques and Problems of Theory Construction in Sociology.* New York: Wiley.

HALL, EDWARD T. 1966. *The Hidden Dimension.* Garden City, NY: Doubleday.

HAMMERSLEY, MARTYN. 1992. *What's Wrong with Ethnography?* London: Routledge.

HAMMERSLEY, MARTYN, and ATKINSON, PAUL. 1983. *Ethnography: Principles in Practice.* London: Tavistock Publications.

HAMNETT, MICHAEL P.; PORTER, DOUGLAS J.; SINGH, AMARJIT; and KUMAR, KRISHNA. 1984. *Ethics, Politics, and International Social Science Research.* Honolulu: University of Hawaii Press.

HANCOCK, J.W. 1940. "An Experimental Study of Four Methods of Measuring Unit Costs of Obtaining Attitudes Toward the Retail Store." *Journal of Applied Psychology* 24: 213–30.

HANNEMAN, ROBERT A. 1988. *Computer-Assisted Theory Building.* Newbury Park, CA: Sage.

HARDING, SANDRA. 1986. *The Science Question in Feminism.* Ithaca, NY: Cornell University Press.

———. 1987. *Feminism and Methodology.* Bloomington: Indiana University Press.

HARRIS, PHILIP R. 1986. "The Influence of Culture on Space Developments." *Behavioral Science* 31: 12–28.

HAWKINS, DARNELL F., ed. 1983. "Social Research and the Courts." *Sociological Methods and Research* 11: 379–536. Special issue.

HAYS, WILLIAM L. 1963. *Statistics*. New York: Holt, Rinehart & Winston.

HEADEY, BRUCE; HOLMSTROM, ELSIE; and WEARING, ALEXANDER. 1985. "Models of Well-Being and Ill-Being." *Social Indicators Research* 17: 211–34.

HEALTH AND WELFARE AGENCY. State of California. 1967. *Survey of Medical Care Resources and Utilization*. Sacramento: State of California.

HEBERLEIN, THOMAS A., and BAUMGARTNER, ROBERT. 1978. "Factors Affecting Response Rates to Mailed Questionnaires." *American Sociological Review* 43: 447–62.

———. 1981. "Is a Questionnaire Necessary in a Second Mailing?" *Public Opinion Quarterly* 45: 102–8.

HEISE, DAVID R. 1965. "Semantic Differential Profiles for 1,000 Most Frequent English Words." *Psychological Monographs* 70, no. 8.

———. 1969. "Problems in Path Analysis and Causal Inference." In *Sociological Methodology 1969*. Edited by Edgar F. Borgatta. San Francisco: Jossey-Bass.

———. 1970. "The Semantic Differential and Attitude Research." In *Attitude Measurement*. Edited by Gene F. Summers. Chicago: Rand McNally.

HENLEY, JAMES R., JR. 1976. "Response Rate to Mail Questionnaires with a Return Deadline." *Public Opinion Quarterly* 40: 374–75.

HERITAGE, JOHN. 1984. *Garfinkel and Ethnomethodology*. Cambridge, Eng.: Polity Press.

———. 1992. "Ethnomethodology." Borgatta and Borgatta (1992). 2: 588–94.

HERZOG, A. REGULA, and RODGERS, WILLARD L. 1988.. "Interviewing Older Adults: Mode Comparison Using Data from a Face-to-Face Survey and a Telephone Survey." *Public Opinion Quarterly* 52: 84–99.

HESS, IRENE. 1985. *Sampling for Social Research Surveys, 1947–1980*. Ann Arbor: University of Michigan, Institute for Social Research.

HILL, A.B. 1957. "The Doctor's Day and Pay." *Journal of the Royal Statistical Society* A. 114: 1–36.

HIMMELFARB, HAROLD S.; LOAR, R. MICHAEL; and MOTT, SUSAN H. 1983. "Sampling by Ethnic Surnames: The Case of American Jews." *Public Opinion Quarterly* 47: 247–60.

———. 1984. "On Werner Cohn's 'What's in a Name'." *Public Opinion Quarterly* 48: 664–65.

HOFFERBERT, RICHARD I., and CLUBB, JEROME M., eds. 1977. *Social Science Data Archives: Applications and Potential*. Beverly Hills, CA: Sage.

HOFFMAN, JOAN EAKIN. 1980. "Problems of Access in the Study of Social Elites and Boards of Directors." In *Fieldwork Experience: Qualitative Approaches to Social Research*. Edited by William B. Shaffir, Robert A. Stebbins, and Allan Turowetz. New York: St. Martin's Press.

HOLDAWAY, SIMON. 1980. "The Police Station." *Urban Life: A Quarterly Journal of Ethnographic Research* 9: 79–100.

HOLSTEIN, JAMES A., and GUBRIUM, JABER F. 1992. "Field Research Methods." In Borgatta and Borgatta (1992). 2: 711–716.

HOLSTI, O.R. 1969. *Content Analysis for the Social Sciences and Humanities*. Reading, MA: Addison-Wesley.

HOLSTI, O.R., and NORTH, R.C. 1966. "Perceptions of Hostility and Economic Variables." In *Comparing Nations*. Edited by R. Merritt and S. Rokkan. New Haven, CT: Yale University Press.

HOPPE, D.A. 1952. "Certain Factors Found to Improve Mail Survey Returns." *Proceedings of the Iowa Academic Society* 59: 374–76.

HORNER, MATINA S. 1969. "Femininity and Successful Achievement: A Basic Inconsistency." In *Feminine Personality and Conflict*. Edited by Judith M. Bardwick. Elizabeth Douvan, Matina S. Horner, and David Gutman. Belmont, CA: Brooks/Cole.

HOROWITZ, IRVING LOUIS. 1965. "The Life and Death of Project Camelot." *TransAction* 3 (November–December): 44–47.

———. 1971. *The Use and Abuse of Social Science.* New Brunswick, NJ: Transaction Books.

HUBBARD, RAYMOND, and LITTLE, ELDON L. 1988. "Promised Contributions to Charity and Mail Survey Responses: Replication with Extension." *Public Opinion Quarterly* 52: 223–30.

HUDSON, HERSCHEL C. 1982. *Classifying Social Data.* San Francisco: Jossey-Bass.

HUGHES, EVERETT C. 1958. *Men and Their Work.* New York: The Free Press.

HULIN, CHARLES L.; DRASGOW, FRITZ; and PARSONS, CHARLES K. 1983. *Item Response Theory: Application to Psychological Measurement.* Homewood, IL: Dow-Jones-Irwin.

HUMPHREYS, LAUD. 1970. *Tearoom Trade: Impersonal Sex in Public Places.* Chicago: Aldine.

HUNT, JANET G., and HUNT, LARRY L. 1977. "Race, Daughters, and Father-loss: Does Absence Make the Girl Grow Stronger?" *Social Problems* 24: 90–102.

———. 1981. "Secondary Analysis: A Personal Journal." In *Readings for Social Research.* Edited by Theodore C. Wagenaar. Belmont, CA: Wadsworth.

HUNT, JENNIFER, and MANNING, PETER K. 1991. "The Social Context of Police Lying." *Symbolic Interaction* 14: 51–70.

HYMAN, HERBERT. 1954. *Interviewing in Social Research.* Chicago: University of Chicago Press.

———. 1972. *Secondary Analysis of Sample Surveys.* New York: Wiley.

INBAR, MICHAEL, and STOLL, CLARICE S. 1972. *Simulation and Gaming in Social Science.* New York: The Free Press.

INTERNATIONAL KINDERGARTEN UNION. 1928. *A Study of the Vocabulary of Children Before Entering the First Grade.* Baltimore: Williams & Wilkins.

JAMES, JEANNINE M., and BOLSTEIN, RICHARD. 1990. "The Effect of Monetary Incentives and Follow-up Mailings on the Response Rate and Response Quality in Mail Surveys." *Public Opinion Quarterly* 54: 346–61.

JANSSEN, JACQUES; MARCOTORCHINO, JEAN-FRANÇOIS; and PROTH, JEAN-MARIE, eds. 1983. *New Trends in Data Analysis and Applications.* Amsterdam: North-Holland.

JAPANESE-AMERICAN RESEARCH PROJECT (JARP). 1967. *Nisei Male Questionnaire Mailed Instrument.* Los Angeles: University of California.

JARDINE, N., and SIBSON, R. 1971. *Mathematical Taxonomy.* New York: Wiley.

JASON, LEONARD A.; McCOY, KATHLEEN; BLANCO, DAVID; and ZOLIK, EDWIN. 1980. "Decreasing Dog Litter: Behavioral Consultation to Help a Community Group." *Evaluation Review* 4: 355–69.

JENCKS, CHRISTOPHER, et al. 1972. *Inequality: A Reassessment of the Effect of Family and Schooling in America.* New York: Basic Books.

JENSEN, ARTHUR R. 1969. "How Much Can We Boost IQ and Scholastic Achievement?" *Harvard Educational Review* 39: 1–123.

———. 1973. *Educational Differences.* London: Methuen.

JOHSON, JOHN M. 1975. *Doing Field Research.* New York: The Free Press.

JOHNSON, ROBERT R. 1976. *Elementary Statistics.* Second ed. North Scituate, MA: Duxbury Press.

JONES, WESLEY. 1979. "Generalizing Mail Survey Inducement Methods: Population Interactions with Anonymity and Sponsorship." *Public Opinion Quarterly* 43: 102–11.

JORDAN, LAWRENCE A.; MARCUS, ALFRED C.; and REEDER, LEO G. 1980. "Response Styles in Telephone and Household Interviewing: A Field Experiment." *Public Opinion Quarterly* 44: 210–22.

JUSSAUME, RAYMOND A., JR., and YAMADA, YOSHIHARU. 1990. "A Comparison of the Viability of Mail Surveys in Japan and the United States." *Public Opinion Quarterly* 54:219–28.

KAHAN, JAMES P., and RAPOPORT, AMNON. 1981. "Matrix Experiments and Theories of N-Person Games." *Journal of Conflict Resolution* 25: 725–32.

KAHLE, L., and SALES, B. 1978. "Personalization of the Outside Envelope in Mail Surveys." *Public Opinion Quarterly* 42: 547–50.

KAHN, R. L. 1962. "A Comparison of Two Methods of Collecting Data for Social Research: The Fixed-alternative Questionnaire and the Open-ended Interview." Ph.D. dissertation. University of Michigan.

KATZ, DANIEL. 1942. "Do Interviewers Bias Polls?" *Public Opinion Quarterly* 6: 248–68.

KAZDIN, ALAN E., and TUMA, A. HUSSAIN, eds. 1982. *Single-Case Research Designs.* San Francisco: Jossey-Bass.

KEISLER, SARA, and SPROULL, LEE S. 1986. "Response Effects in the Electronic Survey." *Public Opinion Quarterly* 50: 402–13.

KELMAN, HERBERT C. 1967. "Human Use of Human Subjects: The Problem of Deception in Social Psychological Experiments." *Psychological Bulletin* 67 (January): 1–11.

———. 1982. "Ethical Issues in Different Social Science Methods." In Beauchamp et al. (1982). Pp. 40–98.

KENNEDY, LESLIE W., and MEHRA, N. 1985. "Effects of Social Change on Well-being: Boom and Bust in a Western Canadian City." *Social Indicators Research* 17: 101–13.

KENT, STEPHEN A. 1992. "Historical Sociology." In Borgatta and Borgatta (1992). 2: 837–43.

KEPHART, W. M., and BRESSLER, M. 1958. "Increasing the Responses to Mail Questionnaires: A Research Study." *Public Opinion Quarterly* 22: 123–32.

KERCHER, KYLE. 1992. "Quasi-Experimental Research Designs." In Borgatta and Borgatta (1992). 3: 1595–1613.

KERLINGER, FRED N. 1964. *Foundations of Behavioral Research.* New York: Holt, Rinehart & Winston.

KERR, JEAN ANNE CORRINNE. 1979. "Space Use by Medical Surgical Hospital Ward Staff." Unpublished Ph.D. dissertation. University of California, Los Angeles.

KIECOLT, K. JILL, and NATHAN, LAURA E. 1985. *Secondary Analysis of Survey Data.* Beverly Hills, CA: Sage.

KIM, JAE-ON. 1992. "Tabular Analysis." In Borgatta, and Borgatta (1992). 4: 2139–59.

KIMMEL, ALLAN J. 1988. *Ethics and Values in Applied Social Research.* Newbury Park, CA: Sage.

KINSEY A.C.; POMEROY, W.B.; MARTIN, C.E.; and GEBHARD, P.H. 1948. *Sexual Behavior in the Human Male.* Philadelphia: Saunders.

———. 1953. *Sexual Behavior in the Human Female.* Philadelphia: Saunders.

KIRK, JEROME, and MILLER, MARC L. 1986. *Reliability and Validity in Qualitative Research.* Beverly Hills, CA: Sage.

KITAGAWA, E., and TAEUBER, K., eds. 1963. *Local Community Fact Book for Chicago Metropolitan Area, 1960.* Chicago: Chicago Community Inventory.

KLECKA, WILLIAM R., and TUCHFARBER, ALFRED J. 1978. "Random Digit Dialing: A Comparison to Personal Surveys." *Public Opinion Quarterly* 42: 105–14.

KLEGON, DOUGLAS. 1981. "*The Social Scientist as Historian: How Important Is It to Look Back?*" In Wagenaar (1981a).

KLEIN, M. W., and MACCOBY, N. 1954. "Newspaper Objectivity in the 1952 Campaign." *Journalism Quarterly* 31: 285–96.

KLEINMAN, SHERRYL. 1993. "The Textual Turn." *Contemporary Sociology* 22: 11–13.

KLENETSKY, MELVIN. 1993. "Without 'Dead White European Males' There Would Be No Civilization." *Executive Intelligence Review* 20: 28–34.

KNUDSEN, D. D.; POPE, H.; and IRISH, D. P. 1967. "Response Differences to Questions on Sexual Standards: An Interview-questionnaire Comparison." *Public Opinion Quarterly* 31 (Summer): 290–97.

KORNHAUSER, WILLIAM. 1962. "Social Bases of Political Commitment: A Study of Liberals and Radicals. In *Human Behavior and Social Processes.* Edited by Arnold Rose. Boston: Houghton Mifflin.

KRATHWOHL, DAVID R. 1985. *Social and Behavioral Science Research.* San Francisco: Jossey-Bass.

KRAUT, ROBERT. 1984, *Telecommuting: Cautious Pessimisim.* Murray Hill, NJ: Bell Communications Research.

KROSNICK, JON A., and ALWIN, DUANE F. 1987. "An Evaluation of a Cognitive Theory of Response-Order Effects in Survey Measurement." *Public Opinion Quarterly* 51: 201–19.

KRUEGER, RICHARD A. 1988. *Focus Groups: A Practical Guide for Applied Research.* Newbury Park, CA: Sage.

KUHN, THOMAS, 1962. *The Structure of Scientific Revolutions.* Chicago: University of Chicago Press.

KVIZ, FREDERICK J. 1978. "Random Digit Dialing and Sample Bias." *Public Opinion Quarterly* 42: 544–46.

———. 1984. "Bias in a Directory Sample for a Mailed Survey of Rural Households." *Public Opinion Quarterly* 48: 801–6.

LABAW, PATRICIA J. 1980. *Advanced Questionnaire Design.* Cambridge, MA: Abt Books.

LAND, KENNETH C. 1969. "Principles of Path Analysis." In *Sociological Methodology 1969.* Edited by Edgar F. Borgatta. San Francisco: Jossey-Bass.

———. 1975. "Social Indicator Models: An Overview." In Land and Spilerman (1975).

———. 1992. "Social Indicators." In Borgatta and Borgatta (1992). 4: 1844–50.

LAND, KENNETH C., and FELSON, MARCUS. 1976. "A General Framework for Building Dynamic Macro Social Indicator Models: Including an Analysis of Changes in Crime Rates and Police Expenditures." *American Journal of Sociology* 82: 565–604.

LAND, KENNETH C., and SPILERMAN, SEYMOUR eds. 1975. *Social Indicator Models.* New York: Russell Sage Foundation.

LANSING, JOHN B., and MORGAN, JAMES N. 1971. *Economic Survey Methods.* Ann Arbor: University of Michigan Institute for Social Research.

LANTZ, HERMAN R., et al. 1968. "Preindustrial Patterns in the Colonial Family in America: A Content Analysis of Colonial Magazines." *American Sociological Review* 33 (June): 413–26.

LARGEY, GALE P.; FEIL, RICHARD N.; and BOK, MARILYN A. 1990. *The Public Mind: Views of Northern Tier Voters—Education, Euthanasia, Smoking, Gun Control.* Mansfield, PA: Mansfield University Rural Services Institute.

LARSON, O. N.; GRAY, L. N.; and FORTIS, J. G. 1963. "Goals and Goal-achievement Methods in Television Content: Models for Anomie?" *Sociological Inquiry* 33: 180–96.

LARSON, R. F., and CATTON, WILLIAM R. 1959. "Can the Mail-back Bias Contribute to a Study's Validity?" *American Sociological Review* 24: 243–45.

LASSWELL, H. D., and KAPLAN, A. 1950. *Power and Society.* New Haven, CT: Yale University Press.

LAVRAKAS, PAUL J. 1987. *Telephone Survey Methods: Sampling, Selection, and Supervision.* Newbury Park, CA: Sage.

LAZARSFELD, PAUL F. 1937. "Some Remarks on the Typological Procedures in Social Research." *Zeitschrift für Socialforschung* 6: 119–39.

———. 1958. "Evidence and Inference in Social Research." *Daedalus* 8 (Fall): 99–130.

———. 1959. "Problems in Methodology." In *Sociology Today: Problems and Prospects.* Edited by Robert K. Merton, Leonard Brown, and Leonard S. Cottrell, Jr. New York: Basic Books.

LAZARSFELD, PAUL F.; SEWELL, WILLIAM H.; and WILENSKY, HAROLD L. 1967. *The Uses of Sociology,* New York: Basic Books.

LEE, A.M. 1952. *How to Understand Propaganda.* New York: Rinehart.

———. 1976. "Valedictory: A Report on the Year 1975–1976." American Sociological Association *Footnotes* 4 (August): 1, 9–10.

LEELAKULTHANIT, OROSE, and DAY, RALPH L. 1992. "Quality of Life in Thailand." *Social Indicators Research* 27: 41–57.

LEITER, KENNETH. 1980. *A Primer on Ethnomethodology.* New York: Oxford University Press.

LENSKI, GERHARD E. 1954. "Status Crystallization: A Nonvertical Dimension of Social Status." *American Sociological Review* 19 (August): 405–13.

LEVY, MARC A. 1985. "Mediation of Prisoners' Dilemma Conflicts and the Importance of the Cooperation Threshold: The Case of the Namibia." *Journal of Conflict Resolution* 29: 581–603.

LICHBACH, MARK IRVING. 1990. "When Is Arms Rivalry a Prisoner's Dilemma? Richardson's Models and 2 × 2 Games." *Journal of Conflict Resolution* 34: 29–56.

LIKERT, R. 1932. "A Technique for the Measurement of Attitudes." *Archives of Psychology* 21, no. 140.

LIN, NAN. 1976. *Foundations of Social Research.* New York: McGraw-Hill.

LINDSKOLD, SVENN; WALTERS, PAMELA S.; and KOUTSOURAIS, HELEN. 1983. "Cooperators Competitors, and Response to GRIT." *Journal of Conflict Resolution* 27: 521–32.

LINDZEY, GARDNER, and BORGATTA, EDGAR F. 1954. "Sociometric Measurement." In *Handbook of Social Psychology.* Edited by Gardner Lindzey. Reading, MA: Addison-Wesley.

LLOYD, CHRISTOPHER, ed. 1983. *Social Theory and Political Practice.* Oxford: Oxford University Press.

LOCKERBIE, BRAD, and BORRELLI, STEPHEN. 1990. "Question Wording and Public Support for Contra Aid, 1983–1986." *Public Opinion Quarterly* 54: 195–208.

LODHI, ABDUL AQIYUM, and TILLY, CHARLES. 1973. "Urbanization, Crime, and Collective Violence in 19th Century France." *American Journal of Sociology* 79: 296–318.

LOFLAND, JOHN. 1971. *Analyzing Social Settings.* Second ed. Belmont, CA: Wadsworth.

LOFLAND, JOHN, and LOFLAND, LYN H. 1984. *Analyzing Social Settings.* Second ed. Belmont, CA: Wadsworth.

LONNER, WALTER J., and BERRY, JOHN W., eds. 1986. *Field Methods in Cross-Cultural Research.* Beverly Hills, CA: Sage.

LORR, MAURICE. 1983. *Cluster Analysis for Social Scientists.* San Francisco: Jossey-Bass.

LOWRY, RITCHIE P. 1974. *Social Problems: A Critical Analysis of Theories and Public Policy.* Lexington, MA: D.C. Heath.

LUCKENBILL, DAVID F. 1981. "Researching Murder Transactions." In Wagenaar (1981a).

LUNDBERG, GEORGE A. 1939. *Foundations of Sociology.* New York: Macmillan.

———. 1947. *Can Science Save Us?* New York: Longmans, Green.

McCAIN, GARVIN, and SEGAL, ERWIN M. 1969. *The Game of Science.* Belmont, CA: Brooks/Cole.

McCLELLAND, DAVID CLARENCE, et al. 1953. *The Achievement Motive.* New York: Appleton-Century-Crofts.

McCLENDON, McKEE J., and O'BRIEN, DAVID J. 1988. "Question-order Effects on the Determinants of Subjective Well-being." *Public Opinion Quarterly* 52: 351–64.

MACCOBY, ELEANOR E., and MACCOBY, NATHAN. 1954. "The Interview: A Tool of Social Science." In *Handbook of Social Psychology,* Edited by Gardner Lindzey. Reading, MA: Addison-Wesley.

McCONAGHY, MAUREEN. 1975. "Maximum Possible Error in Guttman Scales." *Public Opinion Quarterly* 39 (Fall): 343–57.

McDANIEL, WILLIAM C., and SISTRUNK, FRANCIS. 1991. "Management Dilemmas and Decisions: Impact of Framing and Anticipated Responses." *Journal of Conflict Resolution* 35: 21–42.

McDONAGH, EDWARD G., and ROSENBLUM, A. LEON. 1965. "A Comparison of Mailed Questionnaires and Subsequent Structured Interviews." *Public Opinion Quarterly* 29 (Spring): 131–36.

McGRANAHAN, D.V., and WAYNE, I. 1948. "German and American Traits Reflected in Popular Drama." *Human Relations* 1: 429–55.

McIVER, JOHN P., and CARMINES, EDWARD G. 1981. *Unidimensional Scaling,* Beverly Hills, CA: Sage.

MANN, BRENDA J. 1972. "The Great Crowd: Ethnography of Jehovah's Witnesses." In Spradley and McCurdy (1972).

MARCUS, ALFRED C., and CRANE, LORI A. 1986. "Telephone Interviewing in Health Survey Research." Unpublished manuscript. University of California, Los Angeles.

MARIN, GERARDO, and MARIN, BARBARA VAN OSS. 1991. *Research with Hispanic Populations.* Newbury Park, CA: Sage.

MARINOFF, LOUIS. 1992. "Maximizing Expected Utilities in the Prisoner's Dilemma." *Journal of Conflict Resolution* 36: 183–216.

MARKIDES, KYRIAKOS S. 1992. In Borgatta and Borgatta (1992). 3: 1586–95.

MARKLEY, O. W. 1967. "A Simulation of the SIVA Model of Organizational Behavior." *American Journal of Sociology* 73 (November): 339–47.

MARKOFF, JOHN; SHAPIRO, GILBERT; and WEITMAN, SASHA R. 1974. "Toward the Integration of Content Analysis and General Methodology." In *Sociological Methodology 1975.* Edited by David R. Heise. San Francisco: Jossey-Bass.

MARSDEN, PETER V. 1992. "Social Network Theory." In Borgatta and Borgatta (1992). 4: 188–94.

MARSH, CATHERINE. 1982. *The Survey Method.* London: Allen & Unwin.

MARTIN, CHRISTOPHER L., and NAGAO, DENNIS H. 1989. "Some Effects of Computerized Interviewing on Job Applicant Responses." *Journal of Applied Psychology* 74: 72–80.

MARTINDALE, DON. 1960. *The Nature and Types of Sociological Theory.* Boston: Houghton Mifflin.

MARWELL, GERALD. 1992. "Experiments." In Borgatta and Borgatta (1992). 2: 616–20.

MAYNARD, DOUGLAS W. 1985. "Social Conflict Among Children." *American Sociological Review* 50: 207–23.

MAZANEC, JANA. 1992. "Ban's Foes Say They're Hurt, Too." *USA Today,* December 31, pp. 1–2.

MAZUR, ALLEN; ROSA, EUGENE; FAUPEL, MARK, HELLER, JOSHUA, LEEN, RUSSELL; and THURMAN, BLAKE. 1980. "Physiological Aspects of Communication via Mutual Gaze." *American Journal of Sociology* 86: 50–74.

MEAD, MARGARET. 1939. "Coming of Age in Samoa." In *From the South Seas: Studies of Adolescence and Sex in Primitive Societies.* New York: Morrow.

MENDENHALL, WILLIAM; OTT, LYMAN; and SCHEAFER, RICHARD L. 1971. *Elementary Survey Sampling.* Belmont, CA.: Wadsworth.

MERRILL, J. C. 1965. "How Time Stereotyped Three U.S. Presidents." *Journalism Quarterly* 42: 563–70.

MERTON, ROBERT K. 1972. "Insiders and Outsiders: A Chapter in the Sociology of Knowledge." *American Journal of Sociology* 78: 9–47.

———. 1987. "The Focused Interview and Focus Groups: Continuities and Discontinuities." *Public Opinion Quarterly* 51: 550–66.

MERTON, ROBERT K.; FISKE, M.O.; and KENDALL, PATRICIA L. 1956. *The Focused Interview.* New York: The Free Press.

METZNER, HELEN, and MANN, FLOYD. 1952. "A Limited Comparison of Two Methods of Data Collection: The Fixed-alternative Questionnaire and the Open-ended Interview." *American Sociological Review* 17: 486–91.

MICHENER, H. ANDREW. 1992. "Game Theory and Strategic Interaction." In Borgatta and Borgatta (1992). 2: 737–48.

MICHENER, H. ANDREW, and POTTER, KATHRYN. 1981. "Generalizability of Tests in N-Person Sidepayment Games." *Journal of Conflict Resolution* 25: 733–49.

MICHENER, H. ANDREW; SALZER, MARK S.; and RICHARDSON, GREG D. 1989. "Extensions of Value Solutions in Constant-Sum Non-Sidepayment Games." *Journal of Conflict Resolution* 33: 530–33.

MICHENER, H. ANDREW; and YUEN, KENNETH. 1983. "A Text of $M_1^{(im)}$ Bargaining Sets in Side-payment Games." *Journal of Conflict Resolution* 27: 109–35.

MICHENER, H. ANDREW, YUEN, KENNETH; and GEISHEKER, STEPHEN B. 1980. "*N*-Person Side-payment Games." *Journal of Conflict Resolution* 24: 495–523.

MILLER, BRIAN, and HUMPHREYS, LAUD. 1980. "Keeping in Touch: Maintaining Contacts with Stigmatized Subjects." In Shaffir et al. (1980).

MILLER, DELBERT C. 1991. *Handbook of Research Design and Social Measurement.* Newbury Park, CA: Sage.

MILLER, PETER V. 1991. "Which Side Are You On? The 1990 Nicaraguan Poll Debacle." *Public Opinion Quarterly* 55: 281–302.

MILLER, W.S., and ENQUIST, E.J., Jr. 1942. "On the Effectiveness of 'Follow-ups' in Mail Canvasses." *Bulletin of the American Statistical Association* 2: 189–90.

MILVASKY, J. RONALD. 1985. "Early Calls of Election Results and Exit Polls: Pros, Cons, and Constitutional Considerations. Introduction." *Public Opinion Quarterly,* 49: 1–2.

———. 1992. "How Good Is the A. C. Nielsen People-Meter System? A Review of the Report on Nationwide Television Audience Measurement." *Public Opinion Quarterly* 56: 102–15.

MITOFSKY, WARREN J., and WAKSBERG, JOSEPH. 1989. "CBS Models for Election Night Estimation." Paper presented at the Winter Conference of the American Statistical Association. San Diego, CA.

MIZES, J. SCOTT; FLEECE, E. LOUIS; and ROOS, CINDY. 1984. "Incentives of Increasing Return Rates: Magnitude Levels, Response Bias, and Format." *Public Opinion Quarterly* 48: 794–800.

MOERMAN, MICHAEL. 1972. "Analysis of Conversation: Providing Accounts, Finding Breaches, and Taking Sides." In Sudnow (1972).

MOERMAN, MICHAEL, and SACKS, HARVEY. 1974. "On Understanding in Conversation." *Festschrift for E. Voeglin.* The Hague: Mouton.

MOLM, LINDA D. 1990. "Structure, Action, and Outcomes: The Dynamics of Power in Social Exchange." *American Sociological Review* 55: 427–47.

MOLOTCH, HARVEY L., and BODEN, DIERDRE. 1985. "Talking Social Structure: Discourse, Domination and the Watergate Hearings." *American Sociological Review* 50: 273–88.

MONTERO, DARREL. 1974. "A Study in Social Desirability Response Bias: The Mail Questionnaire, the Face-to-Face Interview, and the Telephone Interview Compared." Paper presented at the Annual Meeting of the American Sociological Association, Montreal, August.

MORGAN, CLIFFORD T. 1961. *Introduction to Psychology,* Second ed. New York: McGraw-Hill.

MORGAN, DAVID L. 1988. *Focus Groups as Qualitative Research.* Newbury Park, CA: Sage.

———. ed. 1993. *Successful Focus Groups: Advancing the State of the Art.* Newbury Park, CA: Sage.

MORGAN, DAVID L., and SPANISH, MARGARET. 1984. "Focus Groups: A New Tool for Qualitative Research." *Qualitative Sociology* 7: 253–70.

MOTT, F.L. 1942. "Trends in Newspaper Content." *Annals,* pp. 60–65.

MOURSUND, JANET P. 1973. *Evaluation: An Introduction to Research Design.* Monterey, CA: Brooks/Cole.

MURNIGHAN, J. KEITH, and ROTH, ALVIN E. 1983. "Expecting Continued Play Prisoners' Dilemma Games: A Test of Several Models." *Journal of Conflict Resolution* 27: 279–300.

NAMENWIRTH, J. ZVI, and WEBER, ROBERT PHILIP. 1987. *Dynamics of Culture.* Winchester, MA: Allen & Unwin.

NATIONAL EDUCATION ASSOCIATION. 1930. "The Questionnaire." *National Education Association Research Bulletin* 8: 1–51.

NEDERHOF, ANTON J. 1983. "The Effects of Material Incentives in Mail Surveys: Two Studies." *Public Opinion Quarterly* 47: 103–11.

NIE, NORMAN H.; HULL, C. HADLAI; JENKINS, JEAN G.; STEINBRENNER, KARIN; and BENT, DALE H. 1975. *Statistical Package for the Social Sciences.* Second ed. New York: McGraw-Hill.

NIELSEN, JOYCE MCCARL, ed. 1990. *Feminist Research Methods.* Boulder, CO: Westview Press.

NORTHROP, F. S. C. 1947. *The Logic of the Sciences and the Humanities.* New York: Macmillan.

NORUSIS, MARIJA, J. 1983. *SPSS-X Introductory Statistics Guide.* Chicago: SPSS Inc.

———. 1985. *SPSS-X Advanced Statistics Guide.* Chicago: SPSS Inc.

OLIVER, PAMELA. 1980. "Selective Incentives in an Apex Game: An Experiment in Coalition Formation." *Journal of Conflict Resolution* 24: 113–41.

———. 1984. "Rewards and Punishments as Selective Incentives: An Apex Game." *Journal of Conflict Resolution* 28: 123–48.

OPPENHEIM, A.N. 1966. *Questionnaire Design and Attitude Measurement.* New York: Basic Books.

ORWIN, ROBERT G., and BORUCH, ROBERT F. 1982. "RRT Meets RDD: Statistical Strategies for Assuring Response Privacy in Telephone Surveys." *Public Opinion Quarterly* 46: 560–71.

OSGOOD, C. E., SUCI, G. J.; and TANNENBAUM, P. H. 1957. *The Measurement of Meaning.* Urbana: University of Illinois Press.

OSKENBERG, LOIS; COLEMAN, LERITA; and CANNELL, CHARLES F. 1986. "Interviewers' Voices and Refusal Rates in Telephone Surveys." *Public Opinion Quarterly* 50: 97–111.

PAISLEY, W.J. 1969. "Studying 'Style' as Deviation from Encoding Norms." In *The Analysis of Communication Content: Developments in Scientific Theories and Computer Techniques.* Edited by G. Gerbner, O. R. Holsti, R. Krippendorff, W. J. Paisley, and P. J. Stone. New York: Wiley.

PALIT, CHARLES, and SHARP, HARRY. 1983. "Microcomputer-Assisted Telephone Interviewing." *Sociological Methods and Research* 12: 169–89.

PARRY, H. J., and CROSSLEY, H. M. 1950. "Validity of Responses to Survey Questions." *Public Opinion Quarterly* 14: 61–80.

PEARSON, E. S., and HARTLEY, H. O. 1954. *Biometrika Tables for Statisticians.* Cambridge, Eng.: Cambridge University Press.

PETERSEN, WILLIAM. 1969. *Population.* Second ed. New York: Macmillan.

PEYROT, MARK. 1985. "Coerced Voluntarism: The Micropolitics of Drug Treatment." *Urban Life* 13: 348–65.

PHILLIPS, BERNARD S. 1971. *Social Research: Strategy and Tactics,* Second ed. New York: Macmillan.

———. 1976. *Social Research: Strategy and Tactics,* Third ed. New York: Macmillan.

PHILLIPS, DEREK L. 1971. *Knowledge from What? Theories and Methods in Social Research.* Chicago: Rand McNally.

PINKARD, TERRY. 1982. "Invasions of Privacy in Social Science Research." In Beauchamp et al. (1982). Pp. 257–73.

PIVEN, FRANCES FOX, and CLOWARD, RICHARD. 1971. *Regulating the Poor: The Functions of Public Welfare,* New York: Random House, Vintage.

PLUMMER, KEN. 1983. *Documents of Life.* London: George Allen & Unwin.

POLLNER, MELVIN. 1974. "Sociological and Common-sense Models of the Labeling Process." In Turner (1974).

———. 1987. *Mundane Reason: Reality in Everyday and Sociological Discourse.* Cambridge: Cambridge University Press.

———. 1991. "Left of Ethnomethodology: The Rise and Decline of Radical Reflexivity." *American Sociological Review* 56: 370–80.

POLLNER, MELVIN, and STEIN, JILL. 1993. "Voices of Experience: Oldtimers' Narratives in Alcoholics Anonymous." Unpublished manuscript. Los Angeles: University of California.

POPULATION AND REPRODUCTION GRANTS BRANCH CENTER FOR POPULATION RESEARCH, NATIONAL INSTITUTE OF CHILD HEALTH AND HUMAN DEVELOPMENT. 1971. *Outline: Behavioral and Social Science Aspects of Population and Reproduction Research Program.* Bethesda, MD: Center for Population Research.

POWERS, EDWARD; MORROW, PAULA; GOURDY, WILLIS J.; and KEITH, PATRICIA M. 1977. "Serial Order Preference in Survey Research." *Public Opinion Quarterly* 41: 80–85.

PRESSER, STANLEY, and SCHUMAN, HOWARD. 1980. "The Measurement of a Middle Position in Attitude Surveys." *Public Opinion Quarterly* 44: 70–85.

PRICE, DANIEL O. 1950. "On the Use of Stamped Return Envelopes with Questionnaires." *American Sociological Review* 15: 672–73.

PSASTHAS, GEORGE, ed. 1979. *Everyday Language: Studies in Ethnomethodology.* New York: Irvington Publishers, Halstead Press.

PUNCH, MAURICE. 1986. *The Politics and Ethics of Fieldwork.* Beverly Hills, CA: Sage.

RAGIN, CHARLES C., and BECKER, HOWARD S. 1989. "How the Microcomputer Is Changing Our Analytic Habits." In *New Technology in Sociology: Practical Applications in Research and Work.* E. Brent. and J. L. McCartney, Edited by G. Blank, New Brunswick, NJ: Transaction Press.

RAINWATER, LEE, and YANCEY, WILLIAM L. 1967. *The Moynihan Report and the Politics of Controversy.* Cambridge: MIT Press.

RASER, JOHN R. 1969. *Simulation and Society: An Exploration of Scientific Gaming.* Boston: Allyn & Bacon.

RASINSKI, KENNETH A. 1989. "The Effect of Question Wording on Public Support for Government Spending." *Public Opinion Quarterly* 53: 388–94.

REESE, STEPHEN D.; DANIELSON, WAYNE A.; SHOEMAKER, PAMELA J.; CHANG, TSAN-KUO; and HSU, HUEI-LING.1986. "Ethnicity of Interviewer Effects Among Mexican-Americans and Anglos." *Public Opinion Quarterly* 50: 563–72.

RENSBERGER, BOYCE. 1993. "2.3% of U.S. Men in Survey Report Homosexual Acts." *Los Angeles Times,* Thursday, April 15, pp. A1, A17.

RENZETTI, CLAIRE M., and LEE, RAYMOND M., eds. 1993. *Researching Sensitive Topics.* Newbury Park, CA: Sage.

REYNOLDS, F.D., and JOHNSON, D.K. 1978. "Validity of Focus Group Findings." *Journal of Advertising Research* 18: 21–24.

REYNOLDS, PAUL DAVIDSON. 1979. *Ethical Dilemmas and Social Science Research: An Analysis of Moral Issues Confronting Investigators in Research Using Human Participants.* San Francisco: Jossey-Bass.

RITZER, GEORGE. 1975. *Sociology: A Multiple Paradigm Science.* Boston: Allyn & Bacon.

———, ed. 1990. *Frontiers of Social Theory: The New Synthesis.* New York: Columbia University Press.

ROBERTS, ROBERT E.; MCCRORY, OWEN F.; and FORTHOFER, RONALD N. 1978. "Further Evidence on Using a Deadline to Stimulate Responses to a Mail Survey." *Public Opinion Quarterly* 42: 407–10.

ROBERTSON, IAN. 1987. *Sociology.* 3d ed. New York: Worth.

ROBIN, LEAH. 1993. Personal communication.

ROBINS, DOUGLAS M.; SANDERS, CLINTON R.; and CAHILL, SPENCER E. 1991. "Dogs and Their People: Pet-facilitated Interaction in a Public Setting." *Journal of Contemporary Ethnography* 20: 3–25.

ROBINSON, E., and RHODES, S. 1946. "Two Experiments with an Anti-Semitism Poll." *Journal of Abnormal and Social Psychology* 41: 136–44.

ROBINSON, R. A., and AGISIM, P. 1951. "Making Mail Surveys More Reliable." *Journal of Marketing* 15: 415–24.

RODRIGUEZ, NOELIE, and RYAVE, ALAN. 1990. "Telling Lies in Everyday Life: Motivational and Organizational Consequences of Sequential Preferences." *Qualitative Sociology* 13: 195–210.

ROETHLISBERGER, F. J., and DICKSON, W. J. 1959. *Management and the Worker.* Cambridge, MA: Harvard University Press.

ROGERS, CARL R. 1945. "The Nondirective Method as a Technique for Social Research." *American Journal of Sociology* 50: 279–83.

ROLLINS, M. 1940. "The Practical Use of Repeated Questionnaire Waves." *Journal of Applied Psychology* 24: 770–72.

ROSE, ARNOLD M. 1967. "The Social Scientist as an Expert Witness in Court Cases." In Lazarsfeld et al. (1967).

ROSENBERG, MORRIS J. 1968. *The Logic of Survey Analysis.* New York: Basic Books.

ROSENBERG, MORRIS, and SIMMONS, ROBERTA G. 1972. *Black and White Esteem: The Urban School Child.* Washington, DC: American Sociological Association.

ROSENTHAL, R. 1966. *Experimenter Effects in Behavioral Research.* New York: Appleton-Century-Crofts.

———. 1984. *Meta-analytic Procedures for Social Research.* Newbury Park, CA: Sage.

ROSENTHAL, R., and JACOBSON, L. 1966. "Teachers' Expectancies: Determinants of Pupils' I.Q. Gains." *Psychological Reports* 19 (August-December): 115–18.

ROSSI, PETER H.; BERK, RICHARD A.; and LENIHAN, KENNETH J. 1980. *Money, Work, and Crime: Experimental Evidence.* New York: Academic.

ROSSI, PETER H., and FREEMAN, HOWARD E. 1985. *Evaluation: A Systematic Approach.* Third ed. Beverly Hills, CA: Sage.

———. 1993. *Evaluation: A Systematic Approach.* Fifth ed. Newbury Park, CA: Sage.

ROSSI, PETER H.; FREEMAN, HOWARD E., and WRIGHT, SONIA R. 1979. *Evaluation: A Systematic Approach.* Beverly Hills, CA: Sage.

SABAGH, GEORGES, et al. 1973. *Codebook: Growth of the Mexican-American Family.* Los Angeles: University of California.

SACKS, HARVEY. 1972. "An Initial Investigation of the Usability of Conversational Data for Doing Sociology." In Sudnow (1972).

———. 1974. "An Analysis of the Course of a Joke's Telling in Conversation." In *Explorations in the Ethnography of Speaking.* Edited by J. Sherzer and D. Boumann. Cambridge, Eng.: Cambridge University Press.

———. 1992. *Lectures on Conversation.* Edited by Gail Jefferson, with an Introduction by Emanual Schegloff. Oxford: Blackwell.

SACKS, HARVEY, and SCHEGLOFF, EMANUEL. 1974. "Two Preferences in the Organization of Reference to Persons in Conversation and Their Interaction." In *Ethnomethodology, Labeling Theory, and Deviant Behavior.* Edited by N. H. Avison and R. J. Wilson, London: Routledge & Kegan Paul.

SACKS, HARVEY; SCHEGLOFF, EMANUEL; and JEFFERSON, GAIL. 1974. "A Simplest Systematics for the Organization of Turn-taking for Conversation." *Language* (December), pp. 696–735.

SAXE LEONARD, and FINE, MICHELLE. 1981. *Social Experiments: Methods for Design and Evaluation.* Beverly Hills, CA: Sage.

SCHAEFFER, NORA CATE. 1980. "Evaluating Race-of-Interviewer Effects in a National Survey." *Sociological Methods and Research* 8: 400–419.

SCHEGLOFF, EMANUEL. 1968. "Sequencing in Conversational Openings." *American Anthropologist* 70: 1075–95.

———. 1972. "Notes on a Conversational Practice: Formulating Place." In Sudnow (1972).

SCHEGLOFF, EMANUEL, and SACKS, HARVEY. 1973. "Opening Up Closings." *Semiotica* 8: 289–327.

SCHIFFMAN, SUSAN S.; REYNOLDS, M. LANCE; and YOUNG, FORREST W. 1981. *Introduction to Multidimensional Scaling: Theory, Methods, and Applications.* New York: Academic Press.

SCHUMAN, HOWARD, and DUNCAN, OTIS DUDLEY. 1974. "Questions About Attitude Survey Questions." In *Sociological Methodology, 1973–1974.* Edited by Herbert L. Costner, San Francisco: Jossey-Bass.

SCHUMAN, HOWARD, and PRESSNER, STANLEY. 1979. "The Open and Closed Question." *American Sociological Review* 44: 692–712.

———. 1981. *Questions and Answers in Attitude Surveys.* New York: Academic Press.

SCHUTZ, ALFRED. 1962. *Collected Papers I: The Problem of Social Reality.* The Hague: Martinus Nijhoff.

———. 1964. *Collected Papers II: Studies in Social Theory.* The Hague: Martinus Nijhoff.

———. 1966. *Collected Papers III: Studies in Phenomenological Philosophy.* The Hague: Martinus Nijhoff.

SCHWARTZ, HOWARD, and JACOBS, JERRY. 1979. *Qualitative Sociology: A Method to the Madness.* New York: The Free Press.

SCHWARTZ, MILDRED A. 1987. "Historical Sociology in the History of American Sociology." *Social Sciences History* 11: 1–16.

SCHWARZ, NORBERT; HIPPLER, HANS J.; DEUTSCH, BRIGITTE; and STRACK, FRITZ. 1985. "Response Scale: Effects of Category Range on Reported Behavior and Comparative Judgments." *Public Opinion Quarterly* 49: 388–95.

SCOTT, CHRISTOPHER. 1961. "Research on Mail Surveys." *Journal of the Royal Statistical Society* 124, Series A: 143–95.

SCOTT, JOHN. 1990. *A Matter of Record.* Cambridge, Eng.: Polity Press.

SEARS, ROBERT R.; RAU, LUCY; and ALPERT, RICHARD. 1965. *Identification and Child Rearing.* Stanford, CA: Stanford University Press.

SELLTIZ, CLAIRE; JAHODA, MAIRE; DEUTSCH, MORTON; and COOK, STEWART W. 1959. *Research Methods in Social Relations.* Revised ed. New York: Holt, Rinehart & Winston.

SELLTIZ, CLAIRE; WRIGHTSMAN, LAWRENCE J.; and COOK, STUART W. 1976. *Research Methods in Social Relations.* Third ed. New York: Holt, Rinehart & Winston.

SHAFFIR, WILLIAM B.; STEBBINS, ROBERT A.; and TUROWETZ, ALLEN, eds. 1980. *Fieldwork Experience: Qualitative Approaches to Social Research.* New York: St. Martin's Press.

SHANKS, J. MERRILL; NICHOLLS, WILLIAM L. II; and FREEMAN, HOWARD E. 1981. "The California Disability Survey: Design and Execution of a Computer-assisted Telephone Study." *Sociological Methods and Research* 10: 123–40.

SHELDON, ELEANOR B., and MOORE, WILBERT E. 1968. *Indicators of Social Change, Concepts and Measurement.* New York: Russell Sage Foundation.

SHERIF, M. 1958. "Group Influences upon the Formation of Norms and Attitudes." In *Readings in Social Psychology.* Third ed. Edited by E. E. Maccoby, T. M. Newcomb, and E. L. Hartley. New York: Holt, Rinehart & Winston.

SHIVELY, JoELLEN. 1992. "Cowboys and Indians: Perceptions of Western Films Among American Indians and Anglos." *American Sociological Review* 57: 725–34.

SHURE, GERALD H., and MEEKER, ROBERT J. 1978. "A Minicomputer System for Multi-person Computer-Assisted Telephone Interviewing." *Behavior Research Methods and Instrumentation* 10: 196–202.

SIEBER, JOAN E., ed. 1982. *The Ethics of Social Research: Fieldwork, Regulation, and Publication.* New York: Springer-Verlag.

SIEGEL, PAUL M., and HODGE, ROBERT W. 1968. "A Causal Approach to the Study of Measurement Error." In *Methodology in Social Research.* Edited by Hubert M. Blalock, Jr., and Ann B. Blalock. New York: McGraw-Hill.

SIEGEL, S. 1956. *Nonparametric Statistics for the Behavioral Sciences.* New York: McGraw-Hill.

SINGER, ELEANOR. 1978. "Informed Consent: Consequences for Response Rate and Response Quality in Social Surveys." *American Sociological Review* 43: 144–62.

SINGER, ELEANOR; FRANKEL, MARTIN R.; and GLASSMAN, MARC B. 1983. "The Effect of Interviewer Characteristics and Expectations on Response." *Public Opinion Quarterly* 47: 68–83.

SINGER, ELEANOR, and PRESSER, STANLEY (editors). 1989. *Survey Research Methods: A Reader.* Chicago: University of Chicago Press.

SINGLETON, ROYCE, JR.; STRAITS, BRUCE C.; STRAITS, MARGARET M.; and MCALLISTER, RONALD J. 1988. *Approaches to Social Research.* New York: Oxford University Press.

SIRKEN, M. G.; PIFER, J. W.; and BROWN, M. L. 1960. "Survey Procedures for Supplementing Mortality Statistics." *American Journal of Public Health* 50: 1753–64.

SJOBERG, GIDEON. 1959. "Operationalism and Social Research." In *Symposium on Sociological Theory.* Edited by Llewellyn Gross. New York: Harper & Row.

———. ed. 1967. *Ethics, Politics, and Social Research.* Cambridge, MA: Schenkman.

SJOBERG, GIDEON, and VAUGHAN, TED R. 1993. "The Ethical Foundations of Sociology and the Necessity for a Human Rights Alternative." Pp. 114–159. In *A Critique of Contemporary American Sociology*. Edited by Ted R. Vaughan, Gideon Sjoberg, and Larry T. Reynolds. Dix Hills, NY: General Hall.

SKELTON, GEORGE. 1980. *"The Times* Poll: Carter's Early Concession Had Little Effect on Results." *Los Angeles Times,* November 23, Part I: pp. 1,8,9.

SKOCPOL, THEDA, ed. 1984. *Vision and Method in Historical Sociology.* Cambridge, Eng.: Cambridge University Press.

———. 1987. "Social History and Historical Sociology: Contrasts and Complementarities." *Social Science History* 11: 17–30.

SLAVIN, ROBERT E., and KARWEIT, NANCY C. 1985. "Effects of Whole Class, Ability Grouped and Individual Instruction on Mathematics Achievement." *American Educational Review Journal* 22: 351–67.

SMITH, ERIC R. A. N., and SQUIRE, PEVERILL. 1990. "The Effects of Prestige Names in Question Wording." *Public Opinion Quarterly* 54: 97–116.

SMITH, H.W. 1975. *Strategies of Social Research: The Methodological Imagination.* Englewood Cliffs, NJ: Prentice-Hall.

———. 1981. *Strategies of Social Research: The Methodological Imagination.* Second ed. Englewood Cliffs, NJ: Prentice-Hall.

SMITH, NICK L., ed. 1985. "Special Issue: Moral and Ethical Problems in Evaluation." *Evaluation and Program Planning* 8: 1–76.

SMITH, TOM W. 1987. "That Which We Call Welfare by Any Other Name Would Smell Sweeter." *Public Opinion Quarterly* 51: 75–83.

SNEATH, P. H. A., and SOKAL, R.R. 1973. *Numerical Taxonomy.* San Francisco: Freeman.

SOBAL, JEFFREY. 1984. "The Content of Survey Introductions and the Provision of Informed Consent." *Public Opinion Quarterly* 48: 788–93.

SOKAL, R. R., and SNEATH, P. H. A. 1963. *Principles of Numerical Taxonomy.* San Francisco: Freeman.

SOLOMON, R. L. 1949. "Extension of Control Group Design." *Psychological Bulletin* 46: 137–50.

SOMMER, ROBERT. 1965. "Anchor Effects and the Semantic Differential." *American Journal of Psychology* 78: 317–18.

———. 1969. *Personal Space: The Behavioral Basis of Design.* Englewood Cliffs, NJ: Prentice-Hall.

SPRADLEY, JAMES P. 1970. *You Owe Yourself a Drunk: An Ethnography of Urban Nomads.* Boston: Little, Brown.

SPRADLEY, JAMES P., and MCCURDY, DAVID W., eds. 1972. *The Cultural Experience: Ethnography in a Complex Society.* Chicago: Science Research Associates.

SPROULL, LEE. 1986. "Using Electronic Mail for Data Collection in Organizational Research." *Academy of Management Journal* 29: 159–69.

SQUIRE, PEVERILL. 1988. "Why the 1936 *Literary Digest* Poll Failed." *Public Opinion Quarterly* 52: 125–33.

STEVENS, S. S. 1951. "Mathematics, Measurement, and Psychophysics." In *Handbook of Experimental Psychology.* Edited by S.S. Stevens, New York: Wiley.

STEWART, DAVID W. 1984. *Secondary Research: Information Sources and Methods.* Beverly Hills, CA: Sage.

STEWART, DAVID W., and SHAMDASANI, PREM N. 1990. *Focus Groups: Theory and Practice.* Newbury Park, CA: Sage.

STINCHCOMBE, ARTHUR L. 1968. *Constructing Social Theories.* New York: Harcourt Brace Jovanovich.

STONE, P. J.; DUNPHY, D. C.; SMITH, M. S.; and OGILIVE, D. M. 1966. *The General Inquirer: A Computer Approach to Content Analysis in the Behavioral Sciences.* Cambridge: MIT Press.

STONE, PHILIP J., and WEBER, ROBERT PHILIP. 1992. "Content Analysis." In Borgatta and Borgatta (1992), 2: 290–95.

STOUFFER, SAMUEL A.; GUTTMAN, LOUIS; SUCHMAN, EDWARD A.; LAZARSFELD, PAUL F.; STAR, SHIRLEY A.; and CLAUSEN, JOHN A. 1950. *Studies in Sociology in World War II.* Vol. 4: *Measurement and Prediction.* Princeton, NJ: Princeton University Press.

STRAUS, MURRAY A., and WAUCHOPE, BARBARA. 1992. "Measurement Instruments." Borgatta and Borgatta (1992). 4: 1236–40.

STRAUSS, ANSELM, and CORBIN, JULIET. 1990. *Basics of Qualitative Research: Grounded Theory Procedures and Techniques.* Newbury Park, CA: Sage.

STRICKER, LAWRENCE J. 1967. "The True Deceiver." *Psychological Bulletin* 68: 13–20.

SUCHMAN, EDWARD A. 1967. *Evaluative Research.* New York: Russell Sage Foundation.

SUDMAN, SEYMOUR. 1976. *Applied Sampling.* New York: Academic Press.

———. 1982. "Estimating Response to Follow-ups in Mail Surveys." *Public Opinion Quarterly* 46: 282–84.

———. 1983. "Survey Research and Technological Change." *Sociological Methods and Research* 12: 217–230.

———. 1986. "Do Exit Polls Influence Voting Behavior?" *Public Opinion Quarterly* 50: 331–39.

SUDMAN, SEYMOUR, and BRADBURN, NORMAN M. 1974. *Response Effects in Surveys: A Review and Synthesis.* Chicago: Aldine.

———. 1982. *Asking Questions.* San Francisco: Jossey-Bass.

SUDNOW, DAVID N., ed. 1972. *Studies in Social Interaction.* New York: The Free Press.

SURVEY RESEARCH CENTER (SRC). 1969a. *Student Survey: Questionnaire.* Los Angeles: University of California.

———. 1969b. *The UCLA Student Poll.* Los Angeles: University of California.

———. 1971. *Los Angeles Metropolitan Area Survey: III (LAMAS III): Questionnaire.* Los Angeles: University of California.

———. 1972. *Los Angeles Metropolitan Area Survey: IV (LAMAS IV); Questionnaire.* Los Angeles: University of California.

SWIFT, AL. 1985. "The Congressional Concern About Early Calls." *Public Opinion Quarterly* 49: 2–5.

SWINGLE, PAUL G., ed. 1973. *Social Psychology in a Natural Setting: A Reader in Field Experimentation.* Chicago: Aldine.

SYNODINOS, NICOLAOS E., and BRENNAN, JERRY M. 1988. "Computer Interactive Interviewing in Survey Research." *Psychology and Marketing* 5: 117–37.

TEDIN, KENT L., and HOFSTETTER, C. RICHARD. 1982. "The Effect of Cost and Importance Factors on the Return Rate for Single and Multiple Mailings." *Public Opinion Quarterly* 46: 122–28.

TENHOUTEN, WARREN; STERN, JOHN; and TENHOUTEN, DIANA. 1971. "Political Leadership in Poor Communities: Applications of Two Sampling Methodologies." In *Race, Change, and Urban Society, Volume 5, Urban Affairs Annual Reviews.* Edited by Peter Orleans and William Russell Ellis, Jr. Beverly Hills, CA: Sage Publications.

THOMAS, EWART A. C., and FELDMAN, THOMAS W. 1988. "Behavior-dependent Contexts for Repeated Plays of the Prisoner's Dilemma." *Journal of Conflict Resolution* 32: 699–726.

THOMAS. W. I., and ZNANIECKI, F. 1918. *The Polish Peasant in Europe and America.* Vols. I and II. Boston: Badger.

THORNE, BARRIE. 1980. "'You Still Takin' Notes?' Fieldwork and Problems of Informed Consent." *Social Problems* 27: 284–97.

THORSON, ESTHER, ed. 1979. *Simulation in Higher Education.* Hicksville, NY: Exposition Press.

THURSTONE, L. L., and CHAVE, E. J. 1929. *The Measurement of Attitudes.* Chicago: University of Chicago Press.

TILLY, CHARLES. 1981. *As Sociology Meets History.* New York: Academic Press.

TOIVONEN, TIMO. 1992. "The Melting Away of Class Differences? Consumption Differences Between Employee Groups in Finland 1955–85." *Social Indicators Research* 26: 277–302.

Toops, H. A. 1926. "The Returns from Follow-up Letters to Questionnaires." *Journal of Applied Psychology* 10: 92–101.

Touliatos, John; Perlmutter, David; and Straus, Murray. 1990. *Handbook of Family Measurement Techniques.* Third ed. Newbury Park, CA: Sage.

Traugott, Michael W. 1987. "The Importance of Persistence in Respondent Selection for Preelection Surveys." *Public Opinion Quarterly* 51: 48–57.

Traugott, Michael W.; Groves, Robert M.; and Lepkowski, James M. 1987. "Optimal Call Scheduling for a Telephone Survey." *Public Opinion Quarterly* 51: 540–49.

Traugott, Michael W., and Price, Vincent. 1992. "Exit Polls in the 1989 Virginia Gubernatorial Race: Where Did They Go Wrong." *Public Opinion Quarterly* 56: 245–53.

Treiman, Donald, and Hodge, Robert W. 1966. "Occupational Mobility and Attitudes Toward Negroes." *American Sociological Review* 31 (February): 93–102.

Tull, Donald S., and Albaum, Gerald S. 1977. "Bias in Random Digit Dialed Surveys." *Public Opinion Quarterly* 41: 389–95.

Tumin, Melvin M. 1953. "Some Principles of Stratification: A Critical Analysis." *American Sociological Review* 18 (August): 387–94.

Turner, Jonathan H. 1991. *The Structure of Sociological Theory.* Fifth ed. Belmont, CA: Wadsworth.

Turner, Jonathan, and Maryanski, Alexandra. 1979. *Functionalism.* Menlo Park, CA: Benjamin/Cummings.

Turner, Roy, ed. 1974. *Ethnomethodology.* Harmondsworth, Eng.: Penguin.

Udy, Stanley, Jr. 1958. "'Bureaucratic' Elements in Organizations: Some Research Findings." *American Sociological Review* 23 (August): 415–18.

U.S. Riot Commission. 1968. *Report of the National Advisory Commission on Civil Disorders.* New York: Bantam.

University of California, Los Angeles, Human Subject Policy Committee. 1979. *Protocol for Submission of Proposals to Human Subject Protection Committee at UCLA.* Los Angeles: University of California.

University of Michigan. 1969. *Interviewr's Manual.* Ann Arbor: Institute for Social Research.

van den Berghe, Pierre L. 1967. "Research in South Africa: The Story of My Experiences with Tyranny." In Sjoberg (1967).

Van Maanen, John. 1988. *Tales of the Field: On Writing Ethnography.* Chicago: University of Chicago Press.

Vidich, Arthur J., and Shapiro, Gilbert. 1955. "A Comparison of Participant Observation and Survey Data." *American Sociological Review* 20 (February): 28–33.

Vinson, Donald E., and Anthony, Philip K. 1985. *Social Science Research Methods for Litigation.* Charlottesville, VA: Michie.

Wagenaar, Theodore C., ed. 1981a. *Readings for Social Research.* Belmont, CA: Wadsworth.

———. 1981b. "Social Statistics Without Formulas." In Wagenaar (1981a).

Wallerstein, Immanuel. 1976. "American Slavery and the Capitalist World Economy." *American Journal of Sociology* 81: 1199–1213.

Walsh, John P.; Kiesler, Sara; Sproull, Lee S.; and Hesse, Bradford. 1992. "Self-selected and Randomly Selected Respondents in a Computer Network Survey." *Public Opinion Quarterly* 56: 241–44.

Ward, Hugh. 1990. "Three Men in a Boat, Two Must Row: An Analysis of A Three-Person Chicken Pregame." *Journal of Conflict Resolution* 34: 371–400.

Ward, Victoria M.; Bertrand, Jane T.; and Brown, Lisanne F. 1991. "The Comparability of Focus Group and Survey Results: Three Case Studies." *Evaluation Review* 15: 266–83.

Warner, S.L. 1965. "Randomized Response: A Survey for Eliminating Evasive Answer Bias." *Journal of the American Statistical Association* 60: 63–69.

WARREN, CAROL A. B. 1988. *Gender Issues in Field Research.* Newbury Park, CA: Sage.

WATTS, RONALD K. 1982. "Social, Economic, and Religious Determinants of Jewish Marital Fertility." Unpublished Ph.D. dissertation. University of California, Los Angeles.

WAX, MURRAY L. 1980. "Paradoxes of 'Consent' to the Practice of Fieldwork." *Social Problems* 27: 272–83.

WAX, ROSALIE H. 1971. *Doing Fieldwork.* Chicago: University of Chicago Press.

WEBB, EUGENE J.; CAMPBELL, DONALD T.; SCHWARTZ, RICHARD D.; SECHREST, LEE. 1966. *Unobtrusive Measures: Nonreactive Research in the Social Sciences.* Chicago: Rand McNally.

WEBB, EUGENE J.; CAMPBELL, DONALD T.; SCHWARTZ, RICHARD D.; SECHREST, LEE; and GROVE, JANET BELEW. 1981. *Nonreactive Measures in the Social Sciences.* Second ed. Boston: Houghton Mifflin.

WEBER, MAX. 1949. *The Methodology of the Social Sciences.* Translated by Edward A. Shils and Henry A. Finch. New York: The Free Press.

———. 1958. *The Protestant Ethic and the Spirit of Capitalism.* New York: Charles Scribner's Sons.

WEBER, ROBERT PHILIP. 1985. *Basic Content Analysis.* Beverly Hills, CA: Sage.

———. 1990. *Basic Content Analysis.* 2d ed. Newbury Park, CA: Sage.

WEEKS, MICHAEL F.; KULKA, RICHARD A.; and PIERSON, STEPHANIE. 1987. "Optimal Call Scheduling for a Telephone Survey." *Public Opinion Quarterly* 51: 540–49.

WEEKS, MICHAEL F., and MOORE, R. PAUL. 1981. "Ethnicity-of-Interviewer Effects on Ethnic Respondents." *Public Opinion Quarterly* 45: 245–49.

WEIMANN, GABRIEL. 1990. "The Obsession to Forecast: Pre-election Polls in the Israeli Press." *Public Opinion Quarterly* 54: 396–408.

WEISS, CAROL H. 1972. *Evaluation Research: Methods for Assessing Program Effectiveness.* Englewood Cliffs, NJ: Prentice-Hall.

WELLS, W. D., and SMITH, GEORGIANNA. 1960. "Four Semantic Rating Scales Compared." *Journal of Applied Psychology* 44: 393–97.

WEST, W. GORDON. 1980. "Access to Adolescent Deviants and Deviance." In Shaffir et al. (1980).

WHYTE, WILLIAM FOOTE. 1943. *Street Corner Society: The Social Structure of an Italian Slum.* Chicago: University of Chicago Press.

———. 1984. *Learning from the Field: A Guide from Experience.* Beverly Hills, CA: Sage.

WIASANEN, F. B. 1954. "A Note on the Response to a Mailed Questionnaire." *Public Opinion Quarterly* 18: 210–12.

WIEDER, D. LAWRENCE. 1974. "Telling the Code." In Turner (1974).

WILD, PATRICIA BREYER. 1973. "Child Health Care Survey Questionnaire." Los Angeles: University of California.

———. 1974. *Sociological Determinants of Utilization of a Prepaid Pediatric Health Care Plan.* Unpublished Ph.D. Dissertation. Los Angeles: University of California.

WILLER, DAVID E., and HECKATHORN, DOUGLAS. 1980. "Cumulation, Explanation, and Prediction." In *Theoretical Methods in Sociology: Seven Essays.* Edited by Lee Freese. Pittsburgh: University of Pittsburgh Press, Pp. 111–41.

WILLIAMS, CHRISTINE L. 1991. "Case Studies and the Sociology of Gender." Pp. 224–43 in *A Case for the Case Study.* Edited by Joe R. Feagin, Anthony M. Orum, and Gideon Sjoberg. Chapel Hill: University of North Carolina Press.

WILLIAMS, J. ALLEN, JR. 1964. "Interview-respondent Interaction: A Study of Bias in the Information Interview." *Sociometry* 27: 338–52.

WILLIAMS, NORMA, and SJOBERG, ANDRÉE F. 1993. "Ethnicity and Gender: The View from Above Versus the View from Below." Pp. 160–202 in *A Critique of Contemporary American Sociology.* Edited by Ted R. Vaughan, Gideon Sjoberg, and Larry T. Reynolds. Dix Hills, NY: General Hall.

WILLIAMS, THOMAS RHYS. 1959. "A Critique of the Assumptions of Survey Research." *Public Opinion Quarterly* 23 (Spring): 55–62.

WILLLIAMSON, JOHN B.; KARP, DAVID A.; and DALPHIN, JOHN R. 1977. *The Research Craft: An Introduction to Social Science Methods.* Boston: Little, Brown.

WILSON, EVERETT K. 1971. *Sociology: Rules, Roles and Relationships,* Revised ed. Homewood, IL: Dorsey Press.

WILSON, WILLIAM. 1976. "Slavery, Paternalism, and White Hegemony." *American Journal of Sociology* 81: 1190–98.

WIRTH, LOUIS. 1938. "Urbanism as a Way of Life." *American Journal of Sociology* (July): 3–24.

WOLF, FREDRIC M. 1986. *Meta-analysis: Quantitative Methods for Research Synthesis.* Newbury Park, CA: Sage.

WOLF, MARGERY. 1992. *A Thrice-told Tale: Feminism, Postmodernism, and Ethnographic Responsibility.* Stanford, CA: Stanford University Press.

YAMAGUCHI, KAZUO. 1983. "Structure of Intergenerational Occupational Mobility: Generality and Specificity in Resources, Channels, and Barriers." *American Journal of Sociology* 88: 718–45.

YAMMARINO, FRANCIS J.; SKINNER, STEVEN J.; and CHILDERS, TERRY L. 1991. "Understanding Mail Survey Response Behavior: A Meta-analysis." *Public Opinion Quarterly* 55: 613–39.

YARROW, LEON J. 1960. "Interviewing Children." In *Handbook of Research Methods in Child Development.* Edited by Paul H. Mussen, New York: Wiley.

YOUNG, RUTH C. 1980. "The Quality of Life in the Caribbean: A Political Interpretation." *Social Indicators Research* 8 (September): 299–310.

YOUNG, T. R. 1971. "The Politics of Sociology: Gouldner, Goffman, and Garfinkel." *American Sociologist* 6 (November): 276–81.

———. 1993. "Postmodernism and the Chaos Theory." *Perspectives: The American Sociological Association—The Theory Section Newsletter* 6:3.

YULE, G. UDNEY. 1944. *The Statistical Study of Literary Vocabulary.* Cambridge, Eng.: Cambridge University Press.

ZETTERBERG, HANS L. 1965. *On Theory and Verification in Sociology.* Third ed. Totowa, NJ: Bedminster Press.

ZIMMERMAN, DON H., and POLLNER, MELVIN. 1970. "The Everyday World as a Phenomenon." In *Understanding Everyday Life.* Edited by Jack Douglas. Chicago: Aldine.

ZINNES, DINA A. 1966. "A Comparison of Hostile Behavior of Decision-makers in Simulate and Historical Data." *World Politics* 18: 474–502.

ZUELL, CORNELIA; WEBER, ROBERT PHILIP; and MOHLER, PETER PHILIP. 1989. *Computer-assisted Text Analysis: The General Inquirer II.* Mannheim, Germany: Center for Surveys, Methods, and Analysis (ZUMA).

NAME INDEX

LIVERPOOL
JOHN MOORES UNIVERSITY
I.M. MARSH LIBRARY
BARKHILL ROAD
LIVERPOOL L17 6BD
TEL. 0151 231 5216/5290

SUBJECT INDEX